KT-552-118

RED
&
WHITE

RED
&
WHITE

An unquenchable thirst for wine

OZ CLARKE

Little, Brown

LITTLE, BROWN

First published in Great Britain in 2018 by Little, Brown

1 3 5 7 9 10 8 6 4 2

A CIP catalogue record for this book
is available from the British Library.

Hardback ISBN 978-1-4087-1017-3
C-format ISBN 978-1-4087-1016-6

Typeset in Bembo by M Rules
Printed and bound in Great Britain by
Clays Ltd, Elcograf S.p.A.

Papers used by Little, Brown are from well-managed forests
and other responsible sources.

Little, Brown
An imprint of
Little, Brown Book Group
Carmelite House
50 Victoria Embankment
London EC4Y 0DZ

An Hachette UK Company
www.hachette.co.uk

www.littlebrown.co.uk

To my darling Sophia, with love.
This is Daddy's world.

Contents

The Styles that Shape the World of Wine

List of Maps

SETTING
THE SCENE

Discovering my unquenchable thirst for wine

I started drinking at the age of three. We were having a picnic on the banks of the river. My brother was drowning in the weir. My father was trying to rescue him. My mother was having hysterics. And there was this bottle of my mum's damson wine. No one was looking, so I drank it – delicious.

My brother survived, but I very nearly didn't. After my father had hauled him out of the water, he took one look at the empty bottle, turned me upside down and whacked most of the liquid out of me from whence it had entered. That put me off drinking till I was eighteen. Well, not quite. Later that summer my sister was christened. My father had poured out glasses of South African sherry for when the guests got home from church. Too good to miss, with my brother able to reach them from a chair. Another thick head. Another whack. I think. Actually, it all got a bit blurred by the second glass. And this time I really did get put off drink till I was eighteen. But I've always adored wines that taste of damsons. And I've always been partial to a second glass of sherry.

But that doesn't mean I gave up on flavours, perfumes, scents, sights, emotions and sound. I had a childhood completely packed with all of those. I grew up in the Kent countryside during the 1950s and '60s. I didn't go to school until I was, what, five? I hung around my mum. I ranged through the fields and marshes and woods that surrounded our house. And I loved my dog Chunky. I then became a chorister at Canterbury Cathedral and all the time I was picking up the aromas and enthusiasms of childhood and adolescence. Going off to school so late meant that I was always in the kitchen, cooking with my mother, tasting stuff – stews, roasts, gravies, soups, jams, chutneys, pickles, cakes, buns and bread. We had a sort of market garden and I quickly learned how to pick the ripest strawberries and cherries, blackcurrants, redcurrants, apples, plums and pears. The smell of vegetables mingling with fresh earth as you pull up carrots or potatoes from the soil, the pungency of fresh-cropped parsley or mint or sage, the sultry heavy-lidded odour of Black Hamburg grapes in the greenhouse thickening the air with promise – I revelled in all of these, and I can recall all of them with perfect clarity.

And it wasn't just food and drink. As I grew older, it was the smell of linseed oil and my cricket bat; my wellington boots by the back door; the dust in the lane at high summer; the pile of grass cuttings after spring rain had drenched them; my mother's Calèche perfume when she was going out; my father's study and his workshop – old books, ink, lathes, lubricating oil and wood shavings. Canterbury Cathedral, cold and pallid on a winter morning, the flagstones smelling of a thousand sunless years, or triumphant and exotic as the incense-swathed clerics swept into the vestry after Eucharist. The crisp, chalky smell of freshly starched sheets – and of matron, fresh, crisp and starched. Flavours, scents, emotions, people, places. But no wine.

Quite simply, my parents didn't really drink. This was the 1950s and '60s, and by one reckoning only 5 per cent of Britons drank wine at the beginning of the 1960s. You could just about classify my parents as among them, because about twice a year a bottle of wine did come out at table. The white was Lutomer Riesling from Yugoslavia – and I can easily recall its vaguely sweet-sour fruity fatness from the tiny sips I took. The red was Bull's Blood from Hungary, a furious mighty red in those days; one sip and I puckered up my face with disgust. But then I can also remember the roasted Irish turkey, the sage and onion stuffing, the chipolata sausages, the honey and mustard-glazed ham and the slightly burnt roast potatoes that accompanied it – much more fun than the wine. Why did adults drink it?

The only wine I did enjoy – if you can call it wine – was with the Archbishop of Canterbury. As choristers we would go carol-singing around the cathedral precincts each Christmas, ending up at the Archbishop's Palace in the sure and certain knowledge that there would be a mound of mince pies and trays full of fiery, stinging, acrid-sweet ginger wine – to encourage our flagging vocal cords. Now, if all wine had tasted like that, I could have got interested.

Ah, but there was something else. My mum had a secret. I discovered it one day rummaging through the larder – a proper walk-in job packed full of jars of homemade jam, paper packets of flour and sugar and crystallised fruit and tins of bully beef and Spam, as well as mutton and ham in a meat safe, cheese, cream and butter. Here I go again – that smell – does it exist any more? The near-claustrophobic odour of a monstrously well-packed larder? But my mum's secret. I first saw two bottles at about knee level – my mum's, not mine – behind some Kilner jars. They were bottles of Burgundy. French Burgundy (in those days, most of the 'Burgundy' Britain drank was Spanish, not French). Volnay, its labels illuminated with Gothic script and pictures of monastic cloisters that seemed as exotic and romantic as illustrations from the Book of Kells. We didn't lead a sophisticated life. We didn't go on foreign holidays or throw lots of splendid parties. We didn't dine out at all. And here were these bottles of Volnay, my mum's secret sin.

I never tasted it. But I vividly remember creating an image in my mind of what it would taste like. And this was nothing to do with any flavours I knew. It wasn't all about damsons and

raspberries and apples and pears. I was conjuring an experience
out of nothing. And I never knew when my parents drank the
wine. But I kept checking up on it and I could see the vintage
date on the label changed every year or so. Some late-night
supper for two after we kids were sound asleep ... And I also
found, in my father's study, among his medical textbooks behind
the door, a half bottle of George Goulet Champagne, vintage
1952. I never tasted that either, not physically, but I did imagine
a foaming, golden, honeyed nectar – and that I can still taste
right now.

Did we have a culture of wine at home? Absolutely not. But
did I sense that there *was* a culture of wine, as yet distant but
thrilling, intriguing, soaked with possibilities? Absolutely.

I was very happy as a child. But I led a fairly solitary life
away from the cathedral, and developed some decidedly unusual
views. One, in particular, I remember: at the age of eight, seeing
a picture in the local newspaper of a bald-headed old fellow, his
pate glistening, his Sunday best shining and scuffed all at once,
a brave smile betrayed by his misty eyes. And he was holding
a gold watch given to him by the local gravel works. 'Why's
he so sad?' I asked my dad. 'Well, he's retiring.' 'What's that?'
'You have to stop work when you're sixty-five.' 'But he looks so
sad – he obviously doesn't want to.' 'That's just how it is. You
have to.' 'I'm never going to retire,' I announced. 'Well, you'd
better never have a job then,' my dad replied. 'All right. I won't.'
And I never have.

Oh, I have worked, harder than many people with the most
taxing of jobs. But that declaration that I'd never retire says
a lot about who I am as a person. I had a deep desire not to
grow up. I cried myself to sleep on the eve of my thirteenth
birthday because I thought the good times were finished. I
had an almost perverse determination not to go into business.
I did rather lack confidence in adolescence as I watched other
people go to smart parties, other people go on glitzy holidays,
other people get a girlfriend. But in a strange way it fuelled my

desire to be noticed. And I did have a determination to make a difference in life, to do something in the world that changed how things were.

A determination to make a difference, yet a determination never to enter the fray of business or the professions where I could have made a difference. And a Peter Pan complex – never grow old, never have to settle down or be respectable, can I be immortal? Does it ever have to end? What kind of career could satisfy these desires?

Two that I could think of. The theatre. Here you could be ageless, irresponsible, classless, the eternal outsider of Shakespeare's time. You didn't even have to be a success, so long as you were an ACTOR. So I did that. And wine. What better world than wine, endlessly renewed, always another vintage, always a surprise, never bored, never sated, always a new place, a new person, a new grape, a new method or style. A new vintage. Every year, renewal. And as I saw it, no one could make me retire from something that renewed itself every year – and me with it.

But I wasn't there yet. It was Oxford that did it, and I hadn't got there yet.

I went up to Oxford full of optimism but with very empty pockets. And with a particular interest in girls. So I trawled through the university handbook trying to locate an activity that was a) cheap and b) would render me irresistible to women. Then I saw it. The Oxford University Wine Circle: two pounds a term, four tastings. I would be a wine taster: suave, elegant, worldly. And what's this? You can take a guest, free? That's fifty pence a date. Nirvana beckoned.

My first tasting was red Bordeaux. I remember every detail. Her name was Francesca. She was the favoured recipient of my new-found magnetism. I put on my smart jeans (I had two pairs) and a shirt (I had one of those, too). Francesca wore green. Green hair, green sequins on her face, unfeasibly tight green top, minuscule green leather skirt, and the rest of her – which was most of her – covered in green body paint. I opened the door to the tasting room. Everyone was in a pinstripe suit.

I took four girls to tastings that term. None of them gave me a second date. But something in me had changed. As that Bordeaux evening progressed from basic earthy reds to the mellow joys of St-Émilion and Pomerol and finally up to the glittering delights of classed-growth Pauillac and St-Julien, I listened in awe – not to Francesca; she wasn't talking to me by then – to the wine merchant telling us about how to taste the wines and describing what flavours we might find. This was all making sense.

The final wine was a classic Bordeaux – Château Léoville-Barton 1962. The merchant wanted to give us young bloods a bit of a treat. Just the sight of that name, that vintage, even now fills my brain with a flavour, an aroma, an emotional turmoil. I remember to this day every nuance of the wine's taste. The penetrating blackcurrant fruit was so dry a dragon must have sucked all the sugar from it. A perfume of cedarwood and Havana cigar tobacco as austere as the fruit, and taking the wine to another level of such haunting scented beauty you began to wonder whether there wasn't a little sweetness in the wine after all. At my first-ever tasting the gods of wine had thrown me a classic Bordeaux and said, 'Beat that if you can.'

A flame had been lit in my brain. Flavour and scent, emotions, people, place: memories and experiences reverberated in my mind, criss-crossing dizzily, linking wildly and imaginatively with the wines I was rolling round my mouth. A simple flavour of fruit wasn't enough any more; the spicy odour of barrel-ageing wouldn't do. I was finding that a great bottle of wine wasn't just a nice taste; to get the best out of it I was discovering I had an ability to relate its flavours to everything my life had been thus far.

Roger Bennett was the leader of the Oxford wine buffs, a mighty Melton Mowbray of a man: a cartoonist's dream of a gourmand and an epicure. This jovial Bunter of booze had become the face of undergraduate drinking and ITV sensed an opportunity. Get him on their top current affairs show. Give him a live blind tasting in front of the audience. That'll learn him and his Oxford swells.

I had quickly built a reputation as a bit of a wine swot. The first time Roger spoke to me was when he banged on the door of my room in college. My mother had lent me her car, and obviously I'd told one of the wine bunch. 'Have you got a car?' he said. Not 'Hello, I'm Roger, mind if I come in?' 'Yes,' I said. 'Congratulations. You're a member of the Oxford wine-tasting team. Now, drive to the ITV studios in Birmingham. You're doing a blind tasting.' Live and in front of millions. Tonight! I could be generous and say I was chosen because I was the best. But no: they'd wanted roly-poly Roger. However, he had more sense. And he didn't have a car. 'Get that new squit Clarke to do it. We'll all sit back and watch and have a laugh.'

I'd never done a blind wine tasting. But I thought, if I've tasted it before, I'll remember it. So off I drove. I got there early, and went into the canteen. What are they likely to choose? What's on the canteen wine list? Muscadet, Niersteiner, Soave, red Bordeaux, Rioja and – wow – a five-year-old Beaujolais. I wonder what that's like. Then make-up, five-minute call, check your mike, try to smile – and you're on.

Four glasses of wine: two white, two red. An audience, cameras, heat, glaring light. First impressions, I told myself; if you've tasted it, you'll remember. The first one: pale, almost devoid of any smell or taste. The canteen list – Muscadet? Yes. The next: sweetish. Floral mixed with vomit. It's got to be that Niersteiner. Yes, yes. Then the first red. We'd had a Rioja tasting the week before. The creaminess, the strawberry softness . . . Rioja? Yes, yes, yes. First impressions. Don't stop now. This one – ageing, bricky red, quite light: old Burgundy? Five years old, maybe? The canteen list, you idiot: there's no Burgundy on the canteen list! Beaujolais, five years old, on the canteen list.

I'm not sure anyone had ever done a blind tasting on television before, but it gave me a glimpse of two things: the competitive possibilities in blind tasting and the showbiz. I admit I did like the look of the showbiz.

I returned to Oxford expecting to be fêted. I was studiously ignored. I suppose they thought I would suffer a massive pratfall, bringing me down a peg or two. I suspect they were horrified when I aced the tasting. So, if they represented the world of wine, it didn't look as though they wanted me to be part of it. It was my good luck to come across Metcalfe. We used to meet in the showers at about ten to nine in the evening. I'd scrub him down and he would scrub me down. And then we would put our clothes back on and wait for the curtain call. We were singers in an opera. We both met violent, noisy deaths every night. No one else would scrub the stage blood off us. And we talked about wine and planned a coup. Oxford wine was completely dominated by students from a handful of smart schools, who would turn up to tastings for a few free drinks and a bit of a laugh. And it was totally male. My old instincts revived. 'Wine, women, and song'? We could do it. Metcalfe subtly installed himself as president of the Wine Society and appointed me secretary. We told the hoorays that they were no longer welcome. We canvassed the women's colleges with such success that as much as half the membership the next term was female. And we planned for the Oxford–Cambridge Match.

This was an annual blind wine-tasting match that Cambridge usually won. They would train their team in a somewhat traditional manner – if you shoved enough top-quality Bordeaux and Burgundy from the best college cellars down their throats, the young gentlemen will eventually get the hang of it. We couldn't do that. My college cellar wasn't full of smart red and white wines – Pembroke wasn't known as a 'beer' college for nothing. And so we devised a plan to teach a potential Oxford team to taste wine from scratch, starting from the bottom, building knowledge block by block. From the bottom. It may sound silly now, but that was revolutionary then: in those days you learnt wine from the top.

We would meet around a kitchen table once a week. Everyone brought a bottle or half bottle. None of us were rich but I said it didn't matter. We weren't here to learn about rich men's wine. We were here to learn about flavour – of any sort: about how to recognise it, how to describe it.

I'd serve the wines hidden in brown paper bags and there was only one rule: everyone had to write down what they thought. I kept thinking back to the Birmingham studios. First impressions. Always follow your first impressions. Always immediately note down any flavour that flashed across your mind, however outlandish, because if you had caught sight of a flavour – truly, honestly, not just trying to impress the group – then that flavour *was* there, and it could become your personal recognition trigger in a blind tasting. And always, always be true to yourself and your instincts. Play the ball not the man. Then we all had to say what we thought the wines were – no excuses – out loud in front of the group. Then we would discuss the flavours we'd found – listening to the other tasters' experiences, too – and only then would we rip off the paper bags and reveal the labels. We'd taste again, but this time with our eyes glued to the label so that the flavours we found and the names we read stuck together in our memories.

And the language we talked was of the everyday and of our own everyday life experiences – ordinary life is full of smells, many of them reproduced in different wines. If we could tie the everyday smell and the smell of a wine together we could learn how to put a name to an anonymous glass. So I asked everyone to only use language that meant something to them personally. Here are a few examples: the smell of soft tarmac in the summer heat (Beaujolais often smelled of that); Nivea hand cream (French Gewürztraminer); cat's pee or raw gooseberries (French Sauvignon Blanc); blackcurrant jam and cedarwood or cigars for red Bordeaux; stewed strawberries for red Burgundy; oatmeal and the smell of pee (again!) after eating a Vitamin B tablet for white Burgundy. The Vitamin B tablet wasn't everyday, but I brought along a pack and made everybody take one, and then, an hour or two later, stand in the loo, inhaling the odour, impressing it on the brain. Never to be forgotten. You try it. And in those days, that's what white Burgundy smelled like.

We also used everyday smells to recognise wine faults since there were so many around then. The smell of a wet, shaggy-haired dog just in from a drizzly winter walk would be a joyless white Bordeaux. Vomit? We all knew that one – a Chenin Blanc full of sulphur from the Loire Valley. An old football shirt packed away in a kit bag all damp and dirty at the end of the season and discovered months later festooned with grey mould? That was the smell of a wine destroyed by cork taint – pretty common then, less common now. I knew that one all too well.

And I kept banging on – we must personalise those smells. Not just any old blackcurrant jam – it had to be one that *you* remembered. For me, the one and only, my mum's. The cigars, the cedar box: *you* had to find a personal memory – a generalisation was no good. For me, an old Romeo and Juliet cedar cigar box my dad kept stamps and pencil stubs in. If the hot tarmac didn't do it for you, what about the rubber sole of a running shoe in high summer? Running on a hot tarmac road? Yes, yes, Beaujolais. But you had to find your own personal trigger. Don't just imagine it. Remember it from your own life. Every wine will contain some memory somewhere from your life.

To this day, this is how I teach people to taste. I taught a wonderful girl – and gifted taster – called Rosie like this, and three weeks later she was good enough to be in the Oxford team. Ah yes, the Match. First impressions. Don't try to second-guess the judges. Don't choose the obscure possibility when there's a blatant probability staring you in the face. The self-taught upstarts against the privileged popinjays. We won. And then we won again, and again, and again.

The year after our first win against Cambridge I entered the National Wine Tasting Championships. I came second. The Director-General of the BBC came third. I tasted against Reginald Maudling, the Home Secretary, in the semi-final – the innocence of it all. Everyone said, 'But you can't know about wine: you're too young.' And I said, 'I've just proved that I'm not.' Well, I didn't quite say that, but I thought it. We'd proved that you don't have to be wealthy and brought up on wine to love it and understand it – the guy who won the championship ran a garage. As I stood there beaming with my trophy, I felt like a true radical. Beloved Oxford, hotbed of vinous radicalism. And I've never lost that desire to be radical, to spread the world of wine as wide as I can, by whatever methods I can bring to bear.

But Oxford was soon over. I needed a job. Well, not a job. I became an actor – in England, in Australia and California and Canada, but most of it in London. I was at the National Theatre when my old mate Metcalfe rang and told me a national newspaper was setting up an English wine-tasting team. We had to get into it – and we did. The first match was against France – in Paris. What a wheeze. But as soon as we got into the team, we trained like mad, using the same principles, hidden labels, be true to yourself, first impressions, and you must write it all down. The poor old French were so confident we would fail they had alerted the world's television crews – there was even a crew from Japan. But we won – by a landslide. *Le Figaro* has only twice framed its front page in black since the Second World War. The first time was when Charles de Gaulle died. The second time was . . . yup, to express the national shame at losing to the perfidious English at wine tasting. I was singing at the National Theatre at the time, so I got my picture on the front pages of the newspapers in full costume (dressed as a Welsh druid for some obscure reason), holding a glass of Champagne. The next match was against Germany and we won. I was playing Sweeney Todd at Drury Lane, so it was front pages in costume again. Next up – France again – I was playing *The Mitford Girls* at the Globe (now the Gielgud) with Patricia Hodge. Then the USA – I was doing General Perón in *Evita* by this time, and had become known as 'the actor who knows about wine'.

Which stood me in good stead when a new BBC show called *Food and Drink* needed a wine taster to perform live on television. The guy who was supposed to do it dropped out at the last minute. So the producer simply said 'Get me that actor who knows about wine.' He didn't know my name, he just knew that there was an actor out there who knew about wine, and, being an actor, shouldn't be too fazed about getting up in front of a camera.

I had a cold when I got the message, but you don't say no to anything when you're a young actor. So I drove down to Bristol and presented myself. Baz (Peter Bazalgette), the producer, told me I'd be doing the world's first live television blind tasting. Second, I thought to myself. But I had a cold, so I wouldn't be able to smell properly. Hang on. There would be an audience. Would they know what the wine was? Yes, they would have a big board up with the full name of the wine on it, but I wouldn't be able to see it. Ha. I'd done pantomime, I'd done kids' theatre, I could do this. I'd use the audience.

On I went, and saw this liquid glowing golden and syrupy in the glass. Now, this was in the mid-1980s. Australian wine was extremely rare in the UK, but I'd actually been there – twice. And as far as I knew there were only two Aussie wines on the British high street – Rosemount Chardonnay and Tyrrell's Vat 47 Chardonnay. First impressions. Remember Birmingham. And my first impression was that this was Tyrrell's Vat 47.

And I started playing the audience. Hmm. Very golden. Probably from somewhere warm ... a slight ripple in the audience. It's that Tyrrell's stuff. South Africa's quite warm – nothing. California is hot – nothing. It's the Aussie ... Now Australia is fairly warm – and there's the ripple of sound again. I think it's from ... Australia – and a great wave of applause ... It's that Aussie Chardie. So what's the grape variety? Well, Australia grows lots of different types. Sauvignon ... wait ... silence ... is not that likely. Riesling ... silence ... Now, Chardonnay – and there's the ripple again. I went on like this, teasing the answers out of the audience simply by using long enough gaps in my monologue to listen to their reactions. But the end result was me saying that I thought this wine was a Chardonnay from Australia, vintage 1985, made by a man called Murray Tyrrell in the Hunter Valley near Sydney. It's labelled Vat 47 – and it costs £5.99 in Waitrose. The audience erupted. I exited stage left to be greeted by a delighted Baz. He hadn't realised wine tasting could be showbiz. Would I like to be a regular on the show for the next series? Oh, and one more thing, Baz said. 'Do you realise you forgot to taste the wine?'

Food and Drink became BBC2's most successful programme. I presented the wines with a charismatic, crinkle-haired, batty blonde called Jilly Goolden. We developed a relationship like an old married couple. People used to think we *were* married. They wondered why we had separate hotel rooms on tour. I was basically the hen-pecked hubby. She'd put her hand over my mouth as I was speaking – on screen. She would push me off camera as I was speaking – live. The audience loved it, she loved it, I loved it. She was a truly original, brilliant communicator, coming up with flavours for wines that even my febrile imagination couldn't always match. She understood the hot tarmac road and the rubber-soled gym shoes for Beaujolais, but then she added her own memories of skipping up a Sussex lane with her gymslip flapping in the breeze and a whole nation caught its breath, then tore out to the shops to buy some Beaujolais. When she described a wine as tasting 'of the grease scraped from the inside of a sumo wrestler's thigh' ... yes, I think that one took a bit longer to sell through.

But we both shared the same vision. When we started in the 1980s, Britain still wasn't a wine-drinking nation. Our vision was to transform it into one. Wine was class-ridden in Britain. We set out to democratise it. We needed immediately delicious wines to persuade the millions who thought 'wine's not for the likes of us' to realise wine was a smashing drink – and, of course, it could be for the likes of them. We needed the New World for that; Europe couldn't do it, hadn't been able to produce attractive, basic wines for a thousand years, maybe for ever. Serendipitously, the late 1980s and the '90s were when the New World style of exuberant, juicy, fruity wine became available, attractive and affordable – from Australia, California, New Zealand, South America and the rest. And we needed to get these gorgeous, easy-going drinks to the millions we wanted to persuade into our wine-drinking world. The supermarkets stepped forward at just this moment. They had really only begun to sell wine in the 1970s, but in the 1980s they all set out to dominate the market, both in the UK and in North America. Some just sold slop at rump-end prices, but the important ones – Sainsbury's, Tesco, Marks and Spencer, Safeway and Waitrose – embraced the New World with all the passion of a high-street retailer who sniffs some missing profit margin, and luckily they saw that there was a massive amount of money to be made in persuading millions and millions of non-wine-drinkers to give wine a go. The New World style and the availability of supermarket wine was a potent force that Jilly and I eagerly embraced, much to the fury and derision of a large part of the traditional, stuffy wine world which I wanted to change. I couldn't bear its exclusive snobbishness. I was in the right place at the right time, and with the right partner. It's almost a generation since Jilly and I pranced about together on prime-time television screens. *Food and Drink* ended in 2002. No one who saw Jilly Goolden has ever forgotten her, and I'm sure none of her converts have given up drinking wine. And I was the hen-pecked hubby.

I was writing, too. I got the call from the editor of the *Sunday Express* when I was doing *Sweeney Todd*. I went to see him in his art deco office on Fleet Street. He had been watching the progress of the English wine-tasting team. 'So, you know about wine. Can you write?' You come to that fork in the road. I had no proof that I could write. I could say, 'I don't know.' I said, 'Yes, I can.' 'Excellent,' said the august editor. 'We need a wine column. Would you like to do it?' I left his office thinking, when will the real world kick in? I'm doing major roles in the West End. I'm now a Fleet Street National Newspaper Wine Columnist. Is there anyone as lucky, as cool a dude as me?

And then I met Adrian Webster. We had been actors together at Oxford, but he wasn't a wine guy then, and I hadn't seen him since. He had become a successful publisher while I'd been wandering around the world in the theatre. I suspect he thinks we met up again at some smart wine tasting. This is how I remember it. I was playing General Perón in *Evita* at the Prince Edward Theatre. After a matinée, with full slap still on, I popped out of the stage door in Frith Street on a miserable, drizzly Soho evening to buy a coffee at Bar Italia two doors down. And I saw an unmistakeable gait progressing remorselessly just in front of me. No one walked quite like that. 'Webbo!' I called. And he turned round. He told me he was about to establish his own publishing house. I told him I was governing Argentina eight times a week, twice on Saturdays, and getting a bit tired of it all. He said that he wanted to publish a wine book, so I said let's meet tomorrow. And we did. In a tiny room near the British Museum with only one chair, I think, but Webbo would have had it. We cracked open a bottle of sweet Beerenauslese wine from a place called Rust in Austria and planned to write a book. Planned to write a future, as it happened. We're still doing books together. This one, for a start.

The brave new world of wine
and how we got there

Looking at our first book – a very grand hardback, with *Webster's Wine Price Guide* in big letters and Edited by Oz Clarke in small letters – I realise that I really was making the change from theatre to wine at the right time. And anyway, *Food and Drink* was theatre; all the wine television and live shows I've done, and still do, were theatre; and my shows with the nation's favourite petrolhead, James May from *Top Gear*, were theatre. The book as I see it now was balancing on the very cusp of dramatic change – France took up 206 of the 387 pages and Bordeaux eighty-four of those; Burgundy occupied another forty-nine; California managed just ten pages and Australia four, New Zealand two and Chile and Argentina two pages between them. There was no New Zealand Sauvignon Blanc. There was no Chilean Merlot or Argentine Malbec. There was a bit of Aussie Shiraz, but no Jacob's Creek, no Penfolds Bin 28, no Lindeman's Bin 65 Chardonnay. It was all to come. An open door and someone needed to push it. I thought it might as well be me.

Ten years later, the 1995 *Wine Guide* gives 198 pages to France, Chile now has six pages, New Zealand eight and Australia twenty-two. There's loads of New Zealand Sauvignon now, some Chilean Merlot, but much more Cabernet, and as much Jacob's Creek and assorted Shiraz and Chardonnay from Australia as any sane drinker could swallow. The New World of wine had arrived, and every year it would become more important, not just for the wines it produced, but for the effect it was having on everyone else. Increasingly, the New World was becoming a state of mind rather than a geographical entity. New World meant the search for ripeness became paramount in many parts of the Old World that hadn't previously taken it too seriously. New oak barrels became de rigueur in every wine country, even in parts of Germany. Stainless steel replaced old wood and concrete, winemakers with science degrees replaced hoary old retainers. What used to satisfy well enough was replaced with what could thrill and shock and revolutionise.

Rules and traditions were challenged, nowhere more seismically than in Italy, where Angelo Gaja in Piedmont and Piero Antinori and a host of followers in Tuscany set about dismantling and re-ordering not only Italy's moribund wine laws, but also its hopelessly inward-looking views on what wine could and should taste like. The so-called super-Tuscans, which cast aside the Chianti regulations and produced a string of superlative wines, usually employing French oak and French grape varieties, neither of which were sanctioned by local laws, had an effect far beyond the frontiers of Italy. They showed that France's domination of great wine could be challenged. California had started it. Australia had continued it. Now Europe could do it, Italy leading, with Spain, Portugal and others following behind. And New World meant a change of attitude – the consumer, the wine-drinker, was there to be pleasured. Throughout Europe they had been taken for granted. But in places like California, Australia or New Zealand, there weren't enough locals to drink all the wine they made so they had to search for export markets. And to do that, they had to please people. A revolutionary concept? In wine, yes!

The 1990s was a brilliant decade for me. *Food and Drink* was top of the ratings, and celebrity chefs were the new rock 'n' roll.

Wine may have been the bass guitarist, but I was playing on the same stage. I was writing new books every year and they were selling. The wine world was hungry for new ideas, and just about the most radical was a book I wrote called *New Classic Wines*. I was fed up with places like the USA, Australia and New Zealand always being relegated to the also-ran chapters at the end of the book and often being given less space than the most ordinary of European regions and producers. So in *New Classic Wines* they were all at the front and they took up most of the book. And the only people in the Old World to get a look-in were those who were genuinely prepared to embrace the changing world – people like Miguel Torres in Spain and Angelo Gaja and Piero Antinori in Italy. But they still had to take their place at the back of the book.

And I finally got somewhere to live. I had been leading a peripatetic actor's life, dodging from one flat to another, along with the odd squat. And my wine collection continued to grow, or so I thought. I'd been putting all my spare cash into cases of good Bordeaux throughout my acting years. And I stored them wherever someone with a friendly smile said they would look after them for me until I got somewhere permanent. It's difficult to believe, but I had built up a collection of about a hundred dozen – mostly 1966, '70 and '75 Bordeaux with some Lafite '61 and four cases of Pétrus '64 thrown in. I mention the Pétrus because although it only cost me £3.50 a bottle, it's worth a few thousand pounds a bottle now. Well, it would be if I still had it. When I finally moved into my house with a cellar under the stairs, I was looking forward to filling it with my loot. I learnt a hard lesson. Never store your wine for free. Always pay a professional to cellar it. Or have it under lock and key in your own house.

I started to ring round for my wines. I encountered a strange lack of response on the phone. A university friend told me that, actually, the other 'friend' I'd been storing my 1966 La Mission Haut-Brion and Léoville-Las Cases with had sold them for cash in a layby near Oxford. My musical friend had had the builders in, and he was really sorry, but ... The pharmacist. Why did I ever think the pharmacist was a good idea? Twenty years later I met someone who had gone to the pharmacist's party where he boasted that they should drink as much of Oz Clarke's wine as possible because there was too much for him to cart off to Scotland the next day. Did they enjoy the Lafite '61, I wonder? There was an old flame who knew all too well that revenge is a dish best decanted and served at room temperature.

And there was a guy in Wiltshire with a country house and a cellar full of my Latour, my Ducru-Beaucaillou, my Margaux ... all that. His cellar suffered the worst flood in living memory, so then he said that he had moved my wines to a shed at the bottom of his garden, which proceeded to suffer Wiltshire's worst frost in living memory. All the bottles burst, he said. No, I said, not the port, not the Sauternes. Well, no. He put those in his barn. I rang to arrange a time to pick them up. Too late. His barn had been attacked by terrorists. No, I'm not joking. I couldn't make this up. For some reason he was in a BBC studio and he told me every single bottle of my precious collection was gone, just as I was going on stage to be inter-viewed by Michael Parkinson. God knows what sense I made to Parky. Only Metcalfe could melt the ice around my heart. 'What a relief,' he said. 'You'd have spent the rest of your life drinking wine that was too old.' Yes, but those 1966s, those '70s, those '75s, the Lafite '61, the Pétrus '64 ... someone knows how good they were. I wish it were me.

As the century turned, predictably, the New World pendu-lum swung too far. Wines became too rich, too homogenised, too removed from their roots. But up to a point I could under-stand this. The new 'modern' wine was ripe and soft and fruity. So the natural progression of new wine lovers moving up the scale would be to wines that were riper, richer, softer, fruitier, more dense. Not to traditional flavours, not to wines that are more austere and challenging. The new wine enthusiasts weren't after intellectual challenge; they preferred instant gratification. I find a rather sad intellectual challenge in these oaky monsters by trying to work out what has been lost in the ripening, extracting and oaking, not what is preserved.

One of the biggest complaints about wine at the beginning of this century was that it was all starting to taste the same. Finding different flavours in different wines from different grape varieties grown in different years and in different places is one of the joys and challenges of wine-drinking. Why was everything tasting the same?

To be honest, at the level of widely available, reasonably pleasant cheap wine, I don't think we can fret too much about wines tasting a bit formulaic. The grapes being used are often fairly basic and a rigid, technocratic approach to winemaking at least results in something drinkable.

It was at the higher end that the complaint of homogeneity resonated. Surely Cabernets from Napa Valley, or Argentina or South Africa or Bordeaux should taste different from one another? A super-Tuscan shouldn't resemble a wine from Chile or Australia? Well, they may, if they share the same international wine consultant. There is a small but very influential band of international consultants who have been very influential on wine worldwide. The friendly and engaging Michel Rolland from Bordeaux is the highest-profile of these globe-trotting winemaking consultants. He believes in very ripe fruit and a mellow mouthfeel, and he will show winery owners how to achieve this anywhere in the world. Generally, the owners are delighted at his work because they end up with wines tasting rather similar to other proven high-end successes – many of them made according to the principles of Rolland and a few others. Rolland doesn't necessarily set out to make wines taste the same, but since he and his colleagues mostly work in warm countries where ripening, or overripening, is easy to achieve, and owners are often desperate to make an immediate impact, it isn't surprising they taste a bit similar.

Vineyard consultants can have the same effect, as they take old, traditional, frequently poorly trellised and inefficiently farmed vineyards and transform them into modern, disease-free vineyards with ripeness guaranteed. The fruit is often exposed to an unforgiving sun, and crops are often cut right back, supposedly to intensify flavour and personality in the wine, but this can blank out any nuance the grapes might have possessed. And so, of course, the wines will start to taste the same. An encouraging mark of our current decade is that global consultants appear to be becoming less powerful, local winemakers and vineyard experts are taking more control with a greater local sensitivity – and the move toward biodynamics and 'natural' winemaking simply doesn't suit such wine styles in any case.

And something else was happening. Global warming was kicking in. In 2017 the wine writer Jamie Goode described vineyards as the 'canary in the coal mine'. Grape growers are acutely aware of change in climate and in weather. While politicians wring their hands about limiting the rise of global temperatures to less than 2°C (3.6°F), and realists – or sceptics, depending on your view – think that the temperature could rise by as much as 4.8°C (8.6°F) during this century, grape growers are already at the sharp end. You might think global warming would be welcomed – fifty years ago mediocre to bad vintages in Europe greatly outnumbered good ones – and the sparkling winemakers of England wouldn't have had a business without it. But warming oceans bring ever more extreme weather conditions. The last time the world was this warm was 115,000 years ago; the last time there was this much carbon dioxide in the atmosphere was four million years ago. In many parts of Europe, 2017 was the smallest and most ravaged vintage since the Second World War as frost, hail and fire decimated crops. Nine of the ten hottest Octobers occurring in this century may delight the German and English winemakers, but we are facing a future whereby, even at current rates of warming, up to 73 per cent of vineyard areas in places like the Mediterranean and Black Sea,

Australia, South Africa and Argentina could simply become too hot and too dry to continue producing wine grapes by 2050.

Miguel Torres has been buying land in the Pyrenees foothills because he thinks that his homeland of Penedès in Catalonia will soon be too hot. Growers in Bordeaux's famous St-Émilion area are replanting Merlot with Cabernet Franc because the Merlot simply ripens too fast nowadays, and can produce chewy grape jam rather than succulent yet elegant red wine. Australia's mighty Murray River has sometimes been so short of water in recent years that you could walk across. In 2018 South Africa was so low on water it was feared that the supply in Cape Town would simply run out. In 2015, Sula Vineyards in India picked their vintage on 16 December, two weeks earlier than ever before. The fact that Denmark, Poland, Lithuania, Latvia, Belarus and most of southern England may be covered in vines by 2050 is small recompense for the massive upheaval the wine world may be facing.

I've been banging the drum about preparing for climate change for an awfully long time; I suspect for longer than any other wine writer. And it's been getting me into trouble for at least a quarter of a century. It first came to a head at the New York Wine Experience in October 1993. This was a gathering organised by the extremely powerful *Wine Spectator* magazine. People paid a lot of money for tickets, and everyone big from the wine world turned up. All your target American market in one great ballroom just off Times Square. You didn't send your sales reps. You came yourself. The audience wanted to see the star owners and winemakers standing behind their tables, doling out wine and giving insights into the latest harvest. And the stars did turn out – from Bordeaux and Burgundy and Champagne, Rioja, Port, Barolo, Chianti, Australia and California.

I was the keynote speaker. I'd seen the charismatic larrikin Len Evans from Australia at work earlier in the day. He's not an act you want to follow. But I climbed up to the podium, checked the stopwatch and marched off into the future as I saw it. I talked about rising sea levels and falling river levels, drought and hurricane, panic and lack of planning. And I said the French system of *appellation contrôlée*, the most famous and widely copied wine quality system in the world, might have to be torn up. Even in 1993, I was looking at global warming predictions and saying that winemakers were going to have to change the style of wine they made in Burgundy, or Bordeaux or Rioja. And they were going to have to change their grape varieties, perhaps bringing Spanish varieties like Tempranillo into Bordeaux's vineyards, Rhône Valley varieties like Syrah into Burgundy, and Italian varieties into the Rhône Valley and France's south.

You can hear shock. You can hear resentment and outrage, even if it is just a long, concerted intake of breath. But then the muttering starts, then outrage is vocalised and you struggle to carry on with your speech as chairs are pushed back and rows of French producers and shippers and devotees march out of the lecture hall. That's what happened to me in New York. Four men – Miguel Torres from Spain and Christian Moueix from Château Pétrus, along with Piero Antinori and Angelo Gaja – marched the other way. They stood up and strode to the now-empty front row and pointedly sat down right in the middle, right in front of me – a gesture of solidarity I've never forgotten. Keep going, they were saying. We're listening. The keynote speech was always published in the next issue of *Wine Spectator*. Mine wasn't. I eventually rang the publisher to ask for an explanation. I didn't get one. But the speech was published, without fanfare, in a later edition, perhaps when fewer people were likely to read it, and fewer advertisers likely to get upset.

The obsession with rich, overwrought, overripe wines now seems rather obscene, and I've noticed a distinct shift toward trying to find ways to express vineyard character and preserve fruit flavours at lower alcohols, with many Chardonnays from previously palate-bashing producers like Australia now barely tipping 12.5 per cent. Warm areas are at last planting more heat-resistant grape varieties to stem the relentless flow of the

increasingly unsuitable French classic varieties. We need more
Italian varieties planted, more Spanish, Portuguese and Greek
varieties planted in places like California, Washington State,
Australia, Argentina and southern France. It's happening, but it
needs to happen faster. And the reaction against 'Big is Best' also
shows in the rise of organic and biodynamic grape growing – the
world has never been more aware that we are destroying the very
land that we depend on for life. Whatever you think about the
flavours of 'natural' wines and their 'no additives, no chemistry,
no intervention' kind of winemaking, as a reaction to global
warming and cynical agro-industrial farming they can't be
faulted. In a decade's time they could be positively mainstream.

And this may help us rediscover the flavours of what the
French call terroir – the sense of their place, their vineyard –
that the best wines somehow exhibit. The last generation has
seen a coarsening of wine flavours, as most of the modern
interventions have added flavour and texture to a wine even as
they smothered the delicacy of the true flavours. That's what
most people wanted, that's what most critics wanted, that's what
most people would pay a higher price for. The combination of
a grape variety and a specific place being able to produce a real
sensation of 'somewhere' in a wine is comparatively rare. It
always was. Some vineyards in Bordeaux, Burgundy, the Douro
Valley, the Mosel Valley, Barolo, Somló in Hungary and on the
Greek island of Santorini can do it. Many places can't. That said,
the reaction against monolithic wines, over-processed wines,
over-made-up and confected wines, will produce better, more
sensitive winemaking, and this will reveal more wines with a
sense of place, wines that truly taste of themselves, than we ever
knew existed.

It seems strange to say that the counterfeiting of fine wine has
been a mark of the current decade. Hasn't it always happened?
Pretty much, yes. In Ancient Rome, Falernian was routinely
counterfeited and Pliny the Elder complained that 'not even

our nobility enjoys wines that are genuine'. The *Rubáiyát of Omar Khayyám*, written in twelfth-century Persia, muses 'I often wonder what the vintners buy one half so precious as the goods they sell.' In eighteenth-century England *The Tatler* could write admiringly of English wine merchants 'able to squeeze Bourdeaux [*sic*] out of a sloe and draw Champagne from an apple'. And, good gracious, until 1973, when Britain joined the Common Market, virtually every bottle of Burgundy sold in Britain was a shame-faced lie, quite a bit of it coming out of a giant vat in Ipswich that contained one souped-up mess of southern French and North African wine, which was then sold under whatever label pleased you – Nuits St-Georges, Beaune and Beaujolais were popular.

Modern counterfeiting has become more focused, both in terms of the producer counterfeited and the target market. Rare, famous, high-end wines, from fabled vintages and adulated properties, preferably in larger-than-usual bottles, were during the 1980s and '90s sold predominantly to super-wealthy American collectors, with a few northern Europeans thrown in. The scams hit the front page in 1985, when one of America's richest men, Christopher Forbes, paid what was the world's highest-ever price for a bottle of 1787 Château Lafite-Rothschild initialled by Thomas Jefferson. He paid £105,000 and the bottle turned out to be a fake. In this century the bottles remain big and rare and from fabled vintages, but the target markets have shifted to the latest fountains of ludicrous wealth, Russia and China. The American market faded because several multi-millionaires realised they were being duped and took high-profile legal action.

In places like Russia and China, the fraudsters relied on a relative or total lack of wine knowledge and an extreme desire, for reasons of ego and prestige, to possess the trophy bottles. The cynical realisation also dawned on them that loss of face was a very serious matter in these countries. Even if a fraud were to be discovered, most of these new collectors would prefer to keep quiet. After all, it wasn't the flavours of the wine they had bought, it was the aura of the bottle and the label. A good counterfeit could look just as good as a real bottle; it was only the liquid inside that was different.

And how would anyone know what the old wine was supposed to taste like? Well, when the questionable bottles were from the eighteenth and nineteenth centuries, no one did. There were a couple of world experts on old wine – Michael Broadbent, MW of Christie's was the most famous – but it was largely guesswork. I've had a few of these nineteenth-century Bordeaux and they were all stuffed. I've had similar bottles that were supposed to be fraudulent – and they were a much better drink. If I were rich and keen to make an impression, which one would I prefer to serve to my friends? Probably the bogus one.

Things came to a head with the arrival of a very young but clearly very talented fraudster called Rudy Kurniawan, who was finally sent to prison in 2014. He specialised in slightly younger bottles – twentieth century – where people might have some idea of how the wine might taste. And he was generally reckoned to cook up a fairly good fake wine, too. But when he began counterfeiting wines that had never actually been made – and members of the families concerned were still alive and kicking – he was always going to get into trouble. In 2008 a New York auction house had to withdraw six hundred thousand dollars' worth of Burgundy from a sale because the estate owner, Laurent Ponsot, turned up in New York and said his estate had never made the wines being sold. They had to be forgeries. They were Kurniawan specials. When he was jailed, Kurniawan was made to pay $28.4 million in compensation, and had to forfeit $20 million in assets. And this was just him. Was he really the only one involved?

The general feeling is that it wasn't just him, and that the Fine Old Wine World is probably awash with fakes. Every old bottle without impeccable provenance is now looked at with a very wary eye. One fraud expert reckons that as much as 80 per cent of the top wine circulating in China could be fraudulent. I spent a day in Shanghai a couple of years ago, looking at shops and bars, and I must say, I didn't realise that Château Latour came in so many different-shaped bottles. The top properties now use various secret anti-fraud methods, but it's not the young wines that are generally being faked. And empty old bottles, corks and capsules have a value. I went to an event held by Burgundy's greatest producer, Domaine de la Romanée-Conti, and went round the back afterwards to find the sommelier smashing the bottles with a hammer so that they couldn't be reused. When two bottles of your top wine can sell for a quarter of a million dollars, you don't want to aid the fraudsters by leaving empty bottles lying around.

Nature and nurture

Growing the grapes

If we believe the winemaker who humbly says 'I simply want to express what the grape gives me – perfume, elegance and finesse, or power, structure and lusciousness: I don't want to impose a style, I don't want to transform the grape into something it isn't . . .' – if we believe this statement, then we would surely believe what is now almost a cliché of modern winemaking: that all wine is made in the vineyard. In other words, the winemaker doesn't wish to manipulate or impose, just to let the grapes and their juice and their vineyard yeasts speak. Well, in a perfect world, full of perfect vineyards blessed with perfect vintages, this might be how it is. But in the real world, there's a whole lot of imposing and transforming, exaggerating and obliterating going on in a typical winery. Some of it is to make the grapes speak even more clearly of their place; some of it is to follow a recipe for commercial and critical success based on what is thought to work, not on what the vineyards' fruit would really like to express.

Now, I have quite a lot of respect for all the tricks that can be played in big, modern commercial wineries, turning truckloads of cheaply produced grapes into enjoyable, affordable drinks. But that story would largely be one of winery wizards at work. In my heart, I want whenever possible to drink wines that reflect the place where the grapes grow, but that also means reflecting the people who grew those grapes, and so it also means the decisions they took to bring their crop to harvest, with all its imperfections and angularities, its beautiful flaws and unexpected textures and scents and colours and, when we're lucky, its extraordinary, unpredictable deliciousness. Obviously, the flavour in the grape will be the most important factor. Could anything be more natural? Well, without a good deal of human intervention, that grape might never exist, and would certainly be most unlikely to carry within it the magic spark to make beautiful wine. So let's not get too carried away by talk of everything just being 'natural'; let's take a look at what can be done when humankind and nature come together to make a vineyard.

First select your site. If you're lucky this will be somewhere really beautiful. And you could well be lucky. Vines like slopes, not dull plains, to make delightful wines. Vines like river valleys; vines like cliffs and mountainsides to produce scintillating fruit. The Mosel Valley in Germany, the Douro Valley in Portugal, the sweeping terraces of the Valais in Switzerland make your heart beat faster with their loveliness, and your heart beats much faster still if you attempt to clamber up these daunting yet thrilling crags and cliff faces – the vines that hang above the sweet blue waters of the Mediterranean at Cinque Terre in north-west Italy or those sewn into the rock face above the dappled silver of the Adriatic in Dalmatia tease you to not even try. But great wine can come from the flat and lonely places of the planet. Bordeaux's great Médoc vineyards can seem featureless and friendless. The broad sweeps of Australia's Coonawarra and New Zealand's Marlborough regions make you pine for as much as a bump in the road. But their grapes give good wine. Yet is it as emotional, as heart-searching, as the wines from more beautiful places? Perhaps it isn't.

What these great vineyards will have is a combination of suitable good soil, aspect to the sun, protection from, or exposure to the wind, according to whether you need more warmth or more cool, and the ability to hold on to or to shed water according to need. It rains a lot in the Mosel, so the dark but warm, crumbly slate soils that support the Riesling vines on these slopes let excess water simply drain away. If the soils were wet and heavy the grapes couldn't ripen. The gravels of the Médoc warm the vine and act as a sieve to hurry the Atlantic downpours away from the vine and down to its deeper roots. Where cold and clogged-up clay replaces the gravel, cows replace the Cabernet vine. The blinding white limestone of the Dalmatian cliffs has sucked up and held on to every drop of winter rain as the Plavac Mali grapes face down the fierce blaze of the summer sun. Each place on this earth that hopes to grow grapes is different, but without humans to make the decisions that ambition can't exist. All around the world, experts look for the new Bordeaux, the new Burgundy, the new Champagne. They never find them, because each special area is unique, but in their search they throw up more areas that are also unique. And so the future of wine reveals itself, layer by layer, new precious place upon new precious place for a new generation to devote themselves to, to cherish and to help flourish.

There are just a few soil types that are really good for vines, and it is worth remembering that in most vineyard areas a single hectare can contain all kinds of soils. Soil churns relentlessly. It rebuilds itself, it dies and is born again, it's always shifting. But there are generalisations that are useful. In cool northern European, North American or far-south South American vineyards you need warm, well-drained soil. Gravel and slate do the job, sandstone is OK, so is granite. Limestone and chalk are also excellent because they hold water like a sponge, but never get saturated – any excess passes down through the water table. What you don't want are heavy, cold clays or super-fertile loams. In cool regions you can't ripen grapes on fertile soils because you're only getting enough heat to ripen a small crop. You need infertile soils like gravel to limit the crop and let it ripen. The Romans knew this (along with virtually everything else) and would never plant the vine 'where grain would grow'. Fertile valley floors were fine for fruit and veg and grain. The thin, rocky soil of the slopes was far better for the vine. Pretty much every classic vineyard area established in Europe by the Romans was on a slope or a hillside. But clay is a perfect partner to blend with things like gravel, sand and limestone, and most of France's best vineyards are a combination of these – the clay gives some fertility and organic matter, so long as it is broken up by the other components. As your conditions get warmer, you can cope with more clay, but it still needs a partner to break it up. Clay by itself becomes thick and solid in wet weather, and it becomes desiccated and cracked in drought. Neither is any good for the vine. Mix the clay with limestone or gravel or sand and it becomes a useful soil partner, holding just enough moisture to keep the vine going during warm summers.

So you've got some suitable soil. Now you need to chase the sun, or hide from it. In cool regions you ideally want slopes facing south to south-west to catch the sun's warmest rays, and a protected river valley or lake can give you reflection off the water which helps ripening, while the air movement of a valley should help you avoid frost. But if your vines are caught in a frost pocket – as many vines in Chablis and the Côte d'Or or parts of Bordeaux are – then it might be better to sacrifice a little of the hot afternoon sun for some early-morning warmth which may stop the frost devastating your crop. So, east- to south-east-facing slopes may save your crop, even if the grapes are a little less ripe than those of your south-west-facing neighbours. With global warming you may not want more hot afternoon sun anyway, but the chance of late spring frosts massacring your early-budding vines seems to increase year by year, so east-facing slopes might be better in the long term. In both hemispheres, the idea has always been to face the sun and maximise ripeness, and a slope will catch more direct sunlight in the late summer and autumn than flat land, so aiding the ripening fruit. But in a warming world, more southern hemi-sphere producers are following the example of Chile's Apalta in Colchagua, and planting their slopes looking away from the sun toward the South Pole.

And don't forget the wind. It can be your friend or foe. If you're in a cool area you don't want wind, because it's rarely warm. Wind's only real use is to disturb frosty air and to blow like a benevolent zephyr through your vineyards if there's been rain during the summer and autumn. A nice fresh breeze is called nature's antibiotic, because it blows away all the fungal and rot spores that might otherwise attack your vines. In hot regions like California or Chile or South Africa, strong coastal winds can bring the temperature of your vineyard way down and make it possible to produce light, fresh styles of wine despite the relentless sun. Chile has a whole string of sunny coastal areas cooled by the ocean winds, like Limarí, Aconcagua and Leyda. The winds, sometimes called the Cape Doctor, are cru-cially important for South Africa's Durbanville, Darling and Helderberg vines. If you don't have wind in hot regions, the only other way to keep your vines cool is to plant as high as possible, since the temperature drops by about 0.7°C (1.25°F) for every hundred metres you ascend. You'll know the feeling if you're a skier. The sun is warm down in the village, but it isn't up the mountain. Australia uses altitude for most of its cool mainland vineyards. Tasmania is far enough south not to need any help.

So, which vine? Each variety needs slightly different con-ditions. Some require well-drained soil, others can cope with heavy clay. The most famous example is in Bordeaux, where the late-ripening Cabernet Sauvignon needs the warm gravels of the Médoc, while the early-ripening Merlot revels in the heavy, cool clays of Pomerol. In general, white varieties need less warmth to ripen than reds. That's why in northern Europe reds become rare, while in southern Europe red varieties make up most of the important wines. Even so, there are red varieties like Pinot Noir that don't need – don't want – a lot of heat. They can work well as far north as England. And there are many Mediterranean white varieties that have acclimatised to the heat and after being disregarded for centuries are now producing fantastic, warm-climate whites. Roussanne, Marsanne, Grenache Blanc and Bourboulenc in southern France and Falanghina, Fiano, Vermentino, Greco, Verdicchio and a host of others in Italy prove the point. They are now making some of Europe's most satisfying and fascinating whites. So choose a variety suitable to where you are. In somewhere like France, regulations may do the job for you. If you think you'd like to plant Syrah in Bordeaux, think again. The regulations won't let you, however suitable the vine might be. In the New World you can plant what you like. If you think the grape variety will work, fine, have a go. If the wine is rubbish no one will buy it, but at least you tried.

When you're planting, or replanting, a vineyard, you've got some decisions to make. In an established vineyard, you can take cuttings from the best single vines, propagate them and use the results to replant. This is called massal selection. It's how they always used to do it, and now it's coming back into fashion. Or you can buy clones from a nursery. Each variety has various clones: some have dozens, some have hundreds. They are bred from specific 'mother vines', usually favouring various attributes – high or low yield, resistance to disease, early or late ripening, and, not frequently enough, gorgeous flavours and perfumes. The varieties where you will have the most discussion about clones are Chardonnay and Pinot Noir, where people can become quite obsessive – actually, Pinot Noir producers are almost obsessive by definition. So-called Dijon clones from Burgundy have been the rage for a generation and they have greatly improved wine in cool Burgundy. But they are not always so suitable in warmer New World conditions.

You'll also have to decide whether to plant the vine on its own roots. In most places you can't do this, ever since the nineteenth-century infestation by a tiny, root-sucking aphid called *Phylloxera vastatrix* destroyed most of the vineyards in the world, with the exception of Chile, South Australia and a few other outposts. All over Europe, for instance, the phylloxera is still in the soil – they're nasty little yellow things; I've seen them with a magnifying glass. Usually, you graft your wine vine – the *Vitis vinifera* species – on to the roots of a non-vinifera species which the phylloxera can't or won't destroy. The *Vitis labrusca* is the most common graft, because it's the native vine of north-east America, where the phylloxera came from, and where they co-exist in relative harmony. If you've tasted labrusca wine you'll get some idea why the phylloxera leaves these vines alone.

You can now think about whether to plant your vines closely or far apart. In cool, wet areas close planting is good because the vines will suck up too much water if you let them, and produce loads of leaves and diluted grapes. Close planting makes them compete against each other, reducing their vigour, reducing their crop, increasing their quality. In hot, dry places like southern France or Spain, lack of water may mean you space the vines far apart, and you may even plant them like little bushes to shade the grapes and slow down ripening rather than trellis them on wires, leaving them more exposed to the sun. Most grape growers will train their vines on wires, whether it's hot or cold, wet or dry, because they can exert greater control over the amount of sun the grapes receive by how severely they prune and how they manipulate the number of leaves remaining on the vine. And in cool, wet areas you may not need to irrigate, but in hot, dry areas, you'd probably like to. The vine is a drought plant and can cope pretty well with minimal water – it has to around most of the Mediterranean. Often in Europe, irrigation is banned to discourage over-production, but it isn't in the New World, where many vines couldn't survive without it. Many of those cheap New World brands with gaudy labels come from irrigated vineyards where the yields of grapes per vine get pushed up to unnatural levels. That's why they don't taste of much. Elsewhere, irrigation is used carefully as a tool to regulate quality, and we wouldn't have many of our star wines from Chile or Argentina, or California or Australia without it.

And there's one more big decision, which has become a real talking point. Do you keep your vines free of disease and your vineyards free of weeds and infestations by using chemical methods? Or do you reckon that you can keep control by non-chemical organic methods, or do you go the whole hog and adopt what is called biodynamism? The majority of vineyards in the world use chemical herbicides, pesticides and fungicides. They also use chemical fertilisers to increase production. Without all this, we simply wouldn't have the range of decent, fairly priced wine that we enjoy today. Not only that, but vineyards in regions that are prone to rain and fog and humidity are consequently prone to attack by all kinds of rots and fungus, just like any fruit would be. And I'm talking about seriously famous areas like Bordeaux here. If they didn't use some sort of chemical control, would they be able to produce a crop in a typically damp year?

The traditional answer is no, but this is increasingly being challenged. There are now top producers in Bordeaux who think that they can manage their vines without chemicals. They say it takes a year or two for the vines to learn to defend themselves, and you do lose some grapes, but as the soils become healthier due to the absence of chemicals the vine plant becomes healthier too, and is able to resist most disease attacks. Pests can often be deterred by introducing natural predators or by – my favourite – spraying pheromones to sexually confuse various bugs and stop them reproducing. Even five years ago, the term 'organic' didn't help to sell a wine, especially since it was probably more expensive than a non-organic equivalent and didn't taste any better. Times have changed. There's a new mood abroad. Organic now means a great deal in the world of food, and has become a true selling point for wine. Not because it tastes better – sometimes it does, sometimes it doesn't – but because we are suddenly aware that we're making an awful mess of this planet of ours, the place where we live, the only place where we can live. Increasingly, we see chemical additions in what we eat and drink as toxic, and we increasingly see the casual exploitation and abuse of the world's soils as blatant poisoning of our present and our future. And when we think like that, we begin to taste a difference between organic and non-organic wine, whether it really exists or not. If you're establishing or replanting a vineyard, the organic question matters more and more.

The decision to abandon chemicals will make a dramatic difference to the health of your soil. Some producers can't quite make the leap, but sympathise. They practise 'sustainability', as in New Zealand, or *lutte raisonnée*, which basically means 'we don't use chemicals unless we have to', in France. This is often a big step toward eventually adopting 'organics', and lots of the world's best wine producers follow this route. Some will eventually take the plunge, some will never quite dare. And some will say their vineyard conditions simply don't let them. And some will take the biggest leap of all – into biodynamics. This is 'organics+' and is based on the controversial writings of Rudolf Steiner in the early twentieth century. It lays emphasis on working with the movements of the planets and cosmic forces to achieve balance and consequently health in the soil and the vine. It requires the application of various organic, mineral and herbal preparations in homeopathic quantities. These all then need to be sprayed on the vineyard according to the movement of the stars and planets, and the different phases of the moon, and to whether the day is adjudged to be a fruit, flower, leaf or root day . . . yes, I know. What's it all about? I'm not sure and I'm not sure anyone's sure they're sure. When I hear some biodynamic proselytisers hard at it, my mind rapidly turns to a glass of cool, cleansing ale. But, dammit, it seems to work. Not for everybody. In fact, not for very many growers, because it takes a great deal of personal commitment in terms of time and increased costs – and risk, until you get the hang of it. But the soil gets healthier and healthier. The balance of acids, sugars and tannins supposedly improves year by year. Is it the biodynamics? Or is it the fact that if you adopt biodynamic methods you have to abandon all your lazy shortcuts and give each vine total attention, so you come to know your vineyard intimately? To feel its stresses and challenges, to emotionally respond day by day, hour by hour, to the progress of your grapes toward harvest. Some of the world's greatest winemakers are now biodynamic. Leroy, Comtes Lafon and Domaine de la Romanée-Conti head a long list in Burgundy. Pontet-Canet leads the way in Bordeaux, Chapoutier in the Rhône, Cullen in Australia, Espinoza in Chile, Noemía in Argentina, Reyneke in South Africa and Southbrook in Canada. They all think it works, so who am I to say it doesn't?

Making the wine

In the old days, most winemakers didn't have a lot of say in the grapes they were going to attempt to turn into tasty wine. The carts and trucks would turn up full of grapes at varying levels of ripeness from vineyards the winemaker had never visited. And I'm not talking about a hundred years ago. This was very common during the 1980s and common in the 1990s. Winemakers took what they got. This might help explain why the cult of winemaker as rock star developed during these decades – the winemaker would have been taught loads of tricks at wine school. Davis in California, Roseworthy in Australia, Stellenbosch in South Africa, Bordeaux or Dijon in France, Geisenheim in Germany – these are the famous ones, but there were dozens more. Faced with an entirely unpredictable pile of grapes, he or she would have flexed the muscles, clicked the brain into winemaking mode and set to with yeasts, enzymes, flavourants, colourants and other technical wizardry to produce what could be fairly exciting drinks. That was then. In this century, it's a totally different world.

Today, the winemaker and the vineyard manager live in each other's pockets right through the ripening period. They're discussing vine trellising, management of the leaf canopy, in particular how much the grapes should be exposed to full sunlight – supposed to improve ripening – as against dappled sunlight (much better in my view; the grape loses perfume in direct sunlight). The volume of grapes will also be agonised over. Most wineries now prune generously, then 'green harvest' halfway through the ripening season. This means they cut off any bunches that are ripening less evenly, leaving a smaller crop of grapes, and these are supposed to ripen more fully and quicker. The world's greatest vineyard expert, Richard Smart, isn't convinced it does much to improve the quality, and I rather agree with him, though it once again homogenises flavours.

You could say that the winemaker's most important decision all year is when to harvest. When I used to pick grapes, frankly anything that was vaguely oval and hanging off a vine cane would go in my basket. Anything from pink to purple would do. The picking date was usually decided when the merry band of travellers turned up from northern Spain. They liked to call themselves *gitanes* – that's French for gypsies, for the smokers among you. Here they were. Let's pick before they move off again. The phrase 'physiological ripeness' was one that I never heard. The word 'perfect' really wasn't part of the grape grower's vocabulary any more than the word 'perfect' was used to describe a wine by the winemaker. But science has now come up with study after study showing us the 'perfect' state we could aspire to in a grape's sugar, acid, pH, pulp texture, skin texture, berry texture, seed texture, seed colour, stem lignification, anthocyanin density – you want more? I'm sure there is more. And I'm sure that getting them all to coalesce at precisely the right reading will create a wine that may tick every box – tick, tick, tick toward the nirvana of a 100-point score. Toward perfection, maybe? Science can't tell us what perfect is. Science will make a technically better wine, a wine with deeper colour, softer tannins, richer texture, more seamlessly blended flavours. But it can't make a perfect wine. But then, what is a perfect wine? Is a technically perfect singer the one that touches your heart? Is a technically perfect poet or painter the one who reaches into your soul? Were Maria Callas or Pavarotti perfect? Was Keats perfect? Was Shakespeare perfect? Is there really such a thing as a perfect wine?

I mentioned the 100-point score just back there. This is a reference to the 100-point wine-scoring system brought into being by Robert Parker, the American wine critic who totally dominated wine evaluation from the late 1980s to the beginning of this decade. Initially, he did a lot of good, encouraging people, especially in California and France, to make riper styles of wine. It didn't do him any harm that the 1980s was a golden decade through most of Europe, particularly in Bordeaux. And he did simplify the way wine was judged by marking it out of 100 – no more toffee-nosed mumbo-jumbo. Anyone could understand 100 points. To start with, 80 meant nice, 85 meant pretty good, 90 meant very good and 95 meant outstanding. Anything below 80 was regarded by him as not worth the effort. So, actually, Parker's 100-point system was more like a 20-point system.

It's never a good thing for one mind to dominate any area of activity, and in this case one man's palate, one man's preferences, became absurdly and dangerously powerful. The idea that one drinker's taste buds are an unquestionable gauge of excellence is moronic. All around the world people attempted to make the wines that would score well with Parker rather than the wines that their grapes and soils might be more suitable for. Consultants could bring recipes for Potential Parker Points with them – and they always involved maximising ripeness, max-imising depth and density, maximising new oak barrel ageing, and trying to keep wine's necessary acidity under wraps as far as possible. And they skewed the world view. People started saying 'I can't drink this stuff, but it must be my fault because it's getting 95 Parker Points.'

Well, I'm sure wine is now generally better than it's ever been. Part of that is Parker's legacy. Parker himself cautioned against relying too heavily on scores, when the tasting notes that accompany them are a richer source of information. But wine judging and wine criticism have been ensnared by the 100-point system, whereby all but the bravest feel they need to enter into some kind of contest that approves high scores and derides low ones. Ninety-five is the new 90, so from 'very good' to 'perfect' is only 6 points. Out of 100? I look at the scores for the new wines from, say, Bordeaux 2015 and '16 and I sometimes think, did everybody make a 95+ wine? Really? The trouble is, in this age of social media, you lose followers by marking low. Why would a wine fan say 'Hey, I've got me a 92-pointer' from one app, when the next app makes it 95? Switch apps to the one that gives higher marks. And don't get me started on the grade inflation that now sees 100-point wines appearing from numerous corners of the globe every month. One hundred points means the ultimate, the unimprovable, the 'perfect' wine, right? But next year I make an even better wine, and as others clamber on to the 100-point platform, how do I say mine's better than that? Well, you could give up marking and start expressing the quality through a carefully thought-out use of language. Or . . . oh, where are Spinal Tap when you need them?

Many winemakers won't have to worry about 'perfect'. They will have picked their crop by machine and brought it in to the winery as best they can, minimising the MOG as they go. MOG stands for 'matter other than grapes' – leaves, twigs, mice, mislaid secateurs. There will be one last chance to remove these, then the grapes go into the crusher. Many of the world's most enjoyable wines are made from machine-picked grapes. The New World wouldn't be able to operate without them.

But the winemakers at the best estates in all the leading countries will have an array of devices and machinery at their disposal, to try to make the finest wine possible. And the finest wine won't come from the most expensively endowed cellar. It will come from the winemaker with a vision of flavour, a spark in the soul, a confidence to take risks, and a deep understanding of and love for the land that grew the grapes. It won't always be the most famous land. The vines won't be the most manicured and pampered and cossetted. A vine is a wild thing. The wines that touch your heart never lose sight of that fact.

So. The grapes arrive at the winery. The first selection of decent berries will nowadays have already been made by the pickers. These chosen bunches will then be dumped onto a sorting table, where eagle-eyed employees will remove any other grapes that don't look quite good enough as they pass along on a moving belt. These will usually then go to a machine that pulls off the stems, and they may return for another bout of selection using optics, lasers, high-tech measurements of grape density – I watch these machines at work, picking away at all the marginal deflections from the ideal berry, and wonder if the personality of the wine is also being diminished, as what often seem to me perfectly good berries are cast aside along with whatever personality they could have contributed. What happens to all these berries? They might make very decent wine. I'd love to think that they weren't discarded but put to good use in giving someone pleasure when they pulled the cork.

Anyway. These grapes need to be turned into wine. At its most basic, this involves getting the juice out of the grapes, fermenting it, ageing it and bottling it. It's that simple. And at wine's most basic level it won't even be bottled. So, four stages at the most. Obviously, red, pink, white, sparkling, sweet and fortified wines all have different requirements and are subjected to different techniques. But I want to keep it as simple as possible here, so I'm basically going to talk about red and white wines. So let's get the grape juice in contact with some yeast and get it fermenting.

Usually you will lightly crush the grapes to start releasing the juice, and you'll pull the stems off. But not always. Sparkling winemakers, some ambitious white winemakers and people making white wine from black grapes (the juice in most black grapes is colourless) like to leave the bunches whole while they carefully press out the juice. The stems capture a lot of the solid pulp and the juice that heads off to ferment is thought to be particularly pure. Most red wines are crushed and destemmed and the grape skin, pulp and juice are then all fermented together. Some Pinot Noir and Syrah winemakers like to keep some or all of the stems in the fermentation vat, so these grapes are only crushed, not destemmed. In Beaujolais they often throw all the bunches into the vat uncrushed, which creates a particularly fruity type of red wine. And the stems definitely give a sappy taste to the wine. Too much and the wine is spoilt but, just like seasonings in a soup, a little stem sap can be fabulously tasty.

Now, let's get fermenting. Almost all white grapes have their juice pressed out of them as soon as possible. Occasionally, crushed grapes will be left to stew for a few hours to leach out a bit of flavour from the skins. The resulting wine will be more pungent, if that's what you want. The ancient Georgian method of making 'orange' or 'amber' wines in earthenware jars usually ferments juice and skins, and often stems, all at once. The result is earthy, bitter and strangely attractive. Led by producers in Croatia, north-east Italy and France's Jura region, a significant number of winemakers worldwide are now cautiously experimenting with this style of wine. Watch this space. Black grapes may sit in their juice for a day before fermenting, to extract more colour and flavour from the skins – then off we go.

Most wines are made using industrially cultured yeasts. Hipsters and purists can get in a state about this, but there are hundreds of yeasts that have been developed to facilitate a reliable, consistent fermentation. Some add no extra character, and some can add all sorts of perfumes and flavours. If you're dealing with a vatful of dull grapes, a bit of help from the yeast might be just the thing. But the current mood among top-end producers is to use the yeasts that live on the grapes in the vineyard. This is recommended as being a truer expression of the vineyard's personality. In many cases that's correct. In most cases these 'natural' yeasts do seem to help round out the texture of the wine, sometimes at the expense of perfume. Yet some winemakers say their vineyards are full of terrible yeasts that they would hate to let anywhere near their fermentation vats. Cultured yeasts are a modern phenomenon. The best vineyards don't need them. Less good vineyards often do.

The most important thing in fermentation is to get the temperature right. Fermentation creates heat, which can bolt like a crazed stallion. The temperature can shoot up and a frenzied fermentation could be all over in a couple of days, leaving a red wine that hasn't had time to extract much colour or flavour from the skins, or a white wine whose aromas have disappeared in a haze of hot carbon dioxide. And the yeasts might have been knocked sideways and failed to finish the ferment, which will result in wines of varying sweetness likely to rapidly turn into vinegar.

That's the risk they took with every vintage in the old days. In hot years, they would be piling in blocks of ice to try to keep the lid on the temperature. But the example of Germany, where cold autumns slowed the fermentation right down, taught the world the importance of controlled temperatures, and the introduction of stainless steel made them possible. Some white wines, especially Chardonnays, are fermented in oak barrels; keeping the temperature down is more difficult, but a small 225-litre barrel is a lot easier to control than a monster vat. Some producers are beginning to favour big concrete vats once more, and I do think they are really good for the texture of the southern European-style reds. And some wines are now fermented in concrete eggs. The shape is supposed to help convection currents keep temperatures stable throughout the ferment.

Red wines will ferment on their skins: all the colour, flavour and tannic chewiness – the experts call it 'structure' – are contained in the skins. These skins get forced to the surface of the liquid by waves of carbon dioxide bubbles produced during the fermentation. They are either pushed back down regularly into the liquid, or the liquid is drawn off and poured back into the top of the vat, soaking the skins and extracting more character from them. Extraction was taken to extremes at the beginning of this century, with the skins macerating in the juice before fermentation, being relentlessly pummelled during fermentation and then being left to continue macerating in the wine long after fermentation was finished. The result was frequently wines that were too dense and bitter. The mood nowadays is to ease off, although that post-fermentation maceration is still quite popular before the wine is drained off and the skins are taken to the press to squeeze out whatever wine they still contain. The basic extraction would once have been done by everyone stripping off, piling into the vat and stomping away. I've done it a couple of times. Apart from the very strange sensation of vine twigs getting caught up in my loose bits, I'd say the most important thing is to hold on to the side of the vat – it's very slippery in there. And once the fermentation really gets going, don't even think about it. The carbon dioxide is so acrid you'll choke and then faint, and later everyone will marvel at the meaty character of the wine as they toast your memory.

But just a word more about what fermentation is and what happens to all the sugar in those grapes if the fermentation doesn't convert it to alcohol. Sugar is everywhere in our food and in our drink nowadays. Many dieticians regard sugar as a drug, and the way that food manufacturers routinely add it to so many products, from hamburger buns to 'ready meal' curries and soups and to almost any drink except plain water, rather supports that theory. But in nature, sweetness isn't always available, except when fruits ripen, or if you had the chance to harvest honey, and for thousands of years before the discovery of the sugar cane, and then the sugar beet, both of which made sugar available all year round, and, over time, made it cheap as well, sweet things were prized and jealously protected.

But hang on. Grapes are sweet. Why aren't wines from grapes sweet? Good question. Here's the answer. Fermentation occurs in nature when yeasts attack sugar and devour it. If you watch a tank of wine fermenting it's a riot of froth and bubbles and the air is filled with a heady sweet-sour stink as the yeasts gorge themselves on sugar. The by-products of this ravenous feast are carbon dioxide – all those bubbles and that pong – and alcohol. Yeasts will go on consuming sugar and creating alcohol until the alcohol level in the liquid rises to somewhere around 15 per cent, at which point the yeasts simply can't operate any more and they slump to the bottom of the vat sated and comatose. Sounds all too familiar to me. And the fermentation stops. Now, the more sugar the grapes contain, the more alcohol the yeasts can create up to about 15 per cent or so. Most grapes don't have nearly enough sugar to create 15 per cent alcohol so the yeasts simply gobble up all the sugar they can find, and the resulting wine is dry. And that's the vast majority of the wine we drink. But just occasionally grapes can build up sugar levels so intense that you could create a wine of more than 15 per cent alcohol – 20 per cent, 25 per cent, 30 per cent even. Yet the yeast can't convert all that sugar to alcohol, so when it gives up trying, all the sugar that hasn't been converted into alcohol remains as sweetness in the wine.

Now, there is a very efficient way of creating sweet wines, and that's by adding high-strength spirit to the vat part way through the ferment. This immediately raises the alcohol level to beyond what the yeast can bear, often 18 to 20 per cent; it arrests the fermentation, and you're left with the unfermented grape sugar as sweetness. These wines are called fortified wines. Frankly, you can make fortified wines pretty much anywhere in the world, though only a few places like Spain and Portugal do it well. But naturally sweet wines, without fortification, are a much more tricky proposition. Very few grapes can reach the levels of super-ripeness required, and to do that they either need to be left on the vine to shrivel, or to be attacked by a weird sugar-intensifying fungus, or indeed to be frozen stiff while still on the vine. Or you can intervene and artificially dry the grapes so that their sugar levels concentrate massively. Each of these activities takes a lot of time and effort, and they all involve risk – you can lose your entire crop if something goes wrong. But a few people around the world are stubborn and determined and impassioned. Fortifying wine is a lot easier, but the flavours you get from unfortified sweet wines are some of the wine world's great treats.

Some red and many white wines spend their pre-bottling time in stainless steel tanks. There will be some yeast sediment (lees) left over from the fermentation. If the producer wants to add a little richness and fatness to the wine without any oak taste, leaving the wine on some of these lees and stirring it regularly plumps up the wine pretty effectively. But a fair number of top whites, and nearly all top reds, will get the oak treatment. Oak barrels are made by toasting and bending staves cut from old trees over a flame. Numerous countries grow oak, but French wood is regarded as the most subtle and sophisticated, while American oak gives a richer, more dominating flavour to the wine. How? Well, oak is full of vanillin. When you toast a stave, the vanillin is drawn out of the wood and caramelised on the inner surface of the barrel. When you age a wine in a wooden barrel the flavours of the oak get dissolved in the wine. If you only toast a barrel lightly, the result is a delightful nutty, creamy, spicy, oatmealy flavour that usually enhances a wine. If you toast the barrel heavily you are more likely to get a flavour like chocolate or even mocha coffee. Some people love it on wines like Shiraz or Pinotage. I can take it in very small doses. Just.

And the mood in wine is drifting away from these mocha-chocolate monsters, even in oak infernos like the Barossa and Napa Valleys. It's not long ago that many red wines would as a matter of course be kept in small new oak barrels for a couple of years and emerge into the sunlight at the end of this ordeal riven with bitter wood tannins and sporting a taste halfway between a carpenter's shop and a chocolate factory. Some people must have liked them, because critics would swoon before their stodgy presence and high rollers would hurl wads of money in their direction. These kinds of critics are losing their influence – and their teeth, probably, if this was the kind of wine they drank at home. But oak still plays as important a role as ever, just in a different way.

Most of that intense toasted wood flavour is extracted by the first wine that is aged in the new barrel. If you then use the barrel again, for different wines, the actual flavour of wood becomes less and less evident – it's been sucked out. The barrel's real purpose – of soothing and softening the wine through a gentle interplay with the air outside the cask over a period of one to two years – becomes the main event. And if you use a bigger barrel – 300 litres, 500 litres – even a new one will give less oaky taste, but the subtle softening of the wine will be just as effective. The taste of new wood used to be like a drug for us. It became the hallmark of the New World against the drabness of Europe. Europe then caught on and began whacking the wine into new barrels, too. I didn't know that France had so many forests full of old trees. Perhaps France's geographical extent is a bit wider than I thought. Well, we're in rehab. And we're happy here. Oak barrels are great for wine's texture and character; just let's not taste them: they're the container, not the substance; the support act, not the headliner.

Pretty nearly all red wines will have undergone a second fermentation in vat or barrel. This is called the malolactic fermentation – it doesn't create alcohol; it converts sharp green malic acid into soft, mildly creamy lactic acid. Red wines that don't do the malolactic taste pretty raw. But white wines taste much brighter and fresher without it, so many producers of wines like Sauvignon Blanc and Riesling prevent it from happening. Even Chardonnays don't always go through it, as the fad for big, rich cream-bun mouthfuls fades. There are various other activities that the wine goes through. Red wines often need softening and freshening up and they get aerated by being transferred from barrel to barrel (racking, this is called). Sometimes they get oxygen bubbled through them (micro-oxygenation). At the moment there is a bit of an obsession with trying to smooth out all the rough edges in red wine. I think it's often overdone. A contrast between textures, between rough and smooth, between rich and lean, is one of the challenging delights of red wine. Too much manipulation infantilises the wine. Just as too much sous-vide cooking infantilises a piece of meat by softening it to the point of senile absurdity.

Let's just bottle the wine. But before that we need to talk about sulphur and high-tech. And 'natural' winemaking. Let's do the high-tech first. If you go into many of the top wineries in California or Australia, or even Bordeaux, you'll see impressive-looking chunks of stainless steel – usually pushed pretty far into the shadows when journalists are visiting. One might be a reverse osmosis machine, which removes alcohol, volatile acidity, stray yeasts or water from your wine – molecularly! It can deconstruct your wine, then reconstruct it. Why would anyone want to do that? Another shining steel gizmo might be the vacuum concentrator – this lets you remove water from grape juice before you ferment it. Why would anyone want to do that? And why would anyone want to employ a spinning cone?

These are all devices to alter the composition of your wine. The spinning cone's main job is to lower alcohol – very useful if you've picked your grapes far too ripe, as became the habit in much of California at the beginning of this century. A vacuum concentrator's initial purpose was to help when your vintage was wet and your grapes were bloated and dilute. Take some water out and you'll get a better level of alcohol, and a more concentrated taste – though if the grapes weren't ripe you just get a more concentrated flavour of 'weren't ripe-ness'. Of course, if you'd been setting too big a crop in the vineyards, in the hope that the sun would shine and ripen it all but, as so often, it didn't – well, you can quietly remove some of that tasteless water from that excessive crop you set. Surely no one in Bordeaux would want to do that? And reverse osmosis is such fun. All that molecular re-arrangement. Why, you could even make a wine that didn't taste a bit like the stuff that nature intended: softer, more seamless, more voluptuous – just the kind of thing to please the wine critics and the marketing men.

And sulphur. I would suggest that every single mouthful of wine you've ever enjoyed contained some sulphur. Sulphur dioxide is one of the by-products of fermentation. And sulphur has been used to keep barrels and vats clean, to stop wine oxidising or turning to vinegar and to prepare it for bottling since at least Roman times. When most wine was pretty rancid and most winemaking equally poor, a liberal addition of sulphur could just about get your wine to market. My nostrils still flare and I wince at the memory of that prickly, choking sulphur smell that lay in wait under the cork of most cheap German, Italian and French whites in the last century. Goodness knows how we ever pretended to enjoy such swill.

Sulphur is now under attack. The permitted level of sulphur dioxide (the gaseous form of sulphur generally used in wine production) has dropped continually in the last generation or so, and good winemakers now use far less than the permitted levels. But most still use some – either while the wine is being aged in vat or barrel, or just before bottling, to keep the drink fresh and bright. Winemaking techniques are far more advanced than they used to be. Winery hygiene is now at the kind of level you used to find only in dairies and creameries. Even so, nearly all winemakers feel that two thousand years of experience can't be wrong and a little sulphur is a fundamental safeguard.

However, there is now a movement of 'natural' winemaking, one of whose chief objectives is to make wine with no sulphur additions at all, and certainly no use of enzymes or any other chemical interventions. I think this is an entirely understandable and laudable reaction to the technology and additive-dominated wine world that was ruling the roost at the beginning of this century. Wine was losing touch with its roots. Chemical additions were warping or obscuring the natural flavours that a particular vineyard expressed. Flavour was becoming too focused on winemakers' tricks.

A 'natural' winemaking movement, determined to re-assert purity of vineyard expression, started in France during the 1960s, but really only took off this century and has been zealously promoted by some bloggers, journalists and merchants. Too zealously. Large numbers of so-called 'natural' wines were cloudy, rather feral and tasting more like murky cider than the expression of any vineyard. The thing is that grape juice will turn to vinegar without human intervention. There are good wild yeasts and bad. To turn raw grape juice into enjoyable wine without help from any of the modern aids takes commitment, luck, good hygiene and talent. Especially talent. The 'natural' wine movement has numbers of ideologically committed, ecologically sensitive winemakers, but only some of them have the sheer talent to regularly produce enjoyable, pure wine without the aids they so despise. In fact, some of them do use a little sulphur, and I don't blame them. I keep thinking back to the words of Eben Sadie in South Africa, one of the planet's most thoughtful and ecologically principled winemakers. 'Would you make "natural" wine?' I asked him. 'Only if I only sold it in my own village,' he replied. 'It's simply too delicate a phenomenon to send off around the world.'

I add a plea from the vast majority of wine-drinkers who don't understand the rarified joys of 'natural' wine. Don't demonise us. Don't tell us we are morally degenerate. Don't, please, tell us that the lovingly, carefully produced wines that we enjoy are 'toxic' because they aren't 'natural'. Such grandstanding will get none of us anywhere. One of the great joys of wine is good-natured disagreement. Let's keep the good nature in our disagreements. And I must say, when I go out with friends who are in their late twenties, they do gravitate toward 'natural' wines. 'Why?' I asked. 'Do you like them?' 'That's not the point,' they said. 'They are there to be tried. We want to be surprised. And then we move on. We have to try them.' And did I hear them mutter 'You old people want the same taste every year'?

A white wine might be cold-stabilised – dropping the temperature way down – to get rid of any haze or solids. A red wine might be clarified and have its tannins tamed a bit using egg whites, or casein (from milk), or isinglass (this usually comes from a sturgeon). None of this sounds very palatable, but they're fining agents. They attract the solids in the wine and then precipitate out. All commercial wines get a pretty sterile filtering to make sure that any rogue yeasts and bacteria don't get into the bottle. With high-quality stuff you can do a sterile filtration – some whites have it, most reds don't – or a light filtration or no filtration. This is the mood nowadays. Get your wine pure and clean, then bottle it just as it is. Scientists say filtration doesn't harm a wine. Romantics say it has to. I'm with the romantics.

But I'm not always with the romantics about what stopper to use. I'm pretty keen on screwcaps, but not for all wines. I think they're great for wines where freshness is the whole point. Sauvignon Blanc and Riesling are prime examples. Yet the silly thing is, these will also age much better under screwcap than under cork. I did a tasting a while ago in Australia of Peter Lehmann and Hill-Smith Rieslings under cork and under screwcap going back thirty years. Most of the old cork wines had had it. The thirty-year-old screwcap wines were sublime and tasted about ten years old. The thing is the screwcap is a complete seal. No oxygen can get in and start to decay the wine, so it ages really slowly. A cork gets tired over time and loses its seal and the wine dies. Red Pinot Noir also seems to work pretty well with screwcaps, but I'm not convinced the powerhouse reds like Cabernet Sauvignon really suit them. They need some oxygen coming through the cork to help them soften up. The word is that all the major Bordeaux châteaux have done screwcap trials. I have only tasted the results of one. I think I'd stick to cork. Cork became unpopular around the turn of the century because the producers were sending out vast quantities of cork infected with a fungus, ruining tens of millions of bottles with musty flavours. In 2001 I was judging wines in Australia and New Zealand, and we were sending back 30 per cent of the wines because of mouldy cork taint. I leapt toward screwcap with rude enthusiasm. But the quality of cork has gradually improved and every year or two the producers swear they've finally fixed the problem. Well, they have got much better. And when it comes to a full-on red wine, I still prefer a cork. And I've got about twelve corkscrews. They were getting rusty. Talking of which, on to the real thing. Let's taste some wine.

Some thoughts on wine tasting – everyone can do it

We can do it simply, or we can do it philosophically. Let's do it simply. Think while you drink. That's it? That's it. Think while you drink may be simple, but it is serious. And since we eat and drink several times a day as a necessity, for those of us who are remotely interested in flavour, let's make a necessity into a pleasure.

I adore flavour. I look for flavour in the dullest bread roll and the freshest plucked sprig of thyme. I taste every mouthful of tap water – I do! – every gulp of milk, as well as every sip of beer or cider, gin or wine. I smell the air. I love to walk out of my front door and smell the seasons changing through the aromas carried on the breeze. I can smell the rowdy uncertainty of October as summer still fights off the looming, lumbering beast of winter. I can smell January in its fogs, in its brilliant crystal sunlight, in its sludgy snow and wisps of woodsmoke. I can smell spring. I can smell sap rising, leaves unfolding, dark earth stretching and exhaling, the sweat of a long winter slumber adding its moist brown odour to the optimistic pale scents of early flowers. And I can smell summer. I can smell summer all year. In the dark winter I can smell summer. As the sun rises higher, I can smell the dry, raw heat of summer trampling on the dewy freshness of spring, I can smell dust replace earth. I can smell gold replace green, I can smell the exhausted satisfaction of high summer replace the polished green muscles of May.

And everything we taste we smell. Smell is taste. And smell is memory. Smell is emotion and experience. Happiness has a smell. Sadness has a smell. Grief and triumph, disappointment, hunger and fear, they all have smells. All of these are the bank, the repository, on which we draw when we decide to taste. When we taste food we can taste memories and experiences. But when we taste wine, which has no language of its own, which has no existence in nature before men and women take it in hand and, with greater or lesser sensitivity, begin to mould it; when we taste wine, and search for words to express the wine, search for ways to describe the pleasures, try to understand the unexpected emotions a wine may call up from some distant time, when we *really* taste, and the wine *really* matters to us, then we have the whole of our previous life offering reasons and opinions and descriptors to explain, just a little, what the wine is, and what it is doing to us. And here's me saying I would keep it simple.

Perhaps it would help if I talk about the basics of tasting. But I do mean it when I say think while you drink is a good mantra. You can get pleasure from the simplest food or drink. And, for goodness sake, we are *doing* it, every day of our lives. We are eating and drinking. Every single time we take a mouthful of anything our senses of taste and smell are aroused. We owe it to ourselves to at least take note. Even the most banal mouthful should bring some reaction, if only to make us pine for all the better mouthfuls we have known.

So, I'll try to get down to basics. I am not going to go into the whole palaver of how to store a bottle (nice and cool), how to open it (screwcap? Twist. Cork? Don't use a lousy corkscrew. Fizz? Don't aim it at someone's eye), how to serve it (pour it, not too fast; funnily enough, if you are too careful you are almost guaranteed to spill some – I always do – so relax), and the type of glass (big is better than small, half-full is better than rim-full or bone-empty). That, at least, was fairly simple.

Now we've got half a decent-sized glassful, let's look at it, smell it – and drink it.

Looking

Well, to be honest, the only really important reason to look at the wine is to make sure you have got enough of it in your glass. At some smart tastings you are not given enough to drown a tadpole. And that's certainly not enough either to enjoy the wine or to understand it. Being offered a minute sample is like only being allowed to gaze on the *Mona Lisa* for five seconds, or being read just a single paragraph of *Bleak House*, or hearing the introduction to 'Nessun dorma' but not the aria – and the high Cs. You need to drink a wine to fully understand it. Make sure you have enough in your glass.

Smelling

This is worth doing, because it is our sense of smell that gives us almost all the pleasure we get from eating and drinking. When we think we taste something with our tongue, actually we are smelling the fumes that go up from our mouths to our nasal cavity. Our tongue is only there to detect probable safe foods versus probable dangerous ones. And for this reason, the tongue picks up only five things – sweetness, salt (both safe), sourness (not so good), bitterness (usually a poison in nature) and umami. To show how seriously evolution has taken this, we can detect sweetness at one part in two hundred and salt at one part in four hundred – easy come, easy go. Acid sourness means unripe fruit, which could make us ill, so we pick that up at one part in 130,000. Bitterness could kill us. We detect that at one part in two million. Umami is that indefinably savoury experience, which is in things like mushrooms, soy sauce and Thai fish sauce, but to pinpoint any of those flavours you need your sense of smell. We'll come back to the tongue in a minute.

Our sense of smell is now our least utilised sense, but when we slithered out of the primordial slime it was our only sense, and it grew from being an olfactory bulb at the top of our spinal cortex into what we now know as our brain. We think because we smell. Our sense of smell lost its importance when we learned to stand up on our hind legs on the way to being humans. On all fours you can't see very far, and you're close to the damp, aroma-laden earth, which gives you most of the signals you need to survive and flourish. You stand up. Suddenly vision becomes more important, to seek out food or mates, to warn you of danger.

Yet smell remains the sense most closely related to memory, to our emotions, to those wordless experiences of our lives. Smell is usually the trigger of memory, not touch or sight or sound. And every breath we take activates the five million smell receptors in our nasal cavities. Five million, able to detect ten thousand different odours, maybe more. So why aren't we running around in a riot of delight at every breath we take? Think about it. We breathe, on average, about twelve times a minute – that's 17,280 times a day. If we had to go through the delirium of deconstructing every gulp of air every day, we would go potty. If we don't want to see, we shut our eyes. If we don't want to hear, we plug our ears. But we have to breathe. It would be insufferable to smell everything every time we take a breath. So we have developed the ability to block off our sense of smell. Talk to someone who works in a chocolate factory or an abattoir – do they smell the chocolate or the cow carcasses all the time? No, they block them off.

But we are wine-drinkers. We are wine lovers. *We* can re-activate this sense, just as when we go into a rose garden we can say to ourselves, I *want* to smell those roses. On a mountainside we *want* to smell the herbs and the wild flowers. In the dead of winter, we *want* to smell fresh coffee brewing, fresh bread just baked and oak logs crackling on an open fire.

It's the same with wine. Just casually sniffing some red liquid in a glass may make you think ah, it's wine. So it is. But for good wine, for wine full of the personality of a particular place, full of the aromas and spices of a particular grape variety, full of the vagaries and foibles and ambitions, shortcomings and talents of the men and women who have put their soul into this wine – to discover all that, we must consciously re-awaken our sense of smell. Approach the glass with enthusiasm, curiosity, optimism. Concentrate on the liquid in the glass, swirl it a little, half close our eyes and take a long, satisfying draught of air in through our nostrils. Preferably with a smile playing on our lips, because if our heart and brain know we're smiling they will react to the smile and ready themselves for the pleasure the wine is going to bring.

Am I getting philosophical again? It's just nuts and bolts. I'm just saying, get yourself in the right mood, put your nose into the mouth of the glass and breathe in. Then what? Well, be warned. You may get nothing. I'd love to say that all wines are sizzling with excitement, boiling over with passionate per-fumes dragged from the rocky depths of the vineyard and the scudding clouds above – but they're not. Quite a lot of wines, you'd never really guess that they've come from a vineyard at all. Perhaps they haven't. They do come from grapes, but many cheap commercial wines come from vast expanses of dull earth smothered with a carpet of vines kept alive and delivering the cloddish harvests of their joyless fruit by irrigation, chemical-isation and mechanisation. It's difficult to call such prairies of agro-industry vineyards. The human element is present in as far as some technician has had to press the right button and activate the right piece of machinery.

The worst offenders are probably California, Australia and South Africa. I would have included Italy and Spain, but as the Italians and Spanish drink less and less wine, their basic brews are beginning to taste half-decent. By the way, there is nothing unhealthy about these wines. And when I come across them, I do still 'taste' them, even if there is little there to taste. As I have said before, sometimes you have to remind yourself of how much better the rest of the world of wine actually is. So at least pay them the respect of that first sniff, that first sip. You owe it to them as a wine of any sort. And you owe it to yourself, as a wine taster. If you want to appreciate exciting wine when it comes along, don't sneer too obviously at the cheap stuff.

Quite a lot of us don't think we have a very good sense of smell, but reckon we can taste fairly sensitively. I get that. I often have days when I think, huh, I'm struggling a bit today. I'm not picking much up. Are the wines dull? Or is it just me? It's probably me. I'm good, but I am sure I am not the best. All kinds of things affect the delicate, mercurial sense of smell – tension, nervousness, tiredness, any sort of anger, dehydration. That last one is particularly important. In our air-conditioned world the air we breathe is often artificially dry and this will dry out our nasal cavities. You can feel it in your nostrils. They should be moist, with mucus on the insides. If they are tacky and dry, then your nasal cavity will probably be too dry as well. And without moisture, there is no smell. Volatile aromas need moisture to transport themselves to your nasal cavity, which needs to be moist to receive them. Often in the modern age the air we breathe is relentlessly dry. Which is why many wine tasters – me included – don't always get all the fragrances and delights that the experts say a wine will smell of.

Yet when we put the wine in our mouth – a liquid thrown into contact with our warm, moist mouth – all kinds of fumes laden with every facet of flavour begin to form and rise into our nasal cavity, where our receptors are waiting with open arms, ready to alert our brains to whether the wine is Bordeaux or Burgundy, from Chardonnay or Chenin Blanc grapes, from stainless steel or oak, from a good winemaker or bad, or whether we like it or whether we don't.

Let's recap. Look at the wine – fair enough. Some glassware is lovely. White wines often look rather beautiful in good glass. Most red wines just look red. If you want to check out precise colours, especially in reds, put a sheet of white paper on the table and hold your glass, angled, over it. You'll be able to see as many nuances of colour as the wine possesses.

Then put your nose in the mouth of the glass and take either one good long sniff or several shorter ones and try to form a first impression of the smell. Often you will find words are hard to come by, but a sense of familiarity may flood your mind. I know that smell, I know it . . . You probably do. It's in your memory, it's in your life experience. You can certainly try to pin down the smell – in a white wine you might say to yourself, what about apple, or lemon, or rose petals or mint? – just to see if one of these activates your memory. But a first impression of a good wine is not just one smell: there are normally various aromas all intertwined and endlessly changing their relationship with one another. And do you really have to be able to identify the smell? No. Lots of excellent wine tasters can't put smells into words. Lots of bad wine tasters kid themselves – and try to kid everyone else – by coming up with a list of smells, some of which might be present, that you could just as well have read in a book. And they probably did.

The first taste

A few wines have such a gorgeous smell that you can literally be stopped in your steps, entranced by the wonderful aromas coming out of the glass. That doesn't happen very often. I can remember the first time I tasted one of the greatest Bordeaux reds ever – a Mouton-Rothschild 1959. I was still a student, and the bottle was opened sneakily in a wine merchant's office on the quays in Bordeaux, after everyone except me and my friend who worked there had gone home. I must have smelled it for half an hour without the wine touching my lips. I was mesmerised by the beauty and the power of the wine. And when I finally took a mouthful I was so pent up and bursting with emotion that I almost drowned in the gales of laughter that the wine induced. Not reverence – laughter. Laughter of delight, laughter of sheer, undiluted pleasure at this joyous wine that swept me away. Amazingly, I've still got a tasting note, though I hardly need it, the memory is so fresh – '*a heady, hedonistic and ultimately heavenly brew of sweet blackcurrants, scented with cigar tobacco and cedarwood, invigorated by the cleansing sheen of shingle, and finally splashed and stirred with an irresistible, unlikely marriage of menthol and mint, Vicks VapoRub, eucalyptus and lime*'. Hmm. Not bad for a beginner.

So here we are, wine in mouth, and think while you drink is still the best advice. Even with the simplest wine, take a second or two, and with something exciting take as long as you care to. Hold the wine in your mouth. Roll it around your tongue, sort of chew it slightly if you want. What you are doing is warming the liquid up, releasing all the volatile flavours it possesses. And while you are doing this, you are still breathing in and out. I often close my eyes at this point, to help me concentrate. And I gently breathe out – through my nose, obviously – and try to capture whatever flavours are in the wine, whatever personality, whatever memory and emotion. You'll think your tongue is picking up all this. Think again. Your tongue has about ten thousand little receptors. Sounds a lot? Well, it isn't. A cow has twenty-five thousand. What, for a diet of grass? Maybe that's why the cow needs them. A parrot only has four hundred, yet in Western Australia the little buggers always head unnervingly for the ripest Cabernet Sauvignon grapes at harvest time.

No. It's the five million receptors in your nasal cavity that are working like crazy, sorting out the wine's flavours and scents. We think that we are tasting blackcurrants or mango, cedarwood, cigars or tar with our tongue, but we are not. We are smelling them as the aromas rise up the back of our throat into our nasal cavity. Remember the tongue can only taste four, or, at best, five things. It's easy to prove. Why can't we taste anything when we have a cold? There's nothing wrong with our tongue, but our nasal cavity is totally bunged up.

Try this. Take a mouthful of, say, New Zealand Sauvignon Blanc. And hold your nose tight. Can you taste anything? You will be able to feel some acidity, but not much else. Then release your nose and breathe out. Your *mouth* fills with flavours of lime and green apples and grapefruit. But your tongue couldn't taste these when you were holding your nose. It's the fumes going up to your nasal-cavity receptors which dash off messages about flavour and scent to your brain, which then speedily zaps the message into your mouth, saying 'my tongue tells me this tastes of green apples and lime and grapefruit'. But it doesn't. It's your nasal cavity interpreting those fumes from your mouth. That's why you need to take a few seconds to 'think while you drink'. The wine will reveal itself as you breathe in and out and concentrate – but only if you let it do so. And ten seconds later, after you've swallowed, thirty seconds later, a minute later, you may still be able to taste the lingering perfumes of the wine as an aftertaste. Good wines have an aftertaste. With great wines, with Mouton-Rothschild 1959, you can taste them for the rest of your life.

And what is a great wine? Can a great wine only come from a supposedly supreme vineyard, from the grape varieties that are supposed to be the world's best? Can a winemaker set out with a recipe to make a great rather than a good wine? Are there particular scents and flavours we should look for as we try to track down a great wine, then appreciate it, then remember it and maybe even try to describe it? How would we know when we found one?

If I'm tasting, the wine I remember, the wine that could conceivably change me or my whole relationship to wine, is the one that reflects a truly personal vision of flavour, an emotional desire to express the vineyard and the grapes it grows, and it always includes the indefinable perfumes and promises just over the horizon that a human can rarely put into words, and which can thus never be duplicated, and which cannot be bought and sold like bags of silver. The wealthy owners with their highly paid consultants and winemakers don't deal in words like 'indefinable', 'unpredictable', 'the unknown' as they set out to create so-called icon wines whose flavours reflect a truly personal vision of money and prestige.

There is an inspiring book called *The Emperor of Scent* by Chandler Burr, about the science, the politics and the passion of scent. The great parfumiers take the excitement of human responses a whole lot further than anyone does in wine. And one thing they have no interest in doing is submitting their creations to a norm. In wine, when people pursue this largely self-bestowed title of an 'icon' wine, they generally slide toward the centre of the 'icon' recipe. They look at the latest wines to get the highest marks from the most influential critics, and tell their winemakers to make something like that. The highest praise is often given to a wine because it resembles other successes that went before, not because it doesn't resemble them. In perfume this would be as if all great scent geniuses were ordered by the fashion houses to 'make another Chanel No. 5'. That's a legendary scent. Nowadays, you could recreate it in a laboratory if you wanted to. But the great parfumiers talk a different language of ambition. They are consumed with creating a scent different from the icons; they talk in terms of poetry, emotion and hallucination. The title they crave for their creation is legend, not merely icon. And the scent will smell uniquely of itself.

So, I'm back to thinking, can wine reach those levels of sensory ambition? I suspect not. One of wine's greatest strengths is to be rooted in the earth, while much of its personality is gathered from the sun and the air and the seasons. And wine is ephemeral. It is born, it waxes and shines, and then it fades. And always, it dies. A poem doesn't die, nor does a painting. Music doesn't die, and a scent, once it has been created, doesn't die either. A wine might express greatness, it might be memorable and life-enhancing, but for just a very short period of its life. I agree with Robert Parker that Château Pétrus 1982 tasted from the barrel was one of the most astonishing wines he, or I, had ever experienced. I look at my tasting notes: they just trail away in admiration and an acceptance that I simply don't possess the words to describe the emotional effect it had on me. Parker bought a whole case of 1982 Pétrus and none of the bottles lived up to that promise. So was it a great wine? In the damp darkness of the cellar, surely it was. Poured from an expensive bottle, at its supposed prime, perhaps it wasn't.

Château Cheval Blanc 1947 is one of the fabled wines of the twentieth century. I've never tasted it, but the old-timers go quite dizzy at the very thought. I have read tasting notes, and terms such as 'engine oil', 'port-like' and 'volatile' (as in balsamic vinegar) crop up. I don't much like the sound of it. Was it great at its birth? Or was it merely unusual or astonishing? And if so, if it was a wine that would nowadays have been regarded as faulty and probably never released under its château label, does that actually make it less great? Or is that the very reason it was accorded greatness? And now, of course, the few remaining bottles will either be dying or be dead. But just as a wine from the barrel can shower your palate with a promise of future greatness, so a fading beauty can still leave enough trails and hints of former greatness for you to respect and enjoy it in its decline.

But can greatness be so ephemeral? Can greatness be just a fleeting moment in a wine's life? Shouldn't it somehow be for the ages? A great sportsman can be caught on camera and his greatness preserved, a great musician can be recorded and preserved for posterity, but not a wine. Wine's weakness is that its beauty, its flavours, its personality cannot be preserved, except in the memory of the person who drank the wine. And if the wine was great, it was great for them alone, in their experience of it. A wine's greatness is a truly personal thing. Is that wine's weakness? Or is it, in fact, wine's strength that so-called greatness isn't what critics and wealthy collectors deem it to be, but it is the lucky chance that just a few of us will drink, and experience, and remember a wine that truly reaches into our being and, just maybe, changes our life.

And last, before I forget ... spitting out

Yes, you can spit the wine out. Sometimes you really must. I do tastings that require me to taste perhaps two hundred wines in a morning. Two hundred mouthfuls. Swallowed. What do you think? Upright or comatose? And sometimes I may have to do another two hundred in the afternoon. Still swallowing? Reserve me a place at the nearest hospital. If you are at a big, serious wine tasting with dozens, maybe hundreds of wines, you *have* to spit. There will be loads of spittoons all around the room and you must use them. First, to have any chance of staying sober and remembering where you live; and second, because as your head gets muddled your palate will get muddled too.

But when you spit, do you really get the best out of the wine? Do you really understand it, tease out its nuances, share its emotions, delve into its past, its present and its future? Well, I don't think so. Wine is made to drink. And I think if you are really going to 'get' the wine, you need to drink it.

I've been at grand tastings where they serve forty vintages of some terribly smart Bordeaux or Burgundy or vintage port. I am grateful for the invitation but I often sit there, surrounded by desperately serious, unsmiling wine experts, wondering whether the smear of wine in the glass will allow me two attempts to taste it, or do I have to lick it all up in one tiny go. I am grateful for the invitation. But if I wanted to really understand the wine, I would *so* much prefer to have perhaps half a dozen vintages, half a dozen good-humoured enthusiasts, preferably with a ruddy blush to their cheeks. And half a dozen good full glasses of these wonderful wines, which we would then *drink*, not chisel away at like rodents trying to chew their way through a Doric column.

Wine is for drinking. Even the greatest wines in the world – especially the greatest wines in the world – are supposed to fill us with the gorgeous hilarity of life, the overflowing delight in existence, the exuberance of experiencing and sharing something special. These rare wines are not something to be marked out of 100. Not something to be rated and categorised and deconstructed. Not something to be merely tasted in a competitive, jealous atmosphere. Great wine is to be drunk, with generosity, with subjectivity, with love.

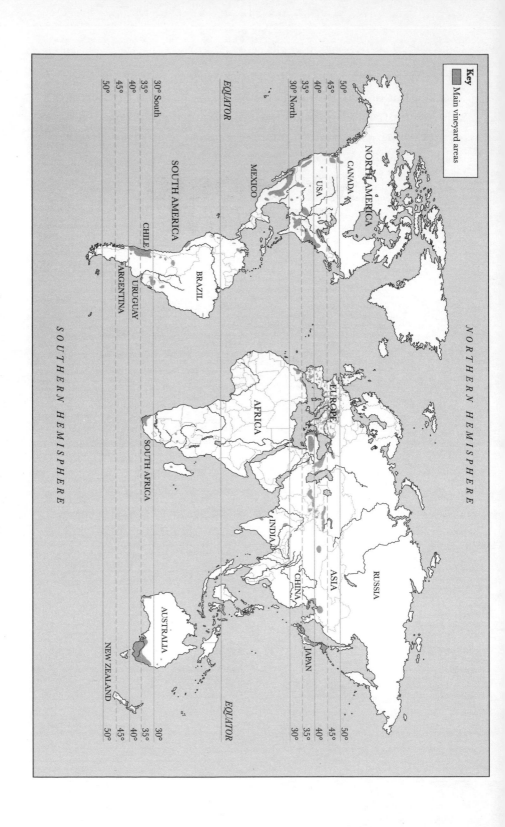

Key
■ Main vineyard areas

NORTHERN HEMISPHERE

SOUTHERN HEMISPHERE

NORTH AMERICA
CANADA
USA
MEXICO
SOUTH AMERICA
CHILE
BRAZIL
ARGENTINA
URUGUAY
EUROPE
AFRICA
SOUTH AFRICA
INDIA
ASIA
CHINA
JAPAN
RUSSIA
AUSTRALIA
NEW ZEALAND

EQUATOR
30° North
35°
40°
45°
50°
30° South
35°
40°
45°
50°

EQUATOR
30°
35°
40°
45°
50°
30°
35°
40°
45°
50°

MY WORLD
OF WINE

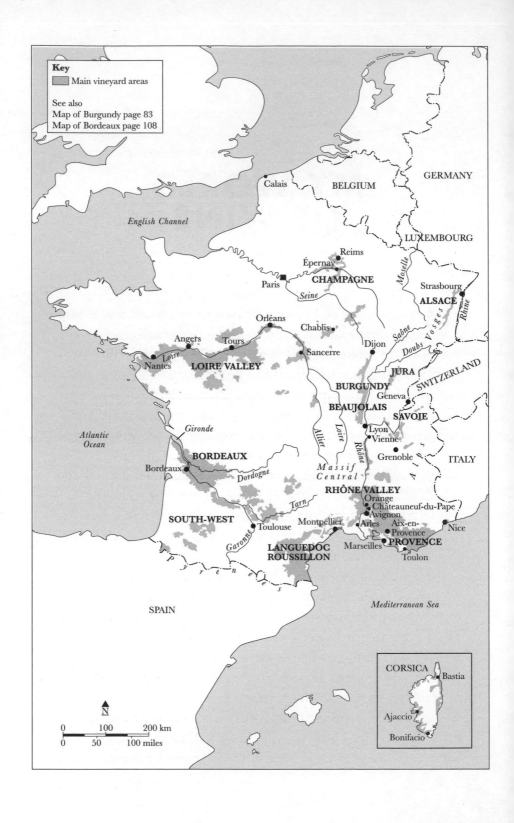

See also
Map of Burgundy page 83
Map of Bordeaux page 108

France

Birthplace of the classic wine styles

My first sight of France was from the top of the White Cliffs of Dover. My father and I had clambered up the pathway to a promontory that stuck out like an academic's nose high above the bustling harbour. And over the Channel, at the last contour of the horizon, I could see France. I could see that France had white cliffs, too. And I could imagine the scuffle and bustle of the port of Calais, as the curve of the world dipped away from me. 'That's where it all starts,' said my father. 'The warm south. The magical south. The mystical south. That's where it all starts.' So when I finally went to foreign lands, I thought this is where I would go. And as I daydreamed in cold, wet Britain, it was about this warm place, this magical place, this southern place called France.

Of course, it wasn't wine to start with. It was the smell and crunch of fresh baguettes, it was the bitter-sweet creaminess of great steaming bowls of café au lait and their hard rectangles of shiny, brittle sugar. It was white peaches, and orange melons, and tomatoes the size of a fist, and butter without salt and slices of strange, sour, oozing cheeses that smelt as though they needed a good wash. And, just a tiny bit, it was wine. We weren't a wine-drinking family. Yet on holiday my father would bring back a litre bottle of what he called 'Onze Degrés' – the basic workman's red – from the market, and he would drink it pensively out of a tumbler at lunch. And I got a splash, well watered down, of this raw, fierce chewy brew. France doesn't make wines like that any more, but I sometimes wish it did. It was my first experience of real wine, and of course I occasionally pine for its rough kiss once again.

So it wasn't the flame of wine's exciting possibilities that France lit for me; it really was the flame of the warm south, of the magic of abroad. Wine became part of it, then wine began to dominate it, but to this day I get as big a thrill from going to France as to any other country. I even like Calais. And I think I'm very lucky, because if any country can claim to be the world's finest, most fascinating, most original, most influential wine producer – now; for the last two thousand years; and into the foreseeable future – it is France. And whereas with many other countries that I have discovered later in my life wine has almost been divorced from the culture and emotion of the country, with France it has all been intertwined right from the start.

Above all, France is in the right place. The northern borders of France are at about 50° North. Although global warming is playing havoc with the old concepts, the general feeling for the last couple of thousand years has been that this is about as far north as the *Vitis vinifera* – the Mediterranean/Middle Eastern species of vine that has produced all the decent wines of the world – will ripen. There is now a vineyard near Calais. And there's a vineyard on top of an old slag heap at a disused coal mine a bit further inland. No one is making any claims for the quality of their wines. And the southern French border is at about 42° North in the torrid, sun-bleached vineyards of Roussillon on the Spanish frontier, where the grapes struggle not to overripen and shrivel on the vine. Between these two latitudes, all the classic red, white and sparkling wine styles of the world developed. And you say, what about Germany and Riesling? Almost all Germany's best vineyards are just below 50° North. And what about Barolo and Chianti in Italy? Barolo is on the same latitude as the best vineyards of

Bordeaux, and Chianti is about level with the mouth of the Rhône Valley.

German wine certainly had considerable prestige in earlier centuries and German winemakers did have an influence in the New World. Italian wine has only developed prestige in the last couple of generations. France, with the Mediterranean on one coast and the Atlantic on another, and possessing the only navigable routes between the south and north of Europe, was strategically placed in terms of trade and political influence. The styles of wine she developed were easy to export and became the models for quality, both in terms of what foreigners would like to drink, and then what they would like to emulate. If you look at modern California, Australia, South Africa, Chile, Argentina and New Zealand, the grape varieties that dominate their quality vineyards are overwhelmingly from the French classic regions, and the styles of wine they make and the methods they employ are based on the French classics – above all, those of Champagne, Burgundy, the Rhône Valley and Bordeaux.

Now, I made my reputation, above all else, as the champion of the new. I embraced Australian Chardonnay, New Zealand Sauvignon Blanc, Californian Cabernet Sauvignon and Chilean Merlot with unseemly enthusiasm. I adored the ripe, boisterous, self-confident and inquisitive way that these new countries took the old classics and reworked them. Their soils were usually different from those of France, which has a positively unjust percentage of the vine's favourite soil – limestone clays. Their climate was always different and the weather was almost always warmer and sunnier and more predictable than in a typical Bordeaux or Burgundy ripening season. And as the twenty-first century has unfolded, it has become increasingly evident that France has been willing to learn from the New World, just as the Californians and Australians and Chileans have always made the pilgrimage back to France to see how the masters did things. A French accent is now just as frequently heard in a Napa Valley winery as an Australian one in a Burgundy or Bordeaux cellar. With climate change, this flow of ideas and experiences will become ever more important. And, for me, I become ever more fascinated by returning to my old tasting haunts in France, to the wine regions that gave me my first thrills and my first understanding of what wine could be – and I still search out the crunchy baguette, the oozing cheese, the juicy white peach and the bowl of steaming café au lait in a roadside bistro to wake me up before my first tasting of the day.

Is Champagne still the best?

I thought I would look at some of the French regions and some of their wines that have moved me the most. I won't be covering every single area. Sometimes I just don't have much to say about them and there are a few that I just don't know very well. So let's start with one I do know well, but with which I've had a troubled relationship. Champagne. I got banned from Champagne. For telling the truth. This was in the 1990s and they didn't seem to be keen on the truth just then. Quality was slipping, prices were rising, and PR was apparently considered to be a good deal more important than the flavour of the drink. So I went out on a limb and did a front-page newspaper article entitled 'Champagne. Who needs it?' I had been tasting the big, well-known labels – they are the same ones now as they were then – and the wines were rubbish. But I had thrown a New World joker into one tasting – Mumm's Napa Valley rosé from California. Cheaper than Mumm's Cordon Rouge Champagne. And much better – and I said so.

This didn't go down well. The PR people said, 'Let's ban him, young whippersnapper. That'll show him. No more samples. No more trips.' Of course, there were a few young whippersnappers in Champagne who were also fed up with how the great name of Champagne was being dragged downward in the pursuit of gold. They sent me all the stuff about how I was to be banned. And they sent me more. The boss of one of the biggest Champagne houses circulated a letter saying 'I don't think the ordinary people should be able to afford Champagne. We must keep it as a deluxe product. Raise the price.' My friends sent me a copy of the letter. And, two weeks before Christmas on BBC prime-time television, I was able to wave the letter and say, 'I tell you what: let's help him. Don't buy Champagne.' And we didn't. British sales of Champagne dropped by nearly 40 per cent in the next year.

Champagne has been about PR and marketing ever since the seventeenth century. Bubbles and fizz, laughter, gaiety, wit and flirtation. I have loved it for that and so have millions of others. But behind the razzmatazz, it can be a really serious wine, made from really serious grapes, grown in individual vineyards that deserve recognition and respect. In other words, we should be prepared to treat Champagne like any other fine wine. Serious wine with bubbles? Yes.

The big Champagne companies have largely concentrated on telling us that all the magic happens in the cellar, that it's only by blending wines from numerous different plots of land and different villages that a delicious end product can be arrived at, and that a wine from a single vineyard won't have the balance and flavour to be enjoyed by itself. To be honest, until this century there might have been some truth in this, but these shortcomings were largely self-inflicted. The general belief is that you need barely ripe grapes to make the best sparkling wine. So Champagne, north-east of Paris and not blessed with too much in the way of clear skies and golden sun, is perfect for that. But in marginal conditions you have to limit your crop. A vine can't ripen any extra fruit. Yet the yields in Champagne's vineyards have been stratospheric. In marginal conditions you should also take great care to cherish your vineyard land, yet Champagne has employed some outrageous techniques to keep the vines pumping fruit, both chemical and, in one now discredited method, by using the rubbish from Paris as fertiliser. And this was for the most glamorous, ritzy wine in the world!

Bizarre. It showed just how removed from agricultural reality Champagne had become.

It's all changing for the better. Global warming, for a start, is making a massive difference. Few of France's vineyard areas seem to be affected quite as much as Champagne. In 2015, the big companies reported that they had to stop picking grapes on several days because it was so hot the juice was literally cooking inside the grapes. But, in general, climate change has meant that producers all over the region who look after their vineyards properly can now get a ripe crop of grapes, even in villages that were deemed inferior in the old days. And the best villages, those classified as Grand Cru or Premier Cru by the authorities, are now producing grapes that give really thrilling flavours and don't need blending at all. All over the region, the growers are growing in confidence and a new generation is treating these much-abused plots of vines with new respect. And the wines are transformed. Until this century, even though so many Champagnes seemed to be devoid of personality, Champagnes being made and sold by the growers themselves were still thin on the ground, and because we'd been brainwashed into thinking the froth, the fizz, the effect, was everything, these sparkling wines with tons of flavour were a bit unnerving. Not any more. Now they're delicious and they're everywhere. Each village offers you numerous chances to look at the vines, meet the maker and taste the wine. Big companies are all very well. Their hospitality suites and tasting chambers, their bilingual guides and silky video presentations, are all very well. But to understand a region and its wines you have to get back to the basics of the land, the growers and the wines they themselves produce. And now, at last in Champagne, you can.

And it's worth the effort. Champagne has three major grape varieties – the black Pinot Noir and Pinot Meunier, and the white Chardonnay – all of which give different flavours to the wines. The Pinot Noir has more weight, more fatness, its flavour is likely to suggest red fruits like strawberry or, if you're very lucky, Morello cherries, even though these might seem slightly bruised. Pinot Meunier sometimes tastes slightly bruised, too, but more like bruised apples, and these might be mildly baked and maybe even have a dash of cream. Chardonnay at its best is more delicate in texture, its bubble seems finer, more like foam than froth, but the cool apple and lemon fruit is often dashed with cream and laid on a bed of baguette crust and hazelnuts. Typically, these three grapes are all blended together, but some of the best Champagnes nowadays don't feel the need to blend and sell themselves as a single-variety wine.

The heart of Champagne is around the city of Reims and the town of Épernay. Between them lies the low, wooded Montagne de Reims, with every patch of sloping land laden with vines and where villages like Bouzy make stern, powerful wines, mostly from Pinot Noir. The River Marne runs through Épernay and has a fair number of vines on its banks, some of them, as at Äy, among the best of all. And south of the Montagne de Reims, a ridge of pale chalk runs away toward the sun. This is the Côte des Blancs, where most of the grapes are Chardonnay and some, from villages like Le Mesnil, are the most fragrant and ethereal in all Champagne. These three areas are the core of Champagne, but so valuable are the grapes that go to make the world's most expensive sparkling wines that pockets of vines crop up to the north of Reims and to the west and south of Épernay. Some of these are now quite substantial. Côte de Sézanne, below the Côte des Blancs, is another good place to find soft, creamy Chardonnay fizz, while there are numerous other scraps of vines until we get to the last sizeable chunk, well to the south, with the Aube and the Côte des Bar and their broad-featured, juicy Pinot Noir.

Alsace – on the French side of the Rhine

You could be excused for wondering what country you were in. The name Alsace sounds French enough, but all the little

towns and villages sound awfully German, with most of their
names ending in –heim or –wihr. And everyone seems to have
a German surname. The wine comes in tall, thin bottles, just
like in Germany. Everybody seems to be growing Riesling, just
like in Germany. They even like sauerkraut. Well, keep your
thoughts to yourself, because for considerable chunks of time
Alsace has been part of Germany and it didn't like it. They do
mostly have German surnames, but they all sport French first
names. And they call sauerkraut *choucroute*, and add *à l'alsacienne*
to make sure you get the message. If the subject ever comes up,
you will find that most Alsatians are fiercely French.

But you can't escape the fact that Germany is right next
door. Alsace is wedged between the Rhine to the east, which
is the German border, and the Vosges Mountains to the west.
In the Middle Ages Alsace was culturally German rather than
French. Napoleon then annexed the left bank of the Rhine,
only for Prussia to retake Alsace in 1870, during the Franco-
Prussian War. France got it back in 1918, lost it again in the
Second World War and only finally retrieved it in 1945. So this
dual identity is properly rooted in history, even if the French
persuasion is in the ascendant at the moment. When it comes
to wine identity, Alsace owes a good deal to its German past.

During the most recent German years its vineyards were
used to provide large amounts of cheap hooch – the Germans
had their own prime vineyards along the Mosel and Rhine;
they didn't have any interest in seeing how good Alsace vineyards might be. Indeed, a lot of the best hillside sites were
abandoned, and some pretty ropey high-volume grape varieties
were planted in fertile fields where they would give the biggest
crop. But this meant that, after 1945, Alsace could virtually
start from scratch without any baggage of wine styles and wine
traditions. Even so, the most important, high-quality grape
varieties Alsace had were German, not French. And there did
seem to be some distaste among the French wine Establishment
for Alsace. To this day, if you try to plant Alsace grape varieties

like Gewurztraminer or Riesling in other parts of France you will feel the full force of the law come down on you in no time. They are not allowed. So why not be different to the rest of France? And that's exactly what Alsace decided to do.

There was no *appellation contrôlée* system in Alsace, so they could decide what suited them best. Nowadays we take it for granted that the grape variety's name will be printed on the label – most of the time we think of wine according to its grape variety rather than its country of origin; it tells us what the wine will taste like. No one in France did that in 1945. When Alsace decided to label its wines by grape variety, and with the one regional appellation, Alsace, rather than loads of sub-divisions like in Burgundy, it was revolutionary. They have now intro-duced some sub-divisions like Grand Cru for the best sites, but most of the wines you come across will still have labels that are a model of simplicity – producer's name, grape variety and Alsace. The producers decided that all Alsace wines would have to be bottled in the region. Again, no other French wine region did that. As to how they wanted to make their wines, well, you could say this harked back to the best traditional German prac-tices, too. Although in the second half of the twentieth century German wines came to be seen as invariably on the sweet side, and increasingly on the bland side, too, this wasn't how German wines used to be. They used to be dry, and as full-bodied as the year's weather would allow. And just occasionally they would be intensely sweet, when the noble rot fungus would strike and shrivel the grapes into a mess of virtually pure sugar on the vine. But innocuous, bland, vaguely sweet? Certainly not.

Alsace wines have typically been a blind taster's delight, because the grape variety's character shone so brightly. The Riesling had such fabulous lime acidity, and positively lickable minerality, drizzled with honey. The Gewurztraminer was unbelievably scented with rose petal, lychee and Nivea Creme, yet would usually have a teasing peppery bite to liven up its waxy texture. The Muscat was the most beautifully grapey wine in France, like crunching your teeth into a Muscat berry picked straight from the hothouse vine. The Pinot Gris allowed you to indulge in louche reveries about exactly what was that intriguing, sweaty dirtiness that only served to make the honey and droopy yellow apple and goldengage plums all the more fascinating. And all the wines would be dry. This was the magic, and sometimes still is. But the bane of Alsace wines now is too much ripeness and too much sweetness. Endless talk of the perfect maturity of grapes and the need to let them hang long into the balmy autumn days has meant sacrificing the irresistible drinkability of the wines for something heavier, possibly more impressive, but definitely less enjoyable. And frequently sweet.

Alsace does make some wines sweet on purpose – there is a category called Vendange Tardive (late harvest) and a much sweeter Sélection de Grains Nobles, which usually means the grapes have been beneficially attacked by noble rot (as in Bordeaux's Sauternes region). But it's the sweetness and the softening of the wines I expect to be dry that gets my goat. Part of this is to do with an entirely commendable involvement with the most ecologically sensitive biodynamic movement you will find almost anywhere on the planet. Part of it is a desire to move the wines away from tasting of their grape variety and toward being more expressive of the vineyards and soils they come from. As such, I have to respect a lot of the current wines without necessarily enjoying them that much. This may be partly my own fault. You have to devote a lot of attention and time to trying to understand many of the new-wave 'back to nature' wines for whom varietal brightness is something the maker may be determined to avoid.

But I rather like varietal brightness. Extra ripening of the grapes and leaving residual sugar in the wine blur the pinpoint loveliness of these flavours. A determination to allow uncontrolled natural fermentations, with the yeast rather than the winemaker in charge of its progress, may produce some impressive gems, but, again, I'm rather fond of the winemaker having a vision of flavour rather than letting the terroir have total say. I have just opened about eight Rieslings, Gewurztraminers, Muscats and Pinot Gris from under my stairs. Just one of them – a Riesling at 12.5 per cent alcohol from a vineyard inside the city of Colmar that I'd never heard of – lifted my spirits. And then I remembered. I had a Trimbach 2010 Riesling – pure, minerally, wonderfully challenging to my palate, just starting to honey up – at 12.5 per cent. And I had a couple of bottles of Domaine Weinbach, a Riesling Schlossberg 2013 as crunchy as green apples and as rasping as peach skin yet scented and almost fat with golden peach yogurt richness, but bone dry; and a Pinot Gris Altenbourg 2013 – wonderfully rich, packed with peach and pear and custard apple fruit, flecked with honey and streaked with the corrupt sharp acid of the slightly burnt brown skin of a baked apple. And dry. And then I remembered why I love Alsace.

The Jura, home of *vin jaune*

I don't go to the Jura much, but I should. In this stressed, urban frenzy of life, the Jura is quite possibly the most relaxing, the most mentally soothing, of all France's wine regions. Tiny villages packed in under the brow of great forest-covered rocks; sometimes the villages actually perch on the rocks, teetering like limestone icing on a geological cupcake. The vineyards spread away beneath the houses and the dark trees, but there aren't many of them; this is France's smallest wine region, the vines dappled among the foothills of the Jura mountains. And though most of the wine is bright and pleasant fizzy Crémant or some frequently impressive Chardonnay that wouldn't look out of place in Burgundy, directly west across the becalmed Saône Valley, what gives Jura its bragging rights is *vin jaune*, or yellow wine.

This isn't one bit like your normal wine. *Vin jaune* sits in a barrel for up to six years, without being topped up, and it grows a thin layer of yeast on its surface, as transparent as an aged diva's skin yet as shifty as an oil slick on fresh water. The cellars are wilfully less than clean, and as you wander from oak barrel to acacia barrel to old whisky barrel to clay amphora and concrete egg, the smells change all the time. They are never clinical or bright, but always risky, adventurous and fascinating – animal, vegetable, fruit, mineral, dirty or washed, each one different but all bound together by the sweet-sour aroma of acetaldehyde, and with an attack on your palate that can be as sharp as a bee sting.

The acetaldehyde is the same smell as dry sherry has, but sherry is soft in comparison to *vin jaune* or its rare star performer, Château-Chalon. The flavours range through citrus fruits like blood orange, grapefruit and Sorrento lemon, but they're not fresh, they're wizened, they're crabby yet concentrated, and the perfumes flirt with exotic oils like bergamot. I'm normally a purist when I taste wine, keeping my palate fresh with wine until I have made up my mind. Yet with *vin jaune*, I cram my mouth with Comté cheese, with its enormous umami of scalded cream, the skin of crème brûlée and the bubbling brown edge of a rarebit. In fact, sometimes I cram the cheese and the *vin jaune* into my mouth together, and they play off each other, because *vin jaune* by itself is exhausting. But sitting on a balcony gazing west over the Saône Valley, already grey with dusk as the pink setting sun still warms you with its last few rays, a glass of *vin jaune* and a sliver of Comté can truly bring you heartsease.

Burgundy – Pinot Noir and Chardonnay nirvana?

Burgundy starts slowly enough. You turn off the Autoroute du Soleil a couple of hours south of Paris in the midst of broad, windswept arable fields. Not a vine in sight. But the road sign says Chablis to the left. So that's where you go. If you're lucky the sun may be shining. It does sometimes. Most of the time it doesn't. Especially in winter. Actually, don't visit Chablis in winter unless you have an unhealthy predilection for the cold.

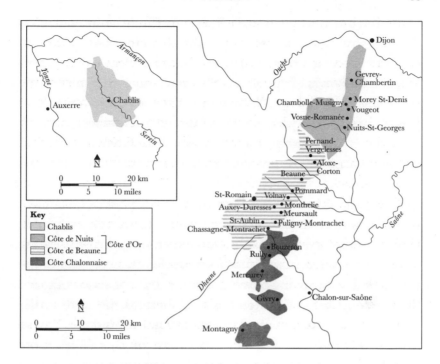

Everything in Chablis is cold. The air is so cold as you descend into the little valley of the River Serein that you expect its dampness to turn to tiny shards of ice on your cheeks. The vines on their river slopes look exhausted and blackened by cold. The wine cellars are so chilly that you need to check your toes and fingers are still alive after half an hour. And the wine – the wine is cold; its very heart is pale and cold.

But this is a coldness that you want to run right through the year. Not just in deepest winter, but in the watery sun of midsummer, too. Because Chablis wine, made from the Chardonnay grape, is, at its best, the coldest, the haughtiest, the least alluring of all Burgundy wines, but, in this warming world, something fantastically precious that simply may not exist in a generation's time. Already too many Chablis wines have added tints of gold to the frosty green that used to warn of the austere, challenging dryness a glass would offer to your palate. Sun and heat have begun, irregularly, to creep into Chablis' fields, and have added oatmeal and even honey to the flavours, nuttiness to the texture, and the strong acidity is being massaged back from its mineral brink. On the top wines, the Grands Crus and the Premiers Crus, new oak barrel sweetness makes me shake my head and say, 'Why would they do this?' To make it taste more like the Meursaults of Burgundy's warmer belly, or even the Chardonnays of another country? Chablis – catch it while you can. But be prepared for the cold. Without it Chablis isn't Chablis.

Your entry into the Côte d'Or, the Golden Slope of Burgundy, is much more dramatic. Speeding down the Autoroute du Soleil from the vines around Chablis, you won't see a hint of anything to do with wine until, suddenly – *wham* – you sweep out of the forests and hills, slicing down a sharp gully, and shoot out into the glorious open. Vines to the left, vines to the right, vines beneath and above you. And in a mere minute it's done. You've driven over one of the wider bits of Burgundy's fabled Côte d'Or, and it's taken you a minute to be past the vines and on to the flatlands beyond. There really isn't very much to the heart of Burgundy at all. At its narrowest it would take more like ten seconds to speed across. And in these tiny vineyards squeezed between the dark woods and the flat, sullen plains, many of the world's most famous wines are made.

So get off the autoroute and head north on the A74. Keep your eyes peeled and almost immediately the hill of Corton with its dark brow of forest rises high above the road to the left. Then forest and rocks and the rough shoulders of hills press in for a mile or two, until at Prémeaux and Nuits St-Georges the real glories start. And they are glories. If you're at all thrilled by Burgundy, above all by red Burgundy, by the history of wine, by the fabled flavours that writers have struggled to describe for a thousand years, then just reading these road signs should excite you. Vosne-Romanée, Clos de Vougeot, Chambolle-Musigny, Morey-St-Denis, Gevrey-Chambertin – they're all here. Read the signs, take the tiny tracks that lead up through the vines into the villages. Stop among the vineyards. If it's late summer, pick a grape and chew on it with your eyes closed, dreaming of the wine it should have become. Would its wine have tasted 'of silk and lace . . . a damp garden . . . a rose and a violet covered in morning dew'? If it was a grape from the tiny vineyard of Musigny, it might have done.

When I first parked my yellow Mini next to the vines of Romanée-Conti and wondered if I dared steal a grape (I did . . .), I don't think I had ever had a great red Burgundy wine. But I had read about them. I had drunk Burgundies, not many, but without much pleasure. And my letters of introduction to local Burgundy merchants didn't seem to be helping. I would taste through ranges of their wines, all dull, none resembling the glorious flavours I had read about in the old-timers' books. Well, I got lucky just once, and it taught me a lesson. I was at a merchant's called Charles Viénot in Nuits St-Georges. Their range was the usual dull stuff, except for one heavenly, savoury, chocolatey, velvety Nuits St-Georges 1966. Of course. They owned some local vines and they had taken care: this was *their* wine. Most of the other stuff appeared to have been bought in at the lowest price they could get away with, regardless of style, and blended away. But not their Nuits St-Georges. They knew these vines and they cared. And from then on, I understood one enormously important principle about Burgundy. You have to deal with the people who own the land and make their own wine. There are some good merchants now in Burgundy, but they also own vineyards and all their best wines come from the vineyards they own.

Pinot Noir is a delicate grape, a moody grape, a transparent grape, an emotional grape. You can't treat it badly. It has a thin skin; it reacts unpredictably to good weather and adolescently to bad. Rough winemaking reveals bitter threads that you didn't imagine the grape could contain. Infinite sensitivity is how you will coax out whatever flavours the grapes might possess. The late Henri Jayer, the greatest red Burgundy master of all, talked of making his wines as if he were extracting just the perfume from a tisane of chamomile or lime leaves or verbena, where you need to cajole the leaves into releasing their scent but you also need to understand that the scent has its roots in the bitter oils of the plant. At the moment you find the most perfect expression of the scent, you will already have roused the bitterness that can swarm out of its lair and spoil the drink even as you are lifting the leaves from the pot.

Henri Jayer is gone, but it's wonderfully reassuring that he was the hero for a whole new generation of Burgundians. I wasn't wrong on my early trips to Burgundy in the 1970s. The wines *were* mostly rubbish; many of the vineyards had been brutalised by chemicals and fertilisers – above all, by those based on potassium. Clones of Pinot Noir that offered massive yields of colourless, flavourless wines had been planted in even the greatest vineyard sites. Professor Claude Bourguignon, Burgundy's most respected soil scientist, gloomily reported in the 1980s that the soil in many of Burgundy's best sites had as much life in it as the sands of the Sahara. Surveying some of the best sites in Vosne-Romanée, he said it would take him ten years to get some life back into these famous soils. Yet Burgundy is where the whole concept of each tiny site being special and different has been developed over a thousand years. How can the site matter so much if the soil is dead? How indeed. One grower with holdings in such superlative vineyards as Chambertin told me during the 1980s, 'My father made great wine, my son will make great wine, but I have never made great wine.' The family had had their vineyards wrecked during the Second World War. He had had a family to feed and he did whatever was necessary to survive. I bought a case of his Chapelle-Chambertin 1985 almost out of pity. I should have spared my tears and saved my money.

But he was right about his son, who is making exceptional wines entirely because he has rejected his father's philosophy, which had put bread on the table in the lean years. When delicacy and perfume and a certain silky or satiny or velvety feel to the wines is what Burgundy devotees crave, and yet the red wine world seems to have been enslaved by the drugs of density and deep colours, high alcohol and insane use of new wood for the best part of a generation, radical steps needed to be taken. And what Burgundy has done, more than any other world-famous wine area, is to embrace the tenets of biodynamic vine cultivation. Which means what?

Well, I talk about it a bit more on pages 38–9, but a lot of it is simply going back to what the old-timers did a century ago. Biodynamism also involves using homeopathic sprays at certain phases of the grapes' ripening period. To be honest, I have no idea if and how these things work, and clearly some of the most articulate and successful Burgundy producers don't know either, even though they are prepared to try the methods out. But many of Burgundy's most fragrant, most succulent, most thought-provoking wines are being produced by this new generation of biodynamic growers. I sometimes wonder whether it's just that the sensitive, the emotionally intelligent producers are the ones who are drawn to biodynamism, and what happens is that they nurture and cherish their vineyards with a positively traditional, compassionate commitment, and that delivers to their winery small crops of really beautiful grapes that a deft touch in the cellar can turn into fabulous wines.

For which they charge you increasingly prodigious sums. Well, there are ways of finding slightly more affordable red Burgundies, even if they don't quite propel you up the stairway to Pinot Paradise. The Côte d'Or is divided into two halves. I've been talking about the northern half, the Côte de Nuits, where the most famous and most compelling red wine villages are, and virtually every vine is Pinot Noir. The southern half is called the Côte de Beaune after the town of Beaune, where, by the way, there is no McDonald's. Not many towns can boast of that. The slope of vines here isn't so narrow or so single-minded as further north. All the best white Burgundies come from this section, from Chardonnay vines growing in villages like Meursault and Puligny-Montrachet. And the reds don't have the amazingly focused personality that the Côte de Nuits can have. The best-known reds come from Volnay, Pommard and Beaune. They are never as expensive as the ones from the north. And there are various little side valleys cutting into the slopes, each with a village or two, each with some lesser-known vineyards which make pretty nice wine for a lot less money. Pernand-Vergelesses, Monthélie, Auxey-Duresses, St-Romain and St-Aubin are all names that just might give you a cut-price Burgundy thrill.

You are even more likely to get at least the cut price if you keep on heading south. The compact slopes of the Côte d'Or become jumbled and thrown about as you continue into the Côte Chalonnaise. Here, it's a lot more difficult to get the conditions just right for ripening red grapes as the vineyards dip and dive, though Mercurey does pretty well. But the soil is limestoney and good, and whites from villages like Bouzeron, Rully and Montagny produce tasty stuff from Aligoté and Chardonnay grapes. Keep drifting south, the countryside becomes calmer, warmer, the gentle slopes roll and dally, except for when a couple of astonishing bull-nosed outcrops of rock loom out above the vines of Pouilly-Fuissé. This is the Mâconnais region. It's lovely. It's relaxing. And the wines are affordable. The wines are chubbier, juicier than they are further north, but they're less expensive too, and as the Côte d'Or prices become sillier, the good whites of the Mâconnais seem to become more attractive every vintage.

And then there's Beaujolais. If ever a red wine was supposed to have a smile on its face, that's Beaujolais. But I wonder how many of us have even tried it? And how many of us have ever had a mouthful of Beaujolais Nouveau, let alone a throatful, a bellyful, a dayful of Beaujolais Nouveau? You had to be there.

Luckily for some of you, you are too young to have the slightest idea what life was like in Britain in the 1970s and '80s. Pretty grim on the whole. And since global warming hadn't yet kicked in, November – gloomy, sullen, damp, chilly November, with the summer now a distant drizzly memory and winter bedding in for another five months at least – was the worst month of all. Wasn't there any way we could cheer ourselves up for the long soggy haul to spring? Well, yes, there was. And it was a wine called Beaujolais Nouveau. The new vintage wine from Beaujolais was offered for sale on 15 November each year. Most of it sploshed its way to the cafés and bars of Lyon and Paris, where it was necked at a great rate, accompanied by platters of sausages and slabs of cheese. It was the first wine of the new vintage. Most of it was never even bottled – a jug would do fine. It was a celebration of whatever bounty nature was in the mood to offer that year. It was all very French, very good-natured and very natural.

Everything was about to change. In 1974 a *Sunday Times* journalist called Allan Hall jokingly offered a prize of a bottle of Champagne to the first person who turned up at his office in London on 15 November with a bottle of the new wine. It was just a wheeze, an afterthought in his weekly column. Perhaps he knew what he was inventing, but I doubt it. Yet there is nothing that strange breed of eccentrics called the British like better than a proper race with a ludicrous objective. Beaujolais to London is at least 800 kilometres (500 miles). He wasn't expecting anyone until somewhere around lunchtime, at which point he would take the winning bottle to meet its fate with his friends around the corner.

The winner panted up the stairs of *The Sunday Times* at 3 a.m. Don't worry – he hadn't driven all that way in three hours. He had flown in a private aeroplane, but hordes of people did drive, at breakneck speed, until three years later the police said 'Obey the law, sunshine, or you will be enjoying your Beaujolais Nouveau at Her Majesty's Pleasure.' And the race just fired the imagination of the nation. Britain took to Nouveau so enthusi-astically that sales increased by 1000 per cent a year. Beaujolais' most canny producer, Georges Duboeuf, saw the global possibil-ities, especially since he had isolated a type of yeast that worked on the Gamay grape to give the wine a banana and bubblegum flavour that didn't really seem like wine at all. It was absolutely a wine of its time. The 1960s generation were tired of a traditional wine world that had to be approached with dumb reverence and an old school tie. They were rule-breakers and they wanted a rule-breaking wine. They wanted a red wine you could chill in the fridge, drink out of a paper cup or a beer mug or a football boot, and which would go with any type of food you threw at it. The restless food of the 1980s – burgers, kebabs, pizza, Thai, Chinese and Mexican – it didn't matter: this sloshable, gulpable fruit bomb of purple-red barely wine could handle the lot.

Well, it made Beaujolais rich, which it deserved. This gen-uinely idyllic region of welcoming villages, vine-strewn slopes and dreamtime hills had been poverty-stricken for long enough, surviving by providing thirsty but parsimonious Lyon with her daily grog. But by the end of the 1980s, 60 per cent of all Beaujolais was sold – and paid for – in November as Nouveau. A shiny BMW could replace your rickety old Citroën 2CV, and it often did, but Nouveau also turned off as many genuine wine lovers as it turned on party animals. Nouveau's brash reputa-tion caused interest in the rest of Beaujolais to slump in North America and Europe. It is only now slowly clambering back. Thank goodness, because Beaujolais, either from the ten top villages or Crus that put their own name on the label (Fleurie, Morgon and Brouilly are probably the most famous of these), or from Beaujolais-Villages or even just under the plain label of Beaujolais, is one of France's most delightful red wines – low in alcohol, full of fruit and rarely using new oak. The French have a word for this – *gouleyant* – to describe wines that just flow down the throat and bring a glint to the eyes. Beaujolais is *gouleyant*.

Meandering through the Loire

I've always had a bit of a soft spot for 1982 reds. I even bought some of them by the case – Pauillacs, St-Estèphes, St-Émilions. But these are Bordeaux wines. Yes, I know, and I have had a lot of pleasure out of them. Yet the 1982 red that has been the most endlessly fascinating, the most unpredictable but marvellously drinkable, is not a wine from Bordeaux. It's an Anjou wine, from a tiny village near the Loire River that few people have heard of called Mazé, and from a grower called Richou. I bought twelve bottles of his Cuvée de Cabernet. I have two left and I trust them more than any of my Bordeaux superstars to thrill me when I finally open them. But those are the only bottles of Loire red I've got under the stairs. Why?

It's the same with Loire whites. When I was starting out in wine, the Loire was one of the only places in France that might offer me a mouthful of something bright and fresh. It looked as though the Loire was about to invent modern white wine in places like Sancerre and Pouilly, with their snappy, leafy, gooseberry and coffee bean-flavoured Sauvignon Blanc. So I should keep stocked up with the new vintage. But I don't. And I taste the Chenin Blancs, dry to sweet, and I taste the rudely fruity red Gamays and the occasionally impressive Pinot Noirs. But I don't buy them. It's as though the Loire always tries to catch my attention when I'm on the way to somewhere else. And perhaps I am.

In which case, I can only blame myself. The Loire is bang in the middle of France. It's France's longest river, plunging out of the Ardèche gorges not far from the southern Rhône Valley before surging northward to Orléans, which isn't far south of Paris, and then looping and lolling on its increasingly indolent way to the Bay of Biscay west of Nantes. In other words, it's easy to get to. If I'm in the Rhône Valley or Beaujolais, Burgundy or Paris, I can get to it. If I am on the way to Bordeaux I can stop off en route. And the Loire is one of the most hospitable wine areas in France, where the image of the generous, jolly *vigneron* ever prepared to open more bottles and settle in for the duration isn't dead. One of my best-ever visits was an afternoon and evening in the deep-dug cellars of Domaine de la Chevalière in Bourgueil. Why don't I have some of this deliciously juicy, earthy red ageing under my stairs? Ah well, more fool me. But I say that, and yet, and yet ... why don't I know the Loire better? One of the reasons may be that some of the wines I knew best have been superseded. Muscadet, the pale, rather stony, dry white wine from around Nantes was once touted as the white Beaujolais. And the Brits did drink a lot of it – unspeakably sulphurous and foul if bottled to a price by the brewery trade, or mild, innocuous but charmingly, forgettably thirst-quenching if bottled on the spot. But when the price went up, and we discovered the New World, that was more or less Muscadet's lot.

Discovering the New World didn't help the Loire's other white wines either. Sancerre and its mouthwatering Sauvignon Blanc wines did show in one appetising glimpse during the 1970s what the future of white wine might be. But the good practitioners were easily outnumbered by the mediocre, and when New Zealand roared onto the wine scene in the 1980s with Sauvignons that were much tastier, and generally cheaper, my head was turned. As places like South Africa and Chile showed that they could do Sauvignon too, and the Loire went into a long funk of making wines that seemed wilfully to avoid the zing and zip that had made them famous in the first place, I stayed away. Just now and then I would delve into Touraine, further down the valley, whose green-flecked Sauvignons at a decent price can still be some of France's most refreshing whites.

And as for Chenin Blanc – well, here's one of the big arguments that wine people used to have. Was it actually a world-class grape variety or not? I have to say, if it was simple majority voting, I would say not. This is a late-ripening grape, which, until global warming came along to hurry things through a bit, frequently lived up to its reputation by not ripening at all. And this reputation wasn't helped by the fact that Vouvray, Chenin's most famous wine from just outside Tours, and, in the hands of a few experts, its most interesting, was available cheap, not quite dry, and always sulphurous, on every supermarket shelf. It was hard work persuading yourself, let alone everybody else, to trade up to the real thing. Even the proper Vouvray can be quite a challenge, but that's because you are supposed to age it. Vouvray does sometimes have a bright, fresh burst of greengage plum fruit right from the start, but that is usually accompanied by some pretty brusque minerality and acidity, and it usually fades after a couple of years and then you just have to wait. And after ten to twenty years, you might be blessed with a wine ebbing toward orange gold but with a remarkable taste of stewed peach and pear skins, a more soothing minerality, like the slipperiness of crumbly chalk after a shower of rain, and maybe, along with an acidity which is now better disguised by age, a unique mixture of buttermilk texture and the unfamiliar richness of quince marmalade. And that *is* worth waiting for.

Even so, I think I'd age the sweet Chenins rather than the dry. Vouvray can be sweet, but there are a couple of areas in Anjou, just south of the Loire Valley, where they get the same sunny, misty, humid vintage conditions as Sauternes in Bordeaux. When everything comes together – morning mist, sunny afternoons, no rain – the Chenin grapes start to develop the same sweetness-intensifying noble rot fungus, and all that peach and quince and goldengage fruit with its screechy grapefruit pith acidity gets scented with bergamot and chamomile, and wrapped in syrup and honey. Bonnezeaux, Coteaux du Layon and Quarts de Chaume are the names to look for. I do have a couple of bottles tucked away. I should have a couple of cases.

It's just that I rarely seem to make a Loire wine my first choice. Saumur, Vouvray and Montlouis make very good sparkling wine, often quite haughty, almost arrogant in their style – hmm, maybe that's why I don't often choose them. The raspberry-scented, pebbly Cabernet Franc reds of Saumur-Champigny,

Chinon and Bourgueil should be exactly the kind of refreshing, low-to-no-oak reds that I might pick first for a summer
lunch, but I've let my enthusiasm for Cabernet Franc be fed by
other countries entirely – like Italy, Hungary, Argentina and
the USA. And it's the same with Chenin Blanc. To be honest,
Chenin isn't usually a first choice for me, except from South
Africa, where it is a bit warmer and sunnier, and then some of
my favourite examples are blended with grapes like Roussanne
and Marsanne, which I rather doubt would ripen in the muddy
fields of Anjou, even if they were permitted.

And yet perhaps there is one area where I do choose the
Loire first. And this is in the contentious but fascinating hinterland of biodynamic and 'natural' wines. I have stood at the
back of crowded rooms and listened to Nicolas Joly of Coulée
de Serrant in Savennières passionately explain why he is a total
believer in biodynamism, and why we all should be, too. And
I have enjoyed some of his wines, although I don't think I
really understand them; or him, for that matter. When a chap
announces, as Joly does, 'Before being good, a wine should be
true,' it doesn't do much for my thirst. And I don't much care
for being placed in a moral bind, as though when I say, 'Actually,
so long as the wine is made with integrity, I think the flavour
is more important than an ideology' this somehow makes me
ethically suspect.

Joly is merely the most visible and vocal of the Loire new
wave – and, fair enough, he's the original. But there is now a
band of brave grape growers and winemakers, particularly in
Anjou, who have decided to take grape growing and winemaking to its ultimate non-interventionist end. And I rather admire
them. I don't buy their wines by the dozen, but I do regularly
look for them when I'm in bars and restaurants and order them
by the glass, frequently being delighted by their self-confidence,
sometimes a little put off by their strangeness, but often reas-
sured by their purity and frankness. And sometimes they are
simply labelled as Vin de France, the lowest rank of French

wine. These unsophisticated hipsters don't need a bureaucrat's rules. Their ethical code is enough for them. And, hopefully, it will also allow them to make a living. On one of my first visits to Anjou in the 1980s, a book had just been published in Paris on all the wines of France. Anjou had been omitted. It was simply not worth writing about. Well, it is now.

The Rhône Valley: where my warm south starts

So where does my warm south start? Where does the chilly, damp north sweeten into the magical, mystical south? Certainly not in Chablis. Not in Burgundy's Côte d'Or, where the sun's rays seem apologetic except in the hottest years. Might it be in the Mâconnais, where the Chardonnays become lush and soft, and the angular defensive roofs of the houses with their storm-coloured slates give way to the confident terracotta warmth of the Mediterranean? Or are we not quite there yet? I don't think *I* am. I'm the one who stood on that windy Kent clifftop with my father, gazing out toward something rare and sweet to the south. I know that if I want to be in my warm south it will take me barely an hour from an airport. But that's too fast for me. I take the car, with my old yellow *Michelin Road Atlas* on the passenger seat beside me. I had the Beast, an old Porsche 911. I used to take it for a holiday on the wide, open, empty autoroutes of France. The fastest speeds I have ever done were in France, when I was giving the Beast her holiday thrills. I'm not proud of it now, but I once hit 210 kilometres (130 miles) an hour somewhere on an empty stretch of road between Calais and my warm south. Ah yes, my warm south.

I can't really feel the kiss of the south until I see the Rhône. And if I'm driving it's not a very pretty first sight. You need to keep calm in the scruffy, ill-tempered, overcrowded streets around Lyon railway station. But the road curves right and there it is – the mighty Rhône, surging through the centre of the city, and if I cling to her banks I'll be carried all the way to the welcoming Mediterranean world. I would stamp my feet on the floor of the Porsche and shout 'I'm going south! I'm going south!' Put me in a car and I still will.

And the knowledge that you're heading south really is the only source of joy for the first hour of your drive. It's as though the whole of Lyon's blotchy industrial lifeblood has been choked together into the river's narrow valley – factories, warehouses, cheap motels, railways, roads and power lines all clutter and jumble your path. But it's all worth it. Soon after Vienne the autoroute soars across the Rhône and out into open countryside. Take the next exit. Stop the car and gaze west to one of the world's most remarkable vineyards, Côte-Rôtie, the Roasted Slope.

This slope is so steep the vines look like a patchwork quilt that has been stuck on to the rock face. And the closer you get to them, the more forbidding they seem. Take any of the tiny single-track roads that twist up to the brow of the vines and I swear you will think your car is about to topple backward, so fierce is the gradient. Apply the handbrake and leave the car in gear. Step out. Way below you are the houses of Ampuis, silent and tiny beside the grand sweep of the Rhône. Don't drop anything, unless you want to decapitate a passing pedestrian at the foot of the hill. Don't try to scramble down the slithery granite rubble in your smart city shoes. The conditions here are so stark that it's difficult to believe anyone would willingly work the vines. Well, they almost didn't. Within living memory the price of a litre of Côte-Rôtie's red wine was less than the price of a kilo of peaches. Abandoned vines outnumbered those still being worked, as children left the village for factory life in Lyon. Just to the south, the almost equally precipitous slopes of Condrieu were virtually abandoned, despite making one of the world's greatest white wines. In 1965 there were only 8 hectares (20 acres) of vineyard left, their old, diseased Viognier vines producing paltry crops – one vintage produced a mere 1900 litres (418 gallons) of Condrieu wine. When I first braved those slopes in the 1980s, the wine was still sufficiently under-appreciated that I was offered it cheap and by the jug as a local restaurant's house white. Côte-Rôtie was the house red. It's now common to see bottles from the south of France, Australia, California, Virginia and South Africa labelled Viognier. It's regarded as one of the leading warm-climate white grape varieties. At its best, Viognier has a fragrance of ripe apricots and juicy Williams pear made more sultry by the scent of springtime flowers, and its texture can be almost as thick as syrup coated with a perilous richness like double cream about to turn sour. It might be from elsewhere, but if it tastes like this it will probably be called Condrieu. Luckily there's a little more of it now.

And a little of its scented, plump-flavoured juice might be blended with Syrah in the red Côte-Rôtie. It's pretty rare in France for the rules to allow producers to blend in white grapes to a red wine, but maybe the legislators took pity on the beleaguered Côte-Rôtie growers. Not all of them use Viognier, but some of the best do, and this would help to explain why Côte-Rôtie at its best is not a powerhouse mouthful of oak and ripeness. The best Côte-Rôtie is delicate, barely touched by new oak, not high in alcohol and with a silken texture more like Burgundy. These aren't the most expensive. These aren't the ones whose grapes hang on the vines late in the autumn until their skins begin to shrivel. These aren't the ones whose charm has been doused by the flavours of new oak and alcohol. But they are the best.

You could head back to the autoroute, but I never do. There's a perfectly good road from Condrieu, which hugs the Rhône and lets you get a feel for the river's power and majesty as it churns its way south, grinding a path out of the unyielding rock of the Massif Central. There are good vineyards here, too, mostly for red wine from Syrah, facing east and taking the name St-Joseph. But the next truly great vineyard is on the far side of the river, on the hill of Hermitage. If you believe the locals, this could be the oldest vineyard in France, planted as long ago as 600 BC, maybe with Syrah grapes, and it is a jaw-jutting outcrop of such granitic self-belief that I don't really want to argue. And although quite a bit of the wine is white and always has been – two hundred years ago it was as famous as Montrachet in Burgundy – I don't usually want to argue with a red Hermitage wine either, certainly not when it's young. The best ones are like a turbulent cauldron of tar and coal smoke, raw herbs, potato peel and savage pepper, but behind the daunting exterior there is beautiful sweet fruit – raspberry, blackberry and maybe blackcurrant – and if you age the wine, for ten to twenty years – and you really should – it takes on a strangely comforting, warming softness of sweet liquorice, cream and the rub of well-worn leather. And Hermitage has one of the world's greatest wine producers, Chave. Every time I leave his cellars, inspired and revived by his wonderful reds and whites, but also by his great common sense, I say, 'This visit makes me realise why I became a wine writer.'

The hill is surrounded by the much broader expanse of Crozes-Hermitage, but you can feel everything is changing. Stand on top of the hill of Hermitage and the south opens out in front of you like a vast plain. Even the river seems to slide side-ways to make room. As it does, the Syrah grape has a last ruddy red hurrah at Cornas and the whites briefly bloom at St-Péray (they sometimes fizz as well), then south of Valence the vine disappears, the river and the roads part company, the mountain slopes retreat to the horizon. Are we done with wine? Not a bit. The real south is about to start. Montélimar is more famous for nougat than wine, but below this sticky-smelling city you won't be able to avoid vines until you're virtually paddling in the Med.

This is the vast, windswept, sun-bleached expanse of the Côtes du Rhône. This name covers the northern vineyards as well, but when you see Côtes du Rhône or Côtes du Rhône-Villages on a bottle it will almost certainly be from these parched acres, which comprise the second-biggest vineyard area in France, after Bordeaux. Most of the wine is produced by co-operatives and blended and sold anonymously. But there are lots of good villages, particularly around the little Eygues River and huddled under the jagged mountain crags of the Dentelles de Montmirail on the eastern side of the valley, like Cairanne, Vacqueyras and Beaumes-de-Venise. Most famous of these villages is Gigondas, whose high-octane wines sometimes manage to exude a freshness and a scent of cinnamon, ginger and orange that they really shouldn't possess in such a hot region, until you realise that quite a few of the best vineyards are high, and facing north, away from the ripening sun.

But if it's fame you are after, well, one of the world's most famous – and most infamous – wines is waiting, back down toward the Rhône River, near the town of Orange. Châteauneuf-du-Pape. This is the place where a local vine-yard owner, Baron Le Roy, laid down the rules for the French system of *appellation contrôlée* that have been imitated all around the world. He did this because he was so fed up with the awful quality of Châteauneuf-du-Pape in the 1920s. It wasn't just Châteauneuf – the whole of France was awash with fake wine. And one of the worst outrages was the continued use of lead.

Lead gets a bad press. Such a lovely sweet taste. Such a delicious, luscious texture when you dissolve a pound or two into your thin, acid wine and transform it into something rich, scented and moreish. The Romans knew all about it. They used to concentrate and sweeten their grape juice by boiling it, and the great Pliny was very particular that you should only use lead pans to boil it in because the resulting liquid was far more succulent. They took the practice with them on their travels, and where the wines were pretty sour and the weather made you rather relish something sweet, the idea caught on. A cookbook written more than a thousand years later was still advocating that you add 'a pound of melted lead in fair water' to any wine you were trying to make.

No surprise, then, that some colder French regions were still using lead in the early twentieth century. Why wouldn't you?

You might call it a no-brainer. Well, you're right there. Lead is one of the most powerful neurotoxins in existence. There's no safe level of lead consumption and the damage to the brain is irreversible. Lead poisoning from drinking sweetened wine probably made Handel go blind and Beethoven go deaf, but it shows how desperate people were for sweetness before sugar became the universally available drug that it is today. But back to Châteauneuf.

The efforts to create *appellation contrôlée* were centred on Châteauneuf-du-Pape because it is such a beguiling name and it seemed to attract an undue share of fraudsters. Forty years later it was still going on. An undercover investigation by *The Sunday Times* in the 1960s discovered that most of the Châteauneuf in Britain came from a vat in Ipswich. The same vat that dispensed the Nuits St-Georges and the Beaujolais, if you preferred those labels, but most people went for the Châteauneuf – a great, big, dark meaty, stewy, porty mouthful – and it did what a red wine is supposed to do. It warmed you up and made you drunk. Well, that type of Châteauneuf maybe, because none of the wine was the real stuff from this parcel of land above Avignon. And the real stuff can be one of the best red wines in France. It is big. It is ripe. The Grenache is a heat-seeking missile of a variety that sucks up sun and spews out alcohol, and although you can use thirteen different grape varieties if you want, Grenache is at the heart of just about every Châteauneuf-du-Pape (there's a little white wine, but not much). Earlier this century there was a bit of an obsession with Prestige Cuvées, creaming off the densest, most alcoholic vats, whacking the wines in new oak barrels, marking them out of 100 and rendering them virtually undrinkable. Thank goodness this fad has faded, because the genius inside a bottle of Châteauneuf-du-Pape is that, despite being big and full of alcohol and soaked in sun, the best ones – such as Vieux Télégraphe, Clos des Papes or Rayas – never lose their perfume. And that's special.

The Med, at last

I'm standing on the bridge in the middle of Arles facing south, bestriding the mighty Rhône as it powers on, almost in sight of the sea. Shall I turn left? Or right? East or west? To the east is the glitter and glamour of Provence, the promise of soignée suppers and midnight swims and dalliance. But what promise of wine? Not nearly enough. To my right is the rough and tumble of the Languedoc, where the sun seems harsher, the wind seems keener, the beach bars are few and the restaurants are little more than café/bars with local fish and salad, but the promise of special wine is tantalising. Which way shall I turn? I turn right, to the west, away from the glamour and the glitz. I don't really feel happy in that world where silver-tongued smoothies are trying to persuade me that their see-through Provence rosés are nectar and surely I don't begrudge them the price. Well, I suppose I don't. A price is what the market will pay. Just don't expect me to recommend to my readers they hand over that much cash for that little substance.

Yet I must give a nod to Provence. In Bandol it has a serious, challenging red from the clifftops near Toulon, more suited to a fully lubricated Scottish Highland evening of well-hung game and the Gay Gordons than anything the French Riviera might offer up. In the bleak, mysterious moonscape of the Alpilles hills near Arles, Eloi Dürrbach at Domaine de Trevallon had been one of the first visionaries in southern France to say to the authorities: your regulations are rubbish. Strip off the corset. Throw away the rule book. Let me do what I know will work. What he wanted to do was to blend Cabernet and Syrah on his unbelievably forbidding stony land overlooking the outcrop of Les Baux where the town seems, from a distance, as though it was hewn from rock at the beginning of civilisation. The authorities said no. It's forbidden. He said yes. Cabernet and Syrah had been successfully blended in the 1860s. He would do it again and label it as humbly as they demanded, yet ask and get a higher price than any other wine south of Châteauneuf-du-Pape.

And there is one more reason I look with affection to Provence, to the east. To a quarry above the fancy yachty port of Ste-Maxime, just around the bay from St-Tropez. A campfire. We're cooking ratatouille livened up by liberal – and affordable – slices of local saucisson. We're students on our first trip to the south. And Bernard Féraud has given us a bottle of his Provence wine that breaks all the rules. It's a Cabernet Sauvignon grown where Cabernet Sauvignon is forbidden. It's a deep dark purple; its thrilling aroma of herbs and blackcurrant storms out of the plastic cup and the rich, ripe fruit wraps itself around our tongues and dazzles our brains with its possibilities. Could the South of France really make wine this exciting? Why was most of it so bad, then? What needed to be done? And we were asking the questions in our quarry campsite before anyone else, thanks to Monsieur Féraud and his brave, illegal wine.

So I turn west, to the Midi, as Languedoc-Roussillon is called. Is this France's New World? Well, yes and no. Is this where France has created a riposte to the New World varietal revolution, led by California and Australia, and followed by almost everybody else? Is this where France took a stand against Australian Chardonnay and California Merlot? It certainly is, and in terms of creating vast vineyards of the popular grape varieties and making simple wines with the grape variety's name in big letters on the front label, that's exactly what France has done. Cheap, branded Chardonnays and Cabernets and Merlots from southern France are in every supermarket. But how good are they? That's a fair question. But we should also ask ourselves how good is the cheap Australian Chardonnay from her hot, irrigated Riverland vineyards? How good is the Californian Merlot from her hot, irrigated Central Valley? How good is the Chilean Cabernet from her hot, irrigated Valle Central? The answers to these questions is that they can be good, but they can also be pretty rubbish. This is the modern commodity wine market.

And France is now a major player in that market. France has always been a massive player in cheap wine. With little competition in Europe, quality was often filthy, and the vines most widely planted were Aramon and Carignan, capable of pumping out vast quantities of thin, sour wine at low alcohol levels which France would then beef up with something gutsier from Italy, Spain, or, in the old days until the loss of her colonies, North Africa. They called it Le Gros Rouge, or the 'Big Red'. No one bought cheap French wine for the flavour. Frequently it was all that was available. Then came the 1980s and the astonishing deal the New World offered. We'll give you cheap wine, but it'll taste good, and it'll be made from the greatest grape varieties in existence – above all, Chardonnay, Cabernet Sauvignon and Merlot, soon to be followed by Sauvignon Blanc and Shiraz. Suddenly, nice-tasting wine had become something simple, but something France couldn't supply.

Well, she could, and the key lay in the Midi. Most of French wine was tightly regulated by the *appellation contrôlée* system, which was very strict about which grape varieties you could plant, where you could plant them and what you could call your wine. Tradition almost always won out over modernity. But the Midi wasn't controlled at all – no one in Paris had thought it was worth the effort. So here we had an area that produced 10 per cent of all the world's wines – in the 1980s it was producing twice as much as all of California, eight times as much as all of Australia – 2800 *million* litres of wine every year. Wine that, increasingly, no one wanted and no one would pay for, except the taxpayers of the EU, who had to subsidise this overflowing wine lake of gut rot.

It took some very enterprising local wine producers like Robert Skalli of Fortant de France, the Jeanjean family and the Mas family (of Domaine Paul Mas) to seize what was an enormous opportunity. Great swathes of feeble vineyard on the lifeless flatlands near Nîmes, Montpellier, Béziers and Narbonne were uprooted, but frequently vast new plantations took their place – of Cabernet, Chardonnay and Merlot. The powerful co-operatives were cajoled and coerced into joining this surge toward France's own New World. And the wine was labelled by its grape variety. This was forbidden in virtually every part of France, except Alsace. It wasn't forbidden in the Midi. Nothing was forbidden in the Midi. And in the cheap wine world, France's Chardonnays and Sauvignons, Cabernets and Merlots are now as important as those of any other country. And they don't stop at these varieties. A chap I know down in the boiling heat of Marseillan where they make Noilly Prat vermouth has planted Riesling and it's not bad. As he said, 'I know I'm going against nature; the Aussies can do it, so why not me?' Perhaps he was on to something. Picpoul de Pinet, the Midi's most lemony, thirst-quenching dry white, is made in the next village.

But the real New World countries don't just make the cheap stuff. They have also led the way in thrilling, imaginative top-end wines, too. Some of the world's best Chardonnays, Cabernets and Merlots come from places like North America, Australia and Chile. Well . . . and France. It's just that in France they are called Burgundy, or Bordeaux; that's where the new-bies got their ideas from. And France is now grateful in return for being shown what can be done at the lower end of varietal wines. But if you get away from the baking plains and their thin, lifeless soils, the Languedoc had a reasonable tradition of making decent wine until the arrival of the railway in 1855 meant that the whole of industrial northern Europe was opened up as a market for cheap red wine – and the Midi obliged. It wasn't until Mas de Daumas Gassac shocked the world with stupendous Cabernet-based reds and Viognier-based whites during the 1980s from grapes grown in the middle of nowhere up a hillside valley north-west of Montpellier that the top-end revolution started.

Many have followed Mas de Daumas Gassac's lead in majoring on internationally acclaimed varieties and some, like the remark-able Grange des Pères just down the road in the same valley, have become global superstars. But it is the effect that international attention has had on the more traditional quality wine villages that I find most encouraging – places like Pic St-Loup, Minervois, St-Chinian, Faugères and La Clape are all starting to shine, with their old traditional grape varieties edging out ones like Cabernet Sauvignon. And, talking of the old grapes, varieties like the red Carignan, Mourvèdre and Cinsault and the white Grenache Blanc, Piquepoul, Bourboulenc, Vermentino and Maccabéo are beginning to show an entirely unexpected talent for super, waxy, deep, unexpected flavours in reds and whites. And often from places where the vines had been given little respect until now. Carignan-based reds from the high, windy valleys of the Corbières wafting smells of mountain herbs out of the glass are some of southern France's most refreshing and original reds. And an area of numbing wind, crumbly granite soil and bleaching sun called the Fenouillèdes reaches up from the Agly Valley into the mountains of the Corbières and produces some of the most thrilling reds and whites in all of southern France. There's a guy up there called Gérard Gauby, who could squeeze nectar from a rock.

The south-west is more than just Bordeaux

The south-west's problem is Bordeaux. Bordeaux is in the south-west and Bordeaux dominates everything that goes on in the south-west. It wasn't always so: the Romans thought it was a much better idea to encourage viticulture in the high country inland and just use Bordeaux as a trading post, because it had this fantastic natural harbour in the Gironde estuary. The Médoc, which is now world-famous for its powerful red wines, was basically a marsh until the Dutch drained it in the seventeenth century. All the best wine came from upcountry. And some pretty good stuff still does. But we hardly see it. The most well-known south-west wine is actually one that didn't exist a generation ago, and only exists now because most of us have given up drinking Armagnac brandy, so they've got a lot of grapes left over. Mostly these are Ugni Blanc and Colombard and you can make an attractively crunchy, green, dryish white from them. Which they do. And which they sell shedloads of for not a lot of money per bottle, as Côtes de Gascogne.

Bordeaux is the boss around here, but she's beset by vineyards to the east and south. A lot of them could easily pass for Bordeaux – they don't taste any different. But, crucially, the border of the Gironde department slices through a lot of them, and to be called a Bordeaux wine you have to be inside the Gironde department. This is no great solace to the growers in Bergerac who see identical grapes grown 4.5 metres (5 yards) over the road in identical soils, but in the St-Émilion satellite appellations and so selling for 25 per cent more. And it's not much solace to producers struggling in Côtes de Duras or Côtes du Marmandais or even Buzet, a few miles up the Garonne. At least Bergerac has the shining stars of the super-sweet Monbazillac and Saussignac, which, from a single estate, can be as exciting as a top Sauternes. And cheaper.

The most interesting wines of the south-west come from further away. Jurançon, down toward the Pyrenees, can be a very individual, tangy, lemony dry or pineapple sweet white mountain wine. Fronton makes a raspberry-scented, silky-textured red out of the Negrette grape to keep Toulouse from dying of thirst. Gaillac produces good fizz up along the River Tarn, but is most important as a preserver of ancient, almost extinct grape varieties and almost extinct winemaking methods, too. The south-west's two most famous and notorious areas are both for reds, and I can't pretend I find either of them easy. Madiran makes frankly brutal wines out of the equally formidable Tannat grape. I've seen them described as Mephistophelean, but have never worked out what treasures they were tempting me with. And after twenty-four years, what will the hell that awaits me resemble? A vat of unreconstructed Tannat? Understandably, Madiran is where they invented the micro-oxygenation system

of trying to soften ferocious red wine tannins by gently bubbling oxygen through the vats. But I'm not that convinced.
And I'm not completely convinced by the modern powerhouse
reds of the Malbec grape in Cahors, either. The Romans *were*
convinced, and these so-called black Cahors wines were very
useful for beefing up pale Bordeaux in the Middle Ages, and
more recently, but I find them pretty hard work. Malbec is
tannic in Argentina, but rich and juicy, too. In Cahors I usually
find rather more of the tannin and less of the juice, and when
long periods of new oak barrel ageing are thrown in as well, as
I said, I find it all a bit hard work.

Bordeaux was my first wine tasting

'You need to have sex in the vineyard before you can fully
understand a wine.' Now, don't get me wrong. This is not my
view. With the number of wines I taste each week I'd have
been dead from exhaustion years ago. No. This was Christian
Moueix waxing lyrical about his precious Château Pétrus, at
that time the most sought-after and valuable red wine in the
world. I was trying to get to the bottom of why Pétrus was
better than its neighbours. I have to say, I hope he didn't try it
on a moonlit night. The Pétrus vineyard is very flat and small.
And it's usually surrounded by hordes of Japanese and Chinese
tourists with their smartphones.

So that's not a bad reason to visit Bordeaux, but there is no
way that anyone who wants to understand the world of wine –
and I mean the whole world – could possibly not visit Bordeaux.
And ideally visit again and again. Bordeaux is the biggest and
most famous red wine area in the world, and it does pretty
well with white wines, too. Bordeaux has been famous – and
kept its fame – longer than any other wine region. The grapes
that Bordeaux grows, led by the red Cabernet Sauvignon and
Merlot and the white Sauvignon Blanc, are grown in almost
every wine country. The style of Bordeaux wine, in particular

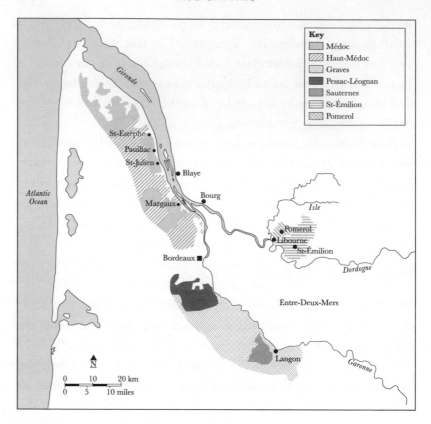

its dark, tannic red wines aged in small French oak barrels, has been copied around the world and in many countries is held up as the exemplar of the very best they can achieve. And yet, in what could seem like a smug and prosperous traditionalists' haven, Bordeaux sits at the very prow of progress – be that in how grapes are grown, how wine is made, what style it is made in, how it is talked and written about, and how it is sold. These are the reasons that I go back again and again.

Bordeaux was my first wine tasting. Bordeaux was my first great wine. My tutors at university never offered us Burgundy, Barolo or even sherry after a really good tutorial. They would treat us with Bordeaux – Montrose 1961, Langoa–Barton 1953 and, best of all, Beychevelle 1961. If we had been very good, one fabulous guy would open a bottle of Beychevelle 1961 and we would all lie around on the floor drinking it. A good tutorial would bring Lagrange 1961 – not quite so stunning, and bottled in Glasgow. A poor tutorial would be either nothing, or cheap Beaujolais. I think he only kept bottles of it to shame us into working harder – he was as keen as we were to down another bottle of Beychevelle 1961.

And Bordeaux was my first wine visit. I had already been twice while I was still a student. I never even thought of visiting anywhere else. I managed to do a vintage at Châteaux Angludet and Palmer. I was in the vineyard. I was among the barrels in the winery. I was carousing with the wine folk, laughing and sing-ing and drinking. At Angludet we reckoned to eat five steaks a day – not difficult if it's steak for breakfast – and drink three litres of wine a day – not difficult if it's wine for breakfast. We didn't have to operate any dangerous machinery. Just secateurs. Any time off and we would pile into my yellow Mini and visit the wineries. We quickly realised that there was one pretty good rule: if the cellarmaster is miserable, the wine will probably be miserable, too. I never liked Rauzan-Gassies, and felt they under-performed, until they changed their cellarmaster. But in general life in Bordeaux seemed to consist of long stretches of hard work, uproarious parties and feasts, and hardly any sleep. If the rest of the wine world was like this, maybe there was a career in it.

It was a hell of a wine baptism. I then visited northern Spain and I don't think I found a single wine I thought was any good; and followed that with a grand tour sweeping around from Bordeaux, along the Mediterranean coastline and all the way up the east of France, enjoying myself, but mostly tasting wines that were wretched. I had had all kinds of good stuff in Bordeaux. Was it the only place in France that could make any-thing decent? In reasonably large quantities, and on a reasonably regular basis – probably yes. Why? OK. Let's take a look at the place. First thing, don't expect scenery. The best wines don't come from memorable landscapes here. The Médoc is dull and flat from top to bottom; the Graves is patches of vines cut out of dark forest or holding the fort against suburban creep. There are some impressive manor houses – the French call them châteaux or castles – and they were mostly built to make the vineyard owner feel important. The town of St-Émilion is lovely, but the vineyards are mostly featureless plateau with just the odd slope. Pomerol – well, you wouldn't even notice you were in it, even though its wines are the most expensive in Bordeaux.

So, no sightseeing. The weather in any case is pretty maritime – the Bay of Biscay is right next door, and it could rain at any moment, although a fairly regular, long balmy autumn period usually helps the grapes to ripen. But let's take a few walks. Let's head into the woods just south of Bordeaux. Into the Graves region. *Graves* means gravel, and in the heartland of Graves, where the best wines come from a sub-division called Pessac-Léognan, the gravel is so dense you sometimes can't see any soil at all. Gravel is warm, so it absorbs heat from the sun, then releases the warmth onto the vines as the sun fades away. That's crucial if you are growing a late-ripener like Cabernet Sauvignon. And gravel is free-draining – all those rain showers ushered in on westerly winds from the Bay of Biscay soak straight through before the grape has time to suck up the liquid and dilute its juice. And gravel has no organic matter, so the vines' roots have to delve deeper for sustenance, which they easily manage. A bed of pebbles won't stop them and older vines with deeper roots always make better wines. These factors are tremendous for wine – particularly for red. The first identifiable wine property in Bordeaux was here: Pape-Clément was given to the city of Bordeaux in 1305. The vineyard is still going. Fantastic reds and a little brilliant white.

Now let's go north of Bordeaux city into the Médoc. We'll take the little back roads that thread their way through meadows and marsh. No vines. This is soggy, low-lying land, but we are about to see what a difference a few feet of height will make. Clumps of vines appear at little villages and they are all on tiny rises of land, and I mean tiny — 3 metres (10 feet), something like that. But that's crucial. Down at sea level the soil is thick clay, but all along the Médoc deposits of gravel, sometimes 3 metres deep, sometimes 6 metres (20 feet), but ideally rising to about 9–12 metres (30–40 feet) above sea level have created ridges of warm, free-draining stony soil. Where there's a gravel ridge you can ripen your Cabernet Sauvignon. Where there's no gravel ridge you can't. Great properties like Château Margaux and Château Latour ripen their grapes on gravel ridges only 9 metres (30 feet) above the muddy waters of the Gironde estuary. You can walk to the edge of the vineyard on gravel. The land drops away. The soil thickens. Cows and sheep take the place of vines. No vines. They couldn't ripen on this sodden clay just metres from the vineyard. In the Médoc the quality of the gravel pretty much equates to the quality of the wine.

Let's go to Pomerol. It's very different. We're further away from the sea here, on the right bank of the Dordogne. Now the main grape is Merlot and the most important soil is clay. Merlot ripens earlier than Cabernet and Merlot positively loves the damp, cool clay. Put it on warmer soils and it will ripen far too fast. So we are in a vineyard that prides itself on its thick, cold blue clay — it's Pétrus — yes, we're here again — and it can make one of the richest wines in the world. Cabernet wouldn't ripen here, but Merlot, held back by the stodgy clay soil, manages to produce fruit here for a sensual red wine like no other. If the soil had been more free-draining and warm, the wine would have been a jugful of jam. Bordeaux is a big place. And a lot of very different things happen here. Sometimes it's the soil, sometimes it's the weather. And sometimes it's the grape varieties.

Cabernet Sauvignon is the most famous of these. It has been the dominant grape of all the top Graves, Pessac-Léognan and Médoc wines for hundreds of years. Famous wines like Margaux, Lafite and Haut-Brion, which travelled first to northern Europe and then across the continents, in particular to North America in the late eighteenth century, owed their character to Cabernet

Sauvignon and gravel. But Merlot is now of equal importance. Most of Bordeaux doesn't consist of precious gravel beds. Most of it is clay, with, when you're lucky, a leavening of limestone. Merlot likes these conditions. They are at their peak in Pomerol and St-Émilion, but over the whole region the early-ripening, clay-happy Merlot is the most-planted grape. Cabernet Franc is also important and works both on gravel and on clay. Petit Verdot ripens very late and needs the gravel. Malbec used to be important, but you rarely see it now. In whites, interestingly the less-known Sémillon leads the more fashionable Sauvignon Blanc, at least partly because Sémillon is more important for sweet wines like Sauternes.

So the weather, the soils and the grape varieties continue to create what we know as Bordeaux. But there's more. A bit of history. The Aquitaine region of south-west France was English between 1154 and 1453. That doesn't do your export trade any harm, and a large number of the most important trading houses were started by British, Irish, Belgian, Dutch and German merchants. This meant that methods for transporting the wine in decent conditions were of paramount importance. So Bordeaux, with numerous local forests to take advantage of, developed the small oak barrel, which to this day is still called the *barrique bordelaise* – the Bordeaux barrel. It's typically 225 litres in volume – that's three hundred wine bottles. This size may have been decided because a single man – a strong one – can just about handle it, rather than because it perfectly suited the maturation of strong Cabernet Sauvignon wine. Who knows? But it became the standard barrel for high-quality wine everywhere in the world, and is still usually made from French oak. Although the spread of Bordeaux's grape varieties has made a massive difference to the world's wines, you could say that the adoption of Bordeaux's barrel had an even greater impact, since it's used for reds and whites, regardless of grape variety.

Traditionally, most of the barrels would be used again and again until they became leaky and worn out. But a new barrel has a very particular effect on wine. The oak wood is full of vanillin. As you toast the staves to help bend them into the barrel shape, this vanillin is drawn out from the wood and caramelises on the inner surface of the barrel. So when you put a tough, dry, young red wine into it, this creamy, toasty, nutty vanillin dissolves in the wine and creates a richness, a roundness, almost a sweetness that during the 1970s and '80s became the hallmark of successful Bordeaux properties. And it was copied right around the world. Anyone can buy a barrel, even if they can't buy a chunk of Bordeaux soil.

The Bordeaux we drink today is very different from the one I started with. The top wines are far richer and riper. Is that better? Not necessarily. What you gain in texture and power you probably lose in perfume and subtlety, but there used to be legions of genuinely unripe wines, red and white. There aren't many today. Producers use a lot more new oak barrels because they can afford to, but also because the critics and drinkers now expect that full oaky flavour, and also have little desire to wait ten years for the wine to soften. Again, is that better? For many wines, yes. The simplest reason is that if people like it, then it's better. And a mixture of stainless steel tanks and carefully monitored oak barrels is likely to give you a clean wine at the very least. There used to be a lot of muddy, dirty Bordeaux reds and sulphurous, stale Bordeaux whites around, but they are pretty rare nowadays. And do I drink as much Bordeaux as I ever did? Yes, I do. I still find both the reds and the whites some of the most fascinating, satisfying, refreshing and companionable wines in the world. I still use Bordeaux wines as references when I'm tasting wines from other countries or even other grape varieties. It's how I learnt wine. It's how I began. It was my first time.

Sweeties, from noble rot to straw wine

If we follow the Garonne River south-east of the city of Bordeaux we come to misty, muggy Sauternes, a tiny area which makes probably the most famous sweet wine in the world.

There is one way to make wine sweet, one that doesn't require you to leave your bunches to freeze in winter's dog days, as in Germany or Canada, or artificially dry them, turning their fresh harvest juice into syrup, as in Italy. This method simply requires that you let the grapes rot on the vine. Now, there are various forms of rot including grey rot, brown rot, white rot, sour rot, bitter rot, the 'black goo' – and lots more. All of these will destroy your grapes and wreck your vintage. But there's one rot that, in a few scattered corners of the wine world, the producers get on bended knee and pray for – noble rot, sometimes referred to by its Latin name, *Botrytis cinerea*. This produces grapes that look just as disgusting as those suffering any other rot – they are shrivelled and covered in foul, furry fungus, so sludgy and slimy that they fall apart in your fingers when you try to pick them. Yuck. But shut your eyes and lick what remains off your fingers. Memorably honeyed, intensely sweet, a celestial syrup. And memorably honeyed, intensely sweet wine is what these ruined-looking grapes will deliver. This is the rot that produces grapes for most of the greatest sweet wines in the world. Noble rot.

Who first discovered that the most repulsive grapes in the vineyard would yield the richest, sweetest wine? Well, numerous wine areas claim they were the first to understand and then to exploit this 'noble rot'. The owner of a Sauternes property in Bordeaux, Château La Tour Blanche, said he introduced the idea from Germany in 1830, but they had been making sweet wine in Sauternes for at least a century before then. The Germans said they discovered how to benefit from noble rot in 1775, but there were instances of noble rot sweet wines on the Rhine right through the eighteenth century. The Hungarians swore that they were utilising noble-rotted grapes in the early seventeenth century for Tokaji. The Austrians even claim they were making noble rot sweet wine as early as 1526. No one really knows, but what is pretty certain is that each of these places discovered, by accident, that their really grotty, rotten grapes could occasionally make sweet wine like they'd never managed before. So let's take a look and see how noble rot operates.

For rot to turn out 'noble', you need quite particular conditions. First, the grapes need to head into autumn healthy and on course for full ripeness. Then you need a warm, sunny autumn, not a wet one, as rain will encourage all the bad sorts of rot. Ideally, your vines should be next to a river or lake. In a warm autumn, mist will form on the water and then creep up into your vineyard overnight, where it will stay until about lunchtime each day, when the sunshine should have burnt it all away. That should mean you are left with vineyards that are now hot but also as stifling and muggy as a Turkish bath – when you're in such a vineyard the steaming humidity will make sweat break out on your brow, and it will encourage the development of noble rot spores, which will dig deep into the grapes, weakening their skins so that the moisture in the grape evaporates and the sugar, the acids and the glycerol all concentrate like mad. With the water largely gone, their sugar level may now reach a potential alcohol of 20 per cent or more. When you ferment this syrupy juice, the yeasts can't operate past about 15 per cent alcohol, so they stop and all the rest of that grape sugar ends up as natural sweetness in the wine.

In France, noble rot strikes quite often in the Loire Valley's watery milieu, especially in Coteaux du Layon, but most often and most famously it strikes in Sauternes, a small region of Bordeaux where the icy little Ciron flows into the sun-warmed Garonne and creates great blankets of morning mist whenever the autumn is warm and sunny. This is where the gold-bedecked Château d'Yquem literally lords it over the world of sweet wine, gazing down its billowing slopes of vines to the Ciron and Garonne rivers. And it is Yquem's kind of lusciousness that most of the world's would-be sweet winemakers look up to, although the German Riesling grape has a better track record in the New World than Sauternes' Sémillon and Sauvignon Blanc grapes.

But most of the New World vineyards aren't situated in places prone to noble rot. And, to be honest, apart from a few 'sticky' fanatics, most New World tyros have their sights firmly set on conquering the dry-wine heights, red, white or fizzy.

In general, just leaving the grapes sitting there in the autumn sunshine to gradually shrivel and concentrate the sugar doesn't make intense enough wines to get very excited about. In the Sauternes region and the surrounding vineyards along the Garonne, such as Barsac, when the conditions to create the all-important noble rot don't appear, they do make fairly sweet but rather nondescript wines by leaving the grapes out on the vine hoping for a bit of shrivel. Jurançon, right down in the south-west near the Pyrenees, is about the only wine to make a name for itself with this style. In these breezy but sunny mountain vineyards the very high-acid Petit Manseng grape sometimes manages to make a delightful sweet wine packed with pineapple fruit and slashed with lemon. The great French writer Colette put it rather better: 'I was a girl when I met this prince; aroused, imperious, treacherous, as all great seducers are – Jurançon.' I think I'd better take another look. Don't wait up.

The 'dried fruit' habit is largely an Italian favourite, but just about hangs on in the rest of the world. France makes *vin de paille* – 'straw wine' – technically from grapes dried on straw but far more likely to be made from grapes dried indoors, with the bunches either hung on hooks or, rather more prosaically, in shallow boxes. The Jura makes a few examples, as does the northern Rhône at Hermitage. They can be quite wild and fretful, with an acidity scratched together from Bramley apples and cider vinegar, but they taste compelling and honeyed and memorable, as the syrup sweetness and the celestial vinegar acid tug at each other in your throat long after you have swallowed.

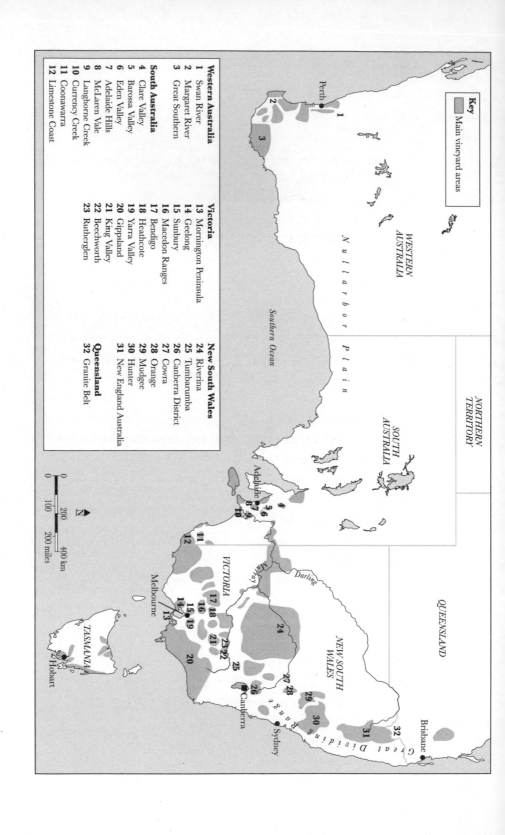

Key
Main vineyard areas

Western Australia
1 Swan River
2 Margaret River
3 Great Southern

South Australia
4 Clare Valley
5 Barossa Valley
6 Eden Valley
7 Adelaide Hills
8 McLaren Vale
9 Langhorne Creek
10 Currency Creek
11 Coonawarra
12 Limestone Coast

Victoria
13 Mornington Peninsula
14 Geelong
15 Sunbury
16 Macedon Ranges
17 Bendigo
18 Heathcote
19 Yarra Valley
20 Gippsland
21 King Valley
22 Beechworth
23 Rutherglen

New South Wales
24 Riverina
25 Tumbarumba
26 Canberra District
27 Cowra
28 Orange
29 Mudgee
30 Hunter
31 New England Australia

Queensland
32 Granite Belt

Australia

Taking on the Old World

M y first trip to Australia? Well, I very nearly didn't make it. It was the mid-1970s, and I was a couple of years out of university. I'd managed to get cast in the Royal Shakespeare Company's world tour of *Hedda Gabler* starring Glenda Jackson. At the same time, I was also offered Horatio in *Hamlet* in Coventry for six weeks at the Equity minimum wage. My agent said I should do the *Hamlet*: it would be good experience. I thought: good experience – Coventry? Or Melbourne, Sydney, Hollywood, Washington DC, New York and who knows where else? So, at the end of the winter, I headed for Australia. But how come I nearly didn't get there?

The answer was a dear friend of mine called Mel Smith. My late lamented friend Mel was a brilliant but troubled comic genius. He was a chum from Oxford. We'd done the Edinburgh Fringe together. It was he who persuaded me I could be an actor. It sounds bizarre now, but when they were looking to create a new *Beyond the Fringe* quartet Mel and I were selected. If only the other two had ever turned up for rehearsals, I wouldn't be writing this now: I'd be luxuriating in a platinum-coated bath full of Dom Pérignon and saying, 'Australia? Where's that?' Anyway, I prefer the life I've actually had.

Mel had a prodigious capacity for alcohol, and wanted to celebrate my great good fortune – a world tour with the RSC.

On the night before I flew we went drinking. That sounded like a really good idea, but I hadn't packed. I hadn't even sub-let my flat – and it was a six-month tour. But we laughed about it a lot as Mel prised the corks from the 1963 vintage ports he'd somehow found. 'Don't open another one, Mel. It's four in the morning and I still haven't packed.'

Mel helped me pack. Well, help is perhaps the wrong word. The RSC bus left the Aldwych Theatre for Heathrow at 10 a.m. We got back to my flat at 9 a.m. The phone started ringing. 'Where are you?' 'Nearly ready. Just need to find my passport.' So Glenda Jackson, and Patrick Stewart, and Timothy West, and – oh dear, Trevor Nunn – had to pick up a dishevelled, disorientated cub actor from the side of the road in Shepherd's Bush Green and race to make the flight.

I had no idea that I was embarking on a voyage that might not transform my life as an actor, but which would turn me into a wine guy. I discovered the New World. And, above all, I discovered Australia.

Touching down into the blinding summer morning's sun after leaving a sodden, foggy England the day before was a massive, glorious shock to the system. I'd just about sobered up, but the amazing sense of liberation at being let loose in this classless, jokey, rough-and-tumble – and sunny, beachy, beery, barbecue-y – world down under was better than any drink. Having plodded through the ill-humoured stuffiness that was 1970s England, Australia seemed like a vigorous, golden promised land for someone with a bit of attitude, some inhibitions to lose and a thirst. God's Own Country. Convert me. I was ready.

Pretty quickly, wine became part of a daily ritual of delight. After rehearsal, after the shows, I was always the one, being the youngest, who was sent off to buy wine for the rest of the cast. So I'd go to a bottle shop – any bottle shop – and pick up an armful of bottles – cheap ones, never pricey – and they had names like Shiraz, Semillon or Riesling. Or sometimes they'd be called Chablis or Burgundy or Claret, but as far as I could make out they'd never been near France. The Aussies weren't too bothered with such details. Most of the wines were from the Hunter Valley near Sydney, made out of whatever grapes they could rip off the vines before the cyclones hurtled through. No, not French at all.

And they didn't taste French either. The Rieslings were a kind of lime green-gold; they literally reeked of freshly squeezed lime juice and spilt petrol (lovely: a childhood 'going-on-holiday' smell for me), and then backed up this citrous pungency with an unnerving flavour like toasted white bread dripping with melted butter. The 'Chablis' was nothing to do with the thin, pale, stony brews that crept out of France in the 1970s. This was golden, thick in the mouth, a wodge of flavour like custard splashed with blood orange and rolled up in shoe leather. The reds were proud, mighty, dense, rippling with fruit and ripeness and swagger, just daring me to take another gulp, and another, and another.

This was cheap wine? I knew cheap wine. I'd been a low-paid actor treading the boards of fortnightly rep theatre in the Midlands. Cheap wine was sour, cheap wine was raw, bitter and bad-tempered. And it was Spanish or Italian or French. I had never drunk any cheap wine like this bargain-basement nectar. If cheap wine could be this good, why on earth were we putting up with such rubbish in Britain? No wonder hardly anyone drank wine. Except for some fancy top-end stuff, it was awful. If we could get basic wines half as good as these 'beaut Aussies', we could become a wine-drinking nation.

The trouble was, we *did* put up with rubbish. In England, wine was more about class than flavour. For the vast majority of Britons, wine was 'not for the likes of us'. Well, if it was for the likes of the taxi drivers and scene shifters and wharfies with whom I drank in the pubs of Melbourne and Sydney, it damn well *could* be for the likes of anyone in Britain with a quid in their pocket and a desire to feel just a little bit happier with their life on any given day. Wine democratised, wine made simple, wine made pleasurable and affordable – all the ideas that led me to crusade against the cobwebby elitism of wine first began to form under those balmy night skies in Australia.

The beach had a part to play as well. I'd done the vintage in Bordeaux when I was a student and I'd met this Australian guy. He'd told me that Australia had vineyard areas as good as the classic areas of France. Some were warmer, some were cooler, some hadn't been discovered yet, but some had flowered a century ago before being discarded and forgotten. And he was going back home to find the coolest of these sites, in Tasmania, to plant Burgundy's red Pinot Noir and white Chardonnay grapes, and begin Australia's cool-climate revolution.

I had his phone number in Sydney. I rang and told him about the thrilling cheap grog I was discovering, and he said, 'OK, I'm going to show you that Australia can make red wines as great as any in Europe.' And, well, I'd met a couple of girls, so we made a picnic foursome. They knew a beach, Obelisk Bay. They'd bring the food and Andrew the drink. It was a bright sunny day, and the girls dashed up to a headland and disappeared as Andrew and I talked wine. As we scrambled down toward the sea we couldn't see the girls ... oh yes, we could! Golden, glistening, helpless with laughter – and stark naked. Obelisk was a nudist beach.

So what would *you* have done? Exactly. Kit off and crash into the surf. Andrew held back just long enough to dig his precious red wines into the sand to keep them cool. And finally, our palates soaked in salt water, we lay back in the sand, breathless and thirsty, while Andrew ripped out the corks from his treasures and I swatted the flies out of the plastic cups. Grange Hermitage from the 1950s – was it the 1955? Wynns Cabernet 1962, Mildara 1963, Rouge Homme, Lindeman's Hunter Burgundy and McWilliam's Mount Pleasant Hermitage. All drunk naked, mixed with sand and sweat and laughter. Red wine never tasted so good. And you wonder why I fell in love with Australia?

I got back home to England eventually, after checking out the USA on the second leg of the world tour and realising that they too found it perfectly normal to expect cheap wine to be nice to drink. I was bursting with excitement about this New World of wine, although I was just about the only one who was. Back home, I looked for Australian wine in the shops. Nothing. Just the same old scrapings from the rump end of Europe's exhausted winelands. And never ripeness. It's as though Britain had been starved of ripeness for a thousand years. And it became blindingly obvious to me that northern Europe had no popular wine culture because it had no enjoyable popular wine. Almost the only place you could find some decent Aussie wine was at the Australian Wine Centre in London's Soho, right next to a sex shop. If you were after a bit of Kanga Rouge, you needed to be sure you stumbled through the right door.

Ah, Kanga Rouge. Believe it or not, there *was* a wine called Kanga Rouge. I've still got a bottle. And Bondi Bleach. And there was a chain of bars that sold Botany Bay white (you could choose sweet or medium) on draught across the country – in half-pint mugs, for all I know. But something *was* stirring. First, Kanga Rouge was surprisingly good; and second, it showed that someone was trying to inject a little humour and populism into the drab, complacent world of wine. It was about time. The 1960s generation, with their politics and their contempt for tradition, were getting older and demanding actual change, not just hot air. Wine was merely one of many dissatisfactions in life they jostled up against.

Well, what was happening in the UK was happening in Australia, too. The 1960s and '70s saw young Australians following the cue of young Americans in travelling the world getting OE (Overseas Experience), as they called it. Sure, they came to England, but they also swarmed over Mediterranean Europe, and found people drinking wine with their meals with as little fuss as if it were water. Trouble was, it tasted pretty filthy. In Italy, in France and in Spain, the cheap wine the locals drank wasn't much different from the feeble fare we were enduring back in England. This was hardly surprising when it was often drunk so copiously, largely because it was safer, and cheaper, than water. But it didn't have to be filthy. Back home in Australia and California, the returning voyagers became fired up with matching and then beating the Europeans at their own game. Not only with the basic wines, but also with the stuff at the top end.

And they had a weapon that no previous generation had possessed – technology. Professors of wine at universities in California and Australia saw that the best European wines were made in marginal areas like Bordeaux and Burgundy, Champagne and the Mosel Valley. The grapes barely ripened most years, vintage conditions were cool and winter set in quickly to chill down the cellars as the wine fermented and settled. Most Californian and Australian vineyards were in hot regions – but they could use science to ape the French. Artificial temperature control with stainless steel vats meant that, even if it was boiling hot outside, you could ferment your wines long and slow, just like the French and Germans, and create the haunting scents and flavours their top wines possessed. Filtration, yeast technology and understanding oak and the flavours it gave to wine, using barrels for your top wines and oak staves or oak chips for the cheaper stuff – they utilised all these. And above all, hygiene. If you lived in a warm place, bacteria attacked your juice as soon as it squelched from the grape – the terrible quality of so much Mediterranean wine was evil-tasting evidence of this. The cooler and cleaner your winery, the purer and cleaner your wine. Nature didn't offer these conditions in Australia and California. Science did.

But why did the Australians make such an astonishing success of it? First, they had a burning desire to learn, to understand and to excel. The Aussies don't like being beaten by anybody or anything – they are some of the world's worst losers. And once they decide to have a go at something, there's no nation in the world that approaches it with such enthusiasm and determination. If one phrase marked out the Australians toward the end of the twentieth century it was 'You gotta have a go!' Once they'd caught the wine bug, they wouldn't rest until they could claim to be the best in the world.

It had been ten years since I returned from my acting trip to Australia and the USA, and I'd been preaching the New World gospel to deaf ears. And then this happened: I was at the London Wine Trade Fair, tasting a forgettable range of, oh, Muscadet, or something like that. And I became aware of this aroma approaching from my right. Not a pleasant one. The aroma of a nylon shirt that's been perspired into for too long. 'Excuse me. Can I have a word?' I was having enough trouble inhaling, let alone starting a conversation. I mumbled that I was too busy, and I got the 'Oh look, don't come the raw prawn with me' treatment. So I turned and gazed at this hairy apparition clad in mucky khaki.

'What do you lot like your wines to taste of?' That was it. Anything to get rid of him and his nylon shirt, so I said, 'Um, what about red wines tasting of blackcurrants and white wines tasting of peaches? Now, please—' 'No, no – one more thing. How much do you want to pay?' '£3.99,' I said, praying he'd leave me to take some deep breaths. And he did.

So, a year later, I'm back at the London Wine Trade Fair. Tasting a turgid range of, I think, Beaujolais this time. And then that odour. Here it comes again. Same nylon. Same soaplessness. But he's got wine with him this time. 'Here, try this.' I can't pretend I was enthusiastic as I took a sip. 'Good God, it tastes of blackcurrants.' 'Yup,' he said, 'that's what you said you liked.' 'How much does this cost?' '£3.99. That's what you said you wanted to pay.' And he had a white wine with him, too. 'Blimey, this tastes of peaches!' 'Yup. That's what you said you liked.' 'How much is this?' '£3.99. That's what you said you wanted to pay.'

This guy must have gone back to Australia and said to his mob, 'OK, I've been to see the Poms, whingeing away as usual, but they say they want to pay £3.99 for a bottle, and they want their reds to taste of blackcurrants and their whites to taste of peaches – so let's get going and make it for them.' Was this the new face of Australia? It was the face of the whole New World.

The Old World view had been 'My family have been making this wine for five hundred years, and if you don't like it, that's not my problem.' The New World approach was 'You're the consumer: what do you like? Tell us, and we'll try to make it for you.' You would find California, New Zealand and, later, Chile, Argentina and South Africa adopting exactly the same approach. And eventually you would see parts of Italy and Spain and the south of France heaving themselves off the floor and grudgingly admitting that making something the wine-drinker actually liked wasn't a bad starting point for a producer. But it was the Aussies with their gutty 'You gotta have a go' attitude who began what became the great Wine Revolution through-out the non-wine-producing nations of northern Europe.

And the 1980s provided the perfect storm. Australia started sending out images of what it was like to be an Australian – well, a certain sort of Australian, epitomised by *Crocodile Dundee* and a string of Foster's Lager adverts for the amber nectar that made the outdoor life of the 'typical' Aussie larrikin look irre-sistible to an awful lot of young men struggling through a tough decade in cold northern Europe. Australia had a dramatic David and Goliath triumph over the mighty United States in the 1983 America's Cup sailing challenge which quite improbably trans-fixed millions of Brits. They followed this up with a joyous, unbridled celebration of their bicentenary in 1988, and after spreading across the wine world with their unabashed, open-faced self-confidence during the 1990s, capped it all in 2000 with the Sydney Olympics, showing the world that the Aussies were champions at celebrating almost anything.

And one more thing. The Australians had planted an awful lot of new vineyards, making an awful lot of new wine. And there weren't enough Australians. The Aussies are mighty drinkers, but even they wouldn't be able to down all the new juice. They were going to have to find someone to sell the stuff to. Let's start with the old enemy – the Poms: they speak the same language – sort of – and they like a drink. If we can make ripe, fruity wines, full of flavour, label them simply according to their grape variety and sell them at a decent price – not too low, not too high – we should be able to shift our wine surplus without having to drink ourselves under the table. Simple.

The Old World fought back, of course it did; quite viciously at times, but normally by pretending that you could not be serious about these parvenus. France, in particular, had held sway for a thousand years. You don't give up your privileges, however ill-deserved, without a fight. So they began an energetic campaign of disinformation. The wines all taste the same. There's no tradition, no history of excellence. There's no regional variation. There's no difference between vintages. There's definitely no terroir, to use the favourite French term of superiority. It's an industrial product, churned out by vast factories. And, as one leading Bordeaux producer sniffed, 'New World wine? Pah! It's Coca-Cola.' Sneer on, old-timers, there's nothing more calculated to spur an Australian to greater heights than the disdain dripping from the aquiline nose of a French aristocrat, or the colonial era–accented derision of a pinstripe-suited Brit.

And it was my good fortune to be strapped in for this roller-coaster ride. I started making wine trips to Australia during the 1980s, and soon I was down there every year, meeting wine people with a blazing passion and a blistering self-confidence unlike any others I'd met. They convinced me that, with their help, I could democratise wine. With Australia's bright, ripe, easy-to-understand, 'sunshine in a bottle' flavours, I could strive to push back the barriers of elitism, to swipe away the snobbery and start to preach a message of the uncomplicated, classless, open-to-all joys that wine possessed. If I was going to do that, I would need heroes, and Australia was full of them.

So I had better go and find them. There was this wine trip being organised to Australia. If I could only get a week off from my duties as General Perón in *Evita*. I got it. Precisely one week. I had to be back for a major photocall exactly a week later. So that's a day to get to Australia and one day back and five days there. Irresistible. Well, the first matter of epic importance was that I sat down in my economy seat next to a frizzle-headed, bubbly, irrepressible blonde called Jilly Goolden. We nattered and bantered and drank Jacob's Creek Shiraz-Grenache all the way to Australia. I arrived in Sydney completely exhausted, but knowing a lot more about life and half-prepared for a TV career with her that would last more than fifteen years. And anyway, we were straight on to a minibus heading for the Hunter Valley. I knew we must be in Australia because our host, Big – and I mean Big – Bob was cracking open the ice-cold tinnies of amber nectar before we'd even caught sight of the Harbour Bridge. Well, if you're half dead, it sure keeps you from getting any worse.

The minibus shuddered to a halt at a hairpin bend on the barely tarmacked track through the forest we were taking north of Sydney. We were ordered out to stand in a line while Big Bob solemnly peeled off the foil, aimed the bottle of Champagne at the rock face and let rip. This was Len Evans Corner. Every time he drove to or from the Hunter Len would stop here and aim a bottle of Bollinger Champagne at the rock face, then toast life and love and Len. We did the same, toasting the most famous man in Australian wine – according to him, the most famous man in Australia. And perhaps he was. I checked the foot of the rock – there were dozens of Bollinger corks lying among the eucalyptus leaves.

But we weren't in the Hunter yet. We got to Wollombi, a one-horse metropolis with a pub. We all piled out again, for another ritual. We each downed a slug of Doctor Jurt's Jungle Juice. Why? There's no point in asking an Australian why he does these ridiculous things with alcohol. Particularly with alcohol that has no redeeming features whatever. Ah well, another ice-cold tinny of fizzy lager will take away the taste – and then we reached the Hunter, the hazy blue Brokenback Mountains to the left, the river and various pimpled outcrops of bright red soil and rock to the right. But not many vines. That's because most of the land in the Hunter is thick pug clay which won't give you a harvest. It's only those red outcrops and mountain slopes that are well-drained enough and sufficiently fertile to support a vineyard, able to resist drought, able to cope with deluge, because you will get both, and you'll get them both when you don't want them – drought in winter when you're desperate for rain, deluge as the cyclones roll down the coast from Queensland at vintage time, usually just before your Shiraz is ripe, sometimes before anything is ripe.

You shouldn't have a vineyard here in this subtropical, humid valley, but as Len Evans said, 'It's only a couple of hours' drive from Sydney, and it's the first half-decent bit of land you come to.' The Hunter doesn't make all that much wine, and nowa-days more people are employed in hotels and bars and on golf courses than in the wine industry. But it's Sydney's own, so it survives, and to a reasonable extent prospers on Shiraz and Semillon and Chardonnay. All of these were on show as we pulled up in our little bus that first day. As was the smoking barbecue, and another coolbox full of lager. And the kings of the Hunter were all there, sunburnt, irreverent, pugnacious, but amazingly friendly so long as we traded insults as lively as theirs – and they were all in shorts. Len Evans, Australia's Mr Wine; Murray Tyrrell, the Hunter champion who brought Hunter Chardonnay and probably Australian Chardonnay to the fore; Max Lake, who swore he modernised and reinvented the Hunter Valley single-handed and then proceeded to give birth to the boutique wine movement all over Australia (but he had a wry side to him. 'We called our winery Lake's Folly. We wanted to call it Lake's Fxxx-Up, but discovered we couldn't register the name because it was in common usage already'); and there was James Halliday, Australia's most energetic wine man in a land of super-energised egos.

It was like turning up in Bordeaux and finding the bosses of Châteaux Lafite and Margaux, Pontet-Canet and Lynch-Bages stripped down for a barbie and a bit of fun. It wouldn't have happened in France but it could, and did, in Australia. And we tasted amazing custardy, biscuity, savoury Semillons, yellow, glyceriney, yeasty, lemon-streaked Chardonnays and wild, rather volatile, earthy but blackcurranty Shirazes, sometimes with their unique whiff of the sweaty saddle that brought a craggy smile to Murray Tyrrell's lips as we slurped oysters and pulled crayfish off the barbie, while Len turned the thick, marbled steaks one more time.

I was finding my heroes all right. Four kings of Australia, no PR people, no marketeers, no flunkies. Just four massive egos and opinions, in shorts. Could all Australia be like this? Well, there's another part to the Hunter – the Upper Hunter Valley – an hour or so's drive to the north, past the gaping open-cast coalmines and the brooding slag heaps. This is where Rosemount set up their stall. It's hotter here and the soils are rich and alluvial. And it catches the cyclones a few hours before they reach Murray Tyrrell and his mob in the Lower Hunter. You can't really do much red up here, but you can do white, and that's what mattered because Rosemount Chardonnay – with its whiff of toasty smoke, its Brazil nut cream, its honeyed spice and almost syrupy texture – was just about to transform the world of wine in northern Europe, and especially in Britain. This was a serious enterprise. But again we bowled up and Philip Shaw, the winemaker, could hardly contain his enthusiasm or his friendliness or his desire to share. We clambered over his new oak barrels, all full of glistening, golden Chardonnay, tasting furiously, jabbering with excitement at getting so close to the action and being made so welcome. And there was a barbie going, just in case we were inclined, and there was a chiller full of beer, just in case. Dizzy with delight, we drifted back to the bus for our trip back to Sydney. But Australia was still showing us how to do it – the back of the bus was now packed with Sydney rock oysters and bottles of cool, dark brown Cooper's Stout. I managed forty-eight oysters, washed down with foaming, chocolatey beer as good as any I could find in Britain. And then I finally hit the sack with the biggest smile the pillows had ever seen. Australia was turning out to be even better than I had hoped.

I am not sure that it would be quite so unrestrained now that corporate rules affect Australian wine like everything else, and when a big company is your host, things can be rather more straitlaced. But luckily, after a decade at the beginning of this century when a multinational un-Australian corporate culture did appear to engulf many of the most famous names like Lindeman's, Wolf Blass, Hardys, even Rosemount itself, the pendulum is swinging once again. Opinionated individuals are reasserting themselves and their wines. Big-brand anonymity is being challenged again. The barbie is being dusted off, the beers – now really tasty craft beers – are being put back in the coolbox and the winemakers are reminding themselves that they got into this game because they like a drink, and they're beginning to wear shorts again when they welcome the foreigners.

New South Wales, Sydney's backyard

New South Wales gets some of the best and some of the worst of both worlds. Because of Sydney's thirst for decent wine, which the Hunter was never able to satisfy by itself, there are quite a few other regions trying to put quality first. In the far north, next to Stanthorpe in the Granite Belt, which is Queensland's best wine region, the New England region was being touted as a site worth developing – or rather re-developing – as long ago as the 1970s: it had contained good vineyards in the nineteenth century. It's been a slow starter, partly because it's really quite a long way from anywhere, but the vineyards are high – some are at 1000 metres (3280 feet), which is very high for Australia – and reasonably cool, and New South Wales is always on the lookout for those. Orange is closer to Sydney, but you have to climb west through the tangled, twisty slopes of the Great Dividing Range to get there. This is tableland, too, a bit like New England, and the town of Orange is a delight – they were considering it as the site of the national capital before they chose Canberra. I bet the locals are glad they were turned down. Since the 1980s it has come up with a string of appetising cool, mostly white wines.

Along this ridge you can go north to Mudgee, which also has vineyards at up to 1000 metres, but most are closer to 500 metres (1640 feet), and are best known for big, fat, slightly earthy reds and whites that are more Hunter Valley than cool climate in style. And you can go south of Orange to Cowra, where the wine style is definitely lusher and whose Chardonnays have been fleshing out numerous well-known brand names for decades. But if you want to taste New South Wales at its true coldest cool, head to the south of the state, where Tumbarumba makes fantastically good, lean but tasty Chardonnays, and to Canberra, where, to everyone's amazement, some of Australia's most exciting Shiraz is appearing from wineries like Eden Road, Collector and Clonakilla.

Victoria, a roller-coaster ride

Victoria suffered mortally from the depredations of the phyl-loxera aphid, the nasty little insect that destroyed most of the world's vineyards in the second half of the nineteenth century. South Australia escaped unharmed – there's never been any phylloxera there to this day – and New South Wales wasn't badly hit, but Victoria got completely thumped. Until phyllox-era arrived in 1875, Victoria was Australia's main vineyard state and exported so much wine to Britain it was called John Bull's Vineyard. Melbourne was lucky to have attracted Swiss settlers who seemed to know about viticulture and set about making some seriously good wine in neighbouring areas like Geelong and Yarra Valley. The rest of Victoria was lucky because of gold. Right the way across the centre and the north of the state came find after find, nugget after great gleaming nugget. Vineyards always follow the gold, and Victoria sprouted vineyards at Avoca in 1848, Bendigo in 1855, Great Western in 1858, Ballarat in 1859 – and, above all, Rutherglen at the end of the 1850s. Here, in the north-east, wine was poured down miners' throats for five pounds a gallon – which was twenty times what the same wine would fetch in Melbourne. Rutherglen must have been a wild place, but it was only a generation before the gold was exhausted and by then the phylloxera was rampant.

In the early twentieth century Victorian wine was largely confined to a rump along the Murray River and in the north-east. I used to judge the Victorian Wine Export Awards in the 1980s and early '90s. Each year I would find one sensational, silky Pinot Noir, one sensuous, plummy Shiraz, one eucalyptus-scented Cabernet, one limey, zesty Riesling, one oatmealy, savoury Chardonnay . . . but just one. These wines were being created at single estates re-established on the remnants of those great old vineyards. But there was rarely another vine for 100 kilometres (60 miles). I'm not sure why these wines, with their hauntingly beautiful flavours, were entered for export awards – they rarely had enough to give their local hotel a supply for its Christmas lunch. But we did make an awful lot of noise about how Victoria seemed to be capable of creating the most exquisite, the most captivating wines in Australia, and we'd love more people to give it a go so that we could buy some. I used to continually say I thought Victoria was perhaps the most thrilling wine state of them all. But I rarely visited because there wasn't much to visit.

And when I did get there, there still wasn't all that much to see, but it was clear that the Yarra Valley, less than an hour out of Melbourne, was where they'd decided to resurrect Victorian wine on a grand scale. This made sense. Melbourne had been

Australia's most prosperous and sophisticated city in the nineteenth century. The Yarra Valley was its local vineyard, mostly managed by the Swiss immigrants who had come from a cool-climate wine culture where delicacy and perfume in wine were valued. They did their best to recreate Switzerland in Victoria and by 1889 were winning gold medals in the Paris Exposition Universelle. By 1890 Yarra's St Huberts Vineyard was the largest in Australia. But Australia was turning away from light table wines toward heavy ports and sherries and beer. It didn't help that Victoria began the twentieth century by electing a government bent on Prohibition; by 1921 the last vines had been pulled out of the Yarra Valley. Big, fat, lazy but succulent cattle idled where the Pinot used to grow.

So I drove out to the Yarra in rather a different mood than on my first trip from Sydney to the Hunter. If you take the side roads out of Melbourne you will feel you've slipped back a century. I drove, dreamily, through thick eucalyptus jungle – hardly out of the suburbs – and the air was pulsing with the cry of the bellbird, like a tumbling cascade of notes on a wooden xylophone. As I unwillingly left the forest behind, things actually got better. Now I was in a landscape of dells and dips, hedgerows and lanes, and tousled, tumbled hillocks that surely came from an English pastoral world of another time. Except for the majestic eucalyptus trees unfurling great fountains of shiny grey-green leaves. However English Australia gets, the mighty gums will always tell you where you really are.

But I drove on, bemused by the calm tranquillity of the place, not at all ready to meet up with James Halliday, one of the Hunter Valley rollickers of my first visit. James had now planted a vineyard in the Yarra and was rapidly becoming Australia's leading wine writer. Rapidly. James does everything rapidly. So surely he was too much of a throbbing gourd of energy and enthusiasms for this mellow place? Well, yes and no. The guy has enough energy to power a small town. The Yarra Valley serenity just about keeps him from exploding. We sat briefly on his porch, gazing across the valley, cattle grazing next to vines, kingfishers darting through the trees and eagles soaring and swooping silently in the high sky. But then this irresistible mixture of a desire to educate and amaze the foreigners about Australia's wines, combined with unbelievable generosity, kicked in. James had got a bit of a feed together, with a few wines. So let's get going.

Well, we started with three sparkling Burgundies from Seppelt, who aged these mesmerising, bubbling reds made like Champagne in deep caves dug into the granite rock by destitute gold miners out in wildest inland Victoria. Did I prefer the 1964, the '46 or the '44? There's something so utterly wicked and improbable about Aussie sparkling Burgundy. These are serious Shiraz red wines – made from one of Victoria's best vineyards at Great Western – which someone has had the audacity to turn into a frothing, dark purple party animal reeking of sweet homemade blackberry jam. And then age it for forty-five years? I was drinking this Seppelt 1944 at forty-five years old! It was as though a queen of the Jazz Age had donned her glad rags and could still trot out a flirtatious Charleston, so long as the beat was slow.

Can you follow that? Of course you can. That's just to wet your whistle for the smoked kangaroo that's coming up. So we had four of Australia's greatest dry Rieslings – Leo Buring from 1973, '71, '70 and '67, showing once again the brilliant individuality of Australian wines. Riesling pinging with a lime acidity that mixed fresh zest with a splash of Rose's Lime Cordial, and wrapped that in crusty white toast dripping with melted butter. 'Ah well, those'll get me ready for the reds.' Only five of the greatest and rarest reds Penfolds had ever made – from the 1967, '63, '62, '61 and '60 vintages. Wines like their Kalimna Cabernet are incredibly rare – Kalimna is the great Shiraz vineyard that is always at the core of Grange, Australia's most famous wine. Kalimna Cabernet and Penfolds 1962 Bin 60A are monumental; people will sell their birthright to catch sight of a bottle.

But we were still warming up. Three great Burgundies came

next. Ahem … Australian Burgundies. From Seppelt again – a 1967, '62 and, just so that no one could accuse us of not respecting age, the 1952 Seppelt Bin I 69/80. (The bin system was a system used by the top wineries to keep track of what were often very limited bottlings of experimental wines.) And I wasn't spitting. And the bellbirds had begun to call from below the porch as a blinding alabaster-white moon rose from behind the far hills. So don't ask me for a tasting note on the three sweet Brown Brothers Spätlese Rieslings from 1973, '72 and '70. They were lovely. Everything was lovely. Australian-style lovely. Not as raucous and as larrikin as the Hunter. But Melbourne has always prided itself on being a sophisticated city, and the Yarra belongs to Melbourne.

I vaguely remember trying to sleep in the next morning. Fat chance if you're staying with James Halliday. This is the guy who said, 'It is a constant aggravation to me the time I lose in sleeping.' So we'll just visit all the Yarra vineyards, then do a tasting – blind (you have to squawk for your supper with these Aussies) – of twenty-four of the world's greatest Pinot Noirs, including stuff like La Tâche from Burgundy for any of you gastroporn enthusiasts – thank goodness, I put his Coldstream Hills Estate Pinot Noir from vines just below the tasting table in fourth place. Oh, then dinner. Oh James, not twice in twenty-four hours. Aussie hospitality. Mixing in a few European beauties this time. Three more fizzes going back to 1964. Four Chablis – one French, but the three Aussies were better, particularly the Seppelt 1956. Three Bordeaux 1961s to put the brilliant Mildara Coonawarra Cabernet on its mettle, but not in its place. Perhaps the Jayer Grands Echezeaux 1934 or the Gouges Nuits St-Georges Pruliers 1934 just about edged the Lindeman's Burgundy Bin 1590, but how delighted the Aussies must have been to be on the same table. And four sweeties with the Yarra next-door neighbour Seville Estate 1980 leading home a Brédif Vouvray 1921. So this was how the Aussie wine buffs spent their weekends.

Frankly, James hasn't changed – his eyebrows are a bit tuftier, but give him half a chance to open his old rarities and he'll be racing for the cellar door waving his corkscrew in anticipation. There's no other wine nation I know so keen to open the special ones, to talk, discuss and disagree – and to drink. If wine was made to drink, then wine was clearly made for Australians. But the Yarra has changed, wine-wise. It's becoming warmer. Some people think it might be getting too warm for Pinot Noir. Yarra Shiraz is now the 'cool' face to reds here, and has a thrilling pepper and wood sap and raspberry fruit that demands you drain your glass. Yarra Chardonnay swings from nutty and oatmealy and capable of standing up to a decent Meursault all the way to lean and smoky and as acrid as a struck match. The pendulum swings, the pendulum swings back. And in Chardonnay, the Yarra Valley is well able to cope.

Victoria still is a state with numerous scattered vineyards, and few real concentrations. There are a few vines in Gippsland, south-east of Melbourne, producing excellent Pinot Noir and Chardonnay – Bass Phillip is one of the most fêted in all Australia. Mornington Peninsula has made a real name for itself with fleshy yet savoury Chardonnay and Pinot Noir, but, as in the Yarra, Shiraz is making its presence felt. Still close to Melbourne, Geelong, Sunbury and Macedon Ranges all play the cool card. And as it warms up as you go north, the sheep-staining ancient red soils of Heathcote grow remarkable Shiraz fabulously rich in fruit yet surprisingly fresh and well-balanced. I once described drinking them as being like watching a fat man with twinkletoes excel at the 'Blue Danube Waltz'. Jasper Hill is a real original. There are real originals, too, at Beechworth, led by Giaconda; the King Valley has Pizzini showing the way with Italian varieties; and Mount Langi Ghiran, Best's and Tahbilk seem to pop up out of nowhere with impressive stuff. But there is one place where the vineyards are concentrated and the style of wine is unique: the great old survivor from the phylloxera plague, Rutherglen, out in the old goldfields of the far north-east, nudging up against the Murray River.

It's not often I arrive at a winery and say, 'Don't show me anything clean, anything new, anything novel. Don't show me your bright, gleaming stainless steel vats and your expensive scented French oak barrels. Show me your cobwebs, show me your dirt, show me the holes in your tin roof. Let me see your house martins and moths dart and flicker above my head in the hot, humid air that is thick with sweetness and let me stroke the sticky leaks and the bulges on your ancient, sagging casks with my fingers. But that's what I say when I visit Rutherglen and turn up at wineries like Morris or Buller or Campbells, family wineries, generation to generation, since the gold-rush days of the nineteenth century. And people like David Morris and Andrew Buller are happy to oblige. They take me into cellars that haven't seen a broom this century, nor maybe last. Rutherglen is where the world's greatest sweet fortified Muscats are made, along with some pretty impressive Muscadelles which now sport the slightly silly name of Topaque. What marketing wizard thought that one up? You can't hurry this fortified wine business. A young Muscat may have a delightful sweetness like chocolate and strawberry syrup and a heavy-lidded scent like orange spice and tea-rose at dusk. And it's a good drink. But it's not a great drink. For greatness, you have to have time on your side, and patience and fortitude. When things are tough, as they mostly have been for the last fifty years, since the public's taste has moved well away from sweet fortified wines, you must be brave and hold on to your old wines. Rutherglen used to boast the largest wine cellars and the largest vineyards in the southern hemisphere. Just a handful of doughty families – led by bloody-minded, hoary-headed chieftains – hang on. Just one new, but equally doughty, producer, Chris Pfeiffer, has arrived in living memory and he knows he will spend the rest of his career building up and ageing the stocks he needs to blend and marry and finally create great Muscat.

I've been in among the barrels with all these guys, and with boyish delight they turn up jewels that literally might have been lost for a decade. And I mean it. They put their precious Muscats and Muscadelles into smaller and smaller barrels as they age and evaporate, and then just hide them away, often up near the hot tin roof, where they will bake themselves to a syrup until one of the wine men remembers they are there – or just stumbles on the tiny cask. I was with David Morris's father, Mick, one morning when he noticed a nine-litre cask jammed into a corner up under the roof. He climbed up with his siphoning hose and dipped it through the bung hole. He told me the air he sucked in almost choked him with its steamy richness. But there was no liquid until he got right to the bottom of the barrel, where he found about a litre and a half of treacle. He humped the little barrel down from the roof. This was an old Liqueur Muscadelle he'd liked the look of a dozen years earlier, so he'd popped it up there for a bit of a bake and then forgotten about it. He wasn't worried. In fact, he was delighted. I scooped a little onto my finger and licked it. I felt dizzy with its richness. 'A dash or two of this will do wonders for a young 'un,' Mick said. And to prove it he poured out a big glass of young Muscadelle, added two drops of the old nectar and gave it a swirl. The young wine was transformed from a glycerol-sweet, rich, blackberry syrup into a much deeper, old cooked raspberry jam. And the old wine, which had been so powerful that it didn't seem to have a taste, only an effect, developed a richness of coffee and dark chocolate and raisins and something appetising and savoury like beef tea. Mick said that he would add one tablespoon of the old beauty to 250 litres of young stuff – and this is what you'd get.

As I left, Mick disappeared, then came back with a dab of sludgily heavy liquid in the bottom of a glass. The almost oppressive perfume uncoiled like a cobra, building up level on level of burning caramel and mint, cocoa and charred hazelnuts and raisins. And then, suddenly, the fruit was gone, the winey sweetness, too, and it smelled like nothing so much as an old,

old painting, and any sweetness it had left was the sweetness of age and wood and oil. It was a nineteenth-century Muscat, laid down by his great-grandfather and briefly freshened up thirty years ago by his father.

South Australia, biggest and sometimes best

I've only got one bottle of Grange, Australia's most famous wine. The 1971. It was given to me by a shaggy-faced chap with a megalithic proboscis in the men's loo at the Adelaide Hilton. Do you want to hear more? Of course you do. Well, it's not terribly salacious. The guy's name was Max Schubert and he had made the wine. And making wine was what he liked doing. Along with a bit of amiable flirtation and a punt on the ponies. What he hated was PR. And he'd sat there next to me at dinner, glumly wishing it was all over and he could go and have a beer. I sensed this, so I followed him to the gents, away from his minders, and struck up an old-fashioned conversation about blondes and horse-racing. We got on like a house on fire after that. And once we had exhausted those topics, he was happy to talk about Grange all night.

Grange is the wine that made Australia famous with the wine highbrows. You could argue that the wine that made Australia truly famous was Lindeman's Bin 65 Chardonnay or Jacob's Creek red and quite a bit of me would agree. Most wine-drinkers have never heard of Grange and hardly any have managed to taste it, whereas the Lindeman's and the Jacob's Creek have transformed the lives of millions of drinkers by their delightful flavours and affordable prices. But what Grange has done is to sway opinion at the very top of the wine-writing, wine-collecting, wine-snobbery tree. You could say, surely the Aussies didn't need any help in letting the world know that their wines equalled the best, but actually they did. Beneath the bluster there was a desperate desire for acceptance at wine's top table. It doesn't affect today's mob too much, but Max Schubert started making Grange in 1951. And you'd find less than a hand-ful of Australians who really thought they could make one of creation's greatest reds in 1951.

I'm not sure Max did either, but he sure as hell knew he could improve on what was then being produced. He made wine for Penfolds and had been sent to Spain in 1949 to study sherry. Everything in Europe was being renewed after the Second World War and one commodity that was being replaced as fast as possible was wood. The old barrels hadn't been looked after during the war years – they were dirty, infected, leaky and ready for the bonfire. You don't smell much new wood in the sherry region of Spain nowadays – they abhor its flavours in their wine. But in 1949 they'd got the required new barrels and vats and you've simply got to use them – season them with wine, tell yourself that this year's sherry will be a bit oaky, but it's all in a good cause long term. And Max smelled the sweet exotic scent of wine fermenting in new oak. He had been making wine since 1931 but had never smelled new oak. From Spain he then went on to Bordeaux and here it was again – the outrageously warm 1949 vintage of Cabernet Sauvignon grapes was being given the new-oak treatment. Max was lucky – 1949 was bringing in super-ripe grapes. If ever a Bordeaux vintage was going to bring in sugar-stuffed fruit similar to what South Australia regularly produced, it was 1949. He was smelling the marriage of two headily exciting aromas – the sweetness of new wood and the sweetness of new wine from ultra-ripe grapes.

Max returned to Adelaide convinced he could do the same thing back home. Then he realised that there probably wasn't a single new oak barrel in South Australia, and there wasn't any Cabernet Sauvignon either. So he would use Shiraz. And by calling in some favours with the brandy producers, he got hold of five 300-litre barrels of new American oak. Max had come back with all kinds of ideas about how to improve Australian red winemaking, which he had realised was unbelievably rudi-mentary. Most importantly, he realised that Australian methods of fermenting red wines were never going to produce what he had in mind. The fermentation was typically tumultuous and uncontrolled, and often only took one and a half to two days, frequently leaving a significant amount of sugar half fermented and likely to turn into vinegar – and how much colour and flavour could you extract from your juicy, ripe, dark black grapes in two days? He found ways to cool the juice and let the wine slowly ferment with its skins for twelve days. The result was dark, thick wine. With eighteen months ageing in new American oak barrels, he would make a wine unlike any Australia had ever produced. The 1951 Grange.

It wasn't plain sailing, though. His wines needed ageing, and tasted sufficiently rough and raw at first that Penfolds gave up on Grange and told him to stop producing it. Max wouldn't. He simply burrowed his way deep into the bowels of the Penfolds cellars and went on making Grange secretly with all the nervous fervour of a prisoner of war digging an escape tunnel out of Colditz. Until, in 1960, those early Granges had softened; the Penfolds bosses tried them, realised what they were worth, and told Max to let rip all over again.

Grange is still Australia's most famous wine, but it's not necessarily the best any more, because Australia now has so many different styles of red wine it excels at. Grange is still mostly Shiraz, although South Australia now has loads of Cabernet Sauvignon if it's required for Grange, and sometimes a dollop or two is. It's still based on Barossa Valley fruit, though Penfolds have never claimed it as such, and if the winemakers find any batches of grapes they are certain are perfect for Grange – anywhere in Australia – well, they can buy them and put them in the mix. And the taste has changed. It has both led the Pied Piper dance toward the great Shirazes Australia now produces, yet also sometimes felt compelled to alter the successful formula to reflect our times, in particular the absurd Gadarene rush toward over-ripeness that affected the world's red wines at the turn of the century. But Grange is still an unforgettable glass of wine and much better at twenty years old than at five. Still full of youthful vigour, with the flavours of leather and black-berry, pine resin and toffee, beef blood and liquorice, and the purest and sweetest of blackcurrants all passionately entwined. Maybe there are now better Australian reds, but there isn't another Grange.

And there isn't another Barossa Valley, which is where most of Grange's grapes come from. Driving up from Adelaide, you don't really appreciate how special the place is for vines. The soils look quite dark and rich, the low mountains to the east don't look too impressive but the little villages and towns are delightful and have an old-fashioned German feel (they should have, as the area was settled by Germans in the 1840s). And there's the key. These religious refugees from Prussia brought vines with them. In particular, they brought Shiraz which they planted out, and in typical German rural manner farmed devotedly and protectively right through the nineteenth century. They probably didn't even know what was going on in the rest of the world. Well, let me tell you. The phylloxera aphid was destroying all the other vineyards on the planet, and that included, eventually, the vineyards of Victoria, South Australia's next-door neighbour.

But the phylloxera has never reached South Australia and no one knows why. And they don't want it. They have fierce, unbribable-looking men with hairy knees and long socks in crisp khaki kit checking vehicles for fruit and vine material on the country roads. Don't try to be smart as the fines run into thousands of dollars. The only way to replace vines destroyed by phylloxera is to graft cuttings on to the roots of different, usu-ally North American, vine species immune to the aphid. These grafted vines don't live so long, and with a different root system are they really the same? And does their wine taste the same?

In the Barossa, they're not intending to find out. Because here – not in France, or Spain, Italy or the Middle East – they have the oldest wine vines in existence. And lots of them. Some of these are the ones planted directly from the settler ships and others are planted from cuttings of these original vines. It's a wonderful feeling to go into the Turkey Flat vineyard and gently rock a vine planted in the 1840s with your hand, or one in the Langmeil vineyards almost as old, or others up in the hills at Henschke, and in dozens of vineyards whose growers sell the precious grapes to a queue of avid winemakers. Those gnarled Methuselahs are like sinewy giants wrestling and tussling in a bizarre balletic embrace, their tiring limbs contorted but not wizened, gaining massive girth as their blood flow thickens to a trickle, and as you cautiously rock the vine you can feel how fragile it has become. Yet they still give a crop of grapes which have unparalleled richness and depth of flavour. Some die each year, but as one proud grower said 'a lot more vines become a hundred years old every year'.

And they are being cherished like never before. Forty years ago the growers struggled to find a winery that could be bothered to turn these grapes into wine, but within a decade, as a bunch of visionaries led by the Baron of the Barossa, Peter Lehmann, suddenly realised their whole birthright was at risk, old-vine Barossa Shiraz became world famous, then far too world famous, as the grapes suffered more abuse at the hands of the overripening brigade crazy for a 100-point wine than any other grapes in Australia. And now they're cherished. A bunch of young winemakers are gaining influence, who want to see more organic grape growing, who are prepared to risk a biodynamic experiment, who don't just choose old-vine Shiraz but old-vine Grenache and Mourvèdre, Carignan, Cinsault, and the white Ugni Blanc, Clairette and Marsanne. And it shows how far we have moved from those arrogant, show-pony Shirazes of the turn of the century that there are more than a few 'back to the future' natural winemakers giving it a go. As Peter Schell at Spinifex, one of the new-generation sensitive Barossa outfits, told me, 'I've made some black monsters. I've picked the Shiraz at 17.5 per cent alcohol. I didn't make Shiraz for seven years from 2001. I was sick to the back teeth of it. Now I'm back in love with it.' And then Tom Shobrooke turned up with a bottle of amontillado 'sherry' he'd made from Nebbiolo. The new Barossa is much more fun than the old.

One grape I should have mentioned is Riesling, but it's not so much a Barossa Valley grape as an Eden Valley grape, just up in the Barossa Ranges and again settled by the Germans, and Riesling is the quintessential German grape. And it's a Clare Valley grape, too, a couple of hours' unhurried driving to the north where people like Jeffrey Grosset create wines of such limpidity and intellectual focus that they make any wine lover's jaw drop, whether they thought they liked Riesling or not. It's one of the experiences I treasure as I take my seat on the plane at Heathrow, about to head off to the far south. That first mouthful of fantastically tangy Clare Valley Riesling, or the equally tangy but just slightly more scented Eden Valley version. It's more a taste of the Australia I'm longing to get back to than any Shiraz or Chardie or Cab.

I'll probably land at Adelaide airport and it'll be roasting. I'll take a taxi into the centre of town and it'll be broiling. I'll stand on the melting tarmac, hemmed in by the bustling traffic, and gaze west up to the Adelaide Hills. It looks cool up there, it looks wooded and sheltered from the glare. It looks as though it might even rain. When you're standing in the centre of what has sometimes, in the last few years, been declared the world's hottest city, you need to leap into a car and head up there. But take your time. There is an impressive, sweeping motorway, but I'd take the smaller roads that twist and turn through eucalyptus forest up to Summertown or Norton Summit, Basket Range or Cudlee Creek. These are intensely beautiful, cramped, tortuous hill valleys; the heavy perfume of the eucalyptus gums envelops you. Stop and look back, and far below Adelaide bakes. Yet up here the pressures of city life fall away with every breath you take. These are the Adelaide Hills. People long to live up here. The parched city of Adelaide drains as much of the Hills' rainwater as it can to slake the city's thirst, and in the patches of old meadow, in glades between the high, narrow, pale gums, where there is still some water to collect and rain to refresh the land, here there are vines. Brian Croser began it all at Petaluma, on his way to becoming Australia's most respected and often most serious wine leader. Cool-climate Chardonnay was what he craved, and he found it at Piccadilly, at 570 metres (1870 feet) up, just about as high as you can go in the Adelaide Hills. It's not just Chardonnay now – Riesling and Sauvignon Blanc are tangy and good; Pinot Noir might well be South Australia's best; and, as a complete alternative to the Barossa style, cool-climate, peppery, sappy, blackberryish Syrah is creating waves as the Hills begin to drop toward the south.

And they drop down on to the McLaren Vale. These are some of the original South Australian vineyards, in a calm, pastoral atmosphere as the land drifts to the coast at Gulf St Vincent. It's almost as though the Germans went north to the Barossa and the English settled south of Adelaide, here in the Vale, where they set about making great big rich beasts of reds, dense and furry with iron, and equally powerful sweet fortifieds that were sent to Britain to keep everyone warm in the nineteenth century. They would have been using Grenache and Syrah for most of these. And as the craze for Chardonnay took off, the Vale planted that too and sold its rich, plump, golden wine all over Australia to whoever needed a little help in cheering up their thinner brews. And now it's become a much more interesting place. So much of Australia has now stood up to the corporate mugging the wine industry was suffering from at the end of the twentieth century, and none more so than here in McLaren Vale. Steve Pannell, the region's leading winemaker, sees the Vale as a hothouse for research as the effects of global warming become ever more alarming in water-deficient South Australia. He still makes a beautiful loganberry and blackberry Shiraz, as well as Australia's best Nebbiolo, but he doesn't think we'll still be drinking McLaren Vale Shiraz/Syrah in twenty years. It'll be the Mediterranean varieties from southern France or Italy, Spain or Greece. Perhaps the Portuguese ones like Touriga Nacional. And that goes for whites, too. If South Australia wants to keep making whites, they're going to need to be investigating varieties like Fiano, Falanghina, Greco or Assyrtiko. Now.

Vines don't stop at McLaren Vale. Langhorne Creek and Currency Creek produce a lot of gentle, easy-going reds just over the hills to the south. But there is one more mighty area way further south that is important. I'd say take a plane because it's a long, dull car journey, but then, I drove. Sometimes you need to drive to remind yourself that even the distance between one small town and the next is so much greater in Australia than it is in Europe. And in most of Australia there won't be dinky little villages to relieve the sense of aloneness you get when you drive off into the hard country. And this isn't the harsh orange of the Outback. As we turn south off the main Adelaide to Melbourne road at Keith, we're entering the Limestone Coast, the largest limestone outcrop in the world. The whole of this southern end of South Australia is one massive limestone resource. Some of the soil is sixty million years old, some is thirty million years old, Coonawarra is one million years old, and there are soils on limestone ridges out by the sea that are only sixty thousand years old. They're all here because of various upsurges, but also because in every ice age the seas retreat, then return and each time create yet another limestone ridge – and there's an ice age about every fifty thousand years. This vast area has barely been scratched for vineyards yet – most of it is still under scrub and forest. Coonawarra is famous, but it's only one of twelve limestone ridges between the Comaum Range Hills and the sea. Vines love limestone. But it's a cool-climate region down here, and the sea isn't that far away. In a warming world we might be seeing a lot more of the Limestone Coast in the next twenty years. We might have to be getting our Shiraz from here, or it might even get too warm for that, even here.

Western Australia, both hot and cool

I've never driven to Western Australia. I don't know anyone who has. It's almost 4000 kilometres (2485 miles) from Sydney to Perth, and for most of that distance you won't see a town, village or house, nor even a tree. You'll be crossing the Nullarbor Plain. Nullarbor means 'no trees' — because there are no rivers to water them. Just an enormous, pancake-flat nothingness. I could take the train, but however keen I am on nothingness (and trains) I think I'd spend rather too much time in the pub car for my health. So this time I do fly, and it's a matter of minutes before I've left the cramped coastal strip around Sydney and breasted the Great Dividing Range. Then a few minutes more of gazing down at the vast spread of square and rectangular blocks of vegetation that make up the blazing hot Riverina Irrigated Area, where a lot of Australia's cheap wine comes from, as well as its most famous sweet wine, Noble One. It's almost easier to make sweet Semillon here than dry, and at Griffith they could never get their Semillon ripe before it rotted. Hopeless. Until a guy called Darren De Bortoli came home from wine school one day and said, 'Don't throw away those rotten old things — that's noble rot. That's what makes Château d'Yquem so sweet.' He made a wine which he called Noble One and, blow me, if their first vintage, 1982, wasn't as sweet as Yquem, and damn near as good, too.

And then I'm into the real Australia, what most of Australia is like, and I think: this is a savage place; everywhere in this angry, orange interior looks bleached of life, shorn of vitality. A glimpse of green way to the south — are those the Clare Valley vineyards, a lonely splattering of green hemmed in by drought and stress? And then once more, this brilliant, awesome humbling nothingness sprawls beneath the wings of the plane, hour after hour.

A few raw signs of human endeavour remain from some brave souls, but it's as though all they have managed to do is to shave the top of this land's skin and leave a pale, salty welt that never heals. It almost gets worse as the plane starts its descent. Even the orange glare seems to have been drained from the soil and vast, balefully bright white salt pans begin to scar the earth like leprosy and warn the humans that this isn't a place for them. And suddenly there are trees, tracks, roads, reservoirs, shacks, then houses, then suburbs and shopping malls, a golf course – and we've landed – in the tiny thin strip of fertile land that clings to the coast of Western Australia, where people live in Perth, the most isolated capital city in the world, closer to Indonesia than it is to the next big city in Australia. To the north, the fertile strip wavers, weakens, then dies, but to the south it spreads cautiously as the Southern Ocean begins to cool the land, but not to water it; that would be asking too much in parched Western Australia.

There are vines near Perth – some of Australia's very first vineyards. They are only a short drive out up the Swan River, but already the desert is making its grab. This is the hottest of any of Australia's major wine regions: the fertile strip is thin indeed. It's a lot more fun to head south and, above all, to the Margaret River. This is where a bunch of obsessive doctors set up vineyards in the 1960s because they had read that the conditions were similar to those of Bordeaux. Well, they may well be; Cabernet Sauvignon is really good here, and they make an excellent, tangy Sauvignon–Semillon white blend just like they do in the Graves region of Bordeaux. And the surf's good, too, just as on the coast to the west of Bordeaux where the golden sands stretch north to Brittany and south to Spain for hundreds of kilometres and waves thud in from the Atlantic Ocean. Just as they do in Margaret River. Surfers career across the breakers' faces. But the sea is much closer in Margaret River. It's right at the end of the road past Moss Wood, or Cullen, or Cape Mentelle, or whichever other winery you're visiting.

And the surf's wonderful. Wineries never have a problem finding vintage helpers. They come from all over Australia, fit, bronzed and bleached blond. And the one thing all winery owners dread is the cry 'Surf's up!' What's more important? A clutch of majestic waves arriving from the Indian Ocean, or getting the Cabernet in? The surf wins every time. I caught my last big wave at Smith's Beach. In it came. 'It's a dumper,' I said. It was high, steep and ugly, frothing at its crest. It's a dumper, don't take it – but I couldn't resist. I've still got the scar.

It's safer further south in what is called the Great Southern. It's colder, too. Western Australia's coastline turns to the east and faces the icy Southern Ocean head on. Not much surfing here; the main town, Albany, made its reputation as a whaling centre. But the cool, dry conditions are fantastic for vines. Brilliantly zesty, tangy Rieslings that seem to spit glinting minerals onto your tongue. Shirazes full of pepper and blackberry, liquorice and squashed violet petals. Cool but flavour-filled Chardonnays and Pinot Noirs, and excellent Cabernet, too, if you like it blackcurranty and stony and dry and full of the promise of cedar. But they're really short of water. Let's see whether climate change starts to bring in more winter rain. If it does, Great Southern could yet prove to be one of Australia's most exciting vineyard regions.

Tasmania, only good for apples

I should have guessed that Tasmania would be good for grapes. The local Department of Agriculture swore it was too cold and only any use for apples. That's always a sign that a classic cool-climate wine region is on its way. That's the tale they told in Marlborough in South Island, New Zealand. That's the tale they told in Elgin in South Africa. That's the tale they told in southern England. Sussex: no good for grapes. Try apples. Luckily, the authorities normally find themselves spouting this risk-averse piffle to people who are too obstinate and obsessive to take any notice. Indeed, it spurs them on. And I was thinking, of these really cool climates that are now modern wine stars, was Tasmania the first? My first Tasmania wine was a 1970 Moorilla Estate Cabernet from the far south of the island – crab apple country, surely? But no, this Cab hummed with sharp, fresh blackcurrant fruit and it was decades before I had another Tassie Cab as good. And I was drinking this before Montana had produced the first Marlborough wine, before Paul Cluver had produced Elgin's first, and before the Mosses had even considered creating Nyetimber in the depths of the Sussex countryside. Was Tasmania actually the first?

I think she probably was, and that would be perfectly fitting – the Aussies like being first at everything, even though I suspect the overwhelming majority of mainland Australian winemakers looked right down their noses at these shivering pioneers as they basked in their superior warmth and poured themselves another mug of their sun-soaked Shiraz. And maybe it was because until fairly recently Australia was so wedded to warm-climate styles that the ultra-cool, knife-edge sorts of flavours that Tasmania was capable of seemed just a step too far south. And to be honest, I half agreed with them. Very few Tasmania table wines convinced me. What was plain was that almost all of the best sparkling wine in Australia was coming from Tasmanian fruit. And usually that means that the grapes aren't quite ripe enough for super still wines. Well, it looks as though Tasmania is sorting itself out. Interestingly, the greatest still wines are coming from the surprisingly dry far south, while the greatest fizz is coming from the wetter, windier north. They've taken a long time about it and progress has been cautious to say the least. But it took Champagne and Burgundy far longer to discover what would work best and where, and whereas some new wine areas blaze briefly and then fizzle as they realise they are trying to run before they can walk, the cliché preferred by the Tasmanians is 'good things come to those who wait'.

And now I need to go. I've spent long enough here in this country that might even mean more to me than France, has definitely meant more to me in finding a purpose in this wine life of mine. Ah, Australia – my distant, addictive lover. As I listen to the last magpie call and watch the dust cloud rise on a country track that may see no more cars all day, as I gaze at the pale, seductive blue sky with a few thin clouds idly splashed across the horizon, as I bid g'day, g'bye, g'see you again soon to the last cheery, abrasive but warm-hearted Aussie ocker, ockie, cockie, whatever, I'm heavy of heart. I must go. Big world out there. But I'll be back.

New Zealand

Much more than Sauvignon Blanc

They nearly called their most famous wine Farewell Spit. At the last minute they saw the funny side and decided on Cloudy Bay. But who would have cared? This was 1985. This was the South Island of New Zealand. Call the wine what you like. No one will ever know. Well, they knew a year later, all right, because this Cloudy Bay 1985 was voted best Sauvignon Blanc in the world in London. Within a couple of years it had become the most sought-after white wine in the world. Queues would form outside any shop that was rumoured to have a supply. Bottles were rationed, then sold and re-sold.

But Cloudy Bay didn't have a vineyard in 1985. It didn't even have a winery. And their winemaker was employed by someone else making their 1985s. The owner picked up his truckload of grapes in Marlborough on the South Island, waited in line at the ferry to get across to the North Island and then drove – I've driven it – another six hours further up the East Coast to a winery in Gisborne. And the phone was ringing when he arrived. It was his winemaker, Kevin, saying 'Right, this is what you do.' He rang at every meal break and tea break until the fermentation was done – not their grapes, not their winery, but it was *their* vision of flavour and that was what won the title of Best Sauvignon Blanc in the World: a wine of lush lychee, nectarine and apricot fruit, shot through with gooseberry, green

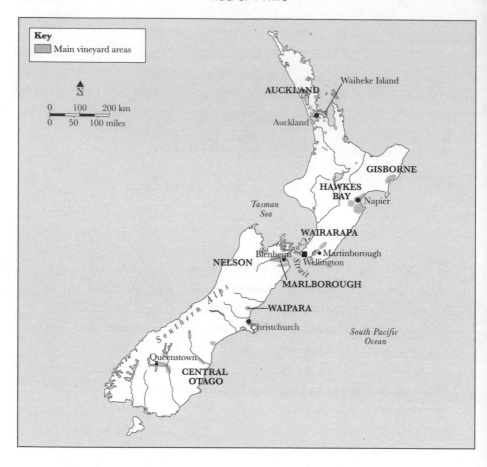

nettle and lime zest acidity, so that your mouth watered with excitement but never puckered from aggression.

New Zealand really was starting from scratch. They had made wine before: indeed, in the 1840s a Frenchman had visited and described the local hooch as 'light white wine, very sparkling and delicious to taste' – high praise from a Frenchman. But any dreams that New Zealand might become a southern hemisphere France disappeared pretty sharpish. Temperance groups were gathering strength, and in 1919 New Zealand actually voted for Prohibition – it was only soldiers returning from the First World War who said, 'Hey, come on, give a bloke a break.' And reversed the vote. But New Zealand's relationship with alcohol was clearly an unhappy one, and decent quality was so clearly not an issue that after the Second World War a Royal Commission visited, tasted their wines and wrote a report saying that most New Zealand wine would be classified as 'unfit for human consumption' in other wine-producing countries. It didn't get much better, either. New Zealand had a prim colonial legacy that distrusted alcohol and made any kind of move toward quality wine extremely difficult. There were still dry areas of the country in 1990 – and that included rugby clubs, for goodness sake. New Zealand was a tense, unconfident little place imprisoned by the tyranny of distance.

How different it is now. In this twenty-first-century world, where everything seems to become noisier, dirtier, angrier, where stress and anxiety are normal states of mind, New Zealand is now blessed by its glorious isolation – a pair of small islands at the bottom of the world, surrounded by the vast expanse of the Southern Pacific Ocean. And as for its murky wine history, when it's that bad, when the only tradition you have is for poisoning people (well, almost), it can be positively liberating.

You have to look forward. There's nothing to look back to. Sweep the old away. Start all over again. Particularly in the South Island where there wasn't a vine when Montana started to plant Marlborough in 1973. Imagine how liberating that must have been. No wonder Cloudy Bay was able to produce a world-beating wine from a standing start, because you really could create visions of the flavours you wanted, with no one to gainsay you.

You could be planting vineyards on land that has never been used to grow anything before. Imagine – you're the first. It must make a difference to grow grapes on virgin land rather than land that has been exhausted by a thousand harvests. What you grow, how you grow it, how you want your wine to taste is up to you. You can create flavours that have never existed before. Good wines taste of their place, where they come from; they taste of somewhere. New Zealand wines shocked and amazed the world because they tasted of a somewhere that no one knew. And that's because New Zealand wines tasted of a somewhere that hadn't existed before. Ever. A winemaker who planted vines in the remote Waitaki Valley way down in the South Island said that when he tasted the wine from his first crop he was dumbstruck. 'It was like tasting a new colour. I knew this flavour had never existed before.'

Well, that's the idea. But on my first trip there – way back in 1987 – reality was a bit more belt and braces. After tasting the shocking, revolutionary Montana Sauvignon Blanc 1983 and the haunting, magical, multi-layered St Helena Pinot Noir 1982 at the same event in 1984, high above London on the top floor of New Zealand House, I knew I was going to have to finagle my way south. In 1987, at the end of October, I flew off just as Europe's last tenuous hours of summer were withering, knowing that twenty-four hours later I would be landing in a distant country in the full optimistic emotional flood of springtime. I'd heard talk of the Land of the Long White Cloud. And here it was, a layer of pale cotton fluff hovering protectively a couple of thousand feet above this fragile sliver of land, lively seas to the east and the west, the crests of the surging waves blindingly white under the glaring purity of this southern sun. It is easy to feel vulnerable, exposed, in New Zealand. Those two islands don't amount to much. You feel that one great earthquake could sink them both, and you'd just be left with the endless expanse of sea. They call New Zealand 'the Shaky Isles'. Two of its major cities, Napier and Christchurch, have had to rebuild themselves after being destroyed by earthquakes. In a reflective mood you can find yourself thinking, one more heave and the whole lot will go.

I climbed off the plane to be met by a rambunctious character called Terry, who seemed to be in charge of New Zealand wine exports, such as they were. 'What do you want to do?' he said. Professional to the last, I replied, 'I want two pints of ice-cold beer and eighteen holes of golf.' And Terry just said, 'It's done.' And it was. I'm going to like this place, I thought. Well, I did, but if I thought I was going to discover a New Age of wine in full swing, I was in for a shock. I was there to judge a wine show. I expected arrays of tingling Sauvignon Blanc. There were just a couple. I expected a flurry of gorgeous scented Pinot Noirs. There were none at all. There were absolutely loads of not-quite-dry Müller-Thurgaus that other judges were raining down gold medals on. They were nice. They were the best Müller-Thurgaus I had ever had. But in Europe we used Müller-Thurgau to make Liebfraumilch. We didn't shower it with gold medals, boasting that it was the nation's best white. Where was the future in all this?

Even further away than I thought, when I discovered a mighty horde of fortified wines to judge, with names like sherry, port, Madeira – you know, Spanish and Portuguese stuff. Except that these were all from New Zealand. I was banging on about how New Zealand wouldn't be taken seriously in the wine world if it gave any gold medals to this mediocre crew. And there was a bunch of old, craggy-jawed fellows chuntering away in the corner. And eventually one of them drew himself up to his not inconsiderable height and lumbered over. He said he heard what I was saying about no gold medals, but this year it was his turn for the Madeira gold medal. And he would sort of like to receive it, if I didn't mind.

It gets better as you head south from subtropical Auckland

After the judging I went off to look around the vineyards and wineries of Auckland. This is where the whole wine industry was based. And I began to understand the problems the new wave would face in New Zealand. Auckland is muggy. It's on a very thin isthmus of land between two oceans. You do get lots of sun, easily enough to dry out the thick sullen clay soils before the next downpour arrives. I went to various wineries and tasted wines that couldn't have been made from healthy grapes. Well, they weren't. All the winemakers happily told me of their different methods for dealing with the flood of rotting grapes they received every vintage. I developed a tasting note that I used for years to describe red wine made from rotting grapes: *Huapai stink*, named after one of the vineyard areas. A strange, disturbing concoction of beef soup, tarmac, malt vinegar and plum skins wrapped in a roll of surgical rubber. Nice.

And yet, the new wave was present in Auckland. Michael Brajkovich at Kumeu River knew how rough his family vineyards were but was so determined to make them work, and so determined not just to up sticks and head for somewhere easier, that he found ways to make his Chardonnay not only the standard bearer for Kiwi Chardie, but for much of the whole southern hemisphere. And at Matua Valley, the Spence brothers knew they could grow decent fruit, but it was 'bloody hard work' as they struggled to domesticate their sodden clay vineyards amid the relentless grape-sapping humidity. They talked about black rot, brown rot, sour rot, trench foot . . . and said they had to use up to twenty times as many sprays on their vines as they would have to in drier regions. And then they pulled out a bottle of Judd Estate Chardonnay – unbelievably good, nutty, intense, savoury – and a Smith-Dartmoor Estate Cabernet Sauvignon, bursting with blackcurrant, damson and strawberry fruit, almost syrupy in its intensity, yet nibbled at by a peppery green acidity and uplifted by a fleeting wild floral scent. Not from Auckland, surely? Absolutely not. They were from the East Coast – the Chardonnay from Gisborne and the Cabernet Sauvignon from Hawke's Bay. The leading wine businesses in New Zealand still have their headquarters in Auckland, but they're not making their reputations on the local grapes.

Gisborne is something of an orphan child in New Zealand wine. Its deep, alluvial silt soils sprawling out into Poverty Bay in the far east of the North Island can and do produce massive crops of fruit. Once it was Müller-Thurgau. Now it's

Chardonnay, much of it for cheap blends and for fizz. They don't get much respect. But all around the edges of the Bay there are less fertile sites, which are simply brilliant for Chardonnay. Judd is one, Dixon is another. Millton Naboth's is another, Ormond is another. These are capable of making some of the greatest Chardonnays in the southern hemisphere, marrying lush texture, finely focused acidity and a brilliant ability to express a rich, nutty, savoury core. I say they are some of the best in the southern hemisphere. Add northern to that.

Drive down the coast for a couple of hours and you're in Hawke's Bay with the art deco city of Napier as its capital. You could pretty much call this the red wine heart of New Zealand. This is where the big beasts congregate – Cabernet Sauvignon, Merlot and Syrah – and it has been claiming to be New Zealand's Bordeaux region since the nineteenth century. This is warm New Zealand, but it is also still wet New Zealand. You get a lot of late summer and vintage rain, more often than not sweeping in from the north-east, threatening to undo all the work of the sunny days. The sun doesn't feel all that hot here, as the coastal breezes, flowing in from the bay, seem to be cooling you down. Don't be fooled. On my first trip I lounged about in late morning without any sunscreen on my hands. By lunchtime they were all blisters, and bloody painful. I almost had to be spoon-fed the local lobster. The ultraviolet penetration around Hawke's Bay is greater than in any other heavily populated place in the world. It is 40 per cent more intense than any equivalent area in Europe. Now this is important because it's not much good for your hands, but it *is* good for grapes. New Zealand red wines, especially from Cabernet Sauvignon, had always been criticised for tasting too green. Hawke's Bay was New Zealand's most successful area, probably aided by the ultraviolet, which helps grape maturity and polymerises tannins but doesn't bake off flavours, so that you ought to be able to ripen the tricky Cabernet Sauvignon fully. Not if you are in the heart of Hawke's Bay, where the soil is too heavy and fertile. You should be able to tell – there are orchards of kiwi fruit and apples everywhere. Fruits love fertile soils. Wine grapes need infertile soils, places where you can't grow much else. Gravel, for instance.

I tracked down that Smith-Dartmoor vineyard, whose Cabernet I had been impressed by up in Auckland. It was in the middle of an old riverbed to the north of the main valley. All gravel. The river had changed course and left behind a field of gravel and little else. Warm, free-draining and infertile. Of course it would be able to ripen Cabernet, though a local told me there was a lot of competition for these infertile soils from asparagus growers. But there was better to come.

I was driving along the Ngaruroro River Valley – broad, fertile, lots of vines too, but they can't have been much good in that thick, dark soil. I turned right after a vineyard village called Fernhill, all nice and prosperous, and suddenly I was in a different world. No greenery. Nothing seemed to grow. There was a rubbish tip and a drag-racing track. But hang on. I stopped the car and leaped over a rusty wire fence. No wonder nothing was growing. This was pure gravel. That's what Cabernet thrives on in Bordeaux – warm, free-draining, infertile. Perfect. Why weren't there any vineyards there? If the New Zealanders were banging on about Hawke's Bay producing Bordeaux in the southern seas – well, they were missing a massive trick. This was Margaux or Pauillac right under my feet – and they were using the land for a rubbish tip and a drag-racing track.

Was anyone listening as I let off steam over a few ice-cold cans later that day? It's possible. Because in 2001 I was back there and early in the morning, barely breakfast time, cold, breezy, the sun hardly past its peachy orange 'good morning everyone' phase, I clambered up a hill just next to where the drag-racing track had been. I looked down and there were vines everywhere. And I witnessed the official designation of this whole area as the Gimblett Gravels. Yes, they had seen the light and designated 800 hectares (2000 acres) to be a protected appellation. In the twenty-first century, Gimblett Gravels Cabernets,

Merlots and Syrahs have been powerful and impressive – easily New Zealand's darkest, ripest reds. But a note of caution – global warming is hitting New Zealand as everywhere else. The problem now in Gimblett Gravels is often to try to hold back ripening rather than hurry it along. Other areas of Hawke's Bay – Esk Valley on the coast north of Napier; Te Awanga, almost on the beach south of Napier; the Red Metal Triangle next to the Gimblett Gravels – they are often producing wines with more perfume, more appetising fruit than they could fifteen years ago. Gimblett Gravels has competition. Good old nature.

At least Hawke's Bay had played some role in New Zealand's wine history, though little of it was glorious. Te Mata, now producer of some of New Zealand's most sought-after Cabernets and Chardonnays, used to be New Zealand's biggest vineyard in the early twentieth century – but it was still only 14 hectares (34 acres) in size, and by the time the current owner, John Buck, bought it in 1974 it had become what he called 'the original Kiwi plonk' winery. Cream sherry was their speciality. It took twenty-four hours to produce – made on a Monday and sold on a Tuesday. It never saw any cream, never saw Spain, never saw a barrel, might never have seen a grape. Industrial drums of Essence de Cream did the tricksy stuff for you.

But Martinborough, an hour's drive north of Wellington, is a 'Johnny-come-lately' based solely on quality aspirations. From now on, from the capital right down to the far south of South Island, it is all new. From now on this really is the new New Zealand; from now maybe it is those dreams of future glory – and to hell with the miserable past – that propel New Zealand wine. Because from here southwards, until the 1970s – and more typically the 1980s – there wasn't a vine. From now on, my heart beats faster the further south I reach. But Martinborough is a good place to start. It's virtually the first bit of cultivable land outside Wellington. You would have thought they would have tried vines ages ago – all those sophisticated civil servants and politicians as a ready market – well, perhaps not. Perhaps beer was easier – Wellington is one of the craft brewery capitals of the world. Wellington lies on a stunning, vast natural harbour, but it is ringed by steep mountains and it's actually pretty difficult to get out of, except by helicopter. Looking east, there is a single, scary road over the commanding Rimutaka Range, and there is a perilous single-track railway – even now, that's it.

However, if you are intrepid enough to make the trip, the Wairarapa Plains spread out before you in pastoral glory and you will think, Why weren't there any vines? Soil is one reason and climate another. The soil is thick, heavy clay, so thick that vine roots would find it impossible to penetrate. And the climate – there's hardly any rain. That's quite a feat in New Zealand. Mountains to the east and west draw off all the rains, and most of the time Martinborough and its neighbours, up the Wairarapa toward Masterston, are in drought. Actually, they do get a bit of rain – the wet southerlies barrel up the valley at just about the time the vines like to flower. If you're setting a crop you want dry air, not drizzly gales blowing all the flowers off your vines. That's if you've got any flowers. The drought conditions mean clear skies in springtime and any buds that do peep forth are likely to get hammered by frost. So it begins to make sense. Why *would* anyone plant here?

Well, around the little town of Martinborough there are a few old, gravelly river terraces, left standing proud when the river changed course centuries ago. And these are as free-draining as any soils in New Zealand. A government report in 1979 said that these terraces would be great for wine – and the author of the report immediately put down his pen, hiked over the mountains and began planting. And, unsurprisingly for New Zealand, the objective was to make superlative Pinot Noir, even if the crops would be tiny. These conditions are entirely unlike Burgundy. And yet you can find what are probably New Zealand's most European Pinots here. Wineries like Ata Rangi, Dry River, Escarpment, Craggy Range, Kusuda and Te Kairanga make startling, dense, thoughtful Pinots. But this is the New World. They don't just make Pinot if they can make other stuff as well. They make superlative Chardonnay, Riesling, Viognier, Cabernet and Syrah ... you get the idea. This is a challenging place to grow grapes. But, weekend after weekend, Martinborough and some spots up toward Masterton now have queues of cool Wellington urbanites pleading for any bottles they can get their hands on.

Across to the cool South

Wellington may not make wine. But it does have two important wine functions. First, it's the port from which the ferry to the South Island departs, and if you have time on a trip, take the ferry. The first hour is across the turbulent Cook Strait, which shows you exactly how brutal the Roaring Forties can be. The last hour is sheer bliss as you glide through the countless islands and coves and cliffs and bluffs of the Marlborough Sounds. Wellington is also where you get the tiny little planes that hip-hop, bounce and bump their way across the Cook Strait to Marlborough, New Zealand's biggest wine area. That's if you can take off. Wellington isn't known as the Windy City for nothing. George W. Bush's Air Force One couldn't land here once because of the gales. The crew said it was too dangerous. Nonsense, said a Kiwi officer, who took the controls and man-handled the plane down to the tarmac. It's a matter of pride with New Zealand fliers never to be beaten by the Wellington weather. And its other wine activity? Every three years it hosts a Pinot Celebration to celebrate absolutely everything to do with — you guessed it — Pinot Noir. After three or four days of relentless Pinot it's amazing how attractive a glass of Sauvignon Blanc becomes. Unless you are a true Pinot nerd, when you might just about neck a drop or two of Nebbiolo, but you'd rather give up drink than admit to pining for a Sauvignon.

Marlborough is Sauvignon heaven — just across the water at

the northern tip of the South Island. If it wasn't for Sauvignon Blanc, Marlborough wouldn't exist as a wine region, and if it wasn't for Marlborough Sauvignon and the global plaudits it has garnered, most of New Zealand would be a vinous backwater, and a lot of those Pinot Noir fancy dans would never have been able to leave their day jobs. Sauvignon matters. Marlborough matters. Indeed, I'll go so far as to say that Marlborough is one of the greatest vineyard areas in the world. And its youth is part of its brilliance. Less than fifty years ago there wasn't a vine here, and no one had the slightest intention of planting. When New Zealand's biggest wine company, Montana, did plant in 1973, it was only because it was the cheapest land in New Zealand – going for as little as NZ $180 a hectare. The sheep starved on it. Everyone was astonished when it began to grow brilliant, mould-breaking Sauvignon Blanc. I know they say that the grape vine likes bad soils, but these were really bad, often nothing more than piles of pebbles.

So what has Marlborough had more than any other great vineyard area? Luck. Being in the right place at the right time. People have spent hundreds of years gradually developing and understanding great vineyard areas like Bordeaux or Burgundy, Germany's Rhine Valley or Spain's Rioja. In the New World, California's Napa, Australia's Barossa or South Africa's Stellenbosch were being studied and cultivated almost as soon as those countries planted vines. And Marlborough does it – *splat* – a mishmash of vines planted with the objective of making cheap plonk like Montana Chablisse Blenheim Dry Chablis out of Müller-Thurgau – but one job lot of Sauvignon Blanc shakes the world of white wine asunder (see Sauvignon Blanc, pages 552–60, for more on this).

First, Montana Sauvignon Blanc leads the way with a brash, fresh, zingy style no winery had ever made before. Then Cloudy Bay in 1986 is crowned Best Sauvignon Blanc in the World with its first vintage of Marlborough wine. Since then Marlborough has been planted with grapes at a furious rate, and from being poor grazing land with a few blocks of vines when I first visited in 1987, it's now almost solid vines with a few blocks of poor grazing land. And most of those vines are Sauvignon Blanc. But not all. There's Chardonnay and Pinot Noir, which both make good white and red wine here, but are also important for good-quality, sometimes excellent, fizz. There are plots of Pinot Grigio, Riesling and Gewurztraminer. There used to be quite a bit of Cabernet Sauvignon and Merlot, but there's not much now. Yet there is some Syrah. And as global warming picks up pace, I think Syrah could be a key red wine for Marlborough in a delightful, sappy, scented, peppery style.

But don't tell me it's just luck. No, of course it's not. Let's talk weather for a moment. Marlborough is dry. Marlborough is sunny – it often has more sunshine hours than anywhere else in New Zealand. Marlborough is also cool. That sun ripens the grapes, but coolness keeps the refreshing acidity high, which is absolutely crucial for Sauvignon Blanc. Normally you can't get cool without wind or rain. And this is the genius of New Zealand's South Island. Its west coast has some of the wettest conditions on earth, but the Southern Alps, a great high spine of mountains, flow down the middle of the island. Most of the dangerous bad weather is brought in on the Roaring Forties westerly storms. The mountains drain off all the rain, leaving the east of the island in a rain shadow – cool, but sunny and dry. Without the Southern Alps, there would be no wine industry in South Island. On the west coast they have trouble ripening cabbages.

And Marlborough is not just one homogenous lump of land. As you come in on the plane, you glide over a fair bit of vineyard. On the right, to the north, you can see the bony bottom of the Wairau River. You also see beautiful mountains, facing south and soaked in green forest. The soils over there are the free-draining gravelly ones. Now look left. You can see the bare, scorched, treeless Wither Hills on the south side, with numerous little dry side valleys dipping into them, all full of vines. These are the Southern Valleys; their soil is heavy and clayish. The grapes ripen about two weeks later on this side of the valley. Mix the riper, more nectariney fruit from the stony soil with the leafier, limier, greener, more citrusy fruit from this side and you have a classic Marlborough Sauvignon Blanc – full, ripe, yet wonderfully zesty. Most wineries try to mix these two styles in a blend, and increasingly they add a third component. Just south over those Wither Hills, there's another valley – the Awatere. It's still part of Marlborough but the valley is no longer protected by the Wither Hills, and is open to the harsh southerly winds. The conditions are cooler still, the flavours leafier, more zesty. Increasingly, wineries add Awatere fruit to maximise the mouthwatering Sauvignon potential. And you can go down on the east coast past Seddon, past the Ure Valley, on down to the Clarence Valley and the whale-watching town of Kaikoura. It's still Marlborough, but it gets colder and windier and the wines get zingier and zestier. It's barely developed yet, but global warming will see expansion all down this coast as Marlborough fights to keep its trademark snap.

There's so much more potential yet to be realised in Marlborough. And it won't all be with Sauvignon Blanc. But they must keep their self-confidence. Even at the world-famous Cloudy Bay winery on my last trip, the boss was saying, 'The worst thing about this valley is people not being as proud of here as they should be. We need people to be big-headed about Marlborough.' It would help. It's a jealous world out there, and I sometimes feel I'm the only one waving the flag for Marlborough.

There are a couple of other small but interesting South Island wine areas. At the northern end, even further north than Marlborough, is Nelson. In many ways it is similar to Marlborough: it often has as much sun but crucially it always has more rain, and that's summer rain, not winter. This hasn't stopped a succession of good wines coming out of Nelson, and from the Neudorf winery you've got some of the most satisfying Chardonnays and Pinot Noirs in New Zealand. Waipara is down the east coast toward Christchurch and it certainly produces some of New Zealand's most remarkably original Pinot Noirs. Not only do you now have fascinating but brilliantly conceived wines from the Pegasus Bay winery, but Waipara is where some of the earliest Pinot thrillers from the 1980s and '90s were grown, and if you head up into the wilds of the Weka Pass you'll find all kinds of wine and vineyard boundaries being pushed back at Bell Hill and Pyramid Valley.

But the place in the south that makes the most noise, that believes in itself the most, that markets itself the best, that sells for the highest price, is Central Otago. And it is worth it. Be prepared to be excited. This is a different world. You can fly there from Christchurch or you can drive. I've done both. If you drive, don't take the main Highway 1: there are cars on it. Head toward the mountains, and when you can't go any further turn left, along the foothills. Drive the country roads. There's no one on them. Drive to the right, drive to the left, drive down the centre – it doesn't matter. No one's there. It makes you realise that there aren't very many people in South Island. Silence really means silence here. When they say, 'Imagine a country where the air is so clear you can see rainbows at night,' well, it's here. South Island, New Zealand.

But if you want to fly, that's cool too. I might say try to book on the biggest plane possible – there's safety in numbers – but big planes can't get into Queenstown airport in Central Otago (they call it Central, by the way). So you'll have to take a small one. And you'll have to wonder whether the pilot knows what he's doing as he gingerly creeps and wobbles up the mist-thick mountain glens that could come straight out of the Scottish Highlands. It *is* like Scotland. How can you grow vines down here? The misty crags, the raw-boned mountainsides, the glum, cold dampness of the air could be a hundred places in Scotland.

But when you finally skid into Queenstown, when you gaze in frank astonishment at the deep brooding blue of Lake Wakatipu and have to scrunch up your eyes to cope with the sudden burst of brilliant sunshine lighting up a ring of lakeside mountains as lovely as anything in Europe's Alps – you know this is different. The wines had better be different. And they are.

If Marlborough Sauvignon Blanc was New Zealand's mighty leap into the world of top-class white, Central Otago Pinot Noir was New Zealand's starburst of world-class red. And it's New Zealand's most recent, only releasing its first wines in 1987. But people have been saying Central Otago should have vines for ages, and because of a nineteenth-century gold rush there were vines planted, but they only lasted as long as the gold rush. If you were canny you could earn a lot more money selling wine to miners than they were likely to make searching for gold. Sam Neill, the Hollywood actor, is a local, and is also an enthusiastic wine producer with his Two Paddocks label. He used to holiday up here as a child and remembers his father saying 'People should be growing grapes here. It's just like the Rhine, just like Burgundy.' Up to a point. In fact, it's more extreme than either. It's worth remembering that this is where New Zealand's ski fields are. It's also worth remembering that the terrible west coast weather is at its worst less than 80 kilometres (50 miles) directly west of here, where the Milford Sound gets 1000 millimetres (394 inches) of rain a year. If it weren't for the good old Southern Alps pushing the rainstorms back, there would be no Central wine. Yet Central Otago is New Zealand's only desert. That means that parts of it get less than 250 millimetres (10 inches) of rain a year. And that, of course, means lots of bright blue skies – and that means heaps of sun.

No, this isn't normal New Zealand, this strange, little, arid oasis hemmed in by mountains. If you're standing in the vineyards and the sun goes behind a cloud, there's a dramatic drop in temperature until the sun breaks out again. So you can imagine that, at night, it gets pretty chilly, even in summer. But that's why Central Otago works — sunny, and often pretty hot days, with a big temperature drop at night means you can easily ripen the grapes but keep fabulous, acid-led intensity. Alcohol levels often hit 14 per cent, but the wines stay fresh-tasting. It's far south — at 45°S it's the furthest south of any of the world's wine regions (barring a few straggly vines in South America). This means that the days are longer, even if the summer is shorter. It's high up — almost 430 metres (1400 feet) in some places — and because it is in a bowl between mountain ranges there is no maritime influence and you are always at risk of frost. I was there in January 2017 — their midsummer — and a great patch of vines had been killed by frost only the week before — a withered brown stain in a sea of prosperous green. You gaze down at the churning turquoise waters of the rivers, flecked with cream foam as they cascade through the gorges. You gaze up at these stern mountain faces, carpeted with wild purple thyme — and you can sometimes smell it in the air and in the wine. You tramp through the ravished, ruined slopes of the old gold sluicings at Bannockburn, or you clamber over the quartz boulders and ancient diggings and shafts at Bendigo, and you know that this is an extreme place, and you should expect the wines to be extreme.

Well, they are. That doesn't mean that they are necessarily aggressive. Scent and fruit can be extreme, too. There are four main areas in Central. Gibbston is a cool, sheltered ledge of vines hanging over the rim of the Kawarau River, and when they survive the frosts and get enough late-summer warmth these Pinot Noirs and Rieslings are the most scented in Central. Seventy-two kilometres (45 miles) east across the trackless mountains, Alexandra is warmer and the wines are sturdier. One hundred kilometres (60 miles) north of Alexandra, Lake Wanaka is a photographer's dream, lush vines swooping down to the southern shores and harsh mountains, snowcapped even in high summer, rising over the dark Prussian blue waters of the lake. This is cool climate, and the vines reach deep into the schistous gravel earth for their character.

And at the heart of it all is Lake Dunstan, the knobbly little town of Cromwell, and most of Central's vineyards. Pinot Noir dominates because everyone here is crazy to make the great Pinot Noir, yet Riesling and Chardonnay can be thrilling, too. Felton Road in Bannockburn, an area of old gold workings facing north toward the lake, makes some of the best Riesling and Chardonnay in New Zealand, as well as thrilling Pinot Noir. Bannockburn is warm and so is Bendigo, a broad, glittery reef of quartz facing north-west further up the lake where there are rumours that Syrah might be the next rising star. The Pinots from these two areas are dense, dark, slow-moving but wonderfully rich, spicy and long-lived, with a brush or two of that wild thyme if you're lucky. The west side of the lake is also warm, but frost-prone – isn't everywhere in Central? – and the areas of Lowburn and Pisa Ranges are making a name for wines of a lusher character, again mostly Pinot Noir but of juicier, sweeter fruit, until you come across something like Burn Cottage, which manages to marry herb scent and sap, ripe blue plum and raspberry fruit showered with mineral dust, and a perfume as timeless as the smell of dry old pews in an ancient church. These pioneers only planted Central to show they could do something different. That's exactly what they do.

I never want to leave New Zealand. And before I head to Auckland airport on my way home, if I have a few hours to spare, I take the ferry across to Waiheke Island out in Hauraki Gulf. They make wonderful wine here, but the beaches are like a siren to me, heading back to the drab north. The waves ripple, the water's warm and salty and swimming is more like floating. And then I can climb up to Te Whau Point and stand with a glass of Man O' War Chardonnay in my left hand and a glass of Stonyridge Pilgrim red in my right. I can see the high-rises and towers of Auckland across the Gulf, reality within reach but delightfully removed. I can sense the rush and the stress but I can't hear it. If I hold my breath, I can't hear anything. If I close my eyes I can see lots. This gentle sun, this friendly place, it's like those childhood summer's days we thought we always had. All that and wine. Why would I want to leave?

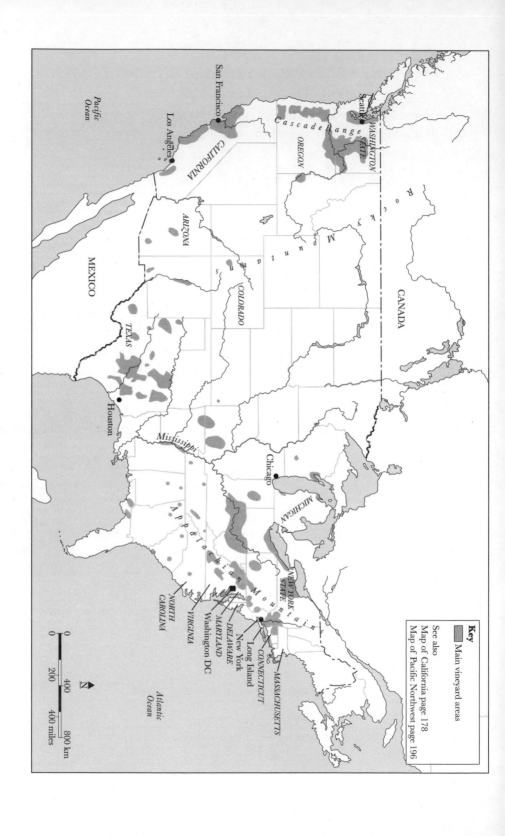

Pacific
Ocean

San Francisco

Los Angeles

CALIFORNIA

ARIZONA

COLORADO

MEXICO

TEXAS

Houston

Mississippi

Seattle

WASHINGTON STATE

OREGON

Cascade Range

R o c k y   M o u n t a i n s

CANADA

Chicago

MICHIGAN

A p p a l a c h i a n   M o u n t a i n s

NEW YORK STATE

NORTH CAROLINA

VIRGINIA

MARYLAND

Washington DC

DELAWARE

New York

Long Island

CONNECTICUT

MASSACHUSETTS

Atlantic
Ocean

0   200   400   800 km
0   400   400 miles

N

Key
☐ Main vineyard areas

See also
Map of California page 178
Map of Pacific Northwest page 196

USA

Out with the old, in with the new

The United States could reasonably claim to make a broader range of wines than any other country. Most countries just use a single species, *Vitis vinifera* – the wine vine – to make their wines. America does that from east to west but also has various other vine species that no one else has. I don't think anyone else in the world makes Scuppernong wines from *Vitis rotundifolia*. The grapes don't even look like grapes, but that doesn't stop them making rich, scented golden wines in North Carolina, Georgia and Alabama. And all fifty states now have wineries. Unbelievably, all of them are supposed to use at least some locally grown grapes – even Alaska, though their Peppermint Mocha Red Velvet Port might suit my needs better. And that doesn't stop pineapples being more successful for wine in Hawaii. North Dakota makes a wine from chokeberries; I can't see that catching on in the wider world.

So, back to the serious stuff. Much as I have enjoyed a lot of wines from less well-known wine states, this book would be twice as long if I went into detail about all of them. So, greatly though I like Black Ankle wines from Maryland – Syrahs, Viogniers and Albariños you ought to seek out if you are down that way – I'm afraid I won't be able to delve too deeply into Maryland and Delaware; and though I have had quite decent Chardonnay from North Carolina, I'll be largely leaving them to their Scuppernong. Michigan has a serious wine industry on land cooled by the Great Lakes. New England makes more wine than you would expect in the icy north-east; I've had good Chardonnays from places like Connecticut and Massachusetts. I narrowly avoided arrest for opening a bottle on air at one Connecticut television station; it's illegal, but in a charming state like Connecticut, how was I to know that? – but that's about it.

And as for the south-west, most of the vineyards are high, arid, windswept and sunny. Sounds perfect, if you can find irrigation water and don't get hammered by frost. Arizona Zinfandel, Colorado Syrah and Gruet's excellent fizz in New Mexico prove that it is worth the effort. Texas also has serious vineyards – what else would you expect? – especially on the High Plains near Lubbock. A whole range of vines, from white Vermentino to red Cabernet Franc and Tempranillo, can do well here. But hail and frost exact a terrible toll. Storms can whip up from nowhere and blast the vineyards in a few minutes of black-skied mayhem. I met one grower who had lost five vintages in a row to hail! So should I stick with a rather good Madeira-style wine from the *Vitis bourquininia* – see what I mean about weird vine varieties: I'd never heard of it – made right down by the Gulf? It's from the Jacquez grape. Banned in Europe for being too weird, but rather tasty. You show 'em, Texas. And now, back to the mainstream.

It might have been the marijuana smoke. It might have been the delightful company. It might have been the time of night. It couldn't have been the flavour of the wine. Could it? Well, perhaps it could. Whatever the reason, I really enjoyed my first experience of American wine. Madison, Wisconsin. The depths of winter, as only Wisconsin knows how. I was on a student acting tour. We'd piled into a bus at New York's JFK airport – cool kids at the back, nerds at the front, me somewhere in the middle by a window. We then drove for the best part of a day across the frozen north – only stopping at Pee Wee's Gin Dive in Zanesville, Ohio, for those of you who know it. And we'd given our *As You Like It* to what we hoped was an ecstatic Madison audience.

Well, they seemed ecstatic as they hauled us up to a great dark room, so thick with spicy smoke you couldn't tell whether it was more dangerous to breathe in or suffocate. And they pinged open these flagons of juicy, fruity, utterly easy to drink red wine. I can remember the flavour, through the haze. I remember thinking, how could a cheap wine have so much plum and black cherry jam fruit? How could students afford something this good? I don't think I had ever had a student wine that was better than barely drinkable.

Oh, I forgot. What was the wine called? Gallo's Hearty Burgundy. That was my introduction, not only to American wine, but to the whole idea that cheap wine could be an excellent drink, not a throat scourer. This was a massive discovery. And Gallo's Hearty Burgundy was a massively important wine. It became America's biggest-selling red, and in those days a significant amount of the fruit was from Napa and Sonoma Valleys – one of today's Pinot Noir stars, Rochioli, used to sell his Russian River Pinot Noir to Gallo for their Hearty Burgundy – and a lot of the other grapes were gutsy, mouth-filling, soul-satisfying varieties like Petite Sirah and Barbera. If America was the land without class, the land of opportunity, the land of the free, it was only right that the first highly drinkable red wine affordable to all, available to all, should be American.

But American wine was transforming at the top end, too. I finally got to California – again, on a theatre tour – but this time it was a world tour with the Royal Shakespeare Company and we were playing a theatre in Hollywood. Trevor Nunn, our director, had a birthday so we all piled into a Chinese restaurant at the seedier end of Sunset Strip to cheer the maestro. It was unlicensed. Disaster? Well, no. An unbelievable stroke of good luck. It was probably Patrick Stewart who crunched a wad of greenbacks into my hand and said, 'Dear boy, go and find us some Champagne!' And there was a bottle shop next door. I looked at the prices of French Champagne. No thank YOU. And I said to the owner, 'Haven't you got anything local?' Serendipity. This little shop was the only Los Angeles outlet for a new but fantastically ambitious Californian sparkling wine outfit called Schramsberg. They set out to match Champagne in style, then beat it on quality. But nowhere near on price. I bought an armful of the Blanc de Blancs and the Rosé and still had change for Patrick. The wine was so good, it reduced a bunch of stargazing actors to silence. I went back to England as an actor. But for how much longer? Something thrilling was happening in the world of wine far away from the tired old continent of Europe. And I wanted to be part of it.

On two acting trips I had discovered a world of delightful cheap wine in America, and now had a glimpse of a top end that really could challenge France. And challenging France would always be the first objective for America. It seemed entirely right and typical that not only should America lead the mass market, but she should also lead the impassioned surge to prove that the New World could make wines to match, and maybe better, those of the Old World. This was the 1970s. Things were about to get a whole lot livelier.

In 1976, on a bright May morning in Paris, a young British wine merchant, Steven Spurrier, set up a blind tasting event to help celebrate the bicentenary of the American Declaration of Independence. All very cordial, but he decided to pit the very best French red Bordeaux against California Cabernet Sauvignon, and the very best French white Burgundy against California Chardonnay – all in the spirit of good-humoured celebration. Hundreds of years of tradition and achievement and defining wine quality versus a bunch of upstarts from the sticks. It would all be jolly good fun. It was. Until he announced the results. The upstarts won. A wine called Chateau Montelena Chardonnay 1973 from the warmer end of the Napa Valley beat the Meursaults and the Puligny-Montrachets. A Stag's Leap

Wine Cellars Cabernet Sauvignon 1973 from the cooler southern end of the Napa Valley beat the Mouton-Rothschild and the
Haut-Brion. These last two were regarded as the greatest red
wines in the world. Haut-Brion had been famous since at least
1663. The Stag's Leap was only that vineyard's second vintage.

This all might have passed unnoticed with a bit of Gallic
huffing and puffing and shoulder-shrugging, except for the fact
that an American journalist from *Time* magazine was at a loose
end that day and thought he would pop by. He couldn't believe
what he was seeing. He wrote a story for the magazine entitled
'Judgment of Paris'. And pretty soon, the whole wine world
knew. The young pretenders of California had beaten the French
elite. The young guns had modelled their wines on the French
classics, and then taken them on in open combat and had won.
In Paris. It was only one tasting result, but its tremors circled the
world, touching off responses in wine region after wine region.
Bordeaux and Burgundy had lived in the belief that they possessed a God-given right to produce the world's finest wines on
ancient sites solemnised by time. Well, they didn't. Not any more.

California: from gold rush frenzy to coastal cool

It had all happened so quickly. It really had. There had
been occasional star wines made in California ever since the
gold-rush days of the nineteenth century. A winery called
Hanzell had pioneered making Californian Chardonnay like
French Burgundy in the 1950s. Wineries like Inglenook and
Beaulieu had made some special Cabernets from the 1940s and
'50s. I've had a couple – an Inglenook called Cask J-12 was a
fantastic, hauntingly dark, cedar-scented wine when I tried it at
forty years old. But by the 1960s Napa Valley had less land under
vine and fewer wineries than at any time since Prohibition
ended in 1933. And then Robert Mondavi arrived. I don't like
to give too much credit to one man, but Mondavi started his
winery in 1966 in a whirlwind of self-belief, ambition and

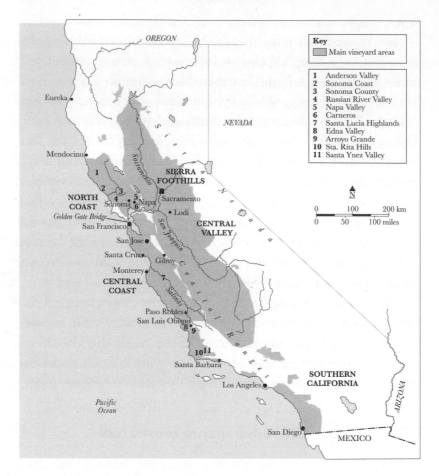

relentless curiosity. He was a bow-legged, mighty molecule of a man, with a forehead as broad as Caesar's and a rasp of a voice that seemed to bypass his vocal cords altogether. Come the time, come the man. This was the 1960s – the decade of JFK, rock 'n' roll, Civil Rights, the decade when the young began to make their voices heard. Mondavi visited Europe in 1962, sucked up all the wine knowledge he could, and by 1966 set out to prove California was Europe's equal. By which, he really meant Europe's superior. It took just ten years to Paris, 24 May 1976.

What Californians did was to learn everything they could from France, then purchase the best and most modern winery equipment, buy as many new oak barrels from France as they were able to load onto a ship, and plant the Burgundy and Bordeaux varieties of Chardonnay and Cabernet Sauvignon and Merlot as if the global supply was about to dry up. And, increasingly, they gave up any pretence of trying to ape the French classics, because they thought they could do it better their way – riper, fuller in flavour, whites of a richness and succulence you wouldn't find in a French Burgundy, reds of a texture and power and mouth-filling intensity they wouldn't recognise in Bordeaux. And pretty soon, Americans weren't fretting about whether their wines matched those of France. They'd superseded them. They didn't need to be judged against anything any more. They were the ideal. Let others attempt to match them.

This was all laudable, but, as always, it does help to see the other person's point of view. Yet California had an institution that didn't see the need of another person's point of view all that often. The Davis outpost of the University of California had been just an adjunct of the Berkeley campus until, in 1959, it was given solo status – and it majored in wine. It put together a strong team of serious scientists and when California wine became a hot subject during the 1970s and '80s, Davis had a production line turning out winemakers tightly schooled in a risk-averse, science-first, unemotional view of how to make the wine California wanted. There was a formula. Follow it. It was the same with vineyards. Soil doesn't matter. It's just there as a medium for holding water. Climate is all that matters.

Davis wasn't alone in this. Roseworthy College in South Australia had a similar doctrine. And given the woeful state of scientific understanding in most of the world's wineries and vineyards, a good dose of science was well overdue. But not an overdose. Wine is made by humans and enjoyed by humans, with all their foibles and fancies, not by machines. Davis was the most important wine school and it still is. And it contributed to a phenomenon, which began in California, of winemakers being seen as rock stars. Rock stars who didn't get their fancy shoes dirty in the vineyards too often. Winemaking and grape-growing became divorced from each other. Tim Mondavi, Robert's son, talked of there being a chasm at Davis between grape growing and winemaking. Winemakers might have talked about vineyards and pruning and trellising and the rest, but in truth they left all that stuff to someone else.

The pendulum always swings. The pendulum always swings back. The wines of the late 1970s were beautifully fruity and balanced and joyously, self-confidently different from those of Europe. I did several California versus France blind tastings. California won every time. And often the wines were at about 12.5 per cent alcohol – equivalent wines today might be 14.5–15 per cent. As we went through the 1980s, I began to sense a brief and barmy flirtation with 'food wines'. Good wines, nice wines go with food. OK? Wines from grapes picked too early, whacked with acidity and stripped of any individuality don't go with anything except Pepto-Bismol. The fad didn't last long – there's only so much heartburn a guy can take – and then the pendulum swung back to where it really wanted to be: riper wines, richer wines, wines made with the attitude of 'We could have left our grapes on the vine for another week or two. Next year we'll try it. If we can get riper fruit, why shouldn't we?' Even though the grapes concerned were the old French favourites like Chardonnay and Cabernet Sauvignon, where balance was everything – 'Well, they couldn't ripen their grapes like this in Bordeaux or Burgundy. We can, so we will.'

During the 1990s money poured into Californian wine and Napa Valley seemed to be nothing but vines from foggy, watery south to hot, steamy north. Cult wines, of often just a few hundred dozen bottles, began to pop up – elitist, exclusive, expensive. Screaming Eagle. Harlan Estate. Bryant Family. Ever tasted them? Don't worry. Very few of us have. Vintages like 1994 and '97 allowed the grapes to hang on the vines, getting riper and riper. Wine critics cooed and crowed and began awarding previously unheard-of 100-point scores to wines that no normal wine lover would ever get a mouthful of. Companies started up, offering a formula that would guarantee a certain score from the top critics. It was increasingly removed from the reality of a piece of land, some grapes, a year's weather and the desire to make a wine as an expression of that relationship.

Just in time, just enough wine-drinkers and wine producers said 'Enough.' Initially it was drinkers and producers of Pinot Noir and Chardonnay who began to say 'This stuff tastes like soup. It has no sense of the vineyard it comes from.' Yes, exactly. The Old World mantra: make a wine that tastes of where it comes from. Don't let the marketing man tell you what to make; you tell the marketing man what you've got. And he'll find some customers for it.

Cabernet and Merlot are more difficult than Pinot Noir and Chardonnay. A massive and, quite probably, perfectly satisfied market has been built on rich, broad, dark flavours increasingly similar to each other, regardless of which patch of land they come from. If critics only reward the richest wines, and if wine-drinkers in general say 'This is what we like, and we're paying good money for it,' who's to say what's right or wrong? But in Napa and Sonoma nowadays you do hear wine producers talk about easing off on the alcohol, toning down the new oak barrels, not trying to squeeze the last ounce out of the grapes. Since a lot of grapes were being picked at potential alcohols of 16–17 per cent and then 'watered back' to about 14.5 per cent by the use of the 'black snake', aka the hose, isn't this the right way? I say yes. A lot of marketers, and indeed consumers, might say no.

Recent movements, like In Praise of Balance, which have promoted a fresher, brighter, lower-alcohol world of wine have mostly had success in Chardonnay and Pinot Noir, as well as encouraging an interest in all the old relic vine varieties that have somehow survived in the numerous nooks and crannies of the Golden State. They acknowledge it is difficult to budge the big Cab mentality, but it will happen. Awareness of climate change is making more and more wine people environmentally sensitive. Overripening grapes is not what nature would do, so nor should you. And remember California is not just the home of money and glamour and self-promotion. It is also the home of the radical, the free-thinker and the eco-warrior bent on preserving this planet.

California has always had enormous potential for variety. It became rather blocked into a two-lane highway mentality based on Chardonnay and the red Bordeaux varietals. The road is beginning to widen, and as it does California will enter a new golden age of variety and change. And it could happen very quickly. It was only ten years between Robert Mondavi setting out to challenge France and the Californian triumph in Paris. The next ten years could be a lot of fun.

So far, I've mostly been talking about California's two important quality areas, Napa Valley and Sonoma County. But there's a lot more to look at. I'm not going to talk about every vineyard area as it is a big place. Some I don't really know that well – North Yuba, I've tasted your wine, but that's it – and some places haven't given me any pleasure. So let's start in the north, in a county thick with mighty redwood forests, warm in the east and creepily cold in the west. But first, a quick geography lesson. Let's talk about fog. Let's talk about ice-cold Arctic currents on the Pacific coast. Let's talk about how you don't go swimming off San Francisco unless you're coated in goose fat and wearing a wetsuit. Why? San Francisco is on the same latitude as southern Spain, so swimming should be a breeze. But then it should also be too hot to grow decent wine grapes. It's the Arctic currents. These are 7–9°C (13–16°F) colder than the surface waters off the coast. They well up during the summer and cause mighty fog banks that can be truly frightening. I've driven toward them and felt I was approaching the edge of the world, with hell just a gear change away to the west.

Cold fogs and icy air sit above the waves. Inland, just like southern Spain, the sun rises, the air heats up and hot air rises into the sky, creating a vacuum. Nature will always fill a vacuum. So wherever there is a dip in the coastal mountain range, you will see cotton-wool bundles of fog being dragged in and settling. And where there's a river valley, fog and cold winds course up it, cooling everything down. And the biggest gap of all in the hills is the Golden Gate gap – a mile of savage waters leading across into San Francisco Bay and San Pablo Bay. Icy winds and fogs pour up the broad delta of the Sacramento and San Joaquin Rivers toward the vast inland spread called the Central Valley, which splays out on both sides of the San Joaquin River halfway south to Los Angeles.

The difference between coastal and inland temperatures is dramatic. Mark Twain said that the worst winter he had ever spent was summer in San Francisco. I've woken up in high summer in San Francisco – I look out of my hotel window and I can't even see the other side of the street. I scrabble my way out to the Golden Gate Bridge, longing to admire its rust-red glory, and I can't see it. And on the awe-inspiring bridge itself, a turbulence of fog and chill winds roars toward the hot interior. The effect of these icy winds can be felt as far inland as 160 kilometres (100 miles), but the closer you are to the coast the cooler it will be, and the more likely you will be able to make great wine. Sonoma Valley, Carneros and Napa Valley all open out on to San Pablo Bay. Without the fogs and the wind, none of them would be making fine wine. They would be better suited to growing prunes. In the Central Valley, as the coastal influences dwindle to nothing, that's what they would grow, if there wasn't more money to be made from grapes.

So, back to the north. I would like to start very far north, at Eureka – simply because it's called Eureka. My friend Keith Floyd started a television series at Eureka for exactly this reason and no other. For the record, I have never found a Eureka wine. What an admission!

There are two little grape areas even further north – Willow Creek anybody? – but no, I haven't visited them, nor tasted the wine. But I have visited the Anderson Valley a bit to the south. This is a very damp, fog-strewn river valley that seems as if it is from a different era. It sort of is: they still mutter in a local language called Boontling if you turn up in flashy clobber and start throwing your weight around. They've had to get used to outsiders – Brightlighters, the locals call them – because the drear, cool, foggy conditions attracted Champagne supremo Louis Roederer. Drear, cool, foggy – just like the weather in Champagne, and there is no doubt that Roederer have made the most Champagne-like fizz in all of California from Anderson Valley grapes.

But I was after something else. Zinfandel is an old grape variety that the Californians adopted as their own. (It actually comes from Croatia, and it isn't even called Zinfandel, but let's leave that.) I had tasted some simply astonishing rich, brambly, briary, peppery, utterly rustic and utterly delicious Zinfandel from old Italian family vineyards up on the ridges, in the deep forest glades where no one ever went. I can see why. On my first visit I noticed that a lot of the agricultural activity I saw close by in these hidden spots didn't seem to be at all related to my Zinfandel, and didn't seem to be the kind of stuff you'd drink. Smoke, maybe. On my last visit, amazed at how the valley had developed as a producer of grapes for fizz, and also as a fantastic producer of cool, clean, delectable Pinot Noir, I heard a gunshot or two. Hunting season, I asked. I think not. The Wild West still rules on the ridges, especially where the price per ounce is on the rise.

Sonoma County is probably the most varied of all the California wine counties, its wines ranging from rich, dark beasts from grapes broiled in the sun and parched by the arid air to delicate, gossamer-light offerings from vineyards that only catch the sun when the fog clears as they creep to a kind of ripeness. And it's one of my favourite counties, because it's not just vines – a lot of other agriculture still goes on, people have lives that aren't totally focused on bottles of Cabernet Sauvignon – and the beer is some of the best in America. When you are in a town like Healdsburg or, above all, Santa Rosa and you're looking for an excuse, just remind yourself that it takes a lot of good cool beer to make a good bottle of wine.

Much of California's early wine history took place in Sonoma. The crazy Hungarian Agoston Haraszthy, who many people reckon was the founding father of modern California wine, set up shop at Buena Vista in the 1850s. It pretty much all began here. If you decide to dally in the little town of Sonoma itself you really can get a feel for those early ambitions and dreams. But the Sonoma area I've been most interested in recently has been further north, along the Russian River Valley, one of California's most famous cool-climate wine areas. That's a bit of a misleading statement, as the Russian River Valley is in fact a classic example of how the coastal cooling effect dwindles as you get further from the ocean. The Russian River flows down from Mendocino County, and until you get to the holiday town of Healdsburg it's a pretty warm valley. Cabernet Sauvignon, Zinfandel and varieties from France's Rhône Valley ripen well. The great Ridge winery makes long-lasting reds from grapes grown at Geyserville and from Lytton Springs, on the ridge to the west that leans into an even warmer valley, Dry Creek.

It isn't until Healdsburg that the Russian River Valley American Viticultural Area (as geographical appellations are called in the States) kicks in, but it still seems pretty warm to me. Cabernet Sauvignon and Zinfandel need quite a lot of heat to ripen and they do fine around here. I'm waiting for the cool winds and the fogs. The Russian River heads on south – Zinfandel and Syrah vines are still happy here – and at last it turns west toward the ocean. But the AVA keeps on going south, across vast flatlands all the way past Santa Rosa. If you were a lawyer you could just about argue that these broad vineyards were affected by the cooling fogs sidling up the valley from the ocean. If you were a lawyer retained by the most powerful drinks producers in America. Then, you could make a very compelling argument for the Russian River Valley AVA to cover 69,000 hectares (170,000 acres) at the last count.

So let's leave the broad acres stuff. The core of Russian River does make fantastic wine and produces what a lot of people think of as perfect Pinot Noir – big, rich, full of black cherry and blackberry fruit, and, if you're lucky, scented with wild strawberries. That richness makes sense. Russian River Valley has some of the warmest places to grow great Pinot Noir anywhere in the world. There's quite a lot of Russian River Pinot Noir nowadays – a lot more than there used to be, and it is often pretty rich stuff. And over 14 per cent alcohol. It's popular. It's good. It's expensive. If you want your Pinot to be more ethereal, more thought-provoking, less ravishing; asking more questions, giving fewer answers, you need to keep heading west, even if you think there are no vineyards left.

Well, there aren't in the river valley itself, but head into the forests and the hills to the north and south, and you'll find sudden splashes of green, glades covered with vineyards. This is the Sonoma Coast. A lot of these vines are close to the ocean, and sometimes you can see it to the west. On the valley floor it would be far too foggy to grow vines, but higher up the fog isn't so dense, or you might be high enough to miss it altogether. And the wind blows relentlessly, tempering the clear, bright sunshine. Sonoma Coast is another of the AVAs that has been seized upon and brutally expanded by giant wine producers well aware that 'Coast' has nice connotations of cool and quality in the minds of us wine-drinkers. You drive the main road south from Healdsburg and you'll see advertising hoardings outside vineyards: 'Gold Medal Pinot $9' and 'Chardonnay and Pinot $5–$9'. Are these wines really Sonoma Coast? The real Coast or the real Russian River? Luckily, they are a feisty lot out on what they would call the Extreme Coast. And it has led to the best producers determinedly pursuing the creation of sub-AVAs that actually mean something. North of the Russian River, Fort Ross-Seaview is the name chosen for some fabulous scented, sappy Pinot Noirs and soft yet beautifully lean and bread-crusty Chardonnay. South of the River, they don't have any new sub-AVAs yet, but they will, because the Pinot Noirs, the Chardonnays and the Syrahs are so startlingly good. If you don't yet see such descriptors as Freestone-Occidental, Sebastopol Hills and Petaluma Gap for some of California's brightest new-wave wines, you will soon. For a thrilling look at the future, seek out single-vineyard wines from Littorai, Wind Gap or Arnot-Roberts.

The southern end of Sonoma drifts away into what used to be a hillocky, hummocky sprawl of dun-coloured land slithering off into San Pablo Bay and good for little but grazing a few sheep or cows. And it is poor stuff – heavy, unfriendly clays, most of which spend half the summer shrouded in fog. Even the sheep need gloves and galoshes. And there's the magic. This is Carneros, slung across the bottom of Sonoma and Napa, the first place to get coated in the fogs off the Bay, the last place for them to burn off, just in time for the chill breezes to take over. Being so close to Napa Valley, it was the first area to be developed in the 1970s and '80s, when wineries were looking for cool conditions to make Pinot Noir and, in particular, sparkling wine, because every step you take north in Napa Valley, conditions get less cool.

But if we drive from Carneros straight up past Napa city on Highway 29, within a space of 50 kilometres (30 miles) we'll go from vineyards cool enough to make good sparkling wine to vineyards hot enough to ripen just about any known red variety. In 50 kilometres. It's a dramatic demonstration of the cooling effect of the Pacific Ocean. The further up the valley toward Calistoga that you travel, the less fog is drawn up along the river banks and the less aggressive the winds off the Bay until, by the time you get to the top, pretty much everything bakes. And in that 50-kilometre stretch you can make more or less any kind of wine you want to, from chilly light and white to rib-sticking rich and red. But the wine that virtually everyone wants to make is Cabernet Sauvignon, or a blend with Cabernet at its heart. And that is what defines Napa Valley. Between the cool of Carneros and the heart of Calistoga you are sure to find some conditions that are perfect for Cabernet to ripen. If you add in the hillside vineyards you'll find a lot more. And what you *should* find is loads of different interpretations of the grape.

Well, you do and you don't. Of course, what you do find is loads of conditions that might be ideal for all kinds of other grapes if they could get a look in. That's easier said than done. The astonishing razzmatazz of Napa Valley is centred on being arguably the world's leading Cabernet site. Arguably means it's worth having the discussion, and the money that has poured into Napa, sending the whole area into a dizzy spiral of increased land costs, increased winery investment and increased obsession with prestige, has meant the cost of wine must spiral too. If you already own your land you can avoid some of these pressures. If you've either bought land or bought a winery you will only survive if you charge a high price for your wine – and that usually means $70 a bottle for starters, rapidly rising through $100. And the only wine that will guarantee that kind of return? Cabernet Sauvignon, by itself or in a Bordeaux blend called Meritage. It's called specialisation. Bordeaux's Haut-Médoc only makes Cabernet Sauvignon blends. They don't get it in the neck. Why shouldn't we decide to do the same? Fair point. Most French classic wines are based on exactly this specialisation argument, so why not Napa?

As in Bordeaux, there are sub-divisions, each claiming the bragging rights to making Napa's finest. The best way to experience these is on a weekday, not a weekend, in, perhaps, February – not in high summer. Napa is America's gold-star wine tourism location. Highway 29, the main road up the valley, is bumper to bumper for most of the summer. Come in February, when winter is ending early. Come in February, when the vines look stark and shorn. Come in February, when the mustard flowers glister between the rows of vines and the pale sun hangs bright but low in the sky, when the Oakville storekeepers have time to chat as you choose your picnic, when the queues are shorter for the mighty burgers at Gott's Roadside in Saint Helena. Come in February, when making wine seems to be at the heart of Napa Valley rather than making money.

Heading north from the city of Napa, the vines come thick and fast – first at Oak Knoll, then at Yountville, two areas slightly disregarded for top red wines, but as global warming kicks in their cooler conditions are being appreciated more. Oakville and Rutherford are next, two scant hamlets; the bigger wineries have more employees than these have inhabitants. But to the left of the highway, barely perceptibly rising toward the wooded hills, are fans of well-drained, generally gravelly soil that attracted the old-timers. Gravel was what made Bordeaux's Médoc area great for Cabernet. Here it is again, and most of Napa Valley's greatest Cabernet sites are west of Highway 29.

Saint Helena is next and is packed with places crying out for your money – restaurants, boutiques, gift shops and galleries. But it's actually a pretty nice town. You don't have to max out your credit card. Ana's Cantina will give you a cheap craft beer with the locals to restore your sense of reality and then you might take a walk up to the town library and gaze at the sudden heartwarming mishmash of old vines. They don't look like Cabernet. They're not. This is called the Library Vineyard. It's what Napa was like before Cabernet. Or follow me, past Spottswoode, down a small road to the mountains. Right at the end is another field on your right. Chaos. Inspiring, tumbledown chaos, surrounded on all sides by manicured vineyards of purring modern efficiency. This is Mrs Rossi's field. I've tramped it with the great radical Sonoma Coast winemaker Sean Thackrey, who buys what fruit he can and at the same time rushes to catalogue the vines, to coax some back to life, to take cuttings and to preserve. This is living history. Some of these vines are trees. What are they? Are they any good? Might there be Napa's next great grape variety hidden among these tired old limbs? Maybe. Sean and his friends are racing against time. On each visit I fear I shall see an empty field, or neat rows of new Merlot destined for the blending pot. And on my next visit, perhaps I shall.

I could just continue on Highway 29 up to Calistoga, but I've got Spring Mountain on my left now, then Diamond Mountain, and around to the east of Calistoga, Howell Mountain. Take the twisting roads to the mountains, through the thick greenery hung with Spanish moss. There are great vineyards up here, and for those who find the valley-floor wines too solid, too chunky, there's a focus and a seriousness to these mountain wines that I think is the real spine of Napa Valley personality. And after Howell Mountain, I can drift down south again on the calmer side of the Valley, on the Silverado Trail. Doesn't that sound more enticing than Highway 29? You will find just as many vineyards, but a lot less hustle, a lot fewer wineries hanging out their shingle, begging for your trade. There are superb vineyards up on the hills above the Silverado Trail as well, and you'll pass Stag's Leap, where the winning Cabernet Sauvignon from the Judgment of Paris was grown, before you get embroiled in the dull suburbs of Napa. But the vines aren't done yet. Two new areas – Coombsville, by the city, and American Canyon to the south – are cooled by San Pablo Bay, and are already producing some of the tastiest Cabernet in the valley. Things are changing in Napa, even if the gilded Establishment would prefer they didn't. In the end, nature is the boss and nature says they must.

It's almost worth heading inland just to experience the unreality of the delta country to the east of San Francisco. Great levees rise above the road, queues form at the bridges as cars wait for the barges and ships to pass, and I always have a slight thrill of foreboding that one day, as I drive through these low-slung fields, the mighty Sacramento River will decide to reclaim all this land for itself. But keep going. Lodi sits at the top of the enormous

Central Valley. With enough cooling from the winds that stray up the delta, yet an ability to produce prodigious crops of grapes if it so desires, Lodi is probably the best value for money area in California. Further south, down the Central Valley, it gets hotter and drier and the wine gets cheaper and worse.

Further east still are the Sierra Nevada mountains, with ancient vines clinging to the foothills making stubborn, toothy reds. This is the heartland of Zinfandel, the most famous of the gold rush varieties, still hanging on in these gold rush hills. The vines only survived because these rugged hills, difficult to farm and miles from any likely tourist route, were simply not worth developing. So the old vines stayed. And Zinfandel itself might have died from lack of attention were it not for that much-abused but actually pretty tasty pink, or blush, wine called White Zinfandel. During the 1970s growers were ripping up old Zinfandel vines and replanting with Cabernet or Chardonnay, yet this party pop became America's most popular wine in the 1980s. Thousands of acres of new Zinfandel vines were planted, but, more importantly, no one was ripping out any more of these century-old historic Zinfandel vines either.

If we're going to keep heading south, we need to stick much closer to the Pacific Ocean. It's the same story: a place on the latitude of California will be too hot for decent wine without the cooling fogs and winds from the coast. With them, there are some magic places to grow grapes south of San Francisco. The Santa Cruz mountains are first up. The area is wild, heavily forested, with steep ravines, challenging craggy slopes and not many people or vineyards. Even so, one of the world's great vineyards is up here – Montebello, where Ridge grows fabulous Cabernet Sauvignon, which it then transforms into a thrilling wine that, as it ages, bestrides the gap of cultures and achievements between California and France. It's one hell of a drive to get up there, so take a little pause.

On my first visit, we finished tasting when it was dark. Well, not really dark. A golden-orange moon rose effortlessly through a haze of smoky purple and couched itself among the silver stars. Gaze awhile. Then turn, and look down the mountain to the seething, clamorous city of San José. How noisy and frantic must it be. Up here? Silence. Repose. A lone light flickers briefly, halfway up the mountain on the far side of the San Andreas Fault. A bird croaks. If you are ever lucky enough to drink Montebello Cabernet Sauvignon, remember: this is where it comes from.

Most of the other Santa Cruz vineyards are famous for their efforts with Pinot Noir, but one of my favourites is something different, from just outside the town of Gilroy, the Garlic Capital of the World. A lot of towns around here proclaim they are the world capital of this or that. You can't mistake what Gilroy is famous for – just roll down your car window. And don't be fooled into buying a bottle of their 'famous' garlic wine. Garlic goes rather well with wine in cooking, but garlic in the wine is truly disgusting. Gilroy might do a roaring trade in garlic wine for first-time buyers, but I doubt anyone has ever bought a second bottle. As you flee the stench up toward the Hecker Pass, you'll see an old vineyard to your right, full of ancient Grenache vines, which one of California's most imaginative winemakers, Randall Grahm of Bonny Doon, makes into one of California's juiciest, glugging reds, Clos du Gilroy.

South of Santa Cruz, you drop down to the vast funnel-like mouth of the Salinas Valley. This is John Steinbeck country, agro-industry in top gear. But the Gavilan Mountains to the north-east contain two of the most pioneering vineyards of the modern era: Calera and Chalone, both famous for Pinot Noir since the 1970s, but both able to produce a range of other wines, too. The south-west slopes, the Santa Lucia Highlands, are also well-known for Pinot Noir, but in a much milder key.

If you've got time, take Highway 1 south of Monterey, cut into the cliff and hugging the coastline, twisting past Big Sur, virtually feeling the spray from the mighty Pacific surf on your cheek. But it's a single-track highway. Don't get stuck behind a fleet of campervans manned by spaced-out hippies trying to remember the words to Jefferson Airplane's 'White Rabbit'. There's nowhere – and I mean nowhere – to overtake. I once took Highway 1 south trying to make a lunch appointment in Santa Barbara. I barely made dinner. You can blithely keep chugging on if you like, or you can turn inland at Cambria to check out Paso Robles. This is a big vineyard area and a good, rough-edged town where the steaks are as big as boxing gloves and the beer is bitter and cold. There are quite a few starry wine operations in Paso, but I'm afraid I find most of their Zinfandels and Syrahs and the like just too rich. They talk about cooling breezes and limestone soils, but most of the wines seem testosterone-fuelled. The most restrained ones come from Tablas Creek, an operation co-owned by the Perrin family from Châteauneuf-du-Pape, who use their Rhône grape varieties to good effect. One local speciality is Petite Sirah, a pretty chewy dark grape with surprisingly rose-scented, juicy fruit that can cope with high alcohol. And red and white Rhône-variety blends also give me pleasure and seem to cope with the high alcohol.

I like the place. I like the people. It's not many winemakers who greet you with 'Oz Clarke! I thought you were dead!', then pile you on to the back of a Harley for a wild ride to try to make it a reality. It's not many places where you conduct a blind tasting while swimming one-armed in a lake (the other arm? It was wine tasting), and your life really does depend on it. Have you tried swimming with one arm? And tried to guess which glass is a Sangiovese and which is a Barbera at the same time? One choke and you're drowned. As I said, I like the place and the people. I'd like to like the wines better. But the beer is local, and good, and cold, and necessary.

The vineyards around San Luis Obispo, the next city south, are extreme examples of the ocean effect. Both Edna Valley and Arroyo Grande manage to produce elegant Pinot Noir and Chardonnay toward the sea; deep, powerful Syrah a mile or two further inland from the likes of Alban; and, a few miles further up the valley, headbanging Zinfandel from vines planted in 1879. We're getting pretty far south here. The effect of the Pacific is getting more intense, not less, as the interior gets hotter. Santa Maria looks particularly unpromising – that is, if you can see it. This forlorn town gets eighty-seven days a year of solid fog – usually in the late summer and autumn – which is dragged up the Santa Maria Valley. Perfect, so long as you are twenty miles inland: great rolling slopes covered in Chardonnay, Pinot Noir and Syrah, famous for their crisp, fresh fruit. Jim Clendenen, one of the pioneers of the cool-climate California movement, arrived here thirty-five years ago and hasn't seen any reason to move yet.

We're in Santa Barbara County now, and wine has one last hurrah, and the icy winds and fogs have one last hurrah before the coastline turns sharply to the east, leaving the fogs and currents flailing about miles offshore. The rest of California is sun-soaked beaches, identikit condos, shiny-skinned bodybuild-ers and smog. This last shout is the Santa Ynez Valley. If you saw the film *Sideways*, well, it happened here. All that bad behaviour and Pinot Noir guzzling. And they guzzled a lot of good wine. I've been to all those wineries. I've been to the one where Miles drank the spittoon. And the boring wine tutor with his wine book was modelled on me. Disgraceful! I know the guy who played me – we used to sing in a choir together. He sent me a copy of 'my' book. Signed by him, and he probably gets my royalties. This is all getting too confusing.

But Santa Ynez is a bit confusing. The main town of Solvang is modelled on a Danish town. Why? Buellton is famous for split-pea soup rather than wine, and that never did your palate much good, but it may not matter. The first winery sign I saw on a trip last year offered 'Artisan Pinot Noir and rustic cookies'. And it's really several wine regions all in one. To the east of Highway 101 the valley is warm, the countryside rolling and relaxing; breeding racehorses seems as important as growing grapes. The wine-tasting crowds pour out from Los Angeles at the weekend. This was where the original wineries were, and you can feel the glitter of showbiz and the glamorous lifestyle. To the west of Highway 101, everything is much more rudimentary. Only real wine geeks should venture there. This is an area now called Santa Rita Hills (though they spell it Sta. Rita to avoid upsetting a large Chilean winery). It's had one famous vineyard since 1976 – Sanford & Benedict – where a lot of the grapes for the fabled Pinot Noirs that first got Californians thinking about Burgundy were grown. Why here?

It's those fogs and winds again. From the western end of the Sta. Rita vineyard area up to the lifestyle east, the temperature difference can be as much as 17°C (30°F) – it's barely warm enough to ripen a grape in the west down by the ocean, hot enough to ripen whatever you please in the east. I like the east, but it's the west that has the exciting vineyards, some of them only managing a few hours of sun a day while the fogs surge and recede as if tied to an elastic band. It may be cool at the western end of the valley, but winter hardly comes. The grapes creep to whatever ripeness you want them to reach. Some are picked in August and some in November. And, amazingly, the Chardonnays and Pinot Noirs at 12 per cent alcohol don't seem under-ripe, while the ones at 15 per cent don't seem overdone. A special place. A special wine place. And we haven't seen the half of it yet.

Was Oregon ever the new Burgundy?

I couldn't have asked for a better introduction to Oregon. I'd driven up from California one August, having been told to take my umbrella and forget the sunscreen. Yet the further north I drove, the hotter it seemed to get. By the time I reached a place called McMinnville in the middle of wine country, where I was attending a Pinot Noir celebration, the exhausted organisers told me it had hit 42°C (107°F) the day before, and that they had suffered eighty-four days of continual sunshine. Suffered!

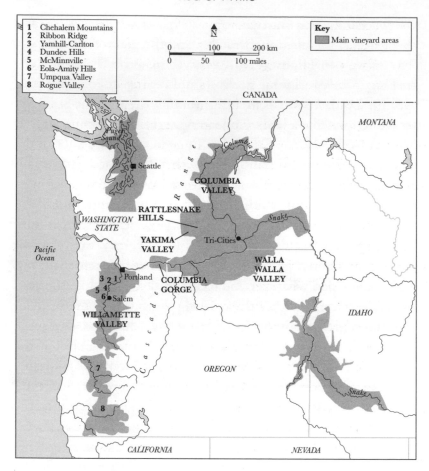

1	Chehalem Mountains
2	Ribbon Ridge
3	Yamhill-Carlton
4	Dundee Hills
5	McMinnville
6	Eola-Amity Hills
7	Umpqua Valley
8	Rogue Valley

In a place like Oregon, which spent its time moaning about lack of sun, surely this was brilliant news. That shows how much I knew about Oregon.

I learnt a bit more when I attended a tasting by David Lett, the state's most famous wine producer, and the winemaker who had basically started the whole Oregon wine scene. I had the first of my several, shall we say, disagreements with him. He was hosting a vertical tasting of just about every Pinot Noir he'd made since 1970. Historically, this was a gem of a tasting – I'd learn masses. Some of the early wines were a bit challenging, but then I picked up the 1978. What a wine! My notes said:

'*A mature wine with a heavenly perfume of rich sweet plums and wild strawberries, a soft, voluptuous feeling of ripe glycerine coats my mouth, as my palate soaks up the giddy fragrance of plums and damsons, of strawberries bulging with the summer sun . . . brilliantly treading the knife edge between sumptuous indulgence and embarrassing lack of manners.*' It was like a really hedonistic, exotic 1978 Burgundy; obviously 1978 was a great year in Oregon, too.

'I loathe the wine.' What? That's David Lett speaking. I actually tried to defend David's own wine to David. He was having none of it. 'Worst wine I've ever made.' He hated it so much he only bottled twenty-five dozen. He was probably grateful we were using a few in the tasting. Now, I got a bit cross. So did he. But it shows how little I understood the motivation of the Oregon pioneers. They had a strong anti-Californian feeling. They had a strong anti-Cabernet Sauvignon feeling. There was a sense, even back in the 1970s, that alcoholic strength, ripeness and 'bigness', in both reds and whites, were being established as the norm for wine flavours by California, and all you needed was Cabernet Sauvignon and Chardonnay. They felt that the all-powerful Davis Wine School in California was refusing to countenance any other way. And David realised that they were teaching a creed to a generation of winemakers which minimised risk and emphasised consistency, efficiency and a positively anal approach to the unexpected. Oregon was the antithesis of everything the Californian profs taught. Oregon, with its risk of insufficient sunshine, its risk of rain during harvest, its risk of failing to set a proper crop. And when David Lett said he wanted to plant Pinot Noir and try to make wines in the delicate, uncertain, risk-drenched way they did it in Burgundy, I'm not sure his professors at Davis even really knew what he was talking about, and they certainly weren't about to be helpful. How could they be? What David Lett wanted to establish in Oregon was the exact opposite of everything they believed in as they sat in air-conditioned comfort and gazed out at California's blazing sun.

So I would turn up for my first visit when Oregon was breaking all its own rules by having a summer even the Californians
might find excessive. And then we had the best salmon bake of
the biggest salmon, and there was music and laughter, dancing
and flirting and ... well, this Oregon place seemed like a syb-
arite's paradise.

It isn't. But it is a really singular, particular place. It has a
mood about it that is understandably magnetic for those who
want a calmer pace to their lives. And if you're looking for a
'new Burgundy' in North America, this does seem to be the
most likely spot. Oregon isn't only about Pinot Noir, although
Burgundy's red grape dominates almost every winery's thoughts.
Chardonnay is less important than Pinot Blanc and Pinot Gris
for many producers. In the south of the state, the Umpqua and
Rogue Valleys even produce Cabernet Sauvignon and on the
Columbia Gorge in the north they can ripen Zinfandel. But it
is the Willamette Valley, south and west of the capital, Portland,
that defines Oregon. And that means Pinot Noir today, just as it
did in the 1960s and '70s when David Lett and a few similarly
hardy ascetic folk set out to create an anti-California beneath
the grey skies and drizzle.

Deciding to be a 'new Burgundy' places quite a burden on the
wine community, especially as California has managed to create
various areas like Anderson Valley, Sonoma Coast, Russian
River and Sta. Rita Hills which make tremendous Pinot Noirs
and Chardonnays, though usually in a fleshier, more indulgent
style than typical Burgundy. And what is a typical Burgundy?
If it was light and ethereal in the 1970s and '80s, it certainly
isn't often like that today. But Oregon is the place that gets the
nod from Burgundy itself. In 1987 the important Burgundy
producer Joseph Drouhin bought 40 hectares (100 acres) of
land in the Willamette Valley's Dundee Hills. There were only
seventeen wineries in Oregon then – there are more than seven
hundred now. And that includes a more recent influx of very
high-powered Burgundians: Dominic Lafon from Meursault;

Louis-Michel Liger-Belair and Jean-Nicolas Méo from Vosne-Romanée; the merchants Louis Jadot and Bouchard Père et Fils are just some of them. They are spread across the valley, and that's refreshing. I have often felt that many Dundee Hills producers sought a kind of mythical, elegant Burgundy style, which often ended up as merely light and hollow. Less well-known sub-regions had more reason to try to establish their wines' personalities with less reference to Burgundy, and I have to admit I generally find more fascinating individual flavours coming from places like Chehalem Mountains, Ribbon Ridge and Eola-Amity Hills in the south. And that'll be the thrill of the future Oregon as sub-divisions really do prove to have different personalities. Just like they do in Burgundy. As Oregon has become less obsessed with Burgundy, it can now begin to achieve that kind of Burgundian focus on all the tiny differences from plot to plot. It took the Burgundians a thousand years. Oregon has only been at it for fifty years. Maybe that's why the modern Burgundians are so keen on a slice of the action.

Desert wines from Washington State, but only in the east

For someone like me, who was obsessed by the possibilities of the New World and was kicking against the elitism and privilege of the Old, Washington State was an absolute natural. Eastern Washington was a moonscape, a desert. It should be impossible to grow anything out there. There shouldn't be cities, just an endless, uninviting prairie of sagebrush and bright red cheatgrass enlivened by the occasional dusty perambulation of tumbleweed. And if I really wanted to get futuristic there was a vast no-go area of nuclear installations to cow any human with thoughts of settling down and making a life. And there was a river. The mighty Columbia River, America's fourth biggest, and you gazed in awe at the imperious surge of its waters and wondered how big the other three must be. This majestic force rolls in confidently from Canada creating a basin of 420,000 square kilometres (260,000 square miles), and inside this arc is an area suited to vines that one local expert put at being five times bigger than California's Napa and Sonoma put together.

But it's still a desert. The Cascade mountains which run down the west of the state create a very effective rain shadow. Seattle, on the coastal side of the mountains, is one of the wettest cities in America. There had been a few attempts to tame this desert in the nineteenth century, and the small Yakima Valley had made some headway in producing grapes for grape jelly as well as very aromatic hops for beer – and equally aromatic marijuana. Yet it wasn't until the 1960s that a couple of visiting wine experts tasted a delightful Grenache rosé made by a professor of psychology at the local university and a Gewurztraminer made by a meteorologist friend of his. They were fantastic. The best Gewürztraminer in America, the experts said. The flame was lit. One of these visiting experts was California's most famous winemaker, André Tchelistcheff, and he was sure he could teach the Washingtonians how to make wine. And there was a local vineyard expert, Walter Clore, who understood the fearsome extremes of such a desert better than anybody: its long stretches of rainless summer and its regular vicious winter freezes that would kill any delicate wine-grape vines that weren't properly prepared. His mantra was 'What doesn't kill you makes you stronger.' And he chose to concentrate on Riesling, the finest cold-climate grape variety he knew, the one with the toughest wood and a fair track record in resisting a deep freeze, as the one to spearhead Washington's ambition to be a quality wine region: 'If you can't grow Riesling and get it to survive, then you shouldn't be planting anything.'

And so there was I, expecting to taste fiery, proud desert wines full of struggle and challenge, but enjoying a delightful, gentle, citrous, flower-scented Riesling that could have come out of Germany's Rhine Valley. Riesling should come from cool, fragile northern European conditions, where the grape creeps to a ripeness of sorts after the summer days are ended. And this lovely stuff was coming from a desert. Well, Walter Clore wasn't wrong when he said, 'Use Riesling as your pathfinder.'

Washington was also lucky that its chief wine-producing company, which emerged rapidly during the 1970s, took his advice and was determined to follow a quality route. Chateau Ste. Michelle was owned by a tobacco giant and they weren't short of resources. They could have looked at this wide, empty expanse of dirt-cheap acres in eastern Washington, done their sums and then set out to mount a challenge to the behemoths of California wine. But they saw there was a gap between the mass market of Gallo and its peers and the emerging top-end stuff of Napa and Sonoma. Filling that gap looked a lot more fun, and more profitable, too. Chateau Ste. Michelle made their mark at a Los Angeles wine show in 1974, with a Riesling that beat all comers, from Germany, Australia and the rest of America. They are now the biggest producers of Riesling in the world and have a close relationship with Ernie Loosen, one of Germany's Riesling luminaries. And Washington now hosts one of the world's grandest Riesling jamborees every three years, where it shows off both sweet and dry Rieslings grown along the banks of the Columbia River.

But most of the wines I now drink from Washington are reds. This is because, although it's important to have a quality big-volume leader like Chateau Ste. Michelle, the fireworks come from the smaller independent producers, and as in most areas of the world where the sun shines, they measure themselves more against the great reds than the whites. Washington makes some outstanding Chardonnay and very good Viognier, but it's Cabernet Sauvignon, Merlot and Syrah that are banging the drum. And they do seem to fit better into the landscape. The locals boast about being on the 46th parallel – similar to the north end of Bordeaux. They boast of having up to seventeen hours of sunlight a day in June and two hours a day more than California through most of the summer. They talk of warm days but very cold desert nights, allowing even slow varieties like Cabernet to ripen yet hold on to great colour and acidity. But there's a frontiersman quality to some of their wine talk. That's not surprising. In some places, like the Yakima Valley and over to the east in Walla Walla, there are communities and a settled quality to the land. But frequently you are gazing in admiration at great slabs of green that really have been gouged out of the desert scrubland, some perched perilously on sprawls above the Columbia River, sometimes on terraces and slopes, but rarely with any sense of other human activity to see or hear. Vineyard regions like Horse Heaven Hills and Wahluke Slope are impressive but lonely.

The two areas that have probably made the biggest mark with red wines are the north side of the Yakima Valley and the south side of Walla Walla. To the north of the Yakima, the Rattlesnake Hills crouch like old lions, their crumpled shanks gaunt but lithe. Beneath them, Cabernet and Merlot flourish and wineries such as Andrew Will make famous reds. East toward the mouth of the Yakima, where its flow spews into the Columbia River, Red Mountain is now carpeted with vines, and wineries include Col Solare, that great Tuscan Piero Antinori's highly successful adventure into Washington wine. Red Mountain is mostly Cabernet Sauvignon and Merlot, with bits of Rhône varieties like Syrah thrown in. This is just about the driest vineyard section in Washington: 130 millimetres (5 inches) of rain is usually all it gets and the wines are dark and dense, with an inky, mineral, bitter bite, brightened with a sensation rather than a taste that has an almost umami effect on your tongue.

The first two superstar Washington wineries I came across were both from Walla Walla – Leonetti and Woodward Canyon. If Washington wine country has a tourist centre, it's Walla Walla, hunched up against the Blue Mountains. This is where the cool bars and restaurants cluster, rather than around the Yakima region. And while Yakima has some very well-established vineyards slowly showing their true worth, Walla Walla seems to be in full flow of trying to work out just how good it can be.

A lot of the best vineyards are actually in Oregon, just across the state line, which is marked by a country road barely more than a track. The superlative Rocks Vineyard is down here on the flat, producing fantastic Syrah but also some Italian varieties keen on the warmth. Results are thrilling – if the frosts don't get you, and down on the flat they often will. But up on the low slopes and then into the foothills of the Blue Mountains things are happening fast. On the Washington side, Mill Creek runs out of the hills and can boast sufficient rainfall to grow grapes without irrigation – Leonetti is already proving their worth. On the Oregon side, Seven Hills is producing a flow of exciting reds from its low slopes, and perched above that, the SeVein development of almost 800 hectares (2000 acres) towers over Walla Walla and promises a new dimension altogether to Washington wine.

New York State, from mellow to extreme

I sometimes think I discovered New York's Long Island wines before New York did. My first thrilling encounter was with Hargrave Sauvignon Blanc in the early 1980s. I followed that with Bridgehampton Sauvignon Blanc and Lenz Chardonnay. They were all unbelievably good. It didn't do any harm that I had a girlfriend in New York and I was dead keen to impress her. But I was bringing these wines over from England! When I tried to replenish stocks in New York City I drew a big, fat zero. None of the liquor stores, none of the bars and restaurants I tried offered any New York wines, and it was pretty clear none of them wanted to. I changed girlfriends. We went to see Buffy Sainte-Marie sing at a club in Millbrook, up the Hudson River, and she brought along a Millbrook Chardonnay – they didn't list it in the club; we swigged it surreptitiously in the dark as Buffy's worn but beautiful voice told us about the American Dream and we tried to live it.

New York City is kinder to New York State's wines nowadays, especially since locavore eating, majoring on local ingredients, has become the rage. But, as elsewhere on the East Coast, drinking the local wine isn't usually first choice for people eating the local food. I suppose we should see New York City's point of view because it has one of the most cosmopolitan and demanding eating and drinking scenes in the world. New York sommeliers are famously hard to impress. Maybe the local wine producers still don't match up to those of the rest of the world. Well, perhaps that's true, but they do make some fascinating wines, usually under challenging conditions. I think we should cut them some slack.

The Hudson Valley is a *very* challenging place to grow wine grapes, but I have a soft spot for it. I had a New York publisher who used to regale me with bottles of wild and wonderful red wines he had made from grapes whose names I barely knew while I was hoping he'd tell me how brilliantly my books were selling. And then he quit. He went back up the Hudson to his grapes and I felt really proud of him. My Buffy Sainte-Marie night was about as epic as they come, and the Millbrook Chardonnay must have had something to do with it. Even so, I can see why the Hudson's somewhat rarefied charms don't find a ready market among the sophisticates of Manhattan.

The Finger Lakes, though, can make some wines as well as anywhere in the world. I'm talking Rieslings, and I'm actually talking about really difficult conditions. You would never know it in midsummer. The Finger Lakes are in the north of the state, just south of Lake Ontario, and in summer they are balmy, and beautiful, and intensely relaxing, the Lakes coaxing out mild, cool zephyrs to flutter through the vines and offer the perfect antidote to any stressed Manhattanite in need of solace. But the summer is short, the winter long and brutal. In the old days no one thought the summer provided enough warmth to ripen the classic wine grapes and no one thought the fragile classics could cope with winter temperatures that always drop below zero centigrade and stick there, but sometimes go as low as −25°C (−13°F). A vine rarely comes back from that kind of temperature alive. So table wines were made out of some pretty rudimentary hybrid vines bred to withstand the Arctic. I used to force them down on upstate camping trips. It's amazing what love will do to your palate.

Luckily for the Finger Lakes, a guy turned up from Ukraine, where they regularly had to wrestle with −40°C (−40°F), and he had a doctorate in how to grow wine grapes in conditions far worse than those of upstate New York. Dr Konstantin Frank thought he could crack the problem of growing high-quality wine grapes if he could find rootstocks like the ones they had in Russia onto which he would graft cold-resistant vines like Riesling. He eventually found what he wanted in a convent garden in Québec, where the winters were even worse than in upstate New York, but where the nuns managed to produce a crop of Pinot Noir grapes one year in three. Dr Frank took back a load of rootstock, grafted on some Riesling and planted it out. In 1957 the temperature dropped to −25°C (−13°F) and even a lot of the hardy hybrids died. Dr Frank's Rieslings grafted onto the Canadian nuns' finest not only survived, but gave a bumper crop of four tons to the acre. By 1961 Frank was making a sweet Riesling from these vines, which ended up being served at the White House.

Riesling is still what the Finger Lakes do best. They can make some nice reds – Cabernet Franc works quite well and I've tried some Syrah and Saperavi, of all things – but Rieslings, dry, medium or sweet, can certainly be the best in North America and can match the opposition in Europe and Australia. Those dry ones would go awfully well with seafood down in New York City, but I think I have seen them more often in San Francisco! And the guys around the fringes of the Lakes have managed to master the 'not quite dry' style. The German winemaker at

Anthony Road said he used to do bone-dry Rieslings, but the fruit was so different from Germany he felt the need to leave a little sugar in the wine to give his palate something to hold on to. Riesling is so often caught in this quandary. Can you go really dry? Will there be enough expression in the fruit without some sugar remaining? Well, the Finger Lakes are in the throes of finding out. While they're at it, they can sometimes produce completely brilliant sweet Rieslings very much in the German mould, and in some years they make stunning ice wines – not surprisingly. If you're not sure whether a New York Riesling is sweet or dry, turn the bottle round – on the back label you will find a graph ranging from bone dry to super sweet, with the taste profile of your bottle very precisely marked. Not knowing if a Riesling is sweet or dry is one of the main problems in trying to persuade people to drink it, and this is a tip-top idea. (Alsace could do the same.)

Long Island gave New York wine legitimacy. Nowhere else in the state could be relied on to ripen Chardonnay enough to resemble a French white Burgundy, and Cabernet Sauvignon and Merlot to resemble a French red Bordeaux. And it's the sea that makes the difference. Long Island stretches east of Manhattan for 160 kilometres (100 miles). Most of the western end is housing, but in the east, at the little town of Riverhead, the island forks and the Great Peconic Bay divides what looks like two narrow lobster claws of land – the North and South Forks.

The South Fork is where the Hamptons are, where the grand, white-slatted beach villas are, where the parties rage and the gossip columnists and paparazzi lurk in hope of an indiscretion. The North Fork is hardworking farmland and, increasingly, vineyards. The land is free-draining, a crucial 1–2°C (1.8–3.5°F) warmer than the South Fork, and it's only a couple of miles wide. This is vital. Water to the south and north tempers the harsh East Coast weather, soothing the humid heat that can send you crazy in a Manhattan summer and warding off the vicious winter freezes that attack vineyards on the mainland. If you said that it sounds a bit like Bordeaux, with the tongue of the Médoc jutting out into the Bay of Biscay, I would agree. And we wouldn't be the only ones. The Hargraves, who started Long Island's first modern vineyard on an old potato field in 1973, thought exactly the same. However, their bank manager obviously wasn't a Bordeaux drinker. He wouldn't give them a loan, but they went ahead anyway and set the ball rolling in the direction of the French classics. Since then, all the New York reds that have remotely resembled those of Bordeaux, and most of the most elegant and tasty Chardonnays, have come from Long Island.

And, usually but not always, that means the North Fork. But at the eastern end of the South Fork a winery called Wölffer has managed to make the reds that are closest to the Bordeaux style – and in price, too. And a winery called Channing Daughters hasn't made anything that resembles anything, to be honest. That's a big compliment. Within leaping distance of the Hamptons and all that jazz, Channing manages to be one of the most original and inspiring wineries in the whole of America. I hope the summer visitors stop chattering and gossiping for long enough to notice.

Four hundred years of trying in Virginia

You can't say the Virginians didn't try. Almost as soon as the first shipload of settlers arrived at Jamestown in 1607 they had a go at planting the vine cuttings they had brought with them. Since most of these settlers died of starvation, surrounded by swamp and unfriendly locals, that first stab at a vineyard didn't get very far. Nor did the second effort, in 1619, when at least the settlers managed to set up the Jamestown Assembly – the first elected assembly in the New World – which decreed that every head of household was required to plant twenty European grape vines on his property. The settlers quickly discovered that tobacco was a native plant they could get their kicks from and harvest for profit far more easily than their vines, which in any case kept dying.

There were loads of native American grape vines which didn't die, but which seemed to make pretty filthy wine. In 1762 a chap called Charles Carter sent some wine made from what was called the American Winter Grape, reportedly 'a grape so nauseous till frost the fowls of the air will not touch it', back to London. The Royal Society for the Arts sent him a hundred pounds, probably out of sympathy. Thomas Jefferson clearly knew the local grapes made terrible wine. In 1771 he started importing vines from Italy and France to plant at Monticello, his estate – he even imported vines and soil (!) from Bordeaux's famous sweet wine property, Château d'Yquem. For thirty-six years he tried. And he never made a bottle. George Washington had a go at his place, Mount Vernon: he tried to make European grape vines give him a crop for eleven years and he never managed a single bottle either. No wonder that when I was a student actor spending Christmas Day at the Colonial Inn in Williamsburg, just down the road from Jamestown, and I asked if they had some Virginia wine, the waiter's answer was blunt: 'No, sir. There's no such thing as Virginia wine.'

Well, there almost wasn't. In 1960 there were only 6 hectares (15 acres) of vines being cultivated in Virginia, and they were basically for table grapes. But people now knew why all those early attempts at planting the classic European wine-grape vine – the *Vitis vinifera* – had failed. There's a nasty aphid called *Phylloxera vastatrix* which is native to north-east America and loves to chomp vine roots. The local varieties have all developed enough resistance to survive. The European varieties had no resistance, and whenever they were planted in America they all died. Eventually, when Europe's whole wine culture was threatened by an invasion of phylloxera from America during the 1860s and '70s, the experts worked out that if you grafted a European vinifera vine onto an American vine rootstock, the

European vine survived phylloxera, and, as far as anyone could tell, made wine that still tasted reassuringly European. And in 1976, 369 years after Jamestown, an Italian called Gianni Zonin decided to give it one more go – with European vines on American rootstock. And this time it worked.

Now, Virginia is one of the most beautiful vineyard areas the world has to offer, with the Atlantic seaboard to the east, the seductive, impossibly blue-hazed Blue Ridge Mountains to the west, and all around you the prosperity of a long-established farming community whose proximity to Washington DC hasn't done the owners of the grand mansions and rolling paddocks full of thoroughbred horses any harm. But this same prosperity has kept the forests and mountains largely undisturbed, except where scars of the American Civil War are solemnly celebrated. It's kept the large towns, and the small, welcoming and reassuringly 'historic'. But it isn't an easy place to grow grapes. Virginia is on the same latitude as southern Italy. That means that the sun is harsh and the winters are harsh, too. Spring starts late, the air heats up but can drip with humidity. Storms build over the Allegheny Mountains to the west. Rain continually threatens from the east, and if the grapes don't ripen quickly, the hurricane season of October can drench whatever crop is left. You might wonder if grape growing is really worth the effort, unless Virginia is able to produce something very particular. Luckily, she can.

I got the message during one explosive hour at the London Wine Trade Fair in 2009. 'Have you been to the Virginia stand?' I didn't know that there was a Virginia stand, but we wine geeks love showing off to each other about our new discoveries at wine shows. Bragging rights and all that. 'You've got to try their Viognier.' It sounded sufficiently unlikely to drive me to their stand. It wasn't one Viognier. It was five – White Hall, Keswick, Barboursville, Veritas and Pearmund. Viognier is a really tricky white grape. In just a few patches of rocky hillside in France's Rhône Valley it makes something ethereal and wonderful, mingling apricot with spring flowers and a smooth texture like crème fraîche. In most of the rest of the world its wines are thick and unrefreshing as the winemakers struggle to unlock its ripe, scented fruit without releasing its chewy oiliness. Yet these Viogniers were fresh, scented, with a wonderfully fascinating flavour like ripe, just-picked apricot skins and the pips in a sugar-ripe pear, the chewiness perfectly balanced by a soothing, waxy, creamy texture, the wine uplifted and perfumed with the white flowers of a warm spring. I'd never had Viognier so delicious from anywhere except the Rhône Valley's Condrieu, and rarely even there. And here were five beauties. Was Virginia really proving it could be a world-beater with Viognier?

Yes, it was. And it also pointed the way for Virginia to make its mark in the wine world. Try the different grapes. Try the ones that Australia and California can't do. With those warm, humid conditions, completely the opposite of typical New World conditions, don't rely on doing typical New World wines. That's why Viognier was such a brilliant choice – its thick skins and loose, unpredictable clusters of grapes resisted the harsh sun, yet also didn't rot in the damp. You can't stop Virginia doing Chardonnay – this is America – but she's making a speciality of bright, melon-fresh unwooded Chardonnay from early-picked grapes. Petit Manseng is a really tricky white grape from south-west France with searingly high acidity, which rarely ripens enough to balance the acidity. Yes, but it bunches are loose, its grape skins are thick and it's perfect for Virginia. You can ripen it way above 14 per cent in Virginia and it stays incisive and nervy, and it finally reveals its intriguing flavour of pineapple chunks, fragrant lemon zest and barleysugar in wines that can be sweet or dry.

You can't stop Virginia doing Cabernet Sauvignon either – as I have said, this is America. But they've taken the Petit Verdot, a really minor player in Bordeaux because it is so difficult to ripen, and put it centre stage. Again, this variety is a late ripener and it has thick-skinned, small berries. It won't rot on the vine in Virginia and gives dense, dark, spicy, black-fruited wines. Tannat is another thick-skinned beast from south-west France that they can tame in Virginia. Nebbiolo, one of the trickiest of all red varieties, shows form here. Barboursville and Breaux create wines of balsam and incense perfume, black raspberry vinegar, celery salinity and stones – cathedral stones, paving stones, graphite – and a biting tannin that seems almost scented. And Virginia draws out the deep raspberry and wet pebble flavours of Cabernet Franc, another red Bordeaux variety that is proving surprisingly successful in the more humid conditions of America's East Coast.

Vines are scattered right across the state. Chatham Vineyards makes delicious light Chardonnay, and Petit Verdot, right on the Eastern Shore. But most of the best vineyards are planted inland, just under or actually on the slopes of the Blue Ridge Mountains. Many of the best are clustered around the college town of Charlottesville toward the south, but you will find a significant number in the north of the state, nearer Washington DC, particularly in Fauquier County. And there's one area that rarely figures for wine tasters – yet. But it will do. The Shenandoah Valley is in the far west, across the Blue Ridge Mountains with the high Allegheny Range glowering on the far side. We are several hundred feet higher here than in the main Virginian vineyard areas and that cools down the days and creates cooler nights. The Alleghenies generate a rain shadow from the west. The Blue Ridge Mountains break up the storms from the east, and whereas most of Virginia's soils are fertile red clays and clay loams, in the Shenandoah limestone ridges poke out right down the valley. Vines love limestone. The locals still worry about frosts and snow and shorter ripening seasons. I know. That's what they said in New Zealand's Central Otago region, in Canada's Okanagan Valley, in Argentina's Tupungato. 'It can't be done,' they said. Look at them now.

Canada

Hot and cold

I really didn't expect it to be Nova Scotia that slapped me across the face with a writhing Atlantic cod and said, 'You have to take us Canadians more seriously. We're making world-class wine.' I sort of knew that already. Chardonnays, Rieslings, Pinot Noirs and Syrahs from Ontario and British Columbia have been clocking up their numbers in my tasting brain for years. Each new vintage brings further proof of wineries that

Some things never change. I still love drinking – though not necessarily tea – and I still pore over books about trains.

Me and my brother planting our first experimental Cabernet Sauvignon vine in the back garden.

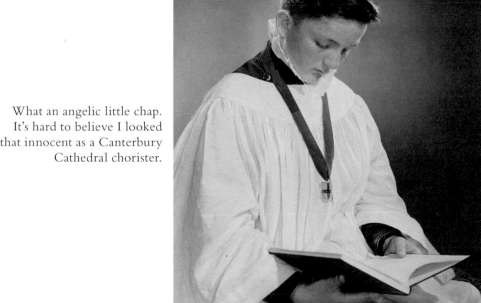

What an angelic little chap. It's hard to believe I looked that innocent as a Canterbury Cathedral chorister.

I got my name 'Oz' in the showers at school for playing cricket like an Australian. (My real name was Owen.) I don't think it was any of these guys. They look far too nice to change a chap's name in the showers. That's me at the back, second from the left, rather boastfully sporting my colours.

What a beautiful bunch of shags! I'm third from the back in what was virtually Pembroke's most successful rowing eight since the Second World War. We got five bumps – four is regarded as a perfect score. Pembroke are much better nowadays; our women are usually the fastest crew on the river.

I've never held back from celebrating – especially when it's with ice-cold Champagne out of a bucket as big as my head. This was when I'd just top-scored in the Oxford–Cambridge tasting match and we'd broken Cambridge's winning streak

A tasteful victory for Oxford palates

A victory drink of vintage champagne for Oxford captain Robert Clarke, who also made the higher individual score.

Bliss. A picnic by the side of a country lane somewhere in France with the girl of my dreams. And a bottle of Beaujolais with a flip-flop on top to keep out the horse flies.

This was my first picture in Spotlight, the Actors' Directory. Very moody, but I'm not sure it ever got me any work. Love the hair.

What on earth is Julian Fellowes doing wearing that dress? I'm playing Face in Jonson's *The Alchemist* at Northampton Repertory Theatre – my first job. I suspect Julian would rather forget which part he was playing – quite a fetching smile, though . . .

The happiest show I ever did – *The Mitford Girls* at the Globe Theatre. That's me at the front with Patricia Hodge and we're just about to do our 'Fred 'n' Ginger' dance routine. Hodge was an unforgettable Nancy Mitford. We all still meet up, and once a Mitford Girl, always a Mitford Girl. And, wow, could those girls knock back the Champagne.

The Big Time. I'm playing General Perón here in *Evita* at the Prince Edward Theatre, with the awesome Stephanie Lawrence as Evita herself. It's wonderful what a bit of make-up and a hairpiece can do. I was also writing for the *Sunday Express* and doing more and more tasting. Something had to give, and, inevitably, it was the make-up and hairpiece.

The newspapers lapped it up when the English winetasting team whacked the French team in Paris. This was a famous JAK cartoon taking the 'michael' out of French haut gastronomy and its sense of its own importance.

"Alas Monsieur, ever since the Evening Standard victory, the customers have demanded English wine waiters!"

Jilly Goolden and I did a series of films for BBC *Food and Drink*; her an exquisitely haughty *Liberté* figure extolling the superiority of French wines, me a raw-boned Aussie ocker telling the world that Down Under grog was the best there is. *Food and Drink* ran primetime for seventeen years and had a massive effect on British eating and drinking.

I hadn't let go of my music interests entirely. The great violinist Tasmin Little and I were chosen to front the *Radio Times* edition celebrating the 100th anniversary of the Proms. My mum thought I was doing something serious at last.

t's a tough life being a winetaster! Hey, I'm not joking. That's a six-bottle jeroboam bottle of Château Pétrus 1990 I'm holding. t's worth about £20,000. You don't think I drank it, do you? I almost had to pay just to hold it.

When I visit wine regions I always say – let me eat what the locals eat. Well, in south-west France, just occasionally, they eat cabbage stuffed with foie gras. A whole cabbage, tightly stuffed. You think I look happy? I was.

This is what a winetaster's glamorous life often consists of – a room like a laboratory and two hundred bottles of young wine (young Bordeaux this time, and young Bordeaux can be a hard ask). And my job is to try to divine which ones will be good in five years', ten years' time, and which ones won't. You really earn your lunch.

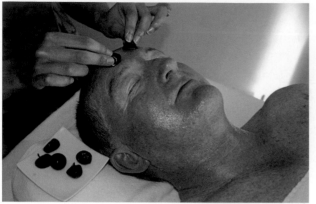

Those are Merlot grapes. They're supposed to be really good for your skin and they play a crucial role in the *vinothérapie* at the Sources de Caudalie at Château Smith Haut Lafitte. They might work. I do look awfully relaxed.

That's more like it – a proper hard-working tongue. There's a lot of dark purple colouring matter in young Bordeaux reds, and a significant amount of it gets embedded in my tongue. It takes days to get back to normal pink.

I was brought up on the Kent coast and the sea was my summer playground. The beaches to the west of Bordeaux are some of the most irresistible in Europe. Bathing Forbidden? Try and stop me.

have settled into star status by being able to repeat early glories, and evidence of wineries I'd never heard of, sometimes from parts of Ontario or British Columbia that I'd never considered, setting out their stall with exciting stuff. But Nova Scotia? That means New Scotland, and no one ever called anywhere New Scotland because it looked like prime vineyard land.

Well, the Atlantic Provinces, as Canada's far eastern regions are known, do yield a few surprises. The northern coast of Nova Scotia calls itself the Sunshine Coast of Nova Scotia, and looks out optimistically to the warmest salt seawater north of the Carolinas – and they are a thousand miles south of here. St John's, Newfoundland, is Canada's third-warmest city, year round. Don't ask me how. And on the Bay of Fundy, a

protected inlet that runs north-east between Nova Scotia and New Brunswick, there are several little valleys and estuaries like Annapolis Valley, Gaspereau Valley and Avon River Valley. My first reaction to these delightful bucolic eddies was that it had to be too cold. Now stop a minute. The experts said Tasmania was too cold. They said South Island New Zealand and southern England were too cold. They are not. And already Pinot Noir and Chardonnay can creep to a sort of ripeness out here. Climate change is relentless and could open hundreds of square miles to grape cultivation along Nova Scotia's coasts.

And barely ripe Pinot Noir and Chardonnay – isn't that what makes the best sparkling wine? Benjamin Bridge are based in the Gaspereau Valley. They started making sparkling wine in 2002. Last year I drank – not for the first time – their 2008 Brut Reserve, fantastically fresh and vigorous at nine years old, a pulsing apple-flesh acidity, slowly building up a soothing, coating richness of roasted hazelnut and brioche and crème fraîche. A magic mouthful that will get better for years yet. And I wondered if this is the best sparkling wine being made in North America. Perhaps it is. In twenty years' time, when Nova Scotia is famous, and the Gaspereau Valley is a hotbed of wine tourism, don't say you weren't told.

It's just possible that the first vineyard I ever visited was in Ontario. My parents had emigrated while I was a student, and my father was a professor at the University of Western Ontario in London. It's barely an hour's drive to the north shore of Lake Erie, and it's only a couple of hours to the Niagara Peninsula. There's a place called Vineland, and it had vines all right – Marechal Foch, de Chaunac, Vidal Blanc and a load of others you wouldn't want to know about. I tasted the wines. Dear, oh dear. My poor old parents, I thought. I visited in midwinter – hellishly cold – and midsummer – hellishly hot. So I got a slightly warped view of what is now Canada's chief vineyard area. Well, perhaps not. As with Nova Scotia, you've got to start somewhere. The boss at one winery told me, 'Most wines can be duplicated here in London. Winemakers are technical people, and they can take a product and rip it apart in their lab and come very close to other brands. That's their job . . . sherry is sherry, just as milk is milk!' Ontario also had to loosen up its post-Prohibition liquor laws and create a framework to encourage quality before these tired old vineyards on the benchland running down to Lake Ontario could join the New World of wine.

This didn't really happen until the 1980s and '90s. But Niagara is now a serious player, for all the classic French varieties, as well as Riesling and a strange hybrid called Vidal which they use for Ontario's sugar-sweet speciality, Icewine. It hasn't been an easy ride, and without Lake Ontario to the north-east and Lake Erie to the south-west, there wouldn't be any vines here, hundreds of miles inland. It would be too extreme: the winters are already long and numbing. They would be worse without the lakes tempering the savage weather by slowly releasing heat from their deep waters on to the peninsula. Spring would be later, fall would be sooner, and midwinter would be colder. And the summers are already short and searing. It's only the cooling lake breezes that temper the heat. As it is, spring only gets going in May and the fall comes to an abrupt end in October. In between, it's generally hotter than Bordeaux and always hotter than Burgundy. But their grapes – the Bordeaux grapes of Cabernet and Merlot, and the Burgundy grapes Chardonnay and Pinot Noir – all do well here, along with Syrah and Riesling.

Ontario's newest high achiever is considerably more tricksy than the Niagara Peninsula. Prince Edward County is a place where I used to picnic on my way to see friends in Kingston, up by the St Lawrence River. Great beaches, no vines, is what I remember. This is on Lake Ontario's north shore and it's a higgledy-piggledy peninsula of enticing inlets and coves. What I didn't know then is that this is the best limestone in Ontario and probably the best in Canada. Just here. Just on this peninsula. Again, the lake's influence is crucial. We are north of Niagara and it's colder – frosts can strike as late as mid-May and again in mid–October. It's nail-biting stuff, getting your plantings just right. You have to be close to the lake for frost protection in spring and winter, but not too close because the lake's breezes will cool you down too much to ripen your fruit. Vines right by the lake will ripen two and a half weeks later than those just 1.6 kilometres (1 mile) inland, but these inland ones will have an unacceptable frost risk. Wherever you are, you will probably have to bury your vines in winter or they will be killed. And under all this lies the limestone plateau, nurturing Chardonnay and Pinot Noir that are often Canada's best. In fact, if you can work out how and where to get a regular crop, this funny, crooked-faced splash of limestone jutting out into the lake may supply the best conditions for Chardonnay in North America.

Or was the first vineyard I visited in British Columbia? Gosh, I wasn't even a student then, but I had hitchhiked my way across Canada, playing the guitar. And one late afternoon I found myself in a sun-soaked orchard at a place called Peachland. How could I resist? With a front-row view of a thrillingly blue lake beneath me, I snuggled down and drifted off to sleep. It was peach trees then. But now it's a vineyard. Looking on the modern maps of the Okanagan Valley I reckon it's now Hainle, and they were the guys who made Canada's first Icewine in 1973. The Okanagan is a ridiculously beautiful deep, thin valley sliced out of the mountains four hours east of Vancouver. Every fibre in your body longs to love every wine that the Okanagan produces. We are pretty far north, from 49° almost to 51°N. That's at the cool end for northern Europe's vineyards. But things are very different here. We are in a rain shadow with the Coastal Mountain Range drawing off most of the westerly damp. It's a short growing season, but a reliably warm one. Up in this mountain valley the days are hot and the nights cold. The colours of the wines are pure and bright. The acids of reds and whites are crisp and mouthwatering. Just what you'd expect in a mountain valley.

Yet the south of the Okanagan Valley dips into Osoyoos Lake on the American border and it is officially Canada's only desert, with more heat in some parts than California's Napa Valley. Even Kelowna, in the cooler north, doesn't have that much less heat than New Zealand's Marlborough region, and it definitely has more than Champagne in France. And this pretty much tells you what kind of wine to expect – fresher, brighter white wines from the north; big, powerful Cabernets, Merlots and Syrahs from the south, where a road sign proclaims 'Welcome to Desert Wine Country'; and balanced, refreshing, limpid, crystalline flavours in reds and whites right through the valley from vineyards perched on ridges above the glittering lake.

But the locals aren't done yet. The Similkameen Valley is a windy, wild, sunny valley that swoops up to the north-west of Osoyoos. Its pristine conditions are making it a hub for organic and biodynamic grape growing in the west and it somehow manages to divide its vineyards between mighty, growling reds and Rieslings so minerally you think you are licking the vineyard rock. And they want to go cooler as well. North of the lake, up into the forests, as the highway and the railway begin the climb toward the Rockies, a few hardy adventurers know that the days are still warm, even if the nights are colder and the summer brief. And that's where they'll plant their vines and make their wine. I wouldn't have expected to find Canadians looking for cooler conditions. But you tell 'em.

It makes sense for Germany to have been the place to invent Eiswein (ice wine, or Icewine, as the Canadians spell it) because it is the coldest of the traditional wine countries, but it's the Niagara Peninsula that now produces most of the world's supply. If there is one thing you can guarantee in Canada it is that winter will come, and it will be harsh. In 1991 some guys in British Columbia made Icewine as early as 29 October. On the other hand, I've discovered one producer who had to wait until April the next year to get conditions right. Is that climate change? It sure is.

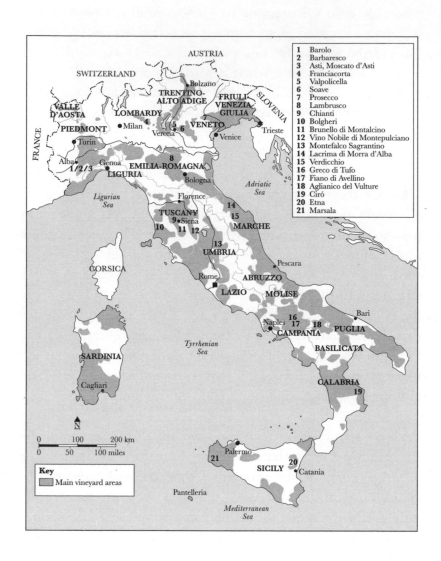

AUSTRIA

SWITZERLAND

SLOVENIA

FRANCE

1 Barolo
2 Barbaresco
3 Asti, Moscato d'Asti
4 Franciacorta
5 Valpolicella
6 Soave
7 Prosecco
8 Lambrusco
9 Chianti
10 Bolgheri
11 Brunello di Montalcino
12 Vino Nobile di Montepulciano
13 Montefalco Sagrantino
14 Lacrima di Morra d'Alba
15 Verdicchio
16 Greco di Tufo
17 Fiano di Avellino
18 Aglianico del Vulture
19 Ciró
20 Etna
21 Marsala

VALLE D'AOSTA

TRENTINO-ALTO ADIGE
Bolzano

FRIULI-VENEZIA GIULIA

LOMBARDY
Milan
Verona **5** **6**
VENETO
Venice
Trieste

PIEDMONT
Turin
Alba **1/2/3**
Genoa
LIGURIA
EMILIA-ROMAGNA
8
Bologna

Ligurian Sea

Florence
TUSCANY
9 Siena
10 **11** **12**

14
15
MARCHE

Adriatic Sea

13
UMBRIA

Pescara

Rome
LAZIO
ABRUZZO
MOLISE

CORSICA

Bari

16
Naples **17** **18**
CAMPANIA
PUGLIA
BASILICATA

Tyrrhenian Sea

SARDINIA
Cagliari

CALABRIA
19

N

0   100   200 km
0   50   100 miles

Palermo
21
20
SICILY Catania

Key
Main vineyard areas

Pantelleria

Mediterranean Sea

Italy

Sangiovese, Nebbiolo and brilliant whites

A couple of years ago I was at Vinexpo, the massive global trade wine fair in Bordeaux. I was sitting in a room crowded with bloggers and wine geeks, but mostly with people whose suits were very well cut and whose shoes were highly polished. And I was tasting a range of the highest-profile red wines from Bolgheri on the Tuscan coast. This is a drab, flat coastal area with absolutely no long wine tradition whatever, but of absolutely massive recent wine renown, created from nowhere by the arrival of Sassicaia Cabernet Sauvignon on the international scene in the 1970s when the 1972 was voted Best Cabernet Sauvignon in the World. Yet, for wine after wine I found myself writing *too much oak, too ripe, fruit too baked, tannins too severe*. Only Sassicaia, the most famous, the least dense, the one with the best balance, with the clearest, cleanest acid and thrilling dark fruit seasoned with herbs and the dryness of rock, shone as a Tuscan wine.

The others could have come from anywhere. The grapes grown were largely the international varieties of Cabernet and Merlot, but, apart from Sassicaia, they weren't making any statement about the vineyards they came from. Except, perhaps, that they were too hot to be growing these French varieties and might do better if they stuck to something local. But, of course, something local is not what Bolgheri is about.

Bolgheri is the international jet set of Italian wine, flavours and styles to match the other glitz bombs around the world. I sat in that room keen to discover more about what I thought was an important part of Italian wine. I left that room thinking that it had almost nothing to do with the rest of Italy. I needed to look elsewhere.

Later that year, in London, I saw a great chance. A broad-ranging tasting of wines from every corner of Italy. A masterclass on Italy's undiscovered jewels of wine, the areas I hadn't vis-ited, the grape varieties I'd never tried. I signed up. I arrived early. Everyone was milling around in a very Italian way. I was directed to one room, then to another. I waited, I enquired, I waited. The masterclass was always just about to start. Now? In which room? No, it wasn't. After a good hour one of the myriad organisers took me to one side and admitted that none of the wines had arrived from Italy. And, actually, the expert giving the masterclass hadn't arrived either. Could I perhaps come back tomorrow, when they were sure it would all be sorted out?

The internationalist Italy of Bolgheri which wasn't the Italy I wanted to discover was so easy to target, the organisation was brimming with marketing expertise. The other Italy, the ribald, ramshackle, uniquely challenging, irresistibly intriguing Italy of flavours and textures and perfumes unlike any others in the world of wine, was just as chaotic as ever. But I now knew the flavours were there, the wines were somewhere there, and I now knew I had to make the effort. I have to as Italy is too important to give up on.

I think I will devote the next ten years of my wine life to finally understanding Italy. It will probably take that long and it is worth doing. It's about time. Ten years ago it wasn't about time, and other countries simply had more to offer. But not now. At last, after, literally hundreds – some might say thousands – of years of underperforming, Italy is finally in exactly the right place, with exactly the right raw materials and exactly the right generation of wine men and women to grapple the title of most interesting wine country in the world from whoever thinks they hold it now. But also the title of most challenging wine country. The old Italy was never easy to understand, unless assuming that you would almost always be disappointed made it easy. The new Italy won't be easy to understand either, but now we have the joy of unpredictability and unfamiliarity frequently leading to something thrilling and unexpected.

And it is about time. No country is more steeped in wine than Italy. Grapes are grown and wine is made in every single one of her provinces – France can't claim that. She has more indigenous grape varieties than France, Spain and Portugal put together – and those are just the ones identified so far. Tuscany alone is supposed to have more than 270 different grape varieties. The whole of France has a mere 204. You look at the map and there's a great spine of mountain running right up the centre, from volcanic Etna in Sicily to the Alps in Piedmont, and then a craggy boundary of mighty south-facing peaks marks her northern frontier round to Slovenia in the north-east. And where there aren't mountains there is sea. The long muscular limb of Italy stretches way down almost to Africa, into the heart of the Mediterranean. With continuous mountain, endless sea coast and the odd river valley there's almost nowhere that cannot grow grapes in Italy, and almost nowhere that doesn't. And, with a little help from the Greeks, this is pretty much where our modern culture of wine began, in the heyday of the Roman Empire. Of course Italy should be the greatest wine country in the world, so why isn't she? Why has it taken until the twenty-first century for this declaration to be seen as anything more than self-deluding and frequently cynical fantasy? Why has Italy been so profligate with her gifts?

I freely admit that I have been one of Italy's biggest critics, but was it my fault that I took so long to 'get' Italy? If Italy doesn't mind, I would suggest it was mostly Italy's fault. When I was getting into wine, no one ever offered me a so-called classic Italian wine. I drank quite a bit of murderous Soave and Valpolicella out of 1½-litre screwcap bottles at student parties, usually because the wine shop had run out of the even cheaper Cypriot stuff – with skull-thudding consequences. I dallied with the odd straw-covered flask of Chianti in gloomy trattorie, peering optimistically at dates who were already silently rehearsing their reasons for not letting me walk them home.

If I was going to be offered something good, it was always French or German, unless, of course, my host was getting the vintage port out. Never Italian. What Italian wine was there to offer? If the classic Barolos and Chiantis were any good, they certainly weren't coming to Britain. I knew nobody who was laying down Italian wines and was eager to share some nicely matured examples with a young wine fanatic desperate to try anything in his fevered dash to experience all the different flavours wine possessed. I did come across the odd Barolo or Chianti – always bitter, usually streaked with an ungenerous sour acidity only partially covered up by the brown oxidised sweet staleness that was suggested as an example of a 'nicely mature' style. Mature, yes, but it wasn't nicely anything. The Italian wine geeks who offered me these wines sometimes verged on the swivel-eyed. It's as though they were members of a club whose password I didn't know. Well, actually, didn't want to know.

So I went back to France, which was entering a golden age of wine in the later years of the twentieth century, burnishing her traditions while embracing the new. And in the 1980s the New World arrived. If I wanted classic I could find it in France, but not in Italy. If I wanted new and modern, I could find it in California or Australia or New Zealand, but not in Italy. I was a wine lover starting from scratch in an era when the world of wine was exploding with excitement. I did keep trying Italy, but got so much more pleasure from so many more places that I never put that much effort into it.

One of the reasons for Italy's failure was also one of her hidden strengths. Though Genoa and Venice had been important trading centres in the Middle Ages, often dealing in the sweet strong wines of the eastern Mediterranean, Italy's own wine culture had a serious flaw. Whereas France, and to a lesser extent Spain and Portugal, traded with countries, particularly in northern Europe, that couldn't grow their own grapes but which adored the taste of wine, all Italy's neighbours could grow grapes perfectly easily and didn't need any topping up. Then add the fact that Islam spread to many of Italy's potential partners in the south and east, which didn't encourage any wine-trading plans that might have helped to make her wines better known, and perhaps persuade producers to try to create something special. And wait a minute – we're talking about Italy here. There wasn't an Italy until 1861, at which time just 2.5 per cent of the population spoke standard Italian. To this day you can struggle to find someone speaking standard Italian in the far south. As one of the leaders of the Unification said, 'We have made Italy; now we must make Italians.' Well, it is still a work in progress. Is that a weakness? In national terms, yes. But in terms of wine and food, absolutely not. It's at the core of understanding Italy; it's fundamental to the new wave that is transforming Italian wine without ever losing sight of tradition, and it's one of the reasons it took me so long.

Note that I said wine and *food*. This is also fundamental in understanding Italy. You can enjoy any New World wine without food. You can enjoy Bordeaux or Burgundy without food. But there is no gastronomic culture in the world where food and wine are more intertwined than in Italy, but it's not any old food and any old wine. It's the local food and the local wine. And by local I don't just mean the province or the city, I mean the village, and sometimes the actual home, the family home where a particular person cooks very particular local food and the grapes for the wine are grown within a stone's throw, within a walk, at worst within a short ride of the gleaming, grinning, raucous dining table. In such circumstances, the wine always makes sense – so long as it is served with its food.

On my last trip to Montalcino, in Tuscany, I was becoming a little confused and exhausted by all the razzmatazz that currently surrounds Brunello di Montalcino. But somehow I hooked up with some Italians going to have supper with a local wine farmer. I was welcomed into a fairly rudimentary home with a rudimentary cellar next door. No one spoke English, but piles of home-cured prosciutto and salami and cheese, followed by a welter of wild boar, meant it didn't matter; I was part of the joyous night. And the wine was wonderfully uncultured – local Rosso di Montalcino splashed from a jug. And the Brunello, unpolished, unsculpted, prising open my jaw, gripping my teeth, then releasing the most delicious, honest heartfelt flow of delight to course down my throat. Did I mark it out of 100? Did I make a concise tasting note? Please. This happy, timeless Italian evening deserved better than that.

This is the core of the traditional Italy. And I did understand this right from the start. On my first tentative trip to Venice, I was sitting in a tatty restaurant lapped by the waters of one of the backwater canals. I had almost too little money in my pocket to raise a smile. Especially when the waiter plonked down a rather smart-looking bottle of Chianti Classico and brandished his corkscrew. No, no. What's your local wine, your everyday drink? And he brought back a jug of a liquid – plumskin purple and still spitting with the unrestrained bubbles of its youth. 'Raboso,' the waiter said. 'That's what we drink.' A crude splash of raw, unsubtle fruit and a sourness that only served to heighten my appetite and craving to eat what they ate, too. Darts of effervescence trailed down my throat as I swallowed. France didn't make wine like this, nor did Spain. But I sort of knew that I could only drink this wine here, beside this canal, with this plate of *fritto misto*. Now.

That was a long time ago. I was learning. I would know different today, wouldn't I? Why would I? Less than a year ago I was in Umbria, getting to grips with the dark, blistering secrets of the black Sagrantino grape in Montefalco. I thought this was a totally red wine town, but as I sat down to rest my weary gums at the edge of the town square I saw someone drinking a liquid the colour of a field of straw, glistening in the late summer sun. No bottle. Just a little jug and a wine that seemed so thick it coiled lazily around the belly of the glass. What was it? Trebbiano Spoletino. You can only get it here. I had never heard of it, so I ordered it. I'm not sure it even tasted of very much, but it was magnificently, exactly what I should have been drinking at that moment, in that place.

You can't do this very often in France any more. Portugal, perhaps, but in Italy I can go from Alpine north to African south and do this a thousand times. And it reminded me of that 1861 Unifier when he said, ' . . . now we must make Italians'. Politically that might be an achievement Italy could well do with. But not culturally and not gastronomically. I realised that more than anywhere I've ever been, Italy is a teeming hive of tiny communities, proud of who they are, not at all keen to be swept up into some rapid sense of 'Italianness', and each one stubbornly, lovingly clinging to the peculiarities and nuances of what they eat and drink.

Globalisation is a phrase we apply to many parts of modern life – fast food, car design, fashion, soft drinks, news providers. Large, powerful, wealthy conglomerates literally take over a section of our life and squeeze the individuality out of it in the name of profit, homogenisation and control. In the world of alcoholic drinks, it's happened with spirits, it's happened with beer, and it's definitely happened with wine. I think at the bottom end you could say, despite so much cheap wine all tasting the same – bland, slightly sugary, inoffensive – that it has been an improvement on some of the terrible swill a previous generation was faced with. But the top end of wine has been mauled by globalisation. Excessive use of new oak barrels to age the wine, Stakhanovite extraction of every last molecule of matter the grape possesses, giddily unnecessary levels of ripeness in the grapes and consequent alcoholic strength – in the first decade of this century we've seen far too many wines from such different sources as France, Spain, California, Argentina, Chile and Australia all seeming to be straining at the leash toward an over-expression that, in fact, robs the wine of its personality rather than accentuates it. In Spain they have a style of Rioja like this called Alto Expresión – it's the most expensive, and it's also the one I avoid.

But the backlash has begun. Drinkers have rebelled. The millennial generation in particular, with its passion for authenticity, integrity, honesty in a product, is fed up with these thick wodges of nowhereness that all taste the same and you can't drink more than a glass of. Where can we find localism, an irresistible, unshakeable belief in the local and the traditional? Where can all the knowledge of the modern vineyard and winery be harnessed, rather than be left to run riot like a crazed robot? What about Italy? The country that isn't a country, the country of a thousand different local prejudices and beliefs and treasures, the country which responded most defensively to globalisation and internationalisation, and is now in the perfect place to be the anti-globalisation hero, the standard bearer for the new post-international age.

Italy probably has a more fascinating but confused and inward-looking past than any other wine country. Italy's new post-modern wine generation, with all their modern knowledge, are poised to unpick this past, strand by strand, and find sensitive ways to offer it to the wider world. Could we soon be smacking our lips over a jug of spitting purple Raboso in New York? Could a lazy swirl of Trebbiano Spoletino be wowing the hipsters in Berlin? Yes, perhaps it could. And Italy will finally prove to the doubters, whose ranks I have only recently left, that she can indeed be the world's most challenging, absorbing and authentic wine producer.

The north-west

Barolo is exactly the kind of wine that would have made you despair of Italy in the past – dispiritingly pale but tinged with brown, about as much fresh fruit as a coal scuttle and enough bitterness to make you check your teeth hadn't come loose. Thank goodness the French invented it. In 1843. Of course there wasn't an Italy then, and Piedmont and its capital Turin were part of the Kingdom of Savoy. This included chunks of south-eastern France, and they drank French wines at court, not the local hooch.

What is now known as the great Nebbiolo grape, arguably Italy's finest, had been growing in the local vineyards since at least the thirteenth century, and some people think they can trace its heredity right back to the original wine grapes of Georgia eight thousand years ago. But it was making rubbish wine. A local landowner called Cavour, who later went on to lead the great movement toward Unification, drank these French wines at court and was so unimpressed by his own Nebbiolo that he planted Pinot Noir to try to ape French Burgundy. It didn't work, but there's a crucial point here which comes up more than once in Piedmont, and in Tuscany further south. Cavour had tasted French wines and that convinced him that his own wines didn't have to be so bad. So, along with another local aristo, the Marchesa di Barolo, he employed a Frenchman called Oudart to come and tell them what they were doing wrong.

Quite a lot. Oudart found chaotic, unpruned Nebbiolo vines laden with fruit that barely ripened by November, if you were lucky, when it was carted off to filthy, antediluvian cellars in the hope that the wild yeasts might ferment the murky juice into something palatable. They rarely did. Winter comes quickly and icily in the Piedmont hills, and you were usually left, after a sputtering fermentation cut short by the raw winter winds, with sweetish, vinegarish, prickly pale red. Oudart swept all the old practices away, cut yields, modernised the cellars and within a couple of years produced the full-flavoured, scented and dry red wine that can be called the first Barolo. Oudart was actually trying to make the wine like they did in Bordeaux – a good idea, since Bordeaux led the world in winemaking in the 1840s. The irony is that it was those puny experimental Pinot Noir vines that Cavour had planted which were the real pointers to the future of Barolo – nowadays numerous experts liken the Nebbiolo grape to the Pinot Noir, and the Barolo hills, along with their neighbours in Barbaresco, to the gentle hillside slopes of Burgundy, the fount of Pinot Noir wine. In France.

The reason they do that is superficially because true Nebbiolo is usually pale and so is Pinot Noir from Burgundy; but most Pinot Noir is marked by a gentleness of texture, an inviting suavity, often described as silky, sometimes velvety, whereas Nebbiolo throws up a defensive palisade of tannin and bitterness quite unlike that of any other world-famous red wine grape. This delicate pale colour beckons, promises scent and allure and dalliance, yet as I take my first mouthful with my eyes half shut in expectation, a foaming Cerberus is set free to maraud my gums. Fight the beast off. Because as your mouth brushes itself down after the tannic assault, you may well be delighted to discover there's a wine of quite unexpected richness of flavour, redolent of loganberry and wild strawberry teased by tangerine acid, a wine of inexplicable fragrant beauty led by summer dusk violets and pot pourri rose petals beginning to spread itself across your tongue, down your throat and up into your memory.

And if you are lucky you will start to fall under the spell that has at the moment made Barolo and Barbaresco into two of Europe's hippest wines. But don't believe the wine gossips who tell you that modern Barolo is now soft, the tannins diminished to positively normal levels. Pinot Noir *can* be criticised (rather ridiculously, in my view) for making a wine that is too deliciously easy to drink. Not Nebbiolo. This is the Italian paradox at its finest. The Nebbiolo in Piedmont can produce wines you will remember all your life. But don't expect that experience to be offered up to you on a plate. Here, you must take the bitter with the sweet, the fragrant with the feral. Recently, drinking a Barolo from the great Bussia vineyard, I thought the tannin tasted like polished pewter. The fruit was dark, almost shrivelled: black cherry, blackberry, sloes and strawberry strewn with mineral shards. The tannin never wavers, but is amazingly well-behaved, like a crusty classics teacher sombrely reflecting on a teenage love, a fleeting smile warming his brooding countenance and reminding you he's human, too. And this is important: if you really want to understand Nebbiolo, a chance sip or two at a tasting won't do. You need to drink the bottle, at table, to allow the wine to lead you into the dark places as well as the light, before you finally decide how much you love it.

But let's go back to the idea that the top vineyard regions of Piedmont resemble Burgundy. It makes sense. After Cavour's creation of modern Barolo and Barbaresco, the next century or so wasn't exactly glorious. A few aristocratic estates might have kept some of their own wine unblended, but the vast majority of wine was bought up by merchants and blended, then sold as if it was divine nectar. That's exactly what used to happen in Burgundy. Merchants used to boast about their 'house style' in Volnay, or Nuits St-Georges, or wherever. What they really meant was that they had obliterated any idiosyncrasies the different wines might have had – but great wine is about idiosyncrasy, not about bland predictability. And in Piedmont not only did they blend and obliterate the characteristics of each tiny plot, they would also age the wine in big, old wooden barrels – literally for ever. Well, for four years, five, six, seven, in the vain hope that this might soften the tannins. Perhaps it did. But it destroyed any fruit the wine might have possessed and aged it beyond redemption. The peerless Barolo producer, the late Aldo Conterno, used to complain that the greatest compliment his father's generation could pay to a Barolo was that it tasted like Marsala, an undistinguished fortified wine, brown and sticky, from Sicily!

Back to Burgundy comparisons. Pinot Noir seems to be a grape that is happiest expressing minute differences between small plots of vineyard land, often right next to one another but subtly different in soil and drainage, elevation and aspect. The heart of Burgundy is all about uncovering and understanding such nuance in a small area of just a handful of villages. Nebbiolo seems to be a grape with the same characteristics. It reacts super-sensitively to tiny changes in soil and aspect and demands very delicate, sympathetic handling in vineyard and winery. Barbaresco and Barolo are two small neighbouring areas with just a handful of villages outside the town of Alba, where Ferrero Rocher make their chocolates and Nutella spread. The town may indeed smell of Nutella through much of the year, but come October the celestial pong of the world's most odorous white truffles invades every cranny of the place. And whereas the heart of Burgundy along the Côte d'Or is almost one slope, with a few dips and dives, Barolo and Barbaresco are all dips and dives, a landscape that looks like a nest of snakes with itchy backs, coiling and twisting to scratch the spot. There are enormous differences in aspect and steepness at every turn, so much so that Nebbiolo won't ripen on much of the land, and the plots where it will ripen are precious and unique, offering the wine that rarest of qualities – the flavour of grapes barely ripe, at the limit of their ability to ripen. All the greatest areas of France were founded at this 'just able to ripen' territorial limit. Barolo and Barbaresco are two of Italy's best examples of this principle.

And now these Nebbiolo plots are treasured and lovingly exploited and their wines are sold, just as those of Burgundy's different vineyard plots are, for a lot of money and under their own names. An impassioned, thunder-browed, self-confident bundle of energy and belief called Angelo Gaja was largely responsible for this transformation, which is as recent as the 1980s and, to be honest, has only spread right through the Barolo and Barbaresco community during this century. People were aghast when Gaja slashed the yields in his vineyards, but the quality leaped. People were aghast when he brought new French oak barrels with all their spicy, vanilla flavours to a community that had never seen a new oak barrel, and certainly never fantasised about the heady, seductive modern flavours it might bring to their wine. And people were aghast at the prices he demanded for his wines. And every time anyone complained, Gaja hiked them still higher. He had learned the painful lesson, which I still hate to accept: that if, as a newcomer in the world of 'fine' wine, you want to be seen as an equal, you must charge the same kind of money as the so-called quality leaders do, regardless of whether you really think the wines are worth such a sum. Sadly, offering a bargain doesn't earn you respect. Surely, in a market-led world, if you can get such a sum, then the wine is worth such a sum. But it doesn't mean you or I have to buy it.

And there is another Piedmont. It's a world of grapes like Dolcetto or Barbera, both within the Barolo and Barbaresco zones and out in the much wider area that encircles these two. These grapes make good strong dry red wines – but when you live in the tight-cossetted world of serious tannic reds, where do you look to let off steam? Frothy, fruity Brachetto; Freisa, fizzy or still; rose-scented Ruché, smelling so sweet and languorous, tasting so dry; and Moscato, the grapiest grape. Most people must have had a mouthful of Asti Spumante, the easy-going, floral, grapey fizz that's perfect with panettone. But Moscato d'Asti is something else. Barely bubbly, with all the crunchy, chin-dribbling joy of the purest Muscat grape flesh, just 5 per cent alcohol. A friend of mine said that the rarest wine he had ever had was a Moscato d'Asti filtered through an old lady's sock. As I said earlier, Italian wine is all about paradox.

Of course, Piedmont has dry white wines too: the top Barolo and Barbaresco producers (such as Aldo Conterno and Angelo Gaja) have excellent modern Chardonnays, but they are ... well, Chardonnay. Much more interesting to me is the local Arneis, mainly grown in Roero, north-west of Alba, with flavours of peaches, green apples and perhaps some citrus – and always my first-choice white when in Piedmont.

Moving east from Alba, the world-famous Gavi white wines are made from the rather uninteresting but reliable Cortese grape. Turns out that Gavi used to be made from the much more characterful but less docile Timorasso, and various local growers, notably Walter Massa, are rebuilding vineyard acreage.

The north-east

Skipping to the north-east, which starts, in wine terms, pretty much on a longitude with Parma, we find winelands – some of them a lot easier than Piedmont, some of them gratifyingly tricky to appreciate. And there are a couple of wines that really aren't difficult at all – Pinot Grigio and Prosecco. Their whole *raison d'être* is that they are easy for anybody to have a bit of fun with. Unless you're a wine buff, of course, in which case you'll get into all kinds of strops, huffing and puffing about them barely being wine. Just as the same people, or their parents, used to huff and puff and say that Lambrusco wasn't real wine, and nor were Soave and Valpolicella for that matter. In which case, that's most of the north-east kicked out of consideration before we've even started. And the north-east is where most of Italy's wine is produced.

OK. We are in the Veneto, hinterland of Venice, everyone's favourite city. And we are talking about Prosecco. It's a fantastic party pop. It's been around for ages – Venice uses it as the base for the Bellini cocktail – but it's only in the last decade or so that it has gone completely mad. It's the 21st Century Fun Fizz. Give me an ice-cold bottle and a couple of chatty friends, and I'm happy. Even so, success does breed a little contempt. Prosecco used to be made in a few villages and valleys up toward the Dolomite Mountains north of Venice. Its bright, easy-going fruity style was clearly too successful. They've now expanded the area that can make Prosecco, from Trieste way out east on the Slovenian border, up north into the ski slopes, down past Venice and west almost to Verona. A lot of grapes. But the stuff makes a lot of people happy. So.

Italy's north-east makes all of Italy's best sparkling wine, whatever style you want. Trentino, in the mountain passes north of Lake Garda, makes delightful fizz led by the Ferrari Company. No, not that one. And Franciacorta, back toward Milan in Lombardy, uses Chardonnay and Pinot Noir to make stunning *metodo classico* fizz, which in the hands of someone like Ca' del Bosco or Bellavista is easily as good as a top Champagne.

There's a worldwide move in sparkling wine to try to make the wines genuinely dry (sparkling wines usually have a little sugar left in them, or added back in the case of Champagne-method wines, to balance the high acidity of sparkling base wine grapes). Franciacorta is proving that bone dry here is a much more attractive proposition than bone dry in most Champagne.

And, as long as we are talking sparkling, here is one more wine, Lambrusco, from Emilia-Romagna. Don't laugh. Don't say yucky, sweet, screwtop fizzy mouthwash. Real Lambrusco is dark purple-red, foaming and violent, chewy, sour, challeng-ing – and absolutely magnificent with Bologna's most famous pasta dish – *tagliatelle al ragù* (bastardised to – also delicious! – spaghetti Bolognese all over the world). I love it. Try it.

If you think Prosecco has rather sprawled over Italy's north-east, most of the other vines you see in the vast flat vineyard spreads around the Po Valley and toward the Adriatic will prob-ably be Pinot Grigio. Oceans of dull, lifeless white wine sold for peanuts? Or, perhaps, glittering streams of simple pleasure, giving millions of non-wine-savvy people the chance to catch a glimpse or two of sophistication and good humour while drinking something entirely innocuous? It's a job that must be done, and previous wines that did this were French Muscadet and German Liebfraumilch. Pinot Grigio does it better than either of these. Even so, the world is so awash with Pinot Grigio that I do sometimes wonder exactly where all the grapes are grown. When the harvests are affected by drought or hail in north-eastern Europe, the supply keeps coming. And sometimes it actually seems to taste better. Funny, that.

That said, the north-east of Italy is the place to go, if you want to find proper Pinot Grigio. Not all Pinot Grigio is just for slosh-ing back. Some of it is really quite serious. Some of it is actually rather challenging. Friuli (Friuli-Venezia-Giulia, to give it its proper name), up toward the mountains and the Slovenian border, makes wines that remind you that Pinot Grigio isn't actually a white grape; it's a pink grape if you let it ripen and don't grossly overcrop it, and some of the best examples do have a warmish, vaguely exotic perfume to them – and a sort of bronze sheen and texture. You'll find these wines up in the hills.

The hills of Friuli and its most easterly zone, Collio, are also where you will find winemakers large and small turning away from the old practice of making a white house blend of local varieties in various combinations, including with Pinot Grigio and Sauvignon Blanc, to concentrate on mono-varietal bottlings of local grape varieties, especially Friulano and Ribolla Gialla. Stick with the top producers like Livio Felluga, Jermann and Vie di Romans and you will find lovely bright clean modern wines; but – with honourable exceptions – too often smaller wineries are trying to combine the use of varieties that may not have huge character in the first place with 'natural' vinification practices which can get out of hand and produce oxidised styles that I'm not always that keen on. Don't be afraid to ask before you order a bottle: in Friuli and Collio these wines are hiding in plain sight!

And if you want a truly original wine – again: caveat emptor – try the local red variety Schiopettino.

And still talking of Pinot Grigio – no wonder it is so suc-cessful: I can't get off the subject – the north-east has another area that arguably makes even better Pinot Grigio: the Alto Adige, the most northerly region of Italy and not really Italy at all. These high valleys squeezed up between the Tyrolean peaks were part of the Austro-Hungarian Empire until Italy was given the Südtirol (Alto Adige is the Italian name) as the spoils of war after the First World War. A century on, you sometimes wonder if the locals have got the message yet – you're Italian now. Tell that to the guy muttering on his porch and picking at the feather in his Tyrolean hat; tell that to the cosy cook ladling out the pork dumplings from her steaming cauldron; and tell that to the proud wine grower who sniffs dismissively and waves southward as he grumbles 'That over there is Italy, not here.'

But it's a wonderful place, as beautiful as any wine region in the world. Every single vineyard seems to be nestling under the protection of steepling crags (even my language is getting a bit gothic), or clinging precariously to scraps of cleared land halfway up the giddy slopes. If the world's best wines were to come from the most beautiful vineyards, a decent number would come from Alto Adige.

This is the first Italian wine region I made a 'professional' wine trip to. I was taking the easy way in to the Italian experience, because these wines owed nothing to the Italy of further south and everything to Austria or even France. The grape varieties were French or German – if you want the world's most pungent, scintillating Müller-Thurgau (am I really saying this?) the Feldmarschall vineyard at over 1050 metres (3445 feet) provides it – or local, in the case of Gewürztraminer (there's even a town called Traminer where they swear the grape originated). The whites were fresh and scented – now that was very un-Italian on my first visit, during the 1980s, when most Italian winemakers barely admitted they made white, and certainly not something with scent and fresh fruit. In reds they could ripen Pinot Noir as well as Cabernet Sauvignon and even the very late-ripening Petit Verdot from Bordeaux, either in the sheltered south-facing suntraps of the hills or on the warm gravel beds further into the valleys. Ah, paradoxes. Yes, Alto Adige *is* part of Italy, the wineland of paradox. During the summer in these mountain vineyards, the daytime temperatures can be as high as in Palermo in Sicily, yet the nighttime temperatures slither back to Alpine chill. There can be as many hours of summer sun here as anywhere in Italy – how does 315 days of sun a year sound? That'll ripen the Cabernet.

Yet it's two local red grapes that I'm fondest of, and they couldn't be more opposite. Lagrein is brooding, dense, dark as a storm cloud gathering at the head of the valley; its fruit is chewy, sharp like strawberry pips, soothing like blackcurrant throat pastilles and at its best dashed with savoury pepper, rolled in liquorice and cured with tobacco spice. A grower told me, as I lapped up his lively twenty-year-old example, 'Lagrein is always starting to age, but it never finishes.' Schiava – or Vernatsch, as the locals still call it – is the opposite: pale, winsome, soothing; at its best, uplifting in its youthful simplicity. The innocence of a wine just made to be a joyful drink. I clambered up the slopes above Bolzano (aka Bozen), the provincial capital of Alto Adige, one spring lunchtime, carrying a litre of Vernatsch and some cheese and wurst (note the language: this is the Südtirol, where both German and Italian are official languages). The sap was dripping off the fresh-pruned wood of the vines. 'Good for the eyes,' my friend said. My eyes? The vine's? The sap had no taste, like melted snow. And we perched among these vines, literally, watching the hubbub of the busy city far below but hearing nothing in the still mountain air. Our wine tasted of strawberries and hickory-smoked almonds, bacon fat and double cream. Silence. And then, at 2 p.m. precisely, a factory siren wafted up from the valley, summoning us back to work and the real world. And I think of the sound of the distant wire snapping in Chekhov's *The Cherry Orchard*.

Talking of the innocence of wines just made to quench thirst and to give pleasure, if you follow the Adige River southward through the forbidding gorge at Salorno, through Trentino and out into the vast Po River flood plain at Verona, then head back into the hills just one more time, you'll find Soave and

Valpolicella, as fresh and mouthwatering and easy-going as anything in Italy.

In fact, come to think of it, Soave and Valpolicella were as influential as any wine you can think of in the modernising of Italian wine. Gone now are the ghastly tired Soaves and Valpolicellas to be found in Italian trattorie all over the world: pioneers like Pieropan in Soave and Allegrini in Valpolicella saw the potential of Garganega and Corvina respectively, and their basic bottlings are my go-to wines in Italian restaurants.

But there are more serious styles too, especially in Valpolicella, where the bright, breezy, young red style is losing favour to something richer and denser and more alcoholic – the Ripasso style in which the wines are re-fermented on the skins of Amarone grapes in the springtime.

And what is Amarone? The king of the dried-grape dry wine styles. It's traditional, but it used to be a rarity made in tiny quantities. Not any more. In this twenty-first-century wine world gone mad for power and density and alcohol, Amarone gives them to you in spades, but unlike most of the blockheaded powerhouses Amarone is brilliantly Italian – it's those paradoxes again – ripe, packed with fruit but bitter too, tannic, sour even. The grapes for Amarone are dried on racks or in crates, which concentrates the sugar but also heightens and changes the acids and the tannins. And if some of them virtually turn into dates, and others start to smell a bit sour, that's all part of the character. In the best examples, this gives a wild, slightly unnerving personality to the wine, which often starts almost sweet with fruit that could be anything from plum and blackberry to baked apple, sweet cherry flesh, sour cherry skins and figs and raisins baked halfway to paste. But the bitterness – the Amarone (*amaro* means bitter in Italian) – always comes back as black chocolate, as woodsmoke, as the burnt bits on the bottom of a roasting pan, and ideally there will be a splash of meat stock and balsamic vinegar sourness to season the final bitterness, which should be as grippy yet affectionate as the lick of a cat's tongue.

Quintarelli, Dal Forno and Allegrini make fabulous Amarone at eye-watering prices, but there are plenty of good producers to choose from these days.

Tuscany and the centre

Central Italy is a pretty substantial chunk, running virtually from the Po River to south of Rome. And it produces a lot of wine. I've never really got excited about Rome's wines. Maybe that's not helped by an evening I spent in the village of Frascati, supposedly the home of Rome's quaffing wine, going from bar to bar vainly searching for a glass of – yes – Frascati.

Abruzzo is a marvellously wild area with a lot of rich, tasty Montepulciano red (that's the grape name: there's also a famous town of Montepulciano which makes a quite different red wine in Tuscany).

The Marche region produces loads of white, and Verdicchio is increasingly one of Italy's best dry whites. The greater part of Verdicchio comes from Castello di Jesi DOC, but I prefer the wines from the smaller hilly area of Matelica. When Burton Anderson wrote his seminal *Vino*, the first really important book in English on Italian wine, in the early 1980s, he suggested that Verdicchio had the potential to age well and to become Italy's greatest white wine. Unfortunately, many producers, with that perhaps in mind, set off down a route of torturing the wines with oak and/or, later, embraced natural and orange wine, to neither of which, judging by results, is Verdicchio suited. It is a very nice grape – which is also confusingly the same as Trebbiano di Soave, which partners Garganega in many top Soaves – with good texture and lovely saline and almond notes, but I'm always keen to ask the excellent local restaurants to point me to completely unoaked and un-mucked-about young wines, which express the true spirit and pleasure of Verdicchio. Try the affordable and widely distributed Casal di Serra from Umano Ronchi to get the idea.

And I just love the strawberry- and rose-scented madcap red of Lacrima di Morra d'Alba. But I don't normally visit. Why? Maybe I'm still smarting from being charged for having a swim in the sea at Rimini. But Rimini is in Emilia-Romagna. I do need to get out more. Maybe to Umbria. Lovely, wild, mountainous Umbria, where you are only allowed to paint your house pink or yellow. Weird, but it works. All of these are in the centre. But the centre of the centre — for many, the centre of Italian wine — is Tuscany.

We'd eloped. Her parents had never approved of me, which I suppose made it all the more exciting, made it all the more critical that we stole away to somewhere full of the certainty of romance and adventure. Italy. Where else? I had never been there. We got off the train at Florence and took a bus to the end of the line, on the southern fringe of the city. We could see the blue hazy hills. We could see a village, so we walked, and grew hungrier and thirstier and more elated.

At the village I bought some fist-sized tomatoes, greasy salami and strange, saltless Tuscan bread. Then I asked for some Chianti. And the shopkeeper asked me, where was my bottle? I didn't know that . . . No matter: there was a pile of dusty litre bottles in the corner and he picked up what might have been the cleanest, moved his bicycle from in front of a bleak-looking barrel, then squirted this jet of frothy, pink-red wine into our bottle and charged us less than for the bread. And out we went, out toward the hills, into a tumbling meadow by the side of the empty road where we opened our throats and swigged our wine.

I had never had any wine so eager, so furiously appetising, so intensely real — so genuine, I suppose. It was prickly, bitter-sweet, sweet-sour, so rasping yet so strangely ripe and right, bubbling with the flesh of cranberries, redcurrants and raw red cherries, yet slapped about with the pips and skin and stalks and twigs of thyme. So utterly full of life. If this was Chianti, why had I waited so long? Ah, yes . . . I can still take you to that village. I can take you to that field. But I can't take you to that wine. Not any more.

Another spring. A lazy Saturday morning in a new, bare flat. We were still in bed. And a glass of wine seemed a natural progression. I only had one bottle, given to me by a friend who had said, 'This will change the world.' Well, it would certainly improve my world that Saturday. I pulled the cork, dashed some wine into a toothmug and we drank to a promising weekend.

And that was my first mouthful of a wine which did change the world. Sassicaia 1968. Tossed back carelessly out of a tooth-mug. I could have drunk it out of a pig's udder and it would still have made my heart leap. I had never tasted a wine of such thrilling purity, such piercingly beautiful blackcurrant fruit. This must be what every Cabernet dreamed of tasting like. The 1968 was the first vintage Sassicaia released to the public gaze. The 1972 was *Decanter* magazine's Best Cabernet Sauvignon in the World, and I'm not surprised. I was only surprised when I found out where this superstar came from. Italy. Tuscany. But not even one of the supposedly good bits of Tuscany. This came from a place called Bolgheri, on the coast. I'd been there. No one had ever even considered growing red wine grapes down on these positively malarial flatlands. The Bolgheri wine classi-fication was only for whites and pinks, and the locals said even those tasted of salt.

You might call my litre of rustic village red and this super-sophisticated Tuscan Cabernet Sauvignon the bookends, between which Tuscany has transformed itself over the last generation or so. The Cabernet was grown on a couple of hec-tares that a marchese had planted during the Second World War when his supplies of Bordeaux were cut off. Until that 1968 vintage it had just been a rough-and-ready brew for personal consumption. But one with a brilliant depth of sturdy fruit, quite unlike anything being produced in Tuscany. And the marchese was uncle to Piero Antinori, who took the reins of Italy's oldest wine company – going since 1385 – in the 1960s.

He had been impressed by Uncle Mario's home brew on holiday visits. It gave him ideas.

But Piero had more serious matters on his mind. He had taken over the family business — in the heart of Chianti country — when Chianti's reputation had hit rock bottom. Basically, the name Chianti covers most red wine in the areas around Siena and Florence — that's a lot of country — and the best villages can be called Chianti Classico. Given that Chianti was the first wine region in the world to be geographically delimited — in 1716 — you would have expected the wines to have built a bit of a reputation. But they hadn't. If anything, the attractive name of Chianti — and the bucolic, straw-covered flasks in which it was generally sold — meant that the wine was mercilessly abused. The local Sangiovese grape will only ripen in the Tuscan hills if it's carefully farmed, yet until the 1960s the vineyards were largely in the unmotivated hands of peasant sharecroppers. When the vineyards were renewed, high-yielding versions of Sangiovese were planted, which were never going to produce fully ripe stuff from their bloated yields. So the regulations allowed winemakers to add up to 30 per cent white grapes to soften the raw red wine. This made it too pale, so you could bring in a dark-coloured bone-setter of a wine from Italy's far south, baked and bruised by the sun, to add colour and body. The result tasted terrible.

It was a mess. Piero Antinori knew it, and was determined to clear it up. And he realised that the road to salvation ran through those Cabernet vines from Bordeaux that his uncle Mario had planted out at the seaside in Bolgheri. Antinori had once said, 'Cabernet seems to have everything that Sangiovese lacks — the body, colour, aroma, plus the longevity.' So he planted 20 per cent of his top Chianti vineyard, Tignanello, with Cabernet. Chianti was traditionally aged in big, old, probably leaky casks. Antinori used small new French oak barrels, just as they did in Bordeaux. Immediately the richness of the Cabernet fruit shone through, and the new small barrels softened the wines and added rich vanilla spice. And for the first time in longer than living memory the world began to go wild about Chianti.

Except it wasn't Chianti any more. The authorities said that you couldn't do that. Antinori said, 'Yes I can, and I don't need you.' He downgraded the classification of Tignanello from Chianti Classico to simple Vino da Tavola (table wine), alongside Sassicaia, and proceeded to charge more than for any Chianti. These were now two of Italy's most famous and most expensive wines, but proud enough and rebellious enough to sell themselves as basic Vino da Tavola. Antinori has much in common with Angelo Gaja in Piedmont: they were both desperate not only to improve their own wines, but to improve the image of their regions, if not that of the whole of Italy. They both realised that French wines ruled the world of quality, so they both decided to go and steal some of Bordeaux's and Burgundy's clothes, totally disregarding what the local authorities might think. Antinori's adoption of frankly Bordeaux-type habits and ambitions led to a flood of similar Cabernet-influenced, or Cabernet-dominated, small-barrel-aged wines in Tuscany; and they earned themselves the brand-new name of super-Tuscans.

Initially they were often fantastically good, somehow threading some Tuscan asperity, some of the herbs and fruit skins and splashes of cherry vinegar that make Tuscan reds so appetising, through the imperious blackcurrant and blackberry power and beauty of the Cabernet. But most of the wines quickly became bigger, heftier, less Italian, more blood-and-thunder international. In many countries – France, the USA, Australia, Argentina – the battle to dial down these steroidal wines is still being fought. But what was remarkable was how quickly Tuscans said, 'We've made the world take notice of us, we have proved we can make delicious, desirable wines by copying the French. Now we'll go back to making Tuscan wines, based on the Tuscan grape Sangiovese.' As Antinori put it, 'It's not a brilliant grape, but it's what we've got, so we'll make the best of it.' Tuscany has come full circle amazingly quickly, and ended up in a far better place because of it. There is still lots of Cabernet Sauvignon – and Merlot, and Cabernet Franc and Syrah – but my greatest delight nowadays is facing up to my prejudices about Sangiovese.

I do think it is a wonderful grape for making young, edgy, crunchy reds. The Australians clearly agree. I was at the Innocent Bystanders bar in Yarra Valley near Melbourne and they were serving litres of Sangiovese from the barrel – to drink there, not to take away. But I don't think it generally reacts that well to the full New World high alcohol, high extract, tons of oak regime that some Tuscans still unfortunately apply to it – and no Australians do! But I think that it's a brilliant success story for 'back to the future'. Leave out the Cabernet, which does taste amazingly dominant in Tuscany reds, blend in one or two old-established black grapes like Canaiolo (which is apparently the 50 per cent parent of Sangiovese) or Ciliegiolo, if you want to, and sell off most of those small barrels and use the money to buy big wholesome casks five, ten, twenty times as big as a French barrel – the same size as a century ago – but this time keep them clean, keep the cellar clean, keep the grapes healthy – and at last we can see what Tuscany, and the Sangiovese, is made of.

Chianti Classico is at the heart of all Tuscan red wines. A couple of months ago I went to a Chianti Classico tasting mostly of 2013, '14 and '15 wines, with the odd 2012 and '16. I couldn't stop smiling. All that curmudgeonly Tuscan charm, its gritty sweet-sour cherry and cranberry and even tomato fruit, its hints of jam and stew, of olive and thyme – and its scent. The wines had scent! The scent of blossom, the scent of orchards, the scent of them feeling good in their skin at long last. I even found myself discussing the merits of the different villages – of Panzano and Gaiole and Castelnuovo Berardenga. That's what I do when I'm in Bordeaux or Burgundy. How exciting that I shall now be able to do this in Italy, too.

Tuscany isn't only Chianti, although Chianti Classico is the heartland for me, in the timeless hills between Florence and

Siena, where, if you half close your eyes and you're far enough from a main road, you really can imagine that you are back in the time of the Medicis, the sight and smell and sound. And then your iPhone rings. Bah. If you want to find a town that you can imagine has barely changed for centuries and whose views surely haven't, Montepulciano is a hilltop jewel. Its wine was clearly good at one time: the popes liked it as far back as the fourteenth century – you don't get called Vino Nobile ('noble wine') without attracting some pretty top-end support. Vino Nobile di Montepulciano wine may have been worthy of the title then, but by the late twentieth century its self-importance was laughable, and most of its wines were some of the most disappointing in Tuscany. Not any more. There is now an array of delicious Vino Nobile di Montepulciano wines, led by estates like Avignonesi, Poliziano and Boscarelli, a little juicier, a little more come-hither than Chianti, showing Sangiovese's marginally more flirtatious side. And the cheaper Rosso di Montepulciano really is a good, bright glugger. A word of advice. Montepulciano is everything you could want a Tuscan hilltown to be. But don't go into the first shop inside the town gates and think that they will have the best bargains. They may not. The higher up the street you go toward the Piazza Grande the better the price:quality ratio generally gets. And I'd apply that rule to just about every tourist town, anywhere, ever.

Montalcino is another fabulous hilltop town, less fairytale than Montepulciano but with one of my favourite wine bars, the Fiaschetteria, on hand to serve countless examples of the local Brunello di Montalcino by the glass. That is, if you can barge your way past the tourists. The wine tourists. Because Montalcino has become an overheated wine mecca in double-quick time. Brunello di Montalcino was barely heard of before the 1960s and barely made. There was only one producer until after the Second World War – Biondi-Santi, the family who in effect invented the wine. They weren't generous with their favours, only declaring four vintages between 1888 and 1945! And the wine was famously hard and dark and supposed to last for ever.

But while Piero Antinori and many others on the other side of Tuscany, to the north, were looking constructively to France, to French classic grapes, French classic methods to lug their region into the modern era, Montalcino was hauled into modern times by an American company called Banfi deciding to use Montalcino vineyards to make a sweet sparkling white Muscat. This was actually what Montalcino was famous for long ago, rather than red wine, but not this time. The plan failed and the company then grafted their pretty vast vineyards over to red grapes and used their commercial nous – and, presumably, their determination not to muck things up twice – to make pretty serious amounts of Brunello di Montalcino. They then proceeded to make Brunello successful and popular, especially in the USA, in a frankly rather richer, oakier style than Biondi-Santi might have recognised. The smell of money began to creep through the streets of Montalcino and what was less than 100 hectares (247 acres) of vines when the Banfi boys arrived is now more than 3000 hectares (7500 acres) today, much of it planted where there was no tradition of fine wine production. The original vineyards were mostly perched around the town of Montalcino itself – pretty high up, and on pretty poor soil. It wasn't always easy to ripen Brunello (the local name for the clone of Sangiovese grown here) – it never is high up – but the wines had scent and style. Most of the new plantings are on richer clay soils and many of them are lower down in the valley and often facing south–west toward the hottest sun of the day. Montalcino is already the driest, and among the hottest, of Tuscany's wine regions. Avoiding the strongest direct sunlight might have been a better option.

Which might explain why I'm looking at a sales blurb inviting me to buy Brunello, and it's boasting of one wine with 'crunching' tannins and 14.5 per cent alcohol, another with 'monstrous' tannins – and this is a sales pitch. I don't really go for all that, I don't think it is what Sangiovese is good at, and it might explain why I'm no great fan of Brunello. I taste examples which are supposed to be pretty smart – often costing £60 or £70 a bottle – and I rarely find much to thrill me. I'm told I haven't tasted the right ones yet. 'So how do I do that?' 'Oh, they're basically unobtainable.' But if I'm in Montalcino I've had offers to lead me to these luminaries. Well, I'd like to, chaps, but I'm not that smitten with the idea that I'll only understand Brunello if I taste wines that are in effect unobtainable by a normal wine lover, even a well-heeled one. I can understand Bordeaux, or Burgundy, the Mosel, or Napa, or Central Otago without having to go anywhere near wines that aren't affordable or available. Oh, and Chianti Classico, too. That's in great nick at the moment and so is Vino Nobile di Montepulciano. They are affordable and they will show me how good Sangiovese can be. And at the Fiaschetteria wine bar, when I get to the front of the crush, I'll drink Rosso di Montalcino, the cheaper, fresher, rather delicious red the locals drink.

Bolgheri, out on the Tuscan coast, is somewhere I used to have a soft spot for, because this is where Sassicaia, one of the most memorable wines Italy has ever produced, comes from. Its soaring global reputation meant that others rushed to plant vines there, led by Piero Antinori and his brother, but also other Tuscans, Piedmontese (Gaja has an estate here), Venetians (Allegrini, the super Valpolicella producer, has an estate here), as well as the French (including Bordeaux classed growth owners) and Californians. You get the message. Rich, successful people dived in to what looked like a bright New World for Italy. Well, up to a point. Sassicaia and the best of the other producers do have vines in the raw, rocky hillsides away from the sea. There's little doubt in my mind that Sassicaia's continuing ability to create smashing wine here is to a considerable extent due to the availability of Cabernet Sauvignon from such stony soil – it's just what Cabernet likes if you're after really strong, focused blackcurrant and blackberry flavours and impressive but digestible tannins. You might even say it's a bit like Bordeaux's Médoc region, where Cabernet thrives. But an awful lot of the other soil isn't stony and isn't sloping and it is hot.

The initial surge of excitement for Bolgheri was during the 1980s and '90s when Cabernet and the Bordeaux template were regarded as the route to greatness for Tuscan reds. This movement has now receded and Bolgheri sometimes seems a bit like a glistening superyacht caught on a mudbank as the tide recedes. With the shining exception of a quite brilliantly palate-caressing wine called Masseto from a tiny plot of vines on dense clay soil at the heart of the Ornellaia estate, Merlot simply isn't the right grape for Bolgheri. It's too hot. But there's a lot of it. Interestingly, Gaja knows this and is quietly grafting over most of his Merlot to two Bordeaux grapes that can cope with heat much better – Petit Verdot and Cabernet Franc. He says, 'Look, Bolgheri is a new area, the styles are still being developed.' Fair enough, but they are still clinging very closely to the new oak and Bordeaux varieties model, with high alcohol thrown in almost as a given.

That's what sells, but the Bordeaux model may not be the right one in the long run. It's mostly getting too hot to produce elegant wines. Wines can be up to 14.5 or even 15.5 per cent alcohol. Surprisingly, Cabernet Franc can hold on to its rich raspberry character at such strengths, but few other grape varieties can. Antinori says that all the best Bolgheris have a significant chunk of Cabernet Franc in them. Bolgheri should consider planting more Mediterranean varieties, properly adapted to the heat. But so should Napa Valley, Stellenbosch and Bordeaux, for that matter. But are they going to? Ooh, was that a pig I just saw flying by the window? The Bordeaux model is still the one that commands the price. Sadly, most of the people who are buying it don't have 'elegant' as part of their wine vocabulary.

The south

I was nearly a Sicilian. No – it's a long story. Oh, all right then.
Back to university. My girlfriend and I had somehow got on
The Sky's the Limit, a fairly downmarket, exceedingly popular
television quiz show hosted by a big star called Hughie Green.
We had written a song and dance routine about Beaujolais –
literally; there was even a tap-dance interlude called 'It's never
too late for Beaujolais' to the tune of 'It's never too late to fall
in love' from *The Boy Friend*, a musical which Glenda Jackson
and Twiggy had just starred in.

God knows what Hughie Green thought when he saw us
two – smart-alec Oxford smoothies – limbering up, but we
hadn't even got the reply to our first question out before he
was ushering us off stage and crushing a hundred pounds' hush
money into our hands, presumably thinking, how on earth did
these two get on to my show?

The winner was a Sicilian restaurant owner from Edinburgh.
He liked wine. And he liked opera. I was singing in a new opera
by the British composer Stephen Oliver at that year's Edinburgh
Festival, so he told me to pop by his restaurant. When I got in
touch he was very excited. The directors of Opera Massima in
Palermo were dining with him. I wasn't stupid. I got them tick-
ets for my opera, and their response was the offer of an audition.
In my friend's restaurant. Over dinner.

So I turned up, and there were these barrel-chested hairy
Hollywood-Sicilian types, heaving spaghetti down their throats
along with rivers of Chianti. And they said, 'Sing.' They went
on eating and drinking. I sang 'Madamina' and 'Notte e giorno'
from Mozart's *Don Giovanni*. Then they said, 'Sit down. Eat.
Drink.' The spaghetti was good, the Chianti was ... well,
Chianti. And that was my audition.

Next day? I got an offer to join Opera Massima as an apprentice
baritone. And it was very, very tempting. My parents had emigrated. I had no home base in England. And this was a chance

to go to Italy and be trained as an opera singer and be paid at the same time. And in somewhere as exotic and mysterious as Palermo in Sicily. Had I gone, I don't think I'd have come back. I think I would have revelled in the southern Italian life and I would be, to this day, a large, pink, sweaty, contented Irish-Sicilian buffo baritone, gargling Marsala to keep his vocal cords sweet.

But I didn't go, and southern Italy disappeared from my life and has never fully re-appeared. I've rarely been excited about its wines – with a few, mostly sweet, exceptions. I've never really understood the southern Italian world, partly because I was never quite brave enough. I did have a go. When I was a young punk wine writer I would often disdain offers of help – particularly from big companies or generic promotional bodies – and say, no thanks, I can look after myself. Southern Italy is not the ideal place for that attitude.

One year I hired a car and my first objective was to find the original vineyards of Falernian wine – one of the all-time classical Roman favourites. I located what I think were the right ones, near Naples. Pretty uninspiring, and their wine even more so. The best stuff I found was unlabelled – not exactly legal, not exactly good for your health, but tasty enough. In fact, it tasted of strawberries. I later discovered that most of the wines around Naples tasted of strawberries, and the locals called them *uva fragola*.

So I went on to Naples. And I really didn't enjoy it. I had hoped to revel in a boisterous southern metropolis, but I felt very ill at ease. OK, I didn't feel safe. It was a classic example of needing some local guidance. I thought I knew best, but I didn't. I headed south and spent an eternity boiling and gridlocked on the coast road. I headed inland to try to locate a) Vesuvius: not difficult, and b) Mastroberardino, the most famous southern wine producer, at least a few of whose wines I had been excited about.

And it kept on being more of the same. I kept getting lost. I couldn't relax and enjoy the wonderful scenery and the disarming chaos. And I learned very little about wine. So I went back home. Now, southern Italy is not easy to understand. But it's a damned sight easier if you have an open mind and don't let the numerous setbacks of life in Europe's far south upset you. And if you've bothered to learn Italian. Even today, not all that many people speak English. When I was trailing about, almost no one did. And I hadn't bothered to learn Italian.

Having said all that, I have kept an eye on the wines but still can't say I get excited by most of them. Puglia, the heel of Italy, was supposed to be Italy's New World of Wine, Italy's California or South Australia. It isn't. Vast swathes of Sangiovese and Trebbiano have been planted, as well as the international varieties – Chardonnay and Merlot – and I was initially optimistic, but it is fiercely hot there and the wines mostly show it. The local varieties fare better – Negroamaro, Malvasia Nera and Primitivo (California's Zinfandel) – but I still don't think they shine and I rarely choose them to drink. I might choose an Aglianico from nearby Basilicata or a Ciró from Calabria, but would I regret it? Probably.

Yet there are two parts of southern Italy whose wines I would choose – indeed, whose wines I frequently seek out in wine lists and enthusiastically wax lyrical about to anyone who will listen. And these are Campania, inland from Naples, and Etna, on Sicily. Sicily isn't just about Etna – the Planeta family have transformed winemaking in several parts of the island, and made a bit of a star out of the excellent, blackberryish local black grape, Nero d'Avola. But Etna has contributed massively to a movement that has really taken off in the last few years, and which is of genuine relevance worldwide: volcanic wines.

I might have seen this coming, because my first trip to Etna was more successful than my first trip to Naples. Simply because the gaunt, thrilling individuality of the place was unmissable. I had hopped off a boat at Catania and headed for the volcano. The vines really did stretch up the looming slopes toward a cone that really did smoke, slumbering and threatening. The soils of the little patches of vines seemed black and crumbly, and sometimes you could pick up dark, twisted chunks of lava rock in your fingers that just had to be magma from an ancient eruption. Well, not that ancient. Etna is active, good and proper, and images in the news periodically show yet another flaming, throat-clogging eruption hurling rocks skywards. On Etna's slopes the word volcanic doesn't just apply to some prehistoric catastrophe. It applies to now. But those early Etna wines did taste prehistoric; it wasn't until well into the twenty-first century that Etna's wines moved toward being some of Italy's most distinctive.

And they do taste volcanic – as far as anyone knows what that means. I'd say the reds really do taste of dust, of ash, of the morning air as it clears of smoke after a fiery night; their colour is pale, the fruit is fleeting, but they have a unique scent halfway between cherry blossom and warm rock. And they're chewy. They have a grainy, saline chewiness that really is different. I know the scientists say the flavours of the minerals that abound in volcanic soil can't be picked up through the roots, but Nerello Mascalese wine made from these grapes, grown high up on lava-strewn slopes which sometimes still seem to be breathing out the warm fumes of the volcano, does talk of its place in a way that relatively few wines do. So thank you, Etna, and Sicily, for giving the wine world something massively original from your ancient vineyards.

Mount Vesuvius also has vines, some increasingly good, but the area of Campania that has transformed the world's view of Italian wine is a little further inland. And the transformative wines are white. For so long, Italian whites boasted little flavour, and apologists would try to wring a few adjectives out of glasses of white Soave, Verdicchio, Pinot Grigio, Orvieto and others that didn't really possess them. Most Italian whites, at their best, had a kind of noble neutrality, a sort of vinous pride that disdained such fripperies as perfume and vibrant fruit. (That's excepting a few wines from the far north.)

And then along came the Campanian trio: Fiano di Avellino, Greco di Tufo and the scented, flowery Falanghina. All fascinating, all memorable, and the Fiano and Greco wines having a quite unexpected power and mineral density. More than any other Italian whites, the Campanian whites woke up the world to the thrilling possibilities of the ancient white varieties that grew in particular along Italy's mountain spine. Grapes that had been dispatched to the local co-operative for distillation are now being made into some of Europe's most memorable, largely unoaked, whites. Angelo Gaja, one of Italy's greatest red winemakers, said a few years ago that Italy's immediate future was coloured white, not red. I agree. And from a guy who often doesn't quite get Italy, that's a big statement.

Italy's traditional sweet wines are different

The dried-grape method, called *passito* in Italian, is the oldest way of creating sweet wine. The Persians and Mesopotamians probably used it; the Ancient Greeks and Egyptians certainly did, as did the Romans. The thinking is pretty clear. Grape juice is a mixture of sugar and water. If you can dry the grapes in the sun, the water will evaporate but the sugar won't; it just becomes more and more concentrated. One way of doing this was to twist the stem of the grape bunch so that no sap and water got through and the grape in effect died on the vine and shrivelled, becoming very sweet and raisined. Another way was to cut the stem, which severed the flow of sap with the same raisining effects.

But the most common method was to harvest the grapes, then lay them out on a frame in the sun covered by reeds. In a week or so they should have shrivelled and intensified nicely. They could then either be pressed and fermented by themselves or added to a clay jar of sweet grape juice, where they would rest for about another week, before the whole mixture was pressed and fermented. The resulting wine was certainly sweet, but, equally important, it was strong. A mixture of high sugar and high alcohol protected the wine from decay and that meant it could travel, and allowed a very lucrative trade to develop around the Mediterranean.

This was most important in the era up to the thirteenth century, when the Venetian Republic dominated trade and acted as a linchpin between the eastern Mediterranean, which made strong, sweet wines, and northern Europe, which craved them. This trade dwindled as Spain and Portugal used their better geographical position to supply the north with dark rich wines to keep the cold at bay, but Italy is the country that still makes most use of the dried-grape method.

From Pantelleria, an island off the southern tip of Sicily, right up to Veneto and into the Tyrolean mountains, wines are made either by drying the grapes on mats or, more usually in the north, by hanging the bunches in drying rooms. The most famous are the sweet red Recioto or dry Amarone wines of Valpolicella (the Soave area also makes white Recioto). The dry wines are in great demand, the sweet wines aren't, which is a real pity because you won't find flavours like these anywhere else.

And there's another Italian special – *vin santo* – which is more infamous than famous, since most of it is sweet, baked slop sold in Tuscany's tourist shops. But real *vin santo* is rare and thrilling, with a yeasty, nutty depth, an acidity just the right side of dangerous, and a gorgeous sweetness of old brown autumn fruit when the wasps have had their fill. The top examples are eye-wateringly expensive: Avignonesi's Occhio di Pernice is twice as expensive as Château d'Yquem.

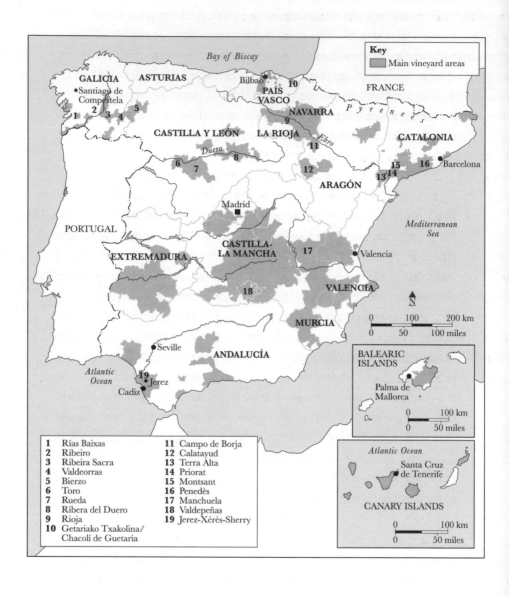

Key

■ Main vineyard areas

Bay of Biscay

GALICIA   ASTURIAS

•Santiago de Compostela

Bilbao

PAÍS VASCO   10

FRANCE

P y r e n e e s

NAVARRA

CASTILLA Y LEÓN   LA RIOJA

9

CATALONIA

Duero

11

Ebro

15   16 •Barcelona

12

13 14

ARAGÓN

6   7   8

PORTUGAL

Madrid ■

Mediterranean Sea

EXTREMADURA

CASTILLA-LA MANCHA

17   •Valencia

N

VALENCIA

18

0   100   200 km
0   50   100 miles

MURCIA

•Seville

ANDALUCÍA

Atlantic Ocean

19
•Jerez

Cadiz

BALEARIC ISLANDS

Palma de Mallorca •

0   100 km
0   50 miles

1	Rías Baixas	11	Campo de Borja
2	Ribeiro	12	Calatayud
3	Ribeira Sacra	13	Terra Alta
4	Valdeorras	14	Priorat
5	Bierzo	15	Montsant
6	Toro	16	Penedès
7	Rueda	17	Manchuela
8	Ribera del Duero	18	Valdepeñas
9	Rioja	19	Jerez-Xérès-Sherry
10	Getariako Txakolina/ Chacolí de Guetaria		

Atlantic Ocean

Santa Cruz de Tenerife

CANARY ISLANDS

0   100 km
0   50 miles

Spain

The Spain you know and the Spain you don't

I can hardly bear to think about it. I was in northern Spain and I got this excited phone call. 'I've got a table at El Bulli. Are you in?' Mmm, let me think about it. A fabulous evening at a restaurant voted number one in the world where you can never get a table? Or a round of golf? 'No thanks. Actually, I think I would rather play golf.' And I didn't even have second thoughts. Someone else probably got the gastronomic experience of their life. I just wandered around in the Spanish rough muttering 'I've really got to take some lessons at this wretched game.'

I wouldn't make the same decision today. El Bulli was newly famous then, but it became one of those restaurants that, every generation or so, completely change the way we think about gastronomy. And in this case, the stardust that El Bulli showered on the eating world helped to transform Spanish food from being a greasy also-ran into a world-beater. And along with Spanish food, Spanish wine in the last decade has leapt forward from being a bit humdrum, a bit too oaky, a bit too one-dimensional, to being one of Europe's real hotspots. Cava and Rioja and sherry are all better than ever, but now there's so much more besides.

It wasn't always like that. In fact, it was never like that. Spain was always seen as bringing up the rear of the major European wine-producing nations, lagging behind even Italy because, although Italy seemed to be chaotic, and so many of the wines we came across were pretty dire, at least there were lots of different wines to come across. In Spain there seemed to be almost none. And this demonstrates that you must be careful if you set out to be a reliable producer of bargain-basement wines – and prove to be good at it. The bargain basement is very difficult to get out of once you're in it.

It may sound slightly bizarre, but a couple of generations ago the wine that Spain was known for was Burgundy. She was also pretty well known for Chablis and Sauternes. And quite well known for claret and Graves. Er . . . aren't those all French wines? Indeed they are. But you would have found Rioja doing the same. Great wine houses like López de Heredia and many others were making their livings selling Rioja Burgundy, Rioja Bordeaux, Rioja Sauternes until the 1950s and '60s.

And if this all suggests that Spanish wine seemed to lack a bit of belief in itself, you'd be dead right. Spain made copies of other wines which were richer, often more tasty than the originals, but which sold for less – except for sherry, where other countries made the copies that were cheaper, and tasted far worse than the Spanish original. Spain was where the big-volume brand owners went for their supplies. You only had to taste the thin, raw offerings of French big brands against the ruddy, cheery, bludgeoning flavours of Spain to realise that Spain was certainly much better at making cheap stuff. But when you've got more vineyards planted than any other country in the world, you're not going to be satisfied with that position for ever.

Spain's rebirth

Some of the seeds of Spain's rebirth could be seen in those 'lookalike' wines. Most of the reds, in particular, may have been ropily made, but, wow, they had power. I've still got a bottle of stuff labelled 'Freelance Spanish Burgundy', imported by an outfit called Burton Sheen in Dorking. It cost me forty-nine pence. The few bottles I dared drink in their youth were Stygian purple and black, and tasted so metallic and furry I worried for my teeth. I pick the bottle up and look at it now and then. I still can't see through the liquid, and when I shake it iron filings clank against the glass.

But if modern winemakers using twenty-first-century methods could get to grips with such daunting fruit, they might do wonders. All over Spain old vineyards of Garnacha, Cariñena, Bobal and Monastrell were filling the vats of local flyblown co-operatives with dark, glowering fruit that might contain flavours of brilliance, if only someone would make the effort to draw them out. Yes, but these are all unglamorous, indigenous varieties, unregarded or unknown in the wider world of wine. In an ultra-conservative world like Spain's, making a better wine from Bobal wasn't going to get you anywhere. Someone needed to come out with one of the big guns – Cabernet Sauvignon, or Chardonnay, preferably. Luckily there was someone just back from studying in France who was itching to take up the challenge.

Miguel Torres didn't have to look far for his Cabernet Sauvignon. Jean Leon, a maverick ex-taxi driver, ex-barista from Hollywood, had planted some vines near Barcelona and in the 1960s Miguel bought cuttings and planted them out in his new vineyard near Vilafranca del Penedès, where his father ran the Torres family wine business with a rod of rough iron. It wasn't classic Cabernet country, to be honest, but his father had a healthy suspicion of his ambitious, imaginative son and wouldn't let young Miguel plant a vineyard he couldn't actually keep an eye on from his tower in the winery.

It didn't matter. Miguel made a wine called Black Label Cabernet Sauvignon in 1970 and in 1979 entered it into a 'Wine Olympics' held by the famous French gastronomic magazine *Gault-Millau*. When the French organise these big wine competitions they apparently only do it to pat themselves on the back. They never seem to expect anything but a French classic to win, and to help things along the competitions are usually judged by, let's say, a 'home-friendly' jury. So when such wines as the Bordeaux superstars La Mission-Haut Brion 1961 and Latour 1970 were entered, people like the Latour general manager popped by to judge. I wonder if he thought the Black Label 1970 was actually the Latour. He certainly didn't when the winner – Black Label 1970 – was revealed. Huh, he sniffed, 'It may be all right for a bawdy night out, but hardly for an elegant luncheon.' And he would have been even less happy if he'd known then that the cuttings Miguel Torres bought from Jean Leon had been quietly removed one dark night from the vineyard of his equally famous Bordeaux neighbour, Lafite-Rothschild. Is that what he meant by a bawdy night out?

Now, it's simplistic to say that one wine can change everything, but in a soporific wine world like Spain's at that time, someone needs to drop a bomb. In fact, Miguel Torres had already done something far more important. He had invented the first modern Spanish white wine. Red wine is all very well, but in such a sweltering place what you desperately craved was a crisp, dry *white* wine. And you couldn't get it. All along the beaches and bars of the Costa Brava, Costa Blanca, Costa del Sol, you couldn't get a glass of decent white. The Spanish themselves didn't drink white wine. They drank yellow – thick, turgid old stuff that was about as refreshing as a lukewarm jacuzzi full of pork fat. Until Miguel Torres, back in 1963, brought out Spain's first modern white wine – Viña Sol. Nowadays, there isn't a bar in Spain that can't offer you a chilled glass of Viña Sol or an equivalent. Miguel has made Torres wine so successful that people think Torres is a wine region, not a family name. Just as people think Rioja is a grape variety, not a wine region. But if you need to pin the thank-you note to just one person for modernising Spanish table wine, Miguel Torres will do nicely.

And what's all this about Rioja being a grape variety? Well, isn't it? In 2017 a consumer survey in Britain discovered not only that Rioja had the best recall of any wine in the public's mind, but that most people thought Rioja was a grape! The Rioja people probably don't know whether to laugh or cry.

So. A fact or two. Rioja is *not* a grape. It's a region in northern Spain, straddling the River Ebro just an hour or so south of Bilbão. And until the last decade or so, if you were talking Spanish red wine to most people, you'd be talking Rioja. Rioja completely dominated Spanish red wine, and had done so since the late eighteenth century.

So Rioja did have some sort of wine reputation when the rest of Spain had none, and this was kept ticking over by a stream of pilgrims heading through the region on their way to Santiago de Compostela. The route still goes through the vineyards. Just a few hours of tramping and I can vouch that you have built up a serious thirst. But this reputation didn't spread far, because decent transport for wine in Spain was close to non-existent. Donkeys laden with pigskins bulging with foetid, gutty wine, ambling for days to the nearest market wasn't going to build up a reputation. If only they had had barrels . . .

If you look at a map, Bordeaux is way down in the southwest of France. Heading south, Spain isn't that far away, and the first wine area you will come to is Rioja. Bordeaux was a very famous wine area by the 1850s, its fame based on longlasting red wines, aged and softened in French oak barrels. In the 1840s a disease called powdery mildew began to lay waste the French vineyards, followed, in the 1860s, by the invasion of the tiny vine-root-chomping aphid phylloxera, which really did destroy just about every vineyard in France. Bordeaux faced complete financial collapse unless an alternative source of sturdy black grapes could be found. And the closest source? Rioja. Just over the Pyrenees, where powdery mildew hadn't yet attacked and phylloxera wouldn't make its unwelcome presence felt until 1901. Bordeaux merchants decamped there in droves. And they brought their up-to-the-minute winemaking methods with them. Above all, they brought the 225-litre oak barrel.

Out went the stinking pigskins, in came the fragrant barrels. The Bordeaux merchants weren't interested in Rioja's reputation, only in its wine. By the late nineteenth century, Rioja was exporting up to fifty million litres of red wine a *month* back to France. Was it sold there as Rioja? Unlikely, I should say. Around then there were lots of excellent French wine names that were a bit short of grapes. Indeed, Marqués de Riscal, the original Spanish bodega in Rioja, called its wine Médoc Alavesa (the Médoc being the main red wine area of Bordeaux). But the understanding of good modern Bordeaux-type wine – and how to make it – had taken root, and through the turbulent first seventy-five years of Spain's history in the twentieth century Rioja quietly built its reputation for oak-aged red in the Bordeaux style, though the grape varieties were different – and so was the wood.

Where Rioja differed from Bordeaux was in its use of American oak for its barrels. Because of trading relationships with the Americas, the Rioja producers found that they could import whole trees from America and make them into barrels in Spain more cheaply than importing French barrels. American oak is of a type called *Quercus alba* and wines that are matured in American oak barrels gain a much more creamy, vanilla-ish flavour than those from French oak. For almost all of the twentieth century and into the twenty-first, when the top producers started switching to French oak, a soft creaminess was the hallmark of Rioja. In places such as Britain and Scandinavia it was the chance to drink red wine without tears, long before the soft, mellow gobfuls of New World sunshine made it to Europe, and at a time when most affordable Italian and French wine was pretty grim.

And the grape variety was Tempranillo. Now this is a good variety. In some places it's very good. And in some parts of Rioja it makes sublime wines, but not in every part. Often Tempranillo is much better blended with either a beefier grape like Garnacha or Mazuelo, a more acidic, livelier variety like Graciano, or a denser, more peppery one like Maturana. Unfortunately the trendy variety, the one the critics knew and the one the market would pay for, was Tempranillo, and great swathes of Rioja that should be – and indeed often were – planted with other varieties are now carpeted with Tempranillo, often giving wine short of character and excitement. In the important but less renowned Rioja Baja, with its deep, silty soils, 23,000 hectares (57,000 acres) of Garnacha – the traditional grape of the area – have been converted to new, high-yielding clones of Tempranillo. Mazuelo and Graciano have also been pushed aside and Rioja is the worse for it. Over 80 per cent of Rioja's vineyards are now Tempranillo.

Luckily, there is a passionate new vineyard-obsessed bunch of winemakers, mostly working apart from the big companies, who are determined to protect and promote all of Rioja's traditional varieties, and to find and cherish all of Rioja's old vineyards and coax them back to life, whatever vine varieties are growing there. Rioja's reputation has been made by large companies blending large amounts of grapes and wine, which they have often bought in from other cellars, to a commendable consistency. The excitement in Rioja now is the rediscovery, just in time, of the precious attributes of the vineyard land in all its eccentricities. In 2017 the Rioja regulators allowed the producers to bottle and label wines from a single vineyard. For the first time. In 2017! That shows you where the political power in Rioja lies – with the big companies and the co-operatives. The next objective is to be allowed to say the wine comes from a single village. No, that's not yet allowed. Honest!

This Tempranillo thing isn't just a Rioja question. Because it seemed to be the one Spanish grape variety with any fame and fashionability, Tempranillo is everywhere. There's too much of it in Spain. In some places it performs with distinction under a variety of names – it can produce beautifully nuanced wines in Ribera del Duero as Tinto Fino, and in Toro where it is called Tinto de Toro it turns into a big-boned bruiser to good effect.

In central Spain, now called Cencibel, it can give attractive sweet fruit to the reds of Valdepeñas. As Ull de Llebre it's widely planted in Catalonia without being very convincing. But it is found in most other areas, too, with the exception of most of the far north-west, regardless of whether or not this early-ripening variety is suitable to places that mostly have too much heat and sunshine rather than not enough.

Up until 2013, there had been an increase of Tempranillo plantings of 70 per cent in just ten years. This is not healthy. Spain has the biggest vineyard area in the world, at about 950,000 hectares (2,350,000 acres), and 210,000 hectares (500,000 acres) of these are Tempranillo. France has slightly less than 800,000 hectares (2,000,000 acres) of vines. Merlot is the most widely planted grape, at 114,000 hectares (282,000 acres), and even that's too much: loads of the early-ripening Merlot is broiling away in the unsuitable suntraps of the south. In Italy, Sangiovese used to be like Tempranillo – far too widely planted – but its area has dropped by almost two-thirds since 1990. Spain does have pockets of traditional grapes languishing in every corner. Now is the time to give them the attention and imagination required to make the best of Spain's red wine potential.

There may be too much Tempranillo around, but along the Duero Valley it does some of its best work. At least, the king of Spain thought so. Vega Sicilia is now one of the most famous wineries in the world, and it sits on the banks of the River Duero in an area called Ribera del Duero. But even when no one really knew where the wine came from, somehow the owner always found ways to get it poured in the smartest dining rooms of Spanish society. Word is that he didn't sell it: he just gave it away to important people. Only very occasionally did the odd bottle surface elsewhere. I had to go to Stockholm to get a taste. Presumably the king of Spain found it easier to obtain – well, up to a point. He wasn't accorded any favours. When he rang to order a case he was told that there was a waiting list and he'd have to wait his turn like everyone else. 'But don't you know who I am? I'm the king of Spain.' 'Yes, yes, sir. And I'm Winston Churchill. Now run along, I've got things to do.'

And it's true. You wait your turn. When the Queen visited Madrid the British ambassador thought it would be a nice idea to serve Vega Sicilia. 'I'm sure Her Majesty would enjoy it, sir, but you will have to wait your turn like everybody else.'

I still remember my first Vega Sicilia. The wine was the 1968. It was certainly different! Intriguing, blackcurrant flavours I couldn't quite fathom, wild scents I couldn't quite place, all carried along on a wave of high acidity that was surely too sharp, too sour. And yet it wasn't. Somehow this shimmering rapier of acid had pierced the fine gauze of fruit and aroma and carried it aloft, tangled and helpless, so that the wine and its fabulously confusing, contradictory flavours simply refused to disappear, and haunts my brain to this day. I asked the winemaker about this javelin streak of acidity, and he said, 'In Vega Sicilia our acidity is our passport to eternity.'

Vega Sicilia is just one winery, and there wasn't even a clearly defined Ribera del Duero region until 1982, but they have made up for the slow start. Several of Spain's greatest wines now come from Ribera del Duero – names like Pingus and Pesquera go alongside Vega Sicilia. There are now more than two hundred wineries in this unlikely Eden. And the intense, focused brilliance of the top wines, darker in fruit and more solemn in perfume than even Rioja's best, makes me wonder whether Ribera del Duero is actually the heartland of Tempranillo, not Rioja. But that would imply that the Tempranillo in Ribera del Duero is the same as in Rioja. It doesn't have to be: grape varieties mutate. The Vega Sicilia winemaker told me that he had isolated eight different Tempranillos in their oldest vineyard, all genetically different.

It's worth staying with the Duero Valley a bit longer. This northern stretch of Spain, between Madrid and the Bay of

Biscay, is gaunt, haughty, severe and challenging. Winters are frighteningly savage – but then you think, how high are we here? And in Ribera del Duera you can be 900 metres (2950 feet) above sea level. It's a useful piece of pub-quiz trivia to know that Madrid is the highest capital in Europe. And what this height means is that you have long, exhausting icy winters, but short, fresh yet very sunny summers. Spring comes late and autumn comes early. You can get frosted in May. You can get frosted in September.

That hardly leaves enough time in between to ripen your grapes. That's why the early-ripening Tempranillo is the most important grape variety here (though not the only one). If you can avoid the late-spring frosts, you can generally ripen your crop before the late-season frosts arrive. That's because the days are hot here – the temperature can reach 40°C (104°F) and are typically 30–35°C (86–95°F) in summer. Ah, but the nights. Remember how high we are. Nights can drop as low as 4–5°C (39–41°F) – that is real woolly-jumper time, even in July. And the extreme shift in temperature keeps a freshness in the fruit, a focus in the flavours and a limpid depth in the colour that, at its best, makes Ribera del Duero worthy of its star status, with Tinto Fino, aka Tempranillo, leading the band.

If you head west toward the bleak Portuguese border, where the Duero River becomes the Douro in Portuguese, the Valley becomes even more of an uninviting moonscape. These are the Toro badlands – the very name suggests somewhere imperious, ill-tempered and unforgiving. Well, Toro wine was pretty much like that until this century. The soils here are sullen clays topped with sand and gravel – you slip about as if you are on a beach sometimes – and the altitude is still high, often over 700 metres (2300 feet) and occasionally up to 800 metres (2600 feet), and there is even more of the scorching sunshine of Ribera del Duero, though still mercifully tempered by cold nights. And you've got yet another version of Tempranillo – this time called Tinto de Toro.

Frankly, it's a brute. Is it really the same variety? But this is about all you can grow out here in the near-desert. They have tried the famous French grapes — who hasn't? — but they just build up enormous alcohol levels and never get their skins ripe in these extreme conditions. That makes sense. Some of the Portuguese varieties work, but the famous French grapes like Cabernet Sauvignon and Merlot are maritime – they come from gentler climes. It is too rough here for such softies. And maybe that's why the relatively good-natured Rioja Tempranillo has had to adapt to these brutal conditions by thickening up, becoming more brutish. There is perfume in a good Toro wine. There is richness of dark raspberry fruit, of almond paste, of gum-drying chocolate, but don't expect the wine to release them without a fight. As the sun sinks fast into the distant hills, you realise the vine doesn't own Toro like it owns some vine-yard places. The vineyards here are visitors, tolerated in this harsh land. I feel quite lonely and I head into the drab little town for supper. Pig's ears, I eat, and pig's snout, and pig's tongue, rudely swamped by draughts of ruddy red Toro. I'm not sure I didn't have bull's testicles too.

The popular answer to the question 'Where is the most important non-Tempranillo red wine in Spain?' would be Priorat. This is dark, dark red that is somehow coaxed out of remarkable terraced mountain slopes — 'slopes' is almost too gentle a term — inland from Tarragona in Catalonia. Garnacha is the main grape, but there are lots of others, and the region was virtually given up as uncultivable – and certainly unprofitable – until the 1980s, when one or two Catalan wine tyros seeking a challenge took on these almost-abandoned terraces.

I've been tasting the wines since the 1990s and I have to admit I have never quite understood their appeal. I loved the endeavour, the commitment, the wide-eyed idealism of some of the Priorat pioneers. What I didn't enjoy was the way these wines were becoming thicker and heavier, and losing the fleet-ing freshness of the mountains in favour of a dense, overripe stew sold increasingly for dense, overripe prices to people who were more interested in how many marks out of 100 the critics gave them. One or two Priorat wines became the most expensive wines in Spain.

Because of the immense efforts and commitment put into such ventures, I felt bad about not appreciating them, but I didn't. I found more pleasure in the far less pricey, lighter, brighter but still very ripe and rich wines of Priorat's neighbours Montsant and Terra Alta. And then, suddenly, a couple of years ago I started finding Priorats which were drinkable again, which were less dense, less shrivelled, and which were almost affordable. What happened, I asked one of the producers as I tasted his 2016s, their argumentative rocky core now wreathed with tobacco leaf and herb sap and gnawed at by the sweet pith of oranges, and he said, 'We suddenly realised we were making wines which nobody really wanted to drink because they weren't really very drinkable.' Hallelujah!

So for me, the most important red wine movement in Spain is indeed led by the Garnacha grape, but it is taking place in such unsung regions as Calatayud and Campo de Borja, or elsewhere in the sprawling forgotten hinterland of Aragon where the vineyard areas don't even have a particular name. But the bony fields are scattered with old, wise bush vines – mostly Garnacha – which modern winemaking is turning into some of Europe's most delicious, most individual and most affordable red wine. The same thing is happening further south with Garnacha but also with Cariñena, Monastrell and Bobal. These are the grapes of the warm south. These are the grapes they used to pick suffocating in their own sugar levels and they would leave the juice and wine to macerate with the skins until January, creating a thick broth of tannin and bitterness. Yet these parts of the east and the south are where the new generation of winemakers, encouraged by the odd Anglo-Saxon and Celtic flying winemaker, is making the most important change in Spanish red wine. As a friend in Manchuela said while we rolled his luscious Bobal red with its wild, reckless flavour over our tongues – well, I rolled the Bobal, he was talking – 'Spain is very old in vineyards, but very new in high quality.' The prospects are exciting.

Yes, but what about Spain's whites?

If you're wondering why I'm not talking about white wines, well, yes, I'm beginning to wonder too. The easy answer would be to say that white wine isn't that important in Spain, and, except for the always welcome ice-cold slug of Torres Viña Sol, it wasn't very important for me either. But that's not true any more – for Spain or for me. Spain is becoming quite an expert at coaxing out impressive white wine flavours from unpromising conditions or grapes. Priorat, the red wine whose pre-eminence I never fully understood, makes small amounts of amazing, oily, excitingly unrefreshing whites that do speak to me. Catalonia has some fresh and lively Chardonnays as well as some disturbing individual wines from white Garnacha and the local Xarel-lo. Rioja, though lumbered with the hardly multi-faceted Viura grape, now allows numerous extra grapes like Chardonnay and Verdejo, and makes quite an array of good dry whites, mostly oaked. These are led by the formidable López de Heredia and Marqués de Murrieta, where they sometimes leave their top white in the barrel for thirty years before they bottle it, and it's simply magnificent.

New developments like the discovery and propagation of the very tasty white Tempranillo should help the cause of unoaked whites in Spain. And along the Duero Valley, in a most unprepossessing, windswept gravel pit of a place called Rueda, some of Spain's freshest and sharpest whites are turned out from Verdejo and Sauvignon Blanc grapes. And to everyone's surprise, Txakoli from the Basque hills behind Bilbão and San Sebastian is proving to be a high-acid star with Spain's new-wave chefs.

And I'm nearly there. I have to traverse one more red wine area – Bierzo, making mouthwatering snappy reds laden with raspberry fruit and the lick of wet rock from the Mencia grape – and I'm in Galicia, the wet, wooded, windy north-west, hardly Spain at all, and with white wine traditions that bear no resemblance to what happens in Spain's vast interior. Yet here I feel at home. I'm a Celt. I understand the drip of cool rain down the collar of my shirt and the long, patient wait for a brief break in the clouds. I understand seascapes flecked with white and salty spray slapped onto my cheeks by the gusty wind. I understand a place where they play the bagpipes (*gaita*) and which they say is wetter than Manchester. The Green Spain is what they call Galicia. Some of the land right on the west coast is as green as Ireland. And it is here that Spain's most thrilling white wines are made, in Rías Baixas. This translates into English as the 'low fjords', coastal valleys that really are a bit like minor Norwegian fjords, and this was one of Spain's most impoverished regions – and there was a lot of competition for that title before European Union membership worked its magic.

The chief magic it worked was in Madrid, which rapidly became a throbbing capital city, full of high-spending sophisticates who liked nothing better than a glass of chilled dry white with their seafood. So that was a double whammy. Spain's best seafood came from Galicia. And there were loads of vineyards there, but the wine was rubbish. Necessity is the mother of invention. This was clearly the coolest part of Spain, the most suitable for delicate white wine production, and there was a local grape that looked promising – the Albariño. Get on with it. Easier said than done, but the Rías Baixas vineyards expanded eightfold, and the amount of wine labelled 'Albariño' expanded by a good deal more, much of it tasting of anything but Albariño. It's taken a generation for things to get back into balance, but now even the biggest, most commercial producers – and one of them is part-owned by E. & J. Gallo of California – are producing zesty, citrous whites, and the individual estates are producing fabulous appley whites, full of flavour, sharpened by lemon peel and green orchard leaves, and, refreshingly often, bringing to mind the spray and spume of the wild ocean as you stand on a rock and gaze out west to Finisterre, the end of the world.

Rías Baixas isn't the only wine-producing part of Galicia, but it is the greenest – things very quickly get drier and warmer as you head inland. Ribeiro makes aromatic whites and intriguing reds. Ribeira Sacra is daunting and beautiful, with really tasty whites and reds. President Obama likes them, and that's good enough for me. And Valdeorras is becoming a positive laboratory for local grape varieties, but its fragrant, almost tropical white Godello has made the most waves so far. Spain needed the north-west's wines to accompany its exploding culinary scene. The north-west is delivering.

Spain's very own fizz

In the meantime, Cava is trying to deliver, but not necessarily managing it. Spain has a powerful and successful Cava industry producing large volumes of decent fizz, and small volumes of excellent, unusual, positively challenging sparkling wine based on the native Catalan grapes of Xarel-lo and Macabeu.

I've always been mildly surprised that one of the world's most successful sparkling wine regions should be in Penedès, to the south-west of the not exactly chilly city of Barcelona. The received wisdom is that you need cool, blustery, damp conditions, like those of Champagne. But you can't fault the Catalans for effort. Two of the world's biggest producers of fizz are Catalan – Freixenet and Codorníu – and instead of merely adopting cheap industrial methods of making wine sparkle, they adopted the expensive, labour-intensive Champagne method of creating bubbles by inducing a second fermentation inside the bottle. But I suspect these pioneers were also realistic. Their local grape varieties were not as interesting as Champagne's

Chardonnay and Pinot Noir. They saw that it might take two or three costly years for each bottle to develop the biscuity, yeasty flavour for which Champagne is famous, but only nine to twelve months for the wine to get a good lively bubble in it. And a light, fresh wine with a good bubble in it could be sold at an affordable price. In a way, affordability has always been both the strong and the weak point of Cava. In many markets Cava became poor man's Champagne – always affordable, always with a decent bubble, but never given great respect. Which meant that it was always susceptible to price-cutting, and over-sensitive to price increases that might have financed finer flavours. When a more sprightly, more party-going rival like Italy's Prosecco turned up at the doorstep in her glad rags, Cava looked positively dowdy in comparison.

But maybe Prosecco's arrival as the favourite party pop isn't such a bad thing. There are a lot of small Cava producers who aren't interested in the cheap disco market. There is now a lot more Chardonnay and Pinot Noir planted in the vineyards used for Cava. Xarel-lo, an earthy, oily, pithy grape in itself, is being paraded with some success as a truly Catalan experience. And just as Cava launches a new classification for single-vineyard wines – how on earth did Cava get there before Rioja? – some of the leading producers have given up on calling their wines Cava altogether. They think the name no longer does justice to the efforts at excellence which they've embarked upon. Having just been drinking – not tasting – Torres's outstanding non-Cava sparkler named, self-effacingly, Cuvée Esplendor, and having been unable to restrain myself from making very flattering comparisons with top Champagne, perhaps they are right. Cava can plod on, trying to improve its wine and its image step by step. Some producers no longer want to be part of the process. They don't want Cava any more, but if Cava has any sense it'll keep hold of those coat tails.

Sherry, Falstaff's favourite tipple

What wine would I most miss from Spain if the grim reaper were to call? Sherry. Without doubt, sherry. But how many of us have ever drunk it? What is it? What does it taste like? Like nothing else on earth. There is no modern wine that approaches these flavours. Sherry delves back centuries to coax out its most implausible and utterly addictive tastes and scents. Of all the world's wines, this is such an adult drink.

So what has sherry meant to me in my drinking life? Well, not enough, quite frankly. I did snaffle quite a bit of it at my younger sister's christening – but that was South African sherry. I did go to a welcoming sherry party on my first day at university. I remember nothing about it. I did have a maiden aunt who used to bring out a bottle of Harveys Bristol Cream when we visited at Christmas. I swear it was the same bottle each time. The level seemed to go down by an inch a year.

But what about those sherry-drinking rituals of British life? Don't you get offered a glass of sherry when you visit friends? No. I don't remember being offered a glass of sherry in twenty years. Don't I offer a glass of sherry when the vicar calls? The vicar has never called. I drink sherry so rarely that before I sat down to write this I thought I'd better open some sherry to remind me of how divine a drink it is. I opened three bottles. Since you ask, they were a Lustau Botaina Amontillado Seco, a Lustau Emperatriz Eugenia Dry Oloroso and a Sánchez Romate Single Butt Dry Oloroso called Miguel Fontádez Florido. If you're not a sherry drinker, those names will mean absolutely nothing to you. They were magnificent. Astonishingly dry. Astonishingly rich. Every brown flavour you have ever had in every food or drink you've experienced – all stuffed into this pungent, inimitable liquid. I'll say. Two days later my study still reeks of sherry. I've had to fumigate my spittoon. I'm sure that if I had a glass of one of these and then walked into a crowded room everyone would know. 'Ooh, he's been on the sherry.

Could smell him a mile off.' And I wouldn't be surprised if you could. Great old sherries have such power and concentration that I suspect they seep into every bone and fibre in your body, and then quietly ooze out of every pore of your skin. People would know if I'd been at these giants of drink.

And maybe that's why I enthusiastically taste sherries at trade tastings and competitions, and frequently give them my highest marks. And then refresh myself with a nice chilled glass of Sauvignon Blanc. And here's me saying I love the stuff. I feel like someone who says he adores Shakespeare yet never goes to the theatre. Someone who adores film yet never goes to the cinema. Fair comment. I should get out more. So let's have a look at what sherry is.

Well, it's a fortified wine. This means that brandy or another high-strength spirit has been added to the wine. As with port, this was done to make the wine strong enough to cope with sea voyages to distant export markets, mostly in northern Europe, but also in North America. But whereas port ended up being made as a sweet wine, almost all good sherry is bone, bone dry. Fino is a bone-dry pale wine. So is Manzanilla. Amontillado and Oloroso are bone-dry brown wines. Sherries called Milk or Cream or Sweet have had sweetness added to them and are rarely much good.

Real sherry can only come from Andalucía in south-west Spain. Even though sherry has been one of the most copied of all wine styles, proper sherry comes from an area near Cadiz, with Jerez as its main town. That's how the name sherry developed, as Jerez is pronounced 'Hereth' in Spanish. I don't expect the English and Dutch sailors picked that up. Jerez would be pronounced 'Jerez' and after a few bumpers out on the swelling Spanish Main, Jerez pretty quickly became 'Sherez'. Slurring that into 'Sherree' would only take another glass or two.

Sherry has been fortified and heading north out of Andalucía for well over six hundred years, but it had an even more important role to play. The great explorers of the Americas set off on their voyages from ports like Sanlúcar de Barrameda, the town which today produces Manzanillas, the most sublime dry sherries. Christopher Columbus set sail from Sanlúcar in 1492, Francisco Pizarro set out to conquer Peru from the same port and Magellan circled the world starting from the quayside at Sanlúcar. And their ships were all packed with sherry wine. Magellan spent more money on sherry than he did on armaments. An ordinary wine would never have survived. Fortified wine could be relied on to survive, and even to flourish. Eventually sherry wines were taken by the empire builders, particularly the British, to South Africa, North America and Australasia, where the settlers quickly decided they would try to make these big, strong wines for themselves.

Even so, it was northern Europe that really made sherry's reputation. In the late fourteenth century Chaucer was writing about the overwhelming 'fumositee' of Andalusian wine (*fumositee* is a brilliant word: fumes of alcohol and heady richness rising up the throat and enveloping the brain in its shrouds). Shakespeare was a whole lot keener on it at the end of the sixteenth century, when sherry's greatest and most enthusiastic imbiber, Sir John Falstaff, was bestriding the English stage in *Henry IV Part One* and *Part Two*. These plays were written in 1597 and 1598, a decade after Sir Francis Drake had 'singed the King of Spain's beard' in Cadiz harbour in 1587 by setting fire to the Spanish fleet and making off with thousands of barrels of sherry wine into the bargain. With the Spanish Armada sailing up the Channel the following year you can imagine how popular Drake's contraband was, and sherry remained a central plank of Britain's drinking culture until the last part of the twentieth century.

Halfway through the nineteenth century, 43 per cent of all the wine drunk in Britain was sherry. Halfway through the twentieth century Harveys Bristol Cream was probably the most famous wine in the land. Nothing stays the same for ever. By the end of the nineteenth century sherry's reputation had been shredded by fraudulent wine, much of it concocted out of potato spirit. And by the end of the twentieth century gross overproduction and dumping of shabby quality wine had pretty much scuppered the British market again. But we need to look on the bright side. Previous revivals had been led by quality. The same is happening now.

But it's not something that can happen in a rush, because good sherry can't be made in a rush. The basic material of sherry is extremely dull, light white wine from an extremely dull grape variety called Palomino, which grows on the pale chalky soils around Jerez. It rarely ripens to more than 12–13 per cent alcohol, but that's OK because it's already losing what little freshness and personality it had by this time. This isn't sounding very encouraging is it? Why would anyone drink this? Well, in its natural state, they wouldn't. But here's where the old habit of fortifying the wine for export comes in handy.

If you fortify this thin, dry wine to about 15–15.5 per cent alcohol and then leave the wine in barrels (called butts) open to the air, some of the yeasts begin to react with the alcohol and form a creamy crust called 'flor'. It's only at this alcohol level that this is a good idea, because the flor also produces acetaldehyde. Below 14.5 per cent alcohol this causes the wine to turn to vinegar, and over 16 per cent the yeast dies, so you've just got this narrow band where the acetaldehyde contributes a thrilling, sourdough, bready richness to the dull Palomino wine. This is what creates the fascinating appetising flavour in Fino and Manzanilla sherry.

This flor yeast crust would die away after a year if you left it alone, but to add depth and intrigue to the wines' flavours the locals have developed what is called a solera system, whereby they keep refreshing the barrels with new wine over a period of five to six years. Typically you would have a stack of barrels full of wine, and you would draw perhaps a third of the wine out of the bottom barrel, then refill that from the barrel above and so on until you get to the top barrel, which will then be topped up with fresh wine. So by the time you get to the bottom barrel, you'll have a mix of perhaps six years of wine, which is what transforms really rubbish Palomino wine into a dry, pungent, refreshing drink like no other.

This is pale dry sherry I'm talking about. But a lot of sherry is brown – called Oloroso. In simple terms, this is wine that doesn't develop the flor yeast. That's easy to organise: you just fortify the base wine up to 18 or 20 per cent alcohol and the flor will never get going. You then use the same solera system of fractional blending, but on a grander scale, and all the flavour comes from the mixing of old with younger, and the controlled oxidation or browning in the barrels. Oloroso soleras can be so extensive as to have component parts decades old; occasionally, the solera will have been started over a century ago and fed with new wine every year.

It's like a stockpot that you throw stuff into and boil up every day. My Auntie Nessie's had only once *not* been boiled up since the Second World War. What catastrophe could possibly have got in the way of the daily boiling? We would go over to Auntie Nessie's for the summer holidays and sit down to eat for the first few days knowing that if we didn't polish off the gruesome green goo that was slapped down in front of us we wouldn't get any of the salmon my Uncle Colm would mysteriously find lying around in the river shallows each morning. We also knew that we would be producing enough methane to keep Ireland's lights on until Christmas.

All of which is not particularly relevant to sherry. Well, yes it is. The stockpot at a day old would have tasted of nothing much, but after thousands of boilings it had a flavour I can feel rising at the back of my throat to this day. The young Palomino wine tastes of nothing, but blended and blended and blended in the solera system it is as dark and mysterious, as challenging and paradoxical, as painful and soothing and uplifting as any wine made. Maybe I don't drink enough of it, because it sweeps other wines aside and reveals the paucity of their ambitions.

Luckily the heroes of the new Spanish cuisine, with their bars and restaurants all over northern Europe and North America, are not so squeamish.

Sherry is a wine full of paradoxes. All of the greatest sherries are bone dry, though some are intense and rich. They can be as clear as water or deep mahogany in colour. And they all share a wild, unexpected palette of flavours and scents that go from the sour and callow and raw right through to slumbering autumnal depths. And somehow it all works. There is no wine in the world like sherry. It is one of the most challenging and adult and supremely satisfying flavours you will ever experience. So here are a few tasting notes of mine from the last few years:

How about this? For a bone-dry Manzanilla sherry from Argüeso: '*Don't come here for delicacy. Come here for a shocking, brilliant haughtiness, an arrogant disregard for dumbing down and smoothing out. This has a high-cheekboned serenity that you will love or hate, a dryness like old lonesome banisters, like house dust settling on ancient floorboards scrubbed clean a thousand times. The fruit is like a pale, unripe apple peering nervously into watery sunlight, and whatever softness it has is that of the creamy sour softness of bread dough before it's baked. Don't ask me why, but it reminded me of the Bates Motel in* Psycho. *The banisters, perhaps . . .*'

On Valdespino's Fino Inocente: '*When you are describing great dry sherry, every term you use seems to rebel against drinking pleasure, yet is crucial to it. This tastes of earth – summer earth, dried out after a brief summer shower. This tastes of dust – dust caught in a shaft of sunlight through the time-bleached banisters of an old staircase. This tastes of an old chest of drawers, of old clean wood, pebbles, apple, cedar and orange, ether – yes, ether – a traditional doctor's surgery, an old, clean Victorian hospital ward. Formaldehyde, the bitter bark of medicinal trees. Paradoxical, confusing, inspiring, glorious.*'

And here's a note for an old brown sherry, Oloroso Muy Viejo, Bodegas Tradición: '*Just as 100 per cent black chocolate shocks you with its dryness, so does this. Its bitterness and asperity rasp like tamarind skin. It really is quite shocking, but excellent too. Deep, dry, you have to peer way past its gaunt exterior to find a richness of nut and chocolate, date and fig, that is stripped and flayed of all sugar, all indulgence, all mellowness and reassuring flesh. This is the Grand Inquisitor of sherries, this is the great ascetic, the flagellator, the moaning, keening hermit of sherries. It is magnificent, but you may have to drink it by yourself, wearing a hood.'*

Key

Main vineyard areas

N

0   50   100 km
0   25   50 miles

MINHO/
VINHO VERDE

TRÁS-OS-
MONTES

Porto

Douro

DOURO
E PORTO

DÃO
E LAFÕES

BAIRRADA

BEIRA
INTERIOR

Tejo

Atlantic
Ocean

LISBOA

TEJO

SPAIN

Lisbon

ALENTEJO

PENINSULA
DE SETÚBAL

Guadiana

Funchal

MADEIRA

ALGARVE

Portugal

Breaking out beyond port

The night before my first trip to Portugal I had just fallen in love – not the ideal thing to do the day before a dawn flight, but there you go. So, to be honest, I was buzzing, and boiled boot polish would have tasted like ambrosia. But shoe leather is pretty much what most of the reds I tried did taste like. At that time – in the 1980s – I had not tasted a single Portuguese red wine that I liked. I hadn't liked the whites any better, and if pressed I'd have to say that pink Mateus Rosé was about my favourite Portuguese wine. (There's another girlfriend story there, but that was in Canada, and a long time ago.) So Portugal for me was simply the home of sweet port and Madeira, possibly fizzy pink and basically nothing else. I suspect that most Brits felt exactly the same.

This first trip didn't do much to change my mind. Everything seemed so old, so tired, so washed out. The country seemed friendly but exhausted and impoverished. This wasn't surprising, as Portugal had been a dictatorship as recently as the 1970s and also a major colonial power. She *was* exhausted and impoverished. There was neither the money nor the will to get involved in the New World wine revolution bubbling up in California and in the southern hemisphere. But the Portuguese would say that there was no need either. They drank almost everything they produced, with the help of Portuguese-speaking countries like

Brazil. Portugal was probably the first country to demonstrate to me that whenever local pundits say, 'Oh, we drink everything we produce,' it is a *bad* sign. The domestic market is always the least critical and most parochial. Quality improves when you need to export and you have to prove you possess a point of difference.

But I did, I think, see some glimmering of what Portugal might become. Although no one there thought for a moment I might be interested in visiting something as rudimentary as a vineyard, I did start to make a list of an impressive number of totally unfamiliar grape names. I didn't taste a single Chardonnay or Merlot or Shiraz on my trip, because there wasn't any. And I got some idea as to what excitement the future might hold for reds from the fact that the Portuguese utterly revered age. The winemakers were old, their clothes were old, their cellars were dark and cobwebby and generally fungal. The youngest wine samples we tasted were usually four years old, and bitter and rough to the tongue. But as the samples got more venerable, as their emaciated flesh slid off their shanks and haunches, did I taste some dusty unfulfilled promise? Just once, I did.

I was in the cellars of an outfit called São João hidden down a backstreet in Oporto, and just as cobwebby and fungal as the others, but when I saw the labels of the wines – made out of cork – with the name of the wine printed roughly across, I realised, yes, I *had* had one Portuguese red wine that I'd enjoyed, years before in a drunken knees-up at the Bristol Wine Fair. What did it taste of? Come on ... but I remembered the cork label with a smile. It had been an old, thoughtful wine intruding on a very raucous night. And here it was again. Dão 1966. Still unbelievably bitter, but this was now the bitterness of sloes and liquorice and Seville orange peel, not the rough kick of a hobnail boot. At eighteen years old, it had a rich, raw-boned power that I fancied might never fade, and the kind of fascinating, completely original flavour that, if you put it under any wine buff's nose, they'd say ah yes, that's Bordeaux, or that's Hermitage, or Barolo, or whatever was their favourite red. They would want it to taste like this. Me? I was dazed and dazzled after a dark week. I plumped for a mixture of the Nebbiolo tar and rose petal and bitterness that Barolo offers, swamped by the lush spicy Merlot indulgence of a mighty Pomerol from Bordeaux. If anyone ever dared to mix those two titans it would taste something like this.

Then in 1986 Portugal joined the European Community. Would this little stub of land stuck on to the edge of Europe like a postage stamp be swept up and homogenised by the mighty European machine? Or would she thank Europe for the money and say 'Now let's show you what we can do?' By the mid-1990s Portugal was enthusiastically spending more European grants and loans than any other country. And if she was modernising her wineries and revamping her vineyards, she wasn't selling her birthright.

Grape varieties you'll never have heard of

Portugal has about 250 different grape varieties, and a refreshing new wave of young wine people made the brave decision to concentrate on these rather than take the easy route of Chardonnay and Merlot and the rest. It means that a lot of us still don't know Portuguese wines as well as we should, because the Portuguese language is, frankly, a bit of a challenge, and if you add to that a bunch of grape varieties we've never heard of it doesn't make it likely that many of us will pick the wine off the shelf in a wine shop or choose it on a wine list.

I'll give you a taster. Have you heard of any of these? Baga? A burly, beetle-browed black grape from Bairrada on the Atlantic coast. Tinto Cão? A blossom-scented delight from Dão further inland. Trincadeira? Juicy, spicy reds from further south, inland from Lisbon. Touriga Nacional? Powerful, imperious, darkly scented reds from the Douro Valley. Castelão makes easy-going reds, pinks and bubbles just about everywhere. Arinto, Antão Vaz and Encruzado make wildly different whites from north to south. And on it goes. Had you heard of any of these?

Well, it gets worse. Or better! Let me translate a few other grape names into English. 'Love me don't leave me' ought to make a nice enough drink. 'Frowning Girl' and 'Ladies' Fingers' might be OK. I'm not so sure about 'Little Puppy Dog' or 'Toad's Eye' or 'Load the Donkeys'. And would I really order a glass of 'Dog Strangler', or 'Fox Strangler' for that matter? 'Boy Strangler'? Er, no ... And what's with 'Bastard'? There's a 'Little Bastard' as well. And two sorts of 'Red Bastard'. As well as a 'Spanish Bastard' and a 'Red Spanish Bastard'. It certainly makes a change from Sauvignon Blanc.

If this is giving you an impression of a strong-willed bunch of wine people, convinced of their own destiny, that's fair enough. And we really are lucky to have Portugal banging a very different drum in European wine. Although the country is roughly scooped out of Spain's western flank, Portugal has historically been isolated, and you only have to experience the high mountains and the bleak desolation on the Spanish border to see how easy it has been for Portugal to spend most of her history as an independent nation. Although some Spanish grape varieties have made the journey over the mountains into Portuguese vineyards – Tempranillo is here disguised as Tinta Roriz – the vast majority are not related to any others anywhere else. How did they get there? Possibly through intrepid Phoenician traders thousands of years ago, who cautiously ventured beyond the Straits of Gibraltar and crept up the Iberian coast, but after a few winters battling the Atlantic gales retreated back to the relative calm of the Mediterranean, leaving vineyards and wine culture behind. The Celts were around at the northern tip of Iberia, and they always liked a drink. The Romans arrived too, and somehow, between them, they established wine traditions completely unrelated to what was happening in Italy, France and Spain, and whatever grape varieties they brought with them evolved in totally independent ways.

A tiny country with everything from damp and chilly to baking

Portugal is tiny, just 600 kilometres (370 miles) long and barely 200 kilometres (125 miles) wide, and within this compact frame almost every climatic condition is present, from chilly to broiling, from dripping wet to desert dry. Let's have a look at some of it.

The north is Portugal's most remarkable area. The majority of the population live here. To the west, it's wet. It's soaking. Sometimes it's wetter than Manchester. In some places it's as wet as the Norwegian fjords. You'll find dripping greenery tangling round your shoulders as you clamber through what seems to be a chilly rainforest. And this is where they make a wine almost water white, hardly visible through the glass but for the tiny beads of effervescence winking at the brim. It will be low in alcohol, citrus in scent and mineral on your tongue like pumice. That's Vinho Verde, the young, green thirst-quencher of Portugal's north, reflecting the rain and the squalls of the wild Atlantic.

Just to the east, Vinho Verde's neighbour is the Douro Valley. There's no dripping greenery here, simply a majestic river gorge that looks so forbidding you can't imagine anyone would cultivate vines on these sheer slopes. But they do. This is where they make the richest, the most luscious, the most overpowering of all the world's sweet fortified wines – port – as well as dry red wine that will soon be lauded as some of the greatest in Europe.

It wasn't always like this. The red wines of the Douro were approached with dread in the old days. A writer in the nineteenth century wrote that Douro table wine was 'strong, rough and comparatively flavourless. If a man were to add six drops of ink to a glass of very common red burgundy, he would get something exceedingly like unfortified port ... the plain truth is that it is an abominable drink.' And that is what Douro red was until recently – a rough, cloddish, bone-dry tooth-stainer made as an afterthought by the grandees who used to create sweet port. They weren't interested in red wine, and when you dined with port shippers they offered their local red apologetically; this dense, chewy, baked slop was only tolerated because the main course required a red to be rushed through en route to a long evening of tales and gossip and witty conversation over decanters of the real point of drinking – sweet red fortified port wine.

The best grapes for sweet port were always those from the hottest slopes – in other words, probably the worst grapes for making fragrant red wines. But the grape varieties of the Douro Valley had had hundreds of years to adapt to the searing conditions and the arid and virtually barren schistous slopes that were often so steep and crumbly that they had to be terraced to make them farmable. As sales of sweet port tumbled in the late twentieth century a group of producers – not the famous port producers who mostly stuck to the sweet stuff, but producers with so-called lesser properties on less favoured slopes, whose grapes didn't get quite so ripe and whose sweet ports were less sought after – began, out of necessity, to try to find out if their black grape varieties could yield wines of freshness, of balance and, above all, of perfume.

There had been one lonely flag bearer for this type of wine – Barca Velha, first made in 1952 and infrequently attempted since. For all we know, it was the first-ever drinkable Douro dry red wine. And it led a lonely existence all right. Way up near the Spanish border. I've been there. No villages, barely a road, just glorious isolation. I scrambled up the hillside and looked back at the shards of schist and slate shining like polished steel under the flare of the sun. Mules still clomp along the terraces down toward the Douro River, which glistens like silver in the heat. Silence. A breeze whispers. A partridge rustles in the hillside scrub. And this is where Douro red wine began. Now everyone makes it. All the famous sweet port producers except Taylor's make some. Its sweet, seductive scent of violets lovingly laid on a bed of rich, ripe damson fruit is unlike any other red in Europe, and makes you wonder how much more beautiful a serious red wine can get.

The joy of irresistible perfumed red wines from the Douro really *is* a new phenomenon. But then remember what I said about my first trip to Portugal: enjoyable reds from anywhere in Portugal is a new phenomenon! Not any more. To the south of the Douro are two areas the Portuguese themselves used to revere most in the old days, even if we could hardly get these rasping wines past our tonsils – Dão and Bairrada. With the cor-uscating exception of my 1966, Dão reds from directly south of the Douro Valley were infamous for their rocky, stony, gravelly, dusty – I know, I'm repeating myself – personality that meant they were virtually indestructible, but who cared? Now they are still rocky and proud; they don't offer any easy pleasures, but if you're in monastic mood they do give you a rather brilliant ascetic satisfaction. Bairrada was equally infamous for its impen-etrable reds made from the haughty Baga grape. They're still not a laugh a minute, but there is a sweet blackcurrant beauty crouched deep inside the Baga carapace, and producers like Luis Pato and his daughter Felipa are coaxing it out like a seafood enthusiast coaxing out a shy winkle with a pin.

Down toward and past Lisbon, on the rainy west coast, in the fertile Tejo Valley or on its low river terraces, and out into the rolling prairie land of golden wheat and scattered vineyards of the Alentejo, are some of the first producers to try to react to the modern demands of attractive fruity reds and, increasingly, soft but bright whites. Above all, these are areas capable of giving hedonistic, powerful reds – less so out on the coast, but in the Alentejo the red wines burst with the sweetness of cherries and blackcurrant, sometimes so ripe and sun-soaked the grapes seem to have half turned to dates and figs and raisins on the vine. I wish I could be as enthusiastic about the wines of the far south, around the Algarve. Even though Cliff Richard made quite nice wine here for a while, this is another example of the curse of the tourist. Roly-poly northern Europeans, all glistening and porcine pink and comatose, don't often request quality when quantity is generally included in the price of the holiday. So the locals don't produce it.

Port, the English Connection

There was one style of Portuguese wine that hardly changed through the dictatorship and revolutions and social chaos of the twentieth century. There was a style of wine that you could explore without ever once despairing of the impenetrability of the Portuguese tongue, because the families who made the wine hardly spoke it, and you as a visitor certainly weren't expected to try. Their houses were as old as those of the Portuguese table wine producers, but these were beautifully furnished; their clothes were also old, but Savile Row suits and Harris tweed jackets age so frightfully well. And as for a reverential approach to age – why, yes. How old do you want us to go? We have wines that go back a century and sometimes more. Which would you like to try?

These are the port producers of the Douro Valley, and, to a lesser extent, the Madeira producers on a lonesome island hundreds of miles out into the Atlantic. It wouldn't be quite fair to say that the main memory of my first trip up the Douro to see the port producers was losing my Greek sandals during a waterskiing escapade fuelled by port cocktails. But we were scudding over the cool, dark Douro waters above the Pinhão dam, laughing and braying in a manner that would have had Evelyn Waugh squealing with delight as he plotted another novel about the foibles of the English partying classes. *Vile Bottles*, anyone? It was very, very English.

And yet this really isn't fair. The prosperity of Oporto and the Douro Valley was established by a very hard-working bunch of northern Europeans over hundreds of years. England and Portugal had been bound by pacts of friendship since the Treaty of Windsor in 1386 (it's still in force: Mrs Thatcher invoked it during the Falklands War in 1982), and wine had become an important part of the trade – in return for English cloth, but particularly for dried and salted codfish, which the Portuguese transformed into their national dish, *bacalhau*. They say that there is a *bacalhau* recipe for every day of the year. A year never seemed so long. But this relationship, helped along by lengthy spurts of hostility with France during the seventeenth and eighteenth centuries, caused the establishment of a tight group of merchants (some were Dutch or German, but most were English – very English) in Oporto at the mouth of the Douro River, all searching for a supply of good, beefy reds.

They found them in the Douro Valley, fierce, gut-wrenching blackstrap stuff, but not stable enough to ship to England without a serious dose of high-alcohol fortifying spirit. It must still have been pretty filthy, but in 1678 the abbot of a monastery at Lamego, his mind clearly on higher things, walloped his wine with fortifying spirit before it had finished fermenting. So suddenly he had a dark purple wine, fortified up to about 20 per cent, but only half-fermented. The high alcohol level had killed off the yeasts and so the wine was stable. And all that grape sugar the yeasts had been devouring was kept in the wine – as rich, heady, gorgeous sweetness. Sweet, irresistible perfumed fruit and head-swingeing alcohol levels. Modern port was born.

The Portuguese do drink port, but prefer a lighter, wood-aged, gentler style that they call tawny, after its colour. Chill that right down and it's a sophisticated delight at the end of a long, hot day. Port's job in northern Europe – Britain, Belgium, Holland, Denmark and Sweden – all points northwards, really – was quite different. Here its job was to warm everyone up under the cold, sullen northern skies. Making you uproariously drunk was an inevitable by-product. And the high alcohol means that you can send it all around the world without it turning to vinegar. As the British Empire expanded, port drinking went along too. Not only in the snowy vastness of Canada, but in the broiling reaches of South Africa, Australia and New Zealand. It was the type of wine that was quickly adopted in these countries as their own vineyards developed. No one considered whether it was the most suitable type of wine to make. But it was less deadly than rum, it could survive in the barrel when wine-making was extremely rudimentary – and life was hard. Really hard. Being sober didn't always seem a particularly attractive proposition. A tankard or two of local 'port' put paid to that.

Port is the easiest of the fortified wines to appreciate. It's rich, it's bursting with sweet fruit, pepper, spice and the warming effects of alcohol. As it ages, the wine becomes mellower, softer, lighter, but stays just as sweet. You can get all involved with the differences between the different styles of port, from expensive vintage to supermarket ruby and more delicate tawny – but the overpowering sweetness of the wine means you can always enjoy port without having to understand it. With sherry, under-standing is critical to enjoyment.

Enjoyment of port is an altogether simpler activity. Sweet fruit, alcoholic power, spice if you're lucky. But here are a couple of tasting notes. This one is for a crusted port from Fonseca: '*This is full of sweet loganberry fruit that's eternally punching above its weight, reaching out longingly toward blackberry . . . there's a nice spicy scent, there's an undertow of metallic minerality, and there's a slight bitter grip which is hardly about wine at all, and more about the pips between your teeth when you're eating raspberries.*' And this one is a ten-year-old tawny port from the Wine Society in Britain: '*The exact opposite of the vintage port style. There's less fire in the belly, more delicacy and charm and calm repose in the glance. The colour isn't bold, but is a mellow tawny, blushed with pink. The pink shows that a little of the youthful blackberry fruit and herb scent still lingers, but the wine is now full of brown beauty, autumnal, reflective, quince and medlar, sultana and date and the dry wood aroma of an Edwardian drawing room.*'

The top port producers sent almost all their produce over-seas, generally to the north, and had very little to do with the Portuguese or even Portugal in general. The producers of Portuguese table wines had to make do with the domestic market and Brazil (where, by the way, they speak a style of Portuguese that is much easier to understand than that of the mother country).

'Have some Madeira, m'dear'

Portugal has a second 'classic' fortified style: Madeira. Madeira's fortunes are similar to those of port. This is a strange, cramped, mountainous island 700 kilometres (435 miles) off the coast of Africa. The cliffs rise sheer out of the threatening ocean, and clouds veering between cheery white and thunderous black heap themselves onto the crag tops like pillars of smoke. The Portuguese navigators who first discovered Madeira in the fifteenth century saw the bank of black clouds billowing above the Atlantic and thought they had reached the edge of the world. It's not that bad nowadays, but you do feel you are an awful long way from anywhere.

The slightly strange style of this wine owes everything to trade. The island of Madeira was uninhabited until the Portuguese took it over, but its geographical position is crucial to its importance. In the days of sail, you couldn't just gaily sail off from Liverpool or Glasgow and head straight across to North America. The powerful westerly winds were full in your face. You'd have trouble even leaving dock. No, you had to tack down the coast of Europe and then the North African coast, waiting for a new wind – the trade wind from the north-east – to arrive. This would propel you across the Atlantic or ease you further down the African coast and on to India and the East Indies.

And where did this change in the wind occur? Around Madeira. So the island became a crucial re-stocking point, for food, but above all for wine. The natural Madeira wine is thin and acid, and rarely used to reach much more than 9 per cent in alcohol strength. This wasn't going to survive a long sea voyage, so bucketfuls of brandy were thrown into the Madeira barrels before they were taken on board. They would have still tasted pretty awful, but all that rolling around in the bilges of the ships seemed to transform the wine. The sour sharpness became a smoky-brown nutty depth of flavour, and the acidity became an appetising citrus-peel nip to freshen up the flavours. And the worse the conditions, the more sordid the ships' bilges, the more time the ship was stuck in the doldrums and the tropics as the sun raged down and sailors' thoughts turned to suicide, the better the Madeira wine turned out.

And as with the port producers, once word got around that there was trade to be done and money to be made, the British quickly established themselves as the island's main shippers. And the main market was the eastern seaboard of the new American nation.

There are now four main styles of Madeira, ranging from the dry Sercial through to the very sweet Malmsey via fairly dry Verdelho and fairly sweet Bual. Modern Madeira is artificially subjected to heat treatment – either by leaving barrels in hot rooms to bake gently, or by actually heating the wine in a vat. The objective is the same: to get that intriguing smoky tang into the wine, without which Madeira simply wouldn't be Madeira.

But what this treatment does is to sort of pasteurise the wine, to make it capable of ageing for generations and centuries, not just the odd year or two. I've never met anybody who's had a Madeira that was too old. I've had a 1797. It was a beast!

So never turn down the chance to go to a Madeira tasting. You'll never taste such old wine anywhere else. When the shippers start bringing out their vintage-dated stuff, don't expect anything from the twenty-first century. The wines from the 1970s and '60s are coming along nicely, slowly finding a way to harmonise such unlikely bedfellow flavours as quince and goldengage, Harrogate toffee and old baked sour lemon slices, walnuts and salt, beef tea and balsamic vinegar.

But the 1950s, '40s and '30s are tasting even better. And while you're at it, don't miss the 1908, or the 1897, the '74, '46 and the '22. My oldest tasting note is for a Terrantez 1795. My tasting note says … Oh no, where *is* my tasting note? Typical. The oldest wine I've ever tasted and I go and lose the tasting note. I'm such an idiot. Well, the 1822 tasted of sweet-sour fruit cake, mint and sweet tomato … but the 1795 … Damn. I can't believe I did that.

One more thing. If you visit a Madeira shipper, they will often ask when you were born. Don't be truthful. It's the only time you will ever want to add twenty years, because they will bring out a bottle of your birth year. '1815,' I said when they first asked me. 'No.' '1914?' 'No. Good try.' Ah well, it's one of the few benefits of getting older.

Here's a tasting note for a Henriques & Henriques fifteen-year-old Bual: '*Sweetness is a relative term here, since acidity always plays a role. Here the acidity is clear – slightly sour and chewy, like tamarind skin. Smokiness also plays its part, but not like a coal fire that won't draw properly; it's more like the fumes that hang around an old winery. And here they trail through a pageant of rich brown flavours: dates, raisins, old brown wood and leather, homemade jam tarts burned in the oven and a rich glycerine syrup of all the fruits that ever began to lose their bloom and turn brown in the still pantry of an Edwardian stately home.*' All this Edwardian stuff! Thank goodness we've had *Downton Abbey* to help the millennials know what I'm talking about.

What is Mateus Rosé?

And that's it for Portugal. Or is it? What that's insistent whisper in my ear. Mum! 'Yes, Mummy, what?' She's right. What is Portugal's most famous wine? It's slightly sweet, slightly fizzy, and it's pink. Mateus Rosé, or Lancers if you live in the USA. OK. Quickly. The reason my mother was such a fan is that when my parents got demobbed at the end of the Second World

War, these two newlyweds went to a smart basement club near Piccadilly called the Bag o' Nails. My father, feeling flush for the first time in his life with his army payoff, ordered Champagne. 'Ooh, no, sir,' said the maître d'. 'No one drinks Champagne any more. Everyone is drinking ... this.' And like a magician flourishing a white rabbit, he lovingly presented them with a bottle of slightly sweet sparkling pink wine. From Portugal. Mateus. For which he charged them rather more than the price of the house Champagne.

Trying to be fair to the maître d', and feeling a bit sorry for my poor old dad – well, he had been away in the jungle for rather a long time, so I suspect his bullshit detector wasn't in full working order – it is *just* possible that Mateus was the coolest wine on the block in the late 1940s. The brand had only been invented in 1942 as a way of clearing the stocks of unsold black grapes in an area next to Vinho Verde and the Douro Valley. No one expected it to be such a success, but it became Portugal's most famous wine, in its dumpy flask with an image of a lovely Portuguese palace on the label.

Ah yes. The Palace of Mateus. Well, the owner of that certainly didn't expect Mateus Rosé to be a world-beater. When the man behind the brand asked if he could use an image of the palace on the label, he offered either a lump sum or a royalty of fifty cents on every bottle sold. The owner took the lump sum. You can visit the Mateus palace at Vila Real, and if you ever wonder what that wailing sound is, it will be the owner beating his head against the wall and moaning, 'Why didn't I take the royalty?'

VENEZUELA

COLOMBIA

ECUADOR

South Pacific Ocean

PERU

Lima ■

Amazon

BRAZIL

North Atlantic Ocean

Recife ●

BOLIVIA
La Paz ●

■ Brasilia

7

PARAGUAY

Rio de Janeiro ●

CHILE

Atacama Desert

Andes

ARGENTINA

6

São Paulo ●

N

| 0 | 1000 | 2000 km |

| 0 | 500 | 1000 miles |

3
5
2
4

Valparaíso ●
Santiago ■

Mendoza ●

Buenos Aires ■

1

URUGUAY

Concepción ●

Montevideo ●

Key

Main vineyard areas

See also
Map of Chile page 296
Map of Argentina page 305

Neuquen ●

River Plate

South Atlantic Ocean

Chiloé Is.

1	Canelones
2	Maldonado
3	Campanha
4	Serra do Sudeste
5	Serra Gaúcha
6	Planalto Catarinense
7	Vale do São Francisco

Cape Horn

South America

The original New World

I wouldn't be surprised if your answer to my question, 'What was the first red wine that you really enjoyed?' is Chilean Merlot or Argentine Malbec. A generation ago it might have been Australian Shiraz or perhaps Spanish Rioja. Not now. Chile and Argentina have made a phenomenal reputation for their red wines in super-quick time. But if you think these two countries are similar just because they're next to each other – think again. France and Germany are next to each other. No one accuses them of being remotely similar.

Chile is a long thin country wedged between the Pacific Ocean and the soaring Andes, with the maritime influences always tempering conditions. Argentina is a vast, broad country whose Andean peaks have created a virtual desert below their eastern foothills. Yet this is where most of the vineyards are. The only way you can cool them down is to head further and further up the mountain slopes. Chile has made a remarkably successful transition from dictatorship to democracy. Argentina is continually at risk of political and financial upheaval as she struggles against an authoritarian Peronist recent past that refuses to go away.

There aren't that many Chileans, and they don't drink masses of wine. Their society was formed on rather formal northern Spanish principles, with the useful addition of French wine expertise in the nineteenth century. Chile quickly became South America's leading exporter of wine made to a high standard of stability. There are far more Argentines, and they were a truly thirsty lot. And most of them came from Italy. Italians were famously good at growing things – vines included – but when it came to making wine, they weren't concerned much with quality, or modernisation or export. Make it red, make it rough, make it available.

And one more thing: the Argentines had a lot more fun. They danced and laughed and sang while their politics and their economy went up the Swanee. The Chileans looked on smugly and disapprovingly from their secure side of the Andes, secretly wishing they'd invented the tango.

World-beating wines from Chile

If someone had described you as boring fifteen years ago, what would you have done? Become less boring, disregarded the barb, fought back? You'd have dealt with it. The one thing you wouldn't be doing is still going on about it now. The longer you go on about it, the more you remind people of the criticism in the first place; in particular, people who thought you were absolutely fine.

Chile was called boring by Tim Atkin, a top British wine writer, fifteen years ago. In fact, he said Chile was the Volvo of wine. I'd always rather wanted a Volvo.

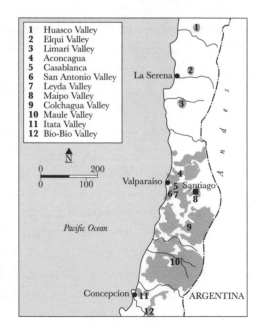

1	Huasco Valley
2	Elqui Valley
3	Limarí Valley
4	Aconcagua
5	Casablanca
6	San Antonio Valley
7	Leyda Valley
8	Maipo Valley
9	Colchagua Valley
10	Maule Valley
11	Itata Valley
12	Bío-Bío Valley

Just the kind of car to cement my position in the upper-middle-class professional hierarchy. But, not surprisingly, I never got myself one. You'd have thought 'Volvo' was a bit of a compliment. And, to be honest, if Chile had been a bit more nimble-footed, she could have spun it to sound positive. Wasn't there a seriously cool Volvo sports, for a start? There are a lot of cars in the world you don't want to be compared to. Super-reliable, high-quality Volvo isn't one of them. But somehow, fifteen years later, Chile's remarkable achievement in providing a veritable flood of nicely flavoured, well-priced wines to fuel the Wine Revolution that has enabled so many northern hemisphere countries to happily and affordably embrace a wine culture is still derided. And the Chileans are still referring to the Volvo incident.

The fact that Chile is making world-beating wines of fantastic, memorable personality that cost a third as much as similar wines would from European countries, from California, or even from Argentina, is not regarded as a wonderful thing we should give thanks for, but as some kind of national failing. I've got more pleasure from Chilean wines, at prices that I can afford, than from wines of almost any other country. I *love* them for that. But on recent trips to the USA and Asia, I found that this very affordability was persuading critics and sommeliers to describe them as lacking prestige, lacking stature, as though price and puffed-up self-importance were the only things that mattered, when the flavour in the glass was telling me the exact opposite.

But look back thirty years. Look at the rest of South America, its economic seesaws, its political fragility and social chaos. Look at where not being boring has led such countries as Venezuela and Brazil and Argentina. Honestly, being boring isn't always such a bad idea. Democracy can be boring, elections that pass off without gunfire and street riots and bloodshed can be boring. But when the Chinese say, 'May you live in interesting times,' they're not wishing you well, they're telling you to watch your step.

I first visited Chile in August 1989. I was there for politics, not for wine. General Pinochet looked as though he would hand back power to the Chilean parliament without bloodshed, obeying the will of the people. I had just been in South Africa as the movement to end apartheid caught fire. The whole of eastern Europe was in a ferment as the Berlin Wall and the Soviet Empire tottered. I leapt at the chance to visit Chile, and decided to take in some winery visits, too. Well, just as South Africa had missed out on the inspiring, liberating transformation of the world of wine because of its pariah status in world politics, Chile was much the same. No one was keen on establishing good relations with General Pinochet, who was seen as a military dictator. No one visited Chile, and the Chileans returned the compliment. The 1970s and '80s were when the modern world of wine was born. But not in Chile.

As one wine producer told me then, 'We are a very small wine industry – only ten or eleven wineries.' He didn't mean Chile wasn't producing much wine, he meant the industry was dominated by a small clique of rich and powerful players. There was a status quo they didn't want disturbed. Santa Rita, an important wine producer, also produced 97 per cent of Chile's glass, controlled 50 per cent of Chile's shipping and operated her largest steel foundry. Valdivieso, among a lot of other things, owned a bank in Brazil. 'We give our workers a pay rise of 9 per cent every Friday,' the boss said. At that time inflation in Chile was 26 per cent. It was 850 per cent in Argentina, 1200 per cent in Brazil and 1600 per cent in Peru. Suddenly a desire to be stable and boring doesn't sound so bad. Just keep doing more of the same.

But what about stainless steel and new oak barrels? We are talking the wine innovations of the 1970s and '80s here? What's wrong with old redwood vats? Well, they're old, they're dirty and they stink. So? In all the cellars I visited there was the same smell, like a mixture of smoky bitumen, sour gherkins and sweet brown sherry. At Concha y Toro I met an ancient retired cooper. He laughed when I asked about the wooden vats. He said they were old when he started work there in 1914! People like Miguel Torres from Spain were trying to modernise the wineries, but the old guard still resisted. A new winemaker turned up at Cousiño Macul, took one sniff at the mouldy old vats and said, 'We've got to throw them all out.' 'Why?' said the owner. 'They've been perfectly good for ninety-two years.'

Well, what about the vineyards? Chile is famous for having arguably the world's healthiest vineyards and they have never been struck by phylloxera. They were in good nick. Up to a point. They had lots of Sauvignon Blanc. Except it wasn't Sauvignon, it was a far less exciting variety called Sauvignonasse, or Tocai Friulano. So they had loads of Merlot. Except they didn't. Most of it turned out to be an obscure Bordeaux variety called Carmenère. The Los Vascos winery had been happily selling Riesling for thirty years. They weren't too pleased when a visiting expert told them it was Chardonnay.

And yet it was Chile that did finally lead the revolution in South American wine. She did possess vast vineyards, especially in her Central Valley, a fertile, sunny, well-watered expanse that was a paradise for vines. Chile had been famous for high-quality, low-cost wine since the seventeenth century. In those days this was regarded as a good thing, not a negative. And it was just so easy to ripen enormous crops of fruit for little cost, so you couldn't really blame that tight-knit bunch of plutocrats who controlled Chilean wine for thinking that the future was in exporting large volumes of simple, low-cost wine to any market with a hard currency to pay in. With that in mind, modern equipment, stainless steel refrigeration, efficient filters, new wooden barrels did gradually appear during the 1990s and, to be honest, Chile became the impecunious wine-drinkers' best friend.

So, perhaps a little unambitious? Well, in terms of fascinating flavours, astonishing flavours, yes – most of those came later. But in terms of setting up a big, efficient modern wine industry, absolutely not. And of that plutocratic bunch that used to rule Chilean wine – well, they're still there, they are still immensely powerful. But two things. First, they have been remarkably positive in encouraging new wine styles, in developing new wine areas and in pushing Chilean wine boundaries as far north and south as it is possible to go. Many of Chile's most gorgeous wines have come from these big producers. And second, human nature being what it is, there has been a reaction – belated but definite – as those without money and influence have begun to make their presence felt. 'The flowers in the pavement' are what the Chileans call them. If you don't cull and kill the flowers in the pavement, they quickly spread. People are positively fertilising these flowers. They've got titles like the Movement of Independent Vintners, the Vignadores de Carignan (Carignan Growers) and Chanchos Deslenguados (Outspoken Pigs), and they are the ginger group, the spur, the radical alternative that will finally persuade critics and experts to give Chile the credit she is due.

You can see it happening already, and those critics who continue to describe Chile as boring should enquire a bit more closely. Some of the world's most remarkable, most extreme, most ambitious vineyard projects are taking place in this 'dull' old country. Chile is 4300 kilometres (2670 miles) long; not long ago you could reasonably state that vines grew for a few hundred of those miles, most of them just to the south of Santiago. Now you can find vineyards to the north and south along almost 2600 kilometres (1600 miles) and there are plans afoot for an even greater spread, from the drizzly, cool Patagonian south to the Atacama Desert, the world's driest place, in the north.

And I'm not joking when I say it's dry. On my first trip to the Atacama, I couldn't sleep at night. I kept waking up with my throat seizing up. I tried wine tasting the next day and I couldn't smell anything. Luckily I had got one of those mineral water sprays that smart hotels sometimes leave hanging around for you to 'borrow'. I had to squirt water up my nose every half an hour to moisten my nasal cavity. Otherwise I couldn't tell Cabernet from a cup of tea.

The most extreme vineyards so far – though madder ventures are planned – are the Tara vineyards in the Atacama's Huasco Valley. (And, by the way, this is a project run not by hare-brained revolutionaries, but by Ventisquero, one of the band of plutocrats.) It hasn't rained in the Huasco Valley for fifty years. Hey, they reckon that in some parts of the Atacama it has *never* rained. Not only that, but the soil is so salty you can see the giant crystals glistening beneath the vines. And the Huasco River? That's salty, too. But it's the only water you've got for irrigation. Vines really don't like salt. Bad luck. You have to use it. Small doses of this brine are worse than big doses – they coat the roots in salt and the vine simply withers away. So you have to literally flood the vines every few weeks with this super-salty water, which briefly washes off the salts, gives the roots a breather, and then, back comes the salt.

Does this really sound like the activity of a bunch of dullards? No one needs to do this. Chile is full of easier places to grow vines, but will they give you a Sauvignon Blanc so nervy and taut that its pithy, leathery grapefruit zest flavours streaked with graphite make you shiver? Or a Syrah with a shockingly intense taste of damson, lime, blackberry and liquorice bristling with the menthol aromas of Vicks VapoRub? That's Tara for you.

So, maybe the desert really is a bit extreme. But even the producers in the easy, fertile areas are keen to start taking risks. The big unknown is how far up the Andes you can plant vines, searching for cool, extreme conditions yet avoiding crippling frosts and storms. So far, less than 0.5 per cent of Chile's vines are creeping up those mountain slopes, though wineries like De Martino, with their Alcohuaz vineyard 2200 metres (7218 feet) up in the Elqui Valley are leading the charge heavenward. But look to the west of Chile's long, lissom form. The Pacific Ocean is Chile's western frontier. And for those of us Europeans who think of the Pacific as a delightful warm, holiday-making kind

of sea, try taking a swim in Chile. I was amazed one morning as
I looked out on a pristine beach, with an inviting aquamarine sea
shimmering beyond. But no one was on the beach. There were
no swimmers. Strange. Still, that didn't put me off. I stripped
down and bounded into the waves. It was probably twenty seconds before I thought, I can't feel my toes. It was probably thirty
seconds before I started to worry about my fingers. I staggered
out, having learnt a very good lesson.

The Pacific off Chile is icy. There is a freezing current that
runs up from the Antarctic called the Humboldt, and it's the
key to most of the exciting new wine regions in Chile. Icy
air sits on the water's surface. As inland Chile warms up each
day – and the summers are mostly very sunny – this icy air is
drawn inland, cooling down every field and vineyard in its
wake. The Central Valley doesn't get much of this ocean effect,
but Limarí, up toward the Atacama Desert, is proving to be a
fabulous area for Chardonnay as the breezes ripple through its
vineyards. Aconcagua, just north of Santiago, was known as a
warm inland region for reds, but its most exciting wines are
now coming from out toward the sea. Casablanca, to the west
of Santiago, was Chile's first cool-climate zone, but San Antonio
and Leyda, where the vines can see the ocean and the wind is
brisk and cold, are giving more exciting results. And Colchagua
literally boils around its main town of Santa Cruz, which is why
the wineries are spreading their wings westward – again, out
to the ocean where the temperature tumbles. And the result is
crisp, aromatic Sauvignons, Chardonnays, Pinot Noirs, Merlots
and Syrahs, unlike anything Chile has produced before.

This is all exciting. And it's all new. But there is another
bright future in Chile: the past. The modern Chilean wine
industry was created in the Central Valley and in Maipo, close
to Santiago. But until about 1860, the engine room of Chilean
wine was further south, in Maule and Itata. And the grapes
they used weren't the modern stars like Cabernet or Sauvignon,
they were old-time red varieties such as Carignan or Cinsault,

dismissed as junk by the experts, or País, the original variety brought over by the Spanish missionaries and, in fact, called Mission in places like the USA, and completely rejected as rubbish by those experts. All over the world, old-vine Carignan and Cinsault are now garnering long-overdue respect. But País is another matter. Good wine from País? Really? Why is it hundreds of years since anybody tried?

Well, they're trying now. And so they should. In Chile, País is the second most planted grape variety. And since no one is exactly replanting País, the vines are mostly old, and mostly in the forgotten south, the border land where settlers battled, and frequently lost, against the local Mapuche people. (Who are still there. They didn't surrender in the last big battle against the Chilean government in 1883, and they still haven't.)

Maule is the biggest of these southern areas, and is an absolute delight after the rather agro-industrial vineyard sprawl of the Central Valley. Maule has more vines than any other region of Chile, yet it's mostly farmed by smallholders and its lonely valleys and slopes are thinly populated and dotted with small plots of vines. In Chile, the land of large vineyards and large corporate wineries, this is so refreshing. But the ruined farm buildings and weed-choked fields show that life was pretty tough down here while everybody was crying out for Chardonnay and Merlot at a keen price. That's not what Maule can do. Most of the País that was made into wine turned up in extremely cheap rosé – not surprising when some growers were being paid as little as five cents a kilo for their grapes.

It's all changing. Maule's País and its Carignan are being scrabbled for, particularly in Cauquenes, where Miguel Torres rescued some ancient Carignan vines and began making stunning rocky reds from them. There's now a whole crowd, led by the banner-waving Vignadores de Carignan, making fabulously tasty reds from this old, unfairly despised variety.

Itata is that bit further south, that bit older, that bit wetter – all things that counted against it a mere generation ago, but as evidence of global warming builds, Itata looks more and more attractive. Again there's País, as well as Cinsault often a century old, and these both make utterly delicious, fresh, rather scented unoaked reds that resemble Beaujolais as much as anything, and are a mouthwatering godsend in this over-oaked wine world of ours. And talking of unoaked, the innovative De Martino make Cinsault and a white Muscat in clay jars called *tinajas*. Pure and delightful, rubbed with the cold scent of stones. Or is it the clay from the *tinajas*?

And you can keep going south. The Bío Bío Valley is colder and wetter still. Riesling, Gewürztraminer and Pinot Noir seem to love it. I've had thrillingly sharp and fruity Sauvignons and Syrahs from way down toward Puerto Montt, a lakes-and-volcanoes resort that you think must be too cold. Obviously not. There's a Pinot Noir now coming from way further south, at Chile Chico in Chilean Patagonia – that's at 46° South. The latest travellers' tales I've heard have got wine producers nosing about out on the island of Chiloé, even further south, whose chief claim to fame is that it might be where the original potato comes from. I bought a bag of Chiloé potatoes from a peasant lady in Puerto Montt's market and smuggled them back to England, where I planted them out. Total failure, all blighted by the next season. If Britain's potato crop is attacked by a new and virulent form of blight, you know who to blame.

Going higher and higher in Argentina

April 1982 wasn't a very good time to launch a new Argentine wine brand on to the British market. But that's what my friend James Rogers did with his 'Andean' range. James was always ahead of any fashions. He looked at Argentina with its extensive, sprawling vineyards and slumbering, rusty wineries crying out for a bit of modern thinking, and saw it as an irresistible source of cheap, ripe, mouth-filling wines to start a New World wine revolution. So he brought in containerloads of red and white wine, convinced that he was going to transform the British wine scene.

And then Argentina invaded the Falkland Islands. I remember it well. I was playing General Perón, Argentina's most famous dictator, in the musical *Evita* at the time. James rather mournfully wondered if I might help him promote his Andean wines in my official capacity. One British regiment asked if I would come down to Portsmouth to cheer

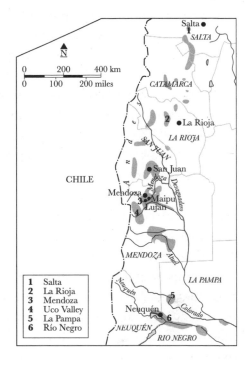

0 200 400 km
0 100 200 miles

1 Salta
2 La Rioja
3 Mendoza
4 Uco Valley
5 La Pampa
6 Río Negro

their ship off in my full Perón regalia. *Evita*'s producer said he knew there was no such thing as bad publicity, but perhaps this was a goosestep too far. It was a bit of a shame. The British and the Argentines had always got on well. Buenos Aires was full of Anglos with their own schools and newspapers. The future King Edward VIII, when Prince of Wales, had to be discreetly corrected when he said he wouldn't mind if Britain lost her Empire, so long as she didn't lose Argentina!

Pretty much the entire shipment of James's Andean wine ended up clogging the drains of south London. You couldn't give it away. And, actually, it wasn't terribly good. The white was a big, yellow, curiously perfumed old thing, lots of flavour, but about as fresh as a football full back after ninety minutes on the pitch. The red wine was a mighty mouthful – rich, ripe, strangely grapey and not bad for a midwinter gut-warmer, but tasting just a bit as if they'd briefly baked the grapes before sending them off to be transformed into this bruiser of a drink.

A few years later the Australians arrived with their Cabernets and Shirazes, juicy and gorgeous. *That* was the New World revolution Britain had waited for. This wasn't.

That 'baked' character, the lack of freshness, the rather tired texture, the flavours that made you wonder exactly which domestic animal it was that the stuff reminded you of – that wasn't just 1980s Argentina. It was the 1990s too. Argentina produced an awful lot of wine – she used to be the fourth-largest producer in the world – and was one of the world's biggest drinkers too – in the 1970s the Argentines knocked back about ninety litres a year each. I'm not sure how they afforded it as inflation was regularly over 100 per cent in the 1970s and in the 1980s touched 1000 per cent!

But this might explain why Argentina seemed neither to have the will nor the finance to modernise her vineyards and wineries. Political uncertainty, inflation, economic collapse – I must admit, I tasted the wines dutifully, but it wasn't until 1998 that I felt any compunction to pay a visit. I didn't choose well. This was the wettest vintage in living memory. Normally in Mendoza, the centre of the Argentine wine world, you can't escape the Andes. At dawn they glow cherry pink above the city. By lunchtime they gleam white as Marilyn Monroe's teeth above the hum and the heat of the streets; and by evening the candy-floss clouds seem soldered together with the snow to form streams of molten silver coursing down the forbidding mountain slopes. I didn't see any of that. I'm not sure I saw the Andes at all as I traipsed from sopping vineyard to dripping winery, tasting wines that were way behind the bright, lively wines that Chile was starting to offer.

It was all about to change. And in a hurry. Argentina has sprinted to make up for lost time. Maybe the sons and daughters look back on their winemaker parents' era with horror yet realise that the economic chaos and political uncertainty could return at any time, and so the modern Argentina of wine is a country in a rush. New wineries sprout in the side valleys of the Andes, on the coast at Buenos Aires and in the far south. Winemaking experiments seem almost everyday as yet another concrete egg or amphora greets you in yet another winery committed to organic or biodynamic principles. And if you can judge the health of a wine culture by the coolness of the dudes, Argentina seems to have more than its fair share of blazing-eyed, passionate, über-cool dudes, with wines as expertly sculpted as their beards.

So let's take a look at what the dudesters are dealing with. For nearly all of Argentina's top wine, it's up to what the Andes will give you, and how you can wheedle just a bit more out of them than nature thinks wise – or natural. If you had to say what really makes these new Argentine wine people tick, it's that they have to try harder. They know it. And they're the first generation that revels in it. Because, while a lot of Chile is a sort of easy-going paradise for vines and wine, none of Argentina is like that.

Mendoza is the major city of Argentina's west, tucked in beneath the highest peaks of the Andes. Seventy per cent of the country's wines come from the Mendoza region. And yet it is a desert. The soil is so sandy you can run it through your fingers, and it would remain desert if it weren't for four mighty rivers that tumble and surge out of the Andes, gorged with melted snow. Yet east of Mendoza city limits, the mighty Mendoza River has barely a trickle of water left in its parched channels. Every litre has been taken to make this desert bloom. Even so, only 3 per cent of Mendoza province is cultivated. But you need the mountains. A lot of Mendoza is flat and it's hot. That 'baked' taste I used to know? You can still find it here, and the further east you go away from the mountains you more you find it. You must cleave to the mountains, or at the very least the slopes that rise up toward them.

Although wine grapes are grown in more than half of Argentina's twenty-four provinces there are three areas that dominate quality and make wines with a truly Argentine flair: the north, reaching high into the Andes toward Bolivia; the centre, around Mendoza (although a lot of grapes are grown further north at San Juan, whose Syrahs are reassuringly good, and La Rioja); and Patagonia, the last frontier on the way to the South Pole. But if you want to experience Argentina at its most memorable you need to get north – to Cafayate and to Colomé, to vineyards closer to the moon than anywhere else on earth.

Getting there isn't easy. A two-and-a-half-hour flight from Buenos Aires to Salta and then a four-hour drive up through the Rios de las Condias Valley is one way. If you want to see what a soaring condor looks like from above, this teetering mountain highway should give you a glimpse. On my first visit I went by air from Mendoza. When someone offers you the use of a private plane you sort of expect luxury. Best to check beforehand. I turned up just after dawn at Mendoza's 'other' airport – or rather, airstrip – weed-strewn, potholed, wind-blown, one rickety old two-seater plane parked by a shed and a pack of stray dogs sniffing and yelping as though I was the only human they had seen for quite some time. I might well have been. Mario finally arrived, not exactly looking like a luxury air chauffeur – a cap and a jacket might have given me more confidence. And, no ... not that old bone-shaker by the shed. But in we clambered. The tiny cockpit stank of gasoline as the engine spluttered into life. There were storm clouds to the west, to the east and to the south. There was a gap to the north, thank goodness. That's our route, is it? Mario's not sure. He's never flown north before. Great. Just great.

I don't feel much better as I notice he's reading the map as he flies. The map's upside down. So I take it and do a reasonable Boy Scout job of orienteering, peering through the propeller blades. Bump by bump we flittered north, like a housefly dwarfed by purple brooding storm clouds spitting with malice. And we skidded onto an airstrip, seemingly the right one, where I transferred to a six-seater plane. With two pilots. Why? Well, it's more of the same – we're only halfway there. We've got to go much higher into the mountains. Yes, but why two pilots? Partly so that one can constantly seek a gap between the clouds that the second can dart through at high speed. And partly to land the plane. As we came down into Cafayate we seemed to accelerate to the speed of a mighty Airbus. Both the pilots were straining back into their seats, tugging at the controls, as I coldly sweated the rest of my life away. And we tore into the airstrip like a boy racer, shuddering to a halt as the blacktop faded away into sand. I got out with shaking legs, thinking that we had had a brush with death. But no, that is why there were two pilots. At this altitude – approaching 2000 metres (6500 feet), with its thin air – you had to attack the runway as you landed or the plane would fall out of the sky. A bit much for one pair of arms to handle. Talk of needing my first drink of the day.

Well, I'd come to the right place for that. Argentina has a native grape called the Torrontes which grows better in the far north than anywhere else, and has a magically refreshing flavour of juicy pear flesh, apple blossom and that pale purple-violet soap of distant memory. It's the altitude that makes the difference. We're over 1700 metres (5577 feet) at the lowest point, and quickly climb to over 2000 metres (6500 feet). This means relentless sun, up to 350 days a year; extreme ultraviolet penetration dramatically affecting the skins of the grape and this skin is what contains the grape's aroma; and enormous fluctuations of temperature between a searing daytime and an icy night – just what grapes need to retain their fresh acidity under cloudless skies. Perfect for Torrontes.

But I had further to travel – higher, wilder, emptier. Route 40 is the only way north. The road quickly dwindles into a sandy, twisty broad track through cherry-red, knobbly cliffs, past razor-sharp layers of pink gingerbread rocks until, two punctures later, we get to Colomé. This estate used to be the heart of a five-million-hectare spread and even now extends to 39,000 hectares (96,000 acres), though its chief claim to fame is phenomenally concentrated red Malbec-based wines from more like 100 hectares (250 acres) of vines, grown at up to 2600 metres (8500 feet), and a tiny, symbolic harvest of grapes like Malbec, Pinot Noir and Sauvignon Blanc from the Altura Maxima vineyard, at 3111 metres (10,207 feet), which is – depending on what may or may not transpire in rival height-hunters Chile and Bolivia – the highest producing vineyard on the planet. But it is extreme. In 2011 they held a 'no frost' party up there, because it was the first time they didn't get hammered by frost. Maybe that's why their vineyard manager comes from Québec.

Mendoza can't match this drama, but it can match and surpass the enthusiasm and obsessive desire to explore and improve all its wines, but above all its Malbec, as it sets out its stall to have Mendoza Malbec judged on the same level as Napa Valley Cabernet, Barossa Valley Shiraz, Bordeaux, Barolo or Ribera del Duero. Mendoza isn't just Mendoza any more. There are all kinds of sub-divisions which are being sought out or rediscovered, defined or redefined, at remarkable speed. But it has been done before. Mendoza has been growing grapes ever since the sixteenth century, but when your main market of Buenos Aires is forty-five days away through blinding heat on the back of a donkey, your wine probably sloshing about in an old pigskin, you don't worry too much about details.

This all changed in 1885 when the railway reached Mendoza. The trains brought waves of immigrants – the governor used to greet the travellers in Italian; everyone who understood was welcomed off the train, the rest were left to soldier on to San Juan. The governor knew that the Italians could make anything grow anywhere, and that's what they did in this mountain-irrigated desert. Most vines were planted for easy ripening and big volumes, but the high, cool valley of the Uco, which clambers up into the Andes to the south-west of Mendoza City, did have vines a hundred years ago. And it did make wine. They used to call Uco wine 'Expedition Wine', the wine to take on the train for the journey to Buenos Aires.

Well, that's where you feel the excitement nowadays. On my first visit I toiled up to an isolated vineyard in Los Arboles, where

I tasted minerally, tingling Chardonnay, completely unlike anything else in Argentina, and crisp, scented red from the Bonarda
grape. The vineyard expert fretted about water supply, about
frosts, and about wildlife eating his crop, but I could see his eyes
gleam with excitement. If he could find a way to ripen and keep
a crop, this isolated patch of vines hugging the mountain slopes
would blaze a trail for Argentina. And it did. But Los Arboles
is not alone any more. The Uco Valley has been scoured by the
young and ambitious and bearded. As one of them said to me
this year, 'The world is saturated with fat and sweet wines. If you
overdo the ripeness and the extraction and the oak you can't taste
what the wine is or where it's from.' Tasting exactly where the
wine is from has become the mission for this Uco brigade. On
my last visit, I started in the highest and most marginal yet most
challenging areas of El Peral and Gualtallary – if you haven't seen
those names on the labels of fresh, tingling, totally untraditional
Argentine reds and whites yet, you will soon – with Sebastian
Zuccardi, one of Argentina's praetorian guard of brilliant hipsters. We stood on the high plateau of Gualtallary, we scrambled
down into the dip below, checking out the different outcrops
of stones, discussing which varieties would work best – from
Sauvignon and Riesling all the way to the mighty Cabernets
and Malbecs. We felt the flatter, more fertile soils slither under
our feet as the river valley teased us, but we looked back to the
difficult stuff, the challenging, rocky, infertile stuff that would
change the world's view of Argentine wine, and he pointed out
how as you got nearer the Andes the slopes bent eastwards and
also gently south. 'Look,' he said, 'the soil here is eighty per
cent stones. In thirty metres it's all rich, fertile soil, and in thirty
metres more it's eighty per cent stones again. In somewhere like
Burgundy or Barolo they would have mapped all the changes out
long ago.' In the Uco, in just a single generation, that's exactly
what Sebastian and his peers are setting out to do.

   This is just one tiny corner of the Uco. I repeated this all the
way to Altamira in the valley's south, where the Andes suddenly

subside and the vines trail away. And then I tasted the wines. Each tiny sub-zone is different, as the altitude, the differing rock and stone and aspect all cut in, here on the marginal uplands of the Andes. This is where Argentina and the Argentines will make their mark in the world of the great wines of tomorrow.

And you should also check out the south. It doesn't possess the sense of urgency and ambition that is enveloping Mendoza and its Uco Valley, but look at the map. You're heading down to Patagonia, to the wild, windswept wastes of the far south that end in the brutal conditions of Cape Horn at the very bottom of the Americas. There's not that much wine made down here, but there's enough to travel for, including a splash made in desert-like La Pampa and the possibilities of future glory in Chubut at 45°S. And if you take the plane down to Neuquén, you can see that this isn't friendly country for the vine. It's not really friendly country for anything human, were it not for one gushing, gurgling resource – the dark, clean, cool Rio Negro, the Black River, which powers its way eastward from the Andes and leaves in its wake a deep sunken valley just crying out to be irrigated. From the city of Neuquén eastward and just a little to the west, this is a windy but sunny paradise for fruit watered by the great river. With the exception of some remarkable old vines – Malbec from Noemía and old vine Pinot Noir from Chacra – the wines don't have the excitement of those of western Mendoza. But stand with me on the south ridge above the river, and look south. That stony, inhospitable terrain stretching to Cape Horn is Patagonia in its natural state. Turn north and gaze at this verdant market garden, the dark green fruit trees packed tight up against the vineyards, the poplars swaying elegantly as they divert the chill winds upwards and away. The evening sun drops low, the heat drains from the air up on this ridge. Would you head further south, or would you sink back into the reassuring embrace of the Black River Valley? I see the sunset shimmering over a dam below. The water is thick and brilliant as mercury streaked with warm mandarin gold, and that's where I go.

Other finds in South America

When you think of the thrilling stuff that's coming out of Chile and Argentina nowadays, and you look at the vastness of the rest of South America, this should be a fertile hunting ground for loads more memorable mouthfuls. It isn't. Why? Well, latitude, mainly. South America tapers off southward and Chile and Argentina own whatever land there is. There's an awful lot that's too cold and windy and wet as the continent peters out at about 55° South, heading for Antarctica. And by the time Chile and Argentina sign off their most extreme, northerly vineyards, you're getting perilously close to the Tropic of Capricorn. That's 25° South. The fatter and broader South America gets heading north, the more unsuitable the conditions become. It's just too hot north of the Tropic of Capricorn. Chile is a desert by this latitude – you can hardly breathe half the time, it's so hot and dry. Argentina has raw and savage Andean peaks, beautiful to gaze at from a distance as the condors glide through fairy rings of bright white cloud and the snow dust glitters, but brutal and unforgiving close up. And most of the rest of South America is tropical jungle above and below the Equator. The whole point about rainforest is that it is wet, all the time! And the sun can't get through the tree canopy. You're not even going to think about growing grapevines there. Chile does have a couple of desert vineyards in the Atacama Desert. Argentina does have one brilliant property high up and north toward Bolivia, which makes a fair bit of exciting wine as well as token amounts from a vineyard planted above 3000 metres (10,000 feet) solely to be able to claim 'top o' the world, ma' status – the highest vines on the planet. But when you plant a vineyard in that state of mind, don't expect rival prospectors to be far behind. Chile already thinks she can better the claim.

And yet there are little droplets of wine activity elsewhere, in the most unlikely places. There's one chunk of land, down in the south-east, at the bottom of Brazil and enveloping little

Uruguay, that might just be on the cusp of making some very good wine indeed, good enough to join the giants Chile and Argentina.

But let's look at the minnows first. Peru is a one-time orca reduced to a tiddler. The first of the South American countries to get the Spanish colonial treatment from Francisco Pizarro, Peru established the original South American vineyards and dominated production for a couple of centuries. I had my first Peruvian wines in the 1980s, from an area called Ica near Pisco. The red was OK. The white wasn't. I've been waiting ever since for an improved offer. There are now some more mountainous, inland vineyards and I'm still waiting for their offerings, too.

Colombia, on the other hand, was never very important as a wine producer, and still isn't, while Ecuador was even less significant, and it's equatorial – yet one of my biggest surprises of 2016 was an entirely delightful Chardonnay called Dos Hemisferios made by an entirely delightful woman – in Ecuador! Just a quarter of an hour from the beach, south of Guayaquil, the country's main port. Well, well. I can't say I've had such luck with Venezuela or Bolivia – which, unsurprisingly, boasts the highest average altitude for any country's vineyards at 2712 metres (8900 feet). They give you altitude sickness pills up there before you start a wine tasting. And I do know someone who has survived Paraguayan wine. Well, I'm not sure I do, actually. I know someone who knew someone who had survived Paraguayan wine. Which brings us mercifully back to the real world of Uruguay and Brazil.

Softening the Tannat in Uruguay

Uruguay didn't seem all that promising, to be honest. A tiny blob of land jutting out into the stormy, uninviting South Atlantic, its only fame seemed to be that for years they had an ex-guerilla president who lived in a shack and drove an old VW Beetle as an example of how he thought politicians should live. And he legalised marijuana. And the only wine they had any reputation for was a grumpy, grizzly old red made from the Tannat grape. The Tannat makes some of the most obdurate, impenetrable reds of France at Madiran, down in the south-west of the country, and I used to think, poor old Uruguay, other New World countries get lucky with Cabernet, or Shiraz, Chardonnay or Sauvignon – and you get stuck with this beast.

So I went there. Again, my visit didn't start well. I travelled over from Buenos Aires on the ferry in the morning. The night before, the Argentine peso had collapsed. In my hotel, the staff were telling us visitors not to go out in the street. But I thought, I played General Perón in *Evita*. I want to go and see the Casa Rosada Palace where Eva Perón used to address the massed hordes of her people from the balcony, exhorting them not to cry. The concierge shook his head and warned me not to take my wallet, but out I went. Into the totally deserted, shadowy, sullen streets. I could vaguely pick up a muffled roar – or was it a moan? – and I headed for it, walking in the centre of these empty streets, not at all sure what the dark alleys might contain. And I passed big bank buildings. Brinks–Mat armoured vans were backed up to the doors. Men with guns stood guard and didn't invite conversation. The Argentines were loading their gold and their dollars and leaving town.

It makes you quite light-headed to be so close to violence, to be so close to history being made, even if it is a shoddy his-tory of rats and sinking ships. But I still followed after the roar, now swelling and clanging and thudding rhythmically into my eardrums. I'd heard of the Argentine way of protest, where wave after wave of housewives take to the streets banging their saucepans in discordant, furious harmony as yet another gang of politicians fails them. Enough, enough . . . thousands of sad, angry men and, mostly, women thronged in front of the Casa Rosada, clashing their saucepans like the cymbals of despair. I wasn't making self-regarding jokes to myself about playing General Perón any more. Reality trumps the theatre stage.

And as I headed back to my hotel and its fretful concierge, the Brinks-Mat armoured vans had gone. Where? To Uruguay. A brief respite, a fugitive on the ferry told me. The land crossing to Uruguay would be clogged with vans and trucks all day, bearing away Argentina's treasure. Uruguay would hold its breath and then, three days later, like a parasite unable to cling to its host, it too would see its economy collapse.

But it was a relief to disembark. Coming from the fervid tension of Buenos Aires, and before that the harsh, semi-tamed desert of Mendoza, Uruguay's air felt like that of a warm summer's day in Suffolk. Uruguay's equivalent of scrub and bush was more like a lush meadow with very little rise and fall, but welcome blocks of mature deciduous trees looking out over the mighty River Plate as sluggish and opaque as lightly milked Darjeeling tea. And cows. It wasn't ten minutes before my car eased to a halt as a herd of at least a hundred brown and white Herefords lumbered casually across the road. 'We are a cow people,' said my driver. He then told me that the Uruguayan barbecue put Argentine and Brazilian efforts to shame, which would be some achievement. And he never mentioned wine.

Which was a pity, because if there is one thing that the Tannat wines need to soften them it is a great slab of bloody red beef. And experiencing these easy-going, warm but frankly quite humid conditions, the tough old Tannat grape made a bit more sense. Uruguay gets a lot of rain, often before the grapes are fully ripe, just like the south-west of France. If you've planted a thin-skinned variety, it'll probably rot on the vine. Tannat is a ruffian, thick-skinned and combative, ready to bat away vintage rains, quite prepared to unashamedly cough up wines that are barely drinkable to a timid modern palate.

But this is fine if you're sitting in Montevideo devouring a platterful of beef. Slightly bloody grilled red meat has a merciful knack of neutralising the toughness, the chewiness in a red wine and of wheedling out any mellowness and friendliness in its heart. But if you're going to try to export your wines to countries a bit less beef-centric than Uruguay, you've got to look for ways to reduce some of that brusque tannic attack. And since they say that Tannat can be perfumed with violets and heady with the syrupy dark fruit of Rosa plums and blueberry jam, how are you going to prove this, and achieve this on anything like a regular basis?

Well, you're not if you only stick to your traditional vineyards. Most of Uruguay's vines are clustered around Montevideo, where over half of Uruguay's population lives. Most countries establish vines right next to their centres of population and then, as things like transport improve, and local drinkers begin to demand better quality, wine growers start looking for more suitable areas for growing finer grapes. But in Uruguay that didn't happen. The mouthwateringly named area of Canelones, sprawled around the edges of the capital, still totally dominates wine production. And, despite some streaks of chalk, these are heavy clay soils. Clay is cold, clay holds moisture, clay retards ripening, clay favours big-boned, stolid red wines. And remember that I said that Uruguay was humid, that rain was frequent as the effects of the River Plate estuary to the south and the blustery wild Atlantic to the east keep things pretty moist.

To be honest, that sounds a bit like the Médoc. That's what the Uruguayans would love you to think. The Médoc is flat, low-lying, surrounded by water, prone to deluge at all the wrong moments, yet making the most famous red wines in the world from a tough old grape like Cabernet Sauvignon. There's one crucial difference. All the famous Médoc wines come from warm, free-draining gravel soils. The downpours rapidly soak through, giving the vines a welcome drink as they pass by and are gone. Uruguay likes to talk of itself as the most European of the New World countries. It prides itself on producing wines with less overt fruit, less buoyant sunny temperament than places like Chile and Argentina. That's true, but you can only push the European angle so far. If you are making wines that lack the New World exuberance, yet which are embittered by roughness and tannin, the European tag won't work. And the Uruguayans know it.

One of the delights of Uruguay is the willingness of wine-makers to discuss every idea of how to improve their wines. There aren't many 'international consultant' types hanging about, but there is a new generation desperate to improve. But if you've invested everything in the heavy old clay soils like everybody else, it takes courage to break away. The first real departure was made by the Carrau family who went right up to the northern limits of the country, where conditions are more desert-like and the soil is sandy. They established a state-of-the-art winery called Cerro Chapeau, and made pretty decent stuff. Scraps of better drained, marginally higher land are being unearthed in the middle of the country. And the best producers among those still glued to the Montevideo clays, like Pisano and Bouza, are straining to achieve ripeness in their Tannat through better methods of pruning and trellising their vines and using smart softening techniques like micro-oxygenation in the winery, but they are also breaking loose by planting Cabernet Franc, Petit Verdot, Tempranillo and whites like Sauvignon Blanc and even Albariño – all easier than Tannat, yet Tannat still remains the soul of Uruguayan wine.

Well, head east. There is gravel in Uruguay, there is granite, there are even slopes rising up to 300 metres (1000 feet) – if you head east. Garzon have gone there. Others must follow. Maldonado is the most exciting region in Uruguay – so far – situated right at the mouth of the River Plate, as the coastline turns northward past the bars and nightclubs of Punta del Este, to face the full force of the Atlantic. And up here, where it is so barren that the few vines have to be covered with hail nets to stop the famished local birds decimating the crop, where you can guarantee wind and rain, but also hectic bouts of sunshine, the thin gravelly soils just might produce the kind of balanced, violet-scented, good-humoured and memorable Tannats to rival, in their different way, anything Chile and Argentina can produce.

Brazil, huge country, huge thirst but tiny wine culture

This was one of my most electric food and wine pairings of the year. Bananas, slathered with an acidic melted cheese, sprinkled with cinnamon sugar and washed down with great gulps of ice-cold fizzy Moscato wine as I gazed out over the sorrel soup sluggishness of the São Francisco River and realised blithely that I hadn't understood a word anyone had said for a good half an hour.

Brazil. The north-east of Brazil. The supposedly parched and impoverished hinterland of Recife. I'm way out of my comfort zone at 8° South. I've come to see a winery and a vineyard. And I'm wondering, when I'm done with the bananas and cheese, will I be looking at the future face of wine? Because this sub-tropical adventure has nothing to do with the old certainties, the rules and preferences that nature has suggested over the centuries. This is man taking control.

An hour's *Mad Max* drive away from the restaurant, Wine Futureworld takes hold. Hundreds of hectares of vines, stretching away across bleached virgin land where it is always summer, the vines never relax, never go dormant – and, if you want, they will give you five crops every two years! If you stagger your plantings you can be picking grapes every single day of the year. They do make vintage wine here, but they have to mark the vats with the month the grapes were harvested, because those same vines will be giving another crop in just a few months' time. The winemaker is tired but content: 'A typical winemaker has thirty harvests in a career. Here I do twenty harvests in single year.'

Is this the future? And is it typical of Brazil? Well, while the São Francisco River continues to shunt vast volumes of water toward the Atlantic, irrigation won't be a problem. Global warming says that too much sun and too much heat is more of a challenge than not enough, but they're already adept at coping with 40°C (104°F). And the wines are pretty good. The reds and whites are tasty, and the fizzy Moscato is irresistible drunk close to frozen in the blinding heat. Could the still wines be better? Maybe, but the winemaker raises the fundamental question of why. 'It's as though everyone is desperate to make wine for holidays and high days and they forget that most days are every day.'

In Brazil? Really? It's easy for us Europeans to latch on to the carnival and samba image of Rio and Copacabana beach. High days every day, surely? But most of Brazil is a far more careworn and downtrodden place where high days are often a distant dream. And wine isn't necessarily a part of it. Brazilians just don't drink very much wine, but icy, fizzy Moscato can at least hold its own against the deluge of beer and *cachaça* spirit that most Brazilians prefer. In which case, something cheap and clean and consistent from just below the Equator *might* be the future.

And yet, and yet . . . our European zeitgeist is to care more and more about provenance, about authenticity, about stories that have integrity and wines that have a sense of somewhereness. But don't these tropical wines have precisely that? Their provenance is unmistakable, their authenticity is transparent, their integrity is unimpeachable. Even their winemaker says, 'I want them to taste of where they come from: the tropics.' Is that any less valid than a winemaker standing in Burgundy or Bordeaux, Barolo or Barossa, and saying precisely the same things?

Brazil. Almost as big as China, stretching from 5° North of the Equator to 33° South, with an endless Atlantic seaboard and a long history of European settlement – Spanish missionaries, Portuguese, German and Italian – there ought to be a thriving wine culture and numerous suitable regions for vineyards. But there are almost none. Between the São Francisco River in the north-east and Rio Grande do Sul in the far south there is barely a vine – São Paolo, surprisingly, has a few. And for what there is, we need to thank the Italians. Way down toward Uruguay, they arrived in droves during the 1880s and discovered that all the best land down by the coast had been taken by the Germans. What a surprise! They had to push inland, up into the densely wooded mountain valleys of Serra Gaucha. That was where I went next. And I could have been bang in the middle of northern Italy, somewhere like Trentino, just south of the Dolomites, or maybe Piedmont. Which is exactly what those early Italians thought, too. Well, I could have been in northern Italy until mid-afternoon, when, with just a few minutes of warning, a most monumental storm blew up and flayed and drenched the grapes that hung on the vines just a day or two short of the harvest. The storm raged. The storm passed. The roads ran red with mud and rainwater. And life went on as usual. The next day it would probably happen all over again.

Humidity. Moisture. Damp. Drizzle. Rain. Call it what you will, even as far south as this you can't escape it in Brazil, and it makes things very difficult if you're trying to produce big red wines from grapes that need to linger on the vines as the storms rage and their skins soften and rot. There are some grape varieties that can resist humidity, but Merlot is not one of them and yet this has been widely planted in our century, with a view to making big, oaky, impressive reds just right for the export market. The trouble is that other countries do this big, heavy style much better, in much more friendly conditions. Brazil is not a natural New World producer. Mostly, they don't control nature. Nature controls them. I was talking about this to a producer and he said, 'We used to make reds at eleven to twelve per cent alcohol, but now, because of globalisation, there's a lot of pressure to overripen grapes. We have to go higher.' No, you don't, I thought. The world doesn't want any more big, oaky clunkers, but it does want tasty, fresh reds at lower alcohol levels, and Merlot, along with its bosom pal Cabernet Franc, can do that very well. I tasted some fresh young reds, no oak, not much alcohol, tingling with raspberry fruit and cranberry acid, brushed lightly with country herbs – and I thought, what a delight. But we'll have to wait a bit longer for the Brazilians to work through their oak and power stage – every wine culture seems to have the same teething troubles.

Some of the wine producers see the problem, and also a solution. As so often, it requires moving away from the traditional vineyard sites. These are huddled into the muggy Serra Gaucha zone – they even have a Vale dos Vinhedos, which they're packing with Merlot – but there are two alternatives – look north, or look south. North is the Planalto Catarinense – much higher, between 900 and over 1400 metres (3000 and over 4600 feet), while Serra Gaucha barely reaches 700 metres (2300 feet). Cooler, very sunny and much drier, it's above the cloud line much of the time. It will be good for Pinot Noir and Sauvignon Blanc but varieties like Cabernet Sauvignon and Carmenère can hang out in the dry air long enough to ripen, too, on these basalt soils. And they've even made an ice wine. In Brazil!

South is way down toward Uruguay. Inland, the hot and, crucially, drier Fronteira or Campanha region with soils that veer between sandy, limestone and granite is producing regular crops of decent ripe reds, but the real excitement is nearer the Atlantic in the rolling hills of the Serra do Sudeste. Lidio Carraro have made it a point of honour to produce wines without oak down there, and the results can be focused and thrilling from such diverse grapes as Touriga Nacional, Teroldego, Nebbiolo and Tannat. I'm sure the Uruguayans have taken note of that one. They've got an Atlantic coast, too.

And there are two other things Brazil does fantastically well. Fizz – she makes some of the happiest, partiest, laughiest sweet Moscato fizz in the world, as well as some tremendous dry stuff led by the guys at Geisse. And no one does grape juice better. The best grape juice comes from various American grape varieties or hybrids which are ridiculously pungent but ripen quickly and are resistant to humidity. It's hugely popular in Brazil and it *is* thrillingly pungent. I can't decide if my favourite is the

Isabella from Valduga or the Niagara from Perini, but at Perini even the soap in the loos is made from Niagara juice – your hands smell of it for the rest of the day. So everyone knows what you've been drinking.

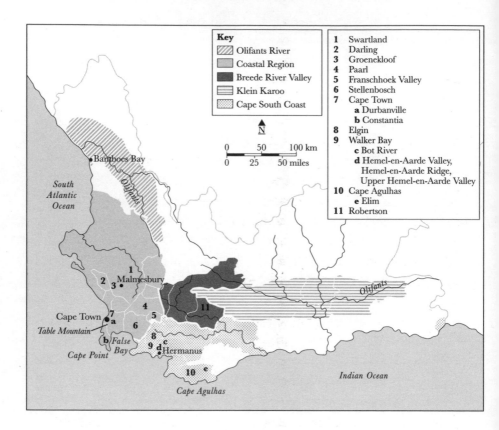

Key
- ▨ Olifants River
- ▨ Coastal Region
- ▨ Breede River Valley
- ▨ Klein Karoo
- ▨ Cape South Coast

N

```
0        50      100 km
0      25     50 miles
```

1 Swartland
2 Darling
3 Groenekloof
4 Paarl
5 Franschhoek Valley
6 Stellenbosch
7 Cape Town
   a Durbanville
   b Constantia
8 Elgin
9 Walker Bay
   c Bot River
   d Hemel-en-Aarde Valley,
      Hemel-en-Aarde Ridge,
      Upper Hemel-en-Aarde Valley
10 Cape Agulhas
   e Elim
11 Robertson

Bamboes Bay

South
Atlantic
Ocean

Olifants

1
Malmesbury
2 3
4
Cape Town
7
a
Table Mountain
6 5
11
Olifants
b False
Bay
8 c
Cape Point 9 d Hermanus
10 e
Indian Ocean
Cape Agulhas

South Africa

Cape of new hope

My travelling companion on my first trip to South Africa was a guy who had been exiled for trying to blow up a train. So you can imagine we didn't come in by the front door. I'm not sure how he got in, but I landed in Zimbabwe en route from Sydney at 2 a.m. The whole of Harare airport was in darkness, the kind of darkness that you know is full of dread. You could feel a pulse, an energy that tells you to stay calm: you're not alone.

And I wasn't. A rogue flash of light showed me where that silent electric energy lay – in army trucks, all lights off, and soldiers, rifles held alert. Silent. Just waiting. Just in case they were needed. Just in case any of us was deemed to be a threat to national security. It's not a nice feeling, presenting your passport to an unsmiling official of an unfriendly regime whose head of state has just survived the latest of several assassination attempts. By white men. 'But I'm only in transit, please.' And so I sneaked into South Africa in the bleak hour before dawn, to have a look at what was going on.

It would be easy to say this was just a wine trip. But it wasn't. This was March 1987, and the 1980s was a very politically active decade for me. I was a member of Solidarity, the Polish anti-Russian movement that played such a massive part in bringing down the Soviet empire. I used to go and picket the

Polish Embassy after finishing my stint in West End shows like *The Mitford Girls* – I was the Actors' Equity representative in London. And I was the only picketer in evening dress. I could feel that change simply had to come soon to South Africa, and from my experience with Solidarity I knew you could change a society with or without a bloodbath. It must be my Irish blood giving me the feeling I can interfere in other countries' politics, but the 1980s were a very politicised decade. A lot of countries wouldn't allow any South African stuff ashore and that included wine. Britain was different. Several supermarkets and high-street retailers *did* boycott South African wine, but others didn't, and you could tell that in some corners of the wine trade there was sympathy with the apartheid government. Some wine writers were openly sympathetic. So the South African wine guys would try to pick us off by offering trips – always in the middle of our winter, the middle of their summer. You didn't have to go straight back home after you'd done your wine work; the sun was still shining, the hotel swimming pool was still cool and inviting – 'Take some time off. Oh, and you don't mind if we take some photos of you, do you?' Legitimacy. Another visit to the beleaguered Cape wine region by this or that 'internationally respected' wine expert.

So I was a bit caught. I'd started doing a few fundraisers for the African National Congress. I wanted to go to South Africa because there was a crucial election coming up that May. But I did also want to see what was happening with their wine, without seeming to endorse it. I admit I sort of half took the king's shilling. I said I would come to South Africa, but that I wished to make my own arrangements. And I wanted no photographs, which explained me arriving in Cape Town from Harare just after dawn to be met by my activist friend rather than the clicking cameras of the local press. He whisked me off to show me that there was a radical, subversive side to South African wine, and there was a small band of outward-looking wine pioneers who had managed to visit and work in overseas wineries (not easy for a South African in those days), and who were determinedly setting South Africa on a modernists' path. And there was also politics to do.

A guy called Chris Heunis was the leader of the National Party in Cape Province, and his constituency was bang in the middle of the vineyard area. The local liberals, led by Denis Worrall, an ex-ambassador to London, were desperate to unseat him, to show that at least some whites yearned to play a part in change. We tasted wine during the day and banged on doors in the evenings. I don't know what the locals must have thought, hearing my accent trying to persuade them not to vote for the local party boss. But it so nearly worked. Heunis kept his seat by thirty-nine votes. One more go around the houses, and who knows.

But it did throw me into the midst of South African society, and not just its wine. I was never a believer that you could keep politics out of sport, and frankly I didn't think you could keep politics out of wine. And this has influenced my views, for better or worse, about South Africa and its wine ever since. It meant that even after my first visit I was very cautious about being enthusiastic about their wines because I was deeply uneasy enjoying myself at the privileged end of an institutionally unequal society. As I now know South Africa so much better, and have been thrilled by the efforts made by so many of the new generation to try to create an integrated society, I find I'm falling over myself with enthusiasm for what the new young South Africa is trying to achieve. I know where they've come from. I know what progress has been made, and what courage was required – and often still is – to do the right thing.

South Africa is still a country that can fill you with unease. You drive out of Cape Town's gleaming airport and within a mile you're cruising past the lean-tos and bivouacs of Nyanga and Khayelitsha townships. They're right there and no one can miss them. As your limo whips you up to Stellenbosch in air-conditioned comfort, you'll swish past countless numbers of people sitting, walking, maybe waving forlornly at you for a lift. Why rush? Time is cheap when you're poor. And do they have a choice?

You'll love Stellenbosch. It's restful, sophisticated, full of entrancing Dutch Cape architecture and quiet tree-lined streets. Quiet enough that as you stand on your balcony before turning in, you can think, Hey, was that a gunshot? Or that? Yes, it probably was, out in the townships on the edge of Stellenbosch; it probably was, another drug deal gone bad.

But I do believe in South Africa and its wine people. And I'm glad my knowledge began with my radical friends way back in 1987. Yet had I just gone to judge the wines I would have been disappointed. The 1980s were the decade when the whole world of wine was blown apart in brilliant fashion by Australia and California. Innovation and excitement tumbled over each other as every year brought quantum leaps in techniques and styles and ambition. This decade was one you *had* to be part of. South Africa wasn't invited to the celebrations. No winemakers visited South Africa in the 1980s, and Cape winemakers weren't welcome in the hothouses of wine brilliance around the world. Most of the Cape wine world retreated into a defensive state of mind, saying, 'We don't care. We don't need you. We don't even like you.' Progress was racing forward at a furious rate; it was passing South African winemakers by and they didn't know it.

Well, a few of them did. I spent time with Jan 'Boland' Coetzee, a famous Springbok rugby player – solid muscle from tooth to toe, you could have used his thighs as pit props. He had managed to work abroad – he did the 1981 harvest with Robert Drouhin in Burgundy – and had also managed to import some decent French oak barrels from Demptos, a well-known French cooper. He spoke English with such an impenetrable Afrikaans accent that the F-word, liberally applied to everything – including me – was about as far as my comprehension stretched. And yet this sporting beast had made a beautifully refined, blackcurranty, cedary Cabernet Sauvignon 1982 that could have come straight out of a top Bordeaux estate.

And down at the southern extremities of the Cape, at Hermanus, Tim Hamilton Russell, a very urbane ad man from J. Walter Thompson in a previous life, was fighting against the dead hand of South Africa's bureaucratic sloth to try to make an African Burgundy. On the last night of this first trip, he delivered one of the most heartfelt, poignant denunciations of racial discrimination and inequality that I have ever heard, and we drank his new 1987 Chardonnay, from vines almost touching the Southern Ocean. It was fat and toasty, and viscous, sumptuously superb. And I noted, *I could be tasting Corton-Charlemagne.* There's Burgundy for you.

It was almost ten years before I was back in South Africa. Mandela was president and everything seemed possible. The world was queuing up to buy South African wine. But was it as good as they thought it was? Well, no, it wasn't. Australia and California had by now been joined in their romp toward an entirely new definition of wine pleasure by New Zealand, and even by countries like France. At the end of 1995 we had very high expectations of wine quality, especially in a New World country which seemed to be bursting with confidence – as South Africa purported to be.

And this confidence led them to issue a challenge – to play a 'Test Match' against Australia. Eleven different categories of wine, including all the important ones like Cabernet, Pinot Noir, Shiraz, Chardonnay, all those. This challenge was called the SAA Shield – South African Airways was sponsoring it. This would show the world how far South Africa had come. It did. And 'not very far' was the answer. Australia won eight of the eleven categories. In terms of scoring, the result was Australia 78, South Africa 21. And the Cape winemakers were astonished. They thought that they were making decent stuff, that they were modernising quite nicely. Well, maybe they were, but the world of wine was leaping ahead, and the Cape had been left way behind.

I'd been an associate judge and I remember giving some TV interviews, trying to explain why the Australian wines had won — more fruit, more perfume, more character — and then there was a commotion at the back of the room and a vast mountain of an Afrikaner strode forward, his broad face as purple as an aubergine. He pointed his finger right in my chest and bellowed, 'Don't you come down here with your pinko ways. Don't come down here and try to tell us to make Australian wine. We've been making wine since 1659.' Well, you haven't learnt much, I thought. But I didn't say.

I was reminded of a leading South African winemaker, who was asked how he thought South African wines compared with the rest of the world. He replied, with as much self-importance as he could muster, 'South Africa produces the best South African wines in the world.' End of story. But this guy at the SAA Shield was angry, he was confused, he was disappointed, and his first reaction was to retreat to the bunker. Like they'd always done. Not so the younger wine people. The young guns, coming into adulthood in the 1990s, surrounded by change their parents could barely comprehend. Their first reaction was to phone the travel agent and say, 'Book me a ticket to Adelaide, or Melbourne, or Sydney. There's a world of wine we don't know about and we need to learn — and learn fast.'

And they did. One of the astonishing things about South Africa now is that there are more young men and women — and I mean twenty-eight to thirty-five-year-olds — in positions of real influence in Cape wine, either in companies or owning their own ventures and making their own wines, than there are in any other wine country. Self-confident, self-critical, self-aware, vocal, each one with a vision of flavour very much their own — the Cape wine scene now hums with their energy.

And is this all because the Australians suckered the South Africans into a contest they could never win? Well, maybe not. The SAA Shield was organised by two of South Africa's most radical, most cosmopolitan wine people, Michael Fridjhon and

John Platter — *Platter's Wine Guide* was then, and is still, the country's wine bible. They'd cooked up the idea of a Test Match on a trip to Chile with the all-time Australian tub-thumper James Halliday. They knew South Africa would get walloped. By a country with whom they had a deadly rivalry in cricket and in rugby. Would a humiliating public defeat by such an old enemy be the kick up the backside to finally make the Cape stop harking back to 1659? Could that have been what these cunning codgers had cooked up? Well, it worked.

New beginnings

It was no easy task. South African wine had been completely dominated by KWV, the growers' co-operative which literally controlled every grape that was grown in the country. You couldn't plant where you wanted, you couldn't plant what you wanted: you took what you were given when it came to vines for planting — or, in some cases, you smuggled decent vine material into the country out of sheer desperation since so much of the local vine population was chronically weakened by virus and disease. Gradually KWV's monopoly was dismantled during the 1990s, but you don't lose the mindset so easily. This was a country used to being strangled by bureaucracy. This was a country that, in apartheid days, had eleven different Departments of Health, and fourteen different Departments of Education. The system supported itself through this tangle of bureaucracy, which is why the surge of the young winemakers has been so important, and why they are now making most of the running in the truly exciting wines flowing out of the Cape. Some of these wines are coming from completely new areas. Some are coming from old, disregarded areas that are now being lovingly nurtured back to their potential. Some are coming from traditional centres like Stellenbosch, still the most important vineyard region in the country. And some are definitely being made by the courageous mentors who set the new South Africa on its path. But youth will have its head, and nowhere more so than here.

South Africa used to be hidebound, endlessly looking back and wondering why the rest of the world didn't respect this ancient wineland of theirs. There wasn't much to respect. Most South African grape growers didn't even drink wine – brandy and Coke was what they downed. The grapes they grew were not judged on quality but quantity, trucked off to the local co-operative to be juiced or made into brandy – and paid for by the tonne. That world still exists. Up in the north-western Cape I met growers only recently who boasted that they could get eighty-three tonnes of Chenin Blanc off one hectare of land! I saw the vines, so weighed down by bulbous fruit that great wooden crutches are needed to support the exhausted branches. Quality? History? No thanks. And I have tasted a fair number of historic Cape red wines, the ones the old-timers were so proud of. With the exception of a Meerlust 1976 and a Nederburg Cabernet from 1974, which I greatly enjoyed for very different reasons, and several Kanonkop wines, there was little to be proud of. The change in attitude now is that the young guns bear no reverence for the old wines, but do bear a great deal of reverence for what's left of the country's old vines. Looking back is not a wine thing now. It's a vine thing.

And one of South Africa's oldest but most neglected regions – Swartland – is leading the charge. As you drive north from the vineyard-rich areas of Paarl and Stellenbosch you feel as though you are leaving the wine realm behind, not driving into a whirlpool of activity and innovation. Golden wheat fields spread out under a blistering sun; the mountains to the east shimmer in a grey-blue haze. It doesn't look promising, but turn to the west: do you see that long, low ridge rising from the wheat? And those ragged patches of green on the gentle slopes? They must be vineyards. They are. This is the Paardeberg hill, not quite a mountain, and those vines are some of the most precious in South Africa – old, straggly, forgotten, unmodernised, unmechanised clumps of varieties like Chenin Blanc, Cinsault and Syrah surviving half-starved on these rocky slopes. And suddenly your eyes see a lot more of them, and you realise that wherever these hills rise, vineyards will cling to the slopes – a little to the north at Riebeekberg, up over the pass to Malmesbury toward the north-west, at Darling and Groenekloof where the high ridge peaks, then tumbles down toward the sea. And there are more hills, like the Piketberg – well, I think you could call that one a mountain – up toward the Olifants River, and those high, heat-hazed crags to the east – they have pools of vineyard too, in the clefts and valleys at their heart.

Swartland is currently South Africa's trendiest region, the home of South Africa's 'natural' wine movement, and, consequently, the wine industry's bushiest beards. Winemakers battle each other to buy these grapes, majoring on old Chenin, Syrah and Cinsault, but being prepared to pay high prices for pretty much any variety whose vines are forty or fifty years old. I tasted wine from eighty-year-old Fernâo Pires vines. How did they survive? Literally not worth ripping out. But it wasn't always like this. Swartland was an area of big co-operatives offering derisory sums for grapes they had no respect for and which would be used as the base for making brandy. Charles Back of Fairview, a leading Paarl winery, was the first person to give respect to – and pay proper money for – the grapes he used in his Spice Route wines. He routinely paid triple what the co-operatives would pay. Triple wouldn't get you these grapes today. Eben Sadie sometimes pays ten times the going rate for the old-vine fruit he needs to make his superlative Columella wine, which he in turn charges a fair bit for. But sometimes the money is still not enough. One winemaker made a thrilling Cinsault from eighty-year-old vines, which sold out in no time. So the next year he went back to find the grower and offer to take his whole crop. Too late: the grower had torn up the vines and planted melons. The grower said the melons tasted amazing. The winemaker was too upset to speak. And this happens every

year. A passionate, inspirational woman called Rosa Kruger has
set out to document every vineyard in the Cape over thirty-five
years old. She reckons old vines have been accorded so little
respect up until now that there are only 1500 hectares (3706
acres) left in the whole country.

But Swartland doesn't have a monopoly on old vines. Paarl,
the traditional centre of the South African sherry business, has
loads of old Chenin, which now can find much better employment in forming the base of some fantastic Cape white table
wine blends. And Stellenbosch, the heart of the modern Cape
wine world, also has a fair whack of the old stuff. Stellenbosch
is famous for Cabernet Sauvignon, by itself or in blends, and
it likes to style itself a bit after Bordeaux or Napa, but despite
there being some top Cabernets, there are top Chardonnays and
Chenins too, as well as Syrahs, and even some exciting Pinotage.

Ah, Pinotage. Be careful of what you wish for. Traditionally
Pinotage has been vaunted as South Africa's very own grape
variety – true – and thus the necessary standard bearer for a
South African style of wine – more debatable. Actually, it's not
even a debate. Many of you will never have tasted a Pinotage
red. Don't all rush at once. Pinotage does indeed have a very
particular character, but few people like it. So why so much fuss
about championing Pinotage reds as the ultimate 'Cape red'
style? Because it's theirs. They really did invent it, or at least it
somehow happened on their watch.

Depending on who you listen to, a certain Professor Perold,
the head of viticulture at Stellenbosch University, set out in 1925
to make a cross between the Pinot Noir and the Cinsault grape
on purpose; or he planted some seeds in his garden, then moved
house and forgot about them, so the seedlings were nurtured
quite fortuitously by the next tenant; or there are much more
colourful stories involving Professor Perold's rugby teammates
and his propensity for wearing non-matching rugby socks as he
strolled through his university vineyard, which had somehow
cross-pollinated a Pinot Noir and a Cinsault vine. All of which

is very well, but it would help if Pinotage tasted nice. At its best it is, I admit, completely unlike any other grape variety. It offers a cavalcade of deep, roaring mulberry, damson and blackberry fruit, sometimes a splash of hot lava, and definitely a perfume like the scents of marshmallows toasted over a bonfire. If we got a bit more of this, I could see Pinotage making a bit of headway in the wine world. But almost none of the wines taste like this – for the most likely chance of catching some Pinotage pleasure, the Beyerskloof and Kanonkop wineries are the best bet. Most examples are tough and stewy, and several are manipulated to taste more like a cappuccino than a glass of red wine.

I think South Africa should have enough confidence by now to let Pinotage sink or swim without any political or ideological baggage. I mean, every viticultural university produces hundreds of different varieties. Almost all drown without trace or survive at the rump end of the wine world. Germany is a dab hand at vine creation. What's their most famous offspring? Müller-Thurgau, the king of Liebfraumilch. France used to spew out endless different vine cuttings. Most of them are now banned, even in France. The Ukrainians and Russians, the Swiss and the Americans all invent varieties. None wear any of them as a badge of honour. None would want to be judged by them.

Mostly coast and a dash inland

So. Back to the vineyards. A simple division would be between the old, established and, generally, inland vineyards, and the newer and, usually, coastal sites. This is a generalisation. Some traditional Stellenbosch vineyards cling to the visually stunning Helderberg mountains as they sink toward the bracing waters of False Bay. And there have been considerable new developments in such areas as the Breede River Valley, not least because places like Robertson, with their bleached limestone soils, have proven to be really effective sources for varieties like the Chardonnay needed to bolster South Africa's booming Cap Classique fizz business. Franschhoek is a glorious valley near Paarl, towered over by handsome mountains on three sides, settled by French religious emigrants in the late seventeenth century. The thin sandy valley soils didn't produce much of note – except, interestingly, some remarkably good Semillon – but recently there has been a dramatic improvement in vineyards and wine, led by Chamonix and Boekenhoutskloof, so nowadays you can laze away lunch and dinner time in the seductive tourist town of Franschhoek with something pretty decent in your glass.

The area which was established even before Franschhoek was Constantia. And if Franschhoek didn't turn out much exciting hooch, Constantia produced what was once the most famous wine in the world. Really. The Cape's first governor, Simon van der Stel, planted vines at Constantia in 1685, on steep, east-facing slopes just over Table Mountain from Cape Town. It's another stunningly beautiful Cape vineyard, and van der Stel might just have established a farm there because he wanted somewhere to relax after a hard week's governing. But luckily he was obsessed with quality and he chose the site not just for the view, but because it had decomposed granite soils – perfect for vines. And while fighting off the baboons – they are still there: don't go dallying in the vines at dusk, when they're hungry – he managed to propagate some Muscadel vines from the original batch that had arrived in 1655 – this wasn't easy, as only three vines had survived – and to make a sweet wine which, within a century, really *was* the world's most famous wine, along with Tokaji from Hungary. Frederick the Great of Prussia guzzled it and so did Bismarck; Russian tsars and British and French kings were also fans. Napoleon was so keen on it that, in exile on St Helena, he was getting through thirty bottles a month! Baudelaire almost preferred it to his lover's lips – and that's saying something for Baudelaire. He wrote, 'Even more than Constantia . . . I prefer the elixir of your mouth, where love performs its slow dance.' A drop or two of Constantia might have caused love to jump and jive a bit more.

Constantia wine became extinct in the late nineteenth century, before being triumphantly revived in 1986 as Vin de Constance on the same soils, from the same grape varieties, and made in the same way, from dried Muscat fruit shrivelled by twisting the stems of the vines. It's a fascinating, greeny-brown sweet wine with an orange-like acidity and the nutty, smoky richness of old Madeira, and I'm delighted it's back.

But Constantia's most important role in South African wine was to revive the idea of cool-climate vineyards being a possibility both for reds and whites. During the 1980s these hillsides, buffeted by the winds from False Bay, and with temperatures on average 4°C (7°F) colder than in Stellenbosch just a little further inland, produced thrilling white Sauvignon Blanc, Semillon, Chenin Blanc and Chardonnay as well as crunchy, crisp, appetising reds from Cabernet Sauvignon, Merlot and even Syrah.

It's the creation of cool, windy weather-challenged vineyards all around the coastline of the Western Cape that gets me most excited. On the west coast above Cape Town, where the Benguela Current is so cold the mackerel need mittens, a succession of hillside and cliffside vineyards gaze out to the glittering ocean. Durbanville and the Tygerberg are almost in Cape Town; Darling and Groenekloof provide the chilly western boundaries to Swartland; and Bamboes Bay in the north is so close to the sea the gales make you fear for your ears.

But the most compelling cool-climate wines are coming from the very southern reaches of the nation, none more so than the tangy, lively whites of Cape Point's vineyards, which dangle like a precarious autumn plum over the raging Atlantic waves. But these aren't South Africa's most southerly vines, though they may feel like it. Elgin is a high, fertile bowl to the east of Cape Town. You drive up a tortuous road to the only gap in the Hottentots-Holland Mountains, playing tag with a spindly single-track railway line. If you can stop at the top of the pass without causing a multiple-car pile-up, you should. The view back across False Bay to Table Mountain is a heart-stopper. You can't photograph it. You have to be there. And then you sweep down the other side of the pass – and where's the sun? Where's the heat? Famous for apples, rather than wines, for most of its existence, Elgin is bounded by mountains that trap cool air, and fogs, and cloud. None of which you would normally want, unless you were growing apples – or nowadays wine grapes. And this is South Africa; the crunchy freshness of the Syrah and Pinot Noir reds and the Sauvignon Blanc, Chardonnay and Riesling whites wouldn't be possible if the sun was able to break through more regularly.

But we've still got further to go. In Elgin we can sense how close the cold sea is, but we can't see it over the coastal hills. As the road corkscrews its way down from the green Elgin bowl out to the broad hot golden expanse of Bot River, and then sweeps south, at last we can see the ocean once again, gently and beautifully at first alongside a broad, inviting lagoon, and then much more rudely as we turn under the towering cliffs into the whale-watching town of Hermanus. It really is too windy to grow vines here, but there's a little road that turns into the cliffs by a liquor store. Follow that. This is the Hemel-en-Aarde Valley – the Heaven and Earth Valley – and, if it initially looks like a sunny Scotland, the vines quickly appear, creeping up the slopes toward a cliff top that drops away vertically to the Atlantic. This is where Tim Hamilton Russell made his lonely white Burgundy lookalike thirty years ago, as he hankered for South Africa to stretch 200 kilometres (125 miles) further south to give him the cooler conditions he craved. With Tim's son Anthony now in charge, the farm still makes superb Chardonnay and still has as its motto the need to explore the limits of unripeness, not the limits of ripeness. Their neighbours have pushed further up the valley, and even renamed the higher sections Upper and Ridge. They're definitely different. Soils change, the weather changes, in just a few miles; Ridge vineyards at the top of the valley ripen three weeks later than those at the bottom and some high vineyards say that their growing season temperatures can be 5°C (9°F) less than those at Hamilton Russell. Pinot Noir and Chardonnay are what everyone shouts about – these are the Burgundian grapes, and with this rapid sub-dividing of small areas and a painstaking fascination with temperature variations, they're starting to behave like Burgundians, too, except that they've also got Syrah and Grenache up on the Ridge. They don't have those in Burgundy, yet.

But we still haven't reached the utter south, the truly last gasp of Africa. That happens right down at Cape Agulhas. You stand on the rocks as the sharks roam barely beyond the breaking surf, and this *is* the end. You can reach it by road from Hemel-en-Aarde – a lot of it dirt tracks through rough grassland and great spreads of wildflowers. Or you can fly. If you know someone with steely nerves and a very small plane, this is the way to arrive. I have a friend called Abrie who qualifies on both counts, and I flew with him down from the Breede River. He handed me the stick and said, 'Here, you fly it.' In a tiny aircraft, everything is so delicate you feel that if you overreact the plane will tumble out of the sky. But the mountain pass is never quite as narrow as you think it is. And in a moment, you're through, out into clear high air, and you can begin to trace the very tip of Africa, its desolate rocky coast, its coves and beaches, where the sharks and whales collect, where the seals bask, and, just here and there, where mankind can find a living. South Africa from a distance, from a height, is very beautiful. It's only close up that you find how much rougher and unsettled it still is. The windsock seems to choke with the force of the gale as we stutter from the sky onto the crunchy landing strip.

No wonder Cape Agulhas and Elim can produce some of the world's most shockingly green Sauvignon Blancs, though their Semillons are almost more pungent still. And yet in these extreme cool conditions the guys are planting warm varieties like Grenache and Mourvèdre and Tempranillo. I'm standing under a night sky so clear it almost seems more silver than black, drinking these 'cool climate/warm variety' reds, and my new friend Dirk explains, 'Whenever the Agricultural Department says, "Don't plant a variety," we plant it.' Just what they say in New Zealand or Australia, or even England. Just with a different accent.

The next morning, he takes me out to see the hippos. An ancestor of his shot the last ones in the Cape. Now he's bringing them back. The old Africa. The new Africa. They need each other. They want each other. They feed off each other. And if there is an Afrikaans wine culture, well, that's changing too, but I understand this Afrikaans culture better with every trip. As one vast, bearded bear of a man said to me, 'We are from this place. We are African. Afrikaans *means* African.'

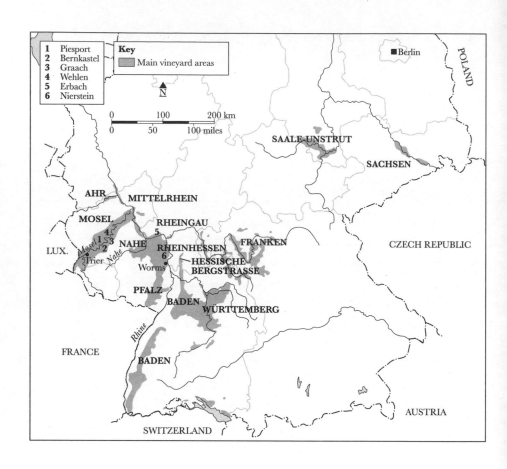

1	Piesport
2	Bernkastel
3	Graach
4	Wehlen
5	Erbach
6	Nierstein

Key

Main vineyard areas

N

0	100	200 km
0	50	100 miles

POLAND

■Berlin

SAALE-UNSTRUT

SACHSEN

AHR

MITTELRHEIN

MOSEL

RHEINGAU

CZECH REPUBLIC

LUX.

4
1 3 NAHE
2

Mosel

Trier

Nahe

5

FRANKEN

RHEINHESSEN

6

HESSISCHE
BERGSTRASSE

Worms

PFALZ

BADEN

WÜRTTEMBERG

FRANCE

Rhine

BADEN

AUSTRIA

SWITZERLAND

Germany, Austria and Switzerland

Big changes in a warming world

Germany and canoeing down the Mosel

German wine got me sacked from my first-ever job as a wine writer. I was still a student, admittedly, but I was doing a pretty good impression of being a world expert on anything to do with wine – and this had landed me a job as the chief columnist on a brand-new wine newspaper called *What Wine?* This column was of fundamental importance, a) to the newspaper, because it was reliably sensationalist – any passing remark I heard at a wine tasting could rapidly be inflamed and inflated into a story that would have made Donald Trump proud; and b) to yours truly, because it provided me with the only hard cash that lay between the college bar flourishing and me dying of thirst.

The previous autumn I had been down in Bordeaux doing the vintage and had met a wild but brilliant wine guy who taught me a good deal about Bordeaux's wine – and above all, how to enjoy it. It rarely involved sitting solemnly around a table in best bib and tucker, reverentially sipping at the region's finest. He had a more basic approach to wine appreciation. Submerge yourself in it – literally. One of our more memorable escapades was the re-invention of all-nude Bacchic rites, which we felt had lain fallow for far too long. Strip off when the moon is full, pour wine into and over yourself by the jugful. Then, stained purple with young Cabernet wine and glistening in the light of the flickering fire, cavort through some pretty smart vines and do God knows how much damage to that year's crop, and to your liver.

And the next day he told me about the perfect summer holiday – very mild in comparison. Canoeing down the Mosel Valley in Germany, stopping at all the *Weinstübe*, tasting everything they had, then on to the next village. No worries about drink and drive. Drink and dunk, maybe, but he swore that the canoes were self-righting.

So when I was short of ideas and gossip for my column, I thought of this wine-canoeing holiday. I hadn't been to the Mosel Valley, but then I hadn't been to half the places I was writing so passionately about. I could wing it. What did the editor know about the Mosel? My piece was full of eyewitness stuff and intimate detail concerning soaring cliff faces and bucolic sweeps of vines weighed down by their golden harvest.

I was particularly proud of giving precise timings for how long it would take to canoe between the different villages. Bernkastel to Graach – twenty-five minutes. Graach to Erbach – fifteen minutes. Never underestimate your editor. He rang and asked, 'Graach to Erbach – was that the river route or the overland route?' Well, by canoe, come on. 'I've measured it,' he said. 'It's eighty-five miles.' And it is. Erbach's not even on the Mosel. I'd meant Wehlen. That *is* fifteen minutes. 'You've never been there, have you?' And that was it. I was done.

It may seem strange now, but there was a time not so long ago when German wine was the height of sophistication in Britain. OK, this was before the New World revolution, it was before the democratisation and simplification of wines brought about by the labelling transformation that simply put the name of the grape variety on the label so that straight away you could identify the probable style of the wine without needing any particular detailed wine knowledge. And it was before the Liebfraumilch boom.

Liebfraumilch, smart wine or scourge?

Liebfraumilch started out as a very smart wine, as did Blue Nun.
During the nineteenth century, Liebfraumilch usually came
from a single vineyard in the town of Worms on the Rhine,
and people thought it was pretty good. Blue Nun was created
in 1921 as a high-grade wine, although the nuns depicted on
the label wore brown habits, not blue. Brown Nun? It would
never have caught on. I've had the 1921 Blue Nun – at seventy
years old – golden, honeyed, scented with autumn richness and
the serene mellowness of measured decay. You would be struggling to enjoy most Liebfraumilch today at seventy weeks old,
let alone seventy years.

But this frankly fabulous quality was what most people
expected of German wine well into the 1970s. Germany is the
most northerly serious wine-producing country in Europe. Its
vineyards are the most marginal, straining for every last ray of
late summer sun to barely ripen their crop; they are often situated on death-defying slopes, expensive and difficult to work
in a high-wage economy. For Germany to become the provider
of vast amounts of bargain-basement plonk made no sense then
and makes no sense now. You should be able to manufacture
basic wine far more cheaply around the southern Mediterranean
or in the mechanised prairie vineyards of the New World. And
you can. Unless the Germans decide that they want to. In which
case – you know the Germans – they can too.

Until fairly recently, German wine was always highly
regarded and its best vineyard sites treasured, right since the
Romans established vines on the Mosel at Trier in the second
century AD. During the Middle Ages, many of the seminal
ideas to improve wine quality came from these cool, northern
valleys, and the idea of ageing wine – often for decades – took
hold in Germany, probably because the high-acid Riesling was
the most commonly grown grape. Acidity helps preserve a wine.
The Germans also knew how to use sulphur – the most efficient

way of stopping a wine from turning to vinegar. During the nineteenth century, it didn't do Germany any harm that Queen Victoria married her adored German first cousin, Albert of Saxe-Coburg and Gotha; and German 'hock' became thought of as the best wine in the world, and the most long-lasting – and the most expensive.

I have two wine lists in front of me as I write, from Berry Bros. & Rudd, London's most distinguished wine merchants. One is from 1896. The oldest wines in this list are German – the 1862 Rhine wines from great vineyards like Marcobrunn being confidently offered, while the oldest Bordeaux wine on offer is from the 1870 vintage. And that 1862 Marcobrunner would have set you back a princely sum of 84 pence a bottle, while such all-time great red wines as Château Lafite-Rothschild in Bordeaux and Romanée-Conti in Burgundy were nearer 75 pence. And let's talk about Liebfraumilch. This sold at 26 pence per bottle – that was more than today's Bordeaux superstar Château Margaux.

The other list I have is from 1909. Nothing much has changed. Hock is still the oldest wine on the list. In fact, you can buy some 1786 Hochheimer – that's from before the French Revolution! Schloss Johannisberg 1893 from the Rhine will cost you – again – 84p a bottle. From Burgundy, Chambertin 1900 is at 23p a bottle and – I'm not joking – Richebourg is 45p a bottle and Romanée-Conti 62p.

How are the mighty fallen. These Bordeaux and Burgundy wines now sell for hundreds, if not thousands, of pounds a bottle. Liebfraumilch will be the cheapest bottle on the shelf in virtually any corner shop or supermarket in the land. But before we spit and scratch at Liebfraumilch's reputation too venomously, there's a silver lining. In the 1950s and '60s, the British weren't a wine-drinking nation. Not much more than 5 per cent of the population professed to being wine-drinkers. There was a small amount of excellent wine being drunk, by a small number of the professional and upper classes. And there was a fair amount of rot-gut filth from the barrel-scrapings of Italy, France and Spain. And North Africa, probably, even if the label didn't say so. You were never going to get the majority of the British population drinking wine when most of it tasted foul.

The supermarkets led the dramatic growth spurt of the 1970s, rapidly coming to dominate the high street. Initially they didn't sell wine, but as more and more British consumers did a weekly shop that included all their food requirements, a couple of canny supermarkets saw the glowing neon sign of 'profit' dangling over wine. There were a few obstacles. The British were bad at foreign languages. No problem. Just make up the wine names. The British didn't really like the taste of most wine – certainly not reds, and most of the cheap whites were yellow, sulphurous and raw. Again, no problem – add sugar and make sure it doesn't taste like wine.

German wines in the 1970s were mostly on the sweeter side, having changed from centuries of dry styles after the Second World War, partly to please American palates, but probably to soothe German palates, too, after the years of deprivation and war. Easy to drink? Certainly. You didn't have to be a wine lover to enjoy these. German wine scientists had invented numerous new grape-variety crossings that gave high yields and high sugar levels without the complication of the wine tasting of very much. Even easier to drink? Yes, and cheap to make. Price shouldn't be a problem, so long as you avoid the tricky-to-grow Riesling. And what about Liebfraumilch for a name? 'The beloved Virgin's milk'? Great name, and you can shorten it to 'Leeb'. Plus a pretty label. That will get the British drinking.

And it did. Liebfraumilch touched a core in Britain and in the USA. The number of wine-drinkers in Britain increased exponentially year on year. The exclusive class-ridden world of wine, awash with pinstripe suits, club ties and Oxbridge accents, was challenged, weakened and then finally overthrown by the irresistible force of the New World and the New Age of wine. But the infantry of this revolution was Liebfraumilch.

Great sweet wines

In general, just leaving the grapes sitting there in the autumn sunshine to gradually shrivel doesn't make intense-enough wines to get very excited about. In France's Sauternes region and in Germany when the conditions to create their famous 'noble rot' fungus don't materialise they do make fairly sweet but rather nondescript wines by just leaving the grapes out on the vine hoping for a bit of shrivel. But Germany gets infections of 'noble rot' fairly frequently on the Rhine, and less frequently in the Mosel Valley and Franken, and can make small quantities of tremendously intense sweet wine. But that's not the only sweetie Germany is famous for. The most extreme form of just letting the bunches sit on the vine is ice wine (or Eiswein in German) and it makes sense for Germany to have been the place to invent it, because it is the coldest of the traditional European wine countries.

Here, the objective is to wait until the grapes freeze solid on the vine — you'll have to wait until November at least, and probably much longer. Knowing nature's sense of humour I'd put money on the conditions usually being perfect somewhere between Christmas Eve and New Year's Day. When the grapes have been subjected to a freeze of at least −8°C (17.6°F) for six to eight hours, all the water in the grape juice will have separated from the sugar and turned into ice shards, creating a very rich sludge that you can turn into a very rich sweet wine, so long as you can press these shivering little jewels without melting the ice. Not only will you have to subject the pickers to unbelievably horrid conditions harvesting the grapes, generally some time between midnight and dawn, but then you have to press the grapes at a similar temperature — often outside in the freezing winery yard. Why? The pressing creates heat, and if the grapes were to warm up the ice might start to melt, the sugars would be diluted and the whole point would be lost.

But what *is* the point? Well, if you want to find a bunch of people prepared to put themselves through the mangle to create something remarkably special, it's usually best to check out the Germans. And they did make the first ice wine. Not on purpose – most leaps forward in wine are by mistake. There was a massive frost in Germany's Franken region in 1794. Making the best of a bad job, the growers gathered the grapes and managed to pummel some thick juice out of them, and the tiny amounts of wine they made were astonishing, with bright, fiery, honeyed fruit scythed through with an acidity like the sharp edge of an ice-skater's blade. For the best part of two centuries, this Eiswein was an occasional but much revered oddity that sold for loads of money. By the 1980s, for some growers it was a badge of honour to try to make Eiswein every year.

A few years back I visited Hermann Dönnhoff in the Nahe region, a brilliant winemaker and the gentlest of family men – unless Eiswein beckoned. He showed me two examples. The first had been picked at 7 a.m. on Christmas Day and the second at 11 a.m. on Christmas Day. Who by? 'Family and friends.' Wow! Just the phone call you want before dawn on Christmas Day – quick, get dressed, get down here, it's Eiswein-picking time. The grapes were so cold they had to whack the bunches with a hammer to try to break them up. They managed to get just 10 litres (17 pints) of juice per load, and it was so cold that on the first day they didn't get any juice out at all. Hermann kept turning the pressure higher and higher – he thought the machine might explode – and it still took twenty-four hours for the first drop to appear. What a lovely day for the Dönnhoff family. But no one seemed to complain about the cold roast goose and flat Champagne. The wine turned out with 350 grams of residual sugar per litre – that's ridiculously sweet – and 19 grams of acid. That's ridiculously acidic. Put them together and that's ridiculously good.

A hotbed of innovation

The whole period from the 1970s to the 1990s, when wines like Liebfraumilch and other cheap concoctions such as Niersteiner and Piesporter were trashing Germany's reputation has led to a massive rethink, and rebirth, of what Germany can and should be as a top wine country.

Today, Germany is a hotbed of innovation. Organic vineyards abound; biodynamism is popping up all over, particularly in the south. The use of sulphur has plummeted. And all the talk is of terroir: taste the place, see the difference between the clay, the granite and the slate. And Riesling is once more the mighty grape – the limpid one, the transparent one, the soil whisperer: see my vineyard through the medium of my grape. And when I taste these wines I do see the vineyard, and the rock and the soil. Sometimes rather more than I want to. And the wines are mostly bone dry, and not short of alcohol. And I think – fair enough – you're proving a point about ripeness and authenticity. But all too often I don't think you're proving a point about pleasure. I don't really drink Riesling wine for its savoury, feral possibilities. Call me old-fashioned, but I drink it for its fruit, for its tingling acidity that delineates vineyard after vineyard for me, neighbours but different, threaded together by a thrilling, humming taut wire of acidity, around which you can wrap so many flavours, so many scents, so many minute but lovely differences of style. And acidity balances sweetness. The sweetness of a Mosel Kabinett with alcohol levels as low as 8 per cent and balanced by finely tuned acidity doesn't seem sweet, is never cloying, and drunk with the right friends in the right place and in the right mood can be a wine more ethereally lovely than any in the world. They are not very fashionable right now, but many good growers still make them. And I still drink them. And when my palate ends up cleansed, scoured, elated and challenged, I know that German Riesling isn't done yet.

But Germany isn't just Riesling any more. Especially in the south, in the Pfalz and Baden, heading down toward France and Switzerland, French grapes like Pinot Blanc and Pinot Gris are making serious, alcoholic and frequently barrel-aged wines. But the biggest surprise is that black grapes now comprise nearly 40 per cent of German plantings. Spätburgunder, aka Pinot Noir, is the leader, but global warming is showing its hand. Merlot and Cabernet Sauvignon are now quite widely planted. And to think that only twenty years ago I had a German friend whose Cabernet Sauvignon vines were ripped out by the police (after he had picked the grapes, obviously; they were local coppers) as they were not allowed. Well, they are now.

The astonishing success of new Austria

Why couldn't Austria have gone for a good, solid, old-fashioned wine scandal? Mixing one region's wines with another. Pretending cheap Pinot Grigio was expensive Chardonnay. Swapping vintages on the label. The usual kind of thing that would well up briefly and be forgotten by the next harvest-time. Why did Austria have to dose its wine with antifreeze? It meant that every tabloid newspaper in the world fought back the giggles as it splashed the story over its pages, their editors competing with each other to heap the biggest pile of steaming ridicule on the country.

This was 1985. Austria was exporting 45 million litres of wine a year. That dropped cliff-like to 4.4 million litres – and you sort of wondered who was taking the 4.4 million. Yet no one died, no one was even made ill. The antifreeze's technical name was diethylene glycol, and in the small doses a few Austrians administered it's not even remotely harmful. Don't try this at home, folks, but I put a dab of diethylene glycol on the tip of my tongue, and the result was fascinating. My whole mouth seemed suffused with richness – not sweetness, but a fat, viscous, shuddering, slabby thickness coating my palate. I could see how a splash or two in a vat of vaguely sweet wine could give

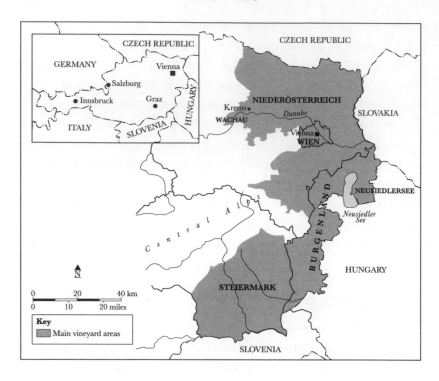

the impression the wine was actually a good deal sweeter. And
so you could sell it for more money. The next year an Italian
scandal surfaced in which more than twenty people died from
adulterated Barbera, but the world barely blinked.

Poor old Austria. Or lucky old Austria. Frankly, with the
exception of the odd dry Riesling from the Wachau gorge on
the Danube west of Vienna – and a bundle of sweet-yet-not-
that-thrilling but, even without the help of the antifreeze, pretty
cheap wines from the humid, sweaty banks of the Neusiedlersee
south-east of Vienna – Austrian wine had almost no reputation
at all. It hadn't shared in the boom times of great German wines,
and its attempts to climb on the Liebfraumilch gravy train were
pretty feeble – their leading brand was called Schluck. I can feel
my taste buds shrivelling.

You might have expected there to be a grand tradition of fine
wine since Vienna was such an important cultural centre, but

that doesn't necessarily follow. Florence was a cultural centre for hundreds of years, but you wouldn't catch the local artists and merchants and aristocrats drinking Chianti if they could get something better. Until 1918 Austria was the centre of the Austro-Hungarian Empire, which included the sweet delights of Tokaj in Hungary and all kinds of wines from the Adriatic coast across to the Italian Tyrol. So there wasn't a massive need for improving the wines in Austria itself. Interestingly, Austria became an important centre for vine cultivation and experiment, and Zinfandel probably arrived in the USA from Croatia via Austria's imperial vine nurseries. But Austria as a nation was ill at ease too. Ever since the loss of its empire at the end of the First World War in 1918, the country had struggled. In 1945 a survey asked whether Austria was a nation. Only 49 per cent of Austrians thought that it was.

The 1985 scandal made the Austrians take a long hard look at themselves. The 1980s were a decade of exciting change and feverish progress in such countries as France and Italy. Dry wines of astonishing quality and personality were appearing almost every vintage. Germany was still caught up in the world of bulk shipments of cheap off-dry whites, and her famous old estates were losing their way. Austria could choose which path to take. And she chose the hard yards. She brought in what was the stiffest wine law anywhere in Europe, with the objective not of reviving old glories, but of creating new glories where none had existed before.

This 'new Austria' has been an astonishing success. Red wines from genuinely Austrian grapes like Blaufränkisch, Sankt Laurent and Zweigelt can be some of the crispest and most drinkable in Europe. (They can also age, but they're truly crunchy and irresistible when young.) Areas like the Burgenland on the Hungarian border can count themselves among the leading red wine areas of central Europe. Sweet wines are now produced legally in considerable quantities from noble-rotted grapes on the shores of the shallow, muggy Neusiedlersee.

Dry whites have leaped even further into the world's wine consciousness. Riesling has been grown on the Danube for generations, and the Wachau is now a world leader for bone dry yet imperious, fleshy, rocky, commanding Rieslings quite unlike those of Germany – or anywhere else. The Wachau is only a 19-kilometre (12-mile) pocket of virtual gorge, with vineyards clinging to the crags way above the rolling Danube, but anyone who wants to pinpoint a taste of 'somewhereness' in a white wine could do worse than amble down this memorable stretch of vines and, well, blue-ish river, stopping at every little village to drink the local Riesling wines and ask for their vineyard sites to be pointed out.

Yet it is a grape supposedly far inferior to Riesling that has really led Austria out of the wilderness – Grüner Veltliner. If you look at the old books, Grüner (as it's usually known) is always being slightly damned with faint praise – good for bright, fresh, slightly peppery, melony young whites, but not to be accorded too much respect. That all changed in London in 2002. A blind tasting pitched Austria's best Grüner Veltliners against an array of top Chardonnays, including such legendary numbers as Le Montrachet and Corton-Charlemagne from Burgundy. Austria walloped them all. These unoaked, unknown Grüners simply swept away the cream of the world's dry whites. From the humiliating scandal of 1985 to this in just seventeen years. Within another five years, Grüner was just about the sexiest white wine in restaurants along America's East Coast. In northern Europe, every self-respecting restaurant or bar now offers examples of Grüner. And as for me? It's often my wine of choice when I'm after a really tasty, refreshing but mouth-filling unoaked white.

And remember I said that you might have expected a grand tradition of fine wine in Vienna? Well, they go one better. Vienna has more vineyards inside its city limits than any other metropolis – over 600 hectares (1482 acres). They've even got a vineyard in the Schönbrunn Palace garden. They may not grow 'fine wine' – but what does 'fine wine' mean when you're having fun? The vineyards are dotted with little wine cellars offering you the new vintage of whatever the owner has grown. These irresistible drinking dens are called *Heurigen*. Don't miss them. And don't drive, as the new wine simply flows down your throat. On my first trip to Vienna, as a singer, not a wine guy, I got lucky. I took the No. 38 tram from the city centre up to Grinzing, in the heart of Heurigen country. How I got back to my hotel, I can't remember. Why would I want to? I woke the next day with a big smile on my face.

Swiss wines 'so silent that it takes time to hear them'

Chandra Kurt, Switzerland's most sensitive wine writer, put it nicely: Swiss wines are 'unique, pure and sometimes so silent that it takes time to hear them'. Spot on. The caricature of Swiss wine is a glass of water-white liquid, maybe with a tiny prickle in it, but almost no flavour of any sort – and it costs as much as a three-course meal would in most other countries. And there's some truth here.

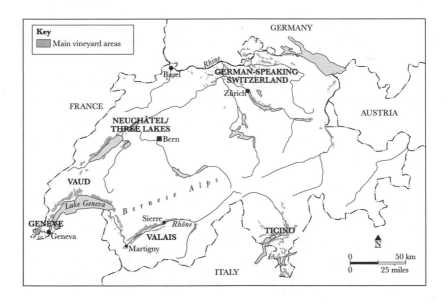

Swiss wine is ridiculously expensive. But so is Switzerland.
To us. To the Swiss, their stratospheric cost of living is presumably perfectly normal. They'd be thrilled by the cost of a
three-course meal in London. And the majority of Swiss wine
is water-white, coming from the Chasselas grape, which is
famous largely for having so little flavour it would make a perfect submissive food–wine match with artichokes and smoked
mackerel and a slice of durian, a really stinky Asian fruit – some
airlines won't even allow you to carry it on board for fear of it
asphyxiating the crew.

But think back to my friend's remark: 'so silent that it takes
time to hear them'. Many Chasselas wines are almost laughably
light. Feather-light almost overstates it. But they are soothingly
soft too. They refresh, they calm, they don't threaten or demand,
and if you're in a bar or on a terrace among the heart-stoppingly
beautiful vineyards that sweep along the shores of Switzerland's
lakes, or climb the rock faces in the Valais region, you will find
hidden flavours, delicate scents, subtle fruits, surprising trails of
minerality in the Chasselas wines. You just have to take the time
to let the wine open out to you. It's a bit like starting to appreciate
Japanese koshu wine, or sake. It's not what's *in* there that gives the
quality, it's what is *not* in there. Our wine world is too full of fire
and thunder, challenge and response. Swiss white wines at their
fragile best take us away to another, gentler place.

But there is a less Zen-like side to Swiss wine, a savage, crag-
clinging, heroic side. The Rhône is one of France's great rivers,
surging and heaving its vast bulk down to the Mediterranean
coast. But the Rhône doesn't start in France. Its source is in
Switzerland. Lake Geneva is like a great bubble, with the Rhône
piling in one end and roaring out the other, hurtling away to
the French border. You could say all the Vaud vineyards on Lake
Geneva's shores are Rhône vineyards, though these produce just
about the most ethereal Chasselas vines in Switzerland.

It might make more sense to follow the Rhône on up to
Martigny, where it executes a ninety-degree turn and for about

35 kilometres (21 miles) you are in one of the world's most star-tling vineyard regions, with hand-hewn rock terraces of vines seeming to climb almost vertically up the face of the Bernese Alps. These south- to south-east-facing cliff ridges soak up the heat in what is Switzerland's sunniest corner and ripen pretty much anything you plant on them. Some of Europe's most scented and enchanting Syrahs are grown here.

There are two ways to experience the thrill. Either take the train from Martigny eastwards to Sierre – and keep your face glued to the windows on the left-hand side. Or go skiing in Verbier. On one of the runs you can stop on a bluff and gaze out over the magnificent Rhône Valley. In the morning you can pick out villages like Chamoson and Vétroz on the slopes across the valley, surrounded by their snow-coated vines. If it's been a sunny day, stop again on your last run of the day. The vines won't be coated in snow any more. Even in late winter the sun is strong enough to melt the snow. In summer and autumn these vineyards are a suntrap, first warning shot of the power matched by the perfume which will mark out the Rhône's wines in France. And though I love the Syrahs, I love all the more the red Cornalins, the Rouges du Pays and the Gamarets, the white Arvines and Humagnes and Amignes. All Swiss. All rare. All full of fire and wit and challenge. Not so silent any more.

Key

■ Main vineyard areas

1 Tokaj
2 Istria & Kvarner
3 Dalmatia

POLAND

CZECH REPUBLIC
Prague ■

GERMANY

SLOVAKIA

UKRAINE

Bratislava ■

1

AUSTRIA

MOLDOVA

Budapest ■

HUNGARY

Chisinau ■

SLOVENIA
Ljubljana ■

ROMANIA

Venice ●

2

Zagreb ■
CROATIA

Belgrade ■

BOSNIA
AND HERZEGOVINA
Sarajevo ■

Bucharest ■

Adriatic Sea

3 ● Split

SERBIA

Danube

Havar

BULGARIA

Black Sea

ITALY

Dubrovnik ●

Sofia ■

MONTENEGRO

ALBANIA

Skopje ●

Istanbul ●

GREECE

*Aegean
Sea*

TURKEY

REP. OF
MACEDONIA

Athens ■

Samos

PELOPONESE

*Ionian
Sea*

Santorini

CYPRUS

▲
N

Crete

0   200   400 km
0   100   200 miles

Mediterranean Sea

Eastern Europe

New beginnings and an old survivor

We don't spend much time thinking about the winelands of eastern Europe, and we only spend marginally more time contemplating those from further east – out past the eastern Mediterranean and into the Middle East and Mesopotamia. But we should. A lot of our wine culture, both young and old, comes from here, and we should relish it.

We should look at the mistakes and tragedies brought about by politics and religion. We should note both the destruction of traditions, and the impassioned rebuilding of half-forgotten or moribund cultures. In wine, the past is the present. The past can be the future. And that is both good and bad. If we look to the east, past the wine worlds that currently boom in western and central Europe, the killing grounds and the laboratories for change and the green shoots of a new vinous spring are all there to see. And we should learn from them all.

We should take note of the effects of Communism on some of Europe's historic winelands, the sapping, the chipping away at the human spirit, and how long it takes to rekindle the spirit in a population. We shouldn't ask for too much too quickly from such countries. I was asking one Bulgarian producer if he was keen on a possible controlled appellation of origin system, and his reply was: 'Not yet. I need to get the toilets done. And the outhouses.' I was talking to another winemaker, in Turkey this time, about how he managed the supply of some of his best grapes from the far south-east, near the Syrian border. 'I carry a gun,' he said. 'Do they try to cheat you?' 'Sure they do. If I'm just dealing with a single village head man, I can argue, tell him that I know he's throwing bricks in among the grapes to add weight. But if he's with a group I have to accept whatever he offers. If I argued, and won, the head man would lose face in front of witnesses, and he'd have to kill me.'

And I asked a Ukrainian winemaker if he thought he would be helping with the vintage in Crimea any time soon. He just looked very, very tired and said nothing.

This corner of the wine world is turbulent for many reasons and in many ways. Because of this, some countries are really not making much impact in the West. Despite this, some countries are. And the most important bunch are members of the old Communist Bloc. They really don't like being called that. But it's the truth. And it is still impacting on the wine industry, because the state of mind inculcated in your childhood and teens can be very difficult to shift.

Here's an example. I was filming a couple of years ago in eastern Europe and had arrived in the Czech Republic. We had a Polish film crew. They were very nice. They were good at their job. But there were three of them for every activity that only required one. And some activities shouldn't even have been part of the shoot. In the old pre-digital days a cameraman might require a focus puller. But not now. We had three. And one morning we discovered we didn't have a tripod for the camera. I could have sworn I had seen one being used, but never mind. We milled about for a bit, and then a guy sidled up. He pointed to his white van on the other side of the square. 'I've got a tripod.' I'm sure he had. Probably ours. The director was working cash in advance. They didn't pay him for the last day, so he upped and left. I ended up directing. Boy, did it show.

When I tell this tale to winemakers they smile and ask the age of the crew. Mostly in their forties. So they would have been in their early twenties when the Berlin Wall came down. Too late. They've imbibed the leaden potion of Communism. Some of my wine friends are in their sixties and some in their twenties, but they all agree that until a truly post-Communist generation takes over, dramatic change will remain a struggle.

Bulgaria, the first 'New World' Cabernet

Why didn't Bulgaria leap out of the traps when Communism collapsed in 1989? During the 1970s and '80s, Bulgarian Cabernet and Merlot were in effect the New World varietals that Europe so sorely lacked. The wines simply pinged blackcurrant flavours at you, and in the 1980s a Bulgarian winemaker said, with a good deal of accuracy, 'If you haven't tasted Bulgarian Cabernet, you haven't tasted Cabernet.' And he was sort of right. Those Bulgarian Cabernets and Merlots were simple, juicy, affordable, utterly recognisable, labelled by their grape varieties, and they never let you down.

Sounds like the New World? It almost was. Bulgaria had managed to get hold of really good Cabernet and Merlot vines from California's top nurseries because their Black Sea beaches were sandy and golden and irresistible to the top end of Soviet society, who wanted some Western pleasures as they lounged lardy and sweaty and pink. And ice-cold Pepsi-Cola was pretty much top of their list. The Bulgarians had no money to buy Pepsi, but Pepsi enthusiastically entered into a contra deal of providing grape-vine varieties that would make just the kind of wine the American market wanted – Cabernet and Merlot. And Pepsi would find a way of selling them. There was also a persistent rumour that South African Cabernet wine, boycotted by most of the Western world during the 1980s, managed to find its way up to the Bulgarian ports, and who knows what happened to it then?

But Bulgaria absolutely failed to keep this momentum going. Wineries got privatised in a rush in the early 1990s, but well into this century people were still arguing about who owned what when it came to vineyards. And when you think about it, Bulgaria didn't really have a proper wine tradition to revive. She was under Ottoman rule from 1386 to 1918. When the Soviets took over they planted vast mechanised prairies with vines to produce cheap stuff for Russia. The Pepsi intervention was a bit of a godsend, however brief. And although Bulgaria is doing its best to find an identity, especially with its own grapes like Mavrud and Melnik, my favourite wine is Enira, made by the German count who owns Château Canon-la-Gaffelière in Bordeaux. Oh, and another thing. By the 1990s we didn't need a cheap, second-division New World situated miles away on the Black Sea. The real New World had arrived.

Romania: can you really make good cheap Pinot?

Romania, to Bulgaria's north, never had such an important presence on export markets during the Communist era, but she had a more deeply rooted wine tradition. This is partly because, although she is sandwiched between largely Slavic countries, Romania has a Latin culture, speaks a Latin tongue and, until Communism, had strong ties with western Europe, especially France. A favourite *fin-de-siècle* tipple in gay 1890s Paris was La Perle de Moldovie. And whereas Bulgaria has failed to become a bargain-basement New World in this century, Romania has succeeded.

German and British investors clearly found Romania a better hunting ground after President Ceauşescu's brutal televised demise on Christmas Day 1989 (I watched it live on television with my mother, between the roast turkey and the Christmas pudding). And they were smart and lucky. Romania had big plantings of Pinot Gris and Merlot – both very useful for decent, budget-priced quaffers. But she also had great swathes of Pinot Noir. Now, half-decent Pinot Noir for a budget price has generally been regarded as an impossible task, particularly by Pinot Noir nerds who don't want their beloved grape to be available and attractive to the masses. But Romania can do it. Big volumes. Lovely, soft-scented strawberry fruit. Low price. Jilly Goolden needed the smelling salts at least once a year when she recommended Romanian Pinot Noir as her top budget red on *Food and Drink*. She was right. And it's even better now.

Romania has some smashing grape varieties of her own, usually with the word 'Fetească' in them. There are some serious private estates re-establishing themselves, and some thrilling new hillside vineyards being carved out, which have every chance of producing memorable reds when they've bedded down. And while we wait, there's no sign of the Pinot Noir getting any worse, or any more expensive.

Moldova, tiny and troubled but bursting with potential

I'm almost tempted to pass over tiny Moldova, a country bursting with vineyards, bursting with potential, but so far finding it very difficult to steer any kind of progressive path toward post-Communist prosperity. I have had two trips there cancelled because of civil strife. They couldn't guarantee my safe passage between the airport and the capital. One joint venture set up by the massive Australian company Penfolds gave up, partly because each year, the day before harvest, they would calculate on getting say 100 tonnes of grapes. They would go to pick and only find 50 tonnes. The other half had 'disappeared' overnight. Well, word gets out that the grapes are ripe. You're hungry; a kilo or two of Chardonnay grapes will get you a loaf or two of bread. Your children need clothes. Twenty kilos of grapes might fix that. And your car is knackered. Twenty kilos of Chardonnay might sort that too. Life is tough. But until they deal with this kind of thing, it won't get any easier.

Yet Moldova was Russia's favourite wine producer, and one bottle that I unearthed in the 1990s tells us why. This was a dusty, misshapen pug of a bottle, with a label hand-scrawled in

Cyrillic. Negru de Purkar was its name, I worked out. 1967. When I opened it, the wine was dauntingly dry, and at first sip it seemed to be fatally cocooned in cobwebs and neglect. But ten hours later – yes, ten hours – this wizened old shrew had shaken its tresses free and blossomed. It now had a heady aroma of cedarwood, the cobwebs were now dust on the cherished volumes in an old bachelor's library, and the fruit was like black-currants, all their sugar sweetness lost in time, but their essence and intensity preserved for eternity. It could have been a great old Bordeaux wine, one of the finest: Château Latour perhaps.

Talking of *Food and Drink*, one year in the 1990s I flashed a Negru de Purkar up on the screen the week before Christmas and told the nation to treat themselves. By God, they did. Not a bottle left within the day. The old Communist chiefs in Moscow would have been furious – the masses getting hold of this jewel. Negru de Purkar was their special occasion wine and they didn't share. When Moldova gets its act together, expect to see some great wines once again.

Hungary, one shining star in a re-awakening wine nation

Hungary never seemed quite so remote and Soviet as these other countries. And in a sort of way it wasn't. Hungary did suffer some very hard-line regimes, and my father used to shake with anger if he ever talked about the 1956 uprising and its suppression by Soviet tanks after thirteen short days of free-dom. Perhaps that's why the only red wine he regularly had in the house was Hungarian Bull's Blood. It was only a couple of bottles a year, but by luck or judgement he'd made a good call. Right up until the 1970s, this dark, robust red wine was astonishingly good. The first twenty-five years of Communism absolutely failed to quench its spirit. Spirit really mattered in Hungarian wine then, and it does now. It's easy to think of a proud, swaggering Magyar red, but it was actually the white wines that were more memorable in most of Hungary. They were quite unlike any modern white I can think of – viscous, almost oily, but tangy and streaked with lemon or lime, fiery and intrusive on your tongue, golden but green – 'stiff', as one writer called them. They surged through your mouth, leaving the jangles and the bumptious din of their contradictory flavours clinging to the sides of your throat. Spirited – yes indeed. And their name should have prepared you for this. You didn't call out for replacement bottles without careful consideration – not when they were tongue-twisters like Debroï Harslevelu, or Badacsonyi Szurkebarat, or Tokaji Szamorodni.

Ah, Tokaji. Well, Hungary may have benefited from being Soviet Russia's economic laboratory, where it gently tried out a few liberalising techniques as it struggled to balance the books. But what kept most non-Hungarians aware of the country and its wine was Tokaji. (It used to be spelt Tokay by Westerners, and that's how it is pronounced.) The wine is generally sweet to very sweet, but marked by an acidity that shimmers through it like the beam of an icy north star, turning simple honeyed sweetness into a dense and raging nectar that pummels your palate with a full spectrum of orange to kumquat to quince and marmalade richness. Most sweet wines make your eyelids droop; Tokaji rubs paprika behind them and makes them smart and sweat.

And it's been famous for, well, almost four hundred years, because it is probably the first wine ever to be made sweet on a regular, intentional basis, relying solely on the sheer concentrated sugar in the grapes. The French reckon they did this first in Sauternes. The Germans reckon they were first in their Rhine Valley, but I reckon it was the Hungarians a good hundred or so years earlier.

And Tokaji certainly was famous. Kings, emperors, tsars – especially tsars – queued up for it. Well, they didn't queue. They were tsars. They just took. It was supposed to have miraculous powers in the – ahem – performance department for ageing potentates with young wives. The tsars of Russia all took it on their deathbeds because it was supposed to bring you back from the dead. Clearly it didn't, but at least the death mask would have had a faint smile playing on the lips.

Britain's oldest wine merchant, Berry Bros. & Rudd, even after the Second World War, had vintages going back to 1811. In a 1930s list they printed a testimonial: 'Your Tokay has given me good nights. I have a wine glass nearly full, then the masseuse sister comes and rubs my back with a special liniment and I curl up like a contented pussy and go to sleep.'

But if it didn't keep you alive for ever, the wine itself seemed indestructible. The Poles were pretty keen on it, and in 1939 Warsaw's leading wine merchant, an outfit called Fukier, had every vintage going back to 1606. They had 326 bottles of that, as well as thousands of bottles of the 1668, the 1682 and the rest. And then, one wretched weekend during the Nazi Occupation, in one soul-destroying drunken rampage, the world's remaining stock of seventeenth-century Tokaji was pissed away.

Well, I doubt if anyone will try to age modern Tokaji for half as long, but the vineyards and wineries were seized by Western wealth in a rush on the fall of Communism. And say what you like about capitalism, but these new Tokajis are new classics, fully worthy of the name.

The Balkans, old and new from the Adriatic and inland

If the only red wine my father had in the house was Hungarian, the only white he had was Yugoslavian – Lutomer Riesling. So I suppose the first white wine I tasted was Lutomer Riesling. Not a bad choice, as it happened – fruity, off-dry, mouth-filling – and made by a bunch of good old-fashioned Communists up near the border with Austria. They kept up the quality for thirty years or so, until the lure of Western gold messed it all up. Just as Hungarian Bull's Blood was wrecked when they sold the rights to a big and greedy British brewing colossus, so Lutomer sold the bottling rights to a crew in London's Docklands. The price sank, the sales sadly rose and, well, let's say my father stopped drinking it, and so did I. The dog didn't.

Lutomer – the wine has changed its name to Ljutomer Rizling by the way, just to make itself sound more attractive – is on the eastern fringe of what is now Slovenia. It's really only these two northern ex-Yugoslav countries – Slovenia and Croatia – that have so far made much of a mark in Europe's wine world. I do taste the odd good wine from Serbia, Macedonia and Montenegro, but there is hardly a torrent. But there is a lot of good wine in the north. Slovenia seemed to have been completely prepared for the break-up of Yugoslavia in the early 1990s and has been making a fair number of good, if pricey, white wines since. One reason for this becomes clear if you look at a map. Western Slovenia seems to slide imperceptibly into Friuli in north-east Italy. I've driven backwards and forwards across this border. There seems no rhyme nor reason for it, especially when you meet people on the Italian side and every single one of them has a Slovenian name. The border happens to cut across many of the best vineyards of Collio, the most famous of Friuli's wine regions. During the Communist era, on nights during the grape harvest when the moon was new and the clouds were thick, the general feeling was that those lorries carefully threading their way along the country tracks to the Italian side were almost certainly lost. Let's hope that they found their way back to the Yugoslavian side before all those good grapes they seemed to be carrying spoiled. That would have been a shame. And many of Italy's best Collio wines would not have been quite so good.

Croatia, on Slovenia's southern border, may be most famous for the Dalmatian coast, with its tiny vineyards clinging to stark white cliffs that tower above a silver sea. Take a boat out from either Split or Dubrovnik and look out for these vineyards – the sight is thrilling, even if the big stolid red wines from the Plavac Mali grape are somewhat unconvincing in the heat of the Adriatic noon. And they are proving almost reassuringly difficult to modernise. There were no roads in most of these coastal vineyards until the 1960s – donkey and boat, or you walked. Well, scrambled. Even on my first trip there in 2011 the roads weren't all paved, and as I clung to an old vine high above the glittering sea, whose reflection on to these bleached white cliff faces blinded and basted me all at once, I remembered what the famous French wine consultant Michel Rolland had said when I asked him whether he knew Dalmatia. He said he'd come to look at exactly this place on the Pelješac peninsula and it was 'the maddest site' he'd ever seen. Not wrong, Michel. Beautiful beyond belief, but mad.

Perhaps that is what UNESCO were thinking when they declared various parts of this Dalmatian coast World Heritage Sites. Certainly they reckon that some of the vines on the island of Hvar have been cultivated continuously longer than any other site in the world. Dalmatia's other claim to fame is that it is the source of California's very own grape – the Zinfandel. This matters a lot if you're Californian. Not so much if you aren't.

But the most exciting Croatian wine area is in a fig leaf of land that pokes provocatively out into the Adriatic just below Slovenia – and that's Istria. When I go to Istria I almost feel I'm in a separate country from the rest of Croatia. And perhaps I am. The road signs are in Italian and Croatian, the architecture reaches out across the Adriatic to Venice. And the wines are entirely different. Istria is different. The peninsula was part of Italy from 1919 until 1945, and before that under the influence of Venice and then Austria. There is an imposing mountain range between Istria and the rest of mainland Croatia. To take the train between Istria and the capital Zagreb you have to go up and around via Slovenia, and it's a long hike. Geographically and emotionally, Istria could be a part of Slovenia, which you might say is much the same as north-east Italy, and in no time you've slid around the Gulf of Trieste to arrive in Venice.

This detachment shows in Istria's most famous wine, Malvasija Istriana – let's just call it Istrian Malvasia. There are many different Malvasia wines around the Mediterranean, some good, some poor. This is a good one. In fact, it's a very good one, and very adaptable. Istria has a fantastic long coastline brimming with seafood and tasty fish, and Malvasia has managed to turn itself into a scented, soft, genuinely juicy and beguilingly different dry white to be downed with platters of shellfish in the summer following vintage. And it is just as good drunk on its own. It's one of the leaders of the European anti-Chardonnay, anti-oak brigade. In fact, it is also a leader of the I'm-fed-up-with-Sauvignon-Blanc brigade. Kiwi Sauvignon has swept the world as the tasty, tangy, no-frills dry white. A softer, more winsome but equally refreshing dry white is waiting on the Istrian coast to make its challenge.

Yet Malvasia has more to it than freshness and gluggability. There is a strong movement of 'old style' Malvasia production – where the wines are fermented on their skins and aged – often still on their skins – for a considerable time in either oak or acacia barrels. The result is wines of a positively orange hue, wild, chewy, exciting, memorable when they are good and, often enough, just too orange, just too wild, just too chewy when they're not. Orange wines have been a cult for a few years now in the rest of Europe's vineyards. The Istrians started early and now produce some of the best examples of all.

Key
Main vineyard areas

1 Galilee
2 Golan Heights
3 Upper Galilee
4 Judean Hills
5 Bekaa Valley
6 Nemea
7 Macedonia
8 Naoussa

POLAND

UKRAINE

MOLDOVA

Chisinau

ROMANIA

RUSSIA

Belgrade

Bucharest

Danube

*Caspian
Sea*

SERBIA

BULGARIA

Black Sea

CRIMEA

Sofia

GEORGIA

Skopje

Tbilisi

8 7 Thessaloniki

Istanbul

ARMENIA

AZERBAIJAN

GREECE

*Aegean
Sea*

Ankara

Athens

Samos

6

TURKEY

PELOPONNESE

*Ionian
Sea*

Santorini

Crete

CYPRUS

SYRIA

IRAN

Mediterranean Sea

Beirut 5

LEBANON

Jezzine

1,2 & 3

ISRAEL

IRAQ

Tel Aviv

Jerusalem

4

JORDAN

LIBYA

EGYPT

N

0   200   400 km
0   100   200 miles

Georgia and the eastern Mediterranean

Where it all began

So that's eastern Europe. But we're not done yet. I'm not sure we've even truly started, because although some of these countries do have venerable old traditions, they're nothing on what exists further east. And, to be gloomy for a moment, if we think the culture of wine was almost throttled by such things as twentieth-century Communism, well, they've had much sterner challenges, and for much longer, out where Europe slips away and Asia takes its place. Much of this area is Muslim and has been for centuries. But the culture of wine has just about survived, and is now undergoing a remarkable revival. And this does matter. Because this is where it all began, In Ancient Persia, in Georgia, in Turkey – somewhere in one of these areas some bunch of ancients made wine – on purpose – for the first time.

How? Well, we're talking six, seven, eight thousand years ago. So details are a bit skimpy. But the legends are colourful. Ancient Persia has a good one. King Jamshid liked eating grapes all year round, so his servants had to carefully pack the grapes in storage jars, without splitting them, which would have caused the grapes to rot and go sour. Yes, but because grape skins have yeast on them, any juice that seeped out would also ferment. If you've never smelled a vat of fermenting grape juice, well, it's sweet-sour, pungent and searing enough to make you want to gag.

So what happened was that one jar hadn't been packed carefully enough; the grapes did split and start to ferment, and whatever hapless servant opened it reeled back in shock, presumed it had been inhabited by an evil spirit and was probably poisonous, and shoved the jar in a corner, marked 'poison'. Meanwhile, one of Jamshid's harem was having a terrible time with nervous headaches, saw this jar and decided to end it all by knocking back the poison. The legend then says that she was overcome and fell asleep, only to awake 'miraculously refreshed and cured of her headaches'. Hmmm. More likely she woke up with an absolute skull-splitter, couldn't remember a thing, but her friends regaled her with her antics, her dirty dancing, her lewd jokes and bawdy songs – all in graphic detail. Was this the first wine? The first hangover, more like. But King Jamshid heard about the shindig, thought it sounded like just too much fun, told his servants to create as much 'poison' as they could – and declared wine to be a sacred medicine, presumably reserved for the king and his chums henceforth.

That was Ancient Persia. The Babylonians, further south in Mesopotamia, had their own legend, the Epic of Gilgamesh, where a wild man, Enkidu, is given his first cup of wine. 'He drank seven times. His thoughts wandered. He became hilarious. His heart was full of joy and his face shone.' Do you see a pattern developing? We've all been there. And in the Bible, the first thing Noah did after the Great Flood was to plant a vineyard; he got clattered the first time he tried his wine and 'was uncovered within his tent'. We don't learn, do we? Don't drink and camp. But we may be slowly creeping toward some factual evidence for that first wine.

Noah's Ark is supposed to have come to rest on Mount Ararat. That's now just inside Turkey, but it used to be in Armenia, where they have discovered a winery that's over 5500 years old.

Georgia, the cradle of wine

Just north of Armenia is Georgia. In Georgia, they've discovered evidence of winemaking going back eight thousand years. And the thing about Georgia is that through a fantastically turbulent history – having Russia to the north and numerous Muslim civilisations to the south – she is still making wine in just the same way as she was eight thousand years ago. There aren't many areas of life where we can recreate something from eight thousand years ago. The Georgians do it every time the grapes ripen and vintage comes around.

These strange, wild Georgian wines are about as far removed from a typical modern wine as wine can be. The brazen, choleric bitterness – particularly of the whites – is threatening and disturbing to anyone whose palate is only attuned to the blandness of so much modern food and wine. But isn't it brilliant that we have this bloodline running back through the centuries? We don't have to like the wines, we don't have to understand them, but we do have to treasure them, emotionally warm to them as they offer a smell, a taste, a feel, a sensation of what people drank eight thousand years ago.

I'd better just fill you in on how these remarkable throwback wines are made. The grapes are basically buried. Literally. Great big faded orange vaguely egg-shaped clay jars called *qvevri* are buried in the ground. At vintage time the bunches of grapes are briskly and roughly crushed, then the whole mishmash – stems, pips, skins, juice, the lot – is thrown into the jars, which can be any size, from a few litres to eight thousand litres and can weigh over five tonnes. They don't add yeast – why would you, when the vineyards' own yeasts have been working perfectly well for eight thousand years? – they just let the fermentation trundle along, then they seal the mouth of the jar with damp clay and leave the whole turbid grape soup to sort itself out, clarify itself, prepare itself to be drunk. This could take three months, six months, a year.

Now, you could just about understand a rough old red wine being given this treatment, but most of Georgia's wines are white. Well, they're not very white after a year buried in a giant clay jar that might be hundreds of years old and might have held hundreds of vintages. I've seen *qvevri* from the fourth century being gently prepared to take another vintage. The colour is far more likely to be orange or even amber.

And the flavour . . . Several of the best wines are made by monks – in fact, my favourite winemaker is a bishop. The wifi password at his monastery is 'Since 1011'. That's how long they've been making wine. One monk said the *qvevri* wines can rearrange your wine universe. My bishop friend said, 'It sets our brains onto different radio waves.' Well, here's a tasting note I made on a 2011 *qvevri* using the Kisi grape (I'd never heard of it, but Georgia reckons to have more than five hundred native grape varieties; I can't know them all): *It emerged from the clay jar bright orange, smelling of chamomile, straw and peaches, tasting as chewy as any red; earthy, as though they should have washed the grapes first; bitter as tarpaulin, zesty as orange peel, rich as dried figs. Enthralling and unnerving. Would I risk a second sip? I'd crave a second glass. Wouldn't you want a second glass of something as close to the wine style of 8000 years ago as you could get?* Ensconced in the twenty-first century, I have to go back eight thousand years to find a truly new wine experience.

I choose Georgia as wine's birthplace because they're still doing it just the same as ever. They've never stopped. UNESCO recognised this in 2013 by awarding the *qvevri* clay-jar fermentation method heritage status. And wine is at the core of Georgia's existence, which is in itself defined by religion. A saint bearing a cross fashioned from a vine brought Christianity to Georgia. Georgian soldiers would carry vine seedlings into battle so that if they died a vine would take root and grow where they fell. My bishop friend said, 'Growing grapes and making wine without praising God doesn't make any sense.' Remarkably, in the twenty-first century most Georgians would agree.

Winelands around the eastern Mediterranean

Clustered around the eastern end of the Mediterranean are several other wine-producing countries, with illustrious wine histories which are now striving, usually with some success, to make their mark in our modern world. Obviously, Israel is one of them. I can't pretend it doesn't make my spine tingle to see names like Galilee, Sumeria and Judaea on the wine labels, sometimes even Bethlehem, Jerusalem or Mount Carmel if you look closely. I was a chorister in Canterbury Cathedral. I prayed about these places, I sang about these places and I read about these places on a daily basis. And as a young whippersnapper my favourite miracle was without doubt Jesus turning the water into wine at Cana. How much praying would I have to do to perform that one? And until AD 636, when the vibrant new faith of Islam, with its prohibitions on alcohol, swept through the eastern Mediterranean lands, vineyards and wine were an important part of Jewish life. But, with the exception of some vineyards established by the Crusaders, Islam put paid to the vine until 1882, when Jews returning to their Holy Land were given a massive fillip by Baron Edmond de Rothschild establishing the area's first modern wineries.

You need to wait nearly another century before the Jewish – now Israeli – wine story gets interesting, and then it's as a result of the spoils of war. Israeli wine traditionally came from sun-baked lowlands – I have tasted a few and my response to such cloddish old trundlers was, well, Israel is one more wine country I don't need to bother about. The Six-Day War in 1967 changed all that. Israel seized the Golan Heights from Syria. Ever since then, politicians have endlessly argued over whether or not Israel should occupy these Heights. You won't find many Israelis in the mood to give them back to Syria, and you certainly won't find any winemakers keen to compromise. These cool, windy acres, reaching as high as 1100 metres (3600 feet) above sea level, revolutionised Israeli wine.

I was shocked, literally, when I tasted the 1983 Sauvignon Blanc from the Golan Heights Winery – fresh, grassy, snapping at my tongue with lemon and green acidity – and only 12 per cent alcohol. I followed this with a gorgeously mouthwatering, blackcurranty Cabernet Sauvignon 1984, which shocked and excited me again. Two further shocks rolled in. One: I saw pictures of the vineyards in the aptly named Valley of Tears. There were rusting carcasses of burnt-out tanks upended among the boulders. These were the reminders of a tank battle in the brutal Yom Kippur War of 1973; 250 wrecked tanks had to be removed before planting could commence. These vineyards have a backstory more bloodstained than any others in the world. And second, they're kosher.

Now, winemaking is a pretty hands-on activity. During vintage, you have to commit yourself to it seven days a week, sometimes twenty-four hours a day. Attention to detail is crucial as ferments wax and wane, sulphides and volatile acidities rise and fall, good and bad flavours appear and disappear. The winemaker must be able to deal with every eventuality, immediately. Easier said than done in a kosher winery, if you're not a kosher winemaker. And Golan Heights was being made by a non-kosher winemaker from America who didn't even speak Hebrew. If you're not kosher, not a practising Jew – you can't touch anything. Nothing. Not the grapes, not the juice, not the filters or the hoses or the tanks. Nothing. They're really serious about it. I was at a kosher wine tasting a few years ago and I absent-mindedly picked up a bottle to read the back label. As soon as I put it down the guy behind the table briskly removed the bottle, put it at the back and opened a new sample. I got the message. The Golan Heights not only showed that Israel could grow grapes good enough for modern wine, but it also showed that, by a mixture of sign language and dogged determination, non-religious winemakers could break the curse of kosher wine being seen as sweet and stale and sometimes barely drinkable.

I still find a lot of Israeli wine too big and brawny. I can taste too much oak and extraction and warmth in a lot of them, but that may partly be because the producers know their audience like that style. And I can now target three areas where Israel is producing a significant number of fresh, balanced wines, many of which are not now kosher, though many still are.

Golan Heights is still growing a lot of excellent, balanced fruit up in its frontier eyrie, gazing nervously one way across to war-torn Syria, or back down toward the uneasy world of the Left Bank. Upper Galilee is another area to look for on the label. The vineyards cluster under the presence of Mount Meron, right on the Lebanese border. This is beautiful hill country, with vines growing in excellent breezy conditions at up to 800 metres (2620 feet) above sea level. But you are on the border, and in Israel that's never a relaxed place to be. And the third area, which may even prove to be the best yet, is the Judean Hills, just 15 kilometres (9 miles) west of Jerusalem. I started taking these hills seriously when I kept coming up against a remarkable, funky, oatmealy Chardonnay called C Blanc du Castel from Domaine du Castel that was halfway to Burgundy in style. When I tracked down the owner and he explained the barren, chalky hillside, some of it north-facing away from the sun, the thin soil, the breezes and the chilly nights, it all made sense. I then tasted a Riesling from Sphera Winery – zesty, citrusy, thirst-quenching and only 12.5 per cent alcohol, and I thought, wow, this is where I'd be if I were planting grapes in Israel.

Lebanon, directly to Israel's north, is in an even more challenging situation. It's predominantly Muslim, for a start. Hezbollah, the Shia Islamist movement with a strong military flavour, is at the heart of power. There are a lot of Sunni Muslims who aren't keen on that, regardless of what the Christians think. All in all, there are reckoned to be nineteen different religious affiliations in Lebanon. Which wouldn't matter if they didn't fight each other. But a civil war between 1975 and 1990 shows that they do. And in the twenty-first century, the threat of a new civil war has erupted at least once.

None of this sounds very encouraging for wine. But Lebanon has a glittering wine history from ancient times up to the Middle Ages, when the Ottoman Empire put a bit of a dampener on things, and for much of the twentieth century French influence dominated a country that is francophone to this day. So that's not bad. And Lebanon had a star. A superstar. A roguish, emotional, poetical, philosophical, irresistible shooting star – Serge Hochar of Chateau Musar. He took over the dilapidated, cobwebby winery in 1959 after receiving a positively classical wine training in Bordeaux. There was never anything classical about Chateau Musar if you think that classical means reminiscent of Bordeaux or Burgundy or some other long-established European luminary. But if you think classical might mean harking back to an altogether more ancient time, to a time of kasbahs and bazaars, of odours and aromas and emotions weaving through the wine like threads of experience from two thousand years ago – well, perhaps that's why Musar was so important. In all my chats with Serge, I don't think we talked about winemaking once. We talked about vineyards, about how he was having trouble getting grape-pickers because the neighbouring hashish producers paid a better hourly rate. We talked about his winery – sometimes of the night during the civil war when bombs and rockets crumped and screamed all around the building and Serge took a magnum of Musar and a supply of cigars and sat and smoked and drank in the heart of the winery, preferring to end it all there rather than be spared cowering in the hills.

And we talked about his wine as we drank – and never spat. He held forth like an elder enlivened by his hookah. And he says that it's the spirit and soul of the vintage that matters. He blends according to the emotional and personal perception he has of the vintage. Not surprisingly, he says, 'Great wine should be dangerously attractive rather than simply enjoyable. What I want is a wine that troubles me.'

Well, Musar certainly troubles tasters who don't know it. Young Musar seems prematurely oxidised and tired. You're certain it can't last. But between their seventh and eighth years, just as you think the only way now is downhill, dammit, Musars break out into a unique maturity that is sometimes as intense as burnt raspberry sauce scraped from the pan, sometimes thick with a dark syrup of black cherries steeped in brandy; sometimes it juggles the sweet sourness of sublime vinegars, sometimes there is a yeastiness as heady as fresh brioche, often wafted through with the scent of cedar, carried on sea breezes from the Bay of Jounieh. But surely it *is* oxidised – that rich fruit reminds me of shrivelled berries dusty with the parched earth of high summer. Yet, yet . . . it *isn't* oxidised. That freshness keeps coming back, a bitter cherry roughness, the cedar now turns to cured tobacco leaves in a warm, muggy loft, and the sweet decay of balsamic vinegar seems to gnaw at the richness, turning the candy of sugared almonds into the tangy intensity of sloes.

Now do you see what I mean when I say that Lebanon's wine flame was kept alight through the most challenging of times by a superstar – Serge Hochar of Chateau Musar? Indeed, a lot of you will know the name Chateau Musar when you couldn't name a single wine from anywhere else in the eastern Mediterranean and the Middle East. That's OK. That's the measure of Musar.

But Serge Hochar died, mysteriously, almost exotically, out in the Pacific Ocean on New Year's Eve in 2014. Musar continues, but the best of the rest of the Lebanese wineries have taken up the baton. And there are quite a few of these, mostly centred in the Bekaa Valley in the east of Lebanon, only a mountain range away from Damascus, Syria's embattled capital. The Bekaa Valley is fertile and high – generally about 1000 metres (3280 feet) and on the hillsides a good deal higher. It's been famous for wine since at least Roman times. The second-century Temple of Bacchus at Ba'albek in the north of the valley still stands glorious and proud, towering over a neighbouring minaret in a Hezbollah hotspot. But as global warming takes its toll – in the last fifty years, vintage dates have moved backwards by as much as a month, sometimes commencing in mid-August, while

alcohol levels have risen – Lebanese winemakers are searching
for cooler conditions.

As in Israel, the only way is up; after all, Lebanon is on the
same latitude as Tunisia. And this move upwards, luckily, has
several destinations that look promising. The hills above the
Bekaa are a start. But the most developed 'new' area is in the
Batroun Mountains that rear up from the coast between Beirut
and Tripoli. These are some of Lebanon's original vineyard sites.
Most of the planting now is about 300–500 metres (1000–1600
feet) above sea level, but drive half an hour further inland and
you'll find likely spots at 2000 metres (6560 feet). The slopes
around Mount Lebanon are encouraging, with vines planted at
up to 1800 metres (5900 feet). And further south, in Jezzine,
they have to terrace the dizzying slopes at heights up to 1400
metres (4600 feet). The first signs are of fresher and brighter reds
and whites than is usually the case with Bekaa fruit. If Lebanon
can hold on to its precarious peace, wineries like Chateau Saint
Thomas, Domaine des Tourelles, Domaine Wardy, Karam and
Ixsir are keen to show us there is Lebanese life after Musar.

Lebanon was lucky if Chateau Musar was the only wine you
knew the name of. Turkey and Greece weren't so lucky. Greece
had retsina, for goodness sake, and for those whose memories
weren't permanently impaired by it, Demestica. And Turkey
had Buzbağ. Now, I used to make as much fun of Buzbağ as
the next guy, normally accompanied by rolling of the eyes,
clutching of the vitals and realistic gagging sounds. I seem to
remember I mostly came across it at actors' parties in the seedier
boltholes of north London and I presumed, probably correctly,
that Buzbağ had been the cheapest red available at the various
Turkish delis in the neighbourhood. But I felt slightly ill at ease
as I mocked the wine, because, beneath the rudimentary winemaking, I thought I could actually taste some rather glorious,
timeless, weary but worthy fruit.

It wasn't enough to persuade me to visit Turkey, but as I
picked up little gobbets of information about the place I realised

I was being lazy by not trying to learn more. Especially when I saw a claim that they'd been domesticating wild vines in south-east Turkey for even longer than in Georgia – as long ago as 9000 BC. And I read that they had fifteen hundred grape varieties in Turkey – at least eight hundred of which were genetically different. I looked up a few: Boğazkere, Kalecik Karası, Narince, Yapincak, Öküzgözü – that one really got me! How many umlauts can you fit into one grape name? And Turkey is big. It wasn't called Asia Minor for nothing. From the balmy shores of the Aegean on the border with Greece to the barren, bleak reaches of tribal lands in south-east Anatolia on the border with Syria, you couldn't find two cultures so widely separated in one giant nation. I have to say, from east to west, Turkish wine people are a doughty bunch. Turkey is still nominally a secular country with a Muslim faith, but the Islamist influence has grown in recent years, and alcohol is increasingly taxed and restricted and prohibited. The wine gang are a brave lot.

And there *is* a wine revolution afoot in Turkey, and their wine world today *is* unrecognisable from that of even ten years ago. Parts of it are genuinely exciting. I admit I'm most thrilled by what's happening with those unpronounceable indigenous grapes. Each time I visit I discover more of them, often saved from extinction by a single passionate producer. But Turkey is also finding ways to create really individual wines from the international warhorses like Cabernet Sauvignon, Merlot and Syrah. The producers complain that we foreigners are biased against these well-known varieties. Well, yes, we are, but only because the hordes of unpronounceables are so challenging and exciting.

And they still make Buzbağ. I tracked down the winemaker, a delightful American called Daniel, who came visiting and never left. Despite my protestations, he laid on a vertical tasting going back fifteen years. He said it had been easy to improve Buzbağ: he just took the bricks out of the boxes of grapes. He was serious. Some of the growers would weight the boxes with hidden bricks to get more money. Some of them also carried guns. Yes . . . The 1995 did taste a little dusty. But I quite liked the 2006 and '08 – Daniel had made those, and there was something rather self-important and serious about them, triggering a flickering memory of my secret admiration for my first Buzbağs. 'The brand has been made since 1944,' Daniel told me. 'It's Turkey's oldest indigenous blend and to make it good stretches my brain more than any other wine.' 'And you should like it.' It's 100 per cent Boğazkere and Öküzgözü from vineyards just about as far east as you can go in the country.

And Greece. Well, let's consign Demestica to the cleaning cupboard under the sink. But let's not forget retsina. There may be more jokes made about this drink than almost any other wine, but retsina is the only link we have between today and the supposedly glorious wines of Ancient Greece. And, by the way, I love good retsina.

If you read some of the nineteenth- and early-twentieth-century wine writers, you get the impression that Ancient Greek wine might have been some kind of nectar. Very rarely, if ever. Just now and then they would have got lucky and made some powerful, sweet wine, luscious and intense, from grapes that had shrivelled their sugary intensity into a viscous syrup of incomparable richness that nature was unable to attack and turn to vinegar.

But mostly the wines of Ancient Greece, and Rome and the other civilisations around the Mediterranean, would have needed all the help they could get to stop them going sour. They would add honey and spices, obviously – saffron, pepper, rose petals, mint – but also potter's earth and powdered marble and bitter wormwood. Sea water was frequently added, though with the lack of any sewerage system I would hope they took their sea water from well offshore – and on a calm day.

But the greatest, most effective preservative was pine resin. The Ancients had discovered that if you smeared the resin of the local terebinth pine on soldiers' wounds, it staved off infection.

So they began smearing resin inside their wine containers – and it worked. Sure, it made the wine taste of pine resin, but you could get used to that, and it was a lot more fun than vinegar. The Greeks started it, and the Romans continued so enthusiastically that their writers sometimes seemed more excited about where the pine resin came from than where the grapes grew. Pliny's favourite resins came from Calabria in southern Italy and from Cyprus. He particularly liked the way little fragments of it stuck to his teeth 'with an agreeably tart taste'. You're not kidding.

So don't knock retsina. Try treating it with reverence. Well . . . But I just want you to know that a) there's nothing better with a great mound of hummus and taramasalata than ice-cold retsina (you can splash in some lemonade if you want); and b) when you drink retsina, you're experiencing just a tiny inkling of what wine might have been like thousands of years ago.

The Ancient Greeks weren't just famous for adding resin to their wine – Greek colonisers carried the vine with them across the Mediterranean. Whether Greek or Roman influence was more important is a moot point, but the modern global wine culture we now enjoy stems from what started in the Mediterranean – and it was the Greeks who brought wine and vine to both Italy and France. So what happened next? Well, just about nothing. A big, fat omega.

If you want the history, you've got the Byzantine Empire, then the Venetians not exactly helping, followed by almost five hundred years as part of the Ottoman Empire. That ended with the First World War and the collapse of the Ottomans. Greece was a free state again, but with zero wine culture. You would have thought Greece's fantastic popularity with tourists in the latter part of the twentieth century might have translated into an enthusiastic export market. But no. The only places where foreigners seemed to want to drink Greek wines was in the local taverna to wash down the moussaka and get ready for an evening of plate-smashing. And they didn't ask for anything expensive.

I'm not surprised; the wine labels were unreadable – proudly offering Hellenic script to an uncomprehending audience.

Well, that was then, but in the twenty-first century we're just beginning to see Greece for what it is: one of Europe's most fascinating wine countries – not remotely like France or Germany, or Italy or Spain. Truly modern in its winemaking, and using ancient grape varieties that *no one else* has. This is the real joy of modern Greece. If we're getting bored of Bordeaux or Burgundy, Riesling or Rioja and we want a genuinely different flavour and style, Greece has got dozens – probably hundreds – of grape varieties stretching back into antiquity. A couple of southern Italian varieties are related because of Ancient Greece colonising the region – otherwise, if you want a walk on the wild side in Europe, Greece is waiting to take you by the arm and guide your taste buds to somewhere you've never imagined existed. The best Greek producers don't force the issue, don't overripen the grapes, don't overoak the wines. As the winemaker at Argyros on the island of Santorini said to me, 'I think the wines have more to say than we do.'

There are famous wine regions – red Naoussa in the north and red Nemea in the south – and they are very different, but don't worry about the geographical designations too much, although it's worth realising that a lot of Greece is not baking hot. Up in Macedonia and down in the Peloponnese south-west of Athens there are high, frequently wet, windy vineyard areas where the grapes can struggle to ripen. Which is exactly what you want for the creation of exciting, taut, appetising, scented wines. And out in the islands, particularly on Santorini and Crete, well, these are sun-baked all right, but the local grapes have been dealing with that for thousands of years.

For red grapes, I'm most excited by the austere, hauntingly ageable Xinomavro and the more gushingly delicious Agiortiko. There are far more white varieties making a mark; these include the heady, blossom-scented Malagousia and Moschofilero, the haughty, mineral and citrusy zest hero Assyrtiko, the pithy, stony Robola, the rosemary- and laurel-scented Dafni of Crete – oh, and sweet Muscat. The island of Samos makes some of the best sweet Muscats in the world. Always did. Except that now we are starting to appreciate them.

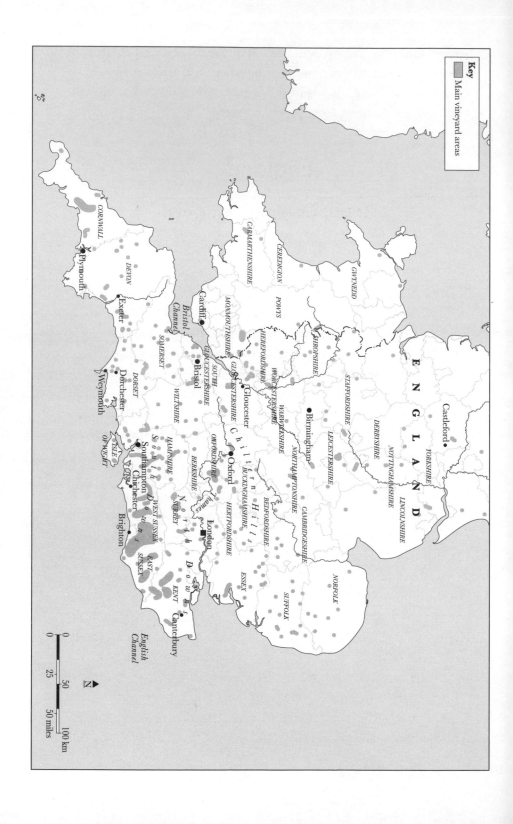

CORNWALL

Plymouth

DEVON

Exeter

Bristol
Channel

Cardiff

CARMARTHENSHIRE

CEREDIGION

GWYNEDD

POWYS

MONMOUTHSHIRE

SOMERSET

Bristol

SOUTH
GLOUCESTERSHIRE

GLOUCESTERSHIRE

Gloucester

HEREFORDSHIRE

WORCESTERSHIRE

SHROPSHIRE

STAFFORDSHIRE

DERBYSHIRE

NOTTINGHAMSHIRE

Dorchester

Weymouth

DORSET

WILTSHIRE

ISLE
OF WIGHT

HAMPSHIRE

BERKSHIRE

OXFORDSHIRE

Oxford

C h i l t e r n   H i l l s

BUCKINGHAMSHIRE

WARWICKSHIRE

Birmingham

LEICESTERSHIRE

NORTHAMPTONSHIRE

BEDFORDSHIRE

E N G L A N D

Castleford

YORKSHIRE

LINCOLNSHIRE

Southampton

Chichester

Brighton

S o u t h   D o w n s

WEST SUSSEX

SURREY

N o r t h   D o w n s

Thames

London

HERTFORDSHIRE

CAMBRIDGESHIRE

NORFOLK

EAST
SUSSEX

KENT

Canterbury

ESSEX

SUFFOLK

English
Channel

N

0   50   100 km

0   25   50 miles

England

At last, Champagne has a rival

The last successful invasion of England by the French was in 1066. William the Conqueror prevailed against the English king Harold and brought some very good ideas on cider-making with him from Normandy. The latest invasion attempt began in December 2015. Taittinger Champagne bought a piece of land at Chilham, near Canterbury, and, before anyone could stop them, they'd planted a vineyard with Chardonnay and Pinot grapes and declared their intention to make sparkling wine. Pommery Champagne then declared a partnership with Hattingley Valley Vineyard in Hampshire. Is this the thin end of the wedge? Has the colonisation of the lush green acres of England's fair south begun in earnest? Are we to become a northern outpost of the ruthless Champagne industry, with all the loss of sovereignty that that entails?

We should be flattered. The only reasons that the Champagne guys are here are, first, that in their most secret moments they believe that they will be able to make great sparkling wine in Kent, Sussex and Hampshire; and second, they are increasingly worried that they *won't* be able to make the world's best fizz in the Champagne region of France for all that much longer. This is to do with global warming. The climatic conditions are changing rapidly in northern Europe. Sparkling wine is at its finest when made from fairly acid grapes that barely reach full ripeness. Champagne, a mere couple of hours' drive from Calais and the English Channel, has always prided itself on walking the tightrope between ripeness and rawness with its Chardonnay, Pinot Noir and Pinot Meunier grapes. Traditionally the temperature during the ripening period in southern England has been about 1°C (1.8°F) cooler than that in Champagne, enough to make it too difficult to even get these varieties barely ripe. But, depending on whose statistics you read, the temperature during the ripening season in Champagne has risen by more than 2°C (3.6°F) since 1990 alone. That is a truly massive increase. Then look north across the English Channel to Kent and Sussex. If these counties are traditionally 1°C (1.8°F) cooler than Champagne, they're now slotting nicely into the 'just able to ripen' position, as Champagne begins to fret that her vineyard conditions are in danger of becoming too warm.

And there's another thing. The soil. Or, rather, the chalk that underlies all the best Champagne vineyards, and the limestone that underpins great French white wine areas like Sancerre and Chablis. It's all part of a geographical system called the Paris Basin (see map, page 572) – with Paris in the centre and a ring of limestone (to the west) and chalk (to the east) that creates a circle of high ridges of this pale, crumbly soil. Dr Richard Smart, one of the world's greatest vineyard experts, is so keen on this ring that he has called it the motherlode of great vineyard soils. Why is this relevant to England? Because this ring isn't just French. The whole northern arc is in England – the English Channel is only about ten thousand years old. Before that, France was part of southern England. Depending on your point of view, of course.

There are two great ridges – the North and South Downs – that run, in effect, from Dover in Kent all the way to Weymouth in Dorset. Pure cretaceous chalk. And this chalk also runs up north of London, creating the Chiltern Hills, and through Norfolk north to Yorkshire. Jurassic limestone butts against cretaceous chalk in Dorset and it too stretches right up through

Leicestershire and Lincolnshire to Yorkshire. Add to that warm gravels through much of the Thames Valley, and greensand running between the North and South Downs where the chalk has been washed away from the ridges, leaving highly suitable vineyard land. There are various other soils, too, but this just shows that if global warming proceeds as rapidly as it is threatening to, England and, to a certain extent, Wales, is packed full of as many suitable vineyard sites as northern France.

If the climate holds. Already vineyard owners in England are reporting that they can harvest their grapes a month earlier than they used to, with twice as much sugar in them. That's not surprising when nine of the ten warmest Octobers ever recorded have been in this century, as well as three of the five hottest Septembers. Each year it should be possible to push vines further north. Yorkshire now finds no difficulty in making decent wine. Twenty years ago I used to describe Yorkshire wine as raw, ferrous and stained by Pennine rain, scarred by the sooty crust of industry. Now there's a delightful professional Yorkshireman called George Bowden at Leventhorpe Vineyards near Castleford, whose wines are mellow, blossom-scented, mildly citrusy whites bursting with cool-climate confidence. I know a guy who's started a vineyard north of Hadrian's Wall, near the Scottish border. And there really is a vineyard in Scotland, too.

As I said, if the climate holds. Britain is only able to take advantage of climate change because of the Gulf Stream. This massive convection system runs through the Atlantic Ocean, sending ice-cold water south from the Arctic and dragging warm water up from the Gulf of Mexico. This warm water laps the beaches and cliffs of western Europe and transforms our weather. Vineyards in southern England are around the 51°N latitude mark. This is the same as the freezing tip of Newfoundland in Canada, but they don't have the Gulf Stream there. It's the Gulf Stream warmth that makes viticulture possible in Britain. You can see the difference its influence makes in the Faroe Islands up toward Norway. The Gulf Stream passes to the west of the islands and the water temperature there is 6°C (11°F) warmer than to the east of the islands.

But the whole Gulf Stream system relies on there being an Arctic ice cap, sending icy water south to fuel the convection system. And the ice cap is shrinking: every few years scientists predict that we will have an ice-free North Pole in midsummer. It hasn't happened yet, but it will. The Gulf Stream will fail one day, and it has failed before. Its flow is already 30 to 40 per cent weaker than it was only a generation ago. If the planet does heat rapidly, the loss of the Gulf Stream's warmth might be just the thing keeping western France and the British Isles pleasant and cool to live in. But that would also spell the end of the English wine industry as we know it now. In which case, let's enjoy it while we can.

And we're certainly doing that. England and Wales (mostly England) are now making more than five million bottles of wine a year. Over two-thirds of this is fizz, as the idea that we can match and maybe better the Champagne producers just over the Channel takes hold. Plantings are increasing at a hectic rate – a million vines were planted in England in 2017 alone and 2018 will be much the same. Wine production is predicted to reach ten million bottles by 2020, most of it sparkling, most of it made from the Champagne varieties – Chardonnay, Pinot Noir and Pinot Meunier – and most of it expensive.

It wasn't always like this. It's true that the Romans made wine in England. It's true that there were significant vineyards during a warm period in the Middle Ages. It's also true that there's not much evidence people liked the stuff, and Britain's last commercial vineyard before the modern era, at Castell Coch in South Wales, was pulled out in 1920. It was in reference to Castell Coch wines that *Punch* magazine famously remarked that it took four men to drink the wine – the victim, two to hold him down and one to thrust the liquid down his throat.

And that was that, until after the Second World War, when tiny amounts of wine began to be made again. I mean *tiny*. The total national crop in 1964 amounted to 1500 bottles; fifty years later, 2014 produced 6.3 million bottles. I tasted various bottles from the 1970s and they were unremittingly challenging. One, from Chilsdown Vineyard near Chichester, I kept for thirty years. I would intermittently hold it up to the light to see if its bleach-white colour had deepened and softened. It never had. At thirty-five years old I opened the bottle and this pale, resentful, indignant liquid forced its way out, as lemon-lipped, as raw, as suitable for paint removal as it had been all those years before. Proud, unbending, just not very nice to ingest.

But the 1980s did show a change. The first International Wine Challenge took place in 1984. English wines and one Welsh wine took the first six places. The competition wasn't intense – the only other entrants were that month's special offers from one high street retail chain – but a win's a win. Winemaking was clearly getting better – there were even one or two people who knew what they were doing! When Stephen Skelton, now Britain's best-known consultant, won the top wine award in 1981, the chairman of the English Vineyards Association was only half-joking when he said, 'Stephen, you cheated really – you were trained,' because Stephen had taken a winemaking course in Germany. The chairman clearly expected the winemakers to be amateurs.

And an English wine style was beginning to form, if erratically, unpredictably – you could never order a wine's new vintage simply because you liked the last one – but there was a cool-climate character emerging, generally based on German grape varieties, which made terrible wine in Germany's warmer conditions, but in cooler England could be delightful. The Müller-Thurgau, Huxelrebe, Ortega and Bacchus varieties could produce still wines with scents of elderflower, of tiny white springtime blossoms, and of the sappy, bright-eyed optimism of an early summer hedgerow. English flavours. Light, low in alcohol, fresh, scented – and no bubbles. Bacchus, at least, is still making delightfully drinkable whites just like these well into the twenty-first century.

And then came the bubbles. The country that gets closest to making a Champagne lookalike is England. And it started with Nyetimber. If a wine country is lucky, there will come a moment when everything changes, an event occurs that has such an effect the past can be abandoned and a glittering future embraced as it suddenly becomes blindingly obvious what sort of wine the country should be making. The most startling example of this was New Zealand's being able to rid itself of its dubious, dowdy past and bask in completely unexpected global adulation when Cloudy Bay won Best Sauvignon Blanc in the World with its first vintage in 1986. From then on, Sauvignon Blanc would define New Zealand. The name of England's prophet, England's revolutionary, was Nyetimber. This winery made sparkling wine using the Champagne grape varieties of Chardonnay, Pinot Noir and Pinot Meunier, and they made it just like they did in Champagne, with the best Champagne equipment and the most qualified Champagne consultants.

Were they the first ones in the UK? They were the first ones. Why hadn't anyone tried it before? There had been some OK English fizz before, but Nyetimber wasn't OK. Nyetimber was magnificent. Nyetimber possessed the lush crème fraîche and brioche richness cut through with piano-wire-taut acidity that the wine buffs would tell you only the very best Champagnes could aspire to. Until now. Nyetimber's first vintage was in 1992; in 1998 the '93 won the trophy for Best International Sparkling Wine in the World – against forty-three other countries. From a standing start. In blind tastings it was routinely identified as a top Champagne. I learned fast, saying 'It's so good, it must be Nyetimber.' Gosh, I felt smug. England would probably have gradually crept toward the realisation that its future lay in top-quality sparkling wine. How long would it have taken?

Sandy and Stuart Moss were from Chicago. They don't creep toward goals in Chicago. They bought the Nyetimber estate in deepest Sussex, with its soils identical to some of Champagne's best, convinced they could make sparkling wine as fine as some Champagne and completely determined to do so. They breezily admitted they decided to do it 'because it was so hard'. Too hard for the home-grown Brits. Lack of confidence, lack of professionalism was pretty rife in England's wine-growing world before Nyetimber. God bless the Yanks. Twenty years later, confidence bubbles through the veins of British grape-growing and winemaking. The Duchess of Cornwall is an enthusiastic and energetic President of WineGB, and Windsor Castle now has its own vineyard. Confidence starts at the top.

Oh, and did I tell you that the English invented Champagne? But that's another story.

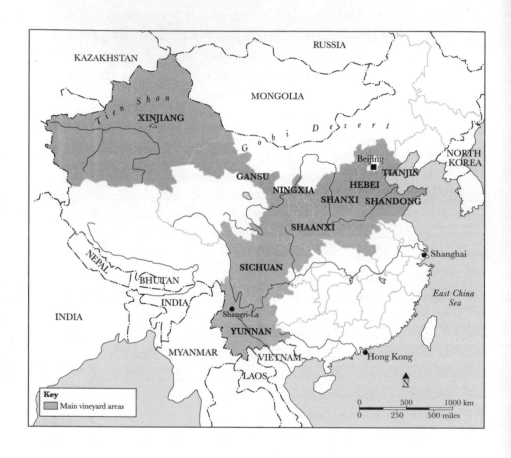

KAZAKHSTAN

RUSSIA

MONGOLIA

Tien Shan

XINJIANG

G o b i   D e s e r t

NORTH
KOREA

GANSU

Beijing

TIANJIN

NINGXIA

HEBEI

SHANXI

SHANDONG

SHAANXI

NEPAL

BHUTAN

INDIA

Shanghai

SICHUAN

INDIA

Shangri-La

*East China
Sea*

YUNNAN

MYANMAR

VIETNAM

Hong Kong

LAOS

N

Key
Main vineyard areas

0   500   1000 km

0   250   500 miles

China and the rest of Asia

The dragon stirs

I could never have said what I am about to say ten years ago. Nor even five years ago. I suspect not even two years ago. So here it is: I have just come from a tasting of forty-nine Chinese wines, nearly all Cabernet and Cabernet blends. With a couple of over-oaked, stewy exceptions, all the wines were good. But I was disappointed. None of the wines were great. I had actually expected some of the wines to be truly magnificent. Surely that's completely unrealistic? When did the first half-decent Chinese red hit the wider world's consciousness? 2011. That was when a 2009 wine from Ningxia, out near the Gobi Desert, called Jia Bei Lan ('Little Feet' in English, named for the winemaker's new baby girl) won the Decanter World Wine Award for Best Red Bordeaux-type Wine Over £10 a Bottle, a category which would include an awful lot of the world's smart red wines, I'd have thought. I managed to wangle a taste and felt the wine was quite good in an edgy kind of way, though I couldn't see how it had beaten such impressive opposition as it must have done in the Awards.

But this was a first wine, from a tiny vineyard. And it was only seven years ago. Give it a break. And now I was tasting the best part of fifty Chinese wines, almost all of them better than the 2009 'Little Feet' which had caused such a fuss. In fact, there were three 2014 wines from 'Little Feet' in the tasting and the evident progress was little short of extraordinary; genuinely classy wines, polished, nicely oaky and somehow staying balanced and mouthwatering at 14.5 per cent alcohol. Not great wine, no. But this was only their sixth vintage. How many examples of great red wines did Australia or California or Chile produce within six years of any kind of international recognition? Not many, if any, I suggest.

China's strength seems to be an astonishing ability to say what they want to do and then do it. Now, I was reading about the director of the Ningxia winery association complaining in 2013 about how local people were telling journalists that his outfit was going to build a wine route – like California's Napa Valley or Bordeaux's in France – and line it with fifty brand new châteaux. Not fifty, he said wearily; we've got plans to build a thousand châteaux. Less than four years later, a friend of mine got back from a visit to this area, which really is on the fringe of the Gobi Desert, and she said there is a new road, hundreds of kilometres long, lined with dozens of château buildings and vineyard after vineyard. All in four years.

This strength of China's does have an Achilles heel: we simply don't or can't believe the progress that's being made. You need intrepid visitors to return to reality back in Europe and say that it's really happening. I shouldn't be so surprised. I go to China often enough, though not usually on vineyard-visiting business, and I am goggle-eyed at the transformation of areas I have known for thirty years. And nearly all that transformation is in the last decade. So when I learn that the vineyards in Ningxia are part of a grand five-year plan to reverse the desertification of the region by the relentless Gobi, I shouldn't be surprised. The government decided vineyards were a good idea, bulldozed away vast stretches of sand dunes, laid down irrigation and planted forest to shelter the vines from the bitter desert winds. The arresting quality of the leading wines is an added bonus. But now that several local wineries have proved that quality is possible and desirable, how many more delights can we expect in the next few years? Which probably explains why I thought six years would be quite enough to go from OK but edgy to magnificent. Well, red wine is not quite that simple, as the Chinese are finding out, but they're impressing the hell out of me as they go about it.

You look at China's vast size and think there must be dozens of suitable places for vineyards. Well, there may be, but not if you're going to use European criteria. Despite Cabernet Sauvignon being by far the most popular grape variety with the wineries, there seems to be only one small section of a region called Gansu, even further inland than Ningxia, which is supposed to have a climate vaguely resembling that of Bordeaux. A very vague resemblance, I'd have thought. Bordeaux doesn't have to bury its vines each winter to protect them from −20 degrees of frost. That's what they have to do in Gansu.

But that's what they've also got to do in Ningxia, an area they actually call the Bordeaux of China, and the Cabernet Sauvignons from wineries like Helan Qingxue (which produces 'Little Feet'), Silver Heights, Ninglan Helan Mountain, Jade Vineyard, Lilan and the French drinks giant Pernod Ricard are impressive. That's some roll call. I haven't even mentioned Grace Vineyards in Shanxi, to the east of Ningxia. I haven't mentioned what is possibly the most remarkable area of them all – Xinjiang. I haven't visited Xinjiang, but I've flown over it and even from 10,000 metres (32,800 feet) up I can sense that it's something special – a sprawling arid plain stretched between high mountains with great blotches of agricultural activity. They could easily be vines. An operation called Jinchuang Suntime established a 10,000-hectare (24,700-acre) vineyard on the slopes of the Tian Shan Mountains, making themselves at a stroke Asia's largest vineyard owner. Pretty nearly the world's, too. How very Chinese. Just do it.

Xinjiang only gets 150 millimetres (6 inches) of rain a year – no problem as the mountains have enough snowmelt to irrigate those 10,000 hectares, and masses more besides. The summer days are very hot, the nights very cold – good for quality – and the sun stays shining right into October, with rain almost unheard of until winter crashes in, snow and all – and the temperatures drop as low as −27°C (−16.6°F). You need a lot of cheap labour to bury 10,000 hectares of vines under the earth in a hurry. Bordeaux it's not, and yet Syrah and the late-ripening Cabernet Sauvignon do get just ripe enough as winter falls at wineries like Zhongfei, Tiansai Vineyards, Sandyland Wine Company and Xiangdu. How are you doing on all these names, by the way?

Xinjiang has been producing grapes and raisins of various sorts for two thousand years without anyone much noticing, and the modern taste for Cabernet, which assails all of China, is recent. Shandong Peninsula, however, south-east of Beijing, is another place which has enjoyed styling itself China's Bordeaux for a while now. Well, it would have to be Bordeaux in a fairly poor vintage. Summer and autumn rain is pretty much endemic, and typhoons have a habit of whipping across the slopes and flattening the vines. It's warm enough to ripen Cabernet Sauvignon, but it isn't dry enough. However, Shandong is very much a tourist centre and its importance was massively boosted when Château Lafite decided to create a joint-venture vineyard here. Their Bordeaux-trained winemaker wasn't all that pleased: he said that he discovered some forms of rot that he'd only read about in textbooks! I've had pleasant Shandong Chardonnays and Rieslings, but that's not what the Chinese drinkers want, yet. The colour of wine is still red.

If I were looking for a place that might make a 'Chinese Bordeaux', I'd head for somewhere even less likely than the wild north-west of Xinjiang. I'd head for Shangri-La. There really is a place called Shangri-La. The area's traditional name is Zhongdian, but, in the understandable desire to get a tour-ist trade going, Zhongdian persuaded the authorities to let it rename itself Shangri-La in 2001. I'm told there was quite a lot of competition from other areas to use this name. China, again!

Shangri-La was the novelist James Hilton's mythical utopia

in the Himalayas, and at the top of the Mekong River Valley, right up by Tibet and long after the last decent road has given out, LVMH, the world luxury multinational, has created a vineyard and a winery called Ao Yun – 'Roaming above the clouds' – about as far removed from the glitz of urban life as any on the planet. LVMH already control two of Bordeaux's fabled First Growth châteaux – Yquem and Cheval Blanc – and they think that these vineyards rising up to 2600 metres (8530 feet) above sea level, surrounded by high mountains that cut off 30 per cent of the sunshine yet also provide a rain shadow from the monsoon, just might be the ones to produce China's first First Growth-quality red. I would never bet against LVMH. After all, their business is putting substance into dreams.

India

I'd like to say that India might rival China in the wine stakes, but I see little sign of it. There are some successful wineries – Sula makes a million cases of wine a year, and has always managed to make an attractive, soft but lemony Sauvignon Blanc. But India is hardly a wine-drinking country – you could barely get a lower per-capita consumption: it's 0.0015 litres of wine per person, per annum. That's about a tablespoon. With 10 per cent annual growth in consumption, it would still take about eight years to get to two tablespoons. Nashik is the main vineyard area, north-east of Mumbai, but it's hard work. The vines never go dormant. It is below the Tropic of Cancer here, heading for the Equator. You get two crops a year, a monsoon vintage and a half-decent one, unless you go in for some pretty creative pruning. White Chenin and Sauvignon can be OK, if sometimes a little sweet; the reds seem to give off a smoky aroma, regardless of whether they're Syrah, Cabernet, Merlot or even Zinfandel, and I really would like a bit less chocolate oak.

Of course, there is one area of India that could probably

produce really good wines, and has even been touted, for what it's worth, as India's Bordeaux. (Does every country have to have their own Bordeaux?) I'm talking about Kashmir, high up in the foothills of the Himalayas. It could be really good. But given that Pakistan and India can't come to any agreement about who actually owns the area, planting a vineyard to grow grapes to make into wine would be seen as provocative to say the least.

Elsewhere in Asia

It's not just India that battles the weather in Asia. Everywhere does. Some of the most successful producers are in the harsh hinterland. Kazakhstan, to the north-west of China, produces pretty pleasant reds as well as surprisingly tasty Riesling and, more predictably, attractive Rkatsiteli.

Thailand has some reputation for such grapes as Chenin and Syrah, although I've never exactly taken to them. Bali makes a bit of rosé that wouldn't go amiss in a beachside bar. And South Korea periodically tries to stir things up quality-wise, but my Korean friends tell me that anyone thinking they can make serious wine in the humid, muggy conditions of the Korean peninsula needs a reality check and a good stiff drink of something entirely different.

And humidity is what dogs Japan, too. I love Japan. I love Japanese culture, especially once you get outside Tokyo. When I'm in Japan I wake up each day convinced that some time between breakfast and bedtime I will discover yet another texture and yet another flavour in my food that I never knew existed. But I rarely drink wine with my meals. Beer, yes – craft brewing is alive and kicking in Japan – sake certainly, warm or cool: I prefer cool. And tea. But I rarely drink koshu, Japan's very own, very delicate wine. It's pretty trendy right now, so I put my tasting hat on whenever there's koshu to be found, but I just don't get lucky.

I suspect it's one of those wines that shines with the very best producers and simply hasn't got enough oomph to survive the merest flicker of mediocrity. And the very best won't be leaving Japan's shores.

I find the same with the classic European varieties like Cabernet and Merlot. Most of the wines I've tried have been from Yamanashi, which is also koshu's heartland. This is a beautiful vineyard area, just west of Tokyo, but when you see fields of vines trained on to head-high pergolas with twee little rain bonnets protecting each bunch of grapes, first you marvel at the Japanese ability to do things properly, but second you realise that ripening the grapes before they rot on the vine is going to be quite a challenge. Japan gets monsoons in spring and summer, from east and west; the rainy season is in June and July, and then the typhoons arrive to keep you company until harvest time. And yet they keep at it. The Japanese swear it's worth it. I'm sure, bit by bit, they'll persuade me. I'm told there's an exciting Pinot Noir being made by Domaine Takahiko in the cooler and drier north island of Hokkaido. The trouble is you have to enter a lottery to try to get hold of a bottle.

THE STYLES THAT SHAPE THE WORLD OF WINE

Wine is now a global village. Ideas about how to make better wine, how to make different wine, which styles might work and which styles won't, can wing around the world at the tap of a smartphone screen. Some countries do have ancient traditions that they still revere, but many countries don't. Many countries, especially in the New World, had no wine tradition, and yet are world leaders in various styles. Even in Europe, old-established wine cultures often needed a dramatic kick to start making any kind of reputation for themselves.

If we look at the wines that have been praised over the last few centuries, they are nearly all French, excepting the Riesling styles of Germany and the fortified styles of Spain and Portugal. The red wines of Bordeaux, Burgundy and the Rhône, the white wines of Burgundy and the Loire, the sparkling wines of Champagne, the sweet wines of Bordeaux. These were the wines that became famous, which were written about, and which were exported throughout Europe and, increasingly, the rest of the world.

So when there was a cautious emergence of a fine wine culture in the New World after the Second World War, followed
by a positive explosion in enthusiasm for better wine at every
quality and price level toward the end of the last century, these
were the wine styles the new producers decided to copy.

Since they couldn't take the soils of Bordeaux or Burgundy
with them, they borrowed the methods and, above all, they
took the grape varieties that had made the wines famous in their
homelands, and planted them, often thousands of miles away, in
very different conditions. The grape variety is at the very heart
of the different flavours in wine. So I have chosen the ones I
think have had the greatest effect on the world of wine. Mostly
this is a story of French classic styles being imitated, and then
flourishing in quite different ways in different countries and in
different continents. But sometimes the story is not so simple.
Sauvignon Blanc may be a French grape, but it became famous
for its unlikely escapades in far-away New Zealand. Syrah is a
French grape, yet it became more famous as Shiraz, and that
was due to Australia's efforts, not those of France. And as for
sparkling wine – was it invented in Champagne? Or could it
have been the English who got there first?

Cabernet Sauvignon and Bordeaux

The empire of King Cab

I n most countries of the world, the first wine that I have tasted has been Cabernet Sauvignon. Not, obviously, from countries like Sweden – although I have tasted a passable example from near Gothenburg (don't ask me how: they manage it in Norway as well). Or Estonia. They make wine there too; unless I'm just having a bad dream regurgitating the flavour. And maybe not in places like Germany or Italy or Spain. But in most countries around the globe, their Cabernet was the first wine I tried. In South Africa it was a very elegant – to use a wine buff's term – example from Meerlust, one of the Cape's most famous estates, and it was delicious. It was also a Cabernet in Zimbabwe, from Stapleford Wines. The trouble with Zimbabwe – well, one of the troubles with Zimbabwe – is that it rains every afternoon during vintage. Cabernet Sauvignon, having loose clusters and thick skins, has at least a beggar's chance of survival against all the fungal infections charging around the vineyard under leaden skies.

My first Algerian wine was Cabernet Sauvignon – from the Atlas Mountain Wine Company; Algeria's expertise had always been in providing vast amounts of blending wine to France from Mediterranean varieties like Grenache, which would have been a bit keener on the North African sunshine than my Mount Atlas Cabernet seemed to have been. But in Lebanon, Chateau Musar made inspiring use of Cabernet Sauvignon, and Britain's leading expert on old wines, Michael Broadbent, writing when he was head of Christie's Wine Auctions, reckoned it was a little bit like a cross between Château Latour, one of Bordeaux's greatest reds, and a Burgundy. Jordan's St George winery must have been listening as they decided to blend Cabernet Sauvignon with Pinot Noir – Bordeaux with Burgundy. You wouldn't have got away with that in France, but it works pretty well in the Middle East and makes a delightfully seamless red. My first Israeli wine was the excellent Golan Heights Cabernet Sauvignon, which managed to taste as though it had been grown in a really cool region, though I knew it had come from an admittedly high but sun-baked patch of land where you had to negotiate the wrecks of bombed-out tanks and armoured cars when you were looking for where to plant your Cabernet Sauvignon. Talking of which, I also tasted Syria's Domaine Bargylus red based on Cabernet Sauvignon. I don't know how, but it was very good, as much for its emotional power and indomitable spirit as for its flavour.

In the Americas, I admit my first red was Gallo Hearty Burgundy, which, of course, could have had Cabernet Sauvignon in it – the Gallos weren't too worried about whether or not French Burgundy had Cabernet in it, or Pinot Noir, for that matter; they certainly weren't worried about Burgundian accuracy with their California version. But then I moved on to Cabernet Sauvignon. Christian Brothers Cabernet, an amazingly juicy, blackcurranty, delicious cheap red wine. I thought California was going to rule the world in good cheap red wine led by Cabernet Sauvignon. But California decided she would rather rule the world in good expensive red wine. The grape was the same – Cabernet Sauvignon – but the price had changed.

And it was Cabernet Sauvignon in South America, too – via Mexico, where I discovered good Cabernet Sauvignon from L.A. Cetto in Baja California. My first, and almost my last, Peruvian wine was Cabernet. The Tacama winery had flown out Bordeaux's greatest wine expert, Émile Peynaud, a guy

who ushered in the modern era in Bordeaux, to tell them how
to do it. I don't think he stayed long enough. In Chile I tasted
a cobwebby, venerable Cabernet from Cousiño Macul. Years
later I went to visit the vineyard. It was now the car park for
two competing supermarkets. Hmm. Come to think of it,
it did have a slight taste of tar. And my first Argentine wine
was Cabernet from an outfit called Weinert. The wine was
impressive in a sort of entirely non-identifiably Cabernet type
of way. And Cabernet Sauvignon was my first Australian red.
I didn't know it at the time – this was the final of the British
National Wine Tasting Championships. I got this wine with a
breezy, joyous, rumbustious burble of ripe blackcurrant fruit
and ridiculous drinkability. I'd never had anything like it. I'd
never had an Australian wine. So I put it down as Australian
Cabernet. Entire careers in wine tasting can be engineered from
intelligent, lucky guesses like this. It was Australian, from just
south of Adelaide: Seaview 1968 Cabernet Sauvignon. I came
second. In the National Wine Tasting Championships. I was
still a student. If I had been any older, I wouldn't have dared put
down Australian Cabernet Sauvignon. So I wouldn't have come
second, either. And New Zealand? My first red was a Cabernet
Sauvignon–Pinot Noir mix. Just like in Jordan. But I think the
Jordanian wine was a little better.

So if I say that Cabernet Sauvignon has had more influence around the world than any other grape, well, there's the
beginning of my evidence. Cabernet Sauvignon *is* the world's
most influential grape. It's the most widely planted wine grape,
and whatever its detractors say, it is the world's top quality red
grape, able to do better, in more places and under more different
conditions, than any other. This easy-to-grow, thick-skinned,
fairly heat-resistant black grape from temperate Bordeaux in
south-west France has been seized upon by virtually every
wine country. And because these countries are all, virtually
without exception, warmer and sunnier than Bordeaux and
consequently better suited to black grapes than white (black

grapes need more sun and heat, and take longer to ripen than most white grapes), their winemakers have seen red Bordeaux as the style they would like to emulate, and which they think they can emulate. A riper version of red Bordeaux seems like an attractive challenge.

But does this mean that Cabernet Sauvignon is the most popular grape variety in the world? No, it doesn't. It depends on who you ask. In many places, Cabernet seems to be the most bitterly resented of grape varieties. Isn't it the most respected grape variety, then? Again, it depends on who you are asking. In many places it seems to be the most reviled. And the reason is, quite simply, its astonishing success and its dominant personality. Some people may see Cabernet as the brightest, most talented high achiever in the playground, while others jealously dismiss this same Cabernet as a bombastic, domineering bully. I suppose there is truth in both views, but I'm much more of an admirer than a mocker. If it weren't for the astonishing success of Cabernet Sauvignon in allowing producers to make marketable, enjoyable red wines in countries and regions with no reputation, all the ancient varieties that are now being rediscovered and lionised would still be footnotes in the history of wine or, indeed, extinct. If it weren't for the lessons in hygiene, extraction of colour and perfume and flavour, and the employment of oak barrels to dramatically improve wine standards that were delivered, along with Cabernet Sauvignon, to many moribund wine regions, the current 'back to the future' craze wouldn't have been possible.

They can complain that Cabernet has colonised everywhere it has set foot. They can complain that it overpowers other varieties when it's added to a blend – and that's true. It does. But its success has meant they can now throw out the Cabernet in Italy or Spain, banish the new oak barrel in Slovenia, Croatia or Greece, because of the massive injection of confidence that Cabernet has delivered to those places. They can kick against Cabernet now in Chile or Argentina, in the south of

France or South Africa, and plead the virtues of almost any other grape precisely because of the vast improvements that Cabernet brought. Cabernet opened the very door that so many Cabernet-haters now march through. And Cabernet taught a whole generation of consumers to love red. Before Cabernet, red wine was usually rough, harsh, indistinct and devoid of fruit flavours. And you could rarely tell from the label what you were in danger of putting into your mouth. Cabernet produced a bright, obvious red wine with flavours of fruit – above all, blackcurrants, black plums and black cherries. Maybe even black olives, if you were in a savoury mood. Whatever country you grew it in, the drinker could recognise the flavour of a Cabernet wine. This burst of fruit meant you could easily cope with the chewy, tannic edge that usually came with Cabernet, especially if the producer had decided to soften it up with oak ageing – barrels, or staves in a tank, or a dousing or two of toasted oak chips in a giant teabag, depending on the budget.

And it said 'Cabernet Sauvignon' on the label. When California decided to lead the way with labelling wines according to their grape variety, the red the public went for was Cabernet Sauvignon. It was the same in Australia, where the more plentiful Shiraz was for a long time dismissed as inferior (it isn't now). Cabernet Sauvignon became shortened to Cabernet, which in turn became shortened to Cab. A bottle of Cab. Napa Cab? Kiwi Cab? Aussie Cab? Cape Cab? Bulgarian, Romanian, Hungarian Cab? Wherever it was grown, however it was made into wine, recognisably Cab.

But does this upfront, easily recognisable style mean that Cabernet doesn't make very interesting wines, intellectually fascinating wines, emotionally arresting wines, wines that bring a sob of pleasure to your throat? This is the barb thrust at Cabernet, particularly by the Pinot Noir brigade. Just as Chardonnay is assailed in white wine by the righteous breast-beating ABC (Anything But Chardonnay), Riesling-lovers who swear, quite wrongly, that Chardonnay doesn't interpret its vineyard birthplace with sufficient precision, so it is with red. Pinot Noir lovers assert that Cabernet bludgeons the palate while Pinot seduces and persuades, that Pinot Noir reveals all the minute facets and possibilities of numerous plots of land while Cabernet strides roughshod over differences in soil and aspect and local weather, extinguishing all subtleties in a blizzard of alcohol and extraction and excessive new oak. It's the oldest rivalry in wine. Is Burgundy, Pinot Noir's homeland, better than Bordeaux, the home of Cabernet Sauvignon? Usually Burgundy holds the moral high ground because of its rarity, its ability to divide an estate of a mere few hectares into numerous different offerings with tantalisingly subtle nuances to delight the taster. And impoverish them, I might add. And frequently confuse them, as they very reasonably wonder whether the emperor's new clothes are quite as fine as they are made out to be. ABC? Anything But Cabernet?

Cabernet and Bordeaux

I think we had better go back to where it all began – in Bordeaux. And we'd also better admit that, in Bordeaux, Cabernet doesn't walk alone. There's a family of grape varieties, all of which are related and complement each other. Cabernet Sauvignon may be the most famous, but the variety is actually the result of a chance cross-breeding between the lesser-known Cabernet Franc and the white Sauvignon Blanc. Cabernet Franc is rarely given enough respect in Bordeaux, but it is increasingly valued elsewhere in the world, where it's always known by its full name: it's only Cabernet Sauvignon that finds itself shortened to Cabernet or Cab. (When I simply write Cabernet, I'm always referring to Cabernet Sauvignon.) Merlot is also descended from Cabernet Franc, and is given much more attention. Even though the most famous wines made in any quantities have all been based on Cabernet Sauvignon, they have also all included some Merlot in their blend, to soften or broaden or fill out the more austere personality that Cabernet Sauvignon can show. But above all, Cabernet Sauvignon is an adult grape. You shouldn't try to soften it too much. That merely serves to infantilise it.

In St-Émilion and Pomerol, on Bordeaux's Right Bank, Merlot is the dominant grape and Cabernet Sauvignon is hardly grown. Cabernet Franc is the most likely partner. But Cabernet Sauvignon and Merlot make a very successful partnership in the vineyard – Cabernet ripens late and needs warm, dry soils like the gravel found in the Médoc region on Bordeaux's Left Bank, whereas Merlot ripens early and can flourish on the cool, clay soils that abound in most of Bordeaux. In cool years the Cabernet needs the juiciness of Merlot, in warm years the Merlot needs the calming restraint of Cabernet Sauvignon.

And there are three other minor players. Carmenère is also the offspring of Cabernet Franc. It was virtually extinct in Bordeaux until recent replantings, but has been of great relevance in Chile. And Malbec and Petit Verdot – at last, something not related to Cabernet Franc – are occasional members of the Bordeaux red band. Petit Verdot is fairly rare everywhere, although Virginia does surprisingly well with it and, if you're lucky, produces dense wine with black cherry fruit and the scent of violets. The other night, tired from writing, I rewarded myself with a glass of Château Kirwan 1983. This has more Petit Verdot than almost any other well-known Bordeaux. The room sang with its heady scent of liquorice and violets. My desire to write a little more was revived by its flavour of black cherries, wet stones and moss rubbed with salt. Malbec is more useful, and more successful up the Dordogne River in Cahors, or, especially, in Argentina.

So does the propensity of Cabernet Sauvignon for seeking out blending partners mean that it is in some way inferior to grapes like Pinot Noir or Nebbiolo? I don't think so. With climate change on a roll, we might see Burgundy's Pinot Noir looking for blending partnerships with grapes like Syrah sooner than we think. And Nebbiolo has often expressed itself best with a bit of help; Barbera often does the job. Cabernet Sauvignon's willingness to take a blending partner has been providing the world with many of its most memorable reds, from over three hundred years ago right up to today.

And if you ask someone like me – someone who is thrilled by flavours, much of whose life seems to be spent in pursuit of scents and perfumes and taste experiences, someone whose mind is always open to something new and unexpected – if you ask what has Cabernet Sauvignon meant to me, in all its forms, with or without its blending partners? Has it meant more than Pinot Noir? Yes, it has. Has it meant more than Syrah? Yes, it has. And has Bordeaux meant more than Burgundy and the Rhône Valley? Yes, it has. But has it meant more than America, Australia, New Zealand ... ah, ha – well, probably yes, it has, but of course Cabernet Sauvignon has been completely funda-mental to the intense pleasure and satisfaction I have gained, and still gain, from the New World. So, back to basics. Back to Bordeaux.

A few properties like Château Haut-Brion had set out in the seventeenth century to sell their own estate wine in premises they controlled. If the barrels in which the wines had been dispatched were sound, and the vintage had been decent, it was clear by the end of the century that Bordeaux red wines greatly improved with a bit of age. The invention in England of tougher glass for bottles, and the utilisation of the cork as a stopper – largely unknown in France, but known in Britain – made it possible to age wines in bottle. By the end of the eighteenth century it was becoming clear which ones were the top estates and they had begun to sort their vineyards out. Some vineyards might have twenty or thirty different varieties, but the best only had three or four, and Cabernet Sauvignon was the most important. The grapes were difficult to ripen, and the wines might often only reach 9 per cent alcohol, but the Cabernet gave the most stable wine.

Cabernet's position was cemented in 1855 when the organisers of the Paris Exposition Universelle asked for a selection of Bordeaux's best wines to be sent for display. The merchants quickly put together a list of fifty-eight red wines and twenty-one sweet white wines and sent it off. It was just a snapshot, based on prices, and it was never meant to be permanent. But the 1855 Classification stuck. All the red wines, bar Haut-Brion in the Graves region, were from the Médoc north of Bordeaux, on the gravel beds where Cabernet Sauvignon reigned supreme. And it's this classification that I grew up with. Despite all its faults, despite half the properties woefully underperforming until this century, the 1855 Classification contained all the red wines I longed to drink.

And I realised that the basic beauty of great Cabernet Sauvignon doesn't have to be complicated. Many writers, myself included, look for extra flavours that aren't really there as they struggle to define differences which are often indefinable, which are often emotional, subjective, more to do with texture and sensitivity than they are to do with flavours. But, of course, flavours lead to a word association that makes some sense on the page, and to really delve into the barely explicable differences of a wine's effect upon you demands that you have something of the poet and the dreamer in your soul. Most people don't. Most wine writers certainly don't.

If I look back to my Bordeaux baptism, at university, with the Cabernet-dominated Château Léoville-Barton 1962, it shows the classic formula, unadorned. Bone-dry blackcurrant fruit, bone dry yet finding some richness in its austerity. And this fruit was seasoned, perfumed by cedarwood, pencil shavings and cigar box – all rather similar scents, all probably interchangeable. And if I had drunk the whole bottle to the dregs the balance of scent and fruit might have changed a little, but the simple, beautiful core, of Cabernet Sauvignon grapes mellowed by just a little Merlot, and picked just at the point of ripeness when a fresh acidity still coursed through the ever-sweetening fruit on the vine, would not have wavered. If people talk of classic claret – and some Britons still do, even using that old-fashioned word 'claret' to describe red Bordeaux – this is the kind of wine they would have in mind. Simple, but lovely. Some of nature's greatest flavour pleasures are simple but lovely. Bacon and eggs, or ham and eggs if you prefer. Roast potatoes and gravy. Apple pie and cream. Cheddar cheese and warm white bread. If you try to complicate flavours such as these, make them more sophisticated, you spoil them. And there's something to be said for pursuing a simplicity with Cabernet, a purity of expression rather than the logical extension *ad absurdum* of a line of adjectives and superlatives.

For the last two centuries Bordeaux with its Cabernet-dominated reds has also been able to show off a quality that is often seen as a pointer toward a wine's potential greatness, or a region's potential for greatness. Longevity. The ability of a wine to age gracefully, maybe transform itself, or maybe merely stick to the truth of its fundamental personality. Among red wines in the nineteenth century and for most of the twentieth, only Bordeaux had much chance of demonstrating this. Good Burgundy and Rhône wines were simply too rare, and Spain and Italy didn't figure. So, of course, this attracted the wealthy, the show-offs, but also the genuine collectors in a way that no other red wine could – and red wine was, and still is, usually regarded as the central attraction when dinners are being planned and executed.

I've benefited too. I'm looking at a few old tasting lists here. A wonderful evening of Château Margaux, from 1953 way into the 1980s – and, by the way, no alcohol levels above 12.3 per cent. I seem to have poured the 1961 onto my strawberries. Here are some Château Latours, from 1949 right into the 1980s. And here's one of every vintage of Latour and Lafite from 1945 and into the 1980s again. Did everything get too expensive after the 1980s for this kind of thing to go on any more? I wouldn't be surprised. Prices went mad in the 1980s, as Wall Street money poured in. I was banned from Bordeaux in the early 1990s for making such a fuss about it. Later, it was Hong Kong and Chinese money. Prices never drop for long, and every new surge means someone like me is less and less likely to see such astonishing line-ups of wine again.

Oh, here's a more recent one. A tasting of wines from vintages ending in −5. Going back to the '65s. The 1865s. I liked the Latour 1865 with its dry black fruit and cedar, its soy sauce and its sweat, its peppery rasp and its pleasing whiff of apple cider. 'The volatile acidity has held it together,' opined an expert. Volatility holding a wine together? It hadn't held the Margaux 1865 together: that was well on its way to life as vinaigrette. Vinegar holding a red wine together? Some experts say the strangest things. But I note that Charles Dickens, writing in 1868, said, 'it is notorious that there is openly sold every year at least one hundred times as much Château Lafite and Château Margaux as is produced' – including mine, by the taste of it. Well, there was no volatility in the Rauzan-Ségla 1865, a startling flavour of raspberry jam, liquorice, jalapeño and tomato concassée, putty and Darjeeling tea. I was amazed. The rest of the table weren't. 'How did they manage that?' How indeed? The savvy wine collectors all chortled knowingly. For me, it was an introduction to the wacky world of fine wine fraud, which had obviously come on a bit since Dickens' time. There are a lot of fraudulent bottles in the rarefied world of old wine. They knew it was a fake. I didn't. I thought it was rather good. Serves me right for being seduced by all those gaudy flavours. Go back to first principles. Blackcurrant, black cherry, cedar, cigar box, pencil shavings. They won't let you down, if you can find them any more.

And it isn't easy. Perhaps people don't even want them any more. The twenty-first century is so far removed from the world of Bordeaux that lasted into the 1980s, but not much later. The dramatic social changes in Europe, America and Asia at the end of the twentieth century brought an entirely new, younger, less humble type of Bordeaux devotee. More demanding, less patient, more eager for an immediate buzz and keen to give the highest praise and offer the highest price to wines that dangled the promise of instant gratification, and, when possible, guaranteed returns on investments.

It's a new Bordeaux world, fuelled in the 1980s by the emergence of Robert Parker as wine's first über-critic. By the end of the century, journalists were wondering whether he wasn't the most powerful critic of any discipline in the world. Robert Parker's view on what was good in Bordeaux, then in California and, less all-embracingly, in other parts of the world, became the only view that the ambitious and the greedy cared about. It changed markets and it changed wine styles. And he started it all off in Bordeaux, with his views on the 1982 vintage. I confess that I also was a great supporter of the 1982 vintage, but I was an actor, not a wine writer, and most of the rest of Europe – and, indeed, of America – said Robert was wrong. He wasn't. The 1982 vintage could be called the first modern vintage, the first marked by what we now know is the relentless charge of climate change. 1982 told us what to expect in the future. And Robert Parker loved it. Above all, he loved what the Merlot grape could do in such a vintage.

The Merlot had always been a junior partner in Bordeaux's hierarchy. Robert Parker didn't pretend to have a subtle, refined, traditional palate like the old-school British writers he so derided. He loved richness, he loved sumptuousness, he virtually invented wine terms like 'plush', 'gobfuls' and 'saturated', 'opaque' and 'blockbuster', 'espresso' and 'mocha', 'searing' and 'Reese's Peanut Butter Cup'. And he found what he wanted in the 1982s all over Bordeaux, but especially in the Merlot fiefdom of St-Émilion and Pomerol, which had never, since Roman times, ever been accorded an equal footing with Pessac-Léognan and the aristocracy of the Médoc, whose top wines had been classified in 1855. Now, a 'meritocracy', including for a while a merry brigade of anti-elitist 'artisans' who virtually made their dense, impenetrable, Parker-adored wines in their garages, were in a position to tell the world: this is the new Bordeaux. We're the leaders now.

Since Parker, and, rapidly, others who followed on his coat tails, awarded the highest marks to the Pomerols and St-Émilions from the Right Bank of the Dordogne, more and more of the Left Bank properties of Pessac-Léognan and the Médoc realised the world had changed, realised that a top 'Parker point' out of 100 was just about the most important factor in their gaining the highest possible price for their wine. In the new age of wine collectors, bargains were not respected; scarily high prices were. And the post-1982 way, the 'Merlot' way wasn't going to disappear. By the twenty-first century it barely mattered, since warming conditions in the vineyards meant that Cabernet Sauvignon on the Left Bank was often able to ripen to previously unheard-of levels, maybe five times in a decade, and Merlot was finding it a bit of a struggle not to produce wines so overripe that they were perilously close to jam. The Cabernet Sauvignon aristos had had to change their style, but a warming world suited them better than the pretender Merlot.

Cabernet and the rest of France

The place where the new belief in an utterly overpowering, rich type of Cabernet Sauvignon became a compelling reality was California. But let's just see how the rest of Europe was being influenced by Cabernet Sauvignon and its family. You couldn't really suggest that the Loire Valley was much influenced, because this is the birthplace of Cabernet Franc, the vine that eventually gave birth to Cabernet Sauvignon. Even so, its traditional, rather leafy, wonderfully refreshing raspberry and river pebbles style of red, probably entirely Cabernet Franc, is a lot less easy to find than it was. I usually head nowadays for Saumur-Champigny when I would have headed for Chinon. There are more new oak barrels, and more sturdy Cabernet Sauvignon than there used to be. Luckily, the Loire is a leader in France's 'back to the future' wine movement, which should result in fewer oak barrels and less sturdy Cabernet Sauvignon than there are now.

Cabernet Sauvignon appears all over the south-west with other members of the Bordeaux family, but it has had a most marked effect in the Languedoc, the Midi, France's grape basket, infamous in the old days for churning out vast amounts of really frightful gut rot, none of which would have contained any Cabernet Sauvignon or Merlot. But now these two grapes crop up all over the place, particularly in the areas not covered by an *appellation controlée*, because growers were encouraged to plant them, along with Syrah, as 'improving' varieties. Merlot has been the least successful. The climate is too hot and you will find an awful lot of pretty feeble, cheap Languedoc Merlot. The Cabernet Sauvignon is slower to ripen and makes a better stab at the torrid, windy conditions down here, but is much more impressive when you push away from the flatlands into the hills.

Its most influential manifestation has been at Mas de Daumas Gassac, tucked away in a forested valley north-west of Montpellier. When Aimé Guibert bought an old farmhouse next to a derelict flour mill he had to cut a road through the rocks and scrub to access the house. He wasn't intending to plant vines. After he had tidied up the place, he started to invite friends. Not a problem, unless one of them happens to be Professor Henri Enjalbert, *the* world expert on vineyard geology at Bordeaux University. Aimé drove him up through the newly cut road with visions of a nice cool G & T waiting at the house. It would have evaporated before they got there. Enjalbert shouted 'Stop! Stop!' as they drove through one of the new cuttings. He leaped out of the car, scrabbled around on his knees as only geologists can, and then pronounced that this virgin land that had never seen a vine before possessed the most perfect soil structure for vines of anywhere in France. And Enjalbert meant anywhere – including Bordeaux and Burgundy.

Enjalbert was from Bordeaux, so Aimé planted mostly Cabernet Sauvignon, and gradually through the 1980s he created a kind of 'Grand Cru' in his valley. He charged a lot of money, he courted the highest opinions and he made sure that everyone had heard of this wine, whose liquid in the early vintages would uncoil in your mouth like a treacle of rubies and the fruit would be almost-baked sweet blackberries and plums cooled by the dry, wind-blown dust of the high, barren hills of the Hérault and glued together with the bitter-black sweetness of molasses. There are several other properties in the valley now, using Cabernet Sauvignon. Some, like Grange des Pères, are world famous. But all over the Languedoc it was Mas de Daumas Gassac and its Cabernet Sauvignon from a virgin hillside vineyard that showed the world that Languedoc had as much right to respect as any other wine region in France.

Cabernet and the rest of Europe

Spain has now got far more Cabernet Sauvignon than I thought, and I can just about see why. Tempranillo often needs a dash of something different to make it a bit more interesting. Tempranillo is an early ripener, Cabernet is a late ripener and so they should hit it off in Spain's warmth. But very few genuinely exciting Cabernet Sauvignon wines have turned up. Miguel Torres in Catalonia did as well as anyone with his Black Label Cabernet 1970, which went to Paris for a competition and whacked the French. But that was in 1979, almost forty years ago. There is a lot of Cabernet Sauvignon planted in Spain, as well as, discouragingly, too much cool-climate Merlot and, encouragingly, quite a bit of heat-loving Petit Verdot. Regions like Navarra have made a big thing out of their Cabernet Sauvignon plantings right next to Rioja, which wasn't supposed to have any Cabernet Sauvignon but did, in fact, have a bit. Yet Navarra Cabernet isn't thrilling. Nor, normally, despite Miguel Torres's skill as a winemaker, is it very exciting in Catalonia. Cabernet does some of its best work in Ribera del Duero, where the world-famous Vega Sicilia first planted Cabernet to blend with Tempranillo in 1864, and the locals have been following suit ever since. And Portugal? Why doesn't one of my favourite countries get its own paragraph? Well, Portugal doesn't need Cabernet. It grows a bit, but I can't think of a single example whose flavour I can remember and that's that.

It took two very ambitious, cosmopolitan Italians to realise that the only way their beloved Italy, this *enotria*, this land of wine with more native grape varieties than any other country in the world, was going to start making anything anyone would want to drink was to turn to France – the old enemy, the great rival. In the 1960s and '70s it was French wines which were making tongues wag, it was French wines which were being copied with ominous success in North America and Australia. And, above all, it was French red wines from Bordeaux. So that is where Piero Antinori of Tuscany and Angelo Gaja of Piedmont decided they would look.

Antinori's championing of Cabernet Sauvignon created waves of excitement in every wine-drinking city around the world, as a whole new style of Cabernet as good as that produced in Bordeaux started flowing out of the Tuscan hills and coastal areas. Not much Cabernet flowed out of Piedmont – although the grape had first been planted there in the 1820s – and Angelo Gaja had the best of red Burgundy as his eventual stylistic target for his Barbaresco vineyards. But Burgundy was a niche interest; Bordeaux was the hot topic, and both Gaja and Antinori needed to grab attention. They weren't trying to prove that Piedmont or Tuscany were necessarily a new paradise for Cabernet, although Tuscany produced a string of examples from the coast and the hills proving precisely that. No, what they wanted to prove was that their land was good land. Gaja's end objective was to prove that Barbaresco was great land for *wine*. He couldn't persuade the outside world of that by using Nebbiolo, the authorised grape, and labelling his wines with Italian titles that meant little to anyone outside the locality. But if he planted the two darling international varieties – Cabernet Sauvignon and

These are some of the most important bottles of wine in my life.

Vieux Château Certan 1952. The last bottle of my first-ever wine tasting prize. I finally drank it a few years ago, very emotionally, as my whole wine life flowed in front of my eyes. I certainly didn't know what I was starting out on all those years ago.

Kanga Rouge was a big brand. And it was seriously good wine, but with a sense of humour. Coonawarra Shiraz is some of the best Shiraz in Australia. And this is the bottle I've still got under the stairs, waiting for the 'right moment'. Don't all rush at once.

The famous Tyrrell's Vat 47 Chardonnay that launched my TV career. Of all the wines in the world, I'm most grateful to this one.

New Zealand's Cloudy Bay Sauvignon Blanc 1985 – the first vintage of what became the world's most famous white wine, and forever changed our view of what white wine could and should taste like.

Some of the great characters who have made a real difference to wine —
and to my enjoyment of it.

The most famous nose in Australia —
belonging to Max Schubert, who invented
Grange Hermitage and catapulted
Australian red wine into the front rank.

Piero Antinori, the Tuscan aristocrat
who realised that the only way for Italian
wine to be taken seriously was to copy
the French, equal the French, if possible
surpass the French, then bid them adieu
and return with pride to a new Tuscan
concept of authenticity and individuality.

Angelo Gaja. Nebbiolo wines from
Piedmont's Barolo and Barbaresco
vineyards are now some of the most
sought-after reds in the world, and it was
Angelo Gaja's single-minded obsession
that has done most to place them there.

Peter Hall, one of England's great
originals, a dreamer who found the
perfect spot for his dreams, then fought
against every travail to doggedly produce
some of England's finest fizz — from his
own little patch of Sussex paradise.

Miguel Torres, the man who invented
modern Spanish reds and whites — and
probably rosés too, and he is still one of
Spain's greatest visionaries.

These photographs show just a little of the fantastic beauty of the French vineyards, just to whet your appetite and persuade you to go and take a look for yourselves.

Clos de Vougeot in Burgundy. My first visit to Burgundy was in my little yellow Mini at vintage time. When the weather holds and the leaves turn gold in the autumn sun there's no more exciting place in France to be.

The Hill of Hermitage. This single hill makes one of France's greatest reds, and has done since Roman times – the mighty, brooding, but ultimately magnificent red Hermitage from the Syrah grape.

Autumn mists linger in the Sauternes vineyards, as the sun warms the vines and the famous 'noble rot' begins to intensify the sugar in the grapes.

Nyetimber makes England's most famous sparkling wine. But the English weather is always a concern, even with global warming, and here storm clouds gather over Sussex's South Downs. Will the storm break, or will the vineyard's luck hold for another day?

The Ürziger Würzgarten ('spice garden') vineyard is probably the hottest suntrap in one of Germany's coolest wine regions – the Mosel Valley. Unbelievably, there are numerous Mosel vineyards even steeper than this, but none so perfectly aligned toward the warmest rays of the sun

If I were to choose one vineyard region you simply had to visit before you died, it just might be Portugal's Douro Valley. UNESCO has already tagged it as a World Heritage site, and with its majestic river valley and its twisting, turning, steeply tumbling slopes with their terraces of vines clinging to the contours, I can see why. This is the little town of Pinhão, but most of the rest of the valley is just vineyards, farmhouses, dusty mountain tracks and the magical Douro River.

Age really does matter when it comes to vines – the older the vine the smaller the crop, but the more intense the flavours. This wizened old beauty, the Freedom Vine, is at Langmeil in Australia's Barossa Valley and dates from 1843. The Barossa Valley probably has more ancient vines than anywhere else in the world.

They say that Rippon Vineyard in New Zealand's Central Otago is the country's most photographed vineyard, with its vines stretching languidly down to Lake Wanaka and the stern mountains of the Buchanan range keeping guard at the back. It's always photographed in the summer, but I love the pearl-like brilliance of the snow and the pale tranquillity of this winter scene.

The Andes create so much drama in Argentina's Mendoza vineyards. The harsh, pale rays of sun break through the storm clouds above Las Flechas de los Andes vineyards like rods of crystal. Do these piles of threatening grey cloud contain hail? Up to 30 per cent of Mendoza's crop can be lost some years to hailstones as big as golf balls.

This really is as dry as it gets. These vines are on the edge of Chile's Atacama Desert, the driest place in the world, and the Huasco River which provides the little nourishment that exists, is full of salt. Somehow the straggly vines survive and make Syrah and Sauvignon Blanc of quite remarkable intensity and excitement.

If it weren't for the prodigious Columbia River powering through the desert of eastern Oregon and Washington State, nothing would grow here. But these remarkable vines show the New World 'can do' attitude at its most triumphant – the Benches Vineyard draped over the bone-dry Horse Heaven Hills and nourished by the mighty Columbia.

The final frontier? It could be. These are the upper reaches of the Mekong River in Yunnan south-eastern China (where it's called the Lancang). Can there be cultivated vines further from civilisation and infrastructure than these? Well, the LVMH luxury goods group are determined to make the best red wine in China, and they reckon these isolated gravel terraces near the legendary paradise of Shangri-La have the best conditions in the whole country. They've named their wine Ao Yun or 'Roaming above the clouds'. Nice.

Chardonnay – and planted them bang in the middle of his best Barbaresco land, people would take note.

And they did. His father, for a start. Angelo planted Cabernet Sauvignon in one of his top Barbaresco vineyards right below the family house. His father would stop every day and gaze at this sacrilege, muttering '*Darmagi*' ('What a pity') at the desecration of this land that had only ever grown Nebbiolo. Angelo thought, What a story. Darmagi – that's what I'll call my Cabernet. And he was unrepentant. 'I knew that initially these Cabernet Sauvignons and Chardonnays would be entered into blind tastings. And when they were, their quality would be recognised.' And then he added, 'This would prove not only that these hills were great for growing Nebbiolo and making Barbaresco wine, but it would be proof of this being a great wine land in general. Making outstanding Cabernet Sauvignon was a way to prove that point.' If he was going to ask the world to agree, he couldn't do it just with Nebbiolo and the name Barbaresco on the label, no matter how great the wine was.

He won the blind tastings. He made people who would never otherwise have listened see the potential greatness of these vineyard lands of Barbaresco and its neighbour, Barolo. And he made people listen when Angelo Gaja spoke. All of Piedmont could thank him for his Cabernet and Chardonnay 'experiments'. And, of course, he became inconceivably famous and successful. But, interestingly, despite his single-vineyard Darmagi Cabernet becoming crazily popular, he always priced it below his single-vineyard Barbarescos, as if to say 'I'm just doing the Cabernet to make you take note. Now buy my Barbaresco, that's where my heart is.'

I sometimes feel that Tuscany is rather ungrateful toward Cabernet Sauvignon. In a blistering run of form, starting with Sassicaia in 1968, followed by Tignanello in 1971 and Solaia in 1978, Tuscany showed that this really is a special place for Cabernet Sauvignon. Sassicaia was as piercingly beautiful as any Cabernet Sauvignon I had ever tasted when I scrambled out of bed to find a glass for my first mouthful of the 1968. Although it's more sophisticated nowadays, it isn't better, though it can still rise to a level as high as almost any Bordeaux. Tignanello was not really supposed to be praised for its Cabernet – the first vintage was 100 per cent Sangiovese from Chianti Classico – it was the rejection of Chianti laws and the adoption of Bordeaux techniques that mattered. Limited periods of ageing in small French oak barrels, as against up to seven years in big old chestnut barrels; no white grapes, as opposed to a typical blend of up to 30 per cent white grapes; the malolactic or second fermentation to take place under control in the barrel, as against haphazardly in the bottle; and when they became available, some Cabernet Sauvignon grapes – usually about 20 per cent. But 20 per cent Tuscan Cabernet Sauvignon completely dominates most Sangiovese – the 1985 Tignanello won the Red Wine Trophy at the 1990 International Wine Challenge. Everyone – including me – thought it was a top Bordeaux.

Solaia was completely different again. Piero Antinori had only been loosely involved with Sassicaia, but Solaia was all his. This was based on the Cabernet Sauvignon from the same vineyard in Chianti Classico as Tignanello, initially just an experiment because they had grown too much Cab for that blend. This 100 per cent Cabernet Sauvignon was as shockingly powerful as Sassicaia, but intriguingly different. Sassicaia would mature, slowly wrapping its remarkable acid-tautened blackcurrant with the richness of creamed marron glacé sweetened with blackberries, plums and hazelnuts, and scented with mint leaves and cedar. Solaia, mixed with a little Sangiovese since the mid-1980s, would sometimes explode with thrilling blackcurrant but would be more likely to develop a rare, brooding marriage of black cherry, black plum, liquorice and sandalwood bark, pine resin and, when you were really lucky, a mouthwatering streak of blood orange acidity.

You would think that the Tuscan world would be falling over themselves trying to repeat this magic. Well, quite a few of them did, for a while. The wave of so-called super-Tuscans in the 1980s relied strongly on the bald statement of Tuscan Cabernet Sauvignon blended with Sangiovese and made in a Bordeaux way. And then, almost as soon as the Cabernets had proved their astonishing power to please, the reaction set in. Thank you, Cabernet, now, if you don't mind we'll revert to our Tuscanness, to our Sangiovese, now that we've shown the world what our vineyards are capable of. Chianti Classico, which had paraded numerous exciting Sangiovese-Cabernet blends which I, for one, had loved, now began to talk down the noble Cabernet, and talk up the peasant Sangiovese. Italian pride. Tuscan pride. Sangiovese was Italian. Cabernet was French. Thanks for the leg-up, now leave us alone.

Only down by the sea did Cabernet and its family continue to be welcome. At Bolgheri, Sassicaia was joined by several other grand, sometimes positively gaudy, estates, led by Ornellaia, whose wines never seem to me to have worried too much about tasting Tuscan, yet whose single-vineyard Masseto Merlot from vines growing on a thick streak of heavy clay running toward the nearby hills is a pulsating example of the fleshy, indulgent, well-fed succulence that Merlot rarely ever achieves outside Pomerol. Still not Tuscan, but you're very grateful for a glass, especially if someone else is paying. The wider area of this bit of Tuscan coastline is called the Maremma, and it has taken to the Bordeaux classics – a bit too wholeheartedly for me. I've seen it called Italy's Napa Valley. Is that a lifestyle comment? If it's a wine comment, I'm not sure it will hold for too long as I find these Bordeaux varieties struggling to cope with the increasing heat. I think in this warm western swathe of Tuscany the sooner they start infiltrating some more heat-resistant Italian grape varieties into the vineyards the better.

There's a lot more Cabernet in Italy, but none of it has caused the same tidal waves as those of Tuscany. The northeast has a fair whack of what is more likely to be Cabernet Franc than Cabernet Sauvignon, and the Veneto is sometimes

positively awash with fairly feeble Merlot. There's even a bit of
Carmenère, but that's usually labelled as Cabernet Franc, except
by the fizz whizz Ca' del Bosco, who make a fantastic una-
shamed example in Lombardy. Sicily used Cabernet and Merlot
in rather the same way as Tuscany to say 'Look at us. See what
we can do.' But Merlot, in particular, is in retreat, thank goodness – there is a lot of sun down in Sicily – as Sicilian varieties
like Nero d'Avola take centre stage. And is there any left around
Barbaresco and Barolo? Well, it depends on who you talk to.

In the rest of Europe, Cabernet makes an appearance in
Austria, and a few growers plant it in Germany – it's even
allowed in the Mosel Valley, one of Riesling's great heartlands.
I can remember when it was banned nationwide and I sym-
pathised with one wine friend who'd had his surreptitiously
planted experimental Cabernet Sauvignon vines ripped out and
destroyed by the local police. Nowadays, they would be asking
for bottles for the tombola at their annual ball. Cabernet is an
oddity in these northern countries and Germany and Austria
both find Merlot a bit easier; so does Switzerland, which makes
a bit of a speciality of rather oaky Merlot in her Italian-speaking
canton of Ticino.

The real importance of Cabernet and co. was in eastern
Europe. Hungary has long had a soft spot for these grapes
down toward the Croatian border. On my last trip I sat on a
sun-warmed hill gazing out across the Pannonian Plain toward
Croatia as a broad rain front seethed eastward. They say this
massive flatland shared between Hungary, Serbia and Croatia is
fertile enough to feed all of Europe. One day we may need it. I
was approvingly swigging a robust, impressive Cabernet Franc-
Merlot from the region of Villány made by a guy called Attila,
while I practised saying 'Two beers please, my friend will pay,'
in Hungarian. Everything made sense.

Romania has an awful lot of Merlot and some Cabernet
Sauvignon, but it has rarely been that exciting and has been
used to suck in some hard currency at the bottom of the market.

Given the excellent quality of Romanian Pinot Noir and Pinot Gris, and given the fact that this Francocentric country can ripen the Cabernet family, you'd think they'd have had a bit more of a go. Bulgaria did. They, too, were desperate for hard currency, but instead of trying to slide into the Western markets with something bland and forgettable, they hit us with the full force of Cabernet Sauvignon and Merlot at their most blackcurranty. Under the Communist flag, it was Bulgaria, not California or Australia, that really showed us Brits that there was a New World of affordable tasty wine sold under the name of its grape variety. And it was sitting next to the Black Sea, not the Pacific. A great big self-confident geezer used to push these wines in Britain. I suspected he traded in all kinds of stuff. I seem to remember he was pretty vast and had a slightly gammy leg, and he reminded me of a cockney version of Sydney Greenstreet in *The Maltese Falcon*: don't mess with me, old son.

He'd beckon to us from his great height with a crooked fore-finger and we'd dutifully line up at the wine shows and taste his Cabernet Sauvignon and Merlot and swoon at the prices – low – and dash off to tell the world. Looking back, I wonder what was really in those bottles. How could they have been so good? And I say this because it is now years since the collapse of the Soviet Union, and those Bulgarian Cabernets and Merlots that alerted us to red wine joy before even the earliest of the New Worlders are still not as good as they used to be then.

Yugoslavia was the other place that initially hit us with some good chunky Cabernet Sauvignon, but not for long: it quickly disintegrated into a desperately tough, poorly made tooth-stainer tasting of grape skins and crushed pips, which was more what we young capitalists expected from a mouldy, fly-blown old Soviet co-operative. Yet Slovenia and Croatia made a much more effective leap into the modern wine world than Bulgaria. Slovenia is best at white wines, but has a fair bit of Merlot and Cabernet Sauvignon up toward the Italian border. Croatia's Istria region is showing that her bright red soils are ideally suited to making low-alcohol, unwooded Merlot of a delightful barbecue-friendly juiciness.

I've rarely been thrilled by Greek Cabernet, much preferring her own grape varieties, but, once again, ambitious people planted Cabernet Sauvignon to get their wine – and their country – recognised and respected abroad. I remember having a late-night meeting with a very glamorous lady who ran Chateau Carras from Halkidiki in the north-east. She had a flat in Knightsbridge, and I turned up there feeling as though I was stepping into a James Bond film. But all she offered was an excellent Cabernet red made by Professor Peynaud of Bordeaux – not even canapés, and certainly not caviar or oysters. She definitely didn't flutter her eyelashes. I was clearly there to taste the wine. But she made her point. Greece could create splendid red wine, even if this one tasted more of Bordeaux than the dark, mysterious Aegean Sea.

Turkey has done the same, and is still doing the same: 'Taste our Cabernet, taste our Merlot and Shiraz. Let us impress you with these. And then you can move on to the blistering delights of our barely intelligible red varieties with their convoluted, incomprehensible names' – of which Turkey just might have more than any other country in the world, most of them still undiscovered, but all of them sure to be unpronounceable.

Cabernet and the USA

If you asked the average American what colour is wine the answer would be Cabernet Sauvignon. That's the colour, that's the wine. It's quite remarkable how the USA has taken Cabernet to its heart and its belly. And this has all happened in the last fifty years. You might even say that it has all happened since Robert Mondavi founded his Napa Valley winery in 1966, along with 12 hectares (30 acres) of vines that were mostly Carignan, not Cabernet Sauvignon, and since the Judgment of Paris tasting in 1976 hurled California wine to the front of the world stage, to their great surprise. This was the tasting set up in Paris to celebrate the bicentennial of the Declaration of Independence in 1776. It was supposed to be a friendly informative vinous stroll in the Paris springtime park. It became competitive when Steven Spurrier, the organiser, decided the tasting should be blind. It became hostile, then mould-breaking, then historic when the California wines scored better than the French classics.

And all the dark California wines were the same colour – Cabernet Sauvignon. The pale ones were coloured Chardonnay. Over the next generation, Cabernet, sometimes abetted by its Bordeaux companion in arms, Merlot, and Chardonnay rose furiously from tiny acreages to completely dominate the vineyards of any part of the country that had enough sun to ripen the grapes. We now can see a reaction as Pinot Noir gains at least the wine buffs' adulation, and at last the relict grape varieties that have been skulking in the ground since Prohibition and before are being coaxed out of their lairs by wine producers who are, frankly, obsessively anti-Cabernet and often anti-Chardonnay – but it is Cabernet that they rail against most. Why?

Cabernet has been too successful. But the reason for that isn't difficult to find. America admires the best. America likes to measure itself against the best and then become the best. A lot of countries suffer from tall-poppy syndrome – they like to cut their champions down to size. America feeds its champions fertiliser and vitamins to make them bigger and stronger and better. So, when in the 1960s and '70s the new brood of Americans decided they would exercise their divine right to be the best at wine, it was to the best that they looked. And all through the twentieth century, and indeed the nineteenth and eighteenth centuries, too, the best red wine had always been that of Bordeaux. And Bordeaux's Cabernet Sauvignon has been the ultimate grape for all that time, aided by Merlot when need be. The California revival was pretty slow to start with – it was as though a couple of generations had been lost to the joys of fine wine through the years of Prohibition, the Depression, the

Second World War – but there were a few precious plots of old
Cabernet Sauvignon, one or two in Sonoma, though mostly in
Napa, around the hamlets of Rutherford and Oakville. The To-
Kalon vineyard in Oakville had been planted with Cabernet in
the 1880s and still survived. There were vines from the grand
old properties of Beaulieu and Inglenook, with the odd bottle of
Cabernet going back to 1892 as proof. I've tasted a rather good
old Beaulieu 'Burgundy' of 1939 – made from Cabernet – as
well as several Inglenooks from the 1950s, which I noted had a
clarity about them almost like spring water. But it was the 'new
men' who would make the difference – Robert Mondavi, Jim
Barrett at Chateau Montelena, Bernard Portet at Clos du Val,
Warren Winiarski at Stag's Leap and Paul Draper at Ridge way
south of San Francisco. Some had old vines to play with, most
had to plant afresh but they were all fired by the ambition to
match Bordeaux and to try to tame the unruly ripeness and
bumptious fruit flavours California naturally gave to its Cabs.
They were perfectly happy with 12.5 per cent alcohol, just
like Bordeaux.

When Stag's Leap Cabernet 1973 won the 1976 Paris tasting
it set off a strange chain reaction. Bordeaux realised it needed
to up its game. It would need to use more new oak, it would
need to rethink ripeness levels and it would need to squeeze
more flavour and colour and structure from its grapes. During
the 1980s, fuelled by the 1982 vintage – dubbed 'Californian'
by many critics, and so popular in America that over half of the
top wines were shipped there – Bordeaux almost seemed to be
trying to make its wines more Californian. It probably was; the
most powerful wine critics were American, not European; the
wealth was in America, not in troubled Europe; and Americans
mostly liked flesh and ripeness in their wines. But up until then
a few Californians with experience of Europe had been trying
to make a style of Cabernet that included the green leafiness
so typical of good Bordeaux Cabernet, which included quite
grainy tannins that needed time to soften, and which included

the desire for the scent of cedarwood and cigar boxes that would only come if you gave the wines time, and if the grapes were not too ripe. Well, a few Californians with experience of Europe were trying to do this. It doesn't sound naturally Californian. And so it proved.

Strangely, there was an initial almost apologetic response to Paris by some Californians, amid the euphoria, which led to a brief flirtation with the frankly ill-conceived concept of 'food wines' – wines made lighter and leaner because they would supposedly partner food better. Whereas the great 1970s Cabernets had managed to effortlessly excel in a beautifully balanced way at 12.5 per cent alcohol, these food wines tasted thin and emaciated at the same strength. And this points to a factor which is both a strength and a weakness in the supreme American self-confidence. Winemakers felt that everything could be achieved by applying technology and science. Making wines richer, riper, stronger – yes, science is in its element here. Making wines lighter, drier, more acid – no, you need subtlety, a great understanding of your vineyard and a vision of flavour. In the second decade of the twenty-first century these things have begun to occur by natural evolution. In the early 1980s they tried to do it by science. It didn't work. In the 1990s and 2000s such subtlety was increasingly submerged by a desire for bigger, lustier wines. Winemakers would tell me that they were just there to make sure that the pure vineyard fruit wasn't screwed up, but it was clear that they were piling on the winery techniques required, in some cases, to soften and enrich the fruit, but others to find a way to make a reasonable drink out of Cabernet and Merlot grapes that had been left to hang on the vine so long they were virtually raisins. Virtually? They *were* raisins sometimes, and many winemakers clearly hated having to try to fashion something out of this over-ripe sludge.

But unfortunately that's what the leading critics seemed to like; and what the owners liked – and needed – were high scores from critics like Robert Parker. Most of the new owners were pretty rich – they needed to be, as prices for vineyard land in Napa rose to hundreds of thousands of dollars an acre, and not that much less in good, warm parts of Sonoma. They could see how to get a high score for their Cabernets: hang the fruit on the vine, tell the winemaker to soften it, fatten it up, deepen it, darken it, use all that expensive gear he'd been given and, often, that expensive consultancy from experts who knew the critics' minds and palates and how to satisfy them. Just get me the points, get me the price, get me the prestige.

It's easy for a European to carp about these wines and their soupy strength. But when I got back home from a tasting of 2015 Bordeaux reds I checked the alcohol levels. A significant number were as high as 14.5 per cent and some were even at 15 per cent. Did they taste like Bordeaux? Not Bordeaux as I knew it. But perhaps they tasted like Bordeaux as people now wanted it to be. My favourite wines were all nearer to 13 per cent alcohol, but that's not where the crowds of tasters were thickest. There is talk of Bordeaux beginning to draw back from some of the super-rich style of this century. I suspect the worst offenders – usually in appellations like St-Émilion – are probably doing so. But the others don't dare to draw back far while critics hold sway and their main markets – China and the USA – rather like the rich style.

And California is in the same bind. The tyranny of the market is that these $100–$200 bottles of Cabernet have to taste really good at their point of release. It's no use saying 'Oh, give it five years, give it ten.' No one wants to. I was talking a while ago to a bunch of the so-called 'kids' of various leading Napa and Sonoma wineries – the children who were beginning to take over from their parents. We got talking about the heady, powerful fruit-first palate whackers. Did they like them? Did their friends like them? It was Dante Mondavi, the son of Tim – famous for the restraint in his Robert Mondavi Cabernets in the old days – who spoke up first. Yes, they did. Would they like the wines fresher or leaner? No. Did they want to age the wines?

No. Would they and their friends pay $100 for these wines, crack open the bottle and happily slurp the purple liquid down? Sure they would. That's exactly what they would like to do. One of the older generation then piped up: 'Professor Peynaud said, "Wine is a cheerful drink. It brings warmth to the heart and soul,"' So if that's what people now like ...

There is a move toward lighter, less oaky, less alcoholic wine styles in parts of California, and with parts of the California wine-drinking fraternity, but not often among the Cabernet makers. But it's much easier to coax grapes like Pinot Noir and Syrah to a cooler style. So much is invested in Cabernet Sauvignon. So many of the best vineyard sites in Napa Valley and the warmer parts of Sonoma are planted with Cabernet Sauvignon. They have to be, as that's the only variety which will make a wine that can get you a high-enough price to service your vineyard and winery debt. Even so, there is a change of mood. Last year the winemaker at Silver Oak – famous for lush Cabernets – told me 'a little bit of greenness is a good thing in a Cab'. I'm not sure I had heard that said in California for twenty years or more. And then winemaker after winemaker began to talk of the search for freshness. Do they mean it? They do in Pinot Noir, in Syrah and in Chardonnay. Can they shift the Cabernet juggernaut? Do the wine-drinkers want them to? Will a wine like Corison Cabernet in St Helena finally come into fashion, with its remarkable dry, intriguing flavours of Fernet Branca Menta, dried thyme, dark treacle and black olives, slowly, thoughtfully, opened out and freshened by red cherry and plum, ripe tomato and a scent of graphite and cedar, and, if there is such a thing, olive blossom? Cathy Corison says, 'It's always going to be powerful here, but it's much more interesting at the intersection with elegance.' And it would be nice to think that's where California Cab is heading.

The Pacific Northwest has been making a more restrained style of Cabernet and Merlot for some time. It immediately set out its stall as making a drier, more Bordeaux style than

California could. But is it really that restrained? Well, increasingly it is and the difference between California and Washington Cabernet is now stark. The first releases of wines like Leonetti and Woodward Canyon Merlot and Cabernet were wonderfully tasty, rich, deeply satisfying reds from Walla Walla, an area in eastern Washington State that no one had ever heard of. It was that ability of their Merlots and Cabernets to be succulent and rich and yet appetisingly fresh – that word again – which made them stand out against the broader, heavier California styles that were developing. But, in fact, the more classic Washington Cabernet style is restrained, dry, dark, brooding; above all in the Yakima Valley, where the arid, barren slopes of Red Mountain boast the hottest, the driest vineyards in this hot, dry desert region, and their Cabernet vines are finally now mature enough to produce challenging but scented reds. They are probably the most tannic reds in Washington, so the dark blueberry and plum fruit, and Italian black chocolate bitter richness is needed to cope with the tannic rasp. Some of Washington's other long-established vineyards are in the Horse Heaven Hills. These great expanses of grassland finally tumble toward the Columbia River and the vineyards risk tumbling even further as they cling to the slopes above the water. More graphite and pepper, rounder, redder fruit, but still quite enough tannin chewiness to make you ask, 'Where's the steak?'

New York's Long Island vineyards were established with the prime objective of saying 'Hey, we can make Bordeaux-style wines on this side of the Atlantic.' Just as Bordeaux's Médoc region is like a tongue reaching up into the Bay of Biscay, Long Island is like a finger pointing eastward into the Atlantic Ocean. They've done a pretty good job, but have realised that Cabernet Sauvignon doesn't usually quite ripen before the autumn storms kick in, though Paumanok's Tuthills Lane Cabernet Sauvignon from the positively Californian year of 2010 is an unbelievably delicious, spicy, glyceriney, ripe black plum mouthful. Hot years like 2010 don't come along too often. Yet! But Wölffer, down by the Hamptons, makes the wackiest, most memorable use of Cabernet in a sweet, rich-sour chocolate, cocoa, spice kitchen, butter, cedar and pheromone madhouse of an Italian Amarone-type called Claletto. Don't spit this out unless you've given the spittoon written warning.

Merlot is a little more likely to work. On South Fork, Wölffer's is always good, and the North Fork wineries can make them fat and glyceriney and liable to smell just slightly of graphite. But if you want scent, Cabernet Franc is the best bet, and increasingly Cabernet Franc is being looked on as the red grape most likely to produce immediately attractive, easy-drinking reds that just might tempt the New Yorkers to support their home brew. A real surprise is that while Cabernet Sauvignon struggles out on the island, Petit Verdot can deliver. It's a late ripener, but those thick skins keep the Atlantic squalls at bay. In 2005 they had 430 millimetres (17 inches) of rain in eight days at harvest time – that had to kill the crop. Not Petit Verdot. Ten days after the downpours, Paumanok picked Petit Verdot at 13.5 per cent alcohol and it made a wonderful dark blackcurrant skins and cedarwood-scented red that was unbelievably good at twelve years old.

Cabernet really isn't the variety for the Finger Lakes in upstate New York, although pioneer Konstantin Frank does make one, but Fox Run show that Merlot can work and they, along with Sheldrake Point, show that Cabernet Franc can *really* work, gushing with irresistible raspberry fruit and peppery bite. Yet again, if you're wondering what to plant in a tricky red wine area, put Cabernet Franc at the top of your list.

Much further south, but still on the eastern seaboard, Virginia also makes very good use of Cabernet Franc, but the surprise package here is Petit Verdot. Virginia's conditions are mostly warm and humid, and late-season rains leading to muggy conditions in the vineyards are always a threat. Petit Verdot doesn't seem to mind if the tail end of a mighty Atlantic storm looms over the vines. Being late-ripening and having a tough skin is the ideal combination if you want to be able to shrug off late-summer rain and get on with the business of maturing your grapes for harvest and developing their black plum and black cherry fruit – and, just occasionally, a lovely wistful scent of violets. Not bad for a grape known in Europe for its chewy power, with the nickname of steakhouse red. It clearly works here. The Governor's Cup is Virginia's most important wine competition. The organisers always put together a case of the top-scoring wines. In 2017 five of these were Petit Verdots.

Cabernet Franc also does well. The European idea that Cabernet Franc ripens early and can't cope with late-season rain is being turned on its head in places like Uruguay, Brazil and Virginia. Here, Cabernet Franc copes better with late rain than Cabernet Sauvignon, and it achieves a harvest of grapes able to make lovely, raspberry-scented wines. These often get blended away into what the locals call Meritage, i.e., Bordeaux blends. They have borrowed this rather clunky name from the Californians. There is more Merlot and Cabernet Sauvignon planted in Virginia, but it's the Cabernet Franc and Petit Verdot that are more exciting.

Cabernet and Canada

It's not humidity and vintage-time rain that gets in the way of the Cabernet family ripening in Canada. It's the fact that winter ends late and starts early, and despite the chance of some fairly torrid summer conditions in both Ontario's Niagara and British Columbia's Okanagan Valley, you can't always get the ripening job done. Some wineries in Ontario don't even try to offer Cabernets or Merlots, and Pillitteri Estate takes the bull by the horns and makes a pretty convincing Cabernet Sauvignon Icewine. I know Cabernet Sauvignon ripens late, but this is ridiculous. They are not the only ones flirting with fantasyland. Inniskillin make a tasty sparkling Cabernet Franc Icewine! And it's Cabernet Franc that I find is most successful in Niagara. One grower told me, when I asked him why there weren't more successful Merlots, that Merlot here gets tannic before any of the other red varieties. Maybe that high-summer sun is just too hot for a coolster like Merlot. Its best place is probably in those Meritage blends – that word again – because Niagara can do these pretty well. I've been watching Southbrook Vineyards Poetica quietly get classier and more convincing vintage by vintage – they even manage to put in a big chunk of Petit Verdot now and then. They'd say it was the biodynamic vineyard practices. Maybe. I'd say it was just as likely to be that if you care enough, and think enough, you'll get it right in the end.

British Columbia finds the Cabernet family a bit easier, especially in the far south of Okanagan where they still get late spring frosts, though the warm lakes help to offset these, and winter arrives suddenly at the end of the season. In between, it is pretty much a desert down by Osoyoos Lake; you're not going to be short of grape-ripening sunshine, and the southerly Similkameen Valley can do a pretty similar job. In fact, they're learning down in the Okanagan area called the Golden Mile that if they aren't careful they can overripen varieties like Merlot. So that Meritage bundle of Bordeaux varieties proves its worth once again, with even true late-ripeners like Petit Verdot and Carmenère contributing to the balance.

Cabernet and South America

It's not exactly Cabernet Sauvignon and the other Bordeaux varieties that South America has to thank for getting its leading wine countries on the road to their current international recognition, but it is south-west France. It's almost as though they all decided to go for the least likely option, the one that really wasn't doing very well on its home patch. Uruguay opted for Tannat, which has made impenetrably dark, bitter-hearted reds in Madiran down toward the French Pyrenees for the last couple of hundred years. No one was trying to export the Tannat vine, but somehow Uruguay ended up with a boatload, along with a bunch of Basque Country immigrants, and it became Uruguay's national grape variety.

Argentina opted for Malbec. There used to be quite a bit of this planted in Bordeaux, but nowadays most Bordeaux vineyard owners go purple in the face (some are purple already, of course) if you recommend planting Malbec. François Mitjavile, one of St-Émilion's great mavericks and owner of the superstar Château Tertre-Rôteboeuf, enjoys lobbing Malbec into the discussion, like a vinous hand grenade, just to watch the sweat rising on the foreheads of his colleagues. No, Malbec's home is up the Dordogne Valley around Cahors. It was and still is popular because it can make very dark wine. (I should know: I did the Malbec harvest on an island in the Gironde once. The grapes burst almost as soon as you touched them, and I was stained magenta from head to toe by the end of the day.) I must say, I find Cahors hard work, and I don't expect they planted Malbec in Argentina because it was first choice. South America mostly took whatever turned up, often on immigrant boats from Italy or the Basque Country.

Malbec may have arrived like this in Argentina. It may have been brought in on purpose by a French agricultural expert called Michel Pouget in 1868. But since there are vineyards dating back to 1861 in the Mendoza wine region up by the Andes, he certainly wasn't the only importer of vines. And actually, no one seems to be quite sure what Argentine Malbec actually is. Just as Uruguayan Tannat seems pretty different from French Tannat, so Argentine Malbec seems so different from French Malbec I often wonder if there hasn't been a mix-up. Thank goodness I'm not alone in thinking this. Argentine scientists have been trying to unravel Malbec's secrets throughout this century, and a couple of years ago concluded that the DNA of Argentine Malbec is completely different to that of French Malbec. So what is it, then? And where did it come from? It's discussions like this that make a wine-writing career the fun it is. I love these controversies, and in a way I never want them to be resolved. Sometimes the scientists say that they have the ultimate proof, and I sit there with my non-scientific palate longing to show them that they don't.

In any case, Argentina may have been a massive producer and consumer of red wine throughout the twentieth century, but the modern Argentine wine world isn't much more than twenty years old. I almost feel as though I was in at the beginning. Except that I was in Chile, in 1997. At the Santiago Hyatt Hotel. I got a message – a plea, almost – could I find the time to meet a Señor Zuccardi? Well, I had a free moment before my pre-dinner pisco sour. 'Send him up,' I said. He wasn't on my list of producers. Of course he wasn't. He wasn't Chilean. Señor Zuccardi had driven over the Andes from Argentina with his startled-looking winemaker and a basket of tank samples. He had bought some new oak barrels and he was trying to install some temperature control. He had started crushing some grapes in the vineyard and rushing the juice to his winery to try to preserve a bit of freshness. But he desperately wanted an opinion, so he drove over the Andes to see me. He didn't speak English. My Spanish was pathetic, so I spoke French with a heavy Spanish accent and added '–ación' to as many words as I could, while he nodded distractedly. And yet I think we got an understanding going.

José Alberto Zuccardi is now one of the most important men in Argentine wine and he and his son make some of the country's most thrilling Malbecs. But then he was an absolute beginner in a ramshackle wine world which had little concept of what was happening in places like California. He had used his precious new oak barrels on his Cabernet and his Malbec – no fruit, lots of tannin, lots of good new oak and going nowhere. Except that it was going somewhere. From then on, year by year, I made sure to taste the Zuccardi wines, to note with surprise and delight how my suggestions were being acted on. Only twenty or so years to go from clutter and chaos to one of the world's most lively and pulsating wine cultures, led by Malbec, but increasingly showing what it can do with Cabernet Sauvignon and Cabernet Franc. Amazing.

Well, surely Chile opted for the mainstream Cabernet and Merlot route – that's what the country is known for. No, even here they didn't take the easy path. Without quite realising it, they built their reputation on one of Bordeaux's varieties, the Carmenère, that was so obscure at the beginning of this century that just a few rows survived in Bordeaux – at the university and in the garden of the manager of Château Haut-Brion. He had to keep the vines in his garden because if he had planted them in the Haut-Brion vineyard the authorities could have declassified the entire crop. Carmenère was banned in Bordeaux. But he knew that before the French vineyards were destroyed by the phylloxera aphid in the nineteenth century, Carmenère had been responsible for some of the greatest wines in Bordeaux. Chile got hold of Carmenère as a job lot when the Chileans turned up and asked for vine cuttings – crucially before the phylloxera arrived in 1867. These healthy vines were taken back to Santiago and planted out – and immediately proved their worth. As Europe's vineyards were decimated by phylloxera, Chile's unaffected vines flourished. Their red wines won gold medals in Europe, in France even. And when the Chilean wine growers were asked what grape varieties they were using, they didn't know. They would reply, 'Oh, the French stuff.' So Chile went on making what seems to have been pretty splendid red wine from 'the French stuff'.

'The French stuff' was whatever they'd managed to pick up in Bordeaux. They'd got Cabernet Sauvignon, and when they planted this south of Santiago in Maipo it produced fabulously blackcurranty rich reds, ideally with a eucalyptus or mint leaf perfume – and that's exactly what Cabernet Sauvignon still does in these same vineyards. And they also had Carmenère. This ripens very late, and wasn't popular in the cool maritime climate of Bordeaux, but when the sun shone, it gave spectacular peppery, savoury, black cherry, blackcurranty wine, which sometimes tasted as though you'd squashed some green peppercorn into soy sauce and splashed it into the vat.

Well, the sun always shone in Chile. You could always ripen your Carmenère. And when the Americans and the British turned up in the 1990s and said, 'Have you got any Merlot?', well, this would do. Who would know? A lot of the vineyard owners already called this Chilean Merlot and the real stuff Merlot Merlot. Anyway, it was much better than the real Merlot. Too right it was. Pretty quickly, Chilean Merlot became known as the tastiest, spiciest, fruitiest Merlot in the world. That's because it wasn't Merlot. It was Carmenère. It was Paul Pontallier of Château Margaux in Bordeaux who eventually got a friend of his at the University of Montpellier to unravel the mystery, because he had established a vineyard in Chile and had been sold two batches of Merlot vines that behaved completely differently. One ripened very quickly and gave rather harsh wine, and the other ripened late and was delicious. The first one was real Merlot, yet again showing that it doesn't like too much sun and heat. The second proved to be what they called in Bordeaux 'the lost grape' – the Carmenère. Here it was, flourishing in Chile, but they called it Merlot, because the British and the American buyers could pronounce Merlot and were paying in cash.

So 'Merlot', aka Carmenère, is what made Chilean red famous. Now they usually separate the two in the winery so the Merlot is worse, but the true Carmenère in its peppery, smoky, savoury, blackcurranty brilliance is better. Even so, the ultimate blackcurrant and mint and sometimes eucalyptus or coal dust performer is Cabernet Sauvignon itself. And those original plantings in Maipo turn out to be on deep gravel beds – exactly what Cabernet Sauvignon likes best. When Chilean red wines enter global competitions and come out top, usually against the old foe, Bordeaux's finest reds, it's the Cabernet from these deep gravels so similar to the gravel beds of Bordeaux that plays the star role.

Cabernet and South Africa

She brought the bottle. I wouldn't have. Meerlust Cabernet
Sauvignon 1976. A quite ridiculously lovely, gentle, scented,
cedary red wine from a hot place like South Africa to drink on
the dewy grass in a London square, and tasting as though it came
from the great cool Bordeaux village of St-Julien. I hardly drank
South African wine in the 1980s – none of us did. But it showed
me that when South Africa finally broke free, there were some
delicious reds still being made there – and that the best were
Cabernet Sauvignon. Well, to be honest, I'd been lucky. There
weren't lots of delicious reds being made. Most of South Africa's
vineyards were of white varieties, with the high-acid Chenin
Blanc the grape of choice. And most of South Africa's red varieties were infected by a virus that caused leaf roll. All the leaves
turned a gorgeous dark, photogenic crimson before the end of
the summer, which meant that they couldn't photosynthesise,
so the grapes could shrivel on the vine in heat but couldn't
physiologically ripen. The result was wines with a curious and
not very appetising mixture of raisined fruit, rough tannin and
raw acidity. I had been lucky with that Meerlust because it was
one of the few classic Cabernets being made.

There were some old-style successes – I've tasted some fifty-
year-old Nederburg Cabernets but they relied crucially on a
big dollop of Cinsault, which in France makes mostly very
pallid rosé, but in South Africa seemed to provide the balance
and structure Cabernet was unable to do by itself. In the New
World, it's wonderful how often European certainties are turned
on their head. Cabernet Sauvignon is still not entirely free of
leaf roll virus in the Cape, but it was the red grape chosen by
the new wave who were preparing for the end of apartheid as it
made what many of them reckoned was the world's best red in
Bordeaux. The newer wave, who came into the wine business
in the 1990s, chose it too. The brave early campaigners like
Thelema, Delaire, Cederberg, Vriesenhof, and the newer stars

like Rustenberg, Le Riche, Vergelegen, Chamonix and Jordan, as well as a whole host of twenty-first-century performers, have all put a big effort into Cabernet and, increasingly, Cabernet blends. Stellenbosch is the absolute humming centre of all this, with areas like Heldenberg, Constantia and Franschhoek chipping in.

Cabernet and New Zealand

New Zealand has made such a noise about Pinot Noir in the last twenty years that you'd think trying to make a Southern Ocean red Burgundy was the original objective down there. But it wasn't. There was the odd Pinot Noir vine planted in the nineteenth century, but Cabernet Sauvignon was there pretty much from the start. James Busby, the guy who brought most of the good grapevines to Australia, then moved to New Zealand in 1832 and planted some Cabernet Sauvignon. A bunch of French settlers near Christchurch planted some Cabernet in the 1840s. Very brave. I doubt if anyone would plant Cabernet near chilly Christchurch today. But then, the French didn't last long in South Island. And nor did grape growing. Everyone said it was too cold (although during the Otago Gold Rush vineyards were planted: they always are during gold rushes). And New Zealand's attempts at viticulture headed north, mostly to Auckland. Here, it was too hot, too humid and too wet to make anything very nice, and the heavy loam and clay soils meant that your chances of getting anything like Cabernet Sauvignon to ripen at all, or Merlot to ripen before the grapes rotted on the vine, were slim.

Eventually it became clear there was only one place that was likely to suit Cabernet Sauvignon and its Bordeaux family, and that was Hawke's Bay on the east side of North Island, clustered around the art deco city of Napier. Most of the land was still too loamy and fertile, but there were a few low, less fertile hills on the south side of the Bay, and although it took them

almost to the twenty-first century to realise it, they had some
land called the Gimblett Gravels about 15 kilometres (9 miles)
inland that was miserably poor stuff. They said you needed 1
hectare (2.47 acres) to raise a single sheep it was so bony. The
local council used it to build a prison and a drag strip, and was
delighted when a concrete company offered to purchase 150
hectares (370 acres) to dig out the gravel.

Well, if you were looking for a little Southern Ocean slice
of Bordeaux, in what was one of New Zealand's sunniest
places, this sounded promising. If you then worked out that
down by the coast it wasn't quite hot enough to ripen Cabernet
Sauvignon on a regular basis, despite the sun and despite the
extreme penetration of ultraviolet rays, but that on the gravels
the temperature was typically 3°C (5.4°F) warmer and you got
heat earlier in the day, and it lasted longer into the evening,
and – wait for it – at 30 centimetres (12 inches) below ground
level, just where your vine roots might be poking about, it
could be 5°C (9°F) warmer than on the coast ... would you
start dreaming of a Pauillac or a Margaux of the Far South?
That's exactly what they did. The concrete company wasn't
allowed to buy its land for digging, and instead every hectare is
now under vine, mostly with Cabernet Sauvignon and Merlot,
and mostly with the objective of making the most Bordeaux-
like wines south of the Equator, and mostly making them that
bit riper than they do in Bordeaux. If anything, the Gimblett
Gravels Cabernets and Cabernet blends can be almost too dark
and powerful, and because many of them are bottled under
screwcap they may age at a glacial pace.

But when I taste the young tank samples, the Gimblett
Gravels reds have unbelievable personality. The Cabernet
Sauvignon has a fabulously pure flavour of ripe, dry blackcurrant and stony – sprinkled, maybe, with rock dust. Cabernet
Franc moves its fruit toward raspberry – really dark raspberry,
almost a raspberry coulis intensity, with a hint of a fresh dusty
leafiness and the rough fur of fresh sage. Merlot, typically, is a

little less focused – it's a less focused grape – but opens out with dark, rich plum and cherry and fudge richness, nicely under-cut with stones and mineral dust. And Petit Verdot – there's even a bit of that – tastes of black plum skins, black cherry, black syrup, black stones, dense, serious, rather magnificent. Bordeaux's best vineyards would be proud to produce any of these flavours.

Cab and Australia

Max Schubert came home from Bordeaux in 1950 determined to create a great, long-lasting, oak-aged red wine in Australia to match the glories of the twenty-, forty- and fifty-year-old wines he had tasted in Bordeaux. And he managed it, except that he didn't use Cabernet Sauvignon. He couldn't find any. He couldn't find any new French oak barrels either – he wasn't sure that there was a single new oak barrel in the whole of South Australia. But there was some American wood he could get made up into barrels. And there was loads of Shiraz. So his attempt to make a world-class New World red Bordeaux based on Cabernet Sauvignon and new French oak barrels ended up as a hugely successful world-class red made from Shiraz and aged in new American oak barrels. And he called it Grange.

I suppose you could say that the Bordeaux ambition and the Bordeaux vision of flavour were at the heart of what Schubert created. The use of new oak barrels – yes – though what he did with them would have caused palpitations in the tradition-bound hearts of the Bordeaux people. But whereas in almost all other New World countries the desire to emulate red Bordeaux and white Burgundy consumed the young and the ambitious, Australia was a lot more laid-back. For a start, they already had what they regarded as world-class white – Riesling in South Australia and Semillon in New South Wales. And as for reds, well, there was a bit of Cabernet Sauvignon hanging around in the armpit of South Australia, in the damp, dismal far south, in Coonawarra, but honestly, if you wanted a red wine Shiraz, Grenache and Mourvèdre were more than enough to satisfy your thirst. They made big, rugged, dry reds, and if that didn't please you they made mighty, sweet ports.

I've just been looking through Max Allen's excellent *The History of Australian Wine* (2012), and from 1900 to 2000 Cabernet Sauvignon is hardly mentioned. It simply wasn't relevant for most of the twentieth century. In the nineteenth century Cabernet had a decent reputation in Victoria, and Coonawarra was established in 1891 with a fair bit of Cabernet. But the Coonawarra project failed. Australians didn't want these light, dry table wines that cool-climate Cabernet would produce. They either wanted big, dry reds better suited to warm areas growing Shiraz and Grenache – or port, which was also better suited to warm areas growing Shiraz and Grenache.

It wasn't really until the 1960s that Australians began thinking about Cabernet Sauvignon seriously, and in the most unlikely of places – the hot, humid, subtropical Hunter Valley, where a Sydney surgeon called Max Lake, inspired by a bottle of Hunter River Cabernet vintage 1930 (they ripped out the vineyard in 1931), decided to replant Cabernet. He called his winery Lake's Folly. He wasn't stupid: the Hunter isn't natural Cabernet country. The really important thing that Lake's Folly did was to show that a non-expert from another profession could set up a small, boutique winery and succeed. Many of Australia's greatest wines now come from such start-ups.

The Margaret River in Western Australia *is* natural Cabernet country, and in the 1960s there wasn't a vine planted in the whole region. Well, there was by the end of the 1960s. A bunch of doctors – what is it with doctors and wine in Australia? – had read reports that said the Margaret River had conditions more like Bordeaux than anywhere else in Australia. Doctor Cullity promptly gave the keys of his surgery to his locum and started Vasse Felix. Doctor Pannell started Moss Wood and Doctor Cullen started Cullen. These are now three of Australia's greatest wineries, and they make some of Australia's greatest Cabernets.

Well, if Australia wasn't that interested in the flavours of Cabernet Sauvignon, I was. That Seaview 1968 from south of Adelaide had won me more bragging rights as a wine taster in the National Wine Tasting Competition than any lucky guess had a right to. On my trip to Australia with the Royal Shakespeare Company in the mid-1970s, I'd had to wait until almost the end of the tour before I was presented with one from an estate called Moorilla in Tasmania. What? Yup. An Italian called Claudio Alcorso had planted Cabernet in the south of the island and printed out a cloth label and here was I drinking it with pasta in a little trattoria overlooking Sydney Harbour. The pinging, assertive, gum-shrivelling raw blackcurrant flavour was enough to make me shiver – with delight. This was the kind of 'in-your-face' fruit no European red wine ever offered. I was heady with excitement.

And so, for a while, was Australia. In the 1970s and early '80s Cabernet suddenly became popular. This fabulously biting, incisive, gloriously focused, blackcurranty wine with the scent of mint and eucalyptus soared through the wine-dark sky, then promptly fell to earth. People said that Cabernet was a dough-nut grape – it had a hole in the middle (that's why, in the old days in Australia, they needed to blend it with Shiraz and call it claret!) – and experts said that mint and eucalyptus were faults in a wine. I was just getting going in the wine world. I bel-lowed my disagreements from the television screens of Britain. We stuck with the blackcurrant and mint and eucalyptus – if we could find it. The Australian producers preferred to listen to their prophets: get rid of the eucalyptus, lose the mint and ripen the stuff up. Which, of course, meant that they lost the skylark clarity of the blackcurrant, too. They didn't mind. They had caught the Shiraz bug by the 1990s. All those old Shiraz vines they were about to rip up because no one wanted their wine were now being fêted as some of the greatest and oldest vines in the world. 'Make it bigger. Make it richer, more treacle, less like a wine, get it marked by the gurus – get me a hundred-pointer!' 'Forget the Cab.' Obviously, the Cab didn't go away – too many vines had been planted, even in warm places like Barossa and McLaren Vale in South Australia – but this did show that, at heart, Australia has been influenced and dominated by Cabernet and co. far less than most other New World countries. And when you think that Cabernet and Merlot are maritime grape varieties and really don't like the conditions to be too hot, their failure to grip Australian red wine culture is probably a good thing. Australia is a hot place; it's the driest continent in the world. It does have cooler spots, places where the air holds just enough dampness, like Coonawarra, and that's where Cabernet thrives. Merlot? No, not even where the air is damp and the soil is heavy has Merlot yet managed to thrive in Australia.

And even in the years of Shiraz mania, Cabernet quietly got on with it. Penfolds Bin 707 was a Cabernet made with as much care and determination as Penfolds' star Shiraz wine, Grange, and it was usually just as good. Wynn's John Riddoch showed that Coonawarra could still make brilliant wine if anyone was listening. Coonawarra's problem was that in the 1970s and '80s, when it looked as though Cabernet would be the Next Big Thing, most of the land was bought by the big companies, and if they couldn't buy vineyards on the fabled but very limited lozenge of bright red soil called Terra Rossa – well, they'd buy the white soil, or heaven forbid, the soggy, sodden black soil where no decent grapes had ever grown. But an awful lot of mediocre grapes now grew there, diluting Coonawarra's reputation with every vintage and those big companies, which moved off the good red soils onto the bad black ones, should not be proud of themselves. But a few individual estates still survived on the red soil. I taste Balnaves Single Estate Cabernet every year and it still has a purity of blackcurrant fruit somewhere between old-style Allen & Hanburys blackcurrant throat pastilles – I think you can still buy them, in a blue and gold tin – and my mum's blackcurrant jam. By definition, my mum's jam is the greatest blackcurrant flavour in the world, but this wine gets close. Then I get more childhood memories – an intriguing mix of peppermint leaf, verbena and Vicks VapoRub – and a steamy winter kitchen memory: the chewy twist of Seville orange marmalade peel. I almost feel as though I've complicated things too much, because the utter joy of Coonawarra Cabernet at its best is its simple purity.

If I want to complicate Cabernet, I could head north to the warmer fields of McLaren Vale and sit down with Joe Grilli as he opens a bottle of his Joseph Moda. This is a Cabernet–Merlot made like an Italian Amarone – he dries the grapes after picking so that they begin to shrivel and a few of them start to split and rot. And my first mouthful is all about Italy and nothing about Australian Cab. I think I'm being faced with a thick mugful of tannic, leathery grape soup. Hold it in your mouth, patience, wait . . . and then the wine begins to unfurl – the freshness of blueberries and late-summer blackberries binds itself into a richness of prunes and fig syrup and chocolate, while the sweet-sour, cream-curdling acidity of plum skins resonates like a taut guitar string and the tannin is as grippy yet affectionate as the lick of a cat's tongue.

Yes, they're making great Cabernet in Australia. In the relative cool of Coonawarra and the Eden and Clare Valleys, in the greater warmth of McLaren Vale and Barossa, and definitely in Margaret River in the far west, where the Cabernets unashamedly offer up deep blackcurrant and plum fruit balanced by an inky graphite dryness, mouthwatering but ripe acidity and grainy, pebbly tannins. And as the lust for enormous Shiraz soup-bombs fades toward a more charming Shiraz–Syrah style, I can see that the austere but awesome delights of Cabernet might once more be given their due. I don't have a problem, of course. I virtually owe my wine-tasting reputation to a Cabernet that doesn't even exist any more – Seaview 1968 – with so much blackcurrant brilliance my mum could have made it into jam.

Cabernet and China

And now we come to China. How much Cabernet Sauvignon is there planted in China? No one seems to know. The experts differ, and explain that national statistics don't necessarily bear any relationship to local statistics. Are some areas bigging up their numbers? Does the Central Authority actually know precisely what is happening around the country? What is unarguable is that red is a lucky colour, and that Cabernet Sauvignon is the most popular, the most revered, the most sought-after quality grape. Most of the best wines in China are based on Cabernet Sauvignon. And it is perfectly possible, given the astonishing rate of growth, and the Chinese ability to decide they want to do something then immediately do it – and on a grand scale – it is possible that China is now growing more Cabernet Sauvignon than any other country in the world. Cabernet Sauvignon is relatively easy to make into an attractive, simple wine as countries like Bulgaria quickly proved. Making it in the more ambitious way that is clearly the objective of such operations as Silver Heights, Grace and Helan Mountain, as well as Château Lafite's operation at Shandong on the coast, and LVMH's Ao Yun in the deep Himalayan south of Yunnan, is taking a bit more time. It took Bordeaux centuries to work it out, it took California decades. It won't take China so long.

Chardonnay

From the sublime to the mundane

C hardonnay is a village in Australia. Isn't it? Well, a lot of people thought so around the turn of the century, when every second bottle you saw in a bar or a supermarket trolley seemed to be Chardonnay from Australia. Or perhaps Chardonnay is a village in California. Or was that Blossom Hill? Blossom Hill really is a place. It's a tram stop on the San José municipal transport system. There were no vines that I could see, which might explain a certain lack of 'somewhereness' in the taste of Blossom Hill Chardonnay. Actually . . . what taste?

So Chardonnay is not a village in Australia, nor in California, nor Chile, South Africa or France – hang on, it *is* a village in France, in southern Burgundy. And they do grow vines there. But I would be surprised if many of us have tasted their wine. You would have thought that they would have tried to market their name a bit harder.

Well, is Chardonnay a wine style then? You know, full and fruity, floods of glistening golden sunshine dripping from the bottle; maybe a taste of peaches and pineapple and cream. But I've got a glass of wine here – and it's sticky and lifeless, and I'm not at all sure it isn't sugary, and it's got a sort of artificial vanilla sweetness that is gumming up my lips. Yuck. But the label says Chardonnay. So Chardonnay isn't just one wine style, and at least some of it is rubbish. And do I hear someone say that Chardonnay at its best is the greatest white wine in the world? And it isn't sticky and drab, but bursting with energy and vigour and supremely, imposingly dry? And this style can come from Australia or California, or half a dozen other countries? But the place you'll find it most often is in Burgundy – not from the village of Chardonnay, but from three or four other villages, further north, which never ever put the word Chardonnay on their labels because the people who make wine in the villages of Meursault, Puligny, Chassagne and Aloxe-Corton say 'We don't make Chardonnay, we make Meursault, Puligny and so on.' You feel that Chardonnay is a necessary evil; they are solely concerned with expressing the character of their patches of land which, because wine needs grapes to turn into wine, happen to grow Chardonnay.

So Chardonnay isn't just a wine style then? But it has become so popular, so famous, and then so infamous that people do think anything with the name Chardonnay on the label will just be in one style. What style that is depends on how much you like Chardonnay in the first place.

Right, let's get this straight. Chardonnay is a grape variety. It's the most famous grape variety in the world. I suspect more people have drunk Chardonnay than the wine of any other variety. For many people, Chardonnay is the only grape variety name they know. People have even called their children Chardonnay. Better than calling them Liebfraumilch, I suppose. A television soap opera called *Footballers' Wives* had a character called Chardonnay, who set light to her own breasts. With a candelabrum. You couldn't make it up.

Despite all this, Chardonnay does manage to make the greatest dry white wines in the world. It also makes some of the dullest and drabbest – and everything in between. Chardonnay has colonised every vineyard region across the globe with enough sunshine and warmth to ripen it, which is just about everywhere.

And fifty years ago it didn't exist. Well, barely. In 1960 California only had 60 hectares (150 acres) of it planted. Australia had a single tiny vineyard. When David Wynn planted 1.6 hectares (4 acres) of Chardonnay in South Australia in 1972 it was, in one stroke, the biggest Chardonnay vineyard in Australia, and the first one in South Australia – the state that now produces the bulk of the vast ocean of Aussie Chardie that pours across the globe every year. On my first trip to Australia, as an actor in the 1970s, I didn't drink a single Chardonnay. I couldn't. There wasn't any. And in France I only tasted it in Burgundy – and the labels never helpfully said it was Chardonnay. That's not the French way. The vast plantations of Chardonnay in southern France didn't exist then, either.

To those of you who now take Chardonnay for granted, and who weren't drinking wine in the 1980s and before, it must sound strange when I say Chardonnay simply didn't exist. White Burgundy, using the Chardonnay grape, existed. Chablis, Meursault and Mâcon Blanc-Villages all existed, and they used the Chardonnay grape. But the word Chardonnay never appeared on the label, and in any case you had no idea what the wine you might pour out was going to taste like. The Chablis might be green–glinting, fresh and snappily appetising; the Meursault might be broad and oatmealy and intriguingly smoky; and the Mâcon might be full of ripe apple flavours and the creaminess of a Brazil nut – but, just as likely, the wines would be dirty, stale and musty. When I first taught my fellow students how to taste wine I told them that if the wine was suspiciously golden, and tasted like the urine of a dog that had overdosed on a Vitamin B supplement, mark it down as Meursault. It never failed.

But in the 1980s a few droplets, then a dribble, then a flood of heady, indulgent, golden liquid began to cascade on to our ripeness-deprived British shores. This wonderful, peachy, lush, seductive, happy juice was simply labelled Chardonnay. And once we learnt that this was the grape variety and that this grape variety offered us pleasure as its first objective, and didn't ask for respect or obeisance, and didn't require we understood it, and didn't demand more money than we could afford, we simply couldn't believe our luck – and we couldn't get enough of it. I was already a wine-drinker. And my world was transformed. And millions of people in Britain and in America and in northern Europe who had never considered the possibility of being wine-drinkers thought, Well, if this lovely, juicy, warm-hearted fruit bomb called Chardonnay is wine, perhaps I *can* be a wine-drinker. And I will.

Chardonnay is actually a relatively neutral-tasting grape variety. It hasn't got the kind of rip-roaring aromas that mark out grapes like Sauvignon Blanc or Riesling or Muscat. You have to do stuff to it – which is just how ambitious winemakers like it. When a grape is too powerful and difficult to tame, a winemaker has trouble imposing his or her personality on the wine. But Chardonnay just lifts its soft, round golden face up to the winemaker and says, 'Do what you want, I'm all yours.' If that winemaker aspires to truly great white wine, Chardonnay offers the best starting point. But, uniquely among white varieties, if the producer wants to make vast amounts of cheap but vaguely distinct white wine, Chardonnay is the best variety for doing that, too. The Australian big brands that hit the world in the 1980s and '90s always over-delivered, because their winemakers, however distantly, had not forgotten the flavours and style of great Chardonnay grown on those few acres of limestone slope in Burgundy. I sat with Philip John, the taciturn Australian who made massive quantities of Lindeman's Bin 65. I couldn't talk marketing jargon with him even if I'd tried. All he cared about was flavour, flavour, flavour. I used to climb over barrels with Philip Shaw, the inspiring but almost horizontally laid-back genius in charge of Rosemount Estate. Marketing strategy? Not interested. Let's go and taste another dozen barrels from different forests and different coopers, all containing subtly different Chardonnays. These were the guys who made those early Aussie Chardies. That's why they over-delivered. Since then, many brands seem never to have heard that distant drumroll of brilliance and are the worse for it.

The initial reason Chardonnay spread around the world was because Burgundy was one of the only European white wines with any reputation, and certainly the only dry French white wine with any renown, so if you were a new-generation wine-maker in a New World country unhappy with the wines a previous generation churned out, trying to imitate France's finest made sense. Several Californians had begun to plant Chardonnay in an attempt to replicate Burgundy as long ago as the 1950s, but when a Californian Chardonnay – Chateau Montelena – beat the cream of white Burgundy in the Judgment of Paris blind tasting contest held in 1976 (see pages 176–7), it did two things. It told the emerging New World that Burgundy was indeed the most revered style of dry white wine, the one to aspire to. It also told anyone who was listening that Burgundy could be beaten. It was California that had done the beating. But they were listening in Australia and New Zealand, and also in Italy and Spain, countries where the old order simply had to change.

The first thing you had to do was to plant Chardonnay. And there wasn't much around. At least California had some source material of vines that went right back to the 1880s, and they were way ahead of everywhere else in planting Chardonnay. But ideally you should plant your vines in conditions similar to those in Burgundy. Tricky. Burgundy is a marginal vineyard region, plagued by pests and hail and too much rain when you don't want it, not enough sun when you do. And it has very particular soils mostly based on a balletic pas de deux of marlstone and limestone that seems to change at every step. Although Calera and Chalone in California found some limestone, they didn't find the marl or the dodgy weather. Hardly anyone found the dodgy weather. The New World was about control, not putting yourself at the mercy of the elements.

So pretty much all the New World vineyards were planted in conditions warmer than Chardonnay was used to, and on soils that Chardonnay wasn't used to. The juice wasn't going to taste the same – and it didn't. But here was where Chardonnay's relatively neutral nature came into play. A Californian could say, 'Let's copy the things the Burgundians do to the juice. Hopefully, that will give us wines that taste like Burgundy – but riper. The kind of flavours Burgundy would like to achieve if the weather was good enough, maybe?'

The Burgundy effect

The most important item was the oak barrel. And oak barrels that were not just used to age the wine, but to ferment the wine as well. For places like California and Australia, which were busy creating a new methodology for winemakers, this was anathema. Their experts had finally persuaded wineries to stop using big, dirty old vats for fermentation. They had replaced them with shiny stainless steel tanks, which could be kept completely free of infection. They had realised that one of the reasons northern European wines, and especially German wines, were so fresh was because in a cold autumn the grape juice would be cold and so it would ferment very slowly. This leisurely low-temperature fermentation preserved fruit freshness in the wine. In hot countries, fermentation was usually fast and furious, and whatever fruit flavours there might have been were blown away in the rush. But you could control the temperature in a stainless steel tank. You could cool the liquid down. And, once again, control was the rallying cry of the New World. The professors at Australia's Roseworthy Wine College and California's Davis School taught their students that only stainless steel should be used for wine fermentation. You could control everything. You should definitely *not* use a wooden barrel. It was so unpredictable, and it might have off-flavours. It might leak. And you couldn't control the temperature.

But the guys in Burgundy fermented their Chardonnay in oak barrels. My first wine visit to California was in 1985. I visited various Napa Valley producers whose Chardonnays were making waves, like Trefethen, Cuvaison and Stag's Leap. I tasted the wines fermented in stainless steel but aged in oak against the same wines fermented and aged in oak barrels. The ones from 100 per cent oak always beat the ones fermented in steel and only aged in oak. Often the owner would be nodding his or her head, while the winemaker, with his or her wine school rule-book, looked distinctly uneasy. Usually, the owners won. The wines actually did taste like riper versions of Burgundy, and that was the point, wasn't it? By the end of the 1980s very few top producers weren't fermenting and ageing in barrels. And there's more. A lot of producers started by using American oak for their barrels. American oak is different from French oak – the trees grow much quicker, and the wood is much looser-grained. You get a lot more spicy, vanilla flavours, and maybe even some resin. The white Burgundy producers only used French oak from slow-growing trees in the centre of France, with a much tighter grain, and hence a much subtler effect on the wine. Clearly French oak barrels were going to be another weapon in the bid to make world-champion Chardonnays.

Cleanliness was a mantra in California and Australia, because the warm climate encouraged all kinds of bacterial and micro-bial activity much more destructively than in the cold conditions of Burgundy, with its long, dark winters and its naturally cool cellars. But the French seemed determined to do everything the dirty way. In Burgundy, the best producers seemed to press the grapes in whole bunches, with the stems still attached. The New World would religiously de-stem the berries, press out the juice and whip it off to the stainless-steel tanks, often protected by sulphur or by some inert gas to stop it oxidising. The Burgundians knew that if you press the whole bunch, the stems act like sieves to catch some of the unwanted solids in the grape juice, and the stalks create drainage channels – the juice runs out quickly and you don't get the bitter flavours the skins and pips can impart when they are being crushed. And then the Burgundians would often leave their juice in the barrel and wait. The juice would turn brown, the colour of cold tea. Oxidised. Ruined, surely? But no. If you allow the air to oxidise the juice early, fermentation scours away all the brown and you're left with beautifully clear young wine that is less likely to oxidise in the bottle later on. The wine-school professors said 'Don't do it' but the ambitious Chardonnay makers did it anyway.

They also left the wine on its lees – the yeast sediment and the leftovers from the fermentation – in the barrel. And they would also take the plug out of the barrel now and then and insert a device that looked like a golf club and waggle it about. This is called rousing the lees. The lees had lots of flavour. The nutty flavour of top Burgundies, the strangely smoky, savoury, almost struckmatch flavour of top Burgundies – it was the lees, the unpredictable, dirty sediment of the fermentation, that held the secret to these flavours. And the texture of the great white Burgundies, so lush yet so dry, so sensual yet so austere – well, there was a microbial second fermentation called the malolactic fermentation, which would convert sharp green apple acid into creamy lactic acid. That's where the texture comes from. All the Burgundians let the malolactic quietly happen in its own time, somewhere between the end of the alcoholic fermentation and the end of winter, maybe even the beginning of summer. You just waited in cool Burgundy. In warm California or Australia you usually tried to stop it happening altogether – unless you were trying to make Chardonnay to rival Burgundy, of course.

These are the fundamentals of the traditional French way of making Burgundy from Chardonnay grapes. There are lots of other twists and turns involving yeasts and blending and filtration – but for now, let's leave those. These fundamentals, which waves of visiting winemakers gradually learned in Burgundy, produced an immense number of good to excellent Chardonnays. It was clear that even when they didn't taste like French Burgundy – and they usually didn't, having much riper fruit flavour and more assertive toasty oak spice – Chardonnay made in this old way from new grapes had produced a truly spectacular new style of wine. Indeed, the ripeness was crucial. The initial intent may have been to make Burgundy lookalikes, and ever since the 1970s there have been a few winemakers in the USA, South America, South Africa, Australia and New

Zealand who keep that as their aim, but the new Chardonnay is a glorious champion drink in its own right. The mixture of ripe fruit – riper than Burgundy could manage – and new oak barrels with lashings of toasty, vanilla-ey, almost chocolatey richness available in their staves if the winemakers decided to coax it out – created a white wine, or should I call it a golden wine, of an indulgent delight that the world had never tasted before.

The giant wine companies, first of California and Australia but gradually of other countries, too, took note and began using French methods of barrel fermentation to make quite a lot, then a lot more, then finally a vast amount of Chardonnay – millions of bottles at a time. And as it became clear that the general public understood the word Chardonnay and knew that its name on the label promised them a lovely, mouth-filling, soft-edged, fruit-laden drink, competition and the battle for market share and profit became more intense. Chardonnay grapes that used to be cropped at four tonnes to the acre were now cropped at six tonnes, or eight, or ten – the flavour wasn't quite so good, but who will notice? We'll just advertise harder. And if you moved your vineyards to the vast flat plains of California's Central Valley or Australia's Murray River Valley, ten tonnes could become twenty tonnes, and at a much lower price.

And the flavour of oak was a delight. Expensive, though, these barrels. Cheaper to hang some toasted oak staves in a stainless-steel tank. The result wasn't that different. But staves were still quite pricey, and so staves could become toasted oak chips – giant teabags of oak chips hung in the vat for a few days, just long enough to leach out the toasty taste. Or, if you're in a hurry, you could always just pour in a few litres of oak essence. Doesn't taste so good, but it is cheap and if you have an order for a million bottles and not much time to fill it, essence will be fine. Oh, and leave some sugar in the wine. I know – the French Burgundies are totally dry, but we're not making Burgundy lookalikes any more, we're making mass-market New World Chardonnays to a very keen price, and the mass market always likes a bit of sugar.

Which is where we are now. We have the sublime. We have
the banal. We have everything in between. And it's all called
Chardonnay. We even have a movement called ABC – Anything
But Chardonnay. This was a snibby-tempered movement started
ages ago by a small bunch of wine buffs, mostly Riesling obses-
sives, who couldn't understand why their beloved Riesling never
got the applause and the acclaim that Chardonnay did. They
thought of Chardonnay as coarse and crude. And oaky. Ah,
there's the rub. Riesling is never oaky. To be honest, ABC should
have been labelled ABO – Anything But Oak. And that's what
the general public picked up on. These little wine fads rarely
get to the public consciousness, but the mass-market producers
overplayed their hand. The Chardonnay fruit became too dilute,
the sugar too evident and the oak too claggy and unsubtle.
And that sugar! One of America's most successful Chardonnay
brands is Kendall-Jackson Vintner's Reserve. At least this one
has some proper barrel ageing, but it always has some residual
sugar. That's why it sells. Australia's Yellowtail brand swamped
both European and American markets. It had a cool label. It also
had sugar. That's why it sold. But sugar and oak-chip vanilla is
not a refreshing combination, and somehow that slogan ABC
slipped into the public consciousness. And an awful lot of the
Chardonnay drinkers migrated upward, as they saw it, to Pinot
Grigio. Same amount of sugar, but no oak, and a sexier name.
Chardonnay is still massively important, but, unbelievably, it is
often now seen to be more downmarket than Pinot Grigio.

All of which should take some of the pressure off Chardonnay
at the bottom end of the market. It's a bit silly that the white
grape variety widely regarded as the best in the world is also the
variety used for a lot of the world's cheapest, most forgettable
wines. But the name was so easy to learn and remember – the
varietal revolution chose Chardonnay as its white knight. The
varietal revolution democratised wine-drinking and made it
simple for millions of new drinkers to understand. The flavour
of the grape variety was the most important factor in how the

wine would taste. Stop using fancy names on the label. Just put the grape variety in big letters. Chardonnay's soft, easy-going golden style of wine was perfect for this. The varietal revolution needed Chardonnay, but the revolution also made Chardonnay into a golden superstar. And the early examples did more than pay lip service to the model of barrel-fermented and -aged French Burgundy, even if few of them could resist cheapening their wines as the marketplace became ever more cutthroat.

And it wasn't just the New World tyros like California and Australia who saw that they could benefit from Chardonnay. The grape itself is easy to grow. The vine can give small yields or big yields depending on what you want. You can grow it on limestone – which it loves – but also on clay or shale, or sand or silt. Pretty much any soil will suit it reasonably well. You can grow it where it's cold – Chablis is cold and a star French Chardonnay area, but Germany is colder, and Belgium and Denmark and England are colder still and they are all growing Chardonnay. You can grow it where it's warm – every European country south of Germany grows Chardonnay and every other wine-growing country in the world whose climate is reasonable grows Chardonnay. And you can grow it where it's hot. Not ideal, and the results may not be special, but if you have a vineyard in India or Ecuador or Israel and want to get the world's attention, offering a Chardonnay is one way to do it.

And Chardonnay is malleable. Fashions change, fads come and go, and Chardonnay can cope with the lot. Sometimes ripeness is all, and if you're skilful you can make Chardonnays at 14.5 per cent alcohol which are still balanced and delicious – they've been doing this for years in California and Australia. But when the ripeness fad fades, and you're told that only the lean and austere will do, if you're skilful you can make linear, taut Chardonnay at 12 per cent and often from the same vineyards that were producing 14.5 per cent fruit bombs a few years before. California and Australia are doing just that right now. When the fashion is for oaky wine – Chardonnay loves oak. But when the fashion turns against oak, then unwooded Chardonnay can be a delightful melon and apple peel style. From the same vineyards. And when the wine buffs crave wines that have that curious, sulphidic, struckmatch smokiness that doesn't sound too attractive, but is an integral part of the white Burgundy experience – well, Chardonnay can have a good stab at that all around the world, too. California and Australia are doing just that right now. And from the same vineyards.

So Chardonnay can rightly be called the most global of grape varieties. None of the red superstars like Cabernet Sauvignon or Merlot or Shiraz have quite the reach that Chardonnay has.

Chardonnay and France

And it did all start in France. As far as we can tell, Chardonnay is a Burgundian grape through and through, and probably did take its name from the southern Burgundian village of Chardonnay. But there is one other part of France where Chardonnay has long been important – and that's Champagne, up to the northeast of Paris. The weather is pretty ropey up here – colder than Burgundy and just as likely to be hit by frosts – and the still wine that Chardonnay makes can be thin, meagre stuff, with a tooth-achingly high acidity. But I've just described the perfect base wine for great fizz. When you're making sparkling wine you need acid, raw base wine to provide the freshness and lift in the final product. Chardonnay makes up about 30 per cent of the vineyards and most of the vines are on an area of blindingly chalky soil called the Côte des Blancs. Often the Chardonnay is blended with Champagne's black grapes to make a single style, but Blanc de Blancs wines, from Chardonnay alone, can have a more tingly acidity, a brighter green apple fruit and an almost creamy texture that makes this one of my favourite Champagne styles.

The southern vineyards of Champagne almost touch those of Chablis, which is more a comment on how far north Chablis is than how far south Champagne stretches. And now we are in

Burgundy, Chardonnay's heartland. Although there is a little Aligoté and Pinot Blanc and Pinot Gris grown in Burgundy, Chardonnay completely dominates the white vineyards, and in Chablis they grow nothing else. But we aren't in the world of warm, golden, oatmealy white wines – this is Burgundy's chilly northern outpost, a good couple of hours' hard driving from places like Meursault. Green is the colour of Chablis, not gold. And green should be the flavour of Chablis. Chablis should have a cold, glinting mineral attack, its haughty austerity should shock your palate, not soothe it. The fruit from this small, chilly, isolated jumble of vineyards should barely creep to ripeness and the wines should taste as if they have dragged the last dregs of nourishment from the cold, chalky soil. You *should* taste and feel this cold, chalky world in the wine. The Grands Crus, supposedly the finest wines, are often aged in new oak barrels. I wish they weren't. Chablis at its best is about challenging your palate, not seducing it.

Seduction starts further south, on the mighty hill of Corton. This is a great, broad forehead of a hill, topped with a tight crop of thick forest like a monk's tonsure, and spreading down to the Burgundian plain with pale rocky slopes gazing east, then south, and just a little west. The hill of Corton sits in the middle of Burgundy's best bit, the Côte d'Or – the Golden Slope. To the north is the Côte de Nuits, where the wines are mostly red. But from Corton to the south, in the Côte de Beaune, there is a clutch of villages that just might make the greatest white wines in the world – and it is these wines that the rest of the world has sought to copy. It is their intricate, paradoxical intertwining of flavours and textures and scents that haunts the dreams of ambitious Chardonnay makers wherever they may be. The whites of this hill are called Corton-Charlemagne. These are the bluntest of the great Burgundies; barely seductive, powerful rather than beautiful or persuasive. The wines are rich and golden, buttery, honeyed, even syrupy when young – fatter than you expect – but bone dry. Could the New World make this style of wine? You would think so, with its fleshy, large-limbed personality.

Yet wait ten years. The flesh is more toned, the bones more finely drawn, the honey is now drained of sweetness, rich, but reserved. The vineyard and its pale, rocky soils begin to speak.

Meursault is probably the best known of these villages. And its wine is the easiest to love. Looking back at my tasting notes, I find that, straight from the grower's barrel in the cool, bright winter sunlight, the young Meursault may still be pale, raw and roughly rubbed with fresh-hewn oak, but its smooth-sided succulence is already clinging to my tongue and cheeks. Tasting it two years later this same Meursault is straw-gold cut with green, honey and hazelnuts languidly wrapped in oatmeal, with a lingering smell of breakfast buttered toast and fresh-brewed coffee. And now the wine is ten years old, more evening gold than straw, and all those suggestions of sweetness have dissolved into something much more savoury, wonderfully rich, but it's the richness of roasted almonds drizzled with cream; the curling brown smoke of toast is still there, and the melted butter still sticks to its crust. Could Burgundy admirers do something like this? Just now and then, from a patch of land in New Zealand or South Africa, California or Australia, they can. Well, they almost can.

The next two villages going south are Puligny-Montrachet and Chassagne-Montrachet, and they share the vineyard of Le Montrachet, which people have been calling the greatest white vineyard in the world for at least three hundred years. There's not much of it – 7.5 hectares (18.5 acres) of rather rocky soil facing to the south-east that comes to an abrupt end in scrub as the hillside turns to the south-west. But it *is* different. I've clambered over the wall and tasted its grapes, which are probably worth about a pound each, the Montrachet wine is so expensive. And they do seem to possess more vibrancy, more intense energy, than grapes from the other vineyards that crowd in on the same slope.

Tasting Montrachet still thick and milky from the barrel, I've been faced with its piercing, stinging richness like an essence coaxed in minute allowance, deep from the vineyard's soul.

Tasting the young wine from the bottle, it has sometimes seemed so thick it clings to the glass, and its power seems bloated and coarse in my mouth as I try to comprehend this elixir of buttered orchard fruit. And then, very rarely, I've tasted Montrachet at ten, and at fifteen years old. The coarseness is gone, but not the concentration, a tantalising scent of drifting woodsmoke mingles with a richness that owes nothing to sweetness and everything to a ripeness of fruit I can't quite put into simple words, and no one ever has, rolled in a cocoon of triple cream. Not dry, not sweet, yet both, not luscious, not lean, yet both ... the most perfect binding of opposites in the world of wine. The beautiful paradox that is great white Burgundy. I've never bought a bottle of Montrachet, or its Grand Cru neighbours. It's far too expensive. But yes, I did own one, once. Chevalier-Montrachet 1966, Domaine Leflaive. Of course. A limpid, golden colour, heavenly aroma of roasted hazelnuts and fresh ground coffee and new bread newly toasted from the grate. And a flavour of honey and of cream, of nuts now smoking from the fire, and the waft of coffee just brewed late on a Sunday morning. And I was in a garden in Hampshire, many summers ago, with my closest friends, part of my first-ever wine-tasting prize. And on that summer's day, at least, the greatest, the happiest bottle of white wine in the world. And maybe someone in Tasmania's Coal River, or on the chilly Sonoma Coast or under the gaze of the Argentine Andes at Gualtallary is feeling their way toward a new Montrachet.

France has a lot more Chardonnay planted, but none like this. Burgundy continues south through the Côte Chalonnaise where the snow-pale limestone soils combat the warming air and produce lean but savoury Chardonnays. The Mâconnais doesn't do lean. This is a rolling landscape, a bucolic mix of orchards, meadows and vines, and the air is drier and brighter than further north, the sun is higher in the sky and more golden, and the wines are richer, rounder, pulsing with yellow peach fruit, juicy melon, sweet ripe apples and the splash of honey. And if you gaze across the plump, contented Saône Valley to the east, a little very tasty Chardonnay is made in the foothills of the Jura mountains and in Bugey, pressed up against the beginnings of the Alps.

Way to the south, all along the Mediterranean coast from the mouth of the Rhône westward almost to Spain, there is far more Chardonnay than you would expect in such warm conditions. But it's these grapes – high-yielding, unambitious, but bearing the precious title of Chardonnay – that go into the watery and often lifeless bottles at the bottom of the price band. The more successful versions are often blends with more heat-tolerant grapes like Viognier. Yet you can make good Chardonnay here: there are cooler spots, there are outcrops of decent soil, and at Limoux, near Carcassonne, some promising limestone pops up high in the hills. There is even the odd roving Australian. They know how to make Chardonnay when it's a bit warm.

Chardonnay elsewhere in Europe and the Mediterranean

Spain and Portugal don't do much with Chardonnay, and I'm quite pleased. Portugal makes much better use of her numerous local grape varieties. She doesn't need Chardonnay. Spain is only recently getting her whites sorted. The best are coming from Rioja, from Rueda and from Galicia in the north-west – and they don't need Chardonnay. But Chivite in Navarra make a good, savoury example. And you couldn't stop Miguel Torres having a go – which he does in style, high up in the Conca de Barbera hills behind Tarragona, where he grows the grapes for his Milmanda Chardonnay, regularly Spain's best. Torres is deeply convinced by the dangers of climate change and has bought much higher land up toward the Pyrenees for when Catalonia becomes too hot for decent grapes. I hope he plants a little plot of Chardonnay.

Italy, on the other hand, grows rather a lot of Chardonnay, some of it impressive, some of it not. The south – that's Puglia and Sicily – is pretty hot and not perfect Chardonnay country. They grow loads of Chardonnay there, but I wish they didn't.

The north of Italy is much cooler and makes a lot more sense for Chardonnay, yet it mostly doesn't dazzle. It should be fragrant and appetising in the high mountain valleys of the Alto Adige, and sometimes it is, but it performs best in Lombardy, near Milan, where it's a crucial component of Italy's best sparkling wine, Franciacorta.

Chardonnay excels – and it really does – in a couple of the most unlikely places, Piedmont's Barbaresco and Tuscany's Chianti Classico. But Chardonnay isn't allowed in these vineyards, surely? No, it isn't. But Angelo Gaja in Barbaresco and Paolo de Marchi at Isole e Olena in Chianti were fed up with the restrictive Italian wine laws, which seemed determined to enshrine mediocrity, and they were fed up with the rest of the world embracing a thrilling new wine revolution while they were stuck in Europe's slow lane. How could they get the rest of the world to take notice? So they said to hell with it. Let's see what our vineyards can do. Gaja's Chardonnays were just perfect for America, where the influential *Wine Spectator* magazine gave them some of the highest marks of any wines they tasted all year. Even a Barolo maestro like the late Aldo Conterno made fabulous nutty, powerful Chardonnay from Barolo vineyards. Paolo de Marchi actually thought he was planting Cabernet, so he was a bit surprised when his grapes turned out to be white, not black. But the Chardonnays he has been making for the last thirty years have all the savoury, nutty, oatmealy flavours that a Burgundy fan could crave, yet they also have a sappiness that Burgundy doesn't have, and an amazingly bizarre sausagemeat savouriness that perhaps some of the great Burgundies do have, but don't want to talk about.

Chardonnay features in all the European countries east of Italy, without particularly excelling in any of them. Hungary manages some full-bodied, nutty examples in the red wine centre of Villanyi and maybe feels that she needs some Chardie while people struggle to understand – and pronounce – her rather good local varieties. A glass of Cserszegi Füszeres, anybody? It's tasty.

Croatia makes appetisingly good, unoaked examples that glint
pale and green in the glass, pining for a platter of Istria's succulent seafood. Romania largely uses Chardonnay as a pleasant
price-conscious quaffer, which might be a route for Bulgaria,
too, as she struggles to find what works best in a modern world
of wine she's still uneasy with. Turkey makes decent enough
Chardonnay in the south-west, but her indigenous grapes like
Narince and Emir are more satisfying. And Greece is the same.
There is some Chardonnay, but the local grapes are so much
better. Israel just about manages to keep some elegance in her
Chardonnays from the coolish Golan Heights and Judean Hills.
Lebanon actually claimed to have the original Chardonnay,
a grape they called Obaideh. The late, great Serge Hochar of
Chateau Musar called it 'the oldest grape on earth, from when
wine made itself'. From the wines I've tried, all I can say is
Chardonnay has clearly benefited from its long stay in France.
Many Lebanese producers prefer to blend their Chardonnay with
grapes like Viognier, and this works pretty well.

The old rule was that Chardonnay wouldn't ripen anywhere
colder than northern France. It will nowadays. Austria is further
south and would dispute being colder anyway and has made a
bit of a speciality of a rather lean, chewy style of Chardonnay
which they call Morillon in the far south of the country. The
Kracher winery in the Burgenland, on the border with Hungary,
manages to make a Chardonnay Trockenbeerenauslese as sweet
as any wine in the land. All the southern regions of Germany
make Chardonnay and you can even find it in the Rheingau,
where there has long been a Chardonnay vineyard called
Rheinhell on an island in the middle of the river, presumably
stuck there to avoid contaminating the local Riesling vines with
Chardonnayitis. Chardonnay vines have been sighted as far north
as Denmark, and Belgium has some positively excellent fresh,
bright, zingy examples from gravelly soils on the banks of the
Meuse River, where there's a world first – an appellation that
spans two countries, Holland and Belgium. The owner of the

Aldeneyck winery in Belgium told me that it's drier there than in Piedmont. Not bad for a country whose national airline, Sabena, used to try to entice tourists by proclaiming Belgium was the wettest country in Europe. From my experience, it still is.

The northern European country that has galloped ahead of the others in Chardonnay plantings is good old England. Once the English worked out that their soils along the south coast were pretty much the same as those in Champagne, and once it became clear that counties like Kent, Sussex and Hampshire really were warming up and climatic conditions were starting to resemble those of Champagne as well, in went the Champagne grapes. In the twenty-first century the quality improvement in English sparkling wine has been nothing short of astonishing, and Chardonnay has played a leading role. Some of the best fizz is Blanc de Blancs, i.e., 100 per cent Chardonnay – sometimes dainty, almost fragile, sometimes shimmering with acidity which is sabre-sharp, sometimes creamy, with the indulgent tongue-coating fatness of good crème fraîche. And Kent is showing that Chardonnay is not only suitable for sparkling wine. A vineyard called Kit's Coty near Maidstone is already creating savoury, nutty, mouth-filling, barrel-fermented Chardonnays, and a new operation, Simpsons, in the Elham Valley near Canterbury is showing that if you're looking for a new Chablis, it might be right here, almost in sight of the cathedral.

Chardonnay and North America

Outside Europe, Chardonnay wasn't a common grape until late in the twentieth century. It's difficult to believe that. New World Chardonnay has become so all-invasive that it can seem like omnipresent alcoholic mouthwash. But it's a very recent phenomenon, and different countries adopted the grape for very different reasons. America turned to Chardonnay for prestige. America had been making Chablis since the nineteenth century. No, I'm serious. I know, Chablis is a village in Burgundy in France. I know Chablis is a dry white wine made from Chardonnay grapes. Yes, yes. But it's such a lovely name. So easy to remember and to pronounce – *Shablee*. It sounds sophisticated, too. Well, the sophisticated image didn't last long. And very little American Chablis ever saw a Chardonnay grape. The Napa Valley's most famous Chablis openly stated it was made from Colombard, Chenin Blanc and a grape called Melon (at least I presume it was the grape not the fruit). The wines weren't even dry, usually. They weren't necessarily white. I've manfully downed ice-cold 'crackling Mountain Chablis'; I've seen bottles of 'pink Chablis'; and I've heard tales of a wine called Italian Swiss Colony Ruby Chablis – which was, naturally, red.

Even if you'd wanted to use Chardonnay, there was very little planted. Some cuttings from Meursault had been planted south of San Francisco in the 1880s and the Wente family planted some more French cuttings in 1912. This so-called Wente clone survived Prohibition and popped up in odd places across the States. A winery called Hanzell in Sonoma County was the first to try to make this Chardonnay taste like French Burgundy, and, crucially, they were the first to import French barrels for fermenting and ageing the wines. An interest in Chardonnay slowly grew – and it *was* slow: in 1960 there were still only 60 hectares (150 acres) of Chardonnay in California. The small band of enthusiasts realised that the smoky, nutty flavour that Hanzell achieved was because of their barrels. American oak didn't give the same flavour at all, and could even make a Chardonnay taste as though it had been dipped in a barrel of Bourbon whiskey. But French oak combined with the riper fruit that California's warm conditions would give was about to become a potent combination.

With the massive publicity of the Judgment of Paris tasting in 1976, when Californian Chardonnays were judged to be better than French Burgundies, every winery needed to make a Chardonnay. And the big beasts of California wine took note. Vineyards were planted at breakneck speed, often regardless of the fact that Chardonnay was a cool-climate variety. So-called

'Chablis' was forgotten. Chardonnay was the new, hip white. This became very apparent during the 1980s, when the so-called Fighting Varietals hit the ground running – Kendall-Jackson, Glen Ellen, Mondavi Woodbridge – they all started out tasting pretty good, a touch on the sweet side but good fruit and a whiff of vanilla oak. Their trouble was that they became wildly successful. The supply of decent grapes couldn't keep up, and I remember tasting each new release of wines like Glen Ellen and Woodbridge and thinking fondly of their early vintages. There was money in Chardonnay. There was a mass market for Chardonnay, and the mass market didn't want to hang around waiting for a wine to mature and mellow. We want it ripe, and we want it now. And a little bit of sugar would be nice, too.

Californian Chardonnay at the top end went through various contortions – one of them being an understandable reaction against creamy oak in the late 1980s, which produced a brief fashion for 'food wines', i.e., lean, acid, and often barely drinkable concoctions – but the general move was to fuller, bigger, broader styles. Even as cool-climate sites were being identified in Sonoma County, in Carneros on San Pablo Bay and in various spots near the coast right down to Santa Barbara, wines were getting richer. Because that's what the audience wanted. I had an excellent session with a bunch of California Chardonnay makers only six years ago. I was trying to argue for the European ideal of a drier, more savoury, less brazen style of Chardonnay – I was talking about wines that tasted of their place. We were sitting in a room full of open bottles of Chardonnay. The air smelt of gorgeous, creamy rice pudding, butterscotch, puffed wheat and toasted crème brûlée. That's what the air smelt of. That's what most of the wines smelt of, too. But I couldn't argue when the winemakers said we think these are the flavours of our terroir, of our place. And we like these flavours. And our customers like them. And they might have added 'And the critics like them.'

I met most of the same guys again last year. There had been a change. We were being hosted by David Ramey, a winemaker

who has never given in to the butterscotch and crème brûlée
brigade, and who has been making some of California's most
appetising Chardonnays right through the century. And suddenly he's not in a minority. The room didn't smell of crème
brûlée and butterscotch and nor did the wines. That oatmealy,
smoky quality that marks out a good Meursault and which
Ramey had always managed to capture was now appearing in
other wines, from Carneros, from Sonoma Coast and Russian
River. Between my two visits a movement called In Praise of
Balance had budded, blossomed, fruited, been harvested and
now had been laid to rest. But its spirit lived on. The movement
challenged the obsession with big, broad flavours, it challenged
the obsession with maximum ripeness and high alcohols, it challenged the powerful wine critics who remorselessly rewarded
wines of power and density over wines of elegance, complexity, intricacy – call it what you will, but what I really mean is
'drinkability'. California wines had got caught in a gustatory
cul-de-sac of ripeness, alcohol and power.

We're only talking about high-end stuff here. But let's see
what happens. High-end Chardonnay is what created the
insatiable demand for low-end Chardonnay, so there is some
connection. And at the high end, the richer, lusher Chardonnays
are easing off, but, interestingly, the leaner, cool-climate
Chardonnays from Sonoma Coast, Anderson Valley and Sta.
Rita Hills are relaxing, too, realising that a bit more weight and
fruit doesn't compromise their appetising, savoury personalities,
but it might find them a wider audience.

Oregon was never much of a Chardonnay paradise. Perhaps
it should have been, with its relative lack of sun and its cool,
damp conditions: it might have become America's real Chablis.
But the Chardonnay the early pioneers planted was stuff they
got from the Davis Wine School in California, designed to give
big yields of so-so flavours in the warm local conditions. Up in
Oregon, the grapes hardly ripened at all, so if the resulting wine
tasted like French Chablis it was French Chablis from a pretty

miserable vintage. The Oregonians got lucky with better clones of Pinot Gris, which ripened just right, so that variety became their flagship white. But the enthusiasm of French Burgundy producers for Oregon as a potential New World Pinot Noir nirvana had the added benefit that new clones of Chardonnay developed in Burgundy for their cool local conditions became available. And the Oregon growers started changing how they approached the business of judging when their grapes were ripe. Josh Bergstrom, who makes fantastic Chardonnay and Pinot Noir, said that when he was testing his Chardonnay grapes' ripeness he used to look for the sweet flavours of peach, apricot and soft Golden Delicious apples. Then he learned that the guys in Burgundy would pick their Chardonnay when it tasted of green Granny Smith apples and lemon flowers, because all the winery techniques employed to make great Burgundy require acid, and not sugar, in the grapes. Josh and his peers are now creating thrilling, oatmealy, Meursault-like Chardonnays, and often at less than 13 per cent alcohol.

Washington State, with its sunny, dry conditions diametrically opposed to those of Oregon, its totally un-Burgundian soils and weather, started off by producing some really tasty, nutty Chardonnays at wineries like Woodward Canyon that woke everybody up. The Chardonnays are a bit more mainstream nowadays, but sometimes I taste a wine from one of the old classic vineyards like Canoe Ridge and the magic is still there.

I thought I would be saying that Long Island is the most exciting place for Chardonnay on the East Coast, but I'm not so sure. Being close to New York City, I suspect they suffered from the Anything But Chardonnay movement, and if they were trying to sell an oaky but naive domestic Chardonnay to your typical New York sommelier at the turn of the century, I wouldn't fancy their chances of earning the train fare home. Perhaps that's why the most attractive Long Island Chardonnays currently are made in an unoaked or barely oaked style. Upstate, the Finger Lakes shouldn't be able to produce New York's best Chardonnays, but wineries like Fox Run and Lamoreaux Landing sometimes do.

If I had to choose the East Coast Chardonnay that has given me most pleasure over the years, it would be Canadian. I used to perform each year at the BBC Good Food Show in a cavernous, soulless exhibition centre in Birmingham. Maybe half a dozen shows a day, rowdy audiences, lousy acoustics and none of my jokes seemed to work. But at the end of an endless day Bill Redelmeier would be standing there at the exit, stroking his beard and holding a full, cold bottle of his Southbrook Vineyards Ontario Chardonnay from the Niagara Peninsula. Nutty, oatmealy, honeyed, it flowed down my throat fast and smoothly enough to persuade me that my jokes weren't that bad, the audience wasn't that sullen, and if Bill was going to be there at the end of tomorrow I could do it all over again. Southbrook Chardonnay is still a smashing drink. I'm still using the same jokes. But Southbrook has a rival. The Chardonnays from Prince Edward County – a hobbity outcrop of limestone poking into the northern waters of Lake Ontario – led by jocund Pied Piper Norman Hardie are so good, and, if you want to use the terminology, so Burgundian, that I think that in the next generation Prince Edward County may prove to be one of the best Chardonnay sites in the whole of North America.

Chardonnay and South America

Chardonnay is important in South America, but in a continent groaning with barbecues of smoking red meat demanding to be scoffed, and with a drinking culture almost completely focused on red wine, whites have only recently got a look in. Argentina, at least, had a spendidly original, scented, citrusy white grape variety called Torrontes if you needed to clear your tonsils out between slabs of beef. But it wasn't until a bunch of radicals decided to test out how high up the Andes foothills they could dare to plant vines before frosts closed them down, that Chardonnay finally got some attention. There isn't much great Chardonnay in Argentina, but the high-altitude limestone soils of Gualtallary have produced enough exciting stuff for me to mark it as one for the future. Catena's White Stone and Ancient Bones Chardonnays are nutty, oatmealy, austere yet lush, lean yet packed with fruit – this is the paradoxical language of Burgundy I'm talking. Well, these two wines deserve the praise. They're the leaders and there are more following behind.

Chile's wine culture was similar to Argentina's, although the Chileans didn't drink so much – nobody drank as much as the Argentines. And they certainly didn't give much thought to whites. At the beginning of the 1980s there wasn't any Chardonnay at all. On my first trip there in 1989, few wineries had any equipment suitable for making white wine – stainless steel, that sort of thing. Few wineries had equipment suitable for red wines either, and the reek of their creaky, leaky old *rauli* wooden vats would greet you at the winery doors. But the forward-looking Errázuriz winery was giving it a go. They had been unable to find any Chardonnay to start with, so they got some French cuttings and grafted them on to forty-year-old Semillon vines. They got hold of a yeast from Champagne and some American oak barrels and I was the first outsider to taste their six-month-old Chardonnay wine. It was explosively good: still cloudy, still prickly on the tongue, but with pinging lime acidity and mouthwatering raw peach and apricot fruit just starting to wrap itself in vanilla. An experiment. It was going to work. Almost thirty years later Errázuriz regularly make one of Chile's best Chardonnays – their Wild Ferment label. They make a lot of it. And it's good every year.

Big wine companies have been more important in Chile's development than in most countries. Until recently, there simply weren't any small producers. In 1989, Eduardo Chadwick at Errázuriz reckoned that there were ten or eleven wine companies of any worth in the whole country. Luckily, big companies like Errázuriz, Concha y Toro and Santa Rita have

seen that quality was the only way they could build a sustaina-
ble export trade, and they also managed to employ and hold on
to Chile's best winemakers. And these people were very keen
to find better vineyard sites. The Casablanca Valley, between
Santiago and the sea, was Chile's first attempt at cool-climate
wine. Sauvignon Blanc was probably more important, but
Chardonnay showed a sharp grapefruity style, which could be
softened down in the winery.

In this century, Chile has realised it has got a whole clutch of
places ideal for cool-climate grape growing – from its Elqui vineyards up near the Atacama Desert down to Malleco in the damp,
chilly south. They call it damp and chilly, but if you were French
or German you wouldn't find the summers too bad, and Malleco
Chardonnay is delicate and delicious. More exciting, though,
are the windy, sunny coastal sites that are spreading up valley
after seaside valley. Leyda and San Antonio, just past Casablanca,
are showing a positively maritime face to Chardonnay, saltiness
seasoning fabulous cling peach and Cox's apple fruit. But the
best of all may be Limarí, way up the coast where an outcrop
of rare Chilean limestone breaks the surface and where the
Chardonnays burst with thrilling pineapple fruit, the cat's tongue
rasp of peach and apricot skins and the juicy cleansing acid of
ripe apples. Don't leave it too long to try them. It's a sign of these
global-warming times that they've said they can't plant any more
vines at Limarí as they're running out of water.

Chardonnay and South Africa

Chardonnay was a very late starter in South Africa, and it didn't
start well. White grapes dominated the Cape vineyards – at one
time it was nearly all Semillon; more recently it was Chenin
Blanc and Colombard that everybody grew. But the chief use for
these grapes was to distill them into brandy. Brandy and Coke
was a far more popular drink than a glass of dry white wine. And
South Africa's political system of ruthless control stretched into

the vineyard business, too. There wasn't any Chardonnay and you couldn't bring it in. An outfit called the KWV controlled the wine world. If that sounds like a secret security organisation out of Soviet Russia, you wouldn't be far wrong. KWV was paranoid about quarantining vines from abroad, and when they said no that meant no. During the 1970s and '80s South Africa didn't get too many visitors, but there was always the same request if the locals heard someone was coming: 'Can you smuggle in some vine cuttings for us, among your undies in your suitcase? And above all, can you find us some Chardonnay?'

Eventually they were all at it. A leading grower was taken to court and the other growers rose up and said, 'If you're going to prosecute him, you'll have to prosecute us as well.' But the scandal that ensued showed that what they thought was Chardonnay was actually an inferior grape called Auxerrois. All that cloak and dagger stuff and they had been smuggling in the wrong grape. Tim Hamilton Russell had managed to sneak in some real Chardonnay. He had pretended that it was advertising material, which he had contrived to get delivered to Swaziland, then surreptitiously dropped off in Johannesburg and finally slipped into his greenhouse in Hermanus, where he was establishing a vineyard a long way from the inquisitive eyes of the KWV, or so he thought. The inspectors kept turning up, and he had to release his first Chardonnays under the name Premier Vin Blanc. I've still got a bottle and I've just checked its colour. It still looks tremendous. Another one to celebrate with when I've finished writing this book. The bottles are piling up.

Those first Hamilton Russell Chardonnays were fantastic – I couldn't believe how much like a succulent Corton-Charlemagne the 1987 was when I gingerly tried it from the barrel at a few months old. But it's not alone any longer. Although Chenin Blanc is at last taking its place as the most talked-about Cape white variety, and its use as a blender with Mediterranean grapes like Roussanne and Marsanne has created an entirely new wine style of mouthwatering originality, Chardonnay in the Cape quietly gets on with making some of the best Burgundy lookalikes in the southern hemisphere. Kershaw's Chardonnays from the cool apple-growing niche of Elgin, high above the sweltering plains, are as delectably oatmeal and nutty as anything in Meursault, and Iona isn't far behind. Chamonix makes a mineral-flecked, citrous-scented, cream-coated Chardonnay that should make the tourist haven of Franschhoek tremble with pride. And the late Tim Hamilton Russell would be proud of his neighbours in the Hemel-en-Aarde Valley if he could settle down on top of the cliff above his mansion with a glass of Restless River Ava Marie or Ataraxia, made by one of his old winemakers, and marvel at what he'd set in motion.

Chardonnay and New Zealand

New Zealand's first riposte to France's stylistic dominance of Chardonnay came from a most unlikely spot – the sodden clay soils under the warm, humid, weeping skies of Kumeu. No one would plant this kind of land with grapes nowadays, but it's right next to the city of Auckland, which would give you the chance of some trade, and that's what persuaded the early Croatian settlers to plant vines, regardless of whether their land was suitable or not. Mostly it wasn't. And most of the grape varieties they planted weren't up to much. Isabella makes pungent, spicy purple grape juice but pretty miserable wine. They certainly weren't planting Chardonnay.

But the Brajkovich family at Kumeu River were a bit different. They did plant Chardonnay. And when Michael Brajkovich came back in 1983 from a stint in Bordeaux and Burgundy horrified at the quality of his winemaking attempts so far but determined to lift his and New Zealand's feeble winemaking up by its own bootstraps, at least he did have some Chardonnay to play with. So he could put into practice things he'd learnt in Burgundy, and which no one was doing in New Zealand. Fermenting wine in a barrel, for a start. The New Zealanders never did that – concrete or stainless steel ex-dairy vats was what they used. Within a year Brajkovich had French barrels in place, imparting their intriguing savoury smokiness to his wine. The acids were very high in New Zealand grapes, and the winemakers routinely chemically de-acidified the juice, which softened the resulting wine, but also took away most of its character. The Burgundians and the Champagne producers had equally high acid in their grapes. They encouraged the second, malolactic fermentation, which converts this excessive sharp malic acid into creamy lactic acid. If New Zealand grapes had very high acid, then the conversion to creaminess would be that much more marked. All of Burgundy did it. That's how they got those creamy, nutty flavours. Brajkovich was doing it within the year. The local wine judges were so shocked that they kicked his wine out of that year's national show. They'd learn.

There were lots of other Burgundian tweaks and twists that Brajkovich introduced to the bemused New Zealanders. And one of the country's greatest weaknesses was a complete isolation from what the rest of the wine world could achieve. 'You can't make decent wine unless you know what decent wine tastes like' was one of Michael's mantras. Well, now New Zealanders could start to find out. And they didn't have to pay for any fancy foreign stuff. It was happening in the muddy acres of Kumeu, just north of Auckland, on the way to the old airfield.

Since then, New Zealand has become one of the most original and enthralling Chardonnay producers in the world. If anything, they're finding that their grapes simply have too much flavour to achieve an exact copy of what they do in Burgundy. But I think that's brilliant. Burgundy characteristics with added peach and pear and apricot, banana, tangerine and fleshy, juicy apple. Choose two or three of these, add some nuttiness, some cream, then bottle and pour. What more could you want? Auckland isn't the centre any more, though the enthralling wines that Man O' War produces on Waiheke Island opposite Auckland Harbour are shockingly good. But the North Island has proved it's got several areas with characters just as strong and different from each other as those Burgundy villages boast. Gisborne produces seductively soft, fleshy wines that adore having the extra savouriness of Burgundy added to their pot. The wines from Hawke's Bay, just down the coast, are a little more austere but wonderfully nutty and dry, and getting very close to Burgundy style when they are on form. Martinborough and Wairarapa add a little mineral and acidity. And every region of the South Island offers different styles. Marlborough more acid but creamy and nutty, Nelson broader, more reserved, but with caramel and oatmeal and bacon fat waiting in the wings. Waipara, as pure and as funky as any in New Zealand. And Central Otago, finding a deft, half-arrogant, intriguing path for its Chardonnay amid the glittering quartz rocks and the fringe of sun-bleached tumbled cotton clouds at the bottom of the world. All different. And not really a new Burgundy. It's a new something else entirely.

Chardonnay and Australia

Australia adopted Chardonnay for strictly commercial reasons. They thought they could make a lot of money out of it, and by God they were right. Chardonnay had never been an Australian speciality. Burgundy was. And Chablis was. OK, here we go again. People used to borrow any name that suited them in the old days. At least the Australians didn't have crackling pink Chablis like the Americans, although they did have sparkling red Burgundy, from 100 per cent Shiraz. Absolutely fantastic if anyone ever offers you a bottle of this sex-on-wheels happy juice. Where was I? Chablis. Burgundy. Of course. Usually from the Hunter Valley north of Sydney. Not France? Was it Chardonnay? How could it be? There wasn't any Chardonnay, but the Aussies reckoned they made a perfectly good Chablis – and Burgundy – in the Hunter Valley without Chardonnay. And they did. If you didn't mind your white wine being the equivalent of a pheasant hung for a month in a steam room rotting on the hook before being roasted – these Chablis and Burgundy wines were sweaty, pheromonal, pulsing with the dark, unspoken undertow of human gustatory experience, hard-squeezed acid, decomposing meat and slobs of custard all hurled together by the sadistic matron at a woebegone boys' school deep in the dales. Yes. Magnificent. It shouldn't be. It can't be. But the ancient Hunter white Burgundies and Chablis were – I'm looking at the notes of a Lindeman's 1965 Bin 2755 Chablis as I write – how could I like this stuff? But I loved it.

Well, you won't make any money out of that. So back to Chardonnay. Throughout most of the twentieth century, Australia had virtually none. A few clumps of vines on the inland side of the Great Dividing Range at Mudgee in New South Wales, and a tiny plot in the Hunter Valley that was used for distilling, not wine, was about it. In the 1970s David Wynn established a small plot in South Australia, then a farmer just south of Mudgee established a rather bigger plot, but nothing to shout about. While California was boasting about how its Chardonnays were beating the French Burgundies in blind tasting competitions, was Australia asleep? Almost, but not quite. Denis Horgan at Leeuwin Estate in Western Australia wasn't asleep when Robert Mondavi turned up and tried to buy his 'cattle and horses' farm. Why did Mondavi want it? To plant grapes and to make great wine. Denis preferred a partnership and in went that Chardonnay, on the way to becoming Australia's ritziest white. 'The Montrachet of Australia', they called it. And it pretty much was. Montrachet with an Aussie twang and an extra lick of fruit and oak. Murray Tyrrell wasn't asleep. He had leapt over the fence of that Chardonnay vineyard in the Hunter Valley one moonlit night and scrambled back with as many vine cuttings as he could stuff into his poacher's pockets. His golden Vat 47 Chardonnay gave me my first blind tasting triumph on *Food and Drink*. I could almost claim it gave me a whole new career. And Rosemount wasn't asleep either.

Rosemount was a different sort of winery. It oozed 'newness' and made no attempt to pretend to any traditional flavours in its wines. It set up shop in what was the distinctly untraditional Upper Hunter Valley. All the famous wines came from the Lower Hunter Valley, an hour's drive toward Sydney. You had to brave the open-cast coal mines and hundred-wagon coal trains to find Rosemount. It's worse now. Their most famous vineyard – Roxburgh – *is* a coal mine. But the owner of Rosemount was a wily international coffee trader called Bob Oatley. He had noticed the surging Chardonnay phenomenon in California in the 1970s and seen that it was being built on lush, ripe, golden fruit and lashings of spicy, creamy, nutty vanilla from new French oak barrels. He saw that none of the big Australian wineries had any Chardonnay at all, and didn't seem to have any plans to plant any. So he brazenly set out to become Australia's Chardonnay baron. He bought every Chardonnay vine he could lay his hands on, planted them out and, by 1982, could send his Rosemount Show Reserve Chardonnay 1980 to the International Wine & Spirits Competition in Britain, where it shocked the judges enough to award it a double gold medal, with its honeyed spice, its Brazil nut cream, its whiff of toasty smoke and its almost syrupy texture. And the colour. High summer, midday sunshine gold. 'Sunshine in a bottle', someone called it. Within a decade, every region of Australia that could ripen a grape was pumping out Chardonnay.

It still is. You would have thought that the vast inland irrigated, mechanised vineyards along the Murray River and its tributaries would be far too hot. Well, they are too hot for smart Chardonnay, but the majority of Australian Chardonnay isn't particularly smart – it's simply a decent drink, although the way the big producers upped the sugar and oak-chip levels in the early part of this century meant that for a while it wasn't a particularly decent drink. And it was claggy, sticky, cheap Australian Chardonnays that wine-drinkers were often trying to avoid as they moved away from Chardonnay altogether. This was a pity. Australia made its reputation by overdelivering, and by not cutting price. In the early days – the 1980s and '90s – wines like Rosemount, Lindeman's Bin 65 or Jacob's Creek were never the cheapest. They were simply the best for the money. And when they offered you sunshine in a bottle, that's what you got.

Paradoxically, most of the serious, high-end Chardonnay producers have spent this century trying not to offer you any sunshine. Cool climate is what the Chardonnay producers crave, and in a hot, dry place like Australia it's not always easy to find. You have to go as high up the hills as you dare without having your crop destroyed by frost. Or as far south as you dare – and, again, hope that the frosts don't get you. But that warm-climate fruit can still creep up and sandbag the most cool-obsessed of wine experts. I was judging the Australian Wine Show one year when, to their shock and surprise, the judges gave the top Chardonnay trophy to a wine called Peterson's – from the subtropical Hunter Valley. As the grower received his prize, he didn't make much of a speech. He just shot a sly grin at the judges and mumbled 'warm-climate fruit'. Another time, a Chardonnay from a large, rambling co-operative out in the hot hinterland won the title Australian Show Wine of the Year. The judges, cool-climate dudes, huddled together later at dinner, shaking their heads in disbelief and moaning 'What have we done?' What, indeed! But they did. Would it happen now? Probably not, but might it happen in twenty years' time? Sure it might. Fashions change, fads come and go, and Chardonnay will effectively make whatever style you want it to – leading fashion, following fashion or deliberately going against the trend. And, Australians being Australians, you can be sure that, as soon as they spy a trend, they'll push it further, and faster, than anyone else.

Queensland's Granite Belt is more of a red wine place, but they do make Chardonnay, and it's as good as you'd expect: quite stony, rocky even, full-bodied but not lush. New South Wales is technically where Yellowtail – the biggest of all this century's brands – comes from. It could come from anywhere in Australia, and, sometimes, perhaps it does. It certainly doesn't have the slightest taste of 'somewhereness' about it. It's not supposed to. But Hunter Valley Chardonnay definitely does taste of the warm, humid conditions the grapes are grown in, even if Tyrrell's Vat 47 has dropped a bit of fat since I first tussled with it. Mudgee and Cowra make pretty good Chardie, but you can still taste the heat. So go higher, up to Orange, up to Canberra, up to Tumbarumba, which occasionally makes some of the best Chardonnays in Australia. In the 2012 vintage, for instance, I couldn't find any better Chardonnays than the incisive, thrillingly balanced wines made by Eden Road. And in the modern world of Aussie Chardonnay, where suddenly everyone is trying to make wines at 12.5 per cent instead of the 14 per cent of a few years ago, high in the hills is the best place to do it.

Or you could go down to the seaside, to Mornington Peninsula in Victoria. I used to think this was a bit of a rich man's playground – an hour or so's drive south of Melbourne, and you sit among your little plot of vines with a glass of cool Chardonnay in hand, gazing out over Western Port Bay as the sailing boats gallantly dodge the white horses breaking on the reef. That's all good. But the Peninsula is now a really serious wine producer and I find my notes on Chardonnay come back again and again to texture – a soft, creamy texture like a celestial porridge of oatmeal and farmer's milk. And they often have a savoury quality that is slightly wild – the French call it *sauvage*, and it really does resemble fresh sausagemeat, uncooked, just mildly spiced. Bizarre? A lot of the best experiences in wine are tinged with the bizarre.

And Victoria does bizarre better than most. Chardonnays from Beechworth, the Grampians and the Pyrenees (which manage to sit right next to each other in Australia), and Gippsland all offer high quality with a certain wildness. The Yarra Valley can be slightly more mainstream, but it's also where some of the most opiniated winemaking goes on. When the current craze for sulphidic, struckmatch, savoury Chardonnays at low alcohol levels took off, it was Yarra boys who pushed the envelope so far you could barely get some of their liquids down your throat. But they have eased back. The Aussies haven't forgotten that making a smashing drink comes before relentless pursuit of an ideology, especially if you intend to do some of the drinking yourself.

South Australia's Chardonnays used to epitomise the rich, gloopy, golden styles, but that's because most of the grapes were coming from the Barossa Valley and McLaren Vale, two areas far more suited to beefy red production. But Eden Valley is cooler, Padthaway to the south is cooler, and, above all, the Adelaide Hills are cooler – and wetter, which is quite an achievement in a state as dry as South Australia. This is where Brian Croser set up shop at Petaluma to bang the drum for restraint and delicacy in South Australia whites. The supremely academic Croser was the flagbearer for a new scientific approach to winemaking in the 1980s and '90s. I was terrified of him when I first went to taste his wines. He asked me which one was the best. I said the young Riesling. He said, well you clearly haven't understood what I've been saying, so let's do the whole tasting again. We missed dinner. A legion has followed him up into the Hills and the leadership has now probably shifted to the equally passionate and visionary Shaw & Smith, who got everyone talking by producing South Australia's first successful, snappy, leafy Sauvignon Blanc. And if your big-brand Chardonnay isn't coming from the Murray River tributaries of New South Wales, it will probably be flooding out from the vast farms that sprawl on both sides of the Murray itself, partly in Victoria, but mostly in the hard, dry bush country of inland South Australia.

In Western Australia, you have to start with Margaret River, and you might as well start with Denis Horgan's Leeuwin Estate. Denis Horgan made his money in the mining-led boom years in Western Australia. Like many of them, he's had a topsy-turvy time, but has doggedly held on to the Leeuwin Estate and stages sensational concerts there every summer. One time, I sat on the grass of his winery lawn with a cool glass of Chardonnay, watching Julio Iglesias at his outrageous, flirtatious best and pinching myself to prove it was real. Leeuwin's Art Series isn't a Chardonnay that bends to the fickle gusts of fashion. It is a sumptuous, waxy-textured, full-fruited blast of beauty. On my last visit, as the lean and consumptive style of barely ripe Chardonnay threatened briefly to erase the sweet memories of the golden oldies I'd learnt to love, Denis did say that he had decided to throttle back his Art Series a little – a tiny nod to the modernists. Then he chuckled. I don't expect too much change any time soon. A lot of the Margaret River Chardonnays are on the full side, and I don't mind a bit. I can always head down to the desolate beauty of Great Southern if I want a bit of mineral rasp and citrusy zip in my Chardie.

Or I could head over to Tasmania. They've been promising to deliver great Chardonnay and Pinot Noir for at least forty years, but progress has been stubbornly slow. Many of the best Tassie wine ended up as fizz. A lot of the early efforts were centred on the north – the Tamar Valley and the wetter, colder Pipers Brook, which Andrew Pirie, the pioneer of modern Tasmania wine, decided was the best place in the island for grapes, precisely because the weather was so bad. He felt that Australian grapes had it too easy, and that they'd never produce wines of European class and style because they weren't stressed enough. Well, the result has mostly been Australia's, and some of the world's, best sparklers, with a few memorable, rather haughty Chardonnays thrown in. You would think that the further south you went in Tasmania, the cooler it would get, but, if you don't get frosted, it's actually warmer and drier in the south. And this is now where the best Chardonnays are coming from. The fruit is so good in places like the Derwent Valley and Coal River that Penfolds' Yattarna – often dubbed the 'White Grange' after Australia's most famous red wine – is sourced mostly from southern Tassie, and with its majestic flavours of baked double cream, brioche bread fresh from the oven and hazelnuts still warm from dry roasting under the grill, I'd agree that Australia's most southerly Chardonnays are often her best. And if the world hopes that there is a new Montrachet out there somewhere, maybe it's here.

Pinot Noir and Burgundy

Looking for the Holy Grail

A word in your ear. Don't worry if you don't 'get' Pinot Noir. A lot of people don't. A lot of people don't 'get' Jane Austen or Henry James. A lot of people don't 'get' Wordsworth or Milton, Handel or Bach or Picasso or Magritte. You're not a less good person because you don't 'get' these writers and composers and artists. I'm sure there's lots of writing and music and art which does speak to you. And for most of us, that's the point. Find something that we like, something that we 'get', and then enjoy the hell out of it. It's the same with wine. For most of us, finding wines that we like, wines that we get is what matters, and then we should enjoy the hell out of them.

And for those of us for whom this easy path to pleasure simply isn't enough, we can join the search for the Holy Grail: the perfect Pinot Noir. Or maybe the very good one. Or just the nice one that isn't a silly price. But while we search – correct me if I'm wrong – er, isn't the whole point of a Holy Grail that you never find it?

A significant minority of the wine world – producers, sommeliers and geeks – is obsessed with Pinot Noir – Pinotphiles, they're called. It's not illegal, but it can be painfully exclusive, especially when you're feeling the urge to wax lyrical about something like a Sauvignon Blanc or a Cabernet Sauvignon, but know that in their company this is akin to declaring you have leprosy. But where did this messianic zeal spring from? Well, Pinot Noir is the grape that makes red Burgundy. Although there are quite a lot of excellent Burgundies made nowadays, and a few great ones, 'twas *not* ever thus. Until, literally, this generation, disappointments from wines with grand Burgundian labels far outweighed delights.

A Burgundy lover of moderate means might go an entire lifetime without, if he was being honest with himself, ever truly tasting a great wine. He would have heard of them, the fabled few; he might have slavered over the gastro-pornography much favoured by writers who did manage to get a slurp or two of the nectar – was it really that ethereal, that transcendant, that apoca-lyptic? How would we know? We weren't there. But he would go perplexedly to his maker thinking, did I really make the best of my wine-drinking life? Should I have chosen Bordeaux, or Rioja, or vintage port instead? Well ... Holy Grail, old chap. You weren't expecting to *find* the Grail, were you? For goodness sake, it's the endless frustrating self-deluding masochistic quest that is the thing.

There's a lot of truth in that. But nowadays there is also a vastly improved chance of finding enough good Burgundy to at least get you on to the stairway to Pinot Noir paradise, even though for every step you achieve the glittering Temple of Ultimate Satisfaction seems to be two steps further away. Yet this still doesn't answer the question – why the obsession? Chardonnay, the white Burgundy grape, hasn't fed such fanat-icism. Cabernet and Merlot, the red Bordeaux grapes, don't foster such a demented tribe. Well, Chardonnay is pretty easy to grow, and as soon as they started people all over the world were able to make something pretty exciting. Not usually much like white Burgundy, but such a good and popular drink it swept away most criticism. Cabernet and Merlot were pretty easy to grow in most New World conditions, so whack the wine in a Bordeaux oak barrel, leave it for a bit, and out popped a whopper. It didn't usually taste like Bordeaux, but it was such a gob-filling bundle of ripeness, nobody cared that much.

But Pinot Noir? Well, it proved difficult to get right in most of the new places it was planted. And it didn't taste like red Burgundy. But this time everyone got really upset and tried ever harder to make red Burgundy from a very capricious grape that came from an area of France — cool, damp, often hit by frost and hail and rain — no New World pioneers would have ever thought suitable for planting a vineyard in the first place. Except that's where red Burgundy came from. And just now and then even the sanest of wine enthusiasts ended up saying things like, 'This is the greatest wine I have ever tasted. My life is changed. From now on . . .' You know what's coming, don't you? Yes, it's that Holy Grail thing again.

The point is you read some writers expressing their reactions to drinking Burgundy, and they can't just be making it up. There was a wonderful Irish writer called Maurice Healy in the first part of the twentieth century. He pledged he was a Bordeaux lover above all. But then the Burgundy effect kicked in and he solemnly swore that the greatest three bottles he had ever tasted were from Burgundy. Here's him writing about one bottle – the mighty Chambertin, which the Emperor Napoleon is supposed to have had a bit of a taste for; indeed, he took barrels of it with him into battle: 'One hears the clang of armour in its depth.' Maybe that's what got Napoleon excited. And as for those 'three best-ever', well, I'm not sure which one this was, but here goes: 'The songs of armies sweeping into battle, the roar of the waves upon a rocky shore, the glint of sunshine after rain on the leaves of a forest, the depths of a church organ, the voices of children singing hymns . . .' A sober-sided Bordeaux lover, swept away. And if I close my eyes and empty my mind of the everyday, I can sort of see what he is getting at. Rather more than I can with Roald Dahl, who wrote that 'to drink a Romanée-Conti is like having an orgasm in the mouth and the nose at the same time'. The mouth *or* the nose would be a miracle, I'd have thought. And I know the owner of Romanée-Conti. He seemed such a nice man.

You see what I mean. Red Burgundy gets to the parts other wines can't reach. And the very best do have an emotional dimension, an ability to engage your palate, but also your heart, your brain, your imagination. And with imagination comes aspiration, and with aspiration come dreams and visions and revelations, and each of these can pull you further away from reality, and further into a fabulous fantasy world of what you would like the wine to be. Red Burgundy can tread this line between reality and fantasy better than any other wine, and its supreme examples have been doing so for a thousand years. And Burgundy lovers have been falling over themselves to express the inexpressible ever since.

Pinot Noir and Burgundy

Let's just look at one or two of the most famous vineyards on this little scrap of land. Burgundy's Côte d'Or, or Golden Slope, as it slinks down southwards on the eastern flank of the Morvan hills for about 48 kilometres (30 miles) before fading away to the west. Let's try to drink in a few of the scents and flavours that might have inspired a thousand years of devotion. South of Dijon, the first fine site is Napoleon's favourite, Chambertin – a great sweep of vines under the stern brow of the dark, wooded ridge. Why is this a wine for soldiers and military metaphor? Well, at its best, this wine alone will explain why the world has been driven to a frenzy trying to recreate red Burgundy with myriad plantings of Pinot Noir, from the chilly valleys of western Canada to the mountains of South Island New Zealand. I suppose you mustn't stop people from aiming high, but great Chambertin is a wine from another era, long before gratification was instant, a wine that has no interest in offering a joyous young mouthful of bright fruit; it's a wine contemptuous of fawning critics who don't have the patience or the knowledge to gaze into its entrails almost more than its heart, to ponder, to admit to a respectful even reverential confusion – and to wait. Are the world's young wine Turks up to emulating that? Young Chambertin is a wine full of grinding teeth and choking, rasping power. What fruit it is prepared to show is like rough sweet juice squeezed from the skins of sloes and damsons and tiny shrivelled black cherries, disdainfully coated with a slap of tar. So wait. Wait ten years. Wait twenty. Wait until you can barely remember the grim unfriendliness of the youthful wine. Wait until you yourself are mature enough for the shock of its majesty. Now you will discover a thick scent, a fume almost, coiling up from the surface of the wine, exotic, darkly sweet, even floral, but like the season's sweetest rose trampled beneath a dashing captain's riding boots. And let the wine linger in your mouth. It may still start out as dark as blood and bittersweet as liquorice and black cherries, but as the wine warms and you relax, the fruit relaxes too, toward the autumn warmth of damsons and plums pendulous with ripeness as the wasps swarm. Wrap this in black chocolate, smear this with the perfumed sweet sludge of prunes, and maybe draw a line through it all of the delicious decay of well-hung game. And now try to recreate this in Australia's Yarra Valley, or California's Russian River Valley, or New Zealand's Central Otago. It only took Chambertin a thousand years or so to sort it out. Off you go. Let us know when you're done.

A few kilometres further south along the Côte d'Or is the village of Vosne-Romanée, where there is a cluster of great vineyards dominated by Romanée-Conti, a fabled vineyard making minute amounts of wine no one ever tastes. Well, almost no one. I'm privileged enough to taste it every year, and I strive to look the wine in the eye and treat it just like every other glassful. Difficult when you're on your knees. But these great wines of Vosne-Romanée are quite different from those of Chambertin. Somehow, there is a redness to the fruit here, the wines have a tantalising savouriness, partly of crisp nut flesh, partly of a chef's pale bouillon, partly of a scrape of cheese rind, that brilliantly offsets the cavalcade of spices, ecclesiastical, cosmetic, culinary – oh, that sounds far too mundane. Can't I do better than that? What do other tasters say? One describes Vosne-Romanée's Richebourg wine as 'all slashed velvet and flamboyant swagger ... with a restless animal power. A siren whose cerebral appeal has become almost physical.' Right. For my part, I was going to say the very name thundered with the opulence of silk-smooth flesh and sumptuous velvet, of tremendous musky scents, of dishes based on fatted calves and cream served to corpulent prelates and priests. I could have continued that the bouquet *'was all flowers – the fragrance of drooping rose petals, panting for the shade, damp springtime moss and sweet, ripe rosehips and red cherry blossom; and in my mouth its syrupy texture was barely roughened by powder-fine tannins and an effortless, lively acidity that leads into an intensity of spice and perfumed plums which with age fattens into chocolate and figs and cream'.*

You see, I am as bad as the rest of them when it comes to the great, rare reds of Burgundy. Romanée-Conti, the utter pinnacle of these fabulous wines, actually has loads of flavour and perfume and excitement, but we are all so thrilled to be anywhere near a glass words start to fail us. I manage phrases like *'a remarkable satiny texture, its bouquet shimmering with the fragrance of sweet briar and its palate an orgy of wonderful scents and exotic opulence'.* Sweet briar? What *is* sweet briar? What does it smell like? I don't know. So why did I write it? Honestly, it's the red Burgundy syndrome: never use one word when five will do. I wonder if this was the wine of which a fellow taster said, 'A real grace which means absolutely nothing and absolutely everything.' I do hope so.

I was going to take you to visit a few more vineyards along the Côte d'Or like Musigny and Corton, and villages like Pommard and Volnay, but honestly, I don't need to. It's wine like these Chambertins and Vosne-Romanées that have had people traipsing back to the ends of the earth, saying, 'I have tasted the greatest wine of my lifetime. I shall devote my existence to trying to recreate it. Now, how do I start? I'd better plant some Pinot Noir. Because that's the grape they have in Chambertin, and Romanée-Conti, and all along the Côte d'Or.' The Burgundy vineyard owners would nod their heads indulgently at your plans, but for them the Pinot Noir is incidental. It happens to be the grape variety that history and a thousand vintages have thrust upon them. But they don't think of the grape as having its own flavour. They regard it as merely the vehicle, the locomotive, to transfer the flavour of their different patches of land, of their terroir, into a liquid that can be drunk and enjoyed.

You may think that sounds a bit precious. But try telling the creator of a good red Burgundy that his wine has a lovely Pinot Noir fruit. If he can bring himself to answer, he'll say, 'I do not make Pinot Noir. I make Chambertin.' (Or Clos de Vougeot, or whatever the wine is that you're tasting.) Aubert de Villaine, the urbane, charming, slightly ascetic owner of Romanée-Conti, pulls no punches: 'Pinot Noir tastes of its own place more than any other variety because it has no taste of its own. It is a sort of ghost. It is like Rosebud in *Citizen Kane*. It is everywhere and yet it is nowhere. Pinot Noir does not exist.' Beat that.

It's a real conundrum. You have to use this grape to make red wines with what might be the most fascinating flavours in the world, yet the high priests of Burgundy say the grape itself does not exist. Are they just trying to be as enigmatic as possible to protect their turf? Well, it's catching. Pinot Noir evinces all kind of sphinx-like declamations around the world. Some Californians call it 'the heartbreak grape', because it just never seems to do what you hope it will. One Californian calls Pinot 'the stuff of which all good suicides are made'. Again, not exactly confidence-boosting. In New Zealand you hear winemakers call Pinot Noir 'the transparent grape'. That's more encouraging. 'You taste it all, especially the spirit.' Which is, sort of, halfway to de Villaine's ghost grape – except it isn't. This transparency has a flavour – something doesn't need to be opaque to have a flavour. And the spirit? Is that in the grape? Or is it the spirit of the vineyard, of the terroir? And how does that match up with another Kiwi, who says 'understanding Pinot Noir is like entering the Heart of Darkness'.

Does everything have to be cryptic with Pinot? Is there no easy discussion of what makes it tick? At least Randall Grahm, a notoriously intellectual American winemaker, thought he'd got Pinot Noir taped. He says the secret of Pinot is that its aroma has the same molecular structure as the male sex pheromone. But I'm not sure. I used to pat some good Californian Pinot Noir behind my ears before going to parties. I always left alone, though I did get followed home by a lot of stray dogs.

So, what have we got? Is Pinot Noir a grape variety with enormous depths of flavour? Or is it transparent and unremarkable? Does it rely crucially on its sense of place, its terroir, or can you coax pleasant flavours out of it almost anywhere? There's truth in all these suppositions. Pinot Noir does often produce pallid, thin wines of no distinction or merit – and it does this in Burgundy just as much as elsewhere. Yet in the right hands, with the right vision of flavour, it can produce wines unlike any other. It may do this most often in Burgundy, but many other parts of the world have taken up the challenge and are producing remarkable wines, often with no real resemblance to Burgundy at all. If they are relying on a sense of place, it is *their* sense of place – not Burgundy's. And can you coax pleasant flavours out of it almost anywhere? Not almost anywhere. But this old protectionist cant continually trotted out by the Burgundians, that Pinot Noir is so tricky to grow and so tricky to make into wine that it's barely worth the rest of the world trying, is clearly untrue. And if you're talking about Pinot Noir being remarkably suited to making simple, fresh, juicy crowd-pleasers – well, the rest of the world is a great deal better at that than they are in Burgundy.

Above all, Pinot Noir is old. Ancient. It might even be the most ancient of all the grape varieties we regularly use for making wine. It's probably descended from wild vines in north-eastern France, or maybe southern Germany, but no one is sure.

Scientists have compiled Pinot Noir's complete genetic code – and that comes to nearly half a billion letters! I have to say, I'm all in favour of this scientific uncertainty for a grape variety that creates so much commotion and emotion. And with this hoary 'oldness' comes instability. Pinot Noir is challengingly genetically unstable. It's always mutating off in one direction or another. The DNA guys say the white Pinot Blanc, the pink Pinot Gris and the black Pinot Noir are all genetically identical. I've seen white, pink and black Pinot grapes – all on the same vine. Hey, I've also seen single grapes that were half white and half black! This is some mixed-up grape – again, quite right, when you consider the fuss everyone makes about it.

But there's no question it has been valued for quality in Burgundy since at least the fourteenth century. And its relative aromatic delicacy seems to have been appreciated against other coarser varieties – not surprising when wine was generally drunk as young as possible and so a light, mellow, scented red would be greatly prized. And Pinot *is* light. It only has one-sixth of the bitter tannins in its skins that Cabernet Sauvignon has, and only one-sixth of the colouring matter, too.

In the late twentieth century, when the Burgundians real-ised that their vineyards were in a mess, and that they had, understandably but ill-advisedly, gone down a fertiliser- and chemical-fuelled route after the Second World War, which beefed up production but inevitably hammered quality, the local scientists decided to isolate and propagate clones of high qual-ity from the vineyards. Initially, these were all taken from one admittedly very good vineyard owned by a Monsieur Ponsot in Morey St-Denis. They're called the Dijon clones and have brought a certain amount of order to Pinot Noir's chaotic life, but in a perfect world you'd go to every high-quality vine-yard in Burgundy and choose material to clone. Those vines in Morey St-Denis had probably adapted over the generations for being just right in that village, not necessarily in a village like Chambolle-Musigny, only half a mile to the south but famous for a far more scented style of Burgundy, or Gevrey-Chambertin, half a mile to the north and famous for something much more virile.

Nothing is simple with Pinot Noir. But this glorious unpredictability is one of the reasons I'm a fan of Pinot. I don't crave predictability in wine. I revel in the uncertainty of every bottle I open. I suppose if I were one of those who pays silly money for rare, top Burgundy, I might want to be certain as to the flavour of what I'd bought. But then, honestly, I shouldn't be buying Pinot, or Burgundy. I should stick to something more undeviating like top Bordeaux, where you can sometimes open a whole case of one wine and all the bottles turn out as you'd expected. With a wine like Burgundy, or top Pinot from elsewhere, with a wine whose silky, tactile character is all-important, whose perfumes and flavours are sultry, seductive, steamy, sinful, but always existing solely to give pleasure, I shouldn't expect predictability as well.

Pinot Noir elsewhere in Europe

So Pinot Noir should be the grape variety of choice for wine-makers in cool areas who want to make their mark. Burgundy has traditionally been thought of as about at the limit of Pinot Noir's ability to ripen well enough to make a decent red wine. There is a lot of Pinot Noir in cooler Champagne, further north past Paris, but it's not there to make red wine (although it makes a little). It's there to provide body and structure to the region's sparkling wines, and when Pinot is a little short of full ripeness it performs that task extremely well, even though attempts to make red wine out of such grapes would taste pallid and thin. Certainly it is the only so-called classic red variety that seems able to perform in genuinely cool regions like northern Europe, but it also has an infuriating, intriguing ability to perform well in areas that really should be too warm. Many of the most exciting vintages in Burgundy have historically been very warm, despite the old Burgundian adage – *Vin Vert, Bon Bourgogne*, or Green Wine, Good Burgundy, i.e., a green, raw, young wine will turn into a good, mature red Burgundy. Well, maybe, but as always with Pinot Noir, no one's putting any money on it. Certainly in the USA, the produce of California's significantly warmer vineyards is applauded by just as many wine fans as the products of the far more Burgundian, cooler, wetter Oregon. And Western Australia and Victoria often seem to produce excellent Pinot Noir within throwing distance of equally good Cabernet or Shiraz vineyards.

So if we're looking at which countries have grabbed Pinot Noir and tried to make something special out of it, not many European nations have. France is where Pinot Noir comes from, and Pinot Noir is quite widely grown there, but there hasn't been any rush to create the great new Pinot. The Loire Valley has a fair bit, and in the nineteenth century Sancerre, in the eastern Loire and home of the tangy white Sauvignon Blanc, used to be largely planted with Pinot Noir. Most of the vineyards reverted to white grapes in the twentieth century, but with global warming the thin, chalky reds of Sancerre and its neighbouring villages are being upgraded to dry, muscular, minerally but very nicely balanced Pinot Noir reds at prices Burgundy can't match. Alsace really should be producing some crackers, but I'm not convinced. There should be a path between wan, pale, rather limp semi-reds, and tough, extractive, chewy and unwelcoming bruisers. Too few Alsace wines find it. The Jura region could do well with Pinot Noir, but theirs is a very hipster world and Pinot gets lost in the rush for the more 'authentic' Poulsard and Trousseau grape varieties. In the Languedoc, Limoux has some success, but my favourite from the dribs and drabs of Pinot Noir dotted about France is the rare, smoky, minerally but surprisingly fruity Côtes d'Auvergne from the middle of nowhere – well, out in the barren hills past Clermont-Ferrand. It's not a movement, just a local delight when you're passing.

Most of southern Europe has no need of Pinot Noir and has had little success with it. Italy, at least, has some form, and the high Dolomite passes of the Alto Adige do produce some quite fragrant pale reds. But the local whites reflect the beauty of the mountains much better. Pinot's part in Franciacorta's fizz near Milan is probably the grape's most meaningful Italian role. Further east, Pinot Noir has found a surprising role in Romania, and, to a lesser extent, Moldova, Bulgaria and Hungary. The grape produces some of Europe's best-value, lush, soft strawberryish reds. There's no attempt to create red Burgundy. This is Pinot Noir with an entirely new job, which it does delightfully well, hurling confusion among those who say Pinot Noir must be complex and expensive, must have low yields, and must be difficult to grow. Not guilty on all counts in eastern Europe.

But, obviously, northern Europe is where Pinot Noir really does have a role to play in spreading the red wine revolution as widely as possible. Switzerland has always made some pretty good Pinot Noir. England, Belgium, the Netherlands and Denmark are creeping toward a refreshing, tasty Pinot style as they all try to create something sublime – well, perhaps not sublime. Oh, why not – you only have to taste the efforts of somewhere like Gusbourne Estate in southern Kent to know they've got sublime in their sights. They've got the will, they've got the weather, and one day soon, on their sandy clays down by the old Royal Military Canal near the windswept coast, they'll crack it.

But Germany is the leader of the northern Europeans. The Germans have been enthusiastic drinkers of serious red wine for ages, but most of their serious red wine came from France and Italy. Pinot Noir could well have been growing in some form in Germany for a thousand years, since the monastic orders that were shaping Burgundy's future were also pretty active there. But the Pinot Noir – or Spätburgunder ('late Burgundy'), as it is known in German – wines weren't up to much: insipid, often sweetish, often with a rooty, smoky, unripe, unhealthy quality. It wasn't until this century that I began to feel the change.

German wines in general had been through the wringer and international interest in them had plummeted. But German pride is a fearsome thing, and as it became evident that global warming was creating climatic conditions in some parts of southern Germany that were becoming increasingly similar to those of Burgundy, so new wave producers saw a way to reassert their importance – on their own domestic market, but also abroad. Through red wine!

The first enjoyable German red I'd had was at an English winery called Lamberhurst. I didn't think much of the English stuff. But Karl-Heinz Johner pressed a glass of pale but surprisingly fragrant red wine into my hands. 'It's not from here,' he said, 'it's from home.' Which was in the warm Baden region of southern Germany. I clocked how nice it was and moved on. To New Zealand a few years later. And here he was again. Another glass of red, a little deeper, the oak less assertive, the almost glyceriney gentleness of the strawberry and red cherry fruit pleasingly chafed by a leafy, herby greenness. Very nice. 'It's from home.' I reckon the wine was about 100 per cent better than his first offering. So I thought I'd better keep an eye out on what was happening in German red wine.

A revolution. And with that, all the good and the bad as a generation tumbles and trips over itself to try to achieve brilliance all at once. You can do that with Sauvignon Blanc: first vintage – might be your best ever. Merlot you might manage it with, but not Pinot Noir. Even so, there was a frenzy, and it was very youth-led. The hipsters had found a cause. Not so long ago I went to the giant German wine show Prowein, resolving to get to the bottom of German red Pinot. I spent all day being jostled and pushed as I struggled to get whatever samples I could beg or steal. The Burgundy stands weren't half as crowded. The crowds were six deep in front of Pinot producers from Ahr, Rheinhessen, the Pfalz and Baden.

I came away bruised yet unconvinced. And over the last few years I've been poking about among the wines of the

Rheinhessen, the Pfalz and Baden, trying to discern a pattern. Well, one pattern is a devotion to the terroir, the vineyard, the place, that is positively Burgundian sometimes, and is absolutely of its time. All over the world I can tell the same story, most especially with Pinot Noir people. But these enthusiasts haven't necessarily made the most enjoyable wines. They might say enjoyable isn't the point – honest and authentic *is*. Fair enough. So long as you don't mind if I sometimes beg to differ. If I'm to generalise, when you're making Pinot Noir wine you can direct its character upward, toward the ethereal skies, toward the world of scent and sunlight and the mildest of springtime breezes wafting the blossom smells across your eager palate. Or you can direct it downward, into the dark, moist mystifying earth, full of secrets and hidden aromas, rich, visceral, clawing a mineral strength out of nature's depths. Two different approaches, two very different styles, with most of Germany favouring the second. As I said, I'm generalising! I am sure we will eventually see some of Europe's greatest Pinot Noirs coming out of Germany. Just for now I find the broader, mellower, cheerily scented styles from the Pfalz the most particular and the most enjoyable.

Pinot Noir and the USA

Given that Pinot Noir likes the cool you might expect that the East Coast of North America would have welcomed the variety with open arms. But the East Coast generally has a pretty extreme climate – mostly freezing winters, but summer heat and storms, and a lot of humidity – and although the Niagara Peninsula and Prince Edward County in Canada's Ontario have had some success, not much has tickled my taste buds from New York, New Jersey and Virginia Pinot-wise. All the real action is on the West Coast, and is led by California, which had a few early maverick pioneer successes, then a lot of failure as Pinot became 'Cabernet-ised', over-ripened, over-scienced, so that the very life was bullied and roasted out of it. Now Sonoma and Santa Barbara Pinot have become the talisman, the blazing brand of the reaction to the domination of California wine by the big Bordeaux beasts of Cabernet and Merlot.

And then there's Oregon. Talk about a reaction against the big, sun-soaked monsters of California. That's why the Oregon wine industry exists. It was the refugees from the brash, brawny, California world seeking somewhere you couldn't make a 15 per cent alcohol Cabernet, or a rich, golden, viscous Chardonnay however hard you tried, who realised that the cloudy, drizzly, cool, unpromising conditions of western Oregon were everything that California was not. Indeed, correct me if I'm wrong, but that sounds precisely like Burgundy most years. Exactly. And if that was so, maybe they could do something California had never managed – make pale, delicate, discreet red wines from the Pinot Noir. Maybe they could make an American Burgundy. Some of them have spent the last fifty years trying to do just that. And I've spent as long as I can remember trying to make up my mind if they've succeeded.

They certainly started out on the right foot. In the 1970s there was little exciting red Burgundy reaching the shores of Britain, but I did have some idea of what it should be like from my extremely limited exposure. The wines could be pale, could be delicate, almost fragile if they wanted. If you were lucky, they might be richer, but above all they mustn't be stewed and coarse and thick. The first Oregon Pinot I tasted was in 1981 – and I was in luck, because it was from the pioneer David Lett, a gruff Ernest Hemingway lookalike who'd established Eyrie Vineyards as early as 1966. I tasted his 1975, a delightful pale, mildly peppery but light, delicate and fragrant Pinot that was very like a gentle red Burgundy. And he told me this had come third in the 1979 *Gault-Millau* Wine Olympiad in Paris. Hang on, didn't the Tyrrell's 1976 from Australia win the Pinot Noir section? Where are France's best Burgundies when you need them? But the French demanded a re-run, with a beefed-up Burgundy section, and this time David Lett's wine came second, ahead of a Chambertin 1961.

This shot Oregon to stardom. It persuaded an unwilling American audience to give the new style a chance. And it also placed Oregon in a quandary. Should it continue to chase a Burgundian dream? Many have, and some of their efforts hardly contain enough colour and flavour to tax a gas chromatograph. Some still have an anti-California rage within them, and the success of a lusher, more sensuous style of California Pinot seems to have fanned the cold flames of vinous puritanism in their winemaking. And some have decided that Oregon is not only totally different from Burgundy – despite the rain – but is also made up of numerous little zones and areas – all different, all needing their own particular sensitive approach. And these are the ones whose wines now shine. The heart of Pinot in Oregon is the Dundee Hills, and, almost predictably, some of the best and some of the most disappointing wines come from here. If I had to choose wines that really tasted of their place, wines where the vineyard character shone through and the passion of the winemaker literally glistened in the glass, I'd go for wines from Eola-Amity Hills, Chehalem Mountains and Ribbon Ridge. Less trendy. Less worried about Burgundy. Much more Oregonian.

There's no denying that California was at the forefront of the new wave wine revolution in the 1970s and '80s. But there's also no argument that their weapons of choice were Cabernet Sauvignon and Chardonnay. These are two thoroughly adaptable grapes that can be manipulated and persuaded to go in various directions by a series of decisions in the winery – what type of stainless steel; what type of destemming machines and pumps, centrifuges and filters; what types of oak barrels – and to tell you what to do with these there were formulae being handed down as dogma by the wine schools, particularly the dominant one at University of California Davis. It was this potential straitjacket that drove the early wine rebels up to cool, drizzly – and undogmatised – Oregon, where, paradoxically, a kind of anti-California dogma developed that actually hindered their progress for quite a while.

And it was only natural that these rebels should choose the grape that refuses to be straitjacketed: Pinot Noir. The grape that, if you somehow managed to grow it properly – difficult in cool-climate, free-wheeling Burgundy, a lot more difficult in warm-climate, ideologically ardent California – then the best philosophy in the winery is leave it alone, leave it alone. Henri Jayer, a brilliant winemaker who produced some of the most heavenly, succulent, scented Burgundies of my lifetime, was always nonplussed when a succession of New World supplicants would ask him, 'What do you do to the Pinot Noir in your winery?' He was only being marginally evasive when he replied: 'Not a lot. Just make sure you have the best grapes you can grow.'

Not all of California's mavericks headed to Oregon. There had been an occasional star Pinot Noir produced, in particular from the Santa Cruz Mountains just south of San Francisco Bay, but most Pinot Noirs heading into the 1980s were pale, prematurely tired, with their brief youthful perfume rapidly replaced by a curious flavour of raisins and plum jam and beetroot, often rounded off with a fair slap of tannic bitterness. Well, there you have it – a cool-climate grape grown in warm conditions and made into wine by the rough-and-tumble intrusive techniques that suited big, burly Cabernet, but didn't suit nervous, fragile, uncertain Pinot Noir at all. The mavericks knew this. But they also knew Pinot Noir had to be the grape chosen to fight against Cabernet's dominance. They knew they had to find cool conditions. They knew they wouldn't find them where all the Cabernet action was – in Napa Valley. Richard Sanford started it by discovering the Santa Ynez Valley north of Santa Barbara. At the coast, the Santa Ynez Valley is so foggy you can't see your own nose. Sixty-five kilometres (40 miles) inland it's so hot you grow rip-roaring Syrahs and Zinfandels. But about 29 to 45 kilometres (18 to 28 miles) up the valley, those fogs creep in overnight and blanket everything until mid-morning, and then the broiling inland end of the valley heats up and draws powerful, cold winds across these gentle, north-facing

river slopes – just for a few miles. But that's where you'll find
Sanford & Benedict Vineyard, quite possibly California's first
'Grand Cru' site. Just a short strip between the dank fog of the
coast and the torrid acres inland. They call this area the Sta.
Rita Hills nowadays, and many of California's coolest Pinot
dudes are growing their grapes right here. Jim Clendenen at
Au Bon Climat, just north of Santa Ynez in the Santa Maria
Valley, which can be even foggier and gloomier than Santa
Ynez at its seaward end, has also made his reputation on grapes
grown where the fog, the wind and the sun just briefly are all in
harmony. You could say the same about Saintsbury, much further north at Carneros, on the tip of San Pablo Bay, where the
fogs dawdle daily, to be cleared away by chilly gales and spurts
of pure-sky sunshine. These and a few others – lone rangers,
non-joiners – lit a Pinot Noir flame and kept it alight until the
long, brutal rule of Cabernet Sauvignon began to crumble in
the twenty-first century.

   They had believed in getting the climate right. Dick Graff at
Chalone and John Jensen at Calera were more concerned about
the soil – above all, limestone. These guys had both worked at
Burgundy's great Domaine de la Romanée-Conti. Whenever
they tried to probe into how winemaker André Noblet achieved
such brilliance in his wines, André would just murmur 'limestone'. Not what Californians want to hear – limestone barely
exists in the Golden West. But Jensen and Graff both found
some, high up on the barren, inhospitable, arid slopes of the
Gavilan mountain range. This was Wild West winemaking.
Hardly any rain – Graff sometimes had to haul water up the
mountain by truck – an awful lot of sun and an awful lot of
bleak, sun-bleached virgin limestone. The other mavericks had
found climates they knew would suit Pinot Noir, and they have
been followed since by the majority of California's modern
Pinot stars. At Calera and Chalone they were determined to
champion the cause of the soil and the gaunt, deep, challenging,
uncompromising, sometimes barely comprehensible characters

and flavours it unwillingly reveals. Most other Californian Pinot Noirs look upwards for the ethereal, the fragrant or for the juicy sweetness of ripe fruit; Calera and Chalone delved deep into some of the rawest vineyard terroir in all America and extracted flavours and characters that, just sometimes, might make you think, Hey, is this a Nuits St-Georges, or a Chambertin, from an unseasonably warm Burgundy vintage of long ago?

In the twenty-first century much of the Pinot Noir attention has shifted north to the Russian River Valley in Sonoma, where conditions get colder and foggier for every mile as you push westward toward the coast, and whose vineyards, led by superstars like Hirsch and Rochioli, have produced cult wines. I love the depth of fruit in these wines, a kind of fruit that keeps the chewy, ripe skin attached. But Russian River is a big area. It makes powerful Zinfandel and Syrah as well as Pinot Noir. It *can* make some of California's greatest Pinots. It can also make some of California's merely richest Pinots.

Indeed, the cutting edge for those trying to square the circle of sunshine, dryness, heat and cool, drinkability and restraint is now more likely to be found in numerous patches of Sonoma coastal land, often in a heavily forested maritime block called Fort Ross–Seaview. And add Anderson Valley in California's far north to that. Much of the States' best fizz comes from Anderson Valley fruit. Now that the movement toward greater balance and freshness in Pinot Noir has begun to gain confidence, Anderson is coming into its own for fragrant, refreshing Pinot Noir. And that original cool-climate haven of coastal Santa Ynez (Sta. Rita Hills) – well, it doesn't seem quite so cool-climate any more. It's a hotbed of Pinot activity, but an awful lot of the top labels are producing fairly heady wines. So? Are they in balance? To my surprise, yes, they are. Are they worthy bearers of the banner proclaiming California is no longer just about Cabernet Sauvignon? Yes, they are. And to the surprise of the entire wine world, Santa Ynez was the setting for the 2005 film *Sideways*, about a Pinot Noir-soaked road trip, which catapulted Pinot lore to the top of the American wine agenda at the expense of Merlot. Miles, the main character, describes Pinot Noir as 'the one varietal that truly enchants me, both stills and steals my heart with its elusive loveliness and false promises of transcendence ... whose flavours are the most haunting and brilliant and thrilling and subtle and ... ancient on the planet'. He should know. I've never seen so much drinking in any film, ever. And it was all Pinot Noir.

Pinot Noir and South America

Pinot Noir is reckoned to be a bit of a shy, blushing type of grape, keen on cool, mellow growing conditions, so the extravagant extremes of the South American climate shouldn't hold out much hope for decent Pinot reds. And they don't. I've been tasting Pinots from Argentina for twenty years and have hardly blinked. Hardly. But I have blinked. Once. Way down south. As far south as the cranky little plane droning over an unspeakably raw, arid, blistering desert would take me. To the snug and well-watered gash of greenery and plenty that is the Rio Negro Valley. The Black River. A deep vein of pure water, clean enough to dip your head into and drink, surging to the sea. But, while it does so, also providing irrigation, prosperity, plenty for a hundred kilometres, hidden from the harsh desert north and from the two thousand kilometres of wind-scorched emptiness running south to the very southern tip of the Americas. I drove up to the Valley ridges, my face smarting under the sun to the north, stung by the wind to the south. And back down the bank, in among the lush green, the high poplars catching the savagery of the wind and handing down cool breezes and a most un-Argentine sense of calm, I found a tiny patch of Pinot magic.

Hans Vinding-Diers is a French-Dutch winemaker of an idealistic nature. He persuaded a local government official to show him all the local land registers, looking for old vines, and he caught sight of this – 1.5 hectares (3.5 acres) of vines dating from

1932. And they were Pinot Noir. It looks pretty woebegone now and it must have looked far worse when Hans trudged up the dirt track to ask the owner if he could buy the grapes. Hans said he couldn't see any grapes, just undergrowth and weeds. And the sour owner said, 'I don't give a s—' when he asked to buy what there was. The owner wanted shot of it all. Hans was desperate to oblige and coaxed the death rattle back out of the exhausted vineyard, so that now, bounded by desert to the north and wilderness to the south, he makes just a few thousand bottles of a Pinot Noir called 1932. Tasting the 2005 and '06 vintages from cask, my head spun. I knew so much about what great Burgundy was supposed to taste like. And I'm here in an adobe bunker in Argentina getting it with both barrels. The intensity of a wild, strawberry perfume, the heady dark cherry fruit, the angelica sweetness, the unsettling, addictive violet aroma ... I start to burble Burgundian Grand Cru language – and the French vineyard manager wags his finger at me. 'No, no, this is not a Burgundy. This is a Pinot de Patagonie.' A Burgundian gone native. But that uplifting perfume of mint and thyme? 'Look,' he says, and I see the vineyard is hemmed in with wild mint and thyme. And that irresistible, probing Poire Williams? 'Ah, yes,' he says, 'this valley grows the greatest Williams pears in the world.' Truly, a wine of its place.

Chile is more blessed than Argentina when it comes to cool places for Pinot Noir. But the Chileans didn't know that until recently. The Casablanca Valley has produced a fair bit of good, sometimes very good, juicy Pinot. But it took a bleak piece of just-planted virgin dirt out on the ridge above the Pacific Ocean to really excite me and show where the future lay. This was the first indication I had that Chile was now aware of the most powerful cooling mechanism any southern hemisphere country possessed: the ferocious, ill-tempered, glacier-cold Humboldt Current that sweeps up the Chilean coast and on to Peru. As the warm inner valleys suck in ice-cold air, anyone brave enough to plant out in the unknown lands toward the sea could find conditions as cool as the famously cool South Island of New Zealand. And in abundance.

I saw the first evidence in wine giant Concha y Toro's laboratory in 2002. I was pestering them to prove to me that they could do better, and at last they conspiratorially brought out some sample bottles of experimental Pinot Noir from a place called Leyda – out toward the ocean, very cool, with a full-on wind every day to draw the heat out of the sun. The wine was crystal clear, limpid, cool, different. By January 2005 I was at Leyda. Most of the landscape there was as parched and thirsty as South Australia. But there were two great slabs of green, the Cahuil and Las Brisas vineyards. Brand new and offering their first fruits. The Brisas Pinot Noir was wonderfully rich, with an intensity of red cherry sauce cut through with the mineral shock of sheared rock. The Cahuil was darker, sweeter, black plum and strawberry fruit but more tannic, too, until exposure to the air opened up its sensuous tongue-coating texture. I was impressed. I was more impressed when they showed the wine of a single hectare in Cahuil, Lot 21 – scented, spicy, rich, utterly seductive. Did they have more single-lot wines? 'Sure. The width of a track makes all the difference here,' said the winemaker. That sounds a bit Burgundian to me. Seven years ago there was dry-grown wheat here. We're 12 kilometres (7.5 miles) from the ocean. Suddenly the keen breeze snapped my clipboard from my hand. 'We'll be much closer to the sea next time you visit. It will be windier, colder, and on a clear winter day you'll be able to see the sea beneath the vineyard, then turn and see the Andes behind you. The whole width of Chile.' And a new sort of Burgundy in between.

Pinot Noir and South Africa

Pinot Noir has played a small but highly significant part in the new South Africa. Fundamentally, South Africa is a bit on the warm side. It is greatly helped by the Benguela Current cooling its coasts down, but generally, we're talking warm to very warm. The Swartland region has made a big noise recently with wines made from patches of old warm-climate varieties scattered across the wheatlands. They're excellent, but they don't prove that South Africa can do cool. For that you need someone to take the great cool-climate red variety – Pinot Noir – and run with it. And both Paul Cluver and Tim Hamilton Russell chose places that reminded them of Scotland. Cluver's fruit farm is in Elgin, a broad, high-altitude, cloud-covered bowl slung between mountains with firs and pines traipsing right down their bouldery slopes. Look to the south. Over that misty ridge is the great, stormy, unforgiving Southern Ocean. This is cool in South African terms. This is where all the best apples are grown. And with Pinot not liking too much heat or direct sunlight, this seemed a sensible place for vines. The savoury, rocky, dense styles of Pinot the Elgin producers are now making tells me this is smart Pinot country, producing a genuinely different Cape style. Then go a little further – out east and then down to the sea and along the base of the cliffs to where a half-hidden valley creeps away to the north. And it's just like a Scottish valley – morning mists that are cleared by cold winds from the sea, with cotton-bright clouds scudding above the rows of pine trees and rocky crags. Tim Hamilton Russell thought this was as far south as he could go as he searched for his 'African Burgundy'. So he planted Pinot Noir, and his valley, Hemel-en-Aarde, is now absolutely the still centre around which the rest of South African Pinotphilia spins. Warm dudes go to Swartland. Cool dudes come to Hemel-en-Aarde. They've planted right up to the top of the valley, as it plateaus then tumbles back to the coast away to the east. They've divided this little valley into three sections, and again, there are real differences: soil, sun, moisture and wind differences – and philosophical differences. Minutiae matter here as the cool brigade begins the long walk toward trying to define and create an African Burgundy. There are some wonderful positive differences between each producer's

wines. Antony Hamilton Russell – Tim's son – says 'Does the
consumer care? Do they care in Meursault or Volnay? We feel
that in fifty years people will care. For our grandchildren we
have to make them care.' Very Burgundian.

Pinot Noir in Australia and New Zealand

Pinot Noir has never played the lead role in Australia. It's not
that they haven't tried – an Aussie not try? – but often I felt
that the egoistic ambition and self-belief that surges through
so many Aussies wasn't really quite the right frame of mind
for untangling the temperamental threads and strands that go
to make up successful Pinot. There wasn't a lot of humility in
evidence. And maybe not a lot of the patience needed to get the
best out of Pinot in the very un-European and generally too
warm conditions of Australia.

And yet Pinot Noir did play a leading role once – in 1979,
when the French *Gault-Millau* magazine held a Wine Olympiad
and awarded the top Pinot Noir prize not to a Grand Cru
Burgundy, but to a Tyrrell's 1976 from the subtropical Hunter
Valley north of Sydney. And then *Time* magazine featured this
wine as one of the World's Top Ten, keeping company with
Romanée-Conti and Chambertin. I've tasted it. And I've
looked Murray Tyrrell, the wily old codger who made it, in the
eye, and said, 'How did you make this?' 'Ah, well, you know ...'
'Look me in the eye, Murray.' Honestly! Still, it put Aussie Pinot
Noir on a pedestal from which it soon tumbled.

There are a few cool spots in the New South Wales Highlands,
but nearly all the action has been in Victoria and Tasmania.
The cooler parts of Western Australia and the Adelaide Hills
in South Australia put in some effort, but the Yarra Valley and
Mornington Peninsula, both close to Melbourne, have spent
the last twenty years slugging it out, cheered on by a few brilliant mavericks in Geelong, Macedon, South Gippsland and
Beechworth. Yarra Valley has tried harder to make a lean,

savoury European style of Pinot Noir, and is now reflecting ruefully that, with global warming proceeding apace, maybe the beautiful Yarra is just a bit warm for the type of Pinot they crave to create. Mornington Peninsula, surrounded by sea, battered by briny winds and with a thirsty, well-heeled populace crying out for the local wine, seems to have been less bothered by any Burgundian constraints and is happy making a richer, rounder and entirely delicious succulent style all its own.

And talking of climate change, Tasmania, for long so disregarded as a wine region that the government refused to give locals any advice about viticulture, telling them to stick to apples and not to get ideas above their station, is now starting to parade itself as Pinot's promised land. I used to agree with critics that most Tassie Pinot was lean and thin, and walking through the vineyards, you'd say, 'What's that?' Sparkling material. 'And that?' Sparkling material. In other words, stuff they couldn't get ripe enough to make into half-decent red. And then I tasted a lush, warm-hearted, scented Pinot from Freycinet, grown behind a protective bluff near Wineglass Bay (I mean it!) on the east coast. Pinots popped up from the Derwent and Huon Valleys in the far south – shouldn't it be even colder down there? No, it's not. If you avoid the frost, it's warmer. Winter often doesn't arrive on the Derwent, near Hobart, until July. That's January in the northern hemisphere! And now there's the Coal River. Way south again, with a special climate, and quite possibly, with Tolpuddle Vineyards, growing the best Pinot Noir in Australia. Not Burgundian. Just exceptional. And the authorities told the locals to stick to apples.

Of all the countries outside France, it is the one furthest away from Burgundy that has had its whole red wine culture defined by Pinot Noir. Maybe that makes sense. Burgundy is in northern France. New Zealand is the last scrap of land before Antarctica. Well, last two scraps. The North Island, which has one remarkably suitable little strip of Pinot Noir land at Martinborough, just over the mountains from Wellington. The other scrap is the South Island, where every place they plant any vines at all immediately proves itself to be suitable for Pinot Noir.

It began with a wine out of nowhere – well, out of a muddy potato field near Christchurch, to be exact. The 1982 St Helena Pinot Noir would never had existed had not blight whacked the potato crop. The farmers were looking for a new crop. Why they picked on tricksy Pinot Noir, I've no idea – potatoes are a lot easier to grow. Their 1982 was wonderful: a deep glycerous richness of blackcurrant pastilles, purple plums and pepper, woven through with tea-rose scent. I didn't taste a better Pinot Noir all year. I don't think I tasted a better Burgundy all year. Then I found nothing much until a Waipara Springs 1990 appeared with the bittersweet brilliance of blackberries, damson and sloes. Then the thoughtful, studious yet silky Neudorfs slunk out from Nelson, the sensuous, intellectual yet beguiling Ata Rangis from Martinborough offering that dark secret world of black cherry and raspberry and balsam that so many Pinots crave but don't find. And finally, the trickle of promise from the desert redoubt of Central Otago in the far south became a flow, if never quite a flood, as a cavalcade strode out of confident swaggerers with many leaders. But for me, with the challenging, thrilling flavours of these ravaged goldfields and the glittering minerality of this land at their core, the haughty benevolent studiousness of Quartz Reef and the wry, precise perfection of Felton Road were leading the noisy band.

The wine enthusiasts in New Zealand bang the drum for Pinot Noir far louder than they bang the drum for Sauvignon Blanc, though Sauvignon's success is what allowed the country to be taken seriously in the world of wine, and, frankly, pays the bills for a lot of the Pinot producers. Indeed, one of the things I find infuriating in New Zealand is the way the Pinot crowd openly deride Sauvignon, sometimes barely concealing their contempt. They should remember who's buttering their bread.

And the wider global village of Pinot producers increasingly supports them. New Zealanders have had a string of successes and seem to produce more and better Pinot every year. This feeds the frenzy: the world is desperate for a new Pinot Noir paradise, more desperate for this than for any other grape because there have been so many failures in this saga of searching for the Holy Grail. And there's another factor – which the Burgundians may not like, but which the rest of the world loves. New Zealand showed that growing good Pinot Noir grapes and making good Pinot Noir wines is not quite as difficult as everyone – especially the Burgundians – was making out. The Marlborough region, famous for Sauvignon Blanc, has even shown that you can produce positively industrial amounts of Pinot with a decent flavour and at a fair price. Only Chile can do this as effectively. Burgundy can't.

On all my trips to New Zealand until 2013, I would endlessly hear Pinot makers saying, 'Oh, Burgundy this, Burgundy that . . .' Always Burgundy. Not any more. On my last trip I hardly heard Burgundy mentioned as New Zealanders revelled in the savouriness that only Martinborough could produce, the funky-hearted richness of the Waipara wines, and the proud, acid-stabbed, herb-strewn, heroic dark fruit of the far south from Central Otago. Nothing like Burgundy. Everything like wonderful, self-confident Pinot Noir.

Syrah–Shiraz

A French–Aussie score draw

So what does Syrah mean to me? A red wine of intellectual fascination, absorbing, sometimes challenging, very likely to speak eloquently of the vineyard from whence it comes. A wine expert's delight, and along with the gentler, milder Pinot Noir, often their favourite red style.

And what does Shiraz mean to me? Liberty. Joy. An explosion of exuberance, a cavalcade of ripeness and sauciness and fun. A ruddy-faced standard-bearer for all that is good about the New World. Red wine without tears! Where's the party? One sounds like a wine-tasting note, the other like a call to arms.

So we're not talking about the same thing here. Well, yes we are. We're talking one grape variety. It's called Syrah in France, and Shiraz in Australia. As for the rest of the world, they can call it Syrah if they want to be taken seriously by wine critics and be applauded for following the more restrained, more cerebral French flavour model. Or they can call it Shiraz to send out the signal that their wine is supposed to be rich and soft, ripe with toffee and chocolate flavours, and set up in the Aussie style for drinking, not pontificating about.

Why the different names? Which is the original? Well, the French would say Syrah, because that's what they call it, and because it has been grown in the Rhône Valley for two thousand years. But the Australians might say, why do you think it is called Shiraz? It was the grape used by the ancient Persians in their wine-growing centre of Shiraz, near the Persian Gulf, where they still grow grapes and, still, in modern Iran, make a little surreptitious wine, and the vine was transported and traded by merchants across Greece and Italy and taken into France by the Romans. Scientists would say this is fanciful nonsense and romantics would say this is a wonderful idea; and since the Romans did take vines with them on their trips north to conquer Europe, who is to say Shiraz/Syrah wasn't one of these? Two thousand years ago the Romans were praising the smoky, tarry flavour of the red wines from Vienne in the Rhône Valley (that's right next to Côte-Rôtie, where some of the Rhône's greatest Syrah red wines are made today). They said the flavour was peculiar to a grape called Allobrogica, named after a local tribe. But Syrah at its best, say, on the Rhône's hill of Hermitage, downstream from Vienne and probably planted by the Romans, is famous for giving dark, smoky, almost tarry wines. And that's today. Who is right? Is it the same grape? What is Syrah? Should it really be called Shiraz?

Well, in the big wide world, away from the rarified milieu of wine experts, Shiraz is much more important. People understand that Shiraz on the label means the wine is going to be round, soft, juicy to jammy, a bit chocolatey, pretty mouth-filling and reassuringly alcoholic. This is the style virtually invented by the Australians and used to spearhead their explosion into the wine world's consciousness during the 1990s. Just about every warm wine-producing country took note and planted Shiraz furiously. And wine-drinkers, particularly those new to wine, lapped it up – its flavour was easy to understand, easy to like, and, at two syllables, the name was easy to pronounce, easy to remember and order another bottle of. To be honest, Shiraz has fallen into the trap of being trivialised by its own success. Nowadays you can get dirt-cheap Shiraz from southern Europe, the Americas, South Africa or Australia, which will be a fairly pallid pastiche of the great trailblazers Australia hit us unsuspecting Europeans with in the 1990s. Australia mostly sticks to the name Shiraz, especially for its big-brand reds, but also for most of its top wines, yet you will find more and more rebels calling their wines Syrah in a quest for both more demanding, intriguing flavours, and in a desire for more legitimacy and respect. And in the rest of the world, Shiraz as a title on the label has largely been dumped into the bargain-basement, high volume, low ambition department. You will find thrilling wines being made from Shiraz in California, Washington State, Chile, South Africa and New Zealand, but they will be calling themselves Syrah. A lot has changed in the last twenty years.

So, we still haven't decided. Which is the original? Syrah or Shiraz? I think I will have to give it to the French, and Syrah. But which is the most influential? That's a much more difficult one to answer, and Australia's Shiraz has at least as strong a claim as France's Syrah, and possibly a stronger one. But this one grape, under either name, has without doubt produced many of the world's most enthralling red wines in the last generation. Cabernet Sauvignon has produced many superb and memorable bottles, usually as variations on a fairly predictable and not necessarily very wide spectrum of flavours. Syrah/ Shiraz revels in the unpredictable, the unexpected, the shock to the palate and the brain. In a way it is a perfect rebel's wine, and the grape is a lot easier to grow than that other rebel's favourite, Pinot Noir. Cabernet Sauvignon and Merlot are the Establishment grapes, and they have stamped their authority on vineyards and wine styles on every continent (well, not Antarctica, not yet – but as climate change is accelerating, just wait a couple of hundred years). But an increasing number of winemakers don't feel at ease in this Cabernet–Merlot world where you are supposed to conform to rules and style parameters. In particular, as we all – a lot of us, anyway – begin to turn away from over-ripeness, from power, from high alcohol, and become intrigued by the variety of flavours and scents and textures possible at lower levels of sugar ripeness, and lower levels of alcohol, from grapes grown in cooler, more challenging conditions, Syrah – note that I have dropped the word Shiraz from this sentence at least – is proving to have brilliant, radical, highly original and unprecedented personality traits to keep us snapping at its heels, demanding more. Shiraz as a hot-climate style, Syrah increasingly as a cool- to warm-climate style? Now we are getting somewhere.

I am looking at a single page from a tasting I did in 2014, and I can see eight different Syrahs or Shirazes, from four different countries – France, Australia, New Zealand and Chile. All France's wines are Syrah, so are New Zealand's as she tries to squeeze out from under Australia's domineering bulk in the red wine stakes. Australia's are Shiraz. What is interesting is that Chile's are both Syrah – Chile sensed that Shiraz as a name was spiralling toward the lower end of the market. But there's another thing. Except for the Australians, all the other wines are from what you would call cool-climate corners of warm countries or, in New Zealand's case, a country they didn't think would ever ripen Syrah twenty years ago. The word is getting through. Over-ripeness is the enemy. Over-ripeness is the coward's way out, flavours and scents and drinkability sacrificed for the thud of power and weight.

I had a look at a couple of my – rather grandiloquent – tasting notes. Here's a Syrah from a chap called Hervé Souhaut on the western edge of the Rhône Valley in France: '. . . *hauntingly scented with lilies and summer night jasmine, a scent that runs right through the lush, juicy, blackberry, pear and peach richness, just tickled with the crunchiness of black pepper and celery, dusted with ginger and nutmeg, and cut through with a gleaming glinting mineral, like quartz caught in the early morning sun.*' See what I mean? Fabulously appetising and contradictory flavours and tastes you would never expect to sit together. Just reading them, I can remember the wine as if I had just finished the glass. Oh, and it's only 11.5 per cent alcohol. Half of those flavours would be lost if you ripened the grapes to 13 per cent.

What about this one? A Chilean Syrah from Aymura in the Elqui Valley, a wild and unlikely vineyard site up toward the Atacama Desert, which, because of the ferocious cold winds that blow up the valley from the icy Pacific, actually manages to be cool. As I said, one of Syrah's greatest gifts is how it reacts to cool conditions in a hot country. I made this note: '. . . *almost shockingly scented for a red wine: a mixture of lilies and a bonfire of the branches from a pepper tree. The taste is simply packed with blackberry and Rosa plum fruit but the bitter-edged brilliance of springtime wood sap hurtles through this heady fruit, trailing after it a summer scent like warm creosote, a hint of talcum powder and a brush of coal dust from a collier's apron.*' Again, flavours you would never put together, or, in some of the cases, would never expect to find in a wine at all. But it works, and with Syrah, expect the unexpected.

And what about Australia? I've got a Tim Adams Shiraz from the Clare Valley, not as hot as the more famous Barossa Valley a bit to the south, but it should showcase the more Australian face of Shiraz. Again, '. . . *wonderfully scented wine, reeking of blackberry juice and the scent of black plums, late into summer, but still on the bough, with a purple bloom bursting over them as they ooze nectar and the merest nudge would knock them to the ground and the wasps would swarm and fight. The flavours wash over your tongue, leaving a trail of sweet mint leaves, blackcurrants rubbed in eucalyptus oil, and all this in a cocoon of coconut and chocolate cream.*'

I wish I had those three bottles open in front of me as I write. They show three very different styles of wine, the cool crispness of the French one through to the lush richness of the Australian, but all connected by Syrah's God-given ability not to be boring and predictable. So I am completely confident in saying that the Syrah/Shiraz is one of the world's great grapes. But if Syrah is this good, and it's French, why wasn't it better known? People have been drinking and talking about Bordeaux and Burgundy for hundreds of years, making their grape varieties like Cabernet Sauvignon and Merlot, Pinot Noir and Chardonnay world famous, yet the Syrah wines of the Rhône Valley, created before either

Bordeaux or Burgundy ever had a vine, were virtually unknown until the 1980s, and so no one knew about the Syrah grape either.

Geography and politics is the answer. The two places that made exceptional Syrah wine, and which are still thought of as probably the world's two best sites, are both tiny. Côte-Rôtie is one single, incredibly steep cliffside teetering above the Rhône as it dips slightly to the west, just south of the old Roman city of Vienne. A couple of kilometres further on, the river curves toward the south again, and this precious, precipitous slope, protected from the violent valley winds – the mistral can whip down the Rhône at speeds of 145 kilometres (90 miles) per hour – angled invitingly toward the morning and midday sun, is gone. The second is Hermitage, a single, haughty outcrop of rock a bit further south, as the Rhône finally fights its way out of the hills and on to the broad plains that stretch away toward the Mediterranean. Its broad-chested slopes catch every ray of sun from dawn to tawny sunset. Just two tiny chunks of challenging, granite hillside. Hermitage has never been more than 136 hectares (336 acres). Côte-Rôtie has been half of that, though recent expansion has brought it up to the giddy heights of 276 hectares (682 acres) and a lot of this not on the historical vineyard land. Some single estates in Bordeaux are over 100 hectares (247 acres). And that puts it into perspective.

So, they are tiny, they don't make much wine and a lot of Hermitage was anyway shipped north to Burgundy or over to Bordeaux to add a bit of beef to their red wines. It obviously worked. Some of Bordeaux's top châteaux, such as Cos d'Estournel, Lafite and Latour, actually planted Syrah in their own vineyards to give their wines some extra oomph, and until late in the nineteenth century, if you offered customers your Bordeaux wine as 'Hermitagé' – i.e., muscled up with good Rhône Syrah from Hermitage – you would get a higher price. And it was difficult to transport your Syrah wine to any of the export markets of northern Europe or further afield on different continents. You could tow a barge north up the swollen Rhône, and I have stood watching the rolling surge of this great river as it hurtles southward. I wouldn't want to have to haul a barge against that current up to Lyon, then up the Saône to Chalons and finally into the river and canal systems that might get you to Paris and the wider world. Stick with Burgundy. Stick with Bordeaux. The odd barrels of Hermitage that did get through to countries like England in the eighteenth century were often more expensive than Bordeaux's best, but they were few, despite Hermitage being described as France's 'manliest' wine.

So when vineyards were developed on the other continents, Syrah rarely figured. Almost no one drank the wine, so they didn't think of Syrah as a useful grape to plant. Cabernet Sauvignon became the go-to, top-quality grape across the globe, because people knew Bordeaux and thought that planting Cabernet would give a pretty good start to their own vineyards. Except in one place. Australia. A man called James Busby came to Europe in 1832 and collected cuttings of 362 different vine varieties, which he planted out back in Australia. Within the decade Syrah had been planted in New South Wales's Hunter Valley, but, more importantly, by the 1840s both this Syrah and also more vines brought out by German religious refugees had been planted all over South Australia's Barossa Valley. But it wasn't called Syrah any more. It was called Hermitage, after the hill in the Rhône Valley, or Shiraz.

To be honest, Shiraz and Barossa didn't necessarily suit one another, but in the young settlement of South Australia you planted whatever you could get, and Shiraz was what you could get. Most of the Barossa soils were heavy loams and clays, some were sand, and none of them remotely resembled the granitic hillside soils of the Rhône Valley. And the vineyards weren't on precipitous slopes – they were mostly on rolling flatlands. So nothing was the same. And the wines they produced didn't taste remotely similar. If you went up into the cooler hills of the Eden Valley, you might eke out a few flavours reminiscent of France, but not down in the Barossa. What you had here was big, rich, dark, often jammy, intense but usually highly drinkable reds. Or rather, in the early days, it was more likely to be sweet and dark and fortified, because although the German Barossa settlers and a few other enlightened souls might like to drink a glass of dry red wine along with their supper, most of Australia drank fortified wine, and most of Australia's exports were fortified wine, too. Probably made out of Shiraz, with a little help from Grenache and Mourvèdre, two hot-climate grape varieties from further down the Rhône Valley.

The thing is, anything vaguely red was probably made out of Shiraz, although, frankly, red, pink, even white, dry, sweet, sparkling or fortified, Shiraz would do the trick. When the market was good Shiraz made most of Australia's wine of any sort and when the market was hard you would end up turning your Shiraz into jam or Shiraz raisin muffins. This doesn't sound like much of a fate for one of the world's great grapes. No, but Australia wasn't much of a place to be a great grape until the end of the last century. One of the saving graces, beginning in 1951, was the creation of Grange Hermitage – you got it, Hermitage. It was a superstar wine made from Shiraz, and it gradually became known nationally, and then internationally, as Australia's greatest red wine, and finally, as a truly great red wine by any reckoning.

The other saving grace, more relevant to the spread of Shiraz around the world, was the rise of the mighty Australian wine brands, starting out with names like Penfolds and Lindeman's, and Wolf Blass, moving on through Jacob's Creek and Rosemount, and ending up in the twenty-first century with Yellowtail. The easy-drinking, juicy, warm, not always completely dry red wines under these names were led by Shiraz. More than any other red grape, with the possible exception of Merlot from California, Shiraz showed the way for the wine-drinking boom that began in the 1980s and gathered pace like a runaway train during the 1990s. And although big, serious, expensive Hunter Valley and Barossa Valley Shirazes have also been accorded more and more respect during the last twenty or thirty years, it was the attempts to recreate easy-going, ripe, approachable and affordable reds that fired other countries around the world to latch on to Shiraz.

French Syrah got its call during the 1980s. First, the most important wine critic of the time, Robert Parker, discovered the Rhône. He loved big, broad flavours, so he was always going to love the wines of the Rhône. He went to town on Hermitage wines from producers like Chave and the La Chapelle from Jaboulet – if any Rhône wines could be said to be well known, these ones were. Great Hermitage was, and still is, rare, but its boiling cauldron of flavours is intoxicating – tar and coal smoke, potato peel, herbs and savage pepper scratch at your tongue and try to mask the gloriously intense fruit flavours of bramble, raspberry and blackcurrant. Sometimes, after tasting young Hermitage, your tongue needs a massage and a lie down. But if you give the wine ten or twenty years, all the crudity mellows into a strange but wonderful warm softness of cream and liquorice, dark fruit syrup and well-worn leather.

Yet it was Côte-Rôtie that knocked Parker into a swoon. Côte-Rôtie is a gentler wine than Hermitage. Sometimes they even add a little white Viognier to make it gentler still. This is just about the most northerly point in France that can ripen Syrah – you're on that magic cusp again, of just being able to ripen the grape. In traditional Côte-Rôtie the colour isn't that deep, the wine has the floral fragrance of violets and even lilies, and the fruit flavour is of raspberries, perhaps cut slightly with the sweet acid of damsons, and seasoned with the grainy burr of apricot skins and pepper. The highest compliment you could pay an old-style Côte-Rôtie producer was '*ça pinotte*' or 'that's starting to taste like Pinot, like Burgundy'. And then along came Guigal, revolutionising winemaking, filling his cellars with new oak barrels for ageing his super-ripe reds, and charging a lot of money for this new breed of Côte-Rôtie.

I remember Parker tasting the 1985s and giving all the

so-called La-Las – three single vineyard wines, La Mouline, La Landonne and La Turque – 100 points, the perfect score. He also gave the Mouline and Landonne 1983s 100 points and he told his rapidly swelling American audience, 'I have never tasted through a greater line-up of wines. I don't believe there is another wine-maker or wine-producing estate in the world that has ever put together such an array of monumental wines as these.' Don't hold back, Robert. Five 'perfect' wines in a single tasting. What do you do to follow that? Guigal's wines may not taste like tradi-tional Côte-Rôtie, but he now leads the way on these roasted slopes, and most of the others follow as best as they can.

And around the world, if people are thinking of the French Syrah, they generally follow Côte-Rôtie, not Hermitage. Some also follow Guigal in ripeness and generous application of oak. But thankfully there is a growing band of enthusiasts who are prepared to look behind the gaudy exterior and into the heart of that old-style Côte-Rôtie – the one that starts to taste like Pinot, like Burgundy, but in many cases tastes just a little bit better, because in many cases Syrah as a grape has a little more to offer than Pinot Noir. In California, in South Africa, in Australia, wine producers are getting the message that you can grow Pinot and Syrah in adjacent fields. That sounds as if Syrah is asking to be considered as a cool-climate grape. Cool conditions but lots of sunshine? Sounds like Switzerland. The Alpine suntrap of the Valais region has made tasty, concentrated Syrah on its south-facing slopes for as long as I can remember. And what that's river at the bottom of the valley? Oh, it's the Rhône, beginning its long tumultuous journey south to the Mediterranean.

Syrah has now spread rapidly around the globe, either with new plantings or with a sudden revival of interest in old ones. But Syrah isn't the only Rhône grape to travel. If we head south to where Châteauneuf-du-Pape is the most famous name, there are a whole bundle of grapes being grown, and indeed Châteauneuf-du-Pape is allowed to use eighteen different varieties of various hues in its blend, but by far the most important of these is

Grenache, sturdily backed up by Mourvèdre. Syrah is impor-
tant, too, but many of the producers there are finding that their
vineyards are becoming too hot for Syrah. The famous Château
Beaucastel has decided to stop using it in its Châteauneuf-du-
Pape. Cinsault is a pale red grape of decreasing relevance in the
Rhône, though increasing relevance in places like South Africa.

Because a lot of the old Syrah vineyards, especially in places
like Australia, also planted Grenache and Mourvèdre (often
called Mataro), there are a fair number of old vines left around
the world. Grenache and Mataro were popular in Australia and
California because they produced good, gutsy fortified wines.
Nobody much drinks these any more, so Grenache and Mataro
have had a spirited revival as crucial components in a new red
wine style called GSM (Grenache, Syrah, Mourvèdre). It's not
really a new style, just a new name; what producers are doing is
to try to make something along the lines of Châteauneuf-du-
Pape, and in Australia and the USA, also in the Languedoc in
France's far south, a fair number of good, rich, balanced GSMs
are turning up. Grenache wine is alcoholic and fleshy when
carefully grown and vinified. Mourvèdre is more bitter, meaty
and feral. As such, they make a very good team to soup up the
ripe, dark fruits of the Syrah. Quite a few of the southern French
appellations use these three as their base.

But back to Syrah. One of the first places it cast its spell
outside the Rhône Valley was France itself. The Languedoc is
the world's largest vineyard region, sprawling from the mouth
of the Rhône right round to Roussillon and the border with
Spain. There have always been some hillside areas that had
decent reputations, but the lumpen majority of Languedoc
wine was raw stuff from the flatlands, usually sold with no
geographical provenance at all. Hillsides almost always make
better wine, but even the hillside stuff could be pretty rough.
But the French have this highly effective system of *cépages
améliorateurs* or vine varieties that will improve things. Top of
this list was Syrah, and its main target: the oceans of murky

rubbish that grapes like Carignan and Aramon were spewing out in the south.

During the 1980s and '90s over 300,000 hectares (741,000 acres) of vines were grubbed up in France's Midi, as the far south is known. That's an area nearly three times as big as the entire vineyard area of the Bordeaux region. Simply vast. But replanting, when it occurred, was frequently with Syrah (as well as other less suitable cool-climate varieties like Merlot and Chardonnay). The hillside areas got their doses of Syrah, too, and I can still remember tasting the early Syrah-dominated wines from places like Faugères, St-Chinian and Minervois – rich, blackberryish, fresh, scented . . . those producers who haven't fallen for the wiles of too much ripeness and too much oak are still creating such delights. But the real transformation happened down in those featureless, unloved plains toward the sea, and if you find yourself enjoying a basic bottle of southern French red, remember Syrah's employment as an 'improver'. Things used to be so bad, you could almost call Syrah an 'enforcer'.

Syrah–Shiraz elsewhere in Europe and the eastern Mediterranean

Syrah has spread almost everywhere, including places it's not really that suited for. Spain has a surprising amount, and I suppose I should be pleased at anything that confronts the unhealthy dominance of Tempranillo. Most of the vines are in the high, hot plateau land of Castilla-La Mancha, and most examples I've seen have been too stewy by half. But recently I've had some juicy blends of Syrah and other stuff from areas I hardly know, like Madrid itself and Ribera del Júcar near Cuenca. (I *have* visited Cuenca. I have sung in a concert there. I've won a *porrón* drinking contest there involving hazelnut liqueur. I've bellowed 'The Laughing Policeman' from up a lamppost as the Easter procession of hooded supplicants with their solemn candles paraded silently beneath me. I've woken up in my dinner jacket with a muddy footprint on the lapel and a headache for the ages. But I've never been invited to visit the vines. Hardly surprising, you may say.) And then I found a very full-flavoured, scented Syrah blend from Cadiz – sherry country. Perhaps Spain is using Syrah more intelligently than I thought.

I can't leave Spain without mentioning that the Grenache and Mourvèdre grapes I was talking about in southern France are actually Spanish – Garnacha and Monastrell. Garnacha not only makes some of the world's tastiest pink wines, but from old scrabby bush vines way off the beaten track in Aragón it makes irresistible raspberry and herb-scented, sappy young reds. From some of Europe's most ancient, unremembered vines come some of its freshest, most modern reds. And if there is a place where we are supposed to go on bended knee to Garnacha it would be Priorat, near Barcelona. This used to be an impenetrable beast of a wine, but it's becoming rather wonderful – lighter, brighter, positively drinkable – and the producers sometimes squeeze in some Syrah, too. Is that what is lightening it up?

Portugal mostly doesn't have much truck with other countries' grape varieties – they have quite enough of their own and I wasn't pleased when I recently discovered an experimental plot of Syrah in the Douro. You don't need it. Kick it out. One place that might need it is the hot centre of the country – again, not if they overripen it into jam, and that's pretty easy to do in the baking conditions of the Alentejo. But I most unexpectedly came across a Danish producer on a property called Cortes de Cima who made a really delightful blackberryish, slightly tarry Syrah, which we drank in the shade while he talked of tennis, and I wondered if I might ask for a cool G & T.

Syrah pops up all through eastern Europe and the Mediterranean, but it hasn't yet taken off as much as I expected in countries like Croatia, Hungary, Romania and Bulgaria. Turkey has quite a lot, though, and when the winemakers lay off the toasty oak it's not bad. Lebanon has a fair bit – the legendary Chateau Musar uses some, but Cinsault is more important. Israel does it quite well – when the grapes are not overripened. How often have I said this? And the coolish Judean Hills manage to keep a bit of perfume in some of their wines. But Italy has made best use of Syrah. Piedmont has had some since the nineteenth century – adding a bit of colour and fruit to their Nebbiolo? Sicily uses quite a bit, often blended with Nero d'Avola, which is such an exciting raspberry- and blackberry-rich wine in its own right it doesn't really need Syrah. Tuscany makes better use of it, and it gives wine of astonishing power yet beauty. Some Chianti producers such as Isole e Olena add some to their Sangiovese to brighten it up. One per cent is fine. That amount can transform a blend. Any more, and the Sangiovese would start to get swamped. The Isole e Olena Syrah by itself is one of the most remarkable in Europe – blueberries and mulberries, greengage and nettles, perfumed cherries and angelica! That's why I love Syrah. Always throwing together flavours you would never think could co-exist. Tuscan Syrah is now quite trendy, but most of it comes from Cortona, well to the south of Chianti Classico, where the flavours are a bit more mainstream, but still dark, spicy and scented.

Syrah–Shiraz and the USA

I would have expected North America to be a real Syrah play-ground, but it isn't. California has a fair bit planted but few star performers. Oregon has a little, surprisingly, but it's pretty good; and in Canada's British Columbia it is showing form, particu-larly in a remarkable starkly beautiful area around the Osoyoos Lake. This is so close to the USA that the frontier runs across the water, and there's the magical balance of loads of sun, not much rain – this is Canada's only desert we are talking about here – and cool, shivery nights. Wineries like Moon Curser and Church and State show that the pursuit of dark-fruited ripeness and lyrical floral scent is alive and well by the lake.

If we are talking real desert, eastern Washington State is a bit more major league. If it wasn't for the mighty Columbia River coursing through its heart, nothing could live out here, nothing could grow. I noticed a cautious increase in Syrah wines from here around the turn of the century, with one or two wineries achieving a crunchy, peppery style, but things have really taken off since then. The extreme conditions of the Yakima and Columbia River Valleys and Walla Walla seem to suit it. Some vineyards like Red Willow – the first Syrah in the state in 1985 – have deserved reputations for wines bursting with ripe, red fruit rather than black, and hinting at scent rather than always delivering. But the air is very dry and a little humidity around the grapes as they ripen will usually give you more scented wines. Remember, this is desert; there shouldn't be vines here. There shouldn't be anything. It's the same in parts of Argentina, Chile and Australia. Desert conditions are good for ripening the fruit, but less good for the nuances that make the wines truly exciting.

Having said that, the bacon-fat flavours that traditional Hermitage used to have, and which modern producers there would love to find again do periodically, and thrillingly, turn up in Washington State. Some of the oldest Syrah plantings – from 1994 – are out in Walla Walla, to the east of the Columbia River. Cayuse is the most famous producer – the owner, Christophe Baron, is French and his winemaking hero is Chave, also French. He chose his first vineyards because the stony soil looked like that of Châteauneuf-du-Pape and he does make fantastic, savoury, meaty, rich Syrahs *à la française*. The exact opposite of Syncline, perched above the Columbia River, off west toward Portland in Oregon, who not only makes the freshest, most floral Syrahs in the state, but has found a source of Grenache, Cinsault and the super-rare Counoise. You can make a Wild West Châteauneuf out of those, whatever your vineyards look like.

I had been eager for Syrah to shine almost as soon as I had discovered Californian wine. California was warmer than Bordeaux, yet the growers planted Cabernet. California was warmer than Burgundy, yet the growers planted Chardonnay. What about Syrah? And what about the other red Rhône varieties? I thought California seemed the perfect place, but I was in a minority of not much more than one. It was Syrah's old problem. We're talking the 1980s here. Syrah and the northern Rhône were just creeping into America's wine consciousness. Cabernet Sauvignon and Chardonnay were firmly embedded – the red Bordeaux and the white Burgundy models – as California buckled down to its task of conquering the wine world. California didn't need any distractions.

And there was very little Syrah to taste, Phelps's rather forthright Napa wine being the best known. But I drank one or two of the early radical fringe creations like Qupé – brilliantly striding across the tightrope between savoury pepper and sweet raspberry, savoury leather and lush blackberry. It was so good I expected a flood of Syrah enthusiasm. But not for the first time in America's relationship with Syrah and the Rhône, the public just didn't seem to want to know. A bunch of wild-eyed enthusiasts headed by Mr Wild Eye himself, Randall Grahm, led a movement called the Rhône Rangers, and plantings did increase. But sales didn't. At one time there were Syrah vines producing eight times as much wine per year as the consumers were drinking. The old joke from the winemakers was, 'It's more difficult to get rid of a case of Syrah than a case of—' Well, you decide … for the sake of decency I'll say influenza, but that's not what the winemakers were calling it. It wasn't a joke for most of them. You really couldn't sell Syrah.

The consumers' preference for Cabernet wasn't the only problem. A lot of Syrah was being made like Cabernet – dark, tannic, tough, surly. One or two brilliant winemakers found ways to match high alcohol with exciting flavours. Alban's La Reva was perennially stunning despite its headbanging strength. Sean Thackrey produced dense, towering wines that made you think, this shouldn't work but it does. Lagier-Meredith created remarkable savoury, chocolatey Syrahs on Napa's Mount Veeder that wouldn't look out of place in a Hermitage line-up. But it was only when the types of winemaker who are more attracted to the intricacies and subtleties of Pinot Noir got interested in Syrah in the early years of this century that the grape at last began to find a place in California.

That still isn't a mainstream place. It's still not an easy sell, but nowadays the producers who are most excited by Syrah are more likely to look for cooler and cooler sources. And they do exist, usually right next to a Pinot Noir vineyard. Carneros was planted as the Great California Hope for Pinot Noir. It hasn't delivered that too often, but Syrah, growing in the same fields, can be savoury yet scented and delicious. Sta. Rita Hills in southern Santa Barbara County is similarly famed for Pinot Noir. Syrahs from producers like Piedrasassi can be equally tasty. But the most surprising wines are coming from isolated clearings in the foggy, damp woodlands that were barely thought of as able to ripen Pinot Noir let alone Syrah, out toward the Pacific Ocean in western Sonoma County.

When I first tasted wines like Wind Gap's Majik Vineyard Syrah – at 11.4 per cent alcohol, from Pinot Noir's heartland in western Sonoma – I thought, have I ever tasted an American Syrah as fascinating as this? Amazingly fragrant with ecclesiastical incense, its deep loganberry and raspberry fruit soaked with chocolate and cream while pepper and saline minerality dart on and off your tongue. At 11.4 per cent alcohol. It shouldn't be possible. So paradoxical. So lovely. So confident in the non-mainstream flavours that Syrah excels at. And then I tasted Arnot-Roberts's Clary Ranch Syrah. 'You definitely wouldn't want to live there,' said the winemaker. 'It's the first place to get the fog and it's the last place the fog leaves each day. You can't ripen tomatoes there.' This cool, saline streak again. The pepper teasing the raspberry fruit as a nip of grainy tannin and cranberry acid tries to assert itself against heady violet scent. I'm not saying the American market is going to clamour for these wines. I'm not saying you could make them in any quantity. But I am saying that this nation that seems not to care about Syrah is actually making some of the most thrilling examples on the planet.

Syrah–Shiraz and South America

There was total silence. People stalled their hands halfway to clapping. People caught their breath and momentarily forgot how to start again. I was awarding the trophy for Best of Show in Santiago at the Wines of Chile Awards in front of a boisterous throng of wine industry heavyweights, each wondering if they would win the big gong. And I gave it to a Syrah, from an area they had never visited – the Elqui Valley, a cool, windy outpost up toward the Atacama Desert – and made by a winery they had never heard of – Viña Falernia. The award was such a shock to the Chilean wine industry that I'm not sure if the owner of Falernia had bothered to turn up. He had no chance of winning against the well-entrenched big boys of the warm valleys to the north and south of Santiago, where they'd been making big, ripe red wines for 150 years. But they didn't win. He did.

I bet those big company bosses were on the phone the next morning saying, 'Get me on a plane to Elqui.' Well, you can't. There isn't an airport. There are some strips of flat earth you could land on if your private plane was small enough, but that's it. How did such an outsider win? This was 2005, and it really marked a coming of age for Chilean wines. Up until then most Chilean wines had what you might call a 'company' stamp on them. This is how we make our wines. This is how we expect them to taste. Chile was already making excellent wines, but the big, warm Cabernet-dominated styles were what the world expected from Chile, and that's what Chile offered.

Not any more. Those 2005 awards also gave trophies to areas of the far south of Chile like Malleco and Bío-Bío, which, again, the big boys knew existed, but never thought of as serious quality regions. And wines from the windy, foggy coastal areas were getting prizes, too. It was a tipping point. And it says a lot for Chile that companies whose whole reputations had been built on ripe, warm styles, quickly realised the game had changed. Big operations like San Pedro, Concha y Toro, Errázuriz and Montes didn't stop making warm-climate wines, but they vowed that a decent chunk of future investment was going to go toward pushing the frontiers of Chilean wine. Chilean wine had been accused of being boring. Not after 2005 it wasn't.

And the red wine that benefited most was Syrah. Like elsewhere in the world, Syrah was regarded as a warm-climate animal. Chile had planted a good deal, in warm places like Colchagua, south of Santiago, and Aconcagua, just to the north. Those vines are still there and they make big, powerful, attractive, smokily ripe wines of that full-bodied, slightly long-simmered, satisfying sort whose flavours you like, but which you can never quite define. The sum is greater than the parts. But it took Falernia's triumph to persuade people that Syrah didn't have to be planted in hot places. This story is beginning to repeat itself. But let me say once again the great traditional Syrah wines of Côte-Rôtie in the northern Rhône Valley were delicate, were scented and were said to resemble Burgundy. That's cool-climate talk.

Cool-climate Chilean Syrah was less delicate, more scented and uniquely different from Burgundy. As with California and its discovery of Syrah's liking for cool conditions, which brought out wines with flavours that no one had previously attained, so it is with Chile. The next valley south from Elqui is Limarí – again barren, swept by icy winds, but sunny and underdeveloped. Here the Syrahs from companies like Tabalí are filled with rich, blackberry fruit, but this time the wine is broad and meaty with a suggestion of charred leather dabbed with fish oil and rubbed with jalapeño chilli, and above all that drifts a mellow floral scent. Syrah again: expect the unexpected.

You can now find intriguing scented Syrahs, sappy, savoury, mouthwatering, all the way down the coast. Leyda and San Antonio are the most fascinating areas, where with every mile the conditions become more radical and challenging as you approach the Pacific. Matetic Vineyards is a few miles inland. Their Syrah is lush, oozing with blackberry and rose petal jam, followed by a savoury whack of grilled meat, old-fashioned gravy and potatoes that would have brought tears to the eyes of a traditional Hermitage producer. Casa Marín is closer to the sea – you can see the waves from their steep, contorted vineyard slopes. Their Syrah barely makes 12 per cent alcohol and the scent is mesmerising – lilies and peppercorn, caraway, cumin and coriander seed, fresh, dry, sun-bleached vineyard stones washed with ripe blackberry and cranberry juice. So savoury, so mineral, yet so scented. Chanel would want to bottle this.

And it's not just Syrah which is benefiting. A lot of Syrah plantations are new, but there are old, forgotten vineyards running away to the south with workhorse grapes from the south of France, like Cinsault and Carignan. Afforded no respect in Europe, they are now the target of Chile's most anti-Establishment, hip winemakers who regard it as an article of faith to protect, propagate and promote these vines whose wines are full of the rasp of herbs, the chewiness of plum skins, the crunchiness of rock dust and, after all that, an intriguing, insistent ripe red fruit and a lingering scent.

There's a lot of Syrah planted in Argentina, but it hasn't caused any great ripples. If anywhere specialises in Syrah, it's the fairly warm San Juan region north of Mendoza, whose wines, even at their best, I have found rather too rich and likely to resemble overheated baked fruit cakes. There is a little planted in the long-established Mendoza regions like Agrelo and Perdriel, but again, it's normally blended away. Way south, Patagonia has a little Syrah, and down here you can just about see a bit of its fresh, peppery personality creeping out. They should make more of it, but Syrah isn't a top priority here. Malbec is.

Syrah–Shiraz and South Africa

Twenty years ago, Syrah occupied less than 1 per cent of South Africa's vineyards. Now it occupies 10 per cent of the winelands and the percentage rises every year. Syrah from South Africa becomes more explosively delicious with each vintage, and it's certainly worth the argument to claim that Syrah produces South Africa's most exciting reds. And one area more than any other has been leading the way. Swartland. Yet as recently as 1992, a guide to South African wines written by one of the country's best wine writers, Michael Fridjohn, didn't feel the need to talk about Swartland as a wine-producing area. As he said, 'Wheat farmers are more evident than grape growers.' But the grapes were there – old vines that farmers had shoved onto bits of infertile scrubland, often on the low mountain slopes, simply because nothing else would grow there. And so the vines matured in unremarkable anonymity.

It's sometimes a good thing to go unremarked, because farmers reckon it's barely worth the effort to replant, so they just leave the vines, year by year, don't bother to mess about with clever pruning or trellising systems, don't waste money on expensive chemical sprays. If they give a crop, cart it off to the local co-operative. If they don't, it barely matters. Such was Swartland until one of South Africa's most visionary wine men, Charles Back, realised this was an untapped resource that could redefine how people thought of South African wine. He started a brand called Spice Route using Swartland grapes, for which he paid a significantly higher price than the co-operatives did, and employed another young visionary called Eben Sadie to make the wine.

Sadie is the man you can credit with giving Swartland its own identity as he set up shop there in 2000 and created the first thrilling, utterly self-confident Swartland red wine called Columella, using Shiraz and Mourvèdre grapes. Because that was what Swartland was full of – old plots of the southern French grapes, not the trendy Cabernet Sauvignons that had made Stellenbosch famous. Syrah, Cinsault, Carignan and Mourvèdre, even Grenache – you can find these vines, old and scrubby, and you can plant more now that people know how good they are. So many 'new' wine countries followed the 'Cabernet is best' route, sometimes for generations, before realising that they'd got more suitable vines, usually from the

Rhône Valley and southern France, sitting in the warm sun of their own backyard just pleading to be rediscovered.

Swartland Cinsault is a remarkable pale but chewy red tasting of sweet stewed apples, red cherries, twig sap and herbs. Sadie says, 'Cinsault is like when you wear your T-shirt inside out with those grainy tannins.' After a long period in the shadows, it's reappearing, along with the other southern French reds that used to be described as 'junk grapes'. But it's Swartland Syrah that is shaking the complacency out of South Africa's reds. There are quite a few good producers now, but none more impressive than Mullineux, who even release two different Syrahs called Granite and Schist to show how the soil changes the wine style. Granite is scented, savoury, smoky, sprinkled with rock dust, and rich with raspberry and blackberry fruit. Schist is deeper, richer, smokier, less scented, but with even riper raspberry and blackberry fruit thrumming through the heart of the wine. Memorable. And if you want to see the new face of Swartland, clamber and stumble up the Porseleinberg hill, so rocky you wonder if there's any soil at all. Just enough, obviously, to plant 30 hectares (74 acres) of new Syrah and Grenache, and the Syrah, with its dark rich red plum and cherry fruit, its liquorice-black core and its trail of smoke, could come right off a prime Syrah slope on the hill of Hermitage.

Swartland may get the most headlines, but every region in South Africa's winelands makes Syrah. The warmer areas still often call it Shiraz, and often choose a richer style, spicy, more beefed up with oak, but impressive. Shiraz is also used as a blender to broaden some of the brute power of the Cabernet. They've had Shiraz/Syrah for generations in the long-established regions of Stellenbosch and Paarl, but it's usually happy to play a supporting role, although some of the young guns sneak in old Syrah from unsung areas to the north and north-east to show they can keep up with Swartland. Constantia also has Shiraz and can sometimes produce wines with a remarkable blend of chocolate richness, white pepper bite and lily scent. Even chilly Elgin and Hemel-en-Aarde have a little. And at Elim, when

nature allows them a crop they won't be left out either, producing dark, dry, mineral wine, heaving with rich but reserved
black fruit folded with savoury cream and mingling smoke and
lily petal scent. Here, in a windswept outpost of humanity on
the southern tip of Africa, Syrah shines.

Syrah–Shiraz and New Zealand

Will Syrah become a star in New Zealand? I feel it should, but
it hasn't yet. But then the idea that you can ripen any sort of
decent red wine in New Zealand is fairly recent. New Zealand
markets itself as being the cool, clean, crisp country lost in the
icy Southern Ocean. Sauvignon Blanc, the archetypal crisp,
green wine style, is clearly the perfect flagbearer for the country.
And if you want a red flagbearer, well, Pinot Noir is by far the
most famous cool-climate red grape. So it makes sense to put
all your efforts into that. The world has been panting for a new
Pinot Noir Paradise. New Zealand provides it, in spades. All
the South Island wine regions, and a couple in the North Island,
produce increasingly individual Pinot Noirs, most of them not
tasting a bit like Burgundy, and all the better for that.

But we have seen in places like California and Chile that
Syrah seems to make fantastic wines in regions that are star
performers for Pinot Noir, and that were thought of as too cool
for Syrah. So why isn't there more Syrah in New Zealand? Well,
think about it. Red Burgundy is one of the most sought-after
wines in the world and Pinot Noir is its grape. It revels in cool
conditions. You are New Zealand, the last scrap of land before
the Antarctic. Your calling card is 'We're cool, we're really
very cool down here. Maybe cooler than any other New World
country. We think we are Pinot Noir Paradise' – and quite a lot
of people agree. Plant Pinot. What about Syrah? Do you want
to make money or don't you? Plant Pinot.

And in areas that are a bit warmer – and New Zealand has a
few – would you plant Syrah? If you are a cool country desperate

to play in the full-flavoured red wine stakes, wouldn't you do like every other country in the world with a half-decent amount of sun and heat? Plant Cabernet Sauvignon and Merlot? Of course you would. That will get you the critical write-ups. And, perhaps more importantly, that's what the wine-drinkers want. Wine buffs love Syrah. Wine-drinkers love Cabernet Sauvignon. There are very few areas of New Zealand warm enough to ripen Cabernet Sauvignon, but Hawke's Bay, on the east coast of the North Island, is one of them. It even made a few famous Cabernets a hundred years ago. Not many, but enough to prove it could be done. In the 1990s an area inland from the sea called Gimblett Gravels was shown to be drier and warmer than the rest of the region. Somewhere you could really ripen Cabernet Sauvignon that would make the world sit up. And that's mostly what it grows, along with Merlot. But there is some Syrah, too. And it can produce the best reds of the vintage. Gimblett Gravels Syrah is dark, packed with dry black chocolate, opaque black fruit and, when it allows itself to behave in a cool-climate way, white pepper spice and a hint of lily sap. Delicious. But the drinkers in New Zealand are no more enthusiastic than they are in California. They prefer Pinot and Cabernet. Wine growers could give up – and the amount of land devoted to Syrah doesn't increase year by year – but New Zealand's climate is warming like everywhere else. Marlborough is Sauvignon Central now, and it makes good Pinot, but there are a few secreted plots of Syrah – even Cloudy Bay has a few hidden vines – and the Syrah wines are already light but delightful. In ten years' time Syrah might be Marlborough's finest red. Central Otago is so wedded to Pinot Noir that any sea change is unlikely, but they've planted a bit of Syrah. I'll be first in line to taste the results. Martinborough is the North Island's finest Pinot producer, but they've got a little Syrah, too – and it's peppery, scented and good.

Maybe Syrah's future is in Pinot land rather than in the Cabernet land of Hawke's Bay. But one of New Zealand's most thrilling Syrahs is made out on Waiheke Island, in the Hauraki

Gulf off Auckland. That's quite warm, but it's wild and windy, too, at the eastern end. And Man O' War Vineyards make a Syrah as scented with lilies, yet as sappy and peppery and laden with ripe black fruit as any in the southern hemisphere. So it seems New Zealand has been lucky, yet again. Her cool areas can do Syrah; so can her warm ones. And she has one more bit of luck. After James Busby had brought all the vine cuttings from Europe to Australia in the 1830s, he moved on to New Zealand. And he brought Syrah cuttings with him. But this Syrah isn't like the modern Syrah, full of juicy fruit and scent. No. The grapes are olive-shaped and the wine they make is dense and dry and shot through with bacon fat. That's what the old guys in France say Hermitage was like 150 years ago. That sounds like the Serine, the old Hermitage form of Syrah that they fear is becoming extinct in Hermitage. And perhaps it is. Well, if the French are interested, they've got some of it in New Zealand.

Syrah–Shiraz and Australia

It's not quite true to say that Shiraz is everywhere in Australia. Sightings of Tasmanian Shiraz are, so far, a bit thin on the ground. But there are sixty-five designated wine areas in Australia, and the vast majority of these will be growing some Shiraz. Or, nowadays, maybe Syrah. I would like to think that there isn't an area I haven't tried. But I can't talk about them all here. So where is the most important Shiraz vineyard of the lot? Barossa Valley, just north of Adelaide? No question. If some people cry 'Hey, Hunter Valley was first.' So? The Hunter has made some smashing wines, and makes more good ones today than it ever used to, but Hunter Valley Shiraz didn't change the world. Barossa Valley Shiraz did.

The thing about Barossa Valley Shiraz was that it represented the complete opposite of what we were mostly drinking in Europe during the 1980s. French and Italian reds were thin; Barossa Shiraz was thick. The European reds were raw, the

Shirazes were juicy, jammy, stewy even – anything but raw. The European reds made you wonder whether the sun ever shone on the vineyards any more, the Barossa wines tasted as though the Aussies had bottled the sun along with the wine, and the wine kept ripening and ripening in the bottle on its long trip to Europe, until it virtually forced the cork out of the neck by sheer exuberance of personality and showered your tongue and throat with black fruit and spice and dark bitter-rich chocolate and liquorice, and if that wasn't enough to make you choke with excitement, there was vanilla and the mouthwatering smoke of toast about to burn under the grill. And did I mention blackcurrants? And blackberries? And aromatic plums, the flesh so sweet and ripe that their skins split trying to contain it?

And this is Shiraz – in all its unabashed glory. No cool-climate scented Syrah here. No French-style delicacy. When the Prussian refugees arrived in the 1840s, they came from a land of very uncertain weather: usually too much rain and not enough sun. The gentle, rolling exposed expanse of the Barossa Valley must have seemed like a paradise – we'd like a bit more rain, but we've got more sun than we ever knew existed, so we are happy. That was in the 1840s. They planted Shiraz and they ripened it as hard as they could. And they planted Shiraz's Rhône Valley bedfellows, Grenache and Mourvèdre, and ripened those as hard as they could as well. And over 150 years no one said, 'Ah, shouldn't we try to make our wines a bit more delicate, more elegant?' These aren't words you will ever find applied to Barossa Shiraz. And frankly, that's a reason for Barossa Shiraz being such a success and being the creator and leader of the 'Shiraz' style. Delicacy and elegance are terms most wine-drinkers don't understand. The 1980s and '90s were the decades of a wine revolution bringing millions into wine for the first time. Give it to them right in their face. They'll understand that. And this message has gone right around the world.

All those big, savoury, dense, oaky Shirazes from countries like Chile and South Africa are based on the Barossa model. But what about all those toffee-sweet, jammy, stewy – and cheap – Shirazes from any countries with a decent amount of sunshine? They seem like very pale Barossa imitations. Well, yes, they are. Just like many commercial Australian Shirazes are very pale imitations of the real thing in the Barossa. Out in the vast, featureless, irrigated and mechanised grape prairies that cling on to the life-giving waters of the Murray River and its tributaries in New South Wales, Victoria and South Australia, Shiraz vines can be planted over hundreds of hectares without a break. Think about this: one hectare is ten thousand square metres. Ten hectares is a square kilometre. Now multiply that by five, by ten. Vineyards out there really do stretch over the horizon. The vineyards aren't glamorous. The wines aren't glamorous. But this is where the fruit for big brands like Yellowtail comes from. Other countries try to imitate its success. And the wine is called Shiraz, not Syrah.

South Australia has other seriously powerful Shiraz heartlands apart from Barossa. McLaren Vale is another beefy operator, just south of Adelaide with significant amounts of rich, old Grenache and Mourvèdre, too. Clare Valley, north of Barossa, is technically a little cooler but its Shirazes are powerful and rather magnificent. Eden Valley, though, in the hills just above the Barossa Valley, is significantly cooler. They grow really good Riesling up there and they grow some of Australia's greatest Shiraz. Henschke are custodians of vines up to 160 years old – and maybe older – at their Hill of Grace vineyard. The Shiraz they make is now frequently Australia's most sought-after wine, more clamoured for even than the Barossa's husky jewel, Penfolds' Grange. And Hill of Grace has all of the intensity of a mighty Shiraz, but as you ponder flavours that move on from the blackest of chocolate and the squashiest of plums into a world of cherries soaked with mint, leather, and peppercorns simmered with blackcurrants – is there a hint of French Syrah complexity just peeping out? Perhaps, perhaps. Is South Australia thinking of flirting with Syrah? Perhaps.

It's difficult to put Hunter Valley Shiraz into any descriptive straitjacket. The Hunter Valley is a subtropical, cyclone-blasted, drought-ridden hellhole for vines – you should never try to establish vines there, unless, of course, you are the closest half-decent site to the great city of Sydney. So that explains it. They grow white and red grapes in the Hunter, and even when the ferocious cyclonic storms roll down the east coast in late summer, the white Semillon is probably ripe enough for you to rip it off the vines before the storms strike and you can make something decent. Red Shiraz ripens later; the rains often dump on the vines before the fruit is ready. One year I was there and I tasted the only red wine – the only one – that had been made in the previous year's disastrous harvest. That was just ten years ago. One of the leading producers gazed at a glass of his 2000 Shiraz and remarked, '2000 is the only benevolent vintage we have had in the last thirty years.' And Hunter Shiraz used to get away with murder because it was Sydney's darling. 'Sweaty saddle' was the descriptor most commonly used for the wine. That's the sweat-soaked saddle on which an unwashed jackeroo has been squelching up and down for a month or two in the Outback. It's horrible now. It was horrible then. Yet the Aussies stoutly supported it. I was judging the National Wine Show one year, when this tired old Hunter Shiraz reeking of cowboys' body odour came up. The judges eyes all glazed over and they all gave it gold. 'You can't,' I said, 'this is undrinkable.' It was clearly some famous wine that should have been retired years earlier, but had been winning golds because no one dared cry 'Enough!' Well, I cried 'Enough!' I appealed to the chief judge, Len Evans, Australia's most famous wine superstar – and a Hunter man. 'Mmm . . . it's a nice old darling . . . Gold.'

Well, modern Hunter Shiraz is surprisingly restrained and a good deal lighter than it used to be. The fruit is ripe but paler, pale red plum, mild red cherry, sometimes even ripe goldengage plums, with now and then something richer and earthier like Brokenwood, or something suffused with sweet, almost brandied black cherries, like McWilliams O'Shea. But the Hunter marches to its own tune and growers like to distance themselves from other Australian Shiraz. Bruce Tyrrell, talking about his Hunter Shiraz and its relative restraint, described Barossa examples as having 'all the subtlety of an oversexed bus'. This restraint was probably in the Hunter's favour toward the end of the 1990s and into the 2000s, when South Australia started to push ripeness levels, strength and cloddish undrinkability to silly levels. It wasn't helped by the American critic Robert Parker discovering the region. It wasn't helped by the trophy-hunting mentality that attached itself to the world's top reds during this time. Not all of the Barossa and McLaren Vale succumbed. I sat with Charlie Melton in the Barossa gloaming, drinking his delightful savoury but scented Shiraz. 'I picked these grapes six weeks before some of my neighbours. And it's still 14.5 per cent alcohol. I used to make my Shiraz at 12.5 per cent.' And he mourned the loss of Barossa identity. 'Shiraz can overripen between lunch and tea. Pick it half a day too late and you've missed it.' And yes, his neighbours were picking their shrivelled, puffy Shiraz grapes six weeks later than Charlie, and, sadly, probably being given higher scores by the über-critics.

But excess always causes a reaction. This time it began in the unlikely locale of the high hills around Canberra, the capital city. A devout theologian called Tim Kirk started making Clonakilla according to the traditions of Côte-Rôtie. He even started to add some Viognier white grapes to the vat. This is memorable wine now – scented with lilies and springtime sap, allspice and almond blossom, and awash with ripe, sweet raspberries, and their bitter pips and the grainy crunch of fragrant peppercorns. Imagine what shockwaves it created in the 1990s.

Victoria's most famous Shirazes had been rich and eucalyptus-scented, and some, like Tahbilk, pretty fierce, too; they came from vines, often old ones, planted away from the cool coast or frostiest mountains. The new wave, when they arrived, thought differently. Most of Victoria's ambitious young winemakers

chose Pinot Noir to make their mark, with the seaside playground of Mornington Peninsula or the tranquil Yarra Valley
(both near Melbourne) as their preferred spots. But if you
looked, the Trojan horse of Shiraz was already there with
Paringa Estate in Mornington and Yarra Yering in Yarra, both
making memorable wines, waiting for the mob to come round
to their way of thinking. One by one, the lightbulbs started
blazing in the Pinotphiles' brains – a good Pinot site is probably
a good Shiraz site. Or rather, a good Syrah site. They started
cautiously, seeking out hotspots among their Pinot plots, but
as global warming crept on remorselessly they began planting
cooler sites, particularly in Yarra Valley, with results that thrilled
the spirit of the rebel and the palate of the hedonist alike.

The Adelaide Hills in South Australia showed that it, too,
could make scented, blackberry- and herb-laden Shiraz, away
from the roar of Barossa and McLaren Vale. And Western
Australia reminded us that it was one of the original cool-
climate Aussie vineyards – not just the famous Margaret River,
but much further south, past Frankland, past Mount Barker,
toward Albany where the whalers used to come to rest after
their Antarctic odysseys and Shiraz can once again amaze us
with its brilliant unpredictability, managing to combine a dark
heart of black treacle, burnt raspberry jam and charred pips with
the lift of floral scent, and tobacco, and the chewiness of leather
and peppercorn – and is that a touch of fluffed-up boiled potato
skins? As the old-timers will tell you, one of the ways to blind-
taste true Hermitage is to look for the potato skins.

Did all this riotous rebellion start with the theologian at
Clonakilla just outside Canberra? Not entirely. There was
'Syrah-type' Shiraz quietly bubbling away far removed from the
brawn of the Barossa. But Clonakilla was the purest example
of the French style in modern Australia. Yet Tim Kirk isn't out
to upset his neighbours. He still labels his Clonakilla as Shiraz.

Sauvignon Blanc

A reverse conquest

Hail to the People's Wine. Hail to the scourge of the wine snob. Hail to the slayer of privilege, the toppler of the great citadels of elitism. The Radical Wine. Well, perhaps I'm getting a bit hot under the collar here; but, honestly, the amount of energy I've expended over the years protecting the reputation of Sauvignon Blanc beggars belief. The amount of sweat I've dripped trying to persuade fellow wine judges that a Sauvignon Blanc deserves a gold medal precisely *because* it's so drinkable. And the number of arguments I have lost as I vainly try to persuade the so-called experts of the wine world that Sauvignon should be lauded precisely *because* it is so popular, when its approachability and its popularity, its directness of taste, its lack of daunting complexity are exactly the reasons this coterie give for damning it with the faintest of praise.

In a way, this fury that Sauvignon Blanc inspires among wine buffs is one of its most important features. They can't bear its popularity. They can't bear the fact that the vast majority of wine-drinkers prefer Sauvignon Blanc to their own favourites like Riesling, or Chenin Blanc or Verdicchio. They can't bear that the vast majority of the drinking populace prefer a wine called Sauvignon Blanc from somewhere like Chile or South Africa, or New Zealand – above all, New Zealand – while, if they must drink this style, at least let the wine be a Sancerre or Pouilly Blanc Fumé.

But this takes us straight to the nub. If I'm not a wine buff, what is Sancerre? What is Pouilly Blanc Fumé? Ah, they are both dry white wines from the eastern end of the Loire Valley in France that happen to be made from the Sauvignon Blanc grape. And they are usually quite grassy, maybe a little leafy, definitely showing a hint of minerality, and ideally made more complex by some lees contact and perhaps a little oak barrel influence . . . in fact, there's a reasonable chance you'll hardly realise they are made from Sauvignon Blanc at all if you're lucky. And they will cost you a bit more, of course – tradition and all that.

Tradition, my eye. Of all the grape varieties that have led the wine revolution of the last thirty years, the one which owes nothing to tradition is Sauvignon Blanc. A little oak barrel influence is not why we drink Sauvignon Blanc with such gay abandon. A bit of complexity from contact with the lees of dead yeast cells is not what lights up the Sauvignon drinker's eyes. And the fact that someone's family has been making a wine for hundreds of years is of no importance in the world of Sauvignon Blanc. This is the wine of a modern age. This is a wine that can be judged solely on the pleasure it gives in the glass and down the throat. And, with respect to the *vignerons* of Sancerre and Pouilly, this is a wine that is labelled Sauvignon Blanc.

So where does this paragon of modernity come from? Well, the grape does in fact come from the Loire Valley. They've known about it since at least the sixteenth century and the little town of Sancerre has certainly been growing Sauvignon for well over two hundred years. But it didn't exactly cause the earth to shake. Until it was discovered by some French journalists on a jaunt from Paris during the 1980s, and achieved a little local success as a bright, fresh young country white to be drunk on the riverside from a jug, no one had ever heard of it. With the almost complete lack of fresh white wines in most of France, Sancerre rapidly achieved a kind of fame, but frankly, it was still much better from the jug. Most bottles tasted earthy and dull. Just like almost every other bottle of French white at the time. And fifty years ago only 20 per cent of the vines in Sancerre's vineyards were Sauvignon Blanc. I wonder where the grapes from the other 80 per cent went, and what the wine was called?

By the 1980s there may have been signs of a red wine revolution peeking over the parapet in Europe, but there was little sign of a white wine revolution. And it was no better elsewhere in the world. To be honest, no one seemed to want a white wine revolution. 'People like what they're used to,' Miguel Torres told me as we surveyed a sullen range of yellow Spanish wines that made his bright, fresh Viña Sol look like a glass of tap water. 'The Spanish would want a wine much more oxidised than this,' he said mournfully.

This became a litany, a dirge, during the 1980s. My first trip to Portugal: 'The Portuguese like their white wines yellow.' My first trip to Italy – well, people hardly wanted to admit white wine existed at all in Tuscany and Piedmont. My first trips to South Africa and Chile – always the same, a few producers hesitantly prodding their way toward a liquid that wasn't yellow, that wasn't as thick as soup and flat as Norfolk, but all saying much the same as the San Pedro winemaker in Chile: 'Oh, the local drinker is used to his good old sherry-style of white. He wouldn't touch the new stuff.' And France was only patchily better. If half the stuff I drank was from any decent recognised grape variety, I'd be amazed.

But, actually, there were some drinkers who might be up for change. It's just they didn't know where to look. The Brits. Except for a lucky few who got their hands on good white Burgundy, the odd Alsace wine and some historically good German single-vineyard wines, the British white wine fare had been pretty drab. That old chestnut, Spanish 'Chablis', was around until the early 1970s. After that those masters of understated, barely drinkable neutrality, Soave and Muscadet, did more trade than they deserved. But their dire quality explained why Britons preferred almost any booze to wine.

And then a new player arrived: cheap German wine, epitomised by Liebfraumilch. It's easy to be sniffy nowadays about Liebfraumilch, but these wines had *fruit*. They may have been fairly spineless, but no mass-market wines before them had possessed fruit. And although it's fashionable to say that the New World ushered in the great democratising wine revolution, in fact all the preliminary skirmishes that showed millions of northern Europeans with no wine culture of their own that wine could actually taste of fruit, and could also be easy to drink and fun, were fought and won by cheap German wines. They were slightly sweet – of course they were, they were sweetened up by additional grape juice called Süssreserve (sugar reserve), but this tasted of fruit! It tasted of the grape juice!

Millions of non-wine-drinkers suddenly realised that they didn't have to say, 'Oh, no thanks, wine is not for the likes of us,' it *was* for the likes of them. Wine could be for the likes of anyone with a mouth. The door to wine pleasure for all had been opened, just a chink, but opened nonetheless. The idea that wine could be drunk simply as a pleasurable drink, which didn't require any book-learning or lucky chance of birth, had been planted. And if people quickly tired of the rather innocuous fruitiness of Liebfraumilch and Piesporter Michelsberg, was there someone ready to take up the baton of a better 'people's wine', a genuinely thrilling 'people's wine', a fabulously refreshing, tangy, zesty, more 'winey' drink – more serious, even, but just as approachable and a lot more exciting? You would look around Europe in vain.

And then, in the vast emptiness of the southern seas, the real revolution began. A vinous volcano erupted on an unregarded, scrawny, wobbly island almost no one had ever visited and which had almost certainly not produced a passably impressive bottle of white wine in the entire twentieth century. Or ever. Down at the rump end of the world, from a patch of land that had never seen a vine and was thought of as so feeble and useless you could virtually barter for an acre with a week's supply of bread; and with a grape variety that was mostly infamous for being a component in France's most ignominious swill – white Bordeaux, which was 1 per cent rather good and 99 per cent so sulphurous and yellow it kept vampires at bay – way down in the vineless South Island of New Zealand, in a bedraggled landscape of starving sheep called Marlborough, someone had actually planted some Sauvignon Blanc vines. And in 1984 the first fruits of this caper crept north. To the seventeenth floor of New Zealand House in London's posh Haymarket.

I shouldn't have been there. I was rehearsing a role in the BBC Shakespeares. But on 1 February an actor had gone missing – on a bender with an Aussie, as it happens – so we couldn't rehearse. And I had an invitation to New Zealand's first wine tasting in Britain. I knew *nothing* about New Zealand wine. Nobody did. Which was sort of why I went. And also, I had never been to the seventeenth floor of anywhere in central London. I reckoned the view would be fantastic. So, at 11 a.m. on the dot, I stepped through the door to a panoramic view of London which was indeed breathtaking. A few polite snifters, and I'll be out on the terrace . . . But not so fast. Give these Kiwis a chance. The view won't change. But my wine world was about to. The table just inside the door. Third wine along. Montana Sauvignon Blanc 1983 from Marlborough, New Zealand, was introducing itself to the world.

My world of wine would never be the same again. And once the word got around, the whole wine world would never be the same again. All because of a wine from a region no one had ever heard of, and a grape variety given the barest modicum of respect in its homeland. I've still got the tasting notes from my first thrilling tryst with Marlborough. They do go on a bit, but I just knew that I was in at the beginning of something truly remarkable. And the lack of oxygen seventeen floors up may have titillated my imagination a bit. So here goes:

Gooseberries. You know how disagreeably sharp and crunchy they are raw? But boil them for half an hour with some sugar syrup – the acidity hasn't budged, but suddenly the rasping green fruit seems ripe and enticing and mouthwatering. Peppers. Take a silver (!) knife and slash into a fresh green capsicum pepper, and breathe in that surge of cold, earthy fragrance before you take your first bite – then the crunch of the crisp flesh, the flow of cool rainwater . . .

I'm not finished. '*Think of the sharpness of just-picked blackcurrants, still smelling of the leaf rather than of the juicy flesh. Think of grass fresh-mown on a spring morning, slightly damp and earthy, but fragrant in the drying sun. Think of new-season asparagus, again the crunch, again the paradox of something vegetal but rich . . .*' And to sweeten out your thoughts, '*think of hints of honey, of apricots and crisp green apples and the spray of acid from a fresh lime*'.

Do you see what I mean? Nowadays we are used to white wines packed with fresh fruit flavours, citrusy scents and overtones of a sultry grove of tropical delicacies. But not then. NO WINE had ever tasted like this before. This was an entirely new type of wine, from an entirely new wine region, completely redefining a grape that had been growing in France with no real distinction for centuries. If we look at most of the great influences in wine, they have flowed outwards from France's classics to be re-interpreted around the globe. Sauvignon Blanc is different. Its incarnation occurred on a scrap of land as far away from France as it is possible to get. It cobbled together a crown of thrilling but unlikely flavours no one had ever put together before, or even conceived of before. And it rode into our own consciousness on 1 February 1984, saying 'Forget everything you knew about Sauvignon Blanc from France. This is how it's going to be from now on.'

You might almost say that the birth of New Zealand Sauvignon Blanc was the birth of wine as simply a damned good drink. A wine that could be described to people in stark, simple language, using flavours they all had a pretty good chance of having experienced. Trying to describe wine in the old days was exhausting because so few wines, red or white, had definable flavours. You read the old-timers' tasting notes, and none of them are specific about anything. The talented tasters weave a delightful tale based on threads and suggestions and whimsy. I'm sure their ability to judge what was good and what was not was just as sure as ours is today, except that the proportion of wines that were actually enjoyable to drink was tiny, and the number of wines that were actually *fun* was infinitesimal.

Sauvignon Blanc introduced the concept of fun into white wine and the idea that a wine didn't have to be complex or intricate to be excellent. This brilliantly green, pungent, acid-streaked yet exotically ripe wine with its outspoken cut-glass purity of flavours hustled in the brand-new concept of wine whose purpose is to be refreshing, pleasurable, mouthwatering, as good a drink and as easy to understand as a perfect gin and tonic or a chilled pint of foaming, hoppy golden ale.

It was a wonderfully classless wine introduced into a world that was becoming very restless about social divisions on a number of fronts. Whether it's relevant or not, this was the era of the deep soul-searching we went through in Britain – with Margaret Thatcher, the miners' strikes, the government versus union confrontations and the traumatic aftermath of the Falklands War. Something new and classless had every chance of succeeding. And you didn't get much more classless than Marlborough Sauvignon Blanc. For a start, there was no tradition, no terroir to worry about, no rules to follow, no pre-conceptions. This land was only bought by a chap called Frank Yukich because it was dirt cheap. No one wanted it. He bought 1600 hectares (4000 acres) of gravel and silt for a few hundred dollars a hectare. With that much land to plant he put out an SOS – I need vines, any vines, just to fill the space. Ideally he wanted Müller-Thurgau, the grape that formed the basis of Liebfraumilch, because his Montana business in New Zealand was pretty much based on the same kind of slightly sweet – and in his case, often slightly sparkling – wine that he could sell shedloads of at bargain-basement prices. It was purely by chance that a sack of Sauvignon Blanc vines turned up to be planted.

Talk about chance. The whole thing was done in such a rush that a good chunk of the vines were planted upside down! These guys weren't experts. And they didn't bring in smart winery equipment and employ top winemakers either. New Zealand had a pretty lively dairy industry – Anchor butter was a massive export brand – so they simply bought secondhand stainless steel dairy tanks, stripped out the stirring mechanisms in the middle and poured in the Sauvignon juice, which was then made into wine by food technologists from the dairy industry. But that was an inspired choice. With milk, you have to be fanatical about temperature, about cleanliness, you need to pursue a ruthlessly antiseptic, sterile, hygienic approach to processing or your vat of milk will quickly turn into a slab of cheese. Such ultra-hygienic winemaking techniques were pioneered in Germany, and were already improving winemaking in California and in Australia. The dairy technologists simply fine-tuned them. And with Sauvignon Blanc, it was a marriage made in heaven. These cool-temperature techniques were exactly what the sharp, green flavour of Sauvignon Blanc craved. And it showed that you could extract and then keep the fabulous fresh flavours of grapes without wrecking them through bad hygiene, uncontrolled fermentation and excessive use of sulphur to obliterate all the potential joys in the wine, which was generally what happened to Sauvignon Blanc grapes in France.

If we now look around the world searching for the classic areas for Sauvignon Blanc, most of them barely boasted a vine thirty years ago. Some were unplanted as recently as ten years ago. Some haven't even been planted yet. And this is another massively important factor in Sauvignon Blanc's effect on the world of wine. Virgin land is often exactly what Sauvignon thrives in. Sauvignon is a cheap wine to make. If you know the recipe, Sauvignon Blanc is an easy wine to make. And if you do it properly, Sauvignon Blanc is an easy wine to sell. It isn't easy to leap to the fore with a new version of Cabernet or Pinot Noir, or Chardonnay for that matter. Vineyards have to be chosen and developed with great care, you have to make numerous choices in the clonal material of vines which you employ, the different methods of cultivation, and then the vinification and maturity of the wine. Mistakes will be commonplace, especially in such matters as the choice and style of wooden barrels, the ideal ripeness for the grapes at harvest, the temperature of fermentation, the amount of maceration of the grapes before and after fermentation – it goes on and on. And you need time as well. With most grape varieties, you need to have mature vines – maybe ten years in the ground, maybe twenty years or more – to allow the full expression of the fruit.

With Sauvignon the first and second crops are often the most exciting, the most pungent, the most arresting. You can buy some oak barrels if you want, but stainless steel is frankly better, and works out much cheaper. And there is one clone of Sauvignon that has proved over and over again to be the tastiest. And it's not one from the Loire Valley. It's from California. It's called CD1 – California Davis clone number one. That's the clone that somehow made its way to New Zealand. That's the one nearly everyone uses, right around the world, if they want to produce green, zesty, tangy, drinkable Sauvignon Blanc.

Now, Sauvignon does need some sunshine to ripen, but it also doesn't like too much heat. This can be seen as a problem or a challenge in most New World countries, where sunshine and heat are in good supply but sunshine and cool conditions are much more difficult to find. This was the unexpected genius of Marlborough. Experts had said the South Island of New Zealand was too cold for grapes, and farmers should concentrate on apples (a lot of the best new areas around the world, from Australia to England, have had to suffer exactly the same official advice). What they hadn't added in to the equation was that Marlborough is incredibly sunny – it's often the sunniest place in the whole of New Zealand.

· No other New World countries are able to plant vines successfully so far south, barring a plot or two in South America, but most of them do have cool areas. Particularly those which are bathed in ice-cold Arctic or Antarctic currents. California with its Alaska current, Chile with its Humboldt Current and South Africa with its Benguela Current are three examples of warm countries with icy waters running up or down their shores, creating all kinds of local conditions near the coastline where their typical sunshine exposure is tempered and cooled by the influence of these chilly stretches of water. California was already well-established by the time the New Zealand phenomenon appeared, but for South Africa and Chile the chance to plant virgin land near the coastline with a grape like Sauvignon, which will create a tasty, saleable wine the whole world recognises, from fairly high, and therefore profitable, yields in the vineyards, was a fantastic bonus. And your very first crop will be bringing you profit and reputation if you do it properly. Those who decry Sauvignon should perhaps reflect that it was the rare opportunity of new countries to make an immediate impact on the world with Sauvignon that provided the financial cushion that permitted the development of the more critically beloved vineyards such as cool-climate Chardonnay, Pinot Noir and Syrah.

And there's another way to make Sauvignon Blanc wine. Pick the grapes early. It's not such a good method as finding sunny but cool nooks and crannies to grow your vines, but it's the method used by a lot of producers in Europe, where Sauvignon is often planted as a bit of a cash cow in areas that are, quite honestly, a bit too hot. The green flavours, the zesty flavours that make Sauvignon such an exciting drink can best be gained by ripening your grapes fully in a cool place, because the cooler the vineyard the more of that lively, mouthwatering acidity the grapes can hold on to. But acidity is also present in under-ripe fruit. It isn't as exciting as ripe acidity from cool vineyards, but if you pick your Sauvignon under-ripe in a warmer vineyard, you can catch flavours like lemon and green apple peel before the sun bakes them away. Again, this is fantastically important financially in places like southern France and central Europe. And it makes even more financial sense when you realise that if you increase the amount of grapes your vineyard produces, the fruit ripens more slowly, so you get a seriously large crop of vaguely appley, leafy wine that you can then sell to supermarkets for cashflow – and, once again, you can use the Sauvignon Blanc money tree to finance your grander projects. Honestly, Sauvignon's critics sometimes need a reality check on a world without Sauvignon. They should remind themselves who's paying the bills for a lot of their vanity projects.

Sauvignon Blanc and Europe

So how has Europe responded to this wave of Sauvignonisation from New Zealand? Usually, countries like France resist such movements, belittle them, denigrate them, and then quietly examine them to see what is worth adopting. Sancerre and Pouilly are making far cleaner wines in far greater quantities than they used to. Their initial response was to dismiss the New World Sauvignons as coarse and one-dimensional and emphasise the subtlety of their own offerings. I don't think subtlety is something I'm searching for very often in Sauvignon Blanc, and I thought most of their efforts from the 1990s into the noughties were just plain bland. With a lot of them I struggled to see why I would drink them, they were so determined *not* to taste like the New Zealanders. Then they began to talk 'minerality' when this was in vogue in the 2000s, and this was definitely an improvement because the limestone soils of Sancerre in particular can seem to give a strong, gaunt and rather attractive character to the wine, and the flint soils of Sancerre and Pouilly can add a certain reckless wildness to the taste. I have to say, in the last few vintages up to 2017 Pouilly and Sancerre do seem to have rediscovered the joys of tangy fruit again. It's taken a while. However, given the way their prices have shot up, I think

Sauvignon de Touraine has been the biggest beneficiary of the New World movement, and now frequently makes the tastiest and best-value Sauvignons in all of France.

Of course, we mustn't forget Bordeaux, which actually has more Sauvignon planted than Sancerre and Pouilly put together. When it's made in the typical bright, fresh, zesty style it rarely has the excitement of even a half-decent Sancerre, let alone a Kiwi palate-pleaser, and by 'bright, fresh, zesty' I generally mean thin, hollow, lemon-ish. But shove the juice into an oak barrel, probably blended with another local variety, the Sémillon, and not only is the result an amazing concoction of blackcurrant leaf, custard, nectarines, sour cream and wax, but these are some of France's best whites. Bordeaux is always about barrels. We couldn't expect them to get the hang of bright, fresh, dry whites when they had the opportunity to complicate matters and produce a far more value-added item. But, in fact, the Sauvignon-Sémillon barrel-fermented wines, despite being as far removed from the typical drinker's view of Sauvignon as a haddock is from a banana, have created a quality niche that France has exported successfully to one or two places like Australia, South Africa and the USA as a slight kick back against the onslaught of New World Sauvignon.

Southern France has planted loads of Sauvignon – I know, it's too hot. Yes, it is, and the wines are mostly fairly forgettable, but they're cheap and quite fresh and pale – and that's a quantum leap from the sulphurous, greasy gut rot that cheap French white used to embody. I suppose somebody used to drink it. Or did everybody use it for unblocking the sink? The only place in the south where Sauvignon really works is over in *la France profonde* of the Gers, in the far south-west, where they've made a bit of a reputation for dry white wines that follow the New Zealand trail – Vin de Pays des Côtes de Gascogne was their most famous label, which tasted snappy and sharp and Sauvignon-like, even though the grapes were the entirely different, and elsewhere pretty miserable, Ugni Blanc and Colombard. So they don't really need Sauvignon Blanc, but you can't blame them for planting some.

Spain has some Sauvignon Blanc, mostly in Rueda, where the tangy 'New World' approach is again led by an entirely different grape, the Verdejo, and, predictably, Miguel Torres makes a brilliant, Bordeaux-barrel type called Fransola near Barcelona. But Spain is too hot. Most of Italy is too hot as well, yet the north-east above Verona and Venice makes a pretty decent stab at Sauvignon. You have to remind yourself that making a white wine with identifiable fruit flavours has only recently stopped being a deportation offence in Italy, so even the good ones can seem a little shy. But just over the border in Austria they make a surprisingly crunchy, grapey Sauvignon that they sometimes hide behind the title Muskat-Silvaner. No one has ever suggested the Sauvignon is related to either of these varieties, but Austrian and Slovenian, and sometimes German, Sauvignon *can* taste grapey – like a fistful of not quite ripe green Muscatels. Ah, there we have it again – not-quite-ripe. You simply can't over-ripen the Sauvignon without it losing all its verve. Over-ripe Sauvignon often tastes of absolutely nothing. The great key with Sauvignon is 'nearly ripe but not quite'.

That's what they try to do in the rest of central Europe, and they do it pretty well in Romania and Moldova, where they don't muck about: they pick it not quite ripe, ferment it cold, bottle it quick and sell it cheap. Hungary is about as central as you can get. They picked up the New Zealand baton before anyone else in Europe. In the early 1990s I was so sure they could match the outrageous, shockingly delicious Sauvignons we were getting from New Zealand that we got an unfinished Hungarian vat sample made by an English guy called Hugh Ryman rushed from Heathrow to the *Food and Drink* studio. I held up this turbid, slimy-looking liquid, with the fermentation bubbles still popping in the glass, and cried 'This is the wine you should be drinking for Christmas! This year, not next year. Don't worry, it'll be ready in time.' And it was.

Sauvignon Blanc in the USA and Australia

New World Sauvignon's effect was felt right through Europe, and not just with Sauvignon wine, because it showed how you could make something fresh and attractive out of almost any grape variety so long as you didn't overripen the fruit, and you kept everything clean and hygienic in a winery preferably dominated by lines of cool, shining stainless steel tanks. The two biggest New World players – the USA and Australia – didn't spawn a surge of lookalikes, partly because they didn't have quite such suitable sites as the South Island of New Zealand, but also because they didn't need to. Although Kiwi Sauvignon has been a big seller recently in the States, this sharp, zesty style didn't find many takers in the 1980s and '90s. There were a few reasonable attempts by wineries like Dry Creek in Sonoma, and some of the boggy land in the centre of the Napa Valley proved to be better for Sauvignon than Cabernet. But this was a period when California in particular was falling in love with the barrel. There was a famous wine called Fumé Blanc made by Robert Mondavi which was Sauvignon-based, but barrel-aged. Mondavi may have started making this because he had some of California's oldest Sauvignon vines on what was coincidentally his best Cabernet block, To Kalon. And, anyway, California looked at New Zealand Sauvignon and thought it was leafy and vegetal. They didn't want to make a version, whether they could or not.

Australia was a bit different. First, Riesling was already providing an exciting, refreshing highly individual unoaked style from as early as the 1950s. Certainly they had a go at the Kiwi style – the Aussies will have a go at anything – but they've never made a great success of it, despite some good stuff coming out of South Australia, and Adelaide Hills in particular. Perhaps it goes against the grain for them to search for sharp, greenish flavours in their Sauvignon when they've spent so much time maximising the ripeness of all their other wines. But with the opening up of a trans-Tasman free trade area with New Zealand in the 1990s, Sauvignon Blanc poured north to Australia, so obviously the Aussie drinkers were pretty keen on drinking it, even if the Aussie winemakers weren't too keen on providing it. Super-ripeness isn't in vogue any more, so most Australian winemakers are quite happy to take the money for Sauvignon but are more interested in creating restrained Chardonnays and Pinot Noirs. The best Aussie Sauvignons come from Western Australia, where they've made a real go of the 'Bordeaux' style, blending in Semillon and fermenting the mixture in the barrel. A lot of the wines are indistinguishable from the better examples from Bordeaux.

Sauvignon Blanc in Chile and South Africa

But there are a couple of New World countries that really did need the New Zealand vision. Chile and South Africa. Chile, in particular. I first got to Chile in 1989, primarily fascinated by what looked like it would be a peaceful transition from dictatorship to democracy – surely a first in South America. But I was keen on the wine, too. Every cellar I went to smelled stale, with an odour halfway between tired tawny port, the bitumen on the roof of our garden shed when I was a kid, and a chicken run. Part of this was awful hygiene, part of this was the use of a wood called *rauli* for all their vats. Smoky, tarry, every wine that went through the *rauli* vats never recovered. But the Chileans knew that political change would not only liberate them, but force them to come to terms with an unpalatable fact. Chile had been a pariah state for the seventeen years of Pinochet's rule. The 1980s were probably the most radical decade in the history of wine. They'd missed it. They would have to catch up in a rush.

So I did find clutches of stainless steel tanks huddled in corners, pleading for attention. They were usually full of Sauvignon Blanc, or were they? The stuff squirted off the vat tasted pretty fresh, lemony, a bit leafy. Yet the bottled 1988s, only a year and a bit old, were all tired and flat — oh, very flat. Why? I didn't get it until I was touring the vineyards with one of Chile's wine gurus called Aurelio Montes. I walked into a vineyard. It *stank* of blackcurrant leaf and nettles and gooseberries. The vineyard did! What's going on? 'Ah, that's our California vineyard,' Aurelio said. All the other vineyards were local Sauvignon. This was imported stuff. California. The CD1 clone. The same one as New Zealand used. So what was the rest? Not Sauvignon at all. It was an old Bordeaux grape variety brought out in the nineteenth century and called Sauvignon — well, why wouldn't you? In fact, its name was similar — Sauvignonasse — but it was a rubbish variety. And the wine it produced was rubbish. Chile hoped to use it for its re-integration into the world of wine. But we'd moved on. We'd had New Zealand.

They got the message. Now, all new plantings are proper Sauvignon Blanc, mostly CD1. And exciting, piquant, stimulating Sauvignon Blanc as good as any in the world has been one of Chile's calling cards. And they've done it by not only planting the right Sauvignon Blanc, but planting it in the right places. I'd heard about this Antarctic current, the Humboldt Current, how the warm interior of Chile sucks in icy air and fog to cool the river valleys way, way down, and provide that tantalising combination, loads of sunshine but cool temperatures. I'd also heard about how it was too difficult to plant the cool coastal areas — there was no infrastructure, there wasn't enough irrigation water, all that. In other words, the Chileans were used to the easy life. They were used to farming the warm, fertile inland areas where heavily irrigated fields produced big crops of ripe red grapes like Cabernet Sauvignon every year. Grape-growing had always been a doddle. Why change?

Change or die, that's why. The Sauvignon revolution set the standard for startling modern whites. Did you want to play or not? Luckily, they did want to play. In which case, head for the ocean. The new generation of Chileans had tasted the new generation of bright, fruit-filled dry whites. Some had even worked in Australia and New Zealand. First, they pushed into Casablanca, between Santiago and the port of Valparaiso. And then they went extreme. Head to that ocean. Don't stop until your face is being blasted by the icy air, until the cooling fogs are tangling in your hair, until you wear a sweater to visit the vineyards in the height of summer and you can see the chill glister of the Pacific waters before the horizon drops away west. Make the effort as far north as the Atacama Desert and as far south as the sun shines. There's the new face of Chile – led by Sauvignon Blanc. The old warm world of Chile looks after itself pretty well. Dark, impressive reds from these regions have never been better, but part of the reason they are better is because of the kick-start given to the whole wine community by those brave radicals heading to the virgin coast.

South Africa faced a similar challenge. The apartheid years had pretty much shut South Africa off from normal intercourse with the rest of the world. Cape wines would creep out now and then, but precious little from the rest of the world crept back in. Precious few bottles. Precious few people. Precious little of the new wine knowledge that was sweeping the rest of the world. All of this was transformed in a rush when Mandela walked free, and by 1994, when the first fully democratic elections were held, the whole world was desperate to give South Africa a helping hand.

This was not as easy as it sounds. There was still a very defensive, self-justifying air in much of the Cape wine industry, and attempts to offer the world South African wines that had been impressive in a previous era but now seemed like mildly interesting period pieces only served to show how much the world of wine had changed and how rapidly the South Africans needed to modernise if they were going to survive. They needed to move out of their comfort zone, which was largely based on fairly old-fashioned reds that tasted increasingly rough against such fare from Australia or California or Europe. Sauvignon Blanc offered a way out.

As with Chile, the Antarctic current that sweeps along the shores of the country was of massive importance. South Africa is pretty hot and only reaches down to just short of 35° South in latitude. In the northern hemisphere that would leave you on the edge of the Sahara Desert. The traditional areas like Stellenbosch and Paarl can suffer temperature spikes way over 30°C (86°F) in the ripening season, which make fresh white wines quite a challenge.

Ha. But the oldest traditional area of all held the secret. Constantia, tucked into the mountains behind Cape Town, and relentlessly battered by the cold south-easterly blasts that sweep in from False Bay, where the Benguela Current loops into what looks as though it should be one of the most perfect crescents of sandy bathing beach in the world. Sunbathing beach, maybe. But stay out of the water: a) it's freezing; b) there's a place called Shark Point just round the headland, and they're not joking. But that icy current and the powerful cold winds that get sucked inland each day are what had made Constantia famous for wine by the eighteenth century, when Bordeaux's Médoc region had hardly been heard of. That original Constantia was a sweet wine, lost in the mists of time, but triumphantly brought back to life in the late 1980s by the Klein Constantia Estate. This was a fantastic historic achievement, a knee respectfully bent to the first Dutch settlers who planted grapes in Constantia in 1655. But I would argue that Constantia's greatest achievement for the present was to plant Sauvignon Blanc on these sunny but nippy slopes, and straight away produce a string of leafy, lime-zesty, nettley Sauvignon Blanc wines, exhilarating in their tangy green scents but with a beguiling mellow warmth of nectarine and ripe dessert apples to bring a flicker of a smile to the lips of even the dourest anti-Sauvignon zealot.

South Africa was already making some impressive, rather Burgundian-style, traditional Chardonnays. She was on the cusp of realising that the great sprawl of old Chenin Blanc vines that lay unloved and barely cultivated across much of the vinelands would actually create world-class, unique white wines in the twenty-first century. But the world was crazy for Sauvignon Blanc at the end of the twentieth century. Cheap to make, quick to sell, were there any other Constantias? Yes, there were, in places far cheaper to develop than the leafy suburbs of Cape Town. Follow the Benguela Current up the west coast to Durbanville and Tygerberg, looking out across the bay to Robben Island, and further north to Darling and Groenekloof, whose very name gets you set for the startling green Sauvignon Blanc flavours that will dance across your tongue from these blustery but sun-swept slopes. East from Cape Town to Elgin, cloudy and cool, the Kent of the Cape where virtually every Cape Granny Smith or Pink Lady apple you've ever bitten into will have been grown. So that'll tell you what a crisp, juicy style of Sauvignon Blanc they can make. And at the very southern tip of the African continent, on the rolling acres of Cape Agulhas, Sauvignon Blanc lets out one more glorious, raucous shout. Stand among these naked vines and look south, into the gales that spit rain in your eyes, toward the vast sullen grey towers of cloud that lower and threaten just off the coast, then taste the Sauvignon Blanc – in all its extreme, citrusy, zesty, gum-scouring glory. One of the world's most uncompromising cool-climate Sauvignons. And it's from Africa.

Riesling and the Germanics

The wine gurus' darlings

You would have thought that the most important word, when I'm talking about Germany's influence around the world of wine, would be Riesling. Of all the famous grape varieties, Riesling is the only German one. There is a band of influential wine critics by whom Riesling is talked about as the world's greatest grape. And in Germany it certainly makes wines, sometimes dry, but also off dry, sweet and intensely sweet, that have a character quite unlike any other.

That's all true. But I wonder whether we shouldn't be dishing out rather more praise to Seitz. Or to Willmes. Or to Munk and Schmitz. Maybe to Geisenheim and Geilweilerhof. Maybe even to Liebfraumilch. None of these are the names of grapes, but they're all of enormous importance to modern wine. Seitz was a German bacteriologist and the Seitz filter, named after him, was the first machine with pores so fine that even bacteria couldn't get through. At last, you could sterile-filter a wine and stop it from going bad. For the first time it became possible to leave a little sugar in your wine in the sure knowledge it wouldn't begin to re-ferment in the bottle. Willmes invented the pneumatic grape press in 1951. Suddenly you could very gently press large amounts of grapes without extracting all the bitterness and rough flavours from their skins and pips. You could create red wines that didn't need ageing to soften them, and you could smooth all the hard

edges off your whites. Munk and Schmitz were manufacturers of
tanks and brewing machinery. They also developed tanks capable of the cold fermentation and pressure fermentation of wines.
They weren't the only ones, but it was Munk and Schmitz who
turned up in Australia in 1952 and sold the first pressure tanks
to Orlando and Yalumba. Fermentation could be slowed right
down – traditionally in Australia it often used to be a furious,
frothing hell's kitchen for just a day or two, with most of the fruit
and perfume from the grapes blown away in the steamy chaos.
Now you could take twelve or even fourteen days to ferment the
juice very gently, preserving all the grapes' scent and character.
Indeed, mimicking the conditions of a cool German autumn was
one of the challenges Australian winemakers were keen to take on
in their fermentations. Some people call Orlando's 1953 Barossa
Riesling the first modern Australian white wine.

And there's more. Geisenheim and Geilweilerhof are both
situated in Germany, and are home to two of the world's most
famous wine research centres, of massive importance in developing rootstocks, better clones of grape varieties – including
Riesling – and in inventing entirely new grape varieties. And
as for Liebfraumilch – well, let's leave that. But without all this
groundbreaking German science it would be well-nigh impossible to make decent Riesling wine anywhere except in a few
German river valleys and the odd mountain redoubt.

But back to the great grape. The Riesling grape. Many have
tried, few have succeeded in emulating the delicate yet piercing, fragile and fragrant Riesling wines that are the glory of
Germany's wine scene. Some of Germany's best Rieslings don't
even reach 10 per cent alcohol and yet are as finely and ballet-
ically balanced as any wines in the world. At this low alcohol
you'd have thought the wines would have to taste raw, but if you
leave some of the grape's natural sugar in the wine it balances
out the acidity in a most ethereal and delectable way.

A world-class style of wine? Certainly. One worth trying to
copy? In this current age, when low-alcohol wines are being

sought after more and more, a really good mouthful at 10 per cent alcohol or less is a pretty attractive proposition.

And there's another thing about Riesling. You can guarantee that it's never been near a new oak barrel. Riesling and the vanilla-ish, spicy, toasty, chocolatey world of new oak barrel ageing absolutely don't get on. I have tried a few Rieslings that had been aged in new wood, and they were foul. The whole point of Riesling is to enjoy the purity of the fruit. Many of its advocates also say that Riesling reflects the terroir – the sense and flavour of the vineyard – better than any other grape. I'm not convinced about this, having had quite a few 'new wave', bone-dry wines from the warmer regions of Germany and France's Alsace that could have done with a bit less vineyard and a bit more fruit and perfume in their flavours. If you cut out the use of new oak, there are a number of white grape varieties in different countries that probably reflect their own particular vineyard conditions just as well.

Even so, this lack of new oak has meant that Riesling has become the darling of the ABC crowd – the Anything But Chardonnay bunch, who are reacting against clumsy, confected, over-oaked wines more than actual Chardonnay itself. It's just that Chardonnay is brutalised by careless oak ageing – or, indeed by the addition of oak staves, or chips, or oak essence in the cheaper versions – more than any other variety.

And yet, Riesling's influence and importance is not nearly as pervasive as its boosters would have you believe. There are several reasons for this. A lot of wines have been called Riesling when there wasn't a single Riesling grape in them. A lot of grapes were called Riesling of one sort or another when they weren't related. And people get confused as to whether Riesling is sweet, medium or dry, so decide to drink something else rather than order a style of wine they didn't expect and look stupid in front of their friends.

And Germany is at the limit of being able to ripen the Riesling grape. This is important for any grape, but especially for Riesling. You don't have to go many miles north of Koblenz and Riesling simply won't ripen any more. The knife edge between ripening and not ripening, the dainty dance of acidity, fruit and perfume, is crucial to its beauty. Well, a few decades ago you might only get three good vintages in ten on Germany's Mosel Valley. Nowadays, you are likely to get nine good vintages in ten. The wines are getting fatter and fuller, however hard the producers strive to keep their delicacy. Indeed, some German critics are wondering whether the Rheingau – the famous swathe of south-facing vineyards on the River Rhine west of Mainz – is now becoming too warm for growers to be able to achieve that balance between acidity and ripeness which has made the area famous for a thousand years.

Now look at the rest of the wine world. All the major European wine countries are further south than Germany, and therefore are going to be warmer, and the Riesling will ripen more quickly and develop less flavour and perfume. The great explosion of New World wine creativity has been based on vineyards getting regular sunshine to promote regular ripening. People established vineyards where the sun shone reliably and relentlessly, not where its pale rays trickle through chilly morning mist rising from the riverbanks. To be honest, most places that grow wine are simply not suited to Riesling, with its need for a long, slow, northern European ripening season. All the New World countries have given it a go. In none of them has it become the kingpin, but that hasn't deterred its fans. Riesling is still being seen as a great challenge by producers who have tried to find cooler, less inviting conditions to ripen this ice maiden satisfactorily. Their success rate isn't high, but there are a few standouts.

In Europe, Austria can make fabulous Riesling wines – fuller, more powerful, more alcoholic than a typical German wine, but on the steepling mountain slopes and cliff edges of the Wachau, a short and intensely beautiful stretch of the Danube River west of Vienna, some truly memorable Rieslings are created.

France allows Riesling in only one area – Alsace, which shares the River Rhine with Germany for about 100 kilometres (60 miles). Twenty to thirty years ago, when dry German Rieslings were few and far between, Alsace's bone-dry examples – lean-limbed, lemony and minerally, with the faint suggestion of a miser's portion of honey – were held up as the great examples of dry Riesling at its best. Too much Alsace Riesling is now broad-featured and sometimes even slightly sweet in a rather clumsy way. You don't quite know what you are getting. One Alsace producer told me you needed to be a Protestant to make a good Riesling. I told him one of my favourites was Trimbach. 'They're Protestants,' he replied. In the rest of Europe, the mountain valleys of Italy's Alto Adige probably make the best stab at Riesling (not surprising, when you realise that the area was once part of the Austro-Hungarian Empire), but Slovakia has one delicious example, made by one of Germany's supreme winemakers, Egon Müller.

Riesling and the rest of the world

Riesling has had very mixed fortunes in other parts of the world and has been planted for very different reasons. Take Australia. Riesling has been a fantastic success, especially in South Australia. But no one chose the grape for its suitability, no one set out to imitate the great German wines. It's simply what the desperate Lutheran refugees brought with them on the boat when they arrived in the 1840s. Pure luck. Riesling, made by the Germans who flocked to the Barossa Valley, and then to the nearby Eden Valley and Clare Valley, became Australia's most famous white wine.

We think Chardonnay is the archetypal Aussie white. It's not. They didn't have any Chardonnay at all in South Australia until the 1970s. Riesling ruled. German families ran the vineyards. German winemakers came out, full of ambition. And some-how, in regions that couldn't in any way pretend to resemble

Germany, they made Aussie Riesling into a classic. There's a good argument for saying that Australian Riesling, bone dry, sometimes floral, sometimes steely, sometimes as taut as piano wire, sometimes streaked with raw minerality, is possibly the greatest dry Riesling in the world. And no other Riesling undergoes such an astonishing transition from pale, zesty, zingy youth to golden green maturity, tasting like white bread toasted, slathered with salty butter melting at the crust, and smeared with West Indian lime marmalade.

The Americas also had a slew of German immigrants, but they didn't imprint themselves so much on the continent's wine consciousness. Midwestern states like Missouri, Wisconsin and, above all, Michigan have had varying levels of success with German grapes and the little peninsulas poking up into Lake Michigan near Traverse City are now producing some serious Riesling wines. Michigan was also responsible for another altogether less tasty German invention – Cold Duck. This was a sweet white, vaguely fizzy abomination loosely named after the German word for leftovers. I have had it once or twice. You couldn't keep it down. They had a red version called Turkenblut. I bet that was a blast. Whoops! I've just made a mess of my shirt.

The Germans pitched up in California, too, along with Italians, Hungarians and French – just about everybody headed west in the craze for gold. Some very famous wineries – Beringer, for instance – are German in origin, and a fair bit of Riesling has always been grown there but, except for some quite compelling sweet wines, dry Rieslings have proved difficult to make.

No problem. Just head north. Oregon's wine business was largely established by Germans planting Riesling and dreaming of making the cool and damp Willamette Valley into America's 'Rhineland', but that didn't last either. Pinot Noir has now become Oregon's focus. Yet Washington State is a surprising success. From grapes grown out in the sun-bleached desert of eastern Washington, watered by the mighty Columbia River, a company called Chateau Ste. Michelle claims to be the world's largest producer of Riesling.

Much of Washington's Riesling is so-so, pleasant and medium dry. But a couple of joint ventures with leading German wine-makers Ernie Loosen (for the Eroica label) and Armin Diel (for Poet's Leap) have shown that, just as in Australia, unpromising conditions can produce something rather thrilling.

But it is New York State that takes the USA's Riesling crown. The Finger Lakes are upstate, just south of Lake Ontario. Summer is nice and warm. Winter is absolutely bloody. It can drop to −20°C (−4°F). That's cold enough to kill off virtually any classic wine vines. But Riesling is used to a fair bit of cold in Germany, and has hard, freeze-resistant wood. Even so, it needed a chap from Ukraine − it can get to −40°C (−40°F) there − called Konstantin Frank and a bit of clever grafting of Riesling on to some vine roots he discovered in a convent in Québec − where it can also get to −40°C − to crack the climate. Now New York makes beautifully focused Rieslings, from dry to sweet, and some of them resemble those of the Mosel Valley, which is quite a feat.

Not only that, but New York has taken on board the fact that wine-drinkers get confused by Riesling. Is it sweet, medium or dry? They've developed a Riesling taste profile for the back labels of the bottles − a graph running from dry to sweet, left to right. It's simple. It works. Now they just have to persuade drinkers to take notice of it.

Canada had the same problem as New York: freezing winters that killed the vines. They did have a wine industry based on various non-wine grape varieties which gave an alcoholic liquid of sorts when fermented, but not something that many would drink unless being held down. But, as in New York, the Canadians worked out how to cope with the climate and have enthusiastically planted the cool-climate Riesling, both in Ontario and British Columbia. They've had a fair bit of success with dry Riesling, although what has made Canada wine famous is, unsurprisingly, Icewine — where the grapes are left to freeze on the vine so that the sugar separates from the ice crystals to create a super-sweet sludge, which is then made into super-sweet wine, often sold in super-small bottles for rather a lot of money. Riesling shares the honours for Icewine with the Vidal variety, but whereas Riesling can make delightful drier wines, for Vidal it's either Icewine or grape jelly.

Riesling hasn't made much of a mark in South America, though Chile's far south, where it is cool and damp, has made some floral, delicate examples, and Bouza make a fascinating, waxy, pithy example in Uruguay, right out on the windy, rainy Atlantic shore. South Africa has one or two excellent producers — Paul Cluver in cloudy Elgin is producing the best — but most of the country is simply too hot and sunny, and the locals don't seem to want to drink it anyway. China might make better use of it, especially in Shandong — a rather damp peninsula south-east of Beijing. The Germans were there long ago, establishing China's most famous brewery, Tsingtao, and the first Chinese wine I ever enjoyed — not experienced, but actually enjoyed — was a light, crisp, lemony Riesling made in Shandong by an Englishman from Hong Kong which I drank at Beijing airport, waiting a very long time for an aeroplane.

But the one country that really should be able to rival Germany is the most southerly of them all — New Zealand. And she does have a handful of outstanding Riesling producers, yet just a handful. To be honest, although New Zealand is as far south as vineyards reach, the regions furthest south can be very sunny. And sometimes very hot. And New Zealanders don't have a particularly positive attitude toward Riesling. There's a reason for that, which is all to do with another of Germany's exports — the Müller-Thurgau grape.

Ah, missed opportunities. There was a time in the 1960s, '70s and '80s when German experts and German wine schools were the gold standard. And, obviously, so were German scientists. And if those white-coated wizards were busy propagating lots of new-fangled grape varieties, let's have them. One of the main objectives of the boffins had always been to create a vine with the quality of the Riesling, but with higher yields and quicker ripening. They've come up with a fair few of these, almost all of them not resembling Riesling in the slightest but capable of ripening vast quantities of dull grapes at breakneck speeds. And the granddaddy of them all, from as far back as 1882, was Müller-Thurgau.

For most of the first hundred years of Müller-Thurgau's existence no one took a blind bit of notice of it. But in the 1960s New Zealand, whose wine, by all accounts from survivors, was unspeakably poor at the time, decided to get a grip. Australia was making a massive success out of Riesling, helped by German expertise and German machinery. Let's get a German expert in to show us the path toward a glorious future for Kiwi wine. Not a bad idea, as German wines were still revered in the 1960s. Wines like Bernkasteler Doctor were some of the most famous in the world – and all the best were from the Riesling grape.

So New Zealand got in touch with the Geisenheim Institute and asked them to send out an adviser. Geisenheim chose Dr Helmut Becker. He was a very nice chap and an excellent scientist, but he was Geisenheim's top man for creating those new grape varieties that were supposed to rival Riesling but never did. He loved the airy, cool conditions he found in this Land of the Long White Cloud. He did think it could become a Mosel or a Rhine of the southern seas. And he said, 'Let's plant Müller-Thurgau.' Which New Zealand did – it quickly became the most planted grape. Müller-Thurgau is the main grape in such dismal brews as Liebfraumilch. Helmut Becker could have said, 'Let's plant Riesling' – with spectacular results in New Zealand's cooler spots. He could have created a great southern Bernkasteler Doctor. But no, he said, 'Let's plant Müller-Thurgau.' New Zealand Müller-Thurgau, frequently mis-labelled as Riesling, rapidly became the best Müller-Thurgau in the world. It probably still is, except that there's only a single hectare of it left in New Zealand. The Kiwis have ripped it up and planted Sauvignon Blanc instead. But that's another story.

And even if Müller-Thurgau wasn't much good in New Zealand or in Germany, it was one of several grapes that helped countries in the cold north of Europe to get a winemaking culture started. Indeed, following the old adage that you should make a grape vine struggle to ripen for best results, vines that overripen in Germany and produce oceans of characterless juice may be capable of something very tasty where the conditions are colder and wetter. England, Denmark and Sweden are some countries that are grateful for such German creations as the white Huxelrebe, Ortega, Bacchus and Reichensteiner, and the red Regent. Varieties such as Solaris and Orion let you make full-flavoured whites in areas of Scandinavia and the British Isles that would have trouble ripening apples.

So let's raise a glass to the Germanic influence. A glass of Champagne, perhaps? Krug or Bollinger, Taittinger or Heidsieck, or Mumm. You think that those are French names? Of course, they're not. They're German, every single one. There wouldn't be a modern Champagne industry without the Germans.

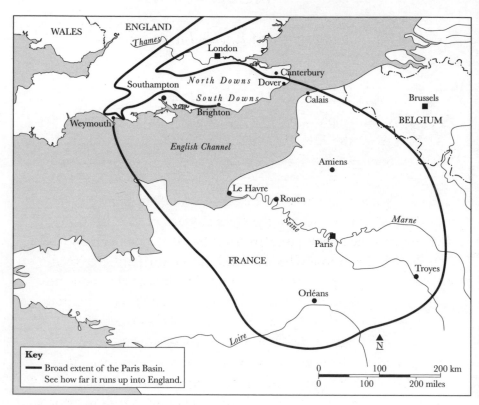

The Paris Basin ring of perfect chalk soil

Fizz

Why Champagne and England reign supreme

Why do people want to make wine sparkle? If we are to believe the UK's University of Surrey, it just might be because it makes the drinker light-headed and fancy free considerably faster than any other wine. The academics there conducted an experiment which 'proved' that if you drank a certain amount of sparkling wine as against the same amount of still wine, after five minutes the bubble-guzzlers had a blood alcohol level 38 per cent higher than those who had stuck to the still stuff. We've all heard about Champagne going 'straight to your head', but now the scientists have proved it! Statistics are wonderful things. I bet the students involved in that 'experiment' couldn't believe their luck.

But the real fact of the matter is that winemakers had been trying to avoid their wines bubbling for about 7650 years, until everything started going mad in Champagne and England in the middle of the seventeenth century. Though that didn't stop Mark Antony trying to create a sparkling wine when Cleopatra came calling. He told his servants to mix wine with fresh grape juice since that would start it fermenting again and create *bullulae* (bubbles) in the ensuing brew. Yes, well, Mark Antony was a bit of a lad and was as likely as anyone to have discovered that bubbles make you 38 per cent more frisky.

But back to – or, rather, forward to – the 1660s, and to England and to Champagne. What's the connection? Well, it was the English who first developed a taste for fizz, and, second, worked out how to make the bubbles happen. And it wasn't until the 1660s that sparkling wine adopted what is now its chief role in life – to be the universal symbol of celebration and fun. How on earth did anyone celebrate before fizz came along? Well, they drank. But it needed fizz to put the fun into wine. And the extra 38 per cent giddiness, obviously.

So, to the basics. For most of its history Champagne wine hadn't had any bubbles. Indeed, at the court of Louis XIV, where Champagne was the favoured wine of the Sun King, the presence of bubbles was a hanging offence. What the king liked was a thin, pale drink that his doctors swore would keep him healthy for decades – he did live an awfully long time – and *no* bubbles, please. Dom Pérignon, who, the Champagne PR machine would have us believe, invented foaming Champagne, did no such thing. He was a Benedictine monk and the cellar-master at Hautvillers Abbey in the Marne Valley, and every year he was up to his elbows trying to beat the bubbles out of the wine. And this wasn't easy.

Champagne is only made in one small region north-east of Paris. It's pretty cold there, and in more years than not it was a real struggle to ripen the grapes. When they picked the grapes and began to ferment the juice, winter usually closed in pretty fast, before the fermentation was finished. Yeasts can't operate if it gets too cold, so they stopped working; halfway through the fermentation they took a winter break.

Now picture this. At the end of winter, the barrels of Champagne wine are loaded onto barges and shipped to their main export market – London. The barrels arrive. It's still cold. The fermentation isn't finished. The barrels are carted off to taverns where this slightly sweet, probably cloudy wine was served by the jug to the thirsty clientele. Then, come April or May, or sometimes even June, the weather warms up, and when you broach the new barrel, the wine is a bit lively. By the end of the week it is frothing and foaming. Word gets round.

Everyone crowds into your tavern, clamouring for jugs of this cascading, riotous happy juice. For a week or two it's bedlam – and men and women lose all their inhibitions in a springtime frolic. You'd better make sure you've sold all your barrels of this boisterous brew as fast as you can, because this is the fermentation starting up all over again. Those bubbles in the wine are the carbon dioxide the yeasts create alongside the alcohol. As soon as the fermentation is finished, the bubbles will be finished, and then you'll just be left with a thin, rather sour – and very still – wine to sell at whatever price you can get.

This might have simply stayed as a delightful English end-of-winter caper. But what if you could have bubbly wine all year round? This is where the cider makers of Gloucestershire and Herefordshire made their contribution to the world of wine. They knew how to make their cider sparkle, and they knew how to make their cider sparkle inside a bottle. They had been doing it for years. But didn't the bottles explode like French ones did when the wine began to ferment in them? Ah. The French were blessed with massive forests whose wood they used for fuel long into the nineteenth century. The unhappy English were running out of trees, partly because all the good ones needed to be reserved for ship-building – usually to fight the French. James I, with an eye to future wars, forbade the use of timber to fuel glass furnaces as early as 1615. God bless King James. God bless the French. This edict forced the English glassmakers to look for a different fuel, and they found one: messy, smoky, asphyxiating – but, wow, did it burn hot! Coal. It burned far hotter than any wood or charcoal. So the glass made was harder, stronger – no matter that it was frequently almost black from impurities. These impurities were often manganese and iron, and they made the glass stronger still.

Now, coal is thought of as a product of the north of England, and most of the early English coal was from the Tyne, around Newcastle. They made a lot of glass up there. But one of the other early coalfields was in the Forest of Dean, alongside the River Severn and the flourishing cider apple orchards of Gloucestershire. Newnham on Severn is a charming little riverside village today, but in the 1630s it was the site of a thriving glassworks using local coal to make the new dark 'English' glass – even the French doffed their caps to it with the term *verre anglais*. And the cider makers were the first customers.

No one ever quite knew who was the first person to bottle his still cider and then notice that, on opening, it had a nice brisk sparkle. But the cider makers quickly caught on. They realised that if you bottled your cider at the end of the winter when it was still slightly sweet, it would develop a delightful foam. If the cider was dry, it wouldn't develop any bubbles at all. If it was too sweet, even the strong new English bottles would be likely to explode. The magic of fermentation and its causes was still a mystery, but these bubbles were real enough. Sweetness? Hmm. Ripe apples are sweet. This new cane sugar that's being imported from the West Indies is sweet. If sweet cider creates bubbles in the bottle, and dry cider doesn't, it's something to do with the sweetness. If we all add a little sugar to the cider and bang a cork in the bottle (that's another massive advantage the English had: they were allies with the Portuguese, who sent them cork. The French weren't, so they had to make do with lumps of wood wrapped in oil-soaked rags to try to stopper their bottles. Yummy.) – will that create bubbles? Yes, it will. They worked out that if you added a lump of sugar the size of a small walnut or nutmeg, this would create just the right amount of bubbles. Interestingly, experts reckon this was the equivalent of about 20 grams of sugar, which is regarded as a fairly typical dose to make a wine sparkle today. A cider maker called Silas Taylor said this would create a cider 'that comes into the glass with a speedy, vanishing nittiness which evaporates with a sparkling and whizzing noise'. I want some of that. And on 17 December 1662, Christopher Merret, well aware of what the cider makers of the West Country had been up to for the last thirty years, delivered a paper to the Royal Society in London, describing how to make wine sparkle by creating a second fermentation. He might even have been aware that John Beale, a ciderman from Herefordshire, had told the Royal Society that a 'walnut' of sugar per bottle produced a lovely fizz – on 10 December 1662, just seven days earlier.

So the first 'sparkling' Champagne, put into the strong glass bottles that are still used today, and using cork, the only natural substance that makes a perfect seal in a bottle's neck – and still used today – these first bottles of bubbly were created from barrels of half-finished Champagne wine, shipped over to London and bottled there. Some merchants just bottled the unfinished wine, which meant that the first fermentation re-started inside the bottle when it warmed up and it was anybody's guess as to how much fizz would be created. Smarter merchants did as the cider makers did – let the wine ferment out dry, then bottle it and add the walnut of sugar. And these guys could sell you sparkling wine all year round.

And this gets right to the heart of sparkling wine. How does it occur? How can you control it? Fermentation wasn't fully understood until first Chaptal and then, crucially, Pasteur discovered its workings in the nineteenth century. But the observations of people like Christopher Merret in England in the 1660s, and, to his credit, Dom Pérignon in France, who realised that sparkling wine would become the rage, so began importing English glass and Portuguese corks in the 1690s, meant that the principles of making wine fizz were well understood.

So here goes. Grape juice is full of sugar. Yeasts are everywhere in the air and many of them will attack grape juice to feed on the sugar. As they do this, they create alcohol and carbon dioxide. If any of you have seen wine fermenting, it's a very lively sight – all churning, heaving waves of bubbles and the acrid smell of alcohol being created. The fermentation finishes when the yeasts have eaten all the sugar and the bubbles die away. What next?

As I said above, if the yeasts can't, or don't, finish that first fermentation, you can shove this unfinished wine into a bottle, cork it up, and hope that the fermentation will quietly finish creating carbon dioxide, which then dissolves under pressure in the wine. This method is still used in a few places and is called by various names, such as *méthode ancestrale*. The wine it produces is generally slightly cloudy because of those yeasts still milling about, and you're never quite sure how much bubble you'll get or what the wine will taste like. Some of the 'back to nature' winemakers aren't too worried about things like that.

Now, this is important. Remember I said 'creating carbon dioxide, which dissolves under pressure in the wine'? Yes. Those bubbles that you see exploding harmlessly into the atmosphere if the wine is fermenting in a vat can be harnessed and preserved in a bottle. Luckily, carbon dioxide is a very soluble gas. So if you take some still wine, bottle it and then add a little sugar – and yeast if need be – to the bottle; if you tightly seal the bottle with a cork; if you then leave the bottle to rest – scientifically, that mixture of wine, sugar and yeast *has* to start fermenting again. The fermentation will create a bit more alcohol, but significant amounts of carbon dioxide which has nowhere to go. There's a whopping great cork in the mouth of the bottle, held down with a wire muzzle. And so all that carbon dioxide dissolves in the wine and when we pull the cork out – *whoosh* – a cascade of foaming fun and laughter fills the glass and sets the party going.

Brilliant. Now do you see why sparkling wine culture couldn't develop until those big, ugly, sturdy English glass bottles came along to deal with a pressure that could be up to twice that in the tyre of a double-decker bus? Now do you see why we could never have bottled sparkling wine until the use of the cork – which expands outwards in the neck of the bottle and hermetically seals it – became commonplace? This second fermentation of wine inside the bottle to create bubbles is now called 'the Champagne method' or the 'classic' or the 'traditional method' or something similar around the world, and is the method used by almost all the people trying to make the best fizz.

But there's still more tweaking to be done. Remember that you added a bit of yeast to the bottle to create the second fermentation? Well, that yeast died off when it had devoured all the sugar, and dropped like a sludge to the base of the bottle. You can leave it there as long as you like; all good Champagnes and Champagne lookalikes make use of the fact that after about eighteen months or so of lying there as an ugly sludge, this yeast deposit starts to break down and to release remarkable creamy, biscuity, nutty, breadcrusty flavours into the wine. These are the flavours that many modern fizz-makers crave. So you can just wait a couple of years for the yeast to do its work, then extract the cork and out will flow this lovely, creamy-tasting bubbly wine.

Up to a point. Lovely, bubbly but *cloudy* wine. The dead yeast is still there. It took the Champagne producers until the nineteenth century to work out how to riddle the yeast down to the mouth of the bottle by a mixture of knocking and shaking the bottle while you gradually upended it on to its head so all the yeast cells are stuck like a plug right next to the cork. I don't want to crow, but the cider makers of Gloucestershire and Herefordshire were already doing this in the 1670s. Crow over. Then you would pull out the cork and turn the bottle upright all in one go, and expel the plug of sediment. That's if you are very good and very experienced. Whenever I've tried it I've wasted at least a third of the bottle and made a dreadful mess of my trousers.

The secret was to freeze the neck of the bottle in frozen brine, so that just the icy plug of sediment shot out. It's important to note here that this method was invented by a Belgian. So when you're asked, 'How many famous Belgians can you name?' Here's another one. 'What was his name?' 'Er . . . I'll get back to you.'

Once you've got rid of the sediment plug, you can add a touch of sugar to sweeten the fizz a bit if you want – there's no yeast left, so don't worry, it won't start fermenting again. A lot of good fizz is quite acid and so a little sweetness improves the flavour. With the effects of global warming and riper, less acid grapes being harvested, more producers are cutting back on this final 'dosage', as the French call it. Some now don't add any sugar at all. It's a matter of taste.

Anyway, we're just about there. Bang a new cork in. Tie it down with a wire muzzle. Decorate the bottle with as much gold as you think you can get away with – and you've got a very attractive, highly marketable bottle of sparkling wine. But we still have to persuade the world that sparkling wine is the ultimate pick-me-up drink, the ultimate good-time gargle and, eventually, the ultimate aspirational drink.

Right from the start this new bubbly wine was about fun. It marketed itself to start with, as there wasn't much of it. Everyone who got some seemed to have a fantastic time. So more and more people wanted it. During the reign of Charles II, the Merry Monarch, those who could get a bottle caroused with it in the pleasure gardens of London. In France, when they finally caught on to its charms, the famously debauched court of the Regency of Louis XV bought up just about every bottle produced to lubricate their orgies. Louis XVI downed a bottle as his last wish before they carted him off to the guillotine. He was very relaxed as the blade descended. But it was the nineteenth century which was the making of Champagne. As the creation of the bubbles became ever more reliable, production of fizz went up from a few hundred thousand bottles to thirty million per annum at the end of the nineteenth century. Suddenly what had been almost unobtainable was now increasingly available. But a succession of remarkable Champagne salesmen, most of them German, as it happens – that's why so many Champagne brands have German names – managed to keep the product tantalisingly attractive and reassuringly expensive. Russia, Germany, Britain, North America – in all those countries Champagne became a symbol of indulgence due to relentless promotion. It goes on to this day. Champagne allies itself to every kind of high-profile event, from Formula One motor racing to theatre first nights, to catwalk fashion shows and celebrity nightclub shenanigans and lottery winners. Marilyn Monroe knew what she was doing for her image when she used to bathe in Champagne. (She would have needed at least 150 bottles for a half-decent bath.) Johnny Depp allegedly tried the same trick in a London hotel. The chambermaid thought the bath water looked a bit strange, so she pulled the plug. I bet she didn't get a tip. That all-time über-smoothie James Bond knew the pulling power of top-notch fizz, and the rappers of today know that the cascade of foaming, golden wine is the perfect bling tipple.

If you want to do something really zany with wine, you choose Champagne. A chic Parisian bootmaker suggests you polish her best boots with Champagne. A very flash Champagne house gets Karl Lagerfeld to design a Champagne glass moulded from the breasts of one of Hollywood's biggest stars. Sex and Champagne all in one? Absolutely. The object of Champagne has always been to make itself the object of desire and it still does so, assiduously and admirably. And right around the world, there are producers who are panting for a bit of this action. They can't call their bubbles 'Champagne', but they can make the wine in the same way, they can give the bottle the same glitzy decoration. And they can sell the story of allure and sophistication, a drop of which is within your reach if you can afford the price of a bottle.

Pretty much every country in the world makes sparkling wine, almost always with the objective of selling party pop. In some countries sparkling wine is a useful way to hoover up unripe grapes, since acid grapes generally make the best fizz. But there are producers who look upon Champagne not just as expensive mouthwash, but as a great classic wine style. And there are corners of the world where they make a damn good stab at producing something similar. They use the same Chardonnay and Pinot Noir grapes. They use the 'Champagne method' of making wine sparkle. And they generally look for the coldest, windiest, often wettest and most miserable patches of land their country possesses to try to ape the conditions of France's chilly north. They make a lot of good wine. They craft a lot of uplifting bubbles encased in delightful flavours. But they are very rarely the same as Champagne. Does that matter?

The country that gets closest is England. Hundreds of years after England worked out the nuts and bolts of how to make wine sparkle, global warming has now meant that her southern counties can ripen Chardonnay and Pinot pretty much every year. And if you look at a map, southern England is just a couple of hours' drive and a short ferry ride from Reims, the capital of Champagne. Add to that soils which are often virtually identical to many of the soils of Champagne, and it all makes sense. It makes sense to the Champagne houses, and Taittinger and Pommery are already involved in English fizz. The word in the shires is that hundreds of acres of Kent and Sussex have already been bought by major Champagne houses, waiting for the day when it starts getting too hot to make the world's best sparkling wine in Champagne.

In Europe, there are various parts of France that fancy their 'Crémant' sparkling wines in a face-off against Champagne. Alsace, Burgundy (Bourgogne) and the Loire all enter the fray, but none of these wins the contest. Italy probably does best, with Franciacorta, made near Milan and mostly drunk in Milan. The top producers here, like Ca' del Bosco and Bellavista, do match Champagne, and those in Trentino, up in the foothills of the Dolomites north of Venice, like Ferrari, aren't far behind. Germany has a considerable bubbles business, mostly based on the Riesling grape and occasionally very tasty. Spain has a powerful and successful Cava industry producing large volumes of decent fizz and small volumes of excellent, unusual, positively challenging sparkling wine based on the native Catalan grapes of Xarel-lo and Macabeu.

It's the New World that gets closest – not often, but just often enough. Canada makes a couple of remarkably good sparklers out of the unlikely – but very cold, so perhaps *not* so unlikely – environs of Nova Scotia. Benjamin Bridge is world-class. The USA makes fizz all over the place, but one foggy, dewy valley in the north of California – Anderson Valley – has done the best job of Champagne-shadowing. Roederer Estate leads the way. You would expect chilly New Zealand to come up with the goods, but her sparklers are nice but rarely completely convincing. South Africa, from less promising conditions, does much better. Australia does seem to have found somewhere sufficiently unattractive and climatically challenged to be just right: Tasmania (House of Arras and Jansz are particularly good). And for a final surprise, an operation called Geisse in rainy, humid, muggy Brazil makes some of the best fizz outside Champagne.

Thinking about Brazil, she also makes some of the best super-fruity, riotously drinkable, slightly sweet, gluggable bubbles out of the Muscat grape, but here we're talking about a different way to make wine sparkle. A way that won't give you such tiny, long-lasting bubbles – but the speed the Brazilians drink their Moscato or the Italians drink their Asti or their Prosecco mean that long-lasting bubbles aren't the point. I'm talking about the 'tank method' of making bubbly – all these wines use the 'tank method' – I know, it doesn't sound that sexy, but it works, it's quick and it's cheap.

Put simply, you fill a big tank with still wine, add yeast and sugar, and seal it up. The second fermentation races away, and under pressure the bubbles dissolve in the wine. You clarify the wine to get rid of the yeast, draw the wine off and bottle it. A simplified, speeded-up version of the 'Champagne method'. You can make your wine sweet or dry, and you can get it out to the partygoers almost before the label's been glued on. I know it's industrial, but isn't all sparkling wine the result of an industrial process, even if some is a cottage industry?

There's an even cheaper method, if you want: 'Vino Pompo' – the 'bicycle-pump' method – whereby the worst wine you can lay your hands on is literally pumped full of gas, bottled and sold to ten-year-old boys on campsites near Barcelona for so little money their dad didn't realise they'd nicked it from the groceries. Well, he realised half an hour later when he heard you and your brother being sick round the back of the tent. Actually, most Vino Pompo wines do taste of vomit. Maybe it's recycled.

Local heroes

Can they go global?

There are ten thousand grape varieties – and counting. The great Swiss grape scientist Dr José Vuillamoz has identified 1368 varieties that we might just conceivably come across somewhere in a lifetime of wine-drinking and concedes that there are many others yet to be unearthed in the fields of Croatia and Greece, Italy and Spain. Of these, about four hundred seem to be responsible for virtually all the wine we drink. And towering above all the other varieties, in every hemisphere at every latitude are an all-powerful, all-conquering array of fewer than ten varieties. They've been the grape varieties at the heart of what have been seen as the great classic wine styles. I've talked about the most important ones extensively in earlier chapters.

And it's very clear to me why countries keen to take part in the remarkable wine revolution of the last half century should have chosen these grapes as the basis for their efforts to join the modern top table of wine. The grapes were almost always French. But during this century countries such as Italy and Spain have enjoyed and endured their own wine revolutions, with a reappraisal of the potential quality of their own indigenous grape varieties very much to the fore. Countries like Portugal and Greece, Austria, the Balkan nations and those ancient wine countries on the very edge of Europe and beyond into Asia have woken up and realised that our modern wine world is looking to them also for a rebirth. And this rebirth has nothing to do with how good they are at making a decent Cabernet or Chardonnay, and everything to do with rediscovering old grape varieties and even old wine styles. In western Europe we now crave more knowledge about wines' distant past. We want to know where our long wine culture came from, and how it evolved. We're open-minded, we're inquisitive, and, at our best, we're non-judgemental.

And there's one more thing: the elephant in the room of so much wine gossip nowadays – climate change. If it's really happening as rapidly as seems likely, one of the best ways to counteract it might be to look at grape varieties from warmer countries like Italy and Spain, Greece and Portugal, and begin to plant these varieties out in the parts of the world that will bear the brunt of any global warming. Which, of course, means pretty nearly every country. It's just that countries like England or Belgium, Denmark, Sweden, Canada and other currently chilly places may feel like they've been given a last-minute invitation to a banquet from which they thought they had been excluded – a banquet whose top table is crowded with the countries that have traditionally been able to ripen the classic, mostly French, grapes. There is sure to be a period when the chilly countries become merely cool, and thus able to do something wonderful with French and German cool-climate classics. But it may not last for long. Some well-considered studies from the Intergovernmental Panel on Climate Change show the whole of the Thames Valley and much of southern England being so hot by 2080 that what vineyards they have will only be fit for growing raisins. Decent Chardonnays will be coming from the high limestone moors of northern Yorkshire. Who knows what will happen, but these guys are the professionals.

There are at last signs that producers are beginning to take the warming seriously. And it could be great news for some grape varieties that I have dubbed local heroes. Not surprisingly, the initial enthusiasm centred on Italian varieties, because there has been a wave of interest, above all in wines made from Nebbiolo and Sangiovese, during this century. But are these the right grapes? Is Spain's Tempranillo the right grape? Have Nebbiolo and Sangiovese only been chosen because producers around the world were obsessed with trying to meet the challenge that few in Italy managed, and yet which gave those few, in places such as Barolo and Montalcino, celebrity and adulation. This sounds like an Italian version of the Pinotmania that has seen so many New World producers break their hearts trying to make exciting 'Burgundian' Pinot Noir. And we are still in denial? Are we still pretending to adapt to changing conditions, but still choosing grape varieties that we have some knowledge of, yet which will not necessarily be able to adapt, and in some cases need relatively cool conditions themselves? It may be that the grapes that will really be necessary to keep decent wine flowing in a warming world have little renown so far, and may even come from regions or countries we barely respect. Well, let's look at a few.

First, let's look at the trendiest of them all, Nebbiolo. This is a grape variety that its supporters ecstatically describe as the finest in the world, yet which most wine-drinkers have never dared to approach. It's the biggest question of all. What do we do with Nebbiolo?

Now that winemaking in north-west Italy's Barolo and Barbaresco regions has transformed itself so that even wine fans who had never enjoyed a Barolo before can see what all the fuss is about – has Nebbiolo got what it takes? Early signs weren't promising. I did a big tasting of pretty much every Italian variety planted in California at a smart San Francisco hotel at the turn of the century, and I might have well as been tasting wines from the end of the nineteenth century, not the twentieth. Most of them were a seething, stewy mass of flavours you couldn't see anyone with any choice in the matter buying further away from the vineyard than the farm gate. The Nebbiolos were thin, reedy and bitter. All the Nebbiolo faults, none of its magic.

But there is a fellow well to the south of San Francisco who knows how to do it. Jim Clendenen is a great straggly haired, jovial wine wizard who cheerfully makes his own way down in the Santa Maria Valley. Pendulums swing wildly from ripe to raw, from too much oak to not enough. Jim just gets some chalk and writes his maxim up on the wall: 'Say no to fads. Don't forget the past. And if you spill use salt and soda water.' And he can make Nebbiolo. Nebbiolo seems to love a mixture of sun and fogs. That's what it gets in Barolo's best vintages. That's what Jim gets every year in the Bien Nacido Vineyards. The Santa Maria Valley's fogs are notorious. They blanket the vines so thickly each morning the vineyard workers need helmet lamps, but the fog always clears, the sun always comes out and Jim makes truly delicious Nebbiolo – sweet and sour, bitter and soft, as though the skins of damsons, black cherries and sloes have been squeezed dry. Jim leaves this in the barrel for five years – that's old school for you. 'Looking for a taste of terroir, a taste of its place?' I asked. 'If you have presence of terroir,' Jim replied, 'it's a miracle. I don't say I don't want terroir to dominate. But if terroir creeps out of the soil, it's a miracle. It's a dark and devilish plot.'

If you're looking for more Nebbiolo in the Americas, follow the Italians. Most of it has been planted in Argentina by Italian settlers, but there is a lot of sun in Argentina and not much fog. The Nebbiolos I've tasted have been pretty stringy. But the Italians also settled in southern Brazil, and right down in the south-eastern corner Lidio Carraro are taking a radical approach to Nebbiolo – no fogs in the vineyard and no oak ageing. And they make a superb red this way – all the flavours squeezed dry again, shrivelled red cherries, plums and prunes sharing the cauldron with sweet tomatoes, stewed buttery carrots, pepper, cumin and oatmeal flapjacks. Barolo this is not. But as an example of Nebbiolo's ability to travel? Absolutely. The winemaker at Lidio Carraro told me that the molecules in urine and honey are almost identical. Why would I want to know that?

And there's one more place the Italians – well, one Italian – has set up his stall: Virginia. Luca Paschina, winemaker at Barboursville, grew up in the Nebbiolo vineyards of Piedmont before emigrating to run Barboursville, an estate based around the ruins of a mansion designed by Thomas Jefferson and surrounded by densely green forested hills. And in October 2013 I stood as the morning dew dripped off the trees at the very top of the vineyard, tasting the brand-new Nebbiolo from an unlabelled bottle perched on the roof of Luca's car. Sharp, rosehip coloured, rosehip and cranberry scented. Fragile but delicious. Luca then brought out his 2008 and his '02. The 2008 was in its youthful prime, with delightful strawberry and cherry fruit touched by rose petal scent but kept in step by some proper Nebbiolo tannin and acid. The '02 was a simply wonderful example of mature Nebbiolo, full of stewed black cherry skins, stewed strawberries, sweet apple peel, long-simmered field mushrooms and just the right bite from a scented sour balsamic vinegar. It's humid in Virginia, it's sunny, but they get fogs. Nebbiolo is famously picky about where it will grow, even in Barolo. You need the odd obsessive to wheedle out little patches of land outside Italy where it might work. A broad-brush approach simply won't do.

Luca understood that, and so do Breaux out toward the Blue Ridge Mountains. They also make Nebbiolo, less delicately than at Barboursville, but shockingly well. I've tasted these wines back to 2001, and they all have this scented sour streak of really fine balsamic vinegar; they have a haughty aroma of graphite and the cold smell of an empty nave at Canterbury Cathedral on a hot summer's day. And they have fruit – black raspberries, black plums, sweet carrots again, with pips and stones and stalks, and this heady scent of heather honey and incense splashed with vinegar.

Pretty much every New World country has tried Nebbiolo, because it attracts the same kind of obsessive determination that Pinot Noir does. Bit by bit, Pinot Noir is showing its brilliance in patches of land all around the world. Nebbiolo is a generation behind – in Italy and elsewhere. Nebbiolo is even more picky than

Pinot Noir. It's an even bigger challenge, and because it didn't have the force of a thousand years of French history pushing it forward, few of the best wine brains have taken up the challenge. Even Australia's efforts have mostly been so-so. I say that, and I can see the indignant features of Steve Pannell in South Australia's McLaren Vale. He is the archetypal Aussie battler, but also one of Australian wine's deepest thinkers, more aware than most of the change that is coming as his world warms and dries out. He has taken up the Nebbiolo challenge. 'Nebbiolo has taught me to embrace the tannic principle in the same way as we embrace the aromatic qualities.' Up in the Adelaide Hills he has found some Nebbiolo nestled among the damp trees, but with enough sun to ripen. He lets his wine spend up to seventy-seven days macerating on its skins – that is a long time – and his gritty, scented, challenging but delicious Nebbiolo, tasting of cigars and leather and a syrup made of dried strawberries and cranberries, is one of the best you'll find anywhere outside Piedmont, and as good as most of the ones in Piedmont. Nebbiolo stirs, and exciting, completely individual wines peep cautiously out of the shadows, still as rare as enjoyable Barolo was a generation ago. And it's up to us to buy them and delight in them if we want to see more of them.

So, is Sangiovese likely to find things any easier? You would have thought so. It doesn't seem nearly so temperamental a grape as Nebbiolo. That depends on who you talk to. By now there should be numerous success stories about Sangiovese around the world. There aren't. There are some countries like Mexico and Argentina that have had Sangiovese planted for generations, but only because many of these vineyard areas were settled by Italians, and Italians liked to plant what they know. And as I taste their Sangioveses in lacklustre line-ups of bottles, I don't get much pleasure from their curious mix of stringiness, skin acidity and rather jammy fruit. But I then remind myself of something a Tuscan producer, Marco Ricasoli-Firidolfi at Rocca di Montegrossi, told me: 'Sangiovese is a wine that at a tasting you should really not like too much. You can only fall in love with Sangiovese over food.'

And he's right. These rather rustic, rough and ready Sangioveses from the Americas were planted, as most Italian varieties were, to provide a red wine with a bit of cut to it, to go with hunks of red meat. You'd have thought that Sangiovese would feature in the outstanding Col Solare red that Piero Antinori of Tuscan fame co-produces in Washington State. But it doesn't. Perhaps he had had his fingers burnt enough by trying to get Sangiovese to work for over twenty years at Atlas Peak in California's Napa Valley.

Australia has made one or two forays into Sangiovese, with wineries like Coriole in McLaren Vale leading the way. I would give the Aussie laurels to the Pizzini label in King Valley, an old tobacco area with lots of Italian families like the Pizzinis. Pizzini makes Sangiovese with the cut and rasp of Tuscany, but just that bit riper and sweeter. It's still crying out for the salami, though. Joe Grilli makes a positively juicy example in McLaren Vale that's a joy on its own and merely enquires about the plate of salami.

To be honest, people in Tuscany are still only slowly working out which clones are any good. There was a much-needed project called Chianti 2000 which made a brave effort to sort the useful from the rubbish. Sangiovese is an old variety with as much genetic variation as that great mutator Pinot Noir, and, despite massive improvements in the clonal material used in Tuscany, the locals know the job is only half done. This is an early-budding, late-ripening variety, so it should be suitable for warmer climates, but it's also a heavy cropper, wilful, self-indulgent and frequently rather coarse. And then you taste a beauty from Vino Nobile di Montepulciano or Chianti Classico and realise that there is quality inside those groaning bunches. But it's not easy to find and few people outside Tuscany have managed it. So is it worth pursuing? I think that if it is going to be of more than peripheral importance around the world, we will need to see a lot more results from the people in Italy who are striving to improve the breed. And we'll need to unearth a few visionaries with a real idea of what kind of flavours they dream of coaxing out of the grape in their distant vineyards under very different skies.

The secret of Tempranillo lies in its name. Temprano is the Spanish for 'early'. That's right. It buds early, then rushes through its ripening period to be ready for a nice early harvest. And actually, although it likes a certain amount of heat, it certainly doesn't appreciate too much, because the grapes will build up enormous levels of sugar very quickly, before the flavour has developed into anything very exciting, and, crucially, before the tannins have had time to mature and soften. Even in Rioja and Ribera del Duero, in northern Spain, where conditions aren't too torrid, bitter tannins can be a real problem, and alcohol levels too frequently reach 14 per cent, and maybe more. Add in some time spent ageing in new oak barrels, which will sweeten and spice up the wine but is quite likely to add even more tannin, and you begin to wonder whether Tempranillo is all that suitable for most of Spain in a warming world, let alone great swathes of the Americas, Africa and Australasia.

Interestingly, one of the roles that has been proposed for Tempranillo is for it to become part of the grape mix allowed in Bordeaux. There has been no visible or audible enthusiasm for such a radical vineyard move in Bordeaux yet – the fact that Tempranillo is a Spanish variety is hardly likely to endear it to the French. But Rioja is pretty much the closest vineyard area to Bordeaux as you head south. And the more open-minded Bordelais might note that Trinity Hills in New Zealand's Hawke's Bay has made an extremely good stab at Tempranillo in the area which is called the Bordeaux of New Zealand. So its most useful role might be in becoming a favoured variety in areas that are currently cooler than northern Spain but are warming up.

The USA has dallied with Tempranillo – Truchard in Carneros and Viader in Napa are California's best players so far – and Washington State and southern Oregon have done quite well with it. Argentina has a lot of Tempranillo – often old stuff planted out in the last century without any fanfare, and frequently called by the female title of Tempranilla. With the exception of some

Tempranillo-based blends from the O Fournier and Zuccardi wineries, the wines are mostly jammy and they are tough. And here we have it again. Mendoza in Argentina is mostly pretty warm. The grapes fill with sugar before the tannins and the skins are ripe, and the result is rather one-dimensional, big, jammy and bitter reds. It doesn't sound like Tempranillo has the formula for a warming world. Australia, not surprisingly, has given it a go. At the turn of the century there was a rush of enthusiastic planting. Wine producers, understandably, liked the fact that Tempranillo can keep its acid quite well in warm conditions, even if the tannins are pretty raw. And the Tempranillo will give you a helluva big crop if you don't rein it in. Although individual estates like Pondalowie and Tim Adams have made rich and even scented examples that are fun to drink despite the tannins, most producers in Australia use Tempranillo as a blender, and you have to ask whether that is to improve the other grapes or whether it is because in Australian conditions you just can't get the right balance in the flavours and texture, so it's best to smooth everything out in a blend. I don't see Tempranillo having a massive role to play in warm areas, though it might be important in currently cool ones.

Not for the first time, the Romans might have the answer. They used to pick Tempranillo (in Spain!) and throw the bunches into a shallow stone trough called a lagar, where a fermentation both inside the grape and of the juice that oozed out from crushed berries took place. That was the basis for what is now called carbonic maceration, the type of fermentation used in France's Beaujolais to make one of the world's juiciest, most appetising, young, gulpable red wines. A few producers in Rioja still make a version of this. They don't sell it off in fancy bottles. They call it bodegueros wine, the 'sort of wine the winemakers drink' and they drink it in the local bars. There's a little street in Logroño, Rioja's main town, with more than twenty bars, each boasting a blackboard with the names of the numerous bodegueros wines – young, vibrant and as gushing as any in Spain. In a warming world, fresh, juicy reds will be at a premium. Perhaps Tempranillo will have a role, but it's for gorgeous gulpers rather than anything majestic and barrel-aged.

If we really want to work out what will cope best with our changing world, it probably isn't anything as well known as these varieties. Many totally obscure grape varieties are being unearthed, or coaxed back to life, all around the Mediterranean basin. Even I haven't heard of the names of many of them. But I will, and so will you. In the meantime, there are quite enough grape varieties that are already widely planted, but often not given much respect. These are usually warm-climate varieties, often already in place across the Americas, Africa and Australasia, yet dismissed as junk grapes. But we will find ways to grow them and make from them wines which will prise out all kinds of personality and flavours. Spain has Garnacha, Monastrell and Mazuelo. These also grow in France as Grenache, Mourvèdre and Carignan. And they've been planted all around the world – but as bulk producers or as the fodder for making fortified wines. Treat them better, find out what makes them tick and they can cope with a warming world. Spain has other varieties like the red Bobal and Graciano, and whites like Verdejo, Godello and Albariño. Albariño has become quite trendy, but it comes from the windy, wet north-west tip of Galicia. I'd give Godello and Verdejo more of a chance.

France is at last taking its non-mainstream grape varieties more seriously. Some of the varieties that were traditionally just used for bulk – Alicante Bouschet and Cinsault – are two examples that have already proved their worth. South African Cinsault is encouragingly fresh and scented from the warm Swartland and Paarl vineyard regions. Tannat is a rough old thing from south-west France, but in places like Uruguay's Maldonado and Argentina's Salta regions, as well as Brazil and Virginia in the USA, it is showing that it can cope with wild weather and reveal a shy but scented heart. The red Trousseau grape from the Jura doesn't sound like a great bet, but it does well in Spain under various names, and in Portugal as Bastardo; California is really picking up on it too.

Count this one in. And talking of Portugal, there are dozens of grape varieties here that are well attuned to the heat and capable of great things. Many are white – look out for Encruzado, Sercial and Arinto – but its most famous are red varieties, led by Touriga Nacional, Touriga Franca, Tinto Cão, Alfrocheiro and Baga. Because these are unfamiliar names, few of the world's vineyards have adopted Portuguese grape varieties. You don't have to learn the language, but you must start trialling these grapes.

Italy has more grape varieties recorded than any other country, but most of her varieties are yet to be documented and there are hundreds of obscure local ones, any one of which might prove to be important in combating climate change. Of the ones we know, I'll just choose a few reds that might have something to offer: Lagrein, Refosco, Terrano, Corvina, Teroldego, Aglianico, Nerello Mascalese and Nero d'Avola. The white Greco, Fiano, Falanghina, Grillo, Vermentino and Verdicchio are just a start; Italy has dozens of high-quality white varieties accustomed to the heat, just waiting for sensitive grape-growing and winemaking to reveal their charms.

This is just a snapshot of some of the varieties that we will need to embrace in the next generation. Other countries have many more. Croatia's Dalmatia has numerous excellent almost – but not quite – extinct varieties. Greece, led by stars such as the white Assyrtiko, Malagousia and Moschofilero and the red Agioritiko and Xynomavro, is at last becoming proud of its vine heritage. Turkey may have as many as one thousand grape varieties. Some of them, especially from Eastern Anatolia, could blossom in a warming world. Saperavi has proved itself to be a superb ancient red variety from Georgia. Who knows how long it has been there. Who knows how many other potential stars are yet to resurface as the world becomes fascinated by the vineyards of what may be our most ancient winemaking culture. It would make absolute sense to me if some of the saviours of our future are quietly waiting, enfolded in our past.

What next?

A future for wine

April brings one of the most exhausting and demanding yet enthralling, fascinating and utterly satisfying periods of my wine year. It's when I judge the International Wine Challenge and I am faced with literally every shape and size of wine that the world can produce. And each year there is a day when I seem to get lucky and flight after flight of wines fills me with joy. And I find myself asking, how much better could wine taste than this? This year it was after a fabulous range of Douro reds; bottle after bottle of superb Champagne teased and goaded by English fizz and by more tasty Cava and Prosecco than I can ever remember; red Burgundy battling it out with New Zealand Pinot Noir; vibrant Galician whites and triumphant Rioja reds from Spain; and white wines from north and central Italy that simply couldn't have been more appetising and mouthwatering, and which came from grapes that half of us have never heard of. If I add in delights from Moravia and Kazakhstan, Georgia, Hungary and Japan, I find myself thinking we are in a good place, a happy place in our world of wine.

Are we? Well, we can be, if we react to the changing world in the right way. Could we make wine taste better than it does today? That depends on how we try to improve it. If we try to force wine into expressions of flavour that the grapes and the vineyards don't possess, then no. In the last generation we have made many wines taste worse by trying to pressure them into being what they aren't, and can't be. But the mood now is to return to a more balanced, natural and respectful view of grapes and the places they grow. Use of oak has lessened, alcohol levels are trimmed and the lazy unnecessariness of casually overripening grapes is being disowned. The result is more and more wines that do what wine is supposed to do. Nourish us, refresh us, provide pleasure in the wide array of flavours that different countries and different grape varieties can provide, and act as open-hearted accompaniments to the astonishing range of different foods that so many of us nowadays consume.

Does wine have to be a perfect match for food? No. What is a perfect match? A lot of nonsense is talked about perfect food and wine pairings. You can spend so much energy on trying to get the perfect balance that you forget to enjoy the meal, to enjoy your friends' company, to relish the occasion, whatever it may be. If you wanted generalisations, what about these? If you're concentrating on the wine, keep the food simple. If you're focusing on the food, keep the wine simple. And if you're in a wine area, eat what the locals eat and drink what the locals drink. In some countries, local food and local wine have been getting to know each other for hundreds of years.

But you can't stop people trying to make wine taste better, surely? Fair enough, but you can ask people not to try to warp wine's basic nature. The reason that this year has brought me more wine joy than normal is because more wines are going back to basics. This doesn't require the use of natural vineyard yeasts for fermentation, although many forward-looking producers do like to use them. This doesn't require that you cut out all use of chemical additives, although a fair number of skilled wine creators worldwide are following that path. And it certainly doesn't mean that you should stop using oak barrels, that you should wilfully under-ripen your grapes, and that you shouldn't keep your winery as hygienic and clean as you care to. But it does mean that you should never lose sight of the fact that wine is a delightful, largely unnecessary but immensely enjoyable member of that group of activities and products that make our lives more fun to live. For most of us, it's no more nor less than that.

But the world is changing. Its climate is changing, its mood is changing, and as the generations change, we shouldn't expect their requirements and obsessions and ambitions to stay the same as ours. Almost more than anything else there is now a very real groundswell of opinion that we are messing up this precious world of ours. David Attenborough's *Blue Planet* television series, with its heartrending images of the creatures of the sea being poisoned and asphyxiated by plastic, has done more to mobilise public opinion than a thousand political speeches. And it chimes very well with these modern times. We will see more natural, 'non-intervention' winemaking. We will see organic wine become commonplace and perhaps even mainstream. We may even find a reaction against such devices as screwcaps for stoppering bottles, just when they appeared to be winning the quality argument against cork. We will probably find an acceptance that some wine needs to be more expensive because water for irrigation is running out. The Murray River in Australia, the winter rains in South Africa, the snowmelt from the Andes – as these begin to fail, the ability to make cheap wines – or, in some cases, any wine at all – in large parts of Australia, South Africa, Argentina and Chile will be called into question.

And as a generation of drinkers matures, who may prefer coffee and tea to wine, who may prefer boutique gin and craft beer to wine, who may question food and drink miles and prefer to eat and drink 'local', where will this leave wine? When Emmanuel Macron, President of France, the world's greatest wine-producing nation, is criticised by doctors for encouraging the French to drink wine, as he was in 2018, is wine really bad for our health, bad for our planet? If 'drink less but drink better' is finally going to be the rallying call of wine; if wine, which has the oldest 'craft' credentials of any alcoholic drink, begins to exploit them and explain them, rather than dumb them down and obliterate them, can we bring a much more canny, a much more ethically sensitive generation into our wine world? And what will we offer them, in a warming world? More wines that are true to their roots, more wines from old grape varieties that long ago proved their worth in warm, dry conditions, and which must now begin to be considered for planting in classic areas of Spain, Italy, Germany and France, whose conditions are changing fast, and also in places like California, Chile and Australia. The old vine varieties of Spain and Italy, of Portugal and Greece, maybe even Turkey and Georgia, will need to be evaluated and trialled and planted in vineyards that used to boast Chardonnay, Sauvignon and Riesling, Pinot Noir and Syrah and Cabernet Sauvignon. These classics can shift north in Europe – to Denmark, England, Holland and even further. A terrifying possibility? The whole phenomenon of climate change is terrifying. But it's also full of opportunity and challenge. Preserving the health of our world as we have it now and preparing to go back to the future as we deal with change will indeed be bewildering and daunting. But we have to do it. For our own good. For the good of future generations of wine lovers. I'm ready. I'm even looking forward to it.

Some of my favourites

The following are some of the wines I've enjoyed most during my life in wine. They're not definitive lists of 'best wines', but all the wines and producers mentioned here are on an exciting roll in terms of quality. Some are easy to find; others are very rare or expensive – but if you get the chance to try them, grab it!

Cabernet Sauvignon and Bordeaux lookalikes

- Castello di Ama, L'Apparita, Toscana, Tuscany, Italy
- Andeluna, Cabernet Franc, Uco Valley, Argentina
- Andrew Will, Champoux, Horse Heaven Hills, Washington State, USA
- Balnaves, Cabernet Sauvignon, Coonawarra, Australia
- Boxwood Estate, Boxwood, Virginia, USA
- Ch. Branaire-Ducru, St-Julien, Bordeaux, France
- Viña Carmen, Gold Reserve Cabernet Sauvignon, Alto Maipo Valley, Chile
- Cheval des Andes/Terrazas de Los Andes, Mendoza, Argentina
- Dom. de Chevalier, Pessac-Léognan, Bordeaux, France
- Col Solare/Chateau Ste. Michelle, Red Mountain, Washington State, USA
- Corison, Kronos Vineyard Cabernet Sauvignon, Napa Valley, California, USA
- Craggy Range, Sophia, Gimblett Gravels, Hawke's Bay, New Zealand
- Diamond Creek, Diamond Mountain, Napa Valley, California, USA

- Les Forts de Latour, Pauillac, Bordeaux, France
- Ch. Grand-Puy-Lacoste, Pauillac, Bordeaux, France
- Grosset, Gaia, Clare Valley, South Australia, Australia
- Ch. Léoville-Barton, St-Julien, Bordeaux, France
- Loma Larga, Cabernet Franc, Casablanca, Chile
- Long Shadows, Pedestal, Washington State, USA
- Ch. Lynch-Bages, Pauillac, Bordeaux, France
- Ch. la Mission-Haut-Brion, Pessac-Léognan, Bordeaux, France
- Ornellaia, Masseto, Toscana, Tuscany, Italy
- Ch. Pichon-Baron, Pauillac, Bordeaux, France
- Ch. Pontet-Canet, Pauillac, Bordeaux, France
- Primo Estate, Moda Cabernet-Merlot, McLaren Vale, South Australia, Australia
- Le Riche, Cabernet Sauvignon Reserve, Stellenbosch, Western Cape, South Africa
- Ridge, Monte Bello, Santa Cruz Mountains, California, USA
- Rustenberg, Peter Barlow, Stellenbosch, Western Cape, South Africa
- Santa Rita, Medalla Real Cabernet Sauvignon, Maipo Valley, Chile
- Spottswoode, Cabernet Sauvignon, Napa Valley, California, USA
- Viader, Napa Valley, California, USA
- Wölffer Estate, Claletto Merlot-Cabernet Sauvignon, New York State, USA
- Woodward Canyon, Walla Walla Valley, Washington State, USA

Chardonnay

- Bergström, Willamette Valley, Oregon, USA
- Bethel Heights, Casteel Chardonnay, Oregon, USA
- Blain-Gagnard, Puligny-Montrachet, Côte de Beaune, Burgundy, France
- Chamonix, Chardonnay, Franschhoek, South Africa
- Cullen, Kevin John, Margaret River, Western Australia, Australia
- Dog Point, Marlborough, New Zealand
- Eden Road, Chardonnay, Canberra, and The Long Road Chardonnay, Tumbarumba, New South Wales, Australia
- Felton Road, Block 2 Chardonnay, Central Otago, New Zealand

- William Fèvre, Chablis Grand Cru, Chablis, Burgundy, France
- Hamilton Russell, Hemel-en-Aarde, Western Cape, South Africa
- HdV, Carneros, California, USA
- Jordan, Nine Yards Chardonnay, Stellenbosch, Western Cape, South Africa
- Kumeu River, Maté's Chardonnay, Auckland, New Zealand
- Littorai, Charles Heintz Vineyard, Sonoma Coast, California, USA
- Maycas del Limarí, Chardonnay, Chile
- Neudorf, Nelson, New Zealand
- Newton Johnson, Chardonnay, Upper Hemel-en-Aarde, Western Cape, South Africa
- Ocean Eight, Mornington Peninsula, Victoria, Australia
- Payten & Jones, Paul's Range, Yarra Valley, Victoria, Australia
- Penfolds, Yattarna, South Australia, Australia
- Pierro, Margaret River, Western Australia, Australia
- Ramey, Hyde Vineyard, Carneros, and Ritchie Vineyard Chardonnay, Russian River Valley, California, USA
- Tolpuddle/Shaw & Smith, Chardonnay, Tasmania, Australia
- La Vougeraie, Clos Blanc de Vougeot, Côte de Nuits, Burgundy, France
- Yabby Lake, Mornington Peninsula, Victoria, Australia

Pinot Noir and Burgundy lookalikes

- Ata Rangi, Martinborough, New Zealand
- Bethel Heights, Willamette Valley, Oregon, USA
- Burn Cottage, Central Otago, New Zealand
- Bergström, Temperance Hill Pinot Noir, Oregon, USA
- Jean-Claude Boisset, Clos de la Roche, Burgundy, France
- Sylvain Cathiard, Nuits St-Georges Aux Murgers, Côte de Nuits, Burgundy, France
- Chevillon, Nuits St-Georges Les Pruliers, Côte de Nuits, Burgundy, France
- Confuron-Cotetidot, Vosne-Romanée Les Suchots, Côte de Nuits, Burgundy, France
- Crystallum, Bona Fide, Hemel-en-Aarde, Western Cape, South Africa
- Domaine Drouhin, Laurène Pinot Noir, Oregon, USA

- B Dugat-Py, Charmes-Chambertin, Côte de Nuits, Burgundy, France
- Felton Road, Central Otago, New Zealand
- Flowers, Camp Meeting Ridge, Sonoma Coast, California, USA
- Ch. Gris, Nuits St-Georges, Côte de Nuits, Burgundy, France
- Kusuda, Pinot Noir, Martinborough, New Zealand
- Comte Liger-Belair, Échezeaux, Côte de Nuits, Burgundy, France
- Littorai, Pinot Noir, Sonoma Coast, California, USA
- Maycas del Limarí, Reserva Especial Pinot Noir, Limarí, Chile
- Moorooduc, Mornington Peninsula, Victoria, Australia
- Neudorf, Home Vineyard Pinot Noir, Nelson, New Zealand
- Ostler, Caroline's Pinot Noir, Waitaki, Otago, New Zealand
- Pegasus Bay, Prima Donna Pinot Noir, Waipara, New Zealand
- Rippon, Emma's Block Pinot Noir and Tinker's Field, Central Otago, New Zealand
- Stoller Family Estate, Reserve Pinot Noir, Dundee Hills, Oregon, USA
- de Villaine, La Digoine Bourgogne-Côte Chalonnaise, Burgundy, France
- Tolpuddle/Shaw & Smith, Pinot Noir, Tasmania, Australia
- Valli, Waitaki, New Zealand
- Williams Selyem, Westside Road Neighbors, Russian River Valley, California, USA
- Yabby Lake, Pinot Noir, Mornington Peninsula, Victoria, Australia

Syrah–Shiraz

- Gilles Barge, Côte-Rôtie, Rhône Valley, France
- Bilancia, La Collina, Hawke's Bay, New Zealand
- Jean-Louis Chave, Hermitage, Rhône Valley, France
- A Clape, Cornas, Rhône Valley, France
- Clonakilla, Shiraz-Viognier, Canberra, Australia
- Collector, Shiraz, Canberra, Australia
- Dom. du Colombier, Crozes-Hermitage and Hermitage, Rhône Valley, France
- Elephant Hill, Syrah, Hawkes Bay, New Zealand
- Henschke, Hill of Grace Shiraz, Eden Valley, South Australia, Australia

- Jamet, Côte-Rotie, Rhône Valley, France
- Jamsheed, Garden Gully Shiraz, Victoria, Australia
- K Vintners/Charles Smith, Shiraz, Walla Walla Valley, Washington State, USA
- Kongsgaard, Napa Valley, California, USA
- Viña Leyda, Reserva Syrah, Leyda, Chile
- Man O' War, Dreadnought, Waiheke Island, New Zealand
- Dom. de Marcoux, Châteauneuf-du-Pape, Rhône Valley, France
- Mullineux & Leeu, Schist and Granite, Swartland, Western Cape, South Africa
- Penfolds, St Henri Shiraz and RWT, Barossa, South Australia, Australia
- André Perret, St-Joseph, Rhône Valley, France
- Porseleinberg, Swartland, Western Cape, South Africa
- Reyneke, Syrah, Stellenbosch, Western Cape, South Africa
- Gilles Robin, Crozes-Hermitage, Rhône Valley, France
- Marc Sorrel, Hermitage, Rhône Valley, France
- Tablas Creek, Esprit, Paso Robles, California, USA
- Trinity Hill, Homage, Hawke's Bay, New Zealand
- Yalumba, Bush Vine Grenache, Barossa, South Australia, Australia

Sauvignon Blanc

- Astrolabe, Sauvignon Blanc, Kekerungu Coast, Marlborough, New Zealand
- Casa Marin, Cipreses, San Antonio, Chile
- Cederberg, David Nieuwoudt Ghost Corner, Elim, Western Cape, South Africa
- Concha y Toro, Terryuno, Casablanca, Chile
- Ch. Couhins-Lurton, Pessac-Léognan, Bordeaux, France
- Dog Point, Sauvignon Blanc, Marlborough, New Zealand
- Gladstone Vineyard, Sophie's Choice, Martinborough, Wairarapa, New Zealand
- Greywacke, Wild Sauvignon, Marlborough, New Zealand
- Ch. Malartic-Lagravière, Pessac-Léognan, Bordeaux, France
- Montes, Outer Limits Sauvignon Blanc, Zapallar, Aconcagua, Chile
- Ch. Smith-Haut-Lafitte, Pessac-Léognan, Bordeaux, France
- Torres, Fransola, Penedès, Catalonia, Spain

Riesling and the Germanics

- Tim Adams, Clare Valley, South Australia, Australia
- Ch. Belá/Egon Müller, Slovakia
- Paul Blanck, Furstentum Vieilles Vignes, Alsace, France
- Bründlmayer, Zöbinger Heiligenstein, Kamptal, Austria
- Dönnhoff, Oberhäuser Brücke, Nahe, Germany
- Grosset, Polish Hill, Clare Valley, South Australia, Australia
- Chateau Lafayette Reneau, Dry Riesling, New York State, USA
- Chehalem, Three Vineyard Riesling, Oregon, USA
- Peter Lehmann, Wigan Riesling, Eden Valley, South Australia, Australia
- Long Shadows, Poet's Leap Riesling, Columbia Valley, Washington State, USA
- Dr Loosen, Erdener Treppchen, Mosel, Germany
- Horst Sauer, Escherndorfer Lump, Franken, Germany
- Weinbach, Schlossberg Cuvée Ste Catherine, Alsace, France

Fizz

- Benjamin Bridge, Brut Reserve, Nova Scotia, Canada
- Breaky Bottom, Cuvée Réservée, East Sussex, England
- Ca' del Bosco, Franciacorta Cuvée Annamaria Clementi, Lombardy, Italy
- Furleigh Estate, Blanc de Blancs, Dorset, England
- Geisse, Brut Rosé, Brazil
- Gusbourne, Brut Reserve, Kent, England
- Hattingley Valley, Rosé, Hampshire, England
- Charles Heidsieck, Champagne, France
- Nyetimber, Classic Cuvée, West Sussex, England
- Quartz Reef, Méthode Traditionelle, Central Otago, New Zealand
- Roederer Estate, L'Ermitage, California
- Schramsberg, Blanc de Blancs, California
- Syncline, Scintillation Blanc de Blancs, Washington State, USA
- Wiston, Rosé, West Sussex, England
- Wyfold, Brut, Oxfordshire, England

Local heroes

- Aalto, PS (Pagos Seleccionados), Ribera del Duero, Castilla y León, Spain
- Alheit Vineyards, Cartology, Hemel-en-Aarde, Western Cape, South Africa
- Allegrini, Amarone della Valpolicella and La Poja, Veneto, Italy
- Barboursville, Nebbiolo, Virginia, USA
- Benanti, Rovittello, Etna, Sicily, Italy
- Breaux, Viognier, Virginia, USA
- Brokenwood, Semillon, Hunter Valley, New South Wales, Australia
- Quinta do Crasto, Reserva Old Vines, Portugal
- CVNE, Imperial Gran Reserva, Rioja, Spain
- De Martino, Cinsault, Maipo, Chile
- DeMorgenzon, Maestro White, Stellenbosch, Western Cape, South Africa
- Fenocchio, Barolo, Piedmont, Italy
- Isole e Olena, Cepparello, Tuscany, Italy
- Quinta da Manoella, Vinhas Velhas, Douro, Portugal
- McWilliam's, Mount Pleasant Lovedale Semillon, Hunter Valley, New South Wales, Australia
- Muga, Rioja Reserva, Spain
- Muhr-van der Niepoort, Spitzerberg Blaufränkisch, Carnuntum, Austria
- Mullineux & Leeu, White Blend, Swartland, Western Cape, South Africa
- Musella, Amarone della Valpolicella, Veneto, Italy
- S C Pannell, Nebbiolo, Adelaide Hills, South Australia, Australia
- Quinta da Pellada, Dão, Portugal
- Dominio de Pingus, Pingus, Ribera del Duero, Castilla y León, Spain
- Riecine, Chianti Classico, Tuscany, Italy
- Quinta dos Roques, Reserva, Dão, Portugal
- Giovanni Rosso, Barolo, Piedmont, Italy
- Sadie Family, 'T Voetpad white, Swartland, Western Cape, South Africa
- Tyrrell's, Vat 1 Semillon, Hunter Valley, New South Wales, Australia
- G D Vajra, Dolcetto and Barbera, Piedmont, Italy
- Quinta Vale Doña Maria, Vinha do Rio, Douro, Portugal
- Wind Gap, Trousseau Gris, Russian River Valley, California, USA

Glossary

AC/AOC/AOP *Appellation d'origine contrôlée/protégée.* The top category of French wines, defined by regulations covering vineyard yields, grape varieties, geographical boundaries, alcohol content and production method. Guarantees origin and style of a wine, but not its quality.

acid/acidity Naturally present in grapes and essential to wine, providing balance and stability, a refreshing tang in white wines and appetising grip in reds. Too much can make a wine taste sharp, too little and it will be flabby.

ageing May take place in vat, barrel or bottle, and may last for months or years. It has a mellowing effect on a wine, but if a wine is stored for too long it may lose its fruit.

alcoholic content The alcoholic strength of wine, expressed as a percentage of the total volume of the wine. Typically in the range of 7–15 per cent.

alcoholic fermentation The process whereby yeasts, natural or added, convert the grape sugars into alcohol (ethyl alcohol, or ethanol) and carbon dioxide.

Amontillado Traditionally dry but rich style of aged sherry.

AVA American Viticultural Area. System of appellations of origin for US wines.

barrel ageing Time spent maturing in wood, usually oak, during which wine may take on flavours from the wood if new barrels are used.

barrel fermentation Oak barrels may be used for fermentation instead of stainless steel to give a rich, oaky flavour to the wine.

barrique The *barrique bordelaise* is the traditional Bordeaux oak barrel of 225 litres (50 gallons) capacity, used for ageing and sometimes for fermenting wine. Used around the world.

biodynamic viticulture This approach works with the movement of the planets and cosmic forces to achieve health and balance in the soil and in the vine. Vines are treated with infusions of mineral, animal and plant materials, applied in homeopathic quantities. An increasing number of growers are turning to biodynamism, with some astonishing results, but it is labour intensive and generally confined to smaller estates.

Blanc de blancs White wine made from one or more white grape varieties. Used especially for sparkling wines; in Champagne, denotes wine made entirely from the Chardonnay grape.

Blanc de noirs White wine made from black grapes only – the juice is separated from the skins to avoid extracting any colour. Most often seen in Champagne, where it describes wine made from Pinot Noir and/or Pinot Meunier grapes.

blending The art of mixing together wines of different origin, style or age, often to balance out acidity, weight etc. Winemakers often use the term *assemblage*.

Botrytis *See* **noble rot.**

brut French term for dry sparkling wines, especially Champagne.

Champagne method Traditional method used for nearly all of the world's finest sparkling wines. A second fermentation takes place in the bottle, producing carbon dioxide, which, kept in solution under pressure, gives the wine its fizz.

château French for castle; widely used in France (and in some New World countries, too) to describe any wine estate, large or small.

claret English term for red Bordeaux wines, from the French *clairet*, which was traditionally used to describe a lighter style of red Bordeaux.

clarification Term covering any winemaking process (such as filtering or fining) that involves the removal of solid matter either from the must or the wine.

clos French for a walled vineyard — as in Burgundy's Clos de Vougeot — also commonly incorporated into the names of estates (e.g. Clos des Papes), whether they are walled or not.

cold fermentation Long, slow fermentation at low temperature to extract maximum freshness from the grapes. Crucial for whites in hot climates.

co-operative In a co-operative cellar, growers who are members bring their grapes for vinification and bottling under a collective label. In terms of quantity, the French wine industry is dominated by co-ops. They often use less workaday titles, such as Caves des Vignerons, Producteurs Réunis, Union des Producteurs or Cellier des Vignerons.

corked/corky Wine fault derived from a cork which has become contaminated, usually with Trichloroanisole or TCA. The mouldy, stale smell is unmistakable. Not pieces of cork in the wine.

crémant French term for traditional method sparkling wine from regions other than Champagne, for example Crémant de Limoux.

Cru French for growth, meaning a specific plot of land or particular estate. In Burgundy, growths are divided into Grands (great) and Premiers (first) Crus, and apply solely to the actual land. In Champagne the same terms are used for whole villages. In Bordeaux there are various hierarchical levels of Cru referring to estates rather than their vineyards. In Italy the term is used in an unofficial way, to indicate a single-vineyard or special-selection wine.

Cru classé The Classed Growths are the aristocracy of Bordeaux, ennobled by the Classifications of 1855 (for the Médoc, Barsac and Sauternes), 1955, 1969, 1986, 1996, 2006 and 2012 (for St-Émilion) and 1953 and 1959 (for Graves). Curiously, Pomerol has never been classified. The modern classifications are more reliable than the 1855 version, which was based solely on the price of the wines at the time of the Exposition Universelle in Paris, but in terms of prestige the 1855 Classification remains the most important. With the exception of a single alteration in 1973, when Château Mouton-Rothschild was elevated to First

Growth status, the list has not changed since 1855. It certainly needs revising.

Cuvée French for the contents of a single vat or tank, but usually indicates a wine blended from either different grape varieties or the best barrels of wine.

dégorgement Stage of disgorgement in the production of Champagne-method wines when the sediment, collected in the neck of the bottle during *remuage*, or riddling, is removed.

demi-sec French for medium-dry.

DO/DOP/DOCa Spain's quality wine categories, regulating origin and production methods.

DOC/DOP Portugal's top-quality wine classification.

DOP/DOC/DOCG Italy's quality wine categories, regulating origin, grape varieties, yield and production methods.

domaine French term for wine estate.

dosage A sugar and wine mixture added to sparkling wine after *dégorgement* or disgorgement, which affects how sweet or dry it will be.

Eiswein Rare, chiefly German and Austrian, late-harvested wine made by picking the grapes and pressing them while frozen. This concentrates the sweetness of the grape as most of the liquid is removed as ice. *See also* **Icewine**.

extraction Refers to the extraction of colour, tannins and flavour from the grapes during and after fermentation. There are various ways in which extraction can be manipulated by the winemaker, but over-extraction leads to imbalance.

filtering Removal of yeasts, solids and any impurities from a wine before bottling.

fining Method of clarifying wine by adding a coagulant (e.g. egg whites, isinglass) to remove soluble particles such as proteins and excessive tannins.

Fino The lightest, freshest style of sherry.

flor A film of yeast which forms on the surface of Fino sherries (and some other wines) in the barrel, preventing oxidation and imparting a tangy, dry flavour.

flying winemaker Term coined in the late 1980s to describe enologists, often Australian-trained, brought in to improve the quality of wines in many underperforming wine regions.

fortified wine Wine that has high-alcohol grape spirit added, usually before the initial fermentation is completed, so preserving sweetness.

Grand Cru French for 'great growth'. Supposedly the best vineyard sites in Alsace, Burgundy, Champagne and parts of Bordeaux (the Médoc, Graves, Sauternes and St-Émilion) – and should produce the most exciting wines.

horizontal tasting A tasting where the wines are all from the same vintage but are from different wineries. *See also* **vertical tasting**.

Icewine A speciality of Canada, produced from juice squeezed from ripe grapes that have frozen on the vine. *See also* **Eiswein**.

late harvest Grapes are left on the vines beyond the normal harvest time to concentrate flavours and sugars. *See also* **Vendange Tardive**.

lees Sediment – dead yeast cells, grape pips (seeds), pulp and tartrates – thrown by wine during fermentation and left behind after racking. Some wines are left on the fine lees for as long as possible to take on extra flavour. Look for the term *sur lie* on the label.

maceration Important winemaking process for red wines whereby colour, flavour and/or tannin are extracted from grape skins before, during or after fermentation. The period lasts from a few days to several weeks.

malolactic fermentation Secondary fermentation whereby harsh malic acid is converted into mild lactic acid and carbon dioxide. Normal in red wines but often prevented in whites to preserve a fresh, fruity taste.

Manzanilla The tangiest style of sherry, similar to Fino.

maturation Term for the beneficial ageing of wine.

Meritage American term for red or white wines made from a blend of Bordeaux grape varieties.

mesoclimate The climate of a specific geographical area, be it a vineyard or simply a hillside or valley.

must Mixture of grape juice, skins, pips and pulp produced after crushing (prior to completion of fermentation), which will eventually become wine.

'natural' wines Movement originating in France and catching on in Italy, California and elsewhere as a counterpoint to the mass of 'industrial' wine. (Artisan) members seek to bring out the true expression of the soil 'naturally', i.e. by minimal intervention both in the vineyard and in the winery, notably without the addition of sulphur dioxide. This process is not yet regulated, resulting in a broad range of quality, from the exceptional to vinegar.

New World When used as a geographical term, New World includes the Americas, South Africa, Australia and New Zealand. And so, it is a term used to describe the fruity, upfront style of wine now in evidence all over the world, but pioneered in the USA and Australia.

noble rot *Botrytis cinerea*. Fungus that, when it attacks ripe white grapes, shrivels the fruit and intensifies their sugar while adding a distinctive flavour. A vital factor in creating many of the world's finest sweet wines, such as Sauternes and Trockenbeerenauslese.

oak The wood most commonly used to make barrels for fermenting and ageing fine wines. It adds flavours such as vanilla, and tannins; the newer the barrel, the greater the impact.

Oloroso The darkest, heaviest style of sherry, usually dry.

orange wine A new style of wine from white grapes, popular with supporters of the 'natural' wine movement, that has ancient origins. The earliest winemakers would very likely have fermented their grapes whole – skins, pips and stalks all thrown in together. From white grapes, the resulting wine would have an orange colour and a rustic flavour. And that's the way some modern winemakers like it. Alternatively, a white wine may be aged in clay amphoras before bottling, which also gives an 'orange' wine. Producers in Georgia prefer to call their claypot-fermented wines 'amber'. A subtler variation is the copper-coloured wine made from darker-skinned white grapes such as Pinot Gris, where the juice is left in contact with the skins for a short time before fermentation; this style is traditional to Friuli in north-east Italy, where it is known as *ramato*, meaning 'coppery'; some US producers now use this term.

oxidation Over-exposure of wine to air, causing loss of fruit and flavour. Slight oxidation, such as occurs through the wood of a barrel or during racking, is part of the ageing process and, in wines of sufficient structure, enhances flavour and complexity.

passito Italian term for wine made from dried grapes. The result is usually a sweet wine with a raisiny intensity of fruit.

phylloxera The vine aphid *Phylloxera vastatrix* attacks vine roots. It devastated vineyards around the world in the late nineteenth century soon after it arrived from America. Since then, the vulnerable *Vitis vinifera* has generally been grafted on to vinously inferior, but phylloxera-resistant, American rootstocks. Quality is supposedly unaffected.

Premier Cru First Growth: the top quality classification in parts of Bordeaux, but second to Grand Cru in Burgundy. Used in Champagne to designate vineyards just below Grand Cru.

racking Gradual clarification of wine: the wine is transferred from one barrel or container to another, leaving the lees behind.

Réserve French for what is, in theory, a winemaker's best wine. The word has no legal definition in France.

ripasso A method used in Valpolicella to make wines with extra depth. Wine is passed over the lees of Recioto or Amarone della Valpolicella, adding extra alcohol and flavour, though also extra tannin and a risk of higher acidity and oxidation.

sec French for dry. When applied to Champagne, it means medium-dry.

sediment Usually refers to residue thrown by a wine, particularly red, as it ages in bottle.

Sélection de Grains Nobles A super-ripe category for sweet Alsace wines, now also being used by some producers of Coteaux du Layon in the Loire Valley.

solera Spanish system of blending fortified wines, especially sherry and Montilla-Moriles. When mature wine is run off a cask for bottling, only a quarter or so of the volume is taken, and the cask is filled up with similar but younger wine taken from another cask, which in turn is topped up from an even younger cask, and so on.

Spätlese German for late-picked (riper) grapes. Often moderately sweet, though there are many dry versions.

spumante Italian for sparkling. Bottle-fermented wines (as with Champagne) are often referred to as *metodo classico* or *metodo tradizionale*.

Supérieur French for a wine with a slightly higher alcohol content than the basic AC.

tannin Harsh, bitter, mouth-puckering element in red wine, derived from grape skins, pips and stems, and from oak barrels. Tannins soften with age and are essential for long-term development in red wines.

terroir A French term used to denote the combination of soil, climate and exposure to the sun – that is, the natural physical environment of the vine.

traditional method *See* **Champagne method**.

varietal Wine made from, and named after, a single or dominant grape variety.

Vendange Tardive French for late harvest. The term is traditional in Alsace. The Italian term is *vendemmia tardiva*.

vertical tasting A tasting where different vintages of the same wine type from the same winery are tasted. This emphasises differences between various vintages. *See also* **horizontal tasting**.

vin de paille Sweet wine found mainly in the Jura region of France. Traditionally, the grapes are left for two to three months on straw (*paille*) mats before fermentation to dehydrate, thus concentrating the sugars. The wines are sweet but slightly nutty and often have an attractive sour streak.

vin jaune A speciality of the Jura region in France, made from the Savagnin grape. Made in a similar way to Fino sherry but not fortified and aged for six years in oak. Unlike Fino, *vin jaune* ages well.

vinification The process of turning grapes into wine.

vintage The year's grape harvest, also used to describe wines of a single year.

viticulture Vine-growing and vineyard management.

Vitis vinifera Vine species, native to Europe and Central Asia, from which almost all the world's quality wine is made.

yield The amount of fruit, and ultimately wine, produced from a vineyard. Measured in hectolitres per hectare (hl/ha) in most of Europe, and in the New World as tons per acre or tonnes per hectare. Yield may vary from year to year, and depends on grape variety, age and density of the vines, and viticultural practices.

Acknowledgements

Without the determination and imagination of Richard Beswick, my commissioning editor, this book would have remained a distant dream of opinions, ideas and memories. Thank you, Richard. And thank you also, Zoe Gullen, for doing such a brilliant job of turning my sometimes rather over-enthusiastic and uncontrolled outpourings into something so much more focused and effective.

And I must thank two other very special people. Fiona Holman has been my helpmate, my organiser, my adviser, my editor and my friend for almost as long as I have been writing books. Her reassuring, warm-hearted presence is something I have treasured while writing this book, as with so many others. And without Adrian Webster, I'm not sure I would ever have started on my career as an author. On this grand project, he has directed, guided and encouraged me, as well as providing the perfect sounding board for the numerous ideas flying around in my brain. Thank you, dear friend.

This is a list of people who have shared their special bottles with me, or who have persuaded me to share my special bottles with them; people who have opened my eyes and my heart to this glorious world of wine I have so enjoyed. Or, indeed, people I simply enjoyed drinking wine with, for no other reason than that we had fun. And I must start with Metcalfe. He got me into this wine business. He's never made any attempt to get me out of it. He's my oldest and truest friend in wine.

Chris Ashton, Tim Atkin, John Avery, Anthony Barton, Michael Bateman, Peter Bazalgette, Joseph Berkmann, Olivier Bernard, Gareth Birchley, Graham Boynton, Julian Brind, Michael Broadbent, Stephen Browett, Steve Burns, Jonathan Butt, Philippe Castéja, Maurizio Castelli, Jean-Michel Cazes, Allan Cheesman, Jeannie Cho Lee, John Clarke, Michael Cox, Brian Croser, Armin Diel, Mark Dorber, Denis Dubourdieu, Terry Dunleavy, Edward Cox, Mark Edmonds, The English Rugby Team, Keith Floyd, Tom Forrest, David Gleave, Colette Gleeson, Jilly Goolden, Bill Gunn, Ron Hall, Ainsley Harriott, Don Hewitson, Michael Hill-Smith, Tony Hodges, William Holmes, Russell Hone, Andrew Jefford, Robert Joseph, Sarah Kemp, Rosie Kerslake, Matt Kramer, The Lads, Tony Laithwaite, David Lane, Geoff Leigh, Ernie Loosen, Mark Lynton, Bob Maclean, James May, Duncan Menzies, Marco Molesini, Christopher Monks, Angela Muir, my mum, Hazel Murphy, Dirk Niepoort, Su Hua Newton, Dee Nolan, Mike Paul, Andrew Pirie, Michael Plumley, Freddie Price, Gavin Quinney, Maggie Ramsay, Ignacio Recabárren, Geoffrey Roberts, James Rogers, Anthony Rose, The Ryder Cup, John Salvi, Jan Samuelson, Mark Savage, Christian Seely, Peter Sichel, Bonnie Simons, Craig Smith, Olly Smith, Steven Spurrier, Tim Stanley-Clarke, Rick Stein, Sarah Stewart-Brown, Patrick Stewart, Jean-Luc Thunevin, Miguel Torres, Will Towers, Julia Trustram-Eve, Aldo Vajra, Pamela Vandyke Price, Christiano Van Zeller, Gary Vaynerchuk, Nils von Veh, Charles Wintour, David Young, Kevin Zraly

And, finally, to my beloved Lola. Where would I be, what would I be, without her.

Credits

Illustrations

Oz Clarke: 1, 2, 4, 5, 9 (*top*)
Sarah Stewart-Brown: 3
JAK/Associated Newspapers Ltd/Solo Syndication: 6 (*top*).
   Courtesy of British Cartoon Archive, University of Kent
Victor Watts/Alamy Stock Photo: 6 (*middle*)
Radio Times: 6 (*bottom*)
Marc de Tienda: 7 (*top*)
Adrian Webster: 7 (*bottom*), 8
Tyrrell's Wines: 9 (*bottom left*)
Cloudy Bay Vineyards: 9 (*bottom right*)
© Mick Rock/Cephas Picture Library: 10 (*top and middle*),
   11 (*top, middle*), 12 (*bottom*), 13
Jon Wyand: 10 (*bottom left*)
Eckhard Supp/Alamy Stock Photo: 11 (*bottom*)
Andrew Hasson/Alamy Stock Photo: 12 (*top*)
Langmeil Winery: 14 (*top*)
© Jane Zwerrenz/Rippon Vineyards: 14 (*bottom*)
© Matt Wilson/Cephas Picture Library: 15 (*top*)
Viña Ventisquero: 15 (*bottom*)
Washington Wine: 16 (*top*)
© Janis Miglavs/Cephas Picture Library: 16 (*bottom*)

Maps
Barking Dog Art

Text
Extract on p. 487 from Road Dahl, *My Uncle Oswald*
   (London: Michael Joseph, 1979)

Index

Canada – *continued*
212–13, 214–16, 434, 472;
Osoyoos Lake 435, 525; Prince
Edward County 215–16, 472,
498; Similkameen Valley 217,
435; sparkling wines 214, 583;
St John's, Newfoundland 213;
Vineland, Ontario 214
Canaiolo grape 243
Canberra 132, 482, 540, 541
Canoe Ridge 471
Canon-la-Gaffelière, Château 362
Canterbury Cathedral 4, 5, 375
Cape Mentelle 149
Carignan (Mazuelo) grape 103, 105,
144, 260, 261, 302–3, 426, 523,
531, 532, 594
Cariñena grape 257, 266
Carmenère grape 411, 423, 435,
438–9
Carrau family (Uruguay) 318
Carter, Charles 208
Casa Marín 531
casein 53
Castel, Domaine du 377
Catalonia 262, 265–6, 267, 269–70,
419, 464, 582–3
Catena 473
Cavour, Count of 227, 228, 229
Cayuse 526
Ceausescu, President 362
Cederberg 440
celebrity chefs 19–20
Cerro Chapeau 318
Cetto, L.A. 406
Chablis 33, 82–4, 121, 136, 256,
388, 451, 459, 460–1, 467–8,
478–9
Chalone 192, 453. 502, 503
Chambertin 346
Chamonix 336, 441, 476
Champagne: drop in British sales
of 75; German influence 570,
580–1; glamour of 581; grapes
used for 75, 76–7, 270, 388, 390,
392, 460–1, 494, 582; history
of 573–5, 577–81; production
methods 233, 269–70, 477,
577–80;
Champagne region: Blanc de Blancs
wines 460; chemical use 75–6;

closeness to southern England
582; Côte des Blancs 77, 460; and
England in seventeenth century
573–5; geography of 77, 388,
460; and global warming 76,
387–8, 582; Grand Cru/Premier
Cru villages 76; and invention of
sparkling wine 404, 574–7; PR
and marketing 74, 75, 76, 574;
River Marne 77, 574; soils of 388,
467, 582; vineyard yields 75–6;
weather in 75, 76, 184, 217, 269,
460, 494, 574
Channing Daughters 207
Chapoutier 39
Chaptal, Jean-Antoine 577
Chardonnay grape: ABC (Anything
But Chardonnay) 409–10, 458,
471, 563; Argentine wines 311,
472–3; Australian wines 15, 25,
73, 102, 122, 129–30, 132, 137,
146, 150, 451–3, 457–60, 478–84;
Blanc de Blancs wines 460, 467;
Burgundy vineyards 87–8, 453,
460–4; Californian wines 176–7,
179–82, 187, 193, 194, 195, 427,
450, 453–60, 468–70, 500, 527;
in Canada 212, 214, 215, 216,
472; Catalonian wines 267, 270,
464; Chablis wine 33, 82–4, 121,
136, 256, 388, 451, 459, 460–1,
467–8, 478–9; for Champagne
76, 77, 270, 388, 460–1, 582;
Chardonnay as a term 449–50,
451; Chilean wines 302, 473–4;
in China 398; clones from
'mother vines' 35; as cool-climate
variety 468–9; critics of 409, 427,
458; as easy to grow 459, 486; in
England 387, 390, 392; in Europe
outside France 464–7; history of
450–3; Italian wines 233, 250,
420, 421, 464–5; Languedoc-
Roussillon wines 102, 103–4; as
malleable 459–60; as most famous
variety in the world 450; neutral
nature of 452, 453–4; New York
State wines 203–4, 206, 207;
New Zealand wines 158, 159,
163, 165, 167, 170, 476–8; and
oak barrels 45, 130, 454–5, 457,

France – *continued*
defeated by English wine tasting
team 13; EU wine lake 103; fake
wine in 1920s 99, 100; golden age
of late twentieth century 222; Le
Gros Rouge 103; Jura region 44,
81–2, 116, 495, 594; Languedoc-
Roussillon (the Midi) 101,
102–5, 418–19, 464, 495, 522–3;
latitudes of wine-growing areas
72; modern commodity wine
market 102–4; and New World
revolution 73–4, 102–4, 127, 428;
non-mainstream grape varieties
594; 'orange' or 'amber' wines 44;
Paris Basin 388; Provence 101–2;
regulations 35, 78–9, 97, 101–2;
south-west 105–7, 112, 116, 315,
411, 417–19, 435–7, 553; world's
most influential wine producer
18, 72, 73; *see also* Bordeaux,
Burgundy, Champagne, Loire
Valley, Rhône Valley; France
wine regions
France wine regions: Bonnezeaux
93; Bourgueil 94; Cahors 107,
411, 436; Châteauneuf-du-
Pape 99, 100, 193, 521–2, 526;
La Clape 105; Corbières 105;
Coteaux du Layon 93, 115; Côtes
de Gascogne 105–6, 553; Côtes
du Rhône 98–100; Faugères
105; Fronton 106; Gaillac 106;
Gigondas 99; Jurançon 106,
116; Limoux 464, 495; Madiran
106–7, 315, 435; Minervois 105;
Montlouis 93; Pic St-Loup 105;
Picpoul de Pinet 104; Pouilly
Blanc Fumé 543, 552–3; Quarts
de Chaume 93; red Gamays 91;
Saumur 93; St-Chinian 105;
Touraine 92; *vin jaune* in Jura
81–2; Vouvray 93, 136
Franco-Prussian War (1870–1)
78
Frank, Dr Konstantin 205, 567;
winery 433
Freisa 231
Freixenet 269–70
Fridjhon, Michael 330, 532
Friulano grape 234

Fukier 366

Gaja, Angelo 19, 20, 25, 230–1, 242,
246, 252, 420–1, 465
Gallo, E. & J. 175, 201, 268, 406
Gamay grape 90
Garganega grape 237, 238
Garzon 318
Gauby, Gérard 105
Gault-Millau (French magazine)
257–8, 499, 508
Geilweilerhof research centre 562
Geisenheim research centre 39, 562,
569
Geisse 322, 583
Georgia *370*, 371, 373, 595; *qvevri*
wines 373–4
Germany 19, *342*, 343–51, 496–8;
Bernkasteler Doctor 569;
Cabernet Sauvignon 351, 424;
Blue Nun 345; Chardonnay
466; climate 45, 345, 454, 497,
563–4; and global warming 23,
351, 497, 564; grape varieties in
345, 347, 391–2; high quality
wines until 1970s 79, 344, 345;
Hochheimer 346; 'hock' 346;
influence in New World 73, 567;
latitudes of wine-growing areas
72, 345, 563–4; Liebfraumilch
157, 233, 335, 344, 345–8, 350,
352, 450, 545, 548–9, 561, 562,
569; Marcobrunner 346; Mosel
Valley 26, 31, 32, 78, 344, 345,
348, 350, 424, 564; Niersteiner
9, 350; noble rot 114, 348; Pfalz
497–8; Piesporter 350, 545; Pinot
Noir (Spätburgunder) 496–8;
Rheingau 466, 564; Rheinhessen
497–8; Rhine Valley 78, 345,
466, 564; sparkling wines 582;
Süssreserve (sugar reserve) 545;
use of science and technology
347, 561–2, 568–9
Gewürztraminer grape 11, 79, 81,
165, 200, 235, 304
Giaconda 137
Gilgamesh, Epic of 372
ginger wine 5
gitanes (gypsies, grape-pickers) 40
Glen Ellen 469

116, 513, 517–18, 520, 526, 536;
Syrah 25, 97–8, 515, 516–18,
520–2; Vienne 513, 517; Viognier
96–7, 104, 163, 201, 209–10, 464,
466, 520, 540
Ribolla Gialla grape 234
Ricasoli-Firidolfi, Marco 590–1
Richard, Cliff 285
Riddoch, John 446
Ridge 191, 428
Riesling grape 561–9; and ABC
(Anything But Chardonnay) 409,
458, 563; and Alsace region 78,
79, 81, 565; Australian wines 53,
121, 135, 136, 145, 146, 150, 443,
538, 555, 562, 565–6, 569; in
Austria 352, 354, 564; in Canada
212, 215, 217, 567–8; in Chile
304, 568; in China 398, 568; as
cold-climate variety 200, 205,
304, 338, 424, 538, 567; dry
wines from 205–6, 350, 563,
565–6; German introduction to
Barossa Valley 565; as high-acid
grape 79, 135, 345–6, 350; and
Icewine 567–8; Israeli wine 377;
in Kazakhstan 400; labelling
in New York 206, 567; lack of
new oak 458, 555, 563; latitudes
of German vineyards 72; as
low-alcohol wine 562–3; and
malolactic fermentation 49; in
the Midi 104; in Mosel Valley
32, 564, 567; New World sweet
wines 115–16, 205; New Zealand
wines 163, 165, 169, 170, 568;
restored as mighty grape in
Germany 350; in Rheingau 466;
ripening of in Germany 200–1,
563–4; and screwcaps 53; South
African wines 338; sparkling
wines 582; in USA 200–1, 204,
205–6, 566–7; the Wachau 354;
Washington State wines 566–7;
Yugoslavian wine 4–5, 366–7
La Rioja grape 308
Rkatsiteli grape 400
Robola grape 385
Rochioli 175, 503
Roederer Estate 583
Roederer, Louis 184, 583

Rogers, James 304–6
Rolland, Michel 22, 368
Romanée-Conti, Domaine de la 29,
39, 502
Romania 362–3, 424–5, 466, 496,
554
Rome, ancient 26–7, 33, 99, 105,
107, 221, 513, 593; English wine
390; Falernian wine 249; German
wine 345; and pine resin 382,
383; and Portugal 282; sweet
wines 252
Rosemount 14, 130, 131, 452, 479–
80, 481, 519
Roseworthy (Australian wine
school) 39, 179, 454
de Rothschild, Baron Edmond 375
Roussanne grape 35, 94, 475
Royal Shakespeare Company 119,
175, 445
Rubáiyát of Omar Khayyám 27
Ruché 231
Russia, counterfeit wine in 27–8
Rustenberg 441
Ryman, Hugh 554

Sadie, Eben 52, 333, 532, 533
Sagrantino grape 225
Saint George 406
Sainte-Marie, Buffy 203–4
Saintsbury 502
Samos, island of 385
San Pedro 529–30, 544
Sánchez Romate 271
Sandyland Wine Company 398
Sanford, Richard 501
Sangiovese grape 241–2, 243, 244,
245–6, 250, 262, 422, 423, 525,
587, 590–1
Sankt Laurent grape 353
Santa Rita 298, 473–4
Santorini 26, 384
Saperavi grape 205, 595
Sassicaia 219, 240–1, 242, 246–7,
421–2, 423
Sauvignon Blanc: acidity levels 165,
376, 551–2; aromas 11; Australian
wines 146, 483, 555–6; bills paid
by 510, 551, 552; Bordeaux wine
107, 112, 115, 553; and Cabernet
Sauvignon's origins 410; CD1

50–1, 181, 247, 429, 430, 459, 470, 515, 540, 562–3, 597; 'all wine is made in the vineyard' cliché 30–1; in ancient Georgia 373–4; in ancient Middle East 371–2; Bordeaux style of 107–8; Chardonnay's emergence in 1980s 451–3, 468–70; cheap commercial wines 59–60, 102–4, 121, 123–4; cold-stabilising of white wines 53; crushing of grapes 43–4; democratised by Australia 121–2; devices and machines 42–3, 45, 50–1, 181, 299, 562; domestic market as always least critical 279–80; early oxidisation of juice 455–6; filtration 53, 124; fining agents 53; future challenges 596–9; *Gault-Millau* Wine Olympiad in Paris 499, 508; and globalisation 225–6, 321, 403; grape selection at winery 43; harvesting of grapes 40, 42, 43; high prices for 'fine' wines 231; homogenisation at turn of century 21–3, 40; hygiene and cleanliness 51, 52, 124, 408, 454, 455, 549, 555, 556, 597; international consultants 22, 23, 41–2; kosher wine 376, 377; latitudes of wine-growing areas 72–3; and lead poisoning 99–100; Loire new wave 94–5; maceration of skins 46, 266, 550, 590; micro-oxygenation system 50, 106–7, 318; 'minerality' in 2000s 552; 'natural' 23, 26, 51–3, 94–5, 333, 598; organic growing 26, 37–8, 144, 350, 598; pneumatic grape press 561–2; pressing the whole bunch 455; process at winery 43–51; provenance and authenticity 226, 311, 320, 350, 495, 498; racking of red wines

50; reverse osmosis machines 50, 51; and science 40–1, 124, 179–81, 429, 454–5, 483, 493, 568–9; spinning cones 50; terroir (sense of place) 26, 81, 127, 350, 469, 491, 492, 498, 563, 588; timing of harvest 40; toasted oak staves/chips/essence 48, 112–13, 124, 409, 457, 480, 563; vacuum concentrators 50–1; varietal revolution 102, 104, 182, 361, 458–9, 469

Winiarski, Warren 428
Wolf Blass 131, 519
Wölffer 207, 432–3
Woodward Canyon 202, 432, 471
Worms (Rhine town) 345
Worrall, Denis 327
Wynn, David 450–1, 479
Wynn's 446

Xarel-lo grape 267, 269, 270, 583
Xiangdu 398
Xinomavro grape 384
Xynomavro grape 595

Yalumba 562
Yapincak grape 381
Yellowtail 458, 481–2, 519, 538
Yugoslavian wine 4–5, 366–7, 425
Yukich, Frank 548–9
Yquem, Château d' 115, 148, 399

Zanesville, Ohio 174–5
Zhongfei 398
Zimbabwe 325, 405
Zinfandel grape 174, 198, 250, 353; in California 184, 185, 191, 193, 194, 501, 503; Croatia as source of 184, 368
Zuccardi, Sebastian 311
Zuccardi, José Alberto 437
Zuccardi (winery) 593
Zweigelt grape 353

About the Author

Oz Clarke had an idyllic childhood in the Kent countryside. He was head chorister at Canterbury Cathedral Choir School. He acted, sang and wine-tasted his way through university, then spent a decade acting with the RSC and featuring in West End musicals – he starred as Perón in *Evita*.

His famous victories in high-profile wine-tasting competitions brought him jobs on two national newspapers, and in 1984 he turned to full-time writing and television work. The BBC's *Food and Drink* made him a household name and was broadcast around the world, as were his later 'Oz and James' wine adventures with James May.

His many books have been translated into sixteen languages, he has won every major wine-writing prize, and he is an Officier de l'Ordre du Mérite Agricole. When he is not visiting vineyards and wineries, chairing wine competitions or presenting innovative concerts with Armonico Consort, Oz lives in London and complains about not playing enough golf.